Brigantine

# PORTHMADOG SHIPS

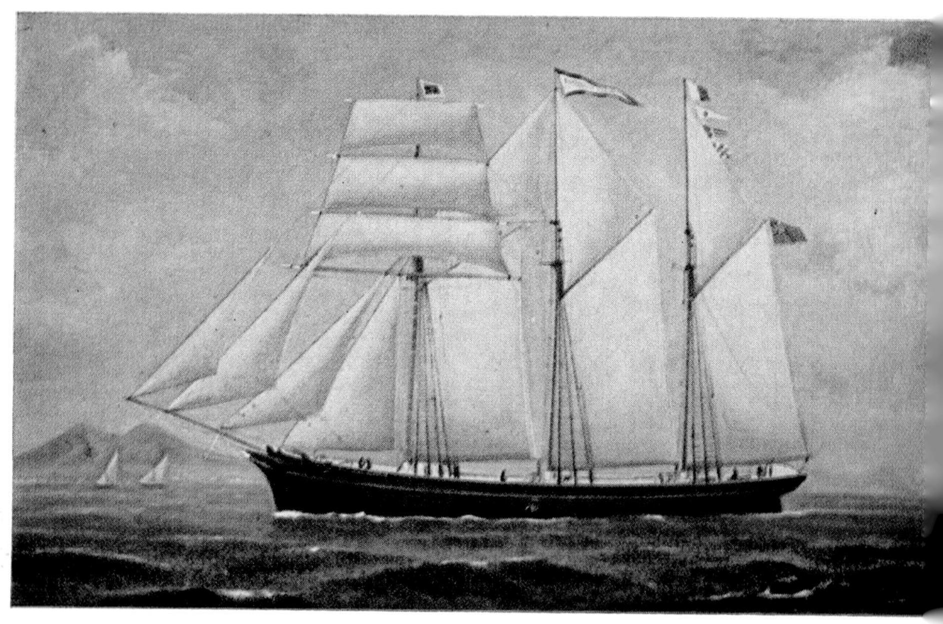

A 'Western Ocean Yacht', the *Elizabeth Eleanor,* built David Williams, Porthmadog, in 1903, Captain John M. Jones, master, entering the Bay of Naples, December 1909.

# PORTHMADOG SHIPS

---

EMRYS HUGHES

and

ALED EAMES

Published by

GWYNEDD ARCHIVES SERVICE

*Printed by Gee and Son, Denbigh, for Gwynedd Archives Service, County Offices, Caernarfon.*

# CONTENTS

# ILLUSTRATIONS

19. The barque *Pride of Wales,* built for Captain David Morris by Simon Jones, 1870. [Eduard Adam, Havre, 1880.]

20. The barquentine *Edward Seymour,* built Griffith Williams, 1876, Captain Henry Hughes, master.

21. The barquentine *Ocean Ranger,* built Appledore, 1875, Captain Davies, Porthmadog, master.

22. The brigantine *Wern,* built J. and Ebenezer Roberts, 1876. [Dr. Jürgen Meyer Collection.]

23. The *Wern* in foul weather. [A. Luzzio, Genoa, 1896.]

24. The *Wern,* after collision with steamer off Dungeness, Captain Thomas Jones, master.

25. The brig *Blanche Currie,* built Porthmadog 1875, lost with all hands 1914.

26. The three-masted schooner (Jack barquentine) *Venedocian,* built Griffith Williams, 1873.

27. The three-masted schooner (Jack barquentine) *C. E. Spooner,* built Porthmadog, 1878, at Le Havre.

28. *C. E. Spooner* and *Venedocian* at Flat Island, Labrador, loading fish for Europe. (Reproduced from printer's block given to late Emrys Hughes by Mr. Arch. Munn, St. John's, Newfoundland.)

29. Wedding day of Captain and Mrs. Hugh Roberts, of the *Evelyn,* 15 February 1893; also in photograph are Captain Hugh Roberts, senior, of the *Constance,* extreme left, and his two other sons, William Roberts, mate/boatswain of the *Evelyn,* the best man, and Captain Thomas Roberts of the *Dorothy.*

30. Brig *Evelyn,* built 1877, at King's Lynn, *c.* 1910.

31. Captain and Mrs. Hugh Roberts and daughter, with crew of *Evelyn,* 1895-6. William Roberts, the mate (standing immediately behind Mrs. Roberts), and Ben Welch, the cook/A.B. (with lifebelt in front of him).

32. Captain H. Roberts and crew of the *Evelyn.*

33. 'Dillad dydd Sul'. Captain H. Roberts and crew of the *Evelyn* in 'Sunday best'.

34. The deck of the *Evelyn*: Captain Hugh Roberts sitting down with the dog, William Roberts, the mate, in foreground.

35. The *Evelyn* (left) at King's Lynn.

36. The *Evelyn* photographed from a passing steamer.

37. The schooner *Sarah Evans,* built 1877, alongside a wharf in the Elbe. [H. W. Short, Hamburg.]

38. The brig *Excelsior* blown inland at Halmstadt, Sweden, and declared a constructive total loss. Captain Evans and crew had to cling to rigging as *Excelsior* dragged anchors in hurricane winds on Christmas Eve 1902, and was driven ashore. All hands saved.

39. Captain Hugh Parry's *Frau Minna Petersen,* built by Simon Jones, 1878. [A. Luzzio, Genoa, 1885.]

40. Schooner *Robert Morris,* built 1876, Captain Thomas Jones, master.

41. Captain and Mrs. D. Davies and crew of *Robert Morris,* sunk by U-boat, November 1917.

42. Built in 1877, the *Edward Arthur* after her conversion to a three-masted schooner.

43. The barquentine *Fanny Breslauer* (built Plymouth 1871), a phosphate trader, Captain Evan Jones, Borth-y-gest, master, at Barbados.

44. David Williams, builder of 'Western Ocean Yachts', and his family.

45. A vessel in frame, *c.* 1900; David Williams (extreme right) and workmen.

46. Partially 'planked up' vessel; David Williams (second from left) and workmen, again *c.* 1900.

47. David Williams (with 'topi' helmet, fourth from right) with workmen inside frame of vessel, probably *R. J. Owens* or *Isallt* (II).

48. Three-masted schooner, *R. J. Owens,* on blocks at Rotten Tare, 1907. David Williams (extreme right) and workmen.

49. The *Isallt* (II) in frame, showing massive oak timbers; David Williams, third from left, and workmen (and small boys, constant and knowledgeable spectators of a vessel's growth).

50. The *Isallt* (II) nears launching day; David Williams extreme right in foreground.

51. Three-masted schooner *Ellen James* (II), built David Williams, 1904, Captain John James Jones, master, at King's Lynn.

52. The three-masted schooner *Isallt* (II) at Copenhagen. Captain R. O. Williams, master and brother of builder, centre, and crew, including David Mark Jones (sitting inside lifebelt), who fell from rigging and was lost overboard in storm some months later. Visiting Englishman (with cricket cap) was schoolmaster at Copenhagen.

53. Three-masted schooner, *John Llewelyn,* built David Jones, 1904, at St. John's, Newfoundland. [Photograph given to late Emrys Hughes by Mr. A. Munn of St. John's.]

54. The *William Morton,* built David Jones, 1905, at Middlefurt, Denmark.

55. The *William Prichard,* built David Jones, 1903, at Bristol on her maiden voyage.

56. The *William Prichard* (centre) towing into Stettin, 1905.

57. The *Jenny Jones,* built Ebenezer Roberts and John Roberts, for Dr. J. H. Lister, 1893.

58. The *Kitty,* built David Williams, 1902, at Papenburg, *c.* 1904-5. [Dr. Jürgen Meyer Collection.]

59. David Jones's three-masted schooner *Blodwen,* built 1891, at Harbour Grace, Newfoundland.

60. Griffith and David Williams's three-masted schooner, *Elizabeth,* built 1891.

61. The *John Pritchard,* built David Williams, 1906.

62. The crew of *John Pritchard;* left to right, Jack Williams, mate, wearing braces, known locally as 'Jack Klondyke', Captain John Watkin Roberts, master, Bill Payne, A.B., David Nicholas, boy, and William Morris Lloyd, Ordinary Seaman.

63. The *Elizabeth Eleanor,* built David Williams 1905, Captain J. M. Jones, master.

64. The *Miss Morris,* three-masted schooner, built David Jones, 1900, one of the largest of the Western Ocean Yachts.

65. The *Dorothy,* built Griffith and David Williams, 1891, towing into Bristol.

66. The schooner *Cariad,* built W. Date, Kingsbridge, Captain John Owen, master, which sailed from Newfoundland to Oporto in ten days.

67. The *Elizabeth* at Leghorn.

68. The *Dorothy* at Leghorn, 1895.

69. The *John Llewelyn* being towed into Bristol.

70. The brig *George Casson,* Captain Hugh Parry, master, entering the Bay of Naples, 5 December 1868.

71. The brig *Fleetwing,* Captain John Roberts, master.

72. The steel barque *Beeswing,* built Greenock 1893, Captain R. Griffiths, master.

73. The barquentine *Martha Percival,* built Ebenezer Roberts, 1877.

74. Captain R. Griffiths and members of crew of the *Beeswing* at Portland, Oregon. Top, left to right, W. Paul, cook; P. Williams, first mate; Captain R. Griffiths; J. Lewis, second mate; R. Roberts, steward. Second row: G. Davies, W. Woodrow, apprentice; A. J. Owens, apprentice; T. O. Jones, boatswain. Bottom row: J. Soly, T. Jones, J. Thomas, J. Williams, R. H. Roberts, M.(?) Jones.

75. The schooner *Dizzy Dunlop,* built 1878, being re-keeled at a Scandinavian port. Captain Thomas E. Williams standing on rudder, Owen Humphreys, the mate, with tall straw hat, standing beside him.

76. The brigantine *Edward Windus,* built 1864, at Harburg, shortly before she was lost through collision in English Channel 1904, with one survivor.

77. The *Cadwalader Jones,* built 1878, at Brixham in 1932. [Then renamed *Mynonie R. Kirby.*]

78. Figurehead of *Cadwalader Jones,* at Brixham, August 1931. [Grahame E. Farr Collection.]

79. *Cadwalader Jones* in Southampton Water, 1908.

80. The three-masted schooner *R. J. Owens,* built David Williams, 1907.

81. Three-masted schooner *Gracie* in course of construction at David Jones's yard, Porthmadog, 1907. David Jones, wearing bowler hat, in centre of picture, with his workmen.

82. The *Gracie* nearing completion, with bowsprit and figurehead shipped. David Jones, the builder, may be seen, dimly, aboard vessel, with workmen in foreground below. Launching day, 31 January 1907.

83. The three-masted schooner *Gracie,* Captain O. H. Owen, master, sailing with ' moonsail ' up.

84. Captain O. H. Owen and the crew of the *Gracie.* [Postcard from Great Yarmouth, May 10, 1913.]

85. The end of the *Gracie,* ashore near Cadiz, shortly after she had been sold to Newfoundland owners in 1916.

86. Launching day photograph: David Williams, the builder, on extreme right, with his family and shareholders in the *Gestiana.*

87. Launching day for three-masted schooner *Gestiana,* last vessel built at Porthmadog, in 1913. A cry of dismay came from assembled crowd when the christening bottle failed to break at first attempt on bows of ill-fated vessel.

88. The *Gestiana* launched ' broadside on ' at Rotten Tare, Porthmadog.

89. The *Gestiana* safely launched at Porthmadog.

90. The German connection (1). Postcard from Robert Leitner, merchant, Harburg, 11 February 1904, to Captain Hugh Roberts, *Evelyn,* asking for names of vessels loading slate at Porthmadog.

91. The German connection (2). Ten Porthmadog master mariners have their photograph taken at Hamburg, where their vessels were unloading slate at the same time. (Left to right, standing) Captain R. A. Jones, *Mary Lloyd;* Captain Lewis, *Mary Casson;* Captain W. Greene, *Tyne;* Captain R. Jones, *M. A. James;* Captain H. Roberts, *Evelyn;* Captain John J. Jones, *Mary Annie;* (seated) Captain J. Morris, *David Morris;* Captain David Roberts, *Michael Kelly;* Captain Owen, *Edwin;* and Captain Roberts, *Ann and Jane Pritchard.*

92. Safe arrival: the *Wave of Life* tows two homeward bound vessels over the bar into Porthmadog on a peaceful evening.

---

## ACKNOWLEDGEMENTS

Unless otherwise stated, the illustrations are from the Gwynedd Archives Service's collections and Emrys Hughes MS. XM/1559 at the Caernarfon Record Office. I am very grateful to the following for permission to reproduce the plates indicated from paintings/photographs in their possession.

Mr. A. Davies, Ship Inn, Porthmadog: 21, 39, 64. Mrs. and Miss Mair Evans, Arenig, Criccieth: Frontispiece, 11, 16, 23, 25, 63, 66, 71, 80. Mrs. E. Edwards, Isallt, Bangor: 44, 47. Mr. S. C. Evans, Osmond Terrace, Porthmadog: 14. Mr. Grahame Farr: 78. Capt. W. H. Hughes, D.S.C., Holyhead: 74. Mr. Ellis Jones, Castle Street, Criccieth: 19, 40, 42. Mr. J. T. Jones, Porthmadog: 64. Mr. Owen Lloyd, 5 Dora Street, Porthmadog: 24. Dr. Jürgen Meyer, Hamburg: 22, 58. Mr. Ronald Owen, Borthwen, Borth-y-gest: 81, 82, 84. Miss Evelyn Roberts, Morannedd, Porthmadog. Miss G. and S. Roberts, Corn Cerrig, Criccieth. Capt. R. Roberts, Criccieth. Mr. David Williams, Largs, Ayrshire: 18, 45, 46, 49, 50, 52, 86.

Also to Mrs. Alma Gill, Pwllheli, for permission to reproduce extracts from the diary of Thomas Evans of Aberdaron, and to Mr. Frank Bright, Mr. E. M. Thomas, Mr. T. H. Jones, Mr. J. T. Jones and Mr. L. McMillan, all of Porthmadog, for tracing much local information.

# FOREWORD

ALTHOUGH, as he makes clear in his preface, he himself regards this book as no more than an introductory study to the history of Porthmadog shipping, most readers will agree that Aled Eames has made a very substantial beginning indeed. Taking the late Emrys Hughes's much-used list of Porthmadog vessels as the basis of his study and developing and expanding it, Aled Eames has added chapters on Porthmadog as a maritime community, on the ships and their builders, and on the seamen, based on his own study of the rich documentary sources available.

The story of Porthmadog is a peculiarly interesting one. The more comprehensible because it has a definite beginning and ending, both in modern times and only a century apart. Moreover, the period is that of the industrial revolution, of the rise of the steamship and the short-lived great iron and steel sailing ships of the late 19th century. During this hundred years, although the scale and scope of its shipbuilding and shipowning activities expanded out of all recognition, Porthmadog remained essentially a locally financed, locally managed shipowning community. It throve and prospered right through to the end. The end was a sudden demise brought about by the stoppage of the slate trade with Germany at the outbreak of the First World War and the nearly coincident development of an economic situation finally adverse to the operation of small merchant sailing ships in world trade, even by such a community as this.

For the other factor of great interest about Porthmadog was that throughout its century of life as a shipping place, it built, owned, and operated small wooden sailing ships in the general range of size which was average in the late 18th century and the first half of the nineteenth. As at Appledore in North Devon, the community of Porthmadog until 1914 remained something apart, almost from before the industrial revolution in the manner of its economic activities and the tools it used. The small wooden sailing ship, locally constructed and having in her fabric and fittings almost nothing which was not made on the spot, in the shipyard proper, in the local foundries, the blacksmith's shop, the rope walks and the sail lofts, the product of a 'carpenter and blacksmith' technology, was a remarkable survival until 1914. She was a survivor to that particular date because she continued to be built until that fateful year.

At Porthmadog, as at Appledore, she continued to be developed right until the very end. One of the few sources of material Aled Eames has not tapped for this preliminary study is the survey reports on these later vessels preserved in the archives of the National Maritime Museum and now available for study. They show that the Porthmadog vessels of the 1890s and the first decade of the present century were superior both structurally and in the materials of which they were constructed to their contemporaries and, indeed, to many of their predecessors. The later Porthmadog schooners were, indeed, as Aled Eames says, quite outstanding vessels, the ultimate development of the small wooden merchant sailing ship in Britain.

This book is a fascinating account, both readable and invaluable as reference material, of a world we have lost.

BASIL GREENHILL.

National Maritime Museum,
London.

# PREFACE

ONE hundred and fifty years ago, in the spring of 1825, Daniel Morris, newly-appointed harbour-master, carefully recorded the first dues on vessels entering and leaving a harbour which, it was enacted, 'shall in future be called or denominated by the name or style of Port-Madoc'. Griffith Griffiths, a Merioneth man, and his four sons had laboured tirelessly for three years to complete the first harbour-works for William Alexander Madocks, whose mile-long embankment across the estuary of Traeth Mawr had already become one of the wonders of early nineteenth century Britain. This massive undertaking had, incidentally, so diverted the flow of the rivers Glaslyn and Dwyryd, 'by means of issuing a large body of inland waters through the main Sluice', that it had 'excavated a commodious and well-sheltered Harbour at a Place extending from Garth Pen y Clogwyn to Ynys y Towyn'. In order to 'afford sufficient security and accommodation to Ships and vessels lying therein', this newly formed harbour was improved by Madocks, who agreed to construct 'a sufficient Pier or Quay thereat for the convenient loading and unloading of ships and other vessels' . . . 'on being paid or allowed a reasonable sum of money by way of Tonnage on all ships and other vessels frequenting the said harbour'. The first stage in the development of the new harbour was completed by October 1824, and, in accordance with the terms of the Act of 15 June 1821, Madocks appointed his first harbour-master, Daniel Morris.

A native of Llanystumdwy, Captain Daniel Morris married a daughter of William Owen, of Ynys Cyngar, the first pilot for the new port, and came to live within a stone's throw of the harbour at the Ship Inn, then situated on the corner of what later became Lombard Street, Porthmadog. As he walked up the little hillock of Ynys Towyn and looked down upon his new harbour, Captain Morris would have gazed across to the gently sloping beach and fields near his new home where Henry Jones, soon to become the port's leading shipbuilder, had recently completed the *Two Brothers*, the first of over two hundred and fifty vessels to be built at Porthmadog — the total is over three hundred if one includes the vessels built in the remoter parts of the estuary.

Unlike many of the ports of Britain whose quays and ropewalks span the centuries, Porthmadog's history is comparatively brief, effectively from 1825 to the First World War. It is due to the grandsons of another of the Morris family, Captain David Morris, Ceylon Villa, Porthmadog, master and owner of some of the most notable vessels of the port, that much of the richness of that story has been preserved. The late Henry Hughes, in his delightfully evocative *Through Mighty Seas* and *Immortal Sails,* brought the port and its little ships to life in a way that only a man who had himself sailed in them and had known the port in its busier days could have done. His brother, the late Emrys Hughes, who also sailed in their grandfather's *Excelsior,* did not live to see the publication of his own work, but it is obvious that much of the detailed research for *Immortal Sails* was, in fact, undertaken by him, as Colonel Henry Hughes readily acknowledged. Henry Hughes's racy and imaginative approach was complemented by the careful, painstaking research of his brother, who set himself the task of compiling a detailed record of all the vessels built at Porthmadog. To my great regret, I never met either brother, but their relationship seems to be well reflected in a letter which Emrys Hughes wrote to his brother in August 1945 when the latter was preparing *Immortal Sails* for publication. They had obviously been discussing the formation of the Mutual Ship Insurance Society at Porthmadog in 1841, and anyone who has read *Immortal Sails* can imagine the exuberant enthusiasm with which Henry Hughes approached the subject. His brother Emrys was more cautious, anxious that his brother's imaginative approach should not distort what had actually taken place:

> 'The deed is based upon an agreement reached at a meeting held at Portmadoc in July 1840.
>
> There is as yet no trace of this agreement. If this agreement could be found, then the exact nature of its foundation could be ascertained. One thing is obvious, that Barnes, Carreg, Casson, Holland, represented the financial interests. The other signatories covenant with these to form the Society.
>
> There is, therefore, no evidence whatsoever to show who were

the first movers in this matter. I think it would be very rash to assume that the 300 and odd would approach Holland or anyone else to ask them to evolve this scheme of insurance.

It was not the first scheme of its kind in the country. There are examples of it on the East Coast, Tyneside, etc., dating back to about 1800.

I trust, therefore, that you will not be too dogmatic when referring to the origins of this Society'.

Emrys Hughes, a surveyor by profession, lived at Delph, near Oldham, but each vacation he would try to get down to Caernarvonshire; whilst his family were safely parked on the beaches, he used to visit the homes of men who had sailed in Porthmadog ships and their descendants, faithfully recording their memories, and photographing any ship-portrait in their possession. The result was a massive tome of some 748 pages, listing the hundreds of vessels (many of them with photographs) in alphabetical order, and including as much material about each of them as could be gleaned from both oral and written sources. Had he lived, Emrys Hughes would surely have wished to continue his researches into the Registers of Shipping which he had realised gave much valuable information regarding the ownership of vessels. Since his death the Record Offices at Caernarfon, Dolgellau and Llangefni have acquired thousands of Crew Agreement Lists and Official Logs of Gwynedd ships, previously held by the Board of Trade. When Mr. Hughes's widow, Dr. Ann Hughes, very kindly agreed to deposit the Emrys Hughes MSS. at the Record Office in Caernarfon, it soon became apparent that the 'Portmadoc Ships' notes were so much in demand, particularly in connection with the newly-acquired maritime records, that it was essential to produce a more readily available, edited version, so that the somewhat fragile but very valuable original manuscript by Emrys Hughes himself might be preserved and not exposed to the constant wear and tear of frequent consultation by a wide range of readers. Moreover, Emrys Hughes MS. M/1559 was already too lengthy a document to be published verbatim. At the suggestion of the County Archivist, Mr. Bryn Parry, I have, therefore, attempted to edit this unique document so that the substance remains, supplemented, as I am certain the late Mr. Hughes would have wished, by any significant details which I have come across in the Custom

House Registers, the Crew Agreement Lists, the Annual Wreck Returns in the Parliamentary Papers, and *Lloyd's Registers*. Much incidental information has also become available since Mr. Hughes compiled his notes from the many papers of the late Henry Parry, school dentist, lifeboatman, and historian, of Nefyn, now deposited on loan at the Record Office, Caernarfon, and those of the late David Thomas, schoolmaster, historian, author of 'Hen Longau Sir Gaernarfon', whose papers are deposited in the Library of the University College of North Wales, Bangor. My indebtedness to them both is apparent throughout the pages that follow; it is because of their tireless research, and that of the late Emrys Hughes himself, that we have the foundations upon which to attempt to develop a fuller maritime history of Gwynedd. This implies a much more ambitious project than this present work. Here, all I have attempted is to provide a background to Mr. Hughes's work, outlining in a general way, some aspects of the growth of the maritime community at Porthmadog, of the ships and their builders, and the lives of the men who sailed them.

It will, therefore, be clear that I regard this as a preliminary investigation of a very rich field. Many facets of the work merit much fuller treatment than has been possible here. To take but one example, the *Western Ocean Yachts*, as they were called, the last of the Porthmadog schooners, deserve at least a book to themselves. As Mr. Basil Greenhill has indicated, the survey reports on these vessels now housed in the National Maritime Museum at Greenwich need to be studied in detail to show how superior these fine three-masted schooners were. So, too, do the surviving ship chandlers' ledgers, the ships' account books and mariners' letters and diaries, a wide range of documents, many of which have come to light whilst this book was, in fact, being printed and, therefore, unfortunately too late to be included here. One hopes that the publication of this preliminary survey will result in other documents and photographs being found and preserved before it is too late; the County Archivist and I recently received a sackful of harbour records and papers which were so damp-sodden that they will have to be carefully dried out before they can be studied. It is also hoped that any who sailed in or had knowledge of Porthmadog ships may be persuaded to record their memories. Some progress has already been made in this context.

During the Autumn Term of 1974, as tutor to a University College of North Wales Extra-Mural class at Porthmadog, I met many descendants of the maritime community of Porthmadog who unearthed documents and photographs and much local information. In the acknowledgements I have attempted to record my indebtedness to some of them individually, but, in fact, every member of the class contributed to this book. One member to whom I am particularly grateful is Mr. J. Lewis Jones of Nefyn, who has himself seen much service at sea, for drawing the outlines of different types of vessels to help a 'landlubber' reader to identify the various rigs and vessels mentioned in this book.

In the Spring Term of 1975, the pupils of 3G of Ysgol Eifionydd, Porthmadog, started their project on the history of their town, and they, too, together with their teacher, Mr. G. Shaw, and the student teachers from the Department of Education, U.C.N.W., Mrs. E. Fox, Miss G. King and Mr. G. Rothera, are recording and researching into the maritime history of the town.

One of the objectives in the publication of this book is to encourage the pupils to trace the history of individual vessels belonging, in some cases, to their ancestors, and thus to fill in the gaps in the alphabetical list of ships; others may wish to trace some of the voyages of the ships — they could, for example, prepare maps based on the cargo book of the *Cadwalader Jones* included in the further studies at the end of this book, and then progress to the preparation of other maps based on their own research on other vessels. It is hoped that the publication of this book will stimulate research into the history of their town by both the members of adult education classes and the pupils in Porthmadog schools.

It is with a deep sense of gratitude that I record my indebtedness to those who have helped to make the work of preparing the book such a pleasant task. Dr. Ann Hughes and the family of the late Emrys Hughes have been most helpful and co-operative. I am also very grateful to Mr. Basil Greenhill, C.M.G., Director of the National Maritime Museum, for his unfailing interest and ready encouragement at all times and for his kindness in writing the foreword to this book. Mr. Greenhill was exchanging information about Porthmadog ships with the late Emrys Hughes as long ago as 1947, and his own masterly account of *The Merchant Schooners* has provided the foundation for all subsequent work in this field. Dr. Lewis Lloyd of Coleg Harlech, who is engaged upon a wide-ranging survey of the maritime history of Merioneth, has kindly contributed the very interesting profiles of the *Deptford,* the *Lady Vaughan,* and the schooners owned by Dr. J. H. Lister, indicating the connections between Porthmadog and the Merioneth ports and their seamen. Captain W. H. Hughes, D.S.C., of Holyhead, Captain Griffith Roberts, O.B.E., and Captain R. Roberts, both of Borth-y-gest, and Mr. J. F. Owen of Chester, who all sailed in the later Porthmadog vessels, have given much time to answering many enquiries; I hope that reading of the vessels they knew so well, and looking at their photographs, will bring back memories of the days of their youth. Miss Evelyn Roberts, Porthmadog, daughter of the late Captain Hugh Roberts of the *Evelyn,* gave generously of her time in tracing photographs, paintings and documents, as did Mr. David Williams of Largs, Ayrshire, and Mrs. E. Edwards of Bangor, son and daughter of the late David Williams, the Porthmadog shipbuilder. Others in Porthmadog who have helped with both documents and photographs include Mr. Owen Lloyd, Mr. S. C. Evans, Messrs. Emrys and Ellis Jones, Criccieth, Mr. M. Morris and Dr. Jones Morris, Mr. Colin Langdown of the Garlandstone Maritime Museum, Mr. and Mrs. Williams, Tu Hwnt i'r Bwlch, and Miss Evans, daughter of the late Captain E. Evans, Arenig, Criccieth. I am grateful to Mrs. Evans and Miss Evans, Arenig, for allowing us to photograph again a number of the paintings in the fine collection of Porthmadog ships brought together by the late Captain E. Evans, paintings which were originally photographed by the late Emrys Hughes. Mr. Owen Jones of Old Windsor and Mr. H. Conway Jones of Southall, Middlesex, have written to me with interesting information about members of their family who sailed in Porthmadog ships, whilst Dr. Jürgen Meyer of Hamburg, and Mr. Grahame Farr of Bristol have very kindly sent me photographs from their own extensive collections, and Mr. R. S. Craig and Mr. Michael Bouquet have both made valuable suggestions, drawing upon their own extensive knowledge of maritime history. Mr. David R. MacGregor, the distinguished naval architect and historian, has generously given permission for the reproduction of the plans of the *M. A. James*, last to survive of the later Porthmadog vessels, based on surveys which he and Basil Greenhill first made of the vessel when she lay as a hulk in the Torridge river in 1948, and from later surveys which Mr. MacGregor himself made at Appledore in 1951 and 1954. Professor J. Darbyshire and Mrs. M. Prichard of the Department of Physical Oceanography at the U.C.N.W. have been most helpful; Professor Darbyshire has readily given information about his recent investigations in the Porth Neigwl (Hell's Mouth) area, and Mrs. M. Prichard has expertly re-drawn the Admiralty Surveys of 1836 and 1889 so that they can be included in this book. I am grateful to the Hydrographer of the Navy for permission to reproduce these surveys. My colleagues at Neuadd Reichel, Mr. A. Vardy of the Department of Plant Biology and Mr. Ifor Jones of the Department of Computing, U.C.N.W., have kindly prepared the statistical materials and advised on their presentation.

Mr. Geoffrey Charles of Bangor has visited Porthmadog and Criccieth several times to photograph paintings and prints of ships, and I am much indebted to him for his encouragement and interest; his infectious enthusiasm for old photographs and his own skill as a photographer makes working with him a considerable pleasure. It would be invidious to name any one member of the staff of the Gwynedd Archives Service, as almost all of them have from time to time helped to prepare this work for the press. In order that the book should be published to coincide with the maritime exhibition to mark the one hundred and fiftieth anniversary of the first year of working of the new harbour at Porthmadog, the Archives staff have frequently set aside their own work to help me. Mrs. Pauline Roberts and Mrs. Christine Owen, both of the Gwynedd Archives Service, have cheerfully undertaken the heavy task of typing the work, and I am very grateful to them, and to Mr. C. Charman and the staff of Gwasg Gee for their kind and ready assistance, and to Mr. Emrys Hughes, M.B.E., Llangefni, who has, at short notice, read the proofs and prepared the index. These good friends have made the publication possible, but I alone am responsible for any errors. Finally, it is appropriate that I should record my gratitude to Mr. Bryn R. Parry, County Archivist of Gwynedd, who first thought of publishing the Emrys Hughes MS., for his constant encouragement and interest; students of local history in Gwynedd have reason to be grateful to Mr. Parry and his staff, and I hope that this book will help, in however small a way, to assist them in their enthusiastic and devoted work of recovering and preserving the records of the past, and making them accessible to students of all ages and interest.

Neuadd Reichel, Bangor,
May 1975.

Porthmadog, 10 July 1876.

# I

# A MARITIME COMMUNITY

ON a calm morning in 1824 the smack *Two Brothers* was launched from the gently shelving beach known as Y Tywyn, amid the open fields of gorse. Directly opposite, across the River Glaslyn, was the small new pier being built for Mr. Madocks and the new wharf soon to be occupied by Samuel Holland. This strip of beach was later known to the people of Porthmadog as Canol y Clwt, and, later still, as Greaves Wharf, but on that day in 1824 it was the *Two Brothers* that caught the eye. Reputed to be the first vessel known as a Porthmadog ship, the *Two Brothers*, 65 tons, had been built for William Parry, mariner, who had 52/64 shares, Daniel Parry, farmer, who had 8/64 — they, presumably, were the two brothers — and David Hughes, slate loader, who had 4/64 shares in her. She was certainly not the first vessel to be built in the area, but as Madocks's first habour works which entitled the area to be called ' Port Madoc ' were not completed by 1824, she can be regarded as the first to bear the new port's name.

Between 1776 and 1824 at least nine sloops and one brigantine were built on the banks of the Dwyfor and ' Aberkin ', another eight sloops at Cricieth, a brigantine, the *Endeavour*, 87 tons, at Borthygest, three sloops at Tywyn, and seven sloops, two snows, two brigs and a brigantine at various sites on Traeth Mawr.[1] Across the bay, at Barmouth, as Dr. Lewis Lloyd, in the first of his series of monographs on the maritime history of Merioneth,[2] has indicated, there was a thriving shipbuilding industry on the Mawddach where well over two hundred vessels had been built, including at least sixty-five snow/brigs. To westward there was the even busier port of Pwllheli, where, between 1759 and 1824, another two hundred and sixty vessels had been built, though the total tonnage was less than that of the Mawddach. Therefore, with the scores of small coasting vessels of Nefyn, Caernarfon, Bangor, Conwy, Amlwch, Holyhead, and the small havens to the south in Cardigan Bay, there had been no shortage of local shipping, despite the French wars, to carry food and equipment for the hundreds of men employed on W. A. Madocks's great embankment scheme. The dramatic nature of Madocks's undertaking has been well told in Elizabeth Beazley's admirable biography of the romantic improver and planner, and his very capable agent, John Williams, Tu Hwnt i'r Bwlch, the Anglesey man who made a considerable contribution to the development of both Tremadog and Porthmadog. The letters which passed between Madocks and John Williams contain frequent references to the coastal vessels which brought, for example, iron rails made at Brymbo from Chester to Ynys Cyngar, gunpowder for blasting from Liverpool and London, timber and other building materials, as well as casks of pickled pork, beef, and herrings to feed the ravenous army of workmen employed on the vast improvement scheme.[3]

It was not a one-way traffic. Ellis Owen, Cefnymeusydd, farmer and antiquary, recorded in his diary for 1825 that in February he was at Tywyn — Port Madoc had not yet come into common usage — arranging for butter to be taken for the London market in the *Elizabeth*,[4] and a few months later he recorded an agreement with Captain Lewis Dedwith to take butter to the Thames, and again in September for Captain H. Davies to take butter, cheese, apples and honey to London in the *Elizabeth*. A month previously, in August 1825, Owen had noted in his diary the sorrow of the many widows and orphans in Tywyn and Tremadog following the loss of several local vessels, when seven of them had sought shelter off Fishguard, only to be driven ashore when the wind backed to the North-West. The *Eleanor* had been lost with all hands and so, too, had 'Evan Ellis y Fleece', of the well-known Tremadoc inn, and all his crew. Jean Lindsay, in her comprehensive *History of the North Wales Slate Industry*, has references to the letters from George Ford, a London slate agent, to his brother-in-law, William Turner, the North Wales quarry owner, in which Ford reported that he was sending furniture, cement, candles and soap by sea for 'Traeth', another of the pre-Portmadoc names.[5] The young Samuel Holland, another quarry owner, in his memoirs, recalled his early days before the harbour was built:

'I got the Quarry Roads improved, and got some of the Farmers to get *Waggons* instead of *Carts,* to carry the slates from the Quarry to the Wharf (*Pentrwyn y Garnedd*) that was near my Cottage from where they were boated to Port Madoc or to the vessels lying afloat in the River at Port Madoc (No quays were built at the Port, then). My father did not consider the Boats then in use of a good construction, so he had *two* built in Liverpool to carry more tonnage and these he sent round from L'pool, under the care of one old sailor, W. Jones — he brought the first that was ready. Then he walked back to Liverpool and brought the other. My father also had a small *sloop* to carry about 20 tons — built in Liverpool called the *Experiment.* This he had laden with wheaten flour and sent under the care of Will Jones and a boy to Port Madoc and up the Traeth to Trwyn y Garnedd where we had two warehouses — this was the first *Wheaten* Flour *imported* to the neighbourhood: other flour brought to the neighbourhood was by carts, over the mountain, from Llanrwst and Bala.'[6]

The building of the harbour at Porthmadog obviated the former practice of loading slates from small boats into larger vessels which lay in that uneasy anchorage at Ynys Cyngar, but the picturesque 'Philistines', as the boatmen of the Dwyryd were known, continued to bring slates by boat to the harbour until the building of the narrow gauge sailway, which they had violently opposed. With their tall black felt hats and knee breeches, the strong men who sailed their open boats from the wharf at Gelligrin made a powerful impression on their contemporaries. The completion of the first stage in building the harbour in 1824 coincided with a wave of speculation in the slate quarries of North Wales, the inevitable consequence of the increased slate prices, which had about doubled between 1798 and 1825. Daniel Morris, the new harbour master, recorded that from January 1 to March 31, 1825, 1,650 tons of slate were shipped by Turner and Company, 753 tons by Lord Newborough, and 741 tons by Holland and Company, whilst in the next three months the same companies shipped 1,285, 757 and 936 tons respectively.[7] Before the end of the year these companies had been joined, in the harbour master's entries for dues paid, by the Welsh Slate Company (whose chairman was Lord Palmerston), and 'Ellis Brondanw', and in all nearly 12,000 tons of slate were exported from the harbour in its first year of effective working.[8]

The building boom and the repeal of the slate tax in 1831 meant

M/531/20

Henry Jones
Ship Builder & owner Portmadoc

His Ship yard was on Canol y Clwt (Now the Greaves Wharf) Portmadoc. Canol y Clwt was situate on a part of Traeth Mawr known as "Y TOWYN". Before the harbour was built and before the Embankment was built this part of the Towyn sloped gently to the water's edge & formed an ideal beach for the building of ships – thus:–

— Rough —
— Sketch Plan —

LINE of DIVERSION
BONT NEWYDD SLUICE GATE
PORT of TRAETH MAWR (Now Llyn Bach)
YNYS TOWYN
OF THE RIVER GLASLYN
MAWR
YNYSTOWYN HOUSE
MADOC ST
A
B
BRIDGE
E
F
C
D
G
Y LONDON
the embankment
Y TOWYN
TRAETH
HOLLANDS WHARF
LINE of NEW WHARVES
CANOL Y CLWT BEACH
CREEK (Now the harbour)
ROTTEN TARE
PIER
CEI NEWYDD
TRWYN PIER
Y BEACH
PEN CEI
NEW COURSE of the GLASLYN

Canol y Clwt was doubtless a building slip before Henry Jones started operating there.

In order to provide for the diversion of the Glaslyn the part hatched A.B C.D. was cut away and the bridge E.F was built with a horizontal sluice which opened & closed automatically with the ebb & flow of the tides. This sluice proved unequal to the direct impact of the incoming tides & during 1848–52. Llyn Bach was built with Bont Newydd & the new sluice gates. Llyn Bach acted as a buffer against the incoming tides & the new vertical Sluice Gates were much more efficient. As the construction of the harbour developed Canol y Clwt was enclosed with the new wharves & ceased to be a ship yard round about 1860. The Pier for which Madocks got statutory power in the Act of 1821 has been built around a spit of Ynys Towyn that sloped down to the sea. Some of the rock can be seen to this day. For some years Trwyn Pier was a well known building slip. the "G.E. Spooner" was the last to be built there. The quay around Rotten Tare was extensively used for ship building later by David Jones & David Williams up to 1914.

P.T.O.

A page from Emrys Hughes's Notes.

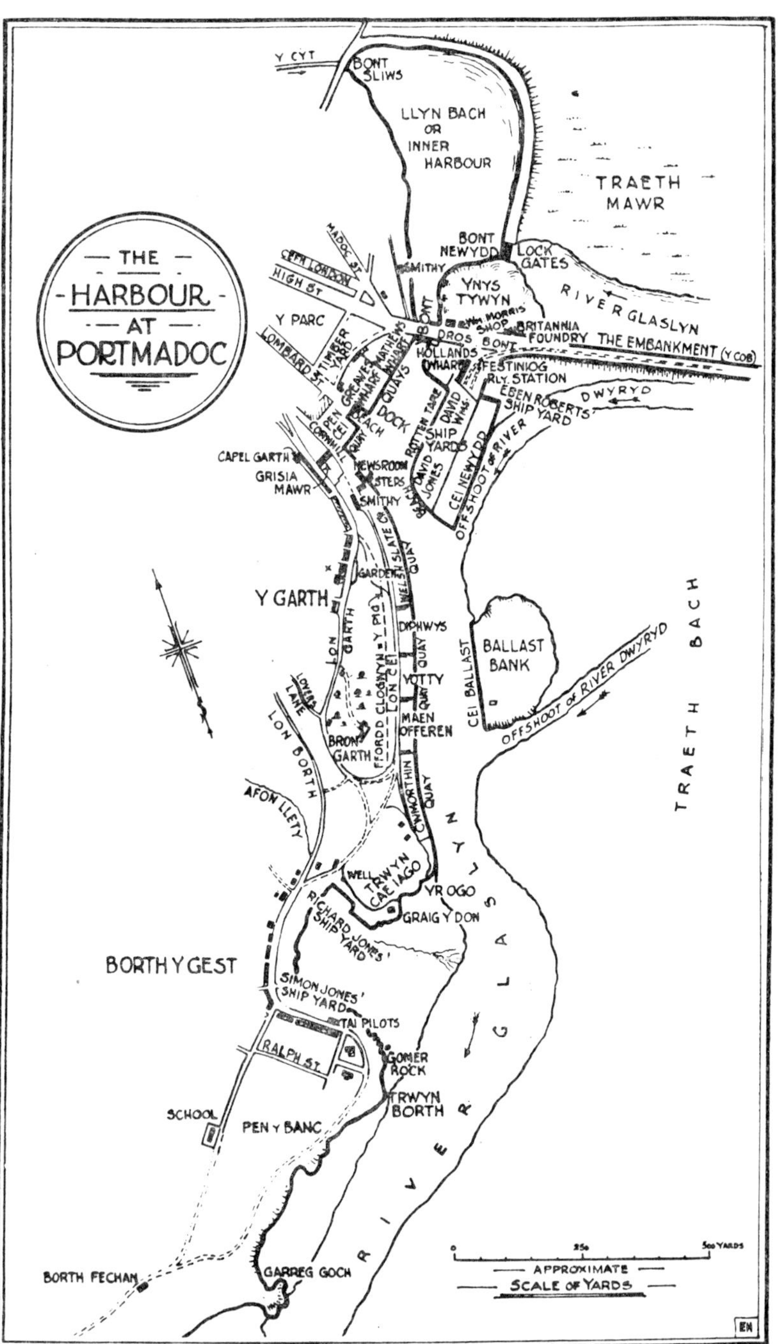
THE
HARBOUR
AT
PORTMADOC
Y CYT
BONT SLIWS
LLYN BACH OR INNER HARBOUR
TRAETH MAWR
BONT NEWYDD
LOCK GATES
RIVER GLASLYN
MADOC ST
CEFN LONDON
HIGH ST
SMITHY
YNYS TYWYN
Y PARC
BONT
Wm. MORRIS' SHOP
BRITANNIA FOUNDRY
THE EMBANKMENT (Y COB)
DROS BONT
LOMBARD ST
TIMBER YARD
MATHEWS WHARF
HOLLANDS WHARF
FESTINIOG RLY. STATION
DWYRYD
GREAVES WHARF
QUAYS
EBEN ROBERTS' SHIP YARD
PEN CEI
BEACH
DOCK
ROTTEN TAPE
DAVID Wms.
SHIP YARDS
CORNHILL
QUAY
OFFSHOOT of RIVER
CAPEL GARTH
GRISIA MAWR
NEWSROOM
STEPS
DAVID JONES
CEI NEWYDD
SMITHY
BEACH
SLATE Co.
GARDEN
WELSH SLATE QUAY
Y GARTH
LON GARTH
DIPHWYS
CLOGWYN Y PIOD
QUAY
LON CEI
YOTTY
LOVERS LANE
QUAY
BALLAST BANK
CEI BALLAST
TRAETH BACH
OFFSHOOT of RIVER DWYRYD
MAEN OFFEREN
LON BORTH
BRON GARTH
FFORDD
CWMORTHIN
QUAY
AFON LLETY
WELL
TRWYN CAE IAGO
YR OGO
GRAIG Y DON
RICHARD JONES' SHIP YARD
BORTH Y GEST
SIMON JONES' SHIP YARD
TAI PILOTS
RALPH ST
GOMER ROCK
TRWYN BORTH
SCHOOL
PEN Y BANC
RIVER GLASLYN
0
250
500 YARDS
APPROXIMATE
SCALE OF YARDS
BORTH FECHAN
GARREG GOCH
EN

that the slate industry entered upon a period of expansion, and although strongly opposed by the boatmen of the Dwyryd, the completion of the Ffestiniog Narrow Gauge Railway in 1836 ensured a busy future for Porthmadog. The stories of the development of the slate quarries and the remarkable engineering achievement involved in the building of the Ffestiniog Railway, now such a tourist attraction, have been told elsewhere; here it is sufficient to note that the tonnage of slates carried across Madocks's embankment from the Ffestiniog quarries to Porthmadog harbour increased from 4,275 tons in 1836 to 120,426 in 1882,[9] and inevitably this had a dramatic effect upon the development of the port.

Samuel Holland's Wharf, to which the new railway brought slates, had a monopoly for some two years, and then quays were built by the Welsh Slate Company, the Rhiwbryfdir Slate Company, and J. W. Greaves, all of them, unlike Holland, having 'To make wharves at their own expense and also pay Madocks Estate a high rent for them'.[10] The rapid expansion of the business of the port and the growing population brought new demands for imported goods — the removal of the duties on coal in 1830, for example, meant that, as a contemporary pointed out, instead of 'a cargo now and then, and that divided amongst the innkeepers, and a few resident gentlemen . . . instead of the 100 tons per annum before imported, 2,000 tons [annually] were discharged at this place in the years following'[11] the repeal of the tax. The registered tonnage of vessels in and out of the harbour increased from 10,075 tons in 1825 to 28,969 tons in 1845; for the most part these were comparatively small vessels engaged in the coastal trade.

At Canol y Clwt, Henry Jones and his son William built at least 30 sloops, representing a tonnage of 1,200 tons, in the period 1825-1860. By the thirties they were building larger schooners as well as the snow *Lord Palmerston,* built in 1828. The 32 barques, brigs and schooners built by Henry Jones, about 3,840 tons, and the 16 vessels, of about 900 tons, by his contemporary, Evan Evans, reflect the growing demand for larger vessels for the slate trade. The census returns for 1841, 1851 and 1861 indicate a growing number of inhabitants described as ship's carpenters, shipwrights and sailmakers; by 1851 there are entries relating to a ship builder employing eight men, a sailmaker employing eighteen men, a master ship carpenter employing five men, fourteen ship's carpenters living at Cornhill, right on the harbour, and then eight in Garth Terrace, six others and one apprentice in Holborn Street, another eight in Nailer's Square, and a ship smith in London Road employing two men and an apprentice. All these lived in the immediate vicinity of the port, but there is evidence that men were tramping in from the surrounding villages, and by 1856 Owen Morris, then a young man working in Samuel Holland's Wharf office, wrote that the shipbuilding industry of the port 'employs as many as 100 carpenters, joiners and smiths, and turns out from £20,000 to £25,000 worth of shipping property annually'. By 1861, in addition to those flocking in daily from both Caernarvonshire and Merioneth, there were close on ninety shipwrights, carpenters and riggers recorded on census night as living in Porthmadog itself, in Britannia Terrace, Wesley Street, Clog y Berth, Lombard Street, Cornhill, Garth Terrace, Ivy Terrace, and London Road.

The admissions register for children newly attending the National School at Porthmadog in 1867 again reflects the now busy life of the port;[12] in addition to the children of master mariners and seamen there are those whose fathers' occupation is given as 'Smith, Pen Quay', 'Sawyer, Foundry Place', 'Rigger, Madock Street' (whose child formerly attended the school at Pwllheli), 'Sailmaker, Britannia Place'. In the sixties the rapid increase in population created an increasing demand for schools; the Nonconformists replaced their first British School, established in 1838 on the present site of the Queen's Hotel, with a new building more convenient for the town and harbour, and among those who made donations towards its cost were William Jones, ship chandler, Captain Peter Jones, ship surveyor, Captain Thomas Jones, shipper, and Captain G. Griffiths, secretary of the Mutual Marine Insurance Society. The Anglicans established the Snowdon Street National School in 1857, and extended it in the sixties, partly because of the ever-increasing population and partly because of its enhanced reputation under the control of Mr. Richard Grindley, an autocratic schoolmaster who appears to have made a considerable impression on his contemporaries, his assistant teachers and his pupils. An enthusiastic report on the school in the seventies stated: 'As usual this school passed a brilliant examination. The Assistants, the Pupil Teachers and the pupils are perfectly under Mr. Grindley's control and therefore the tone and discipline are wonderful '.[13]

The population of Ynyscynhaiarn, which includes Porthmadog, Tremadog, Borth-y-gest and Morfa Bychan, increased from 2,347 in 1851 to 3,059 in 1861, 4,367 in 1871 and a peak of 5,506 in 1881.[14] There was then a slight but steady decline in subsequent decades. A glance at *Slater's Directory* for a few representative years indicates the development of the small business interests in Porthmadog alone.

| | 1829 | 1844 | 1859 | 1868 | 1880 | |
|---|---|---|---|---|---|---|
| Bakers ... ... ... | — | 2 | 2 | 2 | 2 | |
| Bankers ... ... ... | — | 2 | 3 | 3 | 3 | |
| Blacksmiths ... ... | 1 | 4 | 4 | 4 | 4 | |
| Block & Pump Makers ... | — | — | — | — | 4 | |
| Boot & Shoemakers ... | 2 | 4 | 6 | 10 | 14 | |
| Butchers ... ... ... | — | 2 | 6 | 7 | 13 | |
| Braziers & Tinmen ... | — | 2 | 2 | 3 | 2 | (and 7 iron- |
| Coal Dealers ... ... | — | 2 | 5 | 5 | 6 | mongers) |
| Corn & Flour Dealers ... | — | 2 | 2 | 3 | 4 | |
| Grocers & Druggists ... | — | 7 | 14 | 24 | 28 | |
| Joiners & Builders ... | — | 2 | 2 | 6 | 4 | |
| Ship Builders ... ... | 2 | 2 | 4 | 6 | 9 | |
| Ship Chandlers ... ... | 1 | 2 | 4 | 4 | 4 | |
| Slate Merchants & Agents | 6 | 8 | 8 | 14 | 17 | |
| Taverns & Public Houses | 5 | 7 | 8 | 14 | 22 | |
| Tailors ... ... ... | 1 | 4 | 7 | 10 | 8 | |

Between the twenties and late fifties, Porthmadog had developed from a small quay, a few cottages but 'still in a great measure a waste and overrun with gorse' to a town of about two hundred houses; shops, taverns, the harbour and the slate quays were visual evidence of the increasing prosperity of some of its inhabitants. But growth had not been achieved without cost. Owen Morris, writing in 1856, drew attention to the dangers to public health caused by 'the limited space allowed by the Trust Estate as background to the houses — not sufficient, in many instances, to afford room for the erection of privies, ashpits, and other adjuncts necessary to the comfort of a family', and also to the 'grasping avaricious spirit of a section of the Leaseholders, which while forming these damp undrained cellars as habitations, utterly neglected to provide privies etc. for the accommodation of the occupants — thereby causing the nauseous sights too familiar to the eyes and olfactory nerves of the inhabitants and others. On summer mornings the effluvia emmitted from the filthiness is most loathsome and disgusting'. Whilst Osmond and Marine Terraces were 'free from these incumbrances and beautifully clean', London Road and Cornhill were particularly bad. 'The majority of the houses composing London Road have cellars underneath used as dwellings, which are almost invaribly flooded in rainy weather', whilst at Cornhill 'part of the refuse there being thrown into the dock — and another, more economically, collected into an enclosure on the middle of the wharf, for the purpose of being used as manure — and to emit its noxious exhalations for the benefit of the passers by'. Morris recognized that Porthmadog had the problems of a new town which lacked a paternalistic aristocracy to initiate and regulate its gradual development.

> 'Portmadog being a comparatively new and advancing place, its population must necessarily present many of the phases peculiar to newly congragated communities which are generally without the infinity, diversity, and distinction of classes, so characteristic of the society of an old established town . . . The texture of the population of this place is very different — it has not had sufficient time to settle into such nice distinctions, and peculiarities. All of its classes being engaged in trade, and mixing in mutual intercourse — the boundary lines separating them are not easily traceable nor definable, and hence they have an appearance of cohesiveness and uniformity, not often observable in older communities'.[15]

Whilst he welcomed the classlessness — as much, that is, as one would expect from a young man who was obviously on the way to doing very well in the new community — Morris deplored the lack of initiative in improving the 'unpaved, undrained, and, until very recently, unlighted streets, and also the neglect shown of forming sanitary regulations for keeping the town in a decent and decorous aspect, and for the defence of Public Health'.

It was the age of improvement, and Morris's essay, *Portmadoc and its Resources,* intended for an eisteddfod competition in Salem Chapel, and published in 1856, did not go unheeded. In 1857 some forty of the inhabitants petitioned that an enquiry into the water supply, sewerage and drainage of Porthmadog and district be held.[16] Among those whose signatures are on the petition are many directly connected with the maritime interests of the port: John W. Greaves,

Tanyrallt, the quarry owner, David Homfray, Brecon Place, Thomas Christian, the sailmaker, who lived in Brougham Terrace, William Lloyd, draper, William E. Morris, Lombard Street, former harbour master, farmer and limestone dealer, Robert Morris, Samuel Holland's Wharf, William Owen, timber merchant, John Thomas, Greaves Slate Wharf, John Williams, ship smith, William Jones, Lloyd's Surveyor, William Barrow, harbour master, Edward Breese, Ynys-towyn, and the inn-keepers, Mary Evans, Ship Inn, Morris Jones, Blue Anchor, and David Jones, 'Austrilia [*sic*] House'. The report of the inspector, Alfred Dickens, subsequently confirmed Owen Morris's concern for public health standards, and drew attention to the fact that the number of deaths in the parish in 1855 was 87 compared with 34 in 1850. Evidence was given that many of the deaths in 1855 had been due to scarlet fever, and Mr. Jones, the medical officer, reported that he had known 'as many as twenty seven persons living in a six roomed house. This was one of the houses where the fever occurred'. The inspector recorded his gratitude to 'Mr. Morris, the superintendent of the port' for supplying him with the statistics of the annual slate exports from 1849 to 1856, showing an increase from 32,467 tons to 52,463 in the seven years. It was from the same source, no doubt, that he received information regarding the outward shipment of iron ore and other minerals, and the import of 'upwards of 3,500 tons of coal'. The report continued: 'No less than fourteen vessels were built at Portmadoc last year, and at present time there are from twelve to fifteen vessel on the stocks. Thirty new houses were built last year, and several others are now in course of erection'. Overcrowding, unpaved streets, unsatisfactory drainage — the evidence was conclusive, but it took some years to improve matters, and up to thirty before a satisfactory supply of water was brought to the town from Lake Tecwyn. Little wonder that however hard life at sea was, many a mariner breathed deeply and thankfully when once his ship had cleared the Bar, making for the open sea and good fresh air.

The doubling of Porthmadog's population again between 1851 and 1881 reflected the two main factors in the town's development, slate exports and ship building. From 1825 to 1880 it was much cheaper to roof with slates than with tiles; the growth of towns and the construction of railways created a steady demand for slate both in Britain and abroad. By mid-century the slate quarries of Ffestiniog were producing over 50,000 tons of slate a year, and much of it was still going to the home trade. The prizes won by Greaves at the Great Exhibition in 1851 and by Samuel Holland in the 1854 Paris Exhibition indicated that Porthmadog merchants were aiming at wider markets. The Australian gold-rush of 1851 and the rapid growth of Melbourne, for example, had its repercussion on Porthmadog, and Owen Morris, in 1856, recorded that 'In 1852, 1853 and 1854, large quantities [of slate] were forwarded from Portmadoc to Melbourne, Geelong etc. by way of Liverpool where they were reshipped into the Australian liners'. Slate exports to America, in which at least one Porthmadog ship, Captain Richard Prichard's *Gomer*, had been engaged as early as the twenties, had fluctuated considerably, but the most significant increase in exports had been to the European market. Welsh slate had been effectively kept out of the French market by tariffs — in 1859, for example, only 103 tons of slate were shipped from Porthmadog to France — but from 1842 there had been a steady growth in the quantity exported to Germany, where there were no tariff barriers.[17] In May 1842 a great fire destroyed over 2,000 houses in Hamburg, and Mr. Mathews, owner of the Rhiwbryfdir quarry, is said to have gone there shortly afterwards and persuaded the city architect of Hamburg to substitute Porthmadog slate for the Penrhyn slate which had been selected for roofing the new public buildings.[18] Despite a temporary set back during the year of revolutions in 1848, the demand for Welsh slate on the Continent increased steadily until the mid sixties when there was a dramatic surge in demand. The total value of exports of Welsh slate to Western Europe rose from about £5,000 in 1866 to £226,000 to Germany alone in 1876.[19] The Cobden treaty of 1860 substantially reduced the high tariffs on slates to France, and the almost prohibitive duties which had been in force in Norway, Sweden, and Denmark were also repealed, thus bringing about a considerable expansion in the slate exports to these countries. But it was to Germany that the bulk of the trade of Porthmadog now went. The development of the German railway and canal systems meant that slates exported in Porthmadog ships to Hamburg and the other German ports were then transported into central and southern Europe.

The development of shipbuilding and shipping in Porthmadog

in its second phase must be seen, therefore, against the backcloth of the very special relationship with the ports of Germany and the Baltic. Competition in transporting slates for the home market from the railways, which had come to Port Penrhyn (Bangor) in 1848, and to Port Dinorwic and Caernarfon in 1852 — thus challenging the shipping of the Menai Straits — did not reach Porthmadog until 1867, and by that time the German trade was in full swing. Throughout the fifties there had been a steady stream of vessels leaving the yards at Porthmadog, about four or five each year from 1848 to 1855. In 1856, 12 vessels, representing a tonnage of 1,085 tons, were launched, 7 in 1857, of about 760 tons, 8 in 1858, a little over 800 tons, then on an average about 4 annually until 1877 when 10 were built, amounting to over 1,600 tons, and 1878 when 8 more, 1,073 tons, left the blocks. In all, 146 vessels were built at Porthmadog and Borth-y-gest between 1848 and 1878, amounting to a registered tonnage of 18,606 tons.[20]

The young Owen Morris, working in the offices of Samuel Holland, obviously knew the harbour well and rightly concluded that the growth of the shipbulding industry was of the utmost importance, 'its influences ramifying through the whole community and its interest bearing on the well-being and comfort of every class'. He estimated that the shipping belonging to the port in 1856 amounted to the value of approximately £125,000, 'the greatest part of which is owned by the industrial and labouring classes, a fact we have great pleasure in noticing'. Recognizing that the shipping industry was firmly linked with the demand for ships to export Ffestiniog slate, he correctly anticipated the significant growth of the next twenty years:

> 'The opening and increasing productiveness of the Festiniog Quarries created a demand for shipping to carry away their produce, and as every inducement and facility were offered for the building of vessels, and those already built returning such handsome profits (some of them as much as 25 per cent annually on the capital invested in years when trade was brisk), these causes combined to advance the tonnage and value of their property [i.e. shipping] to what they are at present. About £25,000 is annually added to it, and it will, undoubtedly be doubled in a few years hence. Though chiefly employed in conveying slates to English and foreign ports, a great part of its revenue is derived from *back* freight. Besides

1. Porthmadog harbour, 1850; the bow of a vessel neari ng completion at Henry Jones's yard, left of picture, with Holland's Wharf, Slip and Ynys Towyn, centre. [Lithograph, C. F. Williams, 1850.]

2. An early schooner, the *Independent,* Captain Hugh Roberts, senior, and th
sloop *Star,* 1849.

3. Brig *Mary Holland,* built Henry Jones 1843, entering the port of Trieste.

4. Borth-y-gest one hundred years ago from Tai Pilots. In foreground, fishing boat *Pearl,* belonging to John Williams, pilot, and smack *Endeavour,* lying with list to starboard. Across the bay, Richard Jones's building slip with scaffolds showing, and slipway at Craigydon extreme right.

5. Borth-y-gest, looking towards Tai Pilots. *c.* 1900. Simon Jones's vessels had been built on right, near sheds, in photograph (present day parking ground).

14. Grisia' Mawr, Pen Cei/Cornhill, Porthmadog. In this area were ship-broker sail-lofts, William Griffiths's 'navigation school', News Room, and offices of Port madog Mutual Ship Insurance Society.

15. Tug *Wave of Life,* outside the Bar.

16. S.S. *Rebecca* (2) bound Liverpool to Porthmadog [1895, W. H. Yorke].

17. Porthmadog harbour *c.* 1910: left to right, *Edith Eleanor, C. E. Spooner, Wa*
*of Life* and *Elizabeth Pritchard.*

18. David Williams, shipbuilder, Porthmadog.

> enriching the place by its returns, the expenditure of the shipping in repairing, provisioning etc. is considerable — thus proving a resource in a double sense '.[21]

It is perhaps not altogether surprising that with such a shrewd appraisal of the situation, within two years of penning the above words Owen Morris had left his work as a clerk, set himself up in a slate shipping partnership, and steadily began to take shares in the ships being built, eventually taking over the management of some of the most notable vessels of the port.

Working through the Registers of Shipping one soon recognizes the truth of Owen Morris's contention that the ownership of Porthmadog ships was widely spread throughout the community, particularly in the early years. Farmers and quarrymen from the surrounding villages took shares often enough in vessels commanded by their fathers or brothers in much the same way as did the communities around Barmouth, Pwllheli, Nefyn, Caernarfon, Port Penrhyn, Port Dinorwic, Amlwch, and Holyhead. In each of the North Wales ports, however, there was usually a core of master mariners, shipbuilders and a few business men whose energy, enterprise and adventurousness provided the driving force in the development of the shipbuilding programme. This becomes apparent again from the Registers of Shipping: at Amlwch, the Treweeks and Captain William Thomas and his sons; at Bangor, John Parry, Edward Ellis and T. T. Parry; at Pwllheli, William Jones; at Nefyn, Hugh Roberts, the Griffith family and Robert Thomas; at Port Dinorwic, Rees Jones and his son, W. E. Jones, both of whom were significant figures with influence in the ports of North Wales from Barmouth to Holyhead and Bangor. Porthmadog, which had entered the race to build ships somewhat later than the other ports, had inevitably a stronger representation of ' spirited proprietors ' from the slate quarries, but it too had its key men from among the maritime community.

Captain Richard Prichard was surely one of the founders of this maritime community. Born in 1783 at Tŷ Gwyn y Gamlas, Ynys, Llanfihangel y Traethau, across on the Harlech side of the estuary, he sailed the snow-rigged *Gomer,* built at Traeth Bach in 1821, on regular voyages with slates and emigrants to New York in the twenties and thirties. Details of the *Gomer* (built to replace an earlier snow, the *New Liberty,* also built at Traeth Bach in 1810 and sold to

Limerick in 1821) were advertised to intending emigrants thus: 'Brig Gomer (Rd. Prichard, Master), 158 tons, now lying at Portmadoc ballasted with about 100 tons of slates intended to convey to New York 54 adults, 16 under 14 and 24 under 7 years of age: Navigate with 9 men'.[22] The emigrants took their chance, bedding down in the straw amid the slate. There were rumours that Captain Prichard had exceeded the number of emigrants he was allowed to take, but his reputation was high, and the emigrants continued to strive to get aboard the *Gomer*. By 1835 Captain Prichard had come ashore and was in business in Porthmadog; there is the oft repeated story of how, as a good Methodist, he was converted to the cause of temperance and, repenting of carrying porter over from Ireland, and as an earnest of his new-found zeal, he poured a barrel of porter into the streets where a neighbour's sow drank long and deep, and was never sober again. Captain Prichard himself was sober enough to be entrusted with the management of the new National and Provincial Bank at his own premises in Lombard Street, just off the harbour, where for the next twenty years he did much to develop and encourage the shipping interests of the rapidly growing port. He went to sea again in 1855 at the ripe old age of seventy-two, and died in a Californian port.[23] His son-in-law, William Pritchard, and the latter's brother Griffith established themselves as successful shipbrokers in Porthmadog. The Registers of Shipping provide evidence that there were other bankers who played an important part in the development of the port during and after Captain Prichard's days — the Casson brothers had a bank in the house later occupied by the Pritchard brothers at Pen Cei and then in High Street, whilst Hugh Pugh and Robert Jones's names appear in many of the later ship ownership transactions as bank managers advancing mortgages when ships were newly built.

Among the earlier generation, Henry Jones and Evan Evans, the shipbuilders, Captain Daniel Morris, the harbour master, who before his death in 1840 had seen a considerable increase in the number of vessels in and out of the harbour, Thomas Lewis, ropemaker, William Owen, the pilot, Thomas Christian, sailmaker, and William Lloyd, ship chandler, all played important parts in developing the port. The actual date of William Griffith's arrival at Porthmadog to teach navigation is uncertain, but he was sufficiently well established to be the only name under 'Academies and Schools' in *Slater's Directory* for 1844. He had seen service in the Royal Navy, and must have been quite a character for he was still remembered with affection many years later for his cork-leg, his bachelor independence, the hammock in which he always slept, slung from the roof beams, the strongly made slippers he wore, the all-pervading aroma of fried herrings and onions, his favourite dish, and the navigation and seamanship lessons he held, first of all in a room near the foot of Grisia Mawr, the steep steps leading to Pen Cei, and later in the schoolroom of Berea Chapel in Terrace Road.[24] Then there were the successful master mariners, men like Captain David Richards, senior, who came from Barmouth to live at Trwyn Cae Iago, and financed the building of many ships, and Captain David Morris (grandfather of Henry and Emrys Hughes), who commanded the aptly named sloop *Success* in the forties.

It was in 1841 that the vital step of forming the Portmadoc Mutual Ship Insurance Society was taken. Like similar societies established in small ports around the coasts of Britain, this Society was formed in the first place to enable its members to insure their vessels at less expensive rates than those charged by the large London companies, and it is reasonable to suppose that the prime movers were men like Samuel Holland and J. W. Greaves, the slate quarry owners, Captain Richard Prichard, the banker, the shipbuilders and the leading master mariners. Although the other ports had a longer tradition of shipbuilding, Porthmadog was the first in North Wales to have such a society, a venture in which three hundred and twenty Porthmadog people formed a 'Society of persons, interested in ships and vessels belonging to the harbour of Portmadoc, employed in the coasting trade, upon the principle of mutually bearing one another's burdens' which 'would enable the members of the society to effect insurance upon their ship property, upon a more reasonable rate than they had heretofore effected their insurance, and would be beneficial the shipping interest, navigation and commerce of the harbour of Portmadoc'.[25] It was this Society that ensured regular surveys of Porthmadog vessels, thereby maintaining standards of seaworthiness, and made certain that the vessels were commanded by competent masters, examined by experienced members of Porthmadog's maritime community, and this some years before the Merchant Shipping Act of 1854 attempted to provide nationally accepted standards of competency. Fifteen years after its founding, in 1856, Owen Morris reported that the Society's 'premiums have not been above 2 per cent yearly on an average, while from 5 to 7 per cent is exacted by London and other offices. Property to the amount of £100,000 is now insured in it. It has been of very great benefit to the shipping interest affording indemnification for sudden losses, thus giving a desirable stability to this property, which has had a marked effect on its progress. By this influence in increasing its means of communication, the commerce of the place has also been materially benefited. The Society has extended its advantage to Pwllheli and Barmouth — vessels from these ports being insured by it on the same footing, and their owners allowed the same privileges as those of Portmadoc'.[26]

Morris himself, after leaving Holland's office and becoming a partner with Richard Williams in the Slate Works, is probably the man of that name who was a member of the Society's committee and acted as its auditor for a number of years, whilst his former employer, Samuel Holland, always made an effort to preside at the annual meetings of the Society. On 30 January 1865, for example, at the Town Hall, Porthmadog, Holland reported to the Annual General Meeting that the value of vessels insured with the Society was about £130,000, that during the preceding year, including part of the winter of 1863, nine vessels had been lost and twenty-four sustained damage, but eleven new vessels had been received into the Society 'and those of a larger and more valuable class than those lost'. At this meeting Holland proposed that all vessels should be revalued every two years, and this was accepted, together with new bye laws regarding loading and discharging cargoes in winter in Gibraltar Bay, the Mediterranean, the coast of Africa, the Madeiras, Canaries, or Cape Verde Islands. In all, 153 vessels were listed as being insured with the Society on 1 April 1865, and the committee, which now numbered fifty-three (including twenty-nine master mariners), appointed Captain Peter Jones, junior, as their surveyor, twelve additional surveyors at Porthmadog (including five master mariners), two at Barmouth, one at Pwllheli, and one at Port Dinorwic.[27] On 31 January 1868, at the Society's meeting at the News Room, Porthmadog, Holland reported that the value of shipping

## SHIPS BUILT AT PORTHMADOG

| Period | Rig | No. of Ships | Total Tun. | Ave. Tun. |
|---|---|---|---|---|
| 1826-30 | Sp | 8 | 291 | 36.4 |
| | Sn | 1 | 137 | 137.0 |
| | Wh | 1 | 19 | 19.0 |
| | Sr | 1 | 92 | 92.0 |
| TOTALS | | 11 | 539 | 49.00 |
| 1831-35 | Sp | 10 | 313 | 31.3 |
| | Sr | 1 | 92 | 92.0 |
| TOTALS | | 11 | 405 | 36.82 |
| 1836-40 | Sp | 4 | 153 | 38.3 |
| | Sr | 16 | 1468 | 91.8 |
| | Sm | 2 | 87 | 43.5 |
| TOTALS | | 22 | 1708 | 77.64 |
| 1841-45 | Sp | 2 | 112 | 56.0 |
| | Sr | 8 | 607 | 75.9 |
| | Sm | 8 | 338 | 42.3 |
| | Bg | 2 | 506 | 253.0 |
| TOTALS | | 20 | 1563 | 78.15 |
| 1846-50 | Sr | 10 | 920 | 92.0 |
| | Sm | 8 | 313 | 39.1 |
| | Bg | 1 | 171 | 171.0 |
| | Bk | 2 | 700 | 350.0 |
| | Dy | 1 | 48 | 48.0 |
| TOTALS | | 22 | 2152 | 97.82 |
| 1851-55 | Sr | 18 | 1568 | 87.1 |
| | Sm | 4 | 208 | 52.0 |
| TOTALS | | 22 | 1776 | 80.73 |
| 1856-60 | Sr | 32 | 3136 | 98.0 |
| | Sm | 2 | 82 | 41.0 |
| | Bg | 1 | 162 | 162.0 |
| | Bgn | 1 | 177 | 177.0 |
| TOTALS | | 36 | 3557 | 98.81 |
| 1861-65 | Sr | 7 | 807 | 115.3 |
| | Bg | 4 | 712 | 178.0 |
| | Bgn | 7 | 1055 | 150.7 |
| TOTALS | | 18 | 2574 | 143.00 |
| 1866-70 | Sr | 11 | 1345 | 122.3 |
| | Bg | 6 | 1205 | 200.8 |
| | Bk | 1 | 287 | 287.0 |
| | Bgn | 3 | 452 | 150.7 |
| TOTALS | | 21 | 3289 | 156.62 |
| 1871-75 | Sr | 6 | 776 | 129.3 |
| | Bg | 5 | 1075 | 215.0 |
| | Bk | 1 | 402 | 402.0 |
| | Bgn | 3 | 421 | 140.3 |
| TOTALS | | 15 | 2674 | 178.27 |
| 1876-80 | Sr | 10 | 1170 | 117.0 |
| | Bg | 5 | 1042 | 208.4 |
| | Bgn | 1 | 175 | 175.0 |
| | Bkn | 5 | 1097 | 219.4 |
| | Sr3 | 3 | 522 | 174.0 |
| | Cr | 1 | 7 | 7.0 |
| TOTALS | | 25 | 4013 | 160.52 |
| 1881-85 | Sr | 1 | 99 | 99.0 |
| TOTALS | | 1 | 99 | 99.0 |
| 1891-95 | Sr | 1 | 130 | 130.0 |
| | Sr3 | 12 | 1606 | 133.8 |
| | K | 1 | 70 | 70.0 |
| TOTALS | | 14 | 1806 | 129.00 |
| 1896-1900 | Sr3 | 6 | 737 | 122.8 |
| TOTALS | | 6 | 737 | 122.83 |
| 1901-05 | Bkn | 1 | 144 | 144.0 |
| | Sr3 | 8 | 1021 | 127.6 |
| TOTALS | | 9 | 1165 | 129.44 |
| 1906-10 | Sr3 | 5 | 487 | 97.4 |
| TOTALS | | 5 | 487 | 97.4 |
| 1911-13 | Sr3 | 1 | 98 | 98.0 |
| TOTALS | | 1 | 98 | 98.0 |

then insured was £162,000 and warned that one vessel had been lost during the year through negligence, so that it was not perhaps surprising that the meeting passed a resolution tightening the rules regarding the examination and appointment of new masters. The number of vessels insured on 1 January 1868 was 168, at a valuation of £162,000;[28] in 1871 the report stated the insurable value of the Society on 31 December 1870 was £180,578, that the nine vessels lost and paid for during the year amounted to £7,450.14.7, that a deduction of £12,775 had had to be made in the revaluation of ships for 1871, but that as nineteen new vessels were insured at £18,570.3.4, the Society's insurable value amounted to £178,922.4.9. By the following year, the number of vessels insured was 192, with a tonnage of 18,638 and valued at £243,240.[29] The sailing limits for vessels were amended and extended as the years went by, but, unlike the many North Wales mutual marine societies which had been established subsequently, the Porthmadog Society reiterated in 1880 the rule that 'no ship or vessel should be insured with the Society unless the owner or some part owner thereof interested therein to the extent of one fourth part or upwards shall reside within 15 miles from Portmadoc'. The mutual marine insurance societies established at Bangor in 1853, 1870, 1874 and 1881, and at Nefyn in 1857, 1866, 1868, 1872 and 1880, all accepted membership from as far afield as the Clyde, Aberdeen, Liverpool and London.[30] Although the capital involved in the six separate societies at Nefyn in 1876 amounted to two million pounds, Porthmadog owners preferred to keep their Society within the limits which they themselves could supervise and control effectively. In 1866 a second Society was formed at Porthmadog called the North Wales Mutual Ship Collision Insurance Society which insured owners against losses and damage to other vessels, 'third party risks', although in this case membership was extended to vessels belonging to any North Wales port. In January 1875 the Gomerian Freight and Outfit Mutual Ship Insurance Society was formed at Porthmadog: in 1884 120 vessels were insured with this Society.

Nine years later, in 1893, at the beginning of the final phase in the port's building programme, the period of the Western Ocean Yachts, the hundred or so vessels insured are almost all Porthmadog ships. The names of the committee members of the Society for that year suggest the impressive wealth of experience brought to their meetings — and, indeed, to those of all the Porthmadog mutual marine insurance societies — as they deliberated carefully on each claim brought before them at the News Room on Pen Cei. There were the senior master mariners of the port, men like Captain David Morris, Ceylon Villa, sometime master of the *Pride of Wales;* Captain Hugh Parry, Borth-y-gest, the leading shipbroker at Cornhill, at the foot of Grisia Mawr, sometime master of the *George Casson* and the *Frau Minna Petersen,* and father of three master mariners; Captains John Jones, Morris Jones and David Richards, High Street; the very experienced old shipbuilder, Ebenezer Roberts; the shipbrokers, William Pritchard and Griffith Pritchard, now secretary of the Society; Captain Morgan Jones, another shipowner; and a newcomer, Dr. J. H. Lister, the wealthy Barmouth shipowner who had just acquired his first Porthmadog three-masted schooner, the *Jenny Jones,* named after the daughter of his most experienced master mariner-adviser, Captain Evan Lewis Jones of Pen y Cei, Barmouth. Then there were other master mariners, all of them, however, greatly experienced, men like Captains Hugh Roberts, Evan Jones, Owen Morris, John Ellis, David Richards, Dora Street, some of whom attended the meetings when they had a spell home, leaving much of the day-to-day business to the veterans who had come ashore and the shipbrokers. There was a remarkable sense of continuity in the meetings of the societies as the succeeding generations took over their administration, son following father, nephew following uncle. They were dealing with ships they had seen built and about which they knew every detail, commanded by men whom they had grown up with and served with at sea.

One or two brief examples from the minute-books must suffice by way of illustration.[31] Shortly after the *Elizabeth Pritchard* had been completed in David Williams's yard in 1898 there was a meeting of the Gomerian Freight and Outfit Mutual Insurance Society, with Captain Hugh Parry in the chair, and Captains Hugh Roberts, Owen Morris, and David Richards, and Messrs. William Pritchard the broker, Ebenezer Roberts and David Williams, shipbuilders, Thomas Jones and David Lloyd present. As she had been built by David Williams, it was appropriate that it should be another shipbuilder, the vastly experienced Ebenezer Roberts, who proposed that the

*Elizabeth Pritchard* should be accepted for the insurance of her freight. This was seconded by Captain David Richards and passed unanimously. Another vessel proposed on the same day, however, was not admitted as she had not been classed. Masters who survived the loss of their vessels had to appear before a meeting of the committee. On 24 February 1899, with Captain Hugh Roberts in the chair on this occasion, the master of the *Laura* appeared before them. He 'gave a verbal report of the way this vessel was lost in Fishguard Bay . . . and after the usual questions having been asked and replied, it was proposed by Captain John Jones and seconded by Captain Morgan Jones that the report be accepted unanimously' At this same meeting the master of the *Nanhoron* 'also appeared before the Committee and gave a verbal report of the loss of the vessel on Wanjeroog' in the previous January, and in this case it was Captain Morgan Jones and Mr. Ebenezer Roberts who proposed and seconded that the report be accepted unanimously. Membership of the committees of the Porthmadog marine insurance societies carried with it considerable prestige in the essentially maritime community, and not without reason, for these were the men who influenced the appointment of masters and controlled much of the business of the port. The election of the secretaries was also a matter of considerable significance. In February 1877, as the boom period for slates and shipbuilding was ending, a meeting was held at the Assembly Rooms, Porthmadog, to fill the vacancies caused by the resignation of Captain Griffith Griffiths as Secretary of both the Porthmadog Ship Insurance Society and the North Wales Mutual Protection Society. Captain Griffiths, according to the local newspaper, 'had held these offices and previously the office of surveyor for the Society for nearly twenty years, the duties of which offices he discharged with great credit to himself, and with advantage to the Societies'. The secretaryship of the Ship Insurance Society was worth about £130 per annum, and the North Wales Mutual Protection Society £30. Although nine candidates had submitted their names, only three of them were, by the rules of the Society, eligible to stand for election. They were Captain Robert Williams of Merioneth, Captain David Morris, who had now left the *Success* for the *Royal Charter*, and Cadwaladr Williams, ship broker.

'The election occasioned much excitement, and the electorate came together in a great number, there being from one hundred and ninety to two hundred electors present. The election was conducted with great regularity by ballot, Mr. David Homfray, solicitor, being the presiding officer. For the secretaryship of the North Wales Mutual Protection Society, there were two candidates, viz. Mr. Edward Jones, High Street, Portmadoc, assistant secretary to Captain G. Griffiths, and Mr. Griffith Pritchard, broker, Portmadoc. The result was as follows. For the Secretaryship of the Ship Insurance Society, 1. Captain Robert Williams, 83 votes; 2. David Morris, 57 votes; 3. Cadwaladr Williams 49 votes. For the Secretaryship of North Wales Protection Society, 1. Mr. Edward Jones 145 votes; 2. Mr. Griffith Pritchard 45 votes'.[32]

The tighter, more localised control which Porthmadog's maritime community exercised over its mutual marine insurance societies was not, however, the only difference between them and their counterparts in other parts of North Wales. As already indicated, the late sixties and early seventies were years of expansion in the slate quarries of North Wales. There was more money about; it was no accident that the North Wales Quarrymen's Union was formed in 1874, and as their officials claimed in May 1875 'more by upwards of £150,000 has been paid in wages last year in the slate quarries of North Wales than in any other year'.[33] This new-found, albeit brief, affluence among the quarrymen and the shopkeepers and tradesmen who depended on them, coincided with the equally short-lived boom in the building of large sailing vessels in Britain. The opening up of the wheatlands of the American West, and the dramatic growth of the Aremican grain trade after 1874, led to a demand for shipping at a time when the American Civil War had made severe inroads into the American mercantile marine, and encouraged optimism among British shipowners. The obvious financial success of the Davies family of Menai Bridge and William Thomas, the Anglesey-born shipbroker, in Liverpool encouraged people of a wide range of occupational groups in Gwynedd to form companies to purchase large iron sailing ships built at Liverpool and Sunderland.[34] Thus the Gwynedd Shipping Company, based largely on Caernarfon, Llanberis and Port Dinorwic, the Eryri Shipping Company and the Arvon Shipping Company came into existence. Quarrymen, shopkeepers, inn-keepers, accountants, school teachers, ministers of the Gospel and their wives, spinsters — all were tempted to 'have a flutter' by investing in the risky venture of large iron sailing ships, commanded and managed by their countrymen, hoping for quicker and larger profits than those they could expect from the smaller local vessels, in which they had traditionally taken one or two sixty-fourth shares. The investors in William Thomas's ships and those of the Nefyn and Caernarfon based shipping companies came from all parts of North Wales and Liverpool, but in going through the names on their registers it is unusual to find many from Porthmadog. At a time when the building of ships was rapidly drawing to its close in all the other North Wales ports (except Amlwch), when their inhabitants were investing hopefully in 'foreign' built, large iron ships, the maritime community at Porthmadog appear to have decided that they had more faith in the future of their own wooden built vessels, their own shipbuilders, their own master mariners, and their own slate trade with Germany and the Baltic. It is probable, too, that they had already stretched their resources to the limit in meeting the demand for ships for the expanded German trade — between 1860 and 1878 no fewer than 83 vessels had been built at Porthmadog and Borth-y-gest, a crushingly heavy commitment for any small community, however energetic and enterprising.

1873 was the year when the highest tonnage of slate was exported by sea from Porthmadog, and although the Cambrian Railway between Barmouth and Pwllheli, which was completed in 1867, now provided an alternative source of transport, nearly 850 vessels entered and left the port annually in the early seventies. In 1875, 670 vessels, amounting to a registered tonnage of 61,066 tons, were recorded as having paid slate dues; the monthly totals indicate that a definite pattern had been established with most vessels leaving with cargoes in March, April, and May, the larger vessels no doubt intending to proceed from the German ports on a round voyage which would bring them back to Porthmadog about Christmas. There was a steady outward trade in the summer months, and a marked decline in November, December and January.

| | *Vessels* | *Tonnage* |
|---|---|---|
| January ... ... ... ... | 36 | 3,019 |
| February ... ... ... | 50 | 4,498 |
| March ... ... ... ... | 70 | 6,846 |
| April ... ... ... ... | 69 | 6,693 |

| | Vessels | Tonnage |
|---|---|---|
| May ... ... ... ... | 67 | 5,593 |
| June ... ... ... ... | 59 | 5,245 |
| July ... ... ... ... | 61 | 6,160 |
| August ... ... ... ... | 61 | 5,038 |
| September ... ... ... | 49 | 4,486 |
| October ... ... ... | 58 | 5,292 |
| November ... ... ... | 48 | 4,504 |
| December ... ... ... | 42 | 3,690 |
| Total ... ... | 670 | 61,066 |

Details of the little steamship *Rebecca* are included in Emrys Hughes's account, and the impact of her arrival each week on the life of the port is well told in Henry Hughes's *Immortal Sails*. The *Rebecca*'s 'general cargo', mainly groceries, flour, offals, timber and machinery, was destined not only for Porthmadog merchants but also for the surrounding districts, and as she came alongside, the 'hobblers' rushed aboard, and the horses and carts jostled together awaiting their turn to take goods for the shopkeepers of Tremadog, Pentrefelin, Penmorfa, Cricieth, Morfa Bychan, Borth-y-gest and Llanfrothen. The late Professor J. Glyn Davies, who spent his early life working in the office of Thomas Williams's *Cambrian* line in Liverpool, remembered the *Rebecca* well:

> 'I was seasick every time I sailed on her, but I could not keep off her, for she was bound for Lleyn, and that was enough for me. She rolled horribly, even with sails set on a beam wind. I remember her in Bardsey Sound with the wind more or less aft, and the sails no good for steadying her . . . I was see-sawing on my legs aft and trying to calculate the angle of her list. She had an uncomfortable cabin, with pews ranged round and right above the propellor. She looked very small in the Trafalgar Half-tide Dock in Liverpool, but when I went over her side in Aberdaron Bay on a rope hand over hand down to a leaping boat below, she looked like a Cunarder. I have one or two of the *Rebecca*'s passenger tickets amongst my papers . . . first saloon, Liverpool to Pwllheli, 5/-. Second class passengers made for the galley and snoozed on the bench there. Her successor, *Rebecca* No. 2, was a fine boat with a comfortable cabin and bunks in swell state rooms. The master of both *Rebecca*s, Captain Roberts was a dignified man, and rather taciturn'.[35]

The connection between Liverpool and Porthmadog was long established. Samuel Holland's father's first vessel, the *Experiment*, has already been mentioned; in the trade directories of the 1840s the *Miss Madocks*, the *New Dove*, the *Alert*, and the *John and William* were described as regular weekly traders to Liverpool. The first three were still named in 1859, but by 1864 the *Rebecca* had taken over, and in the 1880 edition of *Slater's Directory* she is described as sailing to Liverpool from Porthmadog every Monday. The substantial decline in demand for slate in 1878, which resulted in the temporary halt in shipbuilding in Porthmadog, coincided with the retirement of a number of the pioneers of early Porthmadog — both Samuel Holland, who had been Liberal Member of Parliament for Merioneth since 1870, and Major Edward Windus Mathews, whose father had started the slate connection with Germany, retired in 1878. There were, however, a number of businessmen who had done well during the boom years who now had substantial holdings and influence among the maritime community, among them William Jones, 'Yr Yard', sailmaker and son of Henry Jones, the first shipbuilder; William Pritchard, Cornhill, and Bennett Williams, shipbrokers; Hugh Jones and Thomas Lewis, block makers; William Lloyd, 5 Lombard Street; Thomas Lloyd, Cornhill; Owen Morris, slate shipper; and David Morris, Britannia Terrace, ship chandler. The chandler's account books, which give such a wealth of information about the port, will be referred to again in connection with individual ships, but in passing it is worth noting that over 30 vessels had work carried out by Jones and Morris, the sailmakers, in the first three months of 1875; in the 1888-1891 ledgers of the Morris ship chandlers there were 148 vessels, almost all of them local.[36] By the nineties, David Morris was making payments for goods received from a wide range of companies whose names are still familiar: biscuits from Peek Frean, paint from Goodlass Wall, beef and bonded stores from Cearns and Brown, candles and soap from Price's Patent Candles Company, mustard from Colman and Company, stores, ship's stores, and pipes from Carron and Company, Stirlingshire, cocoa and chocolate from J. S. Fry and Sons, Bristol, and tobacco from W. D. & H. O. Wills, are a few random examples of the goods which Morris in turn sold to his shipping customers.

In practice, these customers were either the ship's husband, the managing owner or sometimes the master himself. At Porthmadog, even as late as the nineties, this did not mean that management was in the hands of a few, for, as a glance at *Lloyd's Register* indicates, in many cases the managing owner was only concerned with one vessel. Thus, for example, in the 1894 *Register,* over sixty different owners of Porthmadog ships are named: Mrs. Ellen Jones, Pennant, Minffordd, was named as owner of the *Wern,* Mrs. J. Jones, Garth, Porthmadog, the *Volunteer,* W. O. Morris, 31 East Avenue, Porthmadog, the *U. Larsing,* John Jones, 44 Madoc Street, Porthmadog, the *Netherton,* and Mrs. M. Lloyd, Llechwedd Ddu, Harlech, the *Mary Lloyd.* In some cases, two vessels were managed: Llewelyn Griffith, 1 Garth Terrace, Porthmadog, managed the *Edward Windus* and the *Oakleys.* There were exceptions — David Morris and Company, the Britannia Terrace ship chandlers, managed the *Cadwaladr Jones,* the *Linus* and the *Robert Morris,* the ship brokers, Pritchard Brothers of Cornhill, managed the *Blanche Currey, Fanny Breslauer, Fleetwing* and *George Casson,* whilst another ship broker, Captain Hugh Parry, also of Cornhill, former master of the *George Casson,* and the *Frau Minna Petersen,* managed a most impressive fleet, including the *Blodwen, Elizabeth, Frau Minna Petersen, Miss Thomas, Phantom, Physician, W. D. Potts* and *Walter Ulric.*

The recession in the slate trade from the late seventies, which had virtually halted the building of ships in North Wales, even in Porthmadog — only the *Richard Greaves* was built in the eighties — came to an end with the temporary boom of 1889, and in 1892 exports from Porthmadog reached their highest level, 98,959 tons by sea and 54,878 tons sent by rail. Inevitably this revival in demand encouraged shipbuilders, shipowners and master mariners of Porthmadog, and created the demand for the beautiful vessels usually known as the ' Western Ocean Yachts ', which marked the final stages in the history of building sailing ships in Gwynedd. A number of well-known Porthmadog vessels had been lost in the eighties and early nineties, the *Anne Catherine, Wave, Sydney, Grace, Confidence, Marie Agathe, Marianne Greaves, Harry Keslake, Patriot, Margaret Owen, Pilgrim, Constance, Arabella, G. & W. Jones, Olga Elkan, Tony Krogmann* among them. Many years in that hardest of trades, phosphate rock from Aruba in the Dutch Antilles, had taken their toll of others which needed repairs and refits. And at Porthmadog

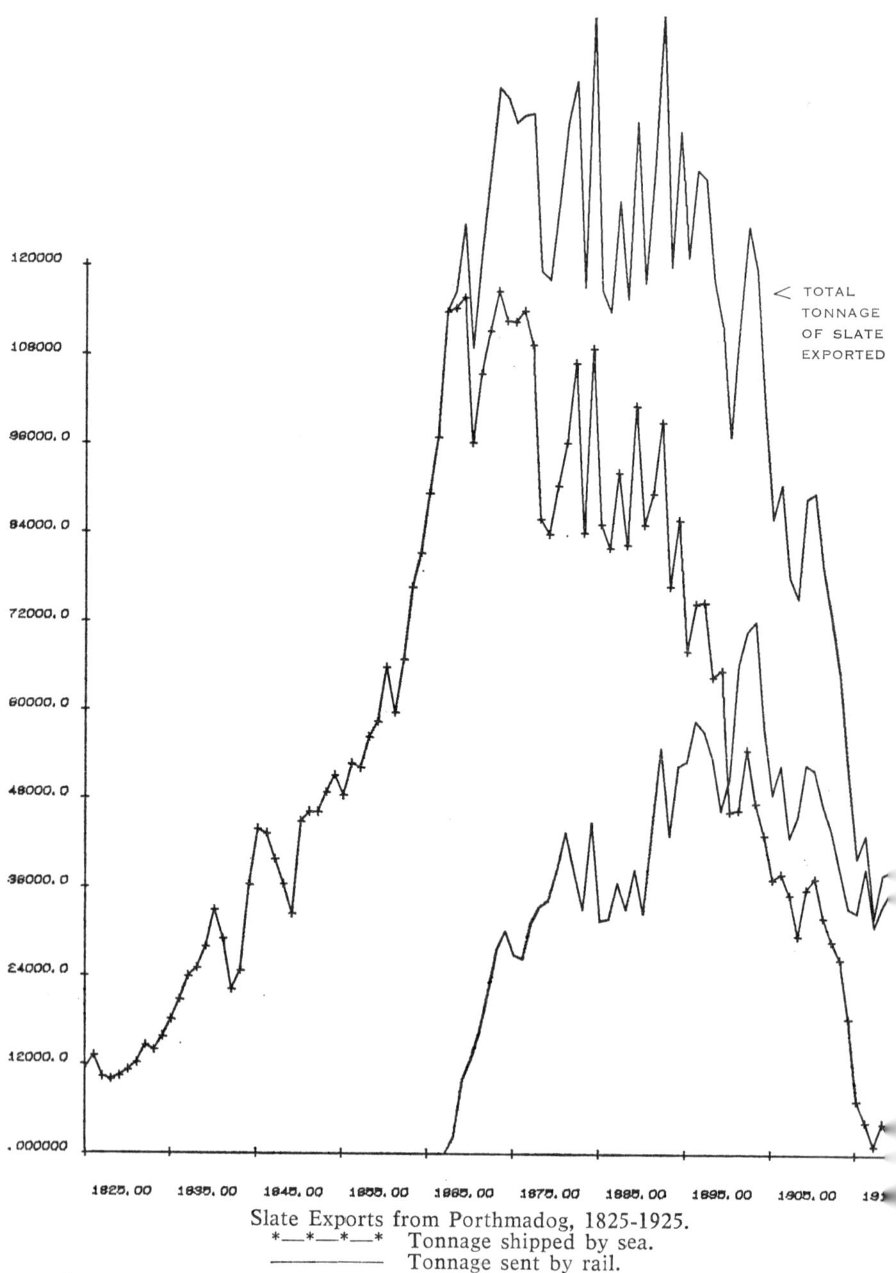


Slate Exports from Porthmadog, 1825-1925.
*—*—*—* Tonnage shipped by sea.
———— Tonnage sent by rail.
Sources: Harbour Records, E. Davies, *Hanes Porthmadog,* and W. M. Richards, N.L.W. 10590.

were a group of very experienced shipbuilders, Ebenezer Roberts, David Jones, Griffith Williams and his nephew, David Williams, experienced master mariners turned ship brokers such as Captain Hugh Parry, Cornhill, and prosperous business men like William Morris, the ship chandler, and the Pritchard brothers, shipbrokers. Moreover, in Germany and in Newfoundland there were merchants who had so come to value both the skill of Porthmadog shipbuilders and the master mariners who commanded their ships that they were willing to invest further in Porthmadog ships. The stage was set for the *Blodwen,* the *Owen Morris,* the *Dorothy,* the *Consul Kaestner* and the almost identical three-masted schooners which followed them from the blocks. When the *Sidney Smith* and the *Elizabeth Llewelyn* were launched, the one built by David Williams, the other by his rival, David Jones, the reporter of the *Cambrian News* judged the mood of the town correctly when he described that March morning in 1895:

> 'On Tuesday morning last two vessels were launched in the harbour amidst the cheers of a large crowd of spectators. It is not simply for the pretty sight of witnessing the vessels slide gracefully from the stocks to take their place so buoyantly and gladly in their new home that the great number of people attend these launches; but everyone feels that it is the surest token of the business prosperity of the place, and the news of the placing of a new vessel upon the stocks is always received throughout the town with pleasure.'[37]

Although the years from 1892 to 1914 saw a gradual decline in the amount of slate exported from Porthmadog, and although the percentage of the total output transported by rail rose steadily compared to the tonnage shipped [See p. 46], the pattern of trade now established by the later Porthmadog schooners encouraged a steady building programme. The Hamburg-Cadiz-Newfoundland, Labrador-Mediterranean voyage was so efficiently carried out that when there was a brief increase in demand for slates in 1902-3 after the depressions of the Boer War and the tragic Penrhyn Strike, the Davies brothers, who were slate merchants in Porthmadog, seriously considered joining with Dawber, Townsley and Company, the Hull slate merchants, and Ellis Partridge and Company of Leicester, to acquire exclusive rights to purchase slates from Newfoundland. Whilst Jonathan Davies, who was President in 1902 of the National

Association of Slate Merchants and Slaters, remained at home in Porthmadog to handle the business, his younger brother, Richard, was sent to investigate various sites at Smith Sound and Hickman's Harbour, Trinity Bay, Black Duck Cove, Placentia Bay and the Bay of Islands.[38] The pencilled comments in his pocket notebook indicate that he was very much aware of their potential as far as shipping was concerned and it is reasonable to suppose that he had the Porthmadog slate schooners very much in mind: 'the slate vein . . . perhaps 300 to 400 feet high, is about 300 yards from the shore of the little cove', 'close to the shore with a good cliff to operate upon rising almost from the water's edge'. In his report to his brother and the Hull and Leicester merchants, he emphasised that the Newfoundland slate vein was 'only of value in my opinion at those points where it is intersected by the Bays and Inlets of the sea, inland the cost of quarrying and marketing the Slate would be prohibitive'. The depression in the home slate industry, which commenced in 1903, decided the Davieses not to proceed with their Newfoundland venture, and so Porthmadog ships had to be content to remain in the salt fish trade there and in Labrador. The Newfoundland connection, however, increased as the years went by — the *Callidora,* the barquentine built by David Jones in 1901, was bought off the blocks by Robert Ehlers of Bristol, 'Newfoundland merchant', who, in turn, sold her to Rorke of St. John's. Of the thirty-four vessels built since the *Blodwen* in 1891, nine were eventually sold to Newfoundland owners. Another three of them were lost in December storms off the coast of Newfoundland.[39]

In contrast to the six hundred and more vessels in and out of the harbour in the boom years of the 1870s, fewer vessels visited Porthmadog harbour each year from 1902, but if one looks at the entries for, say, the month of March 1903,[40] there was still plenty of activity, apart from the lively yards of David Jones and David Williams. During the first week, the *Lizzie* arrived with limestone from Dungarvan, the *Miss Morris* from Dublin with gunpowder, the *Alpha* from Waterford, in ballast apart from a little wheat for J. Williams of Tremadog, the *Walter Ulric, Olwen* and the *Village Maid* arrived in ballast from Irish ports, the *Rebecca* with general cargo, and the *Gomerian* with coal, from Liverpool.[41] That same week the *Victoria* sailed with slate for Harburg, the *Snaefell* with wheat for Wexford,

Total registered tonnage of vessels in and out of Porthmadog Harbour, 1825-1925.
Source: Harbour Records and W. M. Richards, N.L.W. 10590.

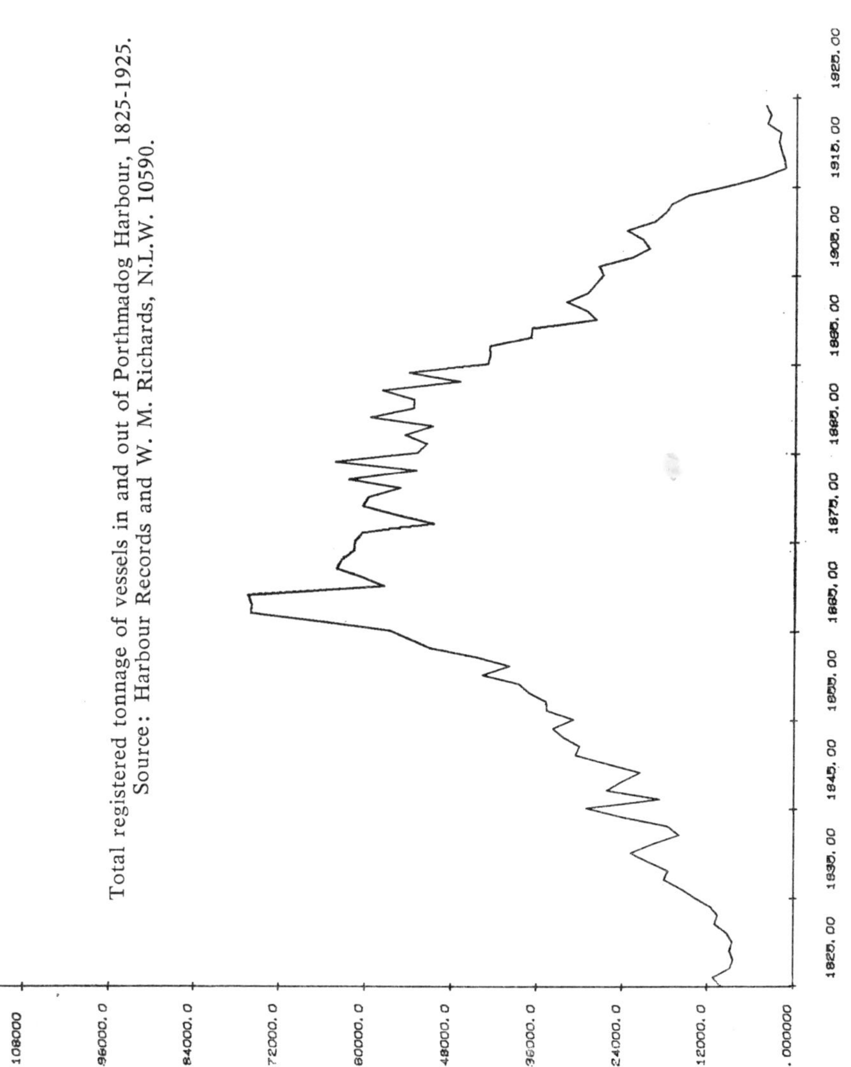

the *David Morris* with slate for Copenhagen, as did the *Elizabeth Pritchard,* whilst the *Volunteer* sailed for Bremen with slate. During the next three weeks the *Tyne, Ann and Jane Pritchard, M. A. James, Evelyn, Cariad, Mary Lloyd, Blodwen, George Casson* and the *Michael Kelly* all sailed for Harburg, the *Ebenezer,* and *Polly Preston* with similar cargoes for Bremen, the *Kitty* and the *Isallt* for Copenhagen, the *Owen Morris* for Kiel and twelve of the coastal schooners for ports in England and Wales. Culm for burning limestone, coal, superphosphates, dynamite, Indian corn, limestone, wheat, timber and potatoes arrived in seven vessels; these, and the inevitable cargoes in the *Rebecca,* were the inward cargoes over the same period. Two more vessels arrived in ballast. The sources for this information are the harbour records, many of which have now disappeared or been dispersed, but, of course, arrivals and departures were regularly recorded in the local newspapers. These sometimes provide a fuller picture for the historian than the bare bones of the harbour records. The arrivals in that first week in March 1903 mentioned above are noted in the *Cambrian News,* but so, too, is the very stormy weather which the vessels that had left the port must have experienced:

> 'The very close relationship of the majority of the inhabitants of Portmadoc to sea faring men naturally gives rise to deep anxiety in the town when stormy weather prevails. So it was last week, but on Thursday night and Friday morning when the storm had assumed the proportions of a cyclone the inhabitants found they had a need to be anxious not only for their sailor relatives, but for themselves . . . Fears were entertained for the safety of the steamship *Rebecca* which left Portmadoc on Thursday morning and put in at St. Tudwal's in the afternoon, but proceeded on her journey to Liverpool in the evening. She seems to have been out during the worst part of the gale, but arrived at Birkenhead without mishap'.[42]

In the same gale, the little steamer *Telephone* dragged her anchor, and ran aground at Abersoch, whilst the lifeboat *Oldham* of Abersoch rescued the crew of the ketch *Seaman* which had gone aground at Castellmarch. Captain Owen R. Hughes, East Avenue, Porthmadog, the master, John O. Hughes, his son, the mate, Thomas Roberts, Lombard Street, Porthmadog, and a young lad from Cricieth, the cook, had taken to the rigging, and after two hours on that wild morning they were hauled, one by one, to safety by the lifeboat crew. The same newspaper reported that the Porthmadog brig

*Fleetwing,* laden with phosphate rock from the West Indies and bound for Amlwch, had been taken in tow in the same storm by the steamer *Kerry,* which had seen her, 'a small sailing vessel pitching in the trough of the heavy seas with her sails blown away, and in a perfectly helpless condition'. When towed into Dublin, the *Fleetwing,* it was reported, had 'lost her bulwarks, stanchions, and all her sails'.

Again the harbour records note briefly the departure of the *M. A. James,* along with the *Ann and Jane Pritchard* and the *Evelyn* in the following week, on 13 March 1903, but the *Cambrian News* a fortnight later bore the following account: 'One of the smartest passages accomplished in recent years by a Portmadoc vessel has recently been performed by the three masted schooner *M. A. James,* Captain Rd. Jones, Borthygest, master. She left Portmadoc on a Saturday with a cargo of slates for Hamburg and succeeded, despite bad weather, to reach her destination by the following Wednesday'[43]

A local newspaper which was read by most of the inhabitants of Porthmadog in the first decade of the century was the Welsh language *Yr Awr,* which came each Saturday from the press of R. Jones Lloyd, 125 High Street, Porthmadog, and sold for a half-penny, 'Pris Dimai'. Alongside the items of local news (in Welsh) and the many advertisements (mostly in English) — 'Richard Jones begs to inform the inhabitants of Portmadoc that he supplies Milk at 3d a quart, twice daily', 'William Morris and Co., Bakery and Ships Biscuit Factory, Chapel Place, Portmadoc, Ships Biscuits a Speciality. These Biscuits are highly recommended to all suffering from Indigestion' (one hardly dares contemplate the comments of seamen when they read that one!) — there was every week a column listing the whereabouts of Porthmadog ships. On Saturday, 21 October 1905, for example, the location of eighty-nine Porthmadog vessels is given thus: enw: [name:] *Fleetwing,* yn, neu wedi gadael: [left:] Port Talbot; am: [for:] Aruba. To Porthmadog readers, Alicante, Stettin, Pernambuco, Papenburg, Aarhus, Leghorn, Genoa and Patras became as familiar as Liverpool, Cardiff or Manchester. The edition for Saturday, 4 May 1907, similarly contains the names of 73 vessels, all Porthmadog owned, and again at ports ranging from Rio Grande, Huelva, and Genoa to Brazil or Copenhagen, but, as usual, there were several at or about to leave Harburg, including the *C. E. Spooner,*

*Evelyn, George Casson, John Llewelyn, Mary Lloyd, M. Lloyd Morris, M. A. James, Tyne* and *William Prichard.* Hard by the columns of shipping news, there were frequently accounts of the latest activities of David Lloyd George, the local M.P., who had so recently scored a notable triumph in his handling of the Merchant Shipping Amendment Act of 1906. It is as well to remember, when reading his speeches during the debates on the Merchant Navy or considering his crucial role in the matter of convoys in the First World War, that Lloyd George had been a young solicitor who had walked the quays of Porthmadog near to his offices, that he had grown up among the seamen who manned Porthmadog ships, and that his sister had married a master mariner from a nearby village. Moreover, when David Williams built the second *Isallt* for his brother, Captain R. O. Williams, in 1909, among those who took a 4/64 share in her was William George, Garthcelyn, Cricieth, the brother whose role in the family firm assisted Lloyd George himself to pursue his political career. In contrast to the investors of earlier years, the shareholders in David Williams's last vessels were drawn almost exclusively from the professional classes. And when the ill-fated *Gestiana,* last of all Porthmadog ships, was built, it is not surprising to find among the shareholders, alongside three physicians and surgeons, a dentist, a quarry owner and a quarry manager, William George and two of his fellow solicitors, the name of ' Margaret Lloyd George of Bryn Awelon, Criccieth, wife of David Lloyd George '. The loss of the *Gestiana* was a sad blow, but its owners were not as dependent upon or as intimately connected with maritime interests as many of those who had previously invested in the ships of the port. The crucial blow to the maritime community came a few months later when the close link of over half a century with Hamburg and the German ports was broken by the outbreak of war in August 1914. It marked the beginning of the end for the maritime community of Porthmadog.

# REFERENCES

[1] The late David Thomas, in *Hen Longau Sir Gaernarfon,* published in 1952, compiled a comprehensive list of vessels built in Caernarvonshire based on his research into the Registers of Shipping of the Custom Houses of Beaumaris, Caernarfon, Aberystwyth, Chester and Liverpool. The late W. M. Richards of Porthmadog and the late Henry Parry of Nefyn helped him to compile his lists by examining the *Lloyd's Registers* and the *Mercantile Navy List.* The numbers of vessels, etc., referred to in this chapter are based upon their painstaking work and my own subsequent research in the *Registers.*

[2] L. W. Lloyd, *Maritime Merioneth:* 1, *The Town and Port of Barmouth* 1565-1973), (Porthmadog, 1974), 16-17.

[3] Elizabeth Beazley, *Madocks and the Wonder of Wales . . . with some account of his agent, John Williams* (1967), 141-147.

[4] I am indebted to Mr. Ivorian Jones of Bangor for drawing my attention to and letting me have transcripts of these extracts from the diaries and account books of Ellis Owen, Cefnymeysydd, now in his possession. Vide *Taliesin,* Gorffennaf 1973, 83, for Mr. Jones's article on the diaries.

[5] Jean Lindsay: *A History of the North Wales Slate Industry* (1974), 187.

[6] W. Ll. Davies: *The Memoirs of Samuel Holland, one of the Pioneers of the North Wales Slate Industry.* Merioneth Historical and Record Society Extra Publications, Series 1, November 1 (1952), 10.

[7] W. M. Richards, 'Some Aspects of the Industrial Revolution in South East Caernarvonshire', *T.C.H.S.,* 4, 71.

[8] ibid., 74.

[9] Lindsay, 121.

[10] *Memoirs Samuel Holland,* 20.

[11] Madog ap Owain Gwynedd (Owen Morris), *Portmadoc and its Resources* (1856), 22.

[12] C.R.O.

[13] C.R.O. Portmadoc National School Log Book: Diocesan report noted in School log-book, 29 January 1875.

[14] E. Davies, *Hanes Porthmadog* (1913), 37, and Lindsay, 121, give slightly different population figures for 1861 and 1871, possibly because of the scattered nature of the parish. According to Davies, the population of Porthmadog itself in 1911 was 3,177, Borth-y-gest and Morfa Bychan 708, and Tremadog 560.

[15] O. Morris, 33.

[16] C.R.O.

[17] Dylan Pritchard: 'The Expansionist Phase in the History of the Welsh Slate Industry', in *T.C.H.S.,* 10, 65-78.

[18] *C.D.H.,* 5 January 1878, account of retirement of Mathew's son, Major Edward Windus Mathew.

[19] Pritchard, 77.

[20] Compiled from David Thomas's lists and Registers of Shipping.

[21] O. Morris, 55.

[22] Quoted by Bob Owen, 'Yr Ymfudo o Sir Gaernarfon', *T.C.H.S.,* 14, 43.

[23] E. Davies, 179. It is said that he was then master of the brig *North Wales,* probably built by Henry Jones in 1852; if so, it is more likely that he died, as some accounts suggest, at Valparaiso, although both Alltud Eifion in *Y Gestiana* (Tremadog, 1892), 86, and Davies, loc. cit., state categorically that his death occurred at one of the Californian ports.

[24] Davies, 152.

[25] The original Deed of Settlement, or Agreement, which came into Emrys Hughes's possession has now been deposited at C.R.O. as MS. XM/2387. Henry Hughes, in *Immortal Sails,* Chapter VIII, describes the formation of the Society. Among those whose signatures appear at the end of the document are Ellis Owen, the diarist, who also signed on behalf of R. R. Williams, Ellis Williams, and Henry Williams, all of London — it was to R. R. Williams that much of the butter sent by Owen in the twenties had been consigned. Also included among the signatures are those of Edward Beck, the Newcastle merchant, who later formed a Shipping Company with Captain Hugh Roberts of Edern which, as 'Hugh Roberts and Company', owned a number of iron steamships in the 1880s, the first of which were the *North Britain* and the *North Wales.* Although there were members of the Portmadoc Mutual Ship Insurance Society who, therefore, lived away from the area, all vessels insured by the Society 'Shall have an agent or Ships Husband who shall reside at Portmadoc or within ten miles thereof'. (Rule 45.)

[26] O. Morris, 55-56.

[27] C.R.O., M/531/50. *Report of the Portmadoc Mutual Ship Insurance Society for the years ending the first day of December 1863-4.*

[28] *Report for year ending 31 December 1867.*

[29] W. M. Richards, *T.C.H.S.* 4, 79.

[30] D. Thomas, *Hen Longau Sir Gaernarfon,* 172-181.

[31] C.R.O. M/531.

[32] *CN,* 2 March 1877.

[33] R. Merfyn Jones, 'A Trade Union in Nineteenth Century Gwynedd', in *T.C.H.S.,* 1974, 91. *C.D.H.,* 25 May 1876.

[34] More details regarding the nature of shareholding in the Shipping Companies of North Wales are contained in the present writer's forthcoming article on 'Shipowners of Gwynedd', 1875-1900, to be published in *Maritime History.* Over a hundred quarrymen had shares in the Arvon Shipping Company in 1875.

[35] J. Glyn Davies, Review of *Immortal Sails* in *T. Cymm. Soc.,* 1948, 212. N.L.W. 12089E-12093E.

[36] The papers of Messrs. Morris and Company, Ship Chandler, are in N.L.W. 12089E-12093E, whilst the Day Books and Rough Day Books of Jones and Morris, sailmakers, Porthmadog, are at U.C.N.W., Bangor, MSS. 13986-13996.

[37] *CN* 15 March 1895.

[38] I am indebted to Mr. and Mrs. J. Williams of Tu Hwnt i'r Bwlch, Porthmadog, for allowing me to peruse these private papers of the Davies family and also the account books of Hugh Jones, Block maker.

[39] Details in the Registers of Shipping now in the care of H.M. Customs at Caernarfon, and I am indebted to Mr. T. W. Lyle and his staff for their kindness and co-operation. A list of the later Porthmadog ships, checked with information for Emrys Hughes, is in Basil Greenhill, *The Merchant Schooners* (1968), II, 213-15.

[40] U.C.N.W., Bangor, 19081.

[41] ibid.

[42] *CN,* 6 March 1903.

[43] *CN,* 27 March 1903.

## II

## THE SHIPS AND THEIR BUILDERS

> '*They were lovely ships. The grace of their hulls and the balance of their tall spars gave them a beauty, both under way and lying to an anchor, not exceeded in all the history of sailing ships*'.[1]

This elegant tribute by Basil Greenhill, Director of the National Maritime Museum, in his masterly books, *The Merchant Schooners,* to the later Porthmadog schooners, and to their builders, David Jones and David Williams, is, and surely will be, the last word. No one could wish for a finer epitaph. How is it that David Jones, with his bowler hat on the back of his head, his pockets bulging with plans and drawings as he stumbled stockily around his yard, and his younger, equally stocky rival, David Williams, who sometimes wore a highly incongruous but strictly practical topi helmet, possibly acquired during his days as ship's carpenter of the full-rigged ship *Havelock* — how is it that such men in remote Porthmadog created such beauty, and, at the same time, such efficiency? For their creations, known to contemporaries as the Western Ocean Yachts, were efficient, probably the finest all round small merchant sailing ships ever built in Britain. As Mr. Greenhill has suggested, they were economical in the crew needed to handle them, they were fast and seaworthy, they faced the icebergs of the North Atlantic and its most violent storms, they sailed to the Baltic and German ports, to the Mediterranean and the Black Sea. Everywhere they went, they were admired. Mariners recognized them as fine sea boats, designers rightly envied their beautiful lines. How is it that a small, tidal harbour, in an out of the way corner of Cardigan Bay, produced such lovely ships?

Firstly, because of the very nature of that port and the Bay in which it was situated. 'A nasty corner of a nasty bay' was the late Professor J. Glyn Davies's apt description in his evocative review of

*Immortal Sails*,[2] and so it was to seamen, whatever the scenic merits of its hinterland. Secondly, the shipbuilders and seamen were the inheritors of an age-old tradition, and, in particular, the accumulated experience in these waters not only of their own immediate predecessors, but of the men of Barmouth, Aberystwyth, Aberdovey, Newquay, Pwllheli, Nefyn, the ports of the Menai Straits, Amlwch and Holyhead. They had learned much from the designs of the North American-built ships so popular with local owners in mid-century. Their frequent visit to the Elbe and the Baltic ports had informed them of the achievements of the builders of schooners in such places as Blankenser and Marstal. Lastly, the shipbuilders and seamen of Gwynedd had gained much from their widespread involvement in the deep-sea trades, both in their own vessels in the phosphate rock trade of the Dutch Antilles and the Newfoundland trades, and also as members of the crews of the full-rigged ships and four-masted barques of Liverpool which knew Cape Horn and almost every teeming port and wind-swept anchorage in the world.

When William Morris, in 1807, decided to publish the surveys made by his father, Lewis Morris, in an extended version of *Plans of the Principal Harbours, Bays and Roads of the St. George's and Bristol Channels*, he added a warning about the dangers of the Welsh coast:

> 'To close the work, it may not be improper in this place to caution those who sail in St. George's channel, to be careful to make a sufficient allowance for lee-way, in forming their course. It is notorious that ten vessels are lost upon the coast of Wales, for one that is lost on the opposite coast of Ireland, yet in the same channel. The reason is obvious, the wind blowing for about nine months in the year from S.W. and W. Quarters; the strong tide of flood and ebb running S.W. by S. and N.E. by N. and the indraughts of deep bays concurring, make a dead heavy swell, that always falls upon the coast of Wales, between Holy-head and St. David's-head; so that in easterly winds we feel the ill effect of it: and it is a remark made by coasters, that in sailing with a fair gale of wind from the coast of Wales to the Westward, a vessel will not make so good way through the water as when she sails thither from the westward. It is no wonder then, that the masters of ships stranded on this coast, and not apprised of these circumstances, are always altogether astonished to find themselves upon a lee-shore, when, by their reckoning, they thought they were several leagues to the westward'.[3]

There was another hazard to which Morris drew attention, Sarn Badrig, that viciously dangerous reef to which wise mariners gave as wide a berth as possible. Morris blamed Captain Greenvile Collins's much heralded survey of the late seventeenth century for adding to the dangers of Sarn Badrig: 'This is a ledge of rocks very narrow and steep on the N.Side, but with regular soundings on the other: it is dry at low water spring tides for about twenty-one miles to sea, stretching out from the coast of Merionethshire, and lies about E.N.E. and W.S.W. The extreme end is about four leagues S.S.W. from St. Tudwal's road. Numbers of vessels have been lost here, owing in a great measure to Captain Collins's chart, which makes ten and seventeen fathom in the very middle of it, when it is correctly ascertained to become dry the last quarter ebb: and he is too closely followed by all on mercenary chart contrivers, few of whom ever saw the places they pretend to describe; this surely is a crime equal to making false lights, to mislead vessels for the sake of the wreck'.

When Madocks had the embankment and, subsequently, the harbour built at Porthmadog, he presented mariners with a considerable challenge, for they had to negotiate the Bar, situated about a mile off Ynys Cyngar, and then, from Ynys Cyngar to Porthmadog itself, a channel of about a mile and a half which vessels drawing more than twelve feet entered with difficulty. According to the 1902 edition of *Sailing Directions for the West Coast of England,* 'in 1889 the bar had a depth of two feet at low water and seventeen feet at high water, springs, but it is subject to constant change, particularly during south westerly gales'. The menace of Sarn Badrig to leeward, and the stormy weather which could be expected frequently off the South Caernarvonshire coast added to mariners' problems. Professor J. Darbyshire of the Department of Physical Oceanography at the University College of North Wales, Bangor, has recently been investigating coastal erosion at Porth Neigwl or Hell's Mouth Bay, where so many sailing vessels ended their days. The South Westerly gales which sweep in directly from the Atlantic into Porth Neigwl, the long fetch reaching into the comparatively narrow area of the bay, and wave refraction cause the unusually stormy seas so familiar to Porthmadog and other seamen in the sailing ships of last century. Professor Darbyshire and his research team are conducting a survey

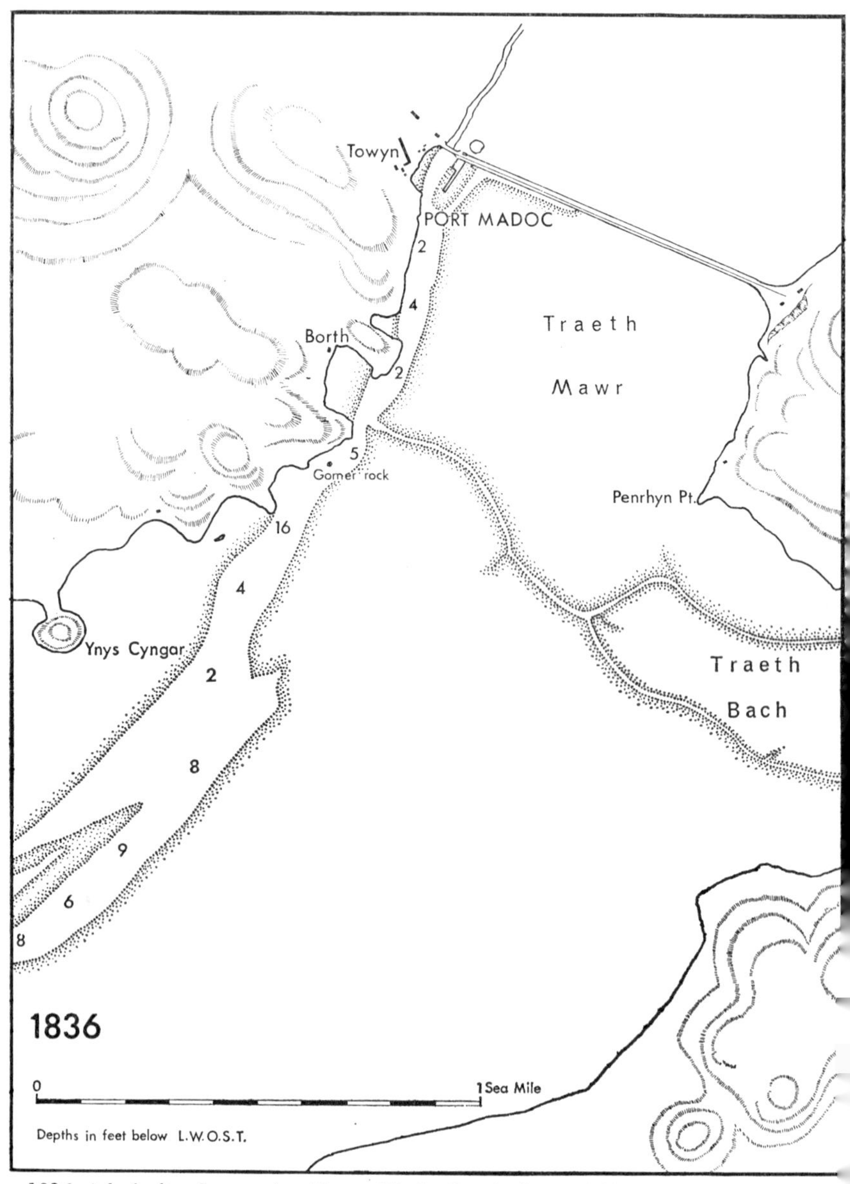


1836 Admiralty Survey by Lieut. W. L. Sheringham, R.N., assisted by Lieut. A Kartright, R.N., 1836. [Reproduced by permission of the Hydrographer of th Navy.]

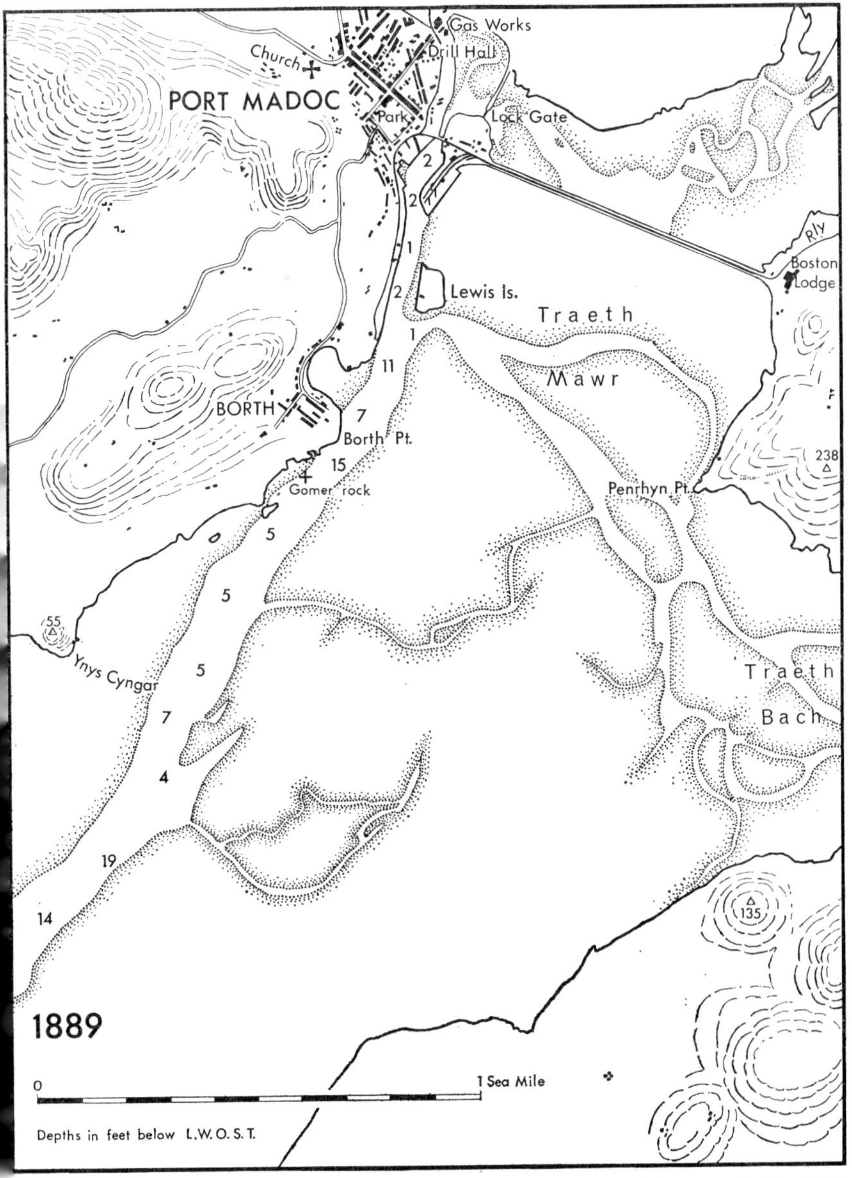


1889 Admiralty Survey by Staff Commander William E. Archdeacon, R.N., 1889. [Reproduced by permission of the Hydrographer of the Navy.]

of the conditions in Hell's Mouth Bay and investigating the effect of bottom topography in refracting waves. During the course of their research they have observed waves of up to twenty feet high, no problem in mid Atlantic rolling seas, but a different matter altogether as short steep waves off the South Caernarvonshire coast. To survive the natural hazards of trading in and out of Porthmadog through treacherous shores, beating out to avoid Sarn Badrig, and surviving South Westerly gales in difficult, dangerous seas, called for stoutly built, seaworthy vessels, and this would have probably been a fair description of the early vessels built by Henry Jones and Evans in the twenties and thirties of the nineteenth century. Owen Morris, writing in 1856, described how, inevitably, the builders of Porthmadog were compelled to change the design of their vessels:

> 'Great improvements have been wrought in the shape of vessels built since so recent a period as thirty years ago. Short, bluff bowed, stout sterned and tub like vessels of a small size were those in vogue then. Provided a vessel had a good stowage room, all was considered well, no regard being apparently paid to her sailing qualities. But gradually a more easy wedge-like overhanging shape was substituted for the bluff perpendicular bow, and a more gradual curvature was adopted for the stern — greater length given — and altogether vessels were modelled with greater regard to sailing and weatherly qualities than heretofore — stowage not being deemed the only essential quality constituting a good vessel'.

The lithograph 'respectfully dedicated to Mrs. Wm. Alexander Madocks and Mrs. Gwynne by their obliged and obedient servant C. F. Williams', dated 1850, shows clearly the yard of Henry Jones where so many of the early vessels were built, and there, if one looks closely, is a vessel in course of construction. It is not possible from the lithograph to identify the vessel, but we know that Henry Jones launched the *Ann Mellhuish* in 1849 and the *Henry Jones* in 1850, both barques of over 300 tons and built for Liverpool owners. On the other hand, as the lithograph was produced in 1850, the vessel in question may be the fifty-nine ton smack *Onyx,* which left the blocks in 1851. If the drawing is an accurate representation, then Henry Jones at this date appears to have retained for some vessels the 'bluff perpendicular bow' which Owen Morris stated had gone out of fashion by the mid-fifties. Whilst examining Williams's lithograph, it is worth noting that the bridge is shown as a weir and footbridge; the new sluice gates and 'Bont Newydd' were constructed in 1851 when it was planned to make 'Llyn Bach' into an inner harbour with more quays and docks, a scheme which never materialised. Opposite to Henry Jones's yard one can see that the rocky spit which jutted out from Ynys Tywyn into the harbour had not yet been transformed and converted by the disposal of ballast and the building of quays on either side into the area known as 'Rotten Tare', where eventually the Western Ocean Yachts and many others before them were to be built. This, too, is where, in later years, many vessels used to come alongside for their repairs and refitting in the winter months from about Christmas to March each year. Beneath the hillock of Ynys Tywyn, Holland's Wharf is clearly shown, a much larger area then, before the building of the Ffestiniog Railway Station. Some little distance from the harbour and Henry Jones's yard are the substantial houses which had already been built in Porthmadog by 1850.

With the development of the harbour, and the need for another slate wharf, Henry Jones's shipyard at Canol y Clwt was converted into Greaves Wharf, and building ceased on this site in the early sixties. But between 1824 and 1860 Henry Jones's output was very considerable. No doubt, in building his first large vessel, the snow *Lord Palmerston,* in 1828, Henry Jones was influenced by the design of the *Gomer,* Captain Richard Prichard's locally famous snow, already mentioned. Mr. Owen E. Jones, now of Old Windsor, has informed me that his ancestor, Captain William Jones, master of the *Harlech Castle,* who was captured by the French in 1796 and eventually escaped from prison in Arras, returned to Merioneth determined to design and build fast cargo vessels based on the French frigate which had captured the *Harlech Castle.* After the wars, Captain William Jones taught navigation and advised on the technical and commercial development of shipping from the Dwyryd and Porthmadog. It was not surprising, therefore, that when Captain Richard Prichard, of Tŷ Gwyn y Gamlas (but described in the Beaumaris Register of Shipping as 'of Tremadoc, mariner'), Ellis Roberts of Beddgelert, mariner, Joseph Williams, senior, Joseph Williams, junior, and Benjamin Williams, all of the City of London, ship agents, and John Pritchard, mariner, Robert Prichard and Richard Roberts, farmers, all of Tŷ Gwyn, Morris Griffith of Tyddyn du, farmer, and

Robert Jones of Plas Ucha, gentleman, all in the County of Merioneth, invested[4] in the new snow, *Gomer,* built at Traeth Bach in 1821, it was said that she was designed along similar lines to a French frigate by Captain William Jones, formerly of the *Harlech Castle.* The similarity between the *Gomer* and the *Lord Palmerston* which Henry Jones built seven years later is apparent from Emrys Hughes's photographs of paintings of both vessels, that of the *Gomer* leaving Trieste, and that of the *Lord Palmerston* in the Mediterranean in 1865. The *Gomer* was some seven feet longer than the *Lord Palmerston* which, in turn, was a slightly larger vessel than the brig *Lady Vaughan,* built at Barmouth by Edward Humphreys about a year earlier — all three vessels certainly had finer lines with much more flare in the bow than the snow/brig *Alice,* built on the Mawddach in 1804. It would appear that Captain William Jones's unfortunate experiences in the *Harlech Castle* some twenty years earlier were turned to advantage by Henry Jones and his contemporaries.

Evan Evans and Francis Roberts also built sloops and schooners at Porthmadog from 1826 to the mid-fifties, and, at Borth-y-gest, Robert Owen and his nephew, William Griffith, who had previously been a farm labourer, built vessels in the forties. Not content with building brigs of under two hundred tons, schooners, sloops and smacks, Henry Jones, in 1843, completed the largest vessel yet built at Porthmadog, the snow *Mary Holland,* in which he, Jones, William Holland of London, John James Mellhuish and two other Liverpool owners had shares. They sold the *Mary Holland* to James Baines, the well known Liverpool shipowner, of Black Ball Line fame, and Thomas Miller in 1854. The painting of her entering Trieste under the command of Captain John Jones gives a good impression of the type of vessel that Henry Jones was building at Porthmadog less than twenty years after his little smack, the *Two Brothers,* in the very first days of the port. Inspired no doubt by his success with the *Mary Holland,* Henry Jones built the two three hundred ton barques *Ann Mellhuish* (1849) and *Henry Jones* (1850). The story of the *Ann Mellhuish* in Australian and New Zealand waters, when she was owned by the brothers known as 'Darkie' Williams, is well told by Emrys Hughes. The *Henry Jones,* like the *Mary Holland* before her, was commanded by Captain John Jones, who may have been a relative of her builder; she was lost by fire off Pernambuco soon after she had been sold by Henry Jones in 1857. The last vessel to be built by Henry Jones was probably the schooner *Ebenezer* in 1858. During his thirty-four years at Canol y Clwt he had built over 60 vessels, ranging from barques to smacks, a registered tonnage of over 5,000 tons, and his son, William Jones, 'Yr Yard', the sailmaker, was well on the way to becoming a very wealthy man, who provided many mortgages for the master mariners of the second half of the century to buy shares in their vessels. It was appropriate that, when Henry Jones died, his body and the funeral party went in small boats from the steps at Pen Cei, Porthmadog, across the bay to Harlech for his burial at Capel Ucha Baptist Chapel.

There were several shipbuilders in competition with Henry Jones in his later years; it is not always easy to identify the actual builder of a vessel as sometimes the name entered in the Register is that of the man for whom the vessel was built, not the man who did the work. Thomas Christian is named as the builder of nine vessels in the late forties and early fifties, but he was, in fact, a prosperous sailmaker for whom one or other of the shipyards had built these vessels, even though Christian is named as the builder in the Register of Shipping. It was Evan Evans who built the schooner *Humility* for Captain David Richards, senior, who later owned a yard at the southern end of Cei Cwmorthin at Trwyn Cae Iago — this is where the schooners *Picton, Patriot* and *Planet,* and the two vessels named *Pilgrim,* were built. Although Captain David Richards, senior, is named as builder, it is said that the actual builders were Robert Williams and Walter Williams, father of Captain Williams, master of the *Walter Ulric.* By the sixties, Daniel Griffith, the shipbuilder, who lived at the Australia Inn, had built a number of vessels, including the *Volunteer, New Blessing, Sarah, Samuel Holland, Anne Holland, Mary Casson,* and the *G. & W. Jones,* all of them, apart from the brigantine *New Blessing,* schooners of between 110 and 150 tons. At Borth-y-gest, William Griffith, the erstwhile farm labourer, had taken over from his uncle, Robert Owen, and built, between 1846 and 1864, on average a schooner a year, the *Daniel Morris* (1), *John Williams, Martha James, Louisa, Elizabeth, Martha Gertrude, Charlotte, Marion, Margaret Jones, Sydney Jones, Elizabeth and*

*Ellen*, *Daniel Morris* (2), *Nathaniel*, and *Ann Griffith*, then the brigantines *Wave* and *Edward Windus*.

It would be tedious and obviously unnecessary, in view of the alphabetical list of ships that follows, to name all the ships built in mid-century by each builder. The increased shipbuilding activity called for a vast amount of timber, and although there was a plentiful supply of good Welsh oak in the neighbourhood, much timber was also imported. In the year 1855, thirty thousand feet of timber were imported, deal, oak, and birch from British North America, Forest of Dean oak from Gloucester, and New Forest oak from Portsmouth and Southampton.[5] As the year went by, the timber droghers which brought timber from St. John's, New Brunswick, Halifax, Nova Scotia and Pensacola became a familiar sight in the harbour. Deck cargoes of timber were notoriously dangerous, particularly in the early years. Many years later, in 1892, the Quebec-built barque *Hope* of Aberystwyth, which had brought timber regularly to Porthmadog, foundered in the North Atlantic in hurricane force winds. She had sailed from Dalhousie, New Brunswick, for Porthmadog on 15 August 1892 with a deck load of thirteen tiers of three inch spruce deals on the starboard side, and fourteen tiers on the port side, the extra tier being taken to counterbalance the cargo under hatches. When the *Hope* encountered the hurricane about sixty miles South East of Cape Race, she began to labour and, with the sea gaining on her pumps, the crew started to cut away the deck load, but, as the official report put it, the timber ' seemed to stick ' in the rigging and lee braces. Whilst the boatswain was cutting away the lee fore braces, the vessel went on her side, and on the next roll she turned keel up.[6] Three of the crew of nine managed to make a raft of some of the deals, from which they were rescued after floating for three days. The lives of the three had been saved by the action of one of them, William Rees, the boatswain, a Porthmadog man, who had seized some rope, part of the fore upper top brace, with which he lashed some of the timber deck cargo together to make the raft. The master, mate and cook, all three of them Aberystwyth men, were drowned, together with an A.B. from Llanbedrog, Humphrey Jones, another A.B., Robert Hughes of Porthmadog, and James E. James, the boy, who came from Pwllheli.[7]

It was not only the timber brought by vessels like the *Hope* and

19. The barque, *Pride of Wales*, built for Captain David Morris by Simon Jones, 1870. [Eduard Adam, Havre, 1880.]

20. The barquentine *Edward Seymour,* built Griffith Williams, 1876, Captain Henr Hughes, master.

21. The barquentine *Ocean Ranger,* built Appledore, 1875, Captain Davies, Porthmadog, master.

22. The brigantine *Wern*, built J. and Ebenezer Roberts, 1876. [Dr. Jürgen Meyer Collection.]

23. The *Wern* in foul weather. [A. Luzzio, Genoa, 1896.]

24. The *Wern* after collision with steamer off Dungeness, Captain Thomas Jon master.

25. The brig *Blanche Currie,* built Porthmadog 1875, lost with all hands, 1914.

26. The three-masted schooner (Jack barquentine) *Venedocian,* built Griffith Williams, 1873.

27. The three-masted schooner (Jack barquentine) *C. E. Spooner*, built Porthmad
1878, at Le Havre.

28. *C. E. Spooner* and *Venedocian* at Flat Island, Labrador, loading fish for Eur
(Reproduced from printer's block given to late Emrys Hughes by Mr. Arch. Mu
St. John's Newfoundland.)

29. Wedding day of Captain and Mrs. Hugh Roberts, of the *Evelyn*, 15 February 1893; also in photograph are Captain Hugh Roberts, senior, of the *Constance*, extreme left, and his two other sons, William Roberts, mate/boatswain of the *Evelyn*, the best man, and Captain Thomas Roberts of the *Dorothy*.

30. Brig *Evelyn,* built 1877, at King's Lynn, *c.* 1910.

31. Captain and Mrs. Hugh Roberts and daughter, with crew of *Evelyn,* 1895-6 William Roberts, the mate (standing immediately behind Mrs. Roberts), and Ber Welch, the cook/A.B. (with lifebelt in front of him).

32. Captain H. Roberts and crew of the *Evelyn.*

'Dillad dydd Sul'. Captain H. Roberts and crew of the *Evelyn* in 'Sunday best'.

*Carpasian,* and the thousands of emigrants who sailed in the ships of Gwynedd, that made British North America's connection with Porthmadog significant. Basil Greenhill, Robert Craig, and Michael Bouquet have in recent years, from different angles, indicated the impact of British North American shipbuilding on British shipping in the nineteenth century. Basil Greenhill and Ann Giffard have shown how James Yeo, the former Cornish village labourer, came to dominate the shipbuilding industry of Prince Edward Island and how some of the wealth created by his activities as lumber baron, shipowner, and the builder of hundreds of ships, in turn flowed back to build the dry dock which has kept Appledore ever since.[8] No such direct links as those of the west countrymen existed between North Wales and North America, but by the mid-nineteenth century the fashion for investing in North American built ships had developed among Welsh shipowners, as in other parts of Britain. Between 1821 and 1874 ninety appear in the local registers, nineteen built in Nova Scotia, ten in Quebec, thirty-eight in Prince Edward Island, sixteen in New Brunswick, four in Canada and three elsewhere in North America. The Davies family of Menai Bridge were probably the best examples of Robert Craig's hypothesis, 'the new kind of shipowner who had become characteristic in Britain after the Napoleonic Wars' who found the product of the British North American yards particularly useful, and 'well suited to the volatile nature of the freight market in Britain'.[9] An examination of the local Register of Shipping indicates that there were many others, such as Nicholas Treweek of Amlwch and Humphrey Owen of Rhuddgaer, Anglesey, who owned the barque *Hindoo.*[10] Although it will be seen in Emrys Hughes's records that Porthmadog owners did have an interest in some North American built vessels, it may be that the influence on Porthmadog of North American shipping was of a more indirect nature. From the twenties, in the days of Captain Richard Prichard, Porthmadog seamen had been involved in the North American trades, and many of them are likely to have served a spell in ships like those of the Menai Bridge Davies family; William Williams of Rhiw had served for some years in the Porthmadog brig *Mystery* before he became mate and then master of the Davies vessels, and later a shipowner on his own account. Such men, serving in North American built ships, and visiting North American ports, could not have failed to be impressed by certain aspects of the design of the hull of American vessels, particularly the design of their schooners. To combat the strong inshore drift of Cardigan Bay, to avoid the crab-like leeway made by bluff-bowed, square-rigged vessels, the schooner, with its sharper bows and a good flare in the run, was most suitable for a port like Porthmadog. Again, the late Professor J. Glyn Davies made the point effectively when he discussed the way in which the adoption of the newer designs affected the landing of lime on Welsh beaches:

> 'I began to see that this coastwise lime traffic had been made possible on the exposed beaches by a new type of ship, which could claw off a lee shore when it came on to blow. These ships could land a cargo of coal or lime stone by dumping it over the side at high water. Carts would fetch it away at low water. I had noticed in several cases that the lime kiln on the beach had a *careg y ring* (*careg yr inn* in one case) and on enquiring I found that they were connected. The ship bringing limestone made fast to the *careg y ring,* a big boulder with a ring bolt driven into it. Whether the ship rove a cable through this ring, or through the ring of a mooring buoy made fast to the boulder, I do not remember . . . If the ship had to scoot from a lee shore while discharging cargo, all that was needed was to hove up short to the ring, fetch the cable in to the waist of the ship, get her beam on the wind, ship the cable out of the ring, and so get a good slant straight away, instead of making a semicircle towards the beach and getting piled up. The old fashioned apple-bowed ships with bellying sails could not claw off; the new American hull with flat sails could. The advance in efficient transport was revolutionary, and affected the agriculture of the western counties profoundly, by supplying lime at cheap rates '.[11]

Many of the Porthmadog coasters were involved in the limestone trade, and, indeed, in so many trades where cargoes had to be discharged on and ballast embarked from open beaches. Even more important, fore-and-aft vessels had the advantage over the square-rigged brigs and brigantines in their ability to beat to windward in short tacks, which often meant a saving of time, and time was so often important if one wished to catch a tide, and, as Glyn Davies said, schooners 'were just the rig for Portmadoc, for beating clear of Sarn Badrig which obstructed long tacks'.

It must also be remembered that, in addition to the influence of North American designs, enterprising master mariners from Porthmadog who visited the Mediterranean and the Baltic would have viewed the ships of other nations with discerning eyes, and made every effort to improve their own. As Porthmadog ships began to take an increasing number of cargoes to the Elbe ports in mid-century, their crews would note the development in design of the barques, brigs, and schooner/brigs being built at Blankeneser where the older traditional fishing boat building had been transformed to meet the demands for an ever-increasing and much more varied shipping industry. A glance through the wonderful collection of photographs in Jürgen Meyer's *150 Jahre Blankeneser Schiffahrt, 1785-1935*[12] and his account of how shipowning developed among the community of Blankeneser, indicates many parallels between Porthmadog and this German port. Thus, by mid-century, Henry Jones and his successors were able to bring together the best of both European and North American traditions in the design of their ships.

One of the outstanding ship builders of Porthmadog, Simon Jones, born at Tŷ Gwair Farm, Penrhyndeudraeth, in 1823, made his name as a shipbuilder in Borth-y-gest in the boom years of the seventies. The story of how he built the barque *Pride of Wales* for Captain David Morris has been told in detail by Henry Hughes in *Through Mighty Seas* and *Immortal Sails*;[13] two years earlier, Ebenezer Roberts had built the brig *Excelsior* for Captain David Morris, and her story has again been told by Captain Morris's grandsons, Henry and Emrys Hughes. Ebenezer Roberts's yard was in Porthmadog, hard by the Ffestiniog Railway Station, on the Dwyryd side, to the east of Holland's Wharf, and here he built some of the graceful and yet most sturdy square-rig vessels to leave the port. Simon Jones, on the other hand, was building his vessels on the southern side of the beach at Borth-y-gest, approximately where the car park is now situated; on the northern side there was the yard which belonged to Richard Jones, a member of the Garreg Wen family. There was another yard in front of the houses where the pilots for the port lived, Tai Pilots, on the southern side of Borth-y-gest, to seaward of Simon Jones's yard. It was from this yard, in 1874, that the barque *Snowdonia* was launched, the same year that the *Fleetwing* left the yard of Richard Jones, also at Borth-y-gest. Built for Morris Owen Morris (known locally as Morris Owen) by his foreman, John Hughes, with advice, some said, from Simon Jones, the *Snowdonia* was regarded by contemporaries as a fine vessel, the largest built in the Porthmadog area. She was lost in 1881 on the north-east coast with all hands at the end of a return voyage with phosphate rock from Aruba. Commanded by Captain John Roberts, a member of a well-known Porthmadog family, the tragedy was heightened in the eyes of contemporaries due to the sad journey of Captain Roberts's bride-to-be, sister of a local minster, who had travelled to meet the ship docking, to be married the next day.[14] The *Fleetwing* had a much longer career, ending her days as a hulk in the Falkland Islands. The *Blanche Currey,* which followed her from Richard Jones's Borth-y-gest yard in 1875, was also a notable vessel, whilst Ebenezer Roberts's next vessel, in the same year, the brig *W. W. Lloyd,* was regarded by many as his finest vessel; Henry Hughes said 'she looked as if she had been carved out of one solid piece of beautiful oak'.[15]

It will be recalled that 1873 saw the highest exports of slate by sea from Porthmadog, 116,567 tons, whilst, in 1875, owing to an abnormal demand for slates, prices in the London market rose sharply, so that in 1877 one hundred square feet of slates, which had cost 33/- seven years previously, now cost 49/-, almost as much as a comparable amount of roofing tiles. With the prospects for their chief export so promising, Porthmadog naturally shared the general optimism regarding the future of sailing ships. 1875 marked the crest of a temporary boom in building sailing ships in Britain, though the fashion was now for large iron ships capable of great carrying capacity, and, as already explained, these were the vessels which tempted a mass of small investors from North Wales. Porthmadog shipowners and shipbuilders had reason to stake their faith in their own small wooden built vessels, which were so stoutly built that they could take the strain of drying out in a muddy tidal harbour like Porthmadog whilst embarking a heavy cargo of slate, could withstand all the strains of the Aruba phosphate rock trade and the problems of long ocean voyages, yet were shallow draughted and manoeuvreable enough to enter their home port and similarily difficult harbours abroad. Thus, in 1876, the year following the launching of the *W. W. Lloyd* and her contemporaries, Porthmadog saw six more vessels leaving the blocks, a schooner, the *Robert Morris,* two brigs, the *Criccieth Castle* and the *Ellen Greaves,* both over 200 tons, two barquentines, the *Anna Braunschweig* and the *Edward Seymour,* and the brigantine, the *Wern*. All six were notable vessels. Ebenezer Roberts built the *Anna Braunschweig* and the *Wern*, and both had long careers in the European and North Atlantic trades; Simon Jones built the *Criccieth Castle* under Tai Pilots for Morris Owen, but her career was short, a mere six years, before she was lost off the Scillies. The *Ellen Greaves*, which he built in the same year at Porthmadog, had a longer life and was lost in the same year as the *Anna Braunschweig*, both of them wrecked in the Aruba phosphate rock trade in 1897.

Evidence of the way the local commercial interests were now investing in the new ships is indicated in the list of owners of the *Ellen Greaves*, for among the shareholders were Morris E. Morris, the chemist (whose account books indicate the range of his business with the shipmasters of the port, containing entries ranging from 'two galls. lamp oil' for Captain Morris Jones of the schooner *Sydney Jones* to 'Feeding Bottle, 2/-, carriage of packet 1/-'[16] for Captain Evan Jones of the barque *Telegraph*), David Jones, Tremadog, auctioneer, Morris Jones, Dolgellau, commercial traveller, and John Williams, Llanystumdwy, miller, who was probably the father or brother of Captain John Williams, Llanystumdwy, the major shareholder. The family involvements are evident also in the case of the barquentine *Edward Seymour,* also named after one of the Greaves family and built by Griffith Williams of Porthmadog, and owned by Lewis Hughes the tailor and his son, Captain Henry Hughes, who became her master. In the case of the *Edward Seymour,* it is possible to see two other points regarding the financing of the building of these vessels. Firstly, Lewis Hughes and Captain Hughes were able to raise a mortgage of £2,000 at 6% from Hugh Pugh and Robert Jones, both described as bankers, Porthmadog, and a further mortgage for £800 in 1877 at an interest rate of 5% from William Jones, sailmaker, the son of Henry Jones, who had built the first Porthmadog ships. Secondly, Hugh Pugh and Robert Jones transferred their mortgage to John Owen, shipowner, Porthmadog, and Griffith Williams, the builder of the vessel, in 1879 — the recession had started, but Hugh Pugh (son-in-law of Sir Hugh Owen, who so influenced the development of Welsh education) was also very much involved by this time as chairman of the Arvon Shipping Company, which, as already mentioned, had been formed to buy large wooden or iron vessels for the ocean trade, and had attracted many investors from other parts of North Wales in the hope of high dividends.

1877 and 1878 were the busiest years of all in the development of Porthmadog shipping. The list of vessels built in these two years immediately arouses interest among ship lovers, for among them were vessels which were still sailing in European waters within living memory, and Porthmadog people remember some of them among the most successful of all the vessels built in the port.

| *Year* | *Name* | *Rig* | *Tn* | *Dimensions* | *Builder* |
|---|---|---|---|---|---|
| 1877 | *Mary Claason* | Bg. | 182 | 104.6/25.1/13.5 | John Jones |
| | *Sarah Evans* | Sr. | 99 | 82.5/22.4/10.8 | Richard Jones |
| | *Olga Elkan* | Sr. | 131 | 90.6/22.5/11.9 | J. & Eben. Roberts |
| | *Marianne Greaves* | Bg. | 185 | 105.8/25.1/13 | Simon Jones |
| | *Evelyn* | Bg. | 202 | 104.9/25.6/13.9 | Hugh Williams |
| | *Edward Arthur* | Sr. | 141 | 95.5/22.9/12.1 | Hugh Williams |
| | *Martha Percival* | Bkn. | 249 | 120.1/26.3/14.5 | Eben. Roberts |
| | *Marie Kaestner* | Sr. | 96 | 83.9/21.5/10.6 | Simon Jones |
| | *Ida* | Bn. | 179 | 103.5/24.2/13.4 | David Jones |
| | *Hilda* | Sr. 3mst | 171 | 100.5/24/12.8 | Griffith Williams |
| 1878 | *Cadwaladr Jones* | Sr. | 93 | 81.5/21.8/10.9 | Morris Owen |
| | *Dizzy Dunlop* | Sr. | 99 | 84.5/22.2/10.7 | Richard Jones |
| | *Osprey* | Cr. | 7 | 33.6/10/5 | R. Ellis |
| | *Tony Krogmann* | Bkn. | 251 | 119/26/14.7 | Eben. Roberts |
| | *Marie Agathe* | Sr. 3mst | 186 | 101/24.5/13.2 | J. & Eben. Roberts |
| | *Frau Minna Petersen* | Sr. 3mst | 165 | 102/24.3/12.6 | Simon Jones |
| | *Florence* | Sr. | 100 | 84.5/22/11.1 | Hugh Williams |
| | *C. E. Spooner* | Sr. 3mst | 172 | 103.2/24/12.7 | David Jones |

Launching day was an important day in Porthmadog, for young and old. In the log book of National School[17] the autocratic Mr. Grindley's usual routine was recorded in such terse statements as 'Taught the School a Song, "Hearts of Oak"', or on another day, 'Peaceful Slumbering on the Ocean', and 'Lesson in Geography to the Upper Standards', 'Voyage round the Black Sea', or 'Visit by Captain O. Jones, *Arabella* at 11 a.m.' In January 1877 he wrote at greater length: 'Jan. 17, 1877. *Ship Launch* at Port. Leave given to whole school to see it. School opened at 10 a.m. Master gave Standard IV a lesson on Regular and Irregular Verbs from 3 p.m.' A fortnight later he recorded: 'Jan. 31, 1877. *Ship Launch* at Borth.

School opened at 9.30 a.m. Few absent from Borth in the morning'. The local newspaper, the *Cambrian News,* reported the launchings in rather more ecstatic terms than the schoolmaster:

> 'On Wednesday morning, January 17, a beautiful launch took place from the yard of Messers Hugh Williams and Co., shipbuilders, Portmadoc. The morning was exceptionally fine, and there was a large number of spectators availing themselves of every vantage ground to see the vessel take to the water. It was impossible to have a more successful launch from every point of view. The ceremony of christening was performed by Miss Griffith, daughter of Dr. Griffith, the vessel being called the Evelyn, in honour of Miss Greaves, daughter of Mr. J. W. Greaves. All competent authorities speak of it as one of the finest vessels ever built at this port. It was drafted by Mr. Daniel Evans, foreman to Messers Hugh Williams and Co., and built for Captain Hugh Roberts, late of the "Constance", and others, and Captain H. Roberts is to command her. She has been classed A1 for fourteen years at Lloyd's; the builders tonnage is 369 tons. The length of its keel is one hundred and seven feet two inches; breadth twenty four feet nine inches; depth of hold, thirteen feet ten inches. It is intended for the general trade'.[18]

The mention of the vessel being 'drafted' by Daniel Evans, the foreman, is particularly interesting; whether this refers to the general design, the half model or a drawing is intriguing. Presumably, Daniel Evans was the loftsman, or 'moulder' as he was called in Appledore, the designer who was responsible for seeing that the vessel developed into a full-size replica of the half model which was the usual first stage in the building of a merchant schooner. Very few yards used drawings instead of the half model as a basis for the design of the schooner, although Emrys Hughes remembered that both David Jones and David Williams used to build from drawings, which were carefully guarded secrets. In a letter to Basil Greenhill in May 1947, Mr. Hughes stated that he had not seen any half-models of the schooners, or drawings, but he had examined and photographed the half-model built to a scale of eight feet to an inch which Simon Jones had made for the barque *Pride of Wales*: 'The model is a longitudinal half of the vessel carved to her exact shape from the gunnals downwards and screwed on to a flat mounting board. At intervals of about five to ten feet a see saw cut is made through the model as far as the mounting board to enable scaled measurements to be taken for the cutting of the templates. Where the curves of the hull are acute the saw-cuts would be at frequent intervals, where the curves are not so acute they would be less frequent '.[19] The whole process of building a schooner has been described in detail by Mr. Greenhill, based on the building in 1903 of the *Katie* at the Bell Inn Yard of the Cock brothers for Robert Pritchard, Porthmadog, and Captain William Griffiths, born at Llanbedr, who later settled in Appledore.[20]

The launching of the *Evelyn* was followed by a series of other similar occasions in the Spring of 1877. From the yard of John and E. Roberts at Borth-y-gest came another vessel described as ' a finely built schooner ' . . . ' This fine vessel is eighty-two feet length of keel, twenty-two feet broad, and twelve feet two inches in depth of hold. By carpenters measure she is to carry two hundred and thirty-three tons and she is one hundred and thirty-nine registered tonnage '.[21] Built for Captain Thomas Griffiths of Sarnfeillteyrn, she was obviously intended for the German slate trade — ' She is called Olga Elkan after the wife of a Hamburgh slate merchant '. A fortnight later the local papers again reported launchings, and confirmed, incidentally, that, although there had been a falling off in the demand for slate, Porthmadog was optimistic regarding the future of its fleet, and however much it rained — slate quarrying communities have always had the rain — the enthusiasm of the spectators was not in any way dampened.

> ' Though last year was one of almost unexampled depression in the shipping trade at Portmadoc, yet seldom has there been a period of greater activity in shipbuilding, for hardly a week passes without their being one or two launches either at Porthmadog or Borth. On Saturday, March 3, two launches took place at Portmadoc, one from the yard of Mr. Ebenezer Roberts, and the other from that of Messers Hugh Williams and Co. The new vessel launched from Mr. E. Roberts was a fine three-masted brigantine, classed A1 for 12 years at Lloyd's. She is two hundred and sixty-eight tons register and will carry about four hundred and sixty tons. The length of keel is one hundred and twelve feet eight inches; breadth twenty-five feet; and depth of hold fourteen feet ten inches. It is one of the largest built at Portmadoc. Its name is the " Martha Percival " after the name of Mrs. Percival of Bodawen, who performed the ceremony of baptism. The owners are Captain Jones (of the Geraldine) and Co., and Captain Jones is to command her. A few minutes before the vessel was launched, another fine vessel was launched close by

> from the yard of Messrs Hugh Williams and Co. The ceremony was performed by Major Mathews, Wern, the ship being called the Edward Arthur after the name of the Major's son. It is a schooner of one hundred and fifty-one tons register, and will carry about two hundred and sixty tons. The length of its keel is ninety-five feet; its breadth twenty-two feet; and depth of hold twelve feet. She is to be commanded by Captain Evan Davies, Portmadoc, and is intended for the coast and foreign trade. The people and neighbourhood of Portmadoc take great interest in these launches, for though the rain was coming down in torrents, the quays were crowded with spectators '.[22]

Not all the vessels launched in 1877 were destined to have a long career despite the great enthusiasm and the high hopes at their launching. The *Marie Kaestner,* built by Simon Jones in 1877 for Captain Richard Pritchard, Borth-y-gest, was destined to have but a brief career, for she was lost in the following year, bound from Liverpool to Porthmadog with a cargo of wheat. Captain Pritchard, her master, and his wife and son, who were aboard for the voyage, were lost with all the crew. The *Marie Kaestner,* however, was significant for another reason: she was the first of the vessels to be launched 'broadside on' at Rotten Tare, a practice which Simon Jones initiated and Griffith Williams and his nephew, David Williams, last of the builders of Porthmadog, continued. The *Hilda* was another vessel whose launching marked a stage in the history of Porthmadog ships. Built for Lewis Hughes, the Porthmadog tailor, who owned the *Edward Seymour,* and commanded by his son, Captain Henry Hughes, who had previously been master of the *Edward Seymour,* the *Hilda* was one of the first of the three-masted schooners, or 'jack barquentines' as they were called in Porthmadog. The *Hilda* and the *Marie Kaestner* were launched on the same day, Saturday, August 17, 1877. In referring to the launch of the *Hilda,* the local newspaper stressed that she 'will carry three hundred and eighty tons of slates . . . the second ship built for Mr. Lewis Hughes during the last two years', a three-masted schooner which 'was a beautiful vessel and nicely launched'. In the case of the *Marie Kaestner,* named 'after Mr. Kaestner a Bremen slate merchant', it was stated that 'This vessel was launched sideways, and this method was attended with risk, yet the launch was very successfully accomplished'.[23]

The experiments of 1877 were continued in the following year; Ebenezer Roberts, and members of his family, with considerable financial support in the shape of mortgages from William Jones the sailmaker, launched the first 'jack barquentine' from their yard, the *Marie Agathe*. She was slightly larger than Griffith Williams's *Hilda,* and, by a curious coincidence, both vessels were lost five years later, in 1883, the *Hilda* in the West Indies in May, and the *Marie Agathe* some three months earlier when on passage from South Wales to La Guyana, Brazil, with a cargo of patent fuel, railway iron, deals, and over three hundred tons of dynamite. She was abandoned in the North Atlantic in a position estimated as 44°N and 11°W, having encountered very heavy weather and strong south westerly gales. Her crew of seven were saved by a passing sailing ship. Better luck was in store for Simon Jones's vessel, launched in the same year, although the omens at her launching were regarded by many as far from promising. The *Frau Minna Petersen* was destined to sail the seas for more years than most of Porthmadog's vessels; few of those who were present on that Saturday morning in 1878 could have foreseen that, under another name, and another flag, she was finally to founder in a gale off the Finnish coast in 1944, and that the news of her end should be brought by a seaman who escaped from Esthonia some years later. Henry Hughes, in *Immortal Sails,* has a lively account of the launching of the *Frau Minna Petersen* and states that following a mishap in her launching 'Simon Jones, however, least disturbed of anyone, secured his craft and triced her back with a heavy purchase to a "square position".'[24] This conflicts somewhat with the account of the launch which appeared in the local press in June 1878, and as the reporter's eye-witness description is equally lively, it is perhaps worth quoting in full as an evocative and detailed description of a launching at Porthmadog a hundred years ago. It was an item of such obvious interest to the readers in those days that, unlike the usually comparatively brief account of a launch among other local news, the editor decided to take up all his space for Portmadoc for that week on this failure to launch a ship, apparently an almost unique event in the history of the port.

'PORTMADOC. FAILURE TO LAUNCH A NEW SHIP. — It had been announced that on Saturday morning, about 7.30 a.m., the new ship which Mr. Simon Jones was building for Captain Hugh Parry, formerly of the George Casson, was to be launched, and there was quite a concourse of people on the wharf before seven a.m. Before eight, the wharves were crowded, the ships in the harbour (where there are now a great many), having flags flying and most of them with crowds of people on their decks and yards. A little before eight, the tugboat steamed out to be ready in case of accident, and at the same time the carpenters began to knock off the blocks. Everything looked most favourable to the ship with its new paint, flags, and handsome figurehead, the usual bottle of wine hanging from the bow by a handsome broad Cambridge blue ribbon. A platform was erected for Miss Morris, of Bank-place, who was to go through the ceremony of naming her Frau Minna Petersen. But through either carelessness, or mistaken zeal, the blocks from under the bow were taken off before those working at the stern had succeeded in taking off those under that part of the vessel. About a quarter past eight there arose a sudden cry, "She's off!" All held their breath as the bow part moved slowly at first, then quicker, the only noise to be heard being the cheers of the lads who were on board, who thought she was properly launched; but after going a little way, and people beginning to hope that although she started unexpectedly she would get into the water all right; it was seen that the stern had moved but very little; and after oscillating backwards and forward once or twice the ship steadied itself on the wharf, the bow being over the wharf, but the stern being about six yards from the edge, the ship being at an angle of about 30 degrees of the edge of the wharf. It was then seen that the only damage done to the vessel was some splinters being knocked off the keel near the bow in going over an iron ring. The bow part in moving by itself, had got off the wood. Captain Richards, the harbour master, made himself most useful after the mishap in seeing that the vessel was steadied safely in its place with timber; the builder, Mr. Simon Jones, being quite overcome at seeing a work on which he had spent so much time and money, and which he expected so very shortly out of his hands, stuck on the wharf and in such a difficult position to launch. Captain Richards and Mr. W. E. Morris tried their best to cheer Mr. Simon Jones, both being confident that the ship could be launched bow first, by taking up a part of the quay and moving the vessels which are now in the way. Great sympathy is felt by everybody with Mr. Simon Jones. The length of the Frau Minna Petersen, is 95ft.; breadth, 23ft. 3ins.; depth, 12ft. 9in.; tonnage about 320 tons. She is being built for Captain Hugh Parry, of the George Casson, who meant to command her himself'.[25]

Captain Hugh Parry has already been mentioned in the preceding pages in his role as ship-broker and chairman of those meetings of the 'Mutual' in the smoke-filled upper room of the News Room, overlooking the harbour at Pen Cei in the closing decades of the nineteenth century. Born in Nefyn, the home of so many outstanding Welsh seamen, he had already spent a lifetime with ships by 1878 and could look back upon several years experience as master of the *George Casson,* built in Porthmadog in 1863 by Pierce and Roberts as a brig, and later converted into a brigantine. In the painting she is seen entering the Bay of Naples, 5 December 1863, commanded by Captain Hugh Parry. On the voyage from Porthmadog to Stettin, for example, four years previously, when he himself was aged thirty-four, he had had in his crew Evan Ebenezer Parry, aged twenty-five, probably his brother, as mate, Owen Roberts, aged twenty-three as boatswain, William Roberts, aged twenty, A.B., Robert Williams, aged sixty-one, cook and A.B., Evan Jones, aged forty, A.B., and Richard Jones, aged sixteen, Ordinary Seaman. The managing owner for the *George Casson* on this and many of her voyages was Owen Morris, Bank Place, and it is, therefore, not surprising that when the *Frau Minna Petersen* was built by Simon Jones for Captain Hugh Parry, and formally registered on 29 July 1878, the registration indicates that two days later Captain Parry obtained a mortgage for £2,200 and interest at 5% from Owen Morris of Porthmadog, described as a slate merchant. When Owen Morris, the sometime clerk in Samuel Holland's office — and author of the valuable essay already referred to on Porthmadog, which he wrote as a young man of twenty-five in 1856 — died intestate in April 1884, administration was granted to Jane Morris, 9 Bank Place, Porthmadog, spinster. On 11 November 1895 Captain Parry received his receipt for the discharge of this mortgage, and in February 1901, a few months before his own death, he sold the *Frau Minna Petersen* to Cornish owners. The bald outlines of their transactions have been included here to illustrate a fairly typical example of the way in which shipbuilding had developed in Porthmadog by 1878. Simon Jones, the experienced builder, had been commissioned to build for the shrewd and experienced master mariner, Captain Parry, a new three-masted schooner, rigged in accordance with the new style in fashion in the port, with the financial backing of the astute and intelligent slate shipper, Owen Morris, who had seen the port grow from the quiet coastal trade of the forties to the feverish activity of the seventies. Owen Morris was still a comparatively young man, aged forty-eight, and Captain Hugh Parry was aged thirty-nine. No doubt in the hope of maintaining good relations with their German customers, they called the new vessel *Frau Minna Petersen.*

Exports of slate shipped to Germany, however, were about 23,000 tons lower in 1878 than they had been in 1877, and this, together with the fact that the mishap in launching had put back her sailing, meant that the *Frau Minna Petersen* did not go immediately into the German slate trade. Instead, in October 1878, Captain Hugh Parry sailed his new vessel from Irvine to Algiers and back to Liverpool. In the spring of 1879 he took a slate cargo from Porthmadog to Stettin. There then followed two voyages through the Mediterranean to Asia Minor at a time when the air was full of the tension caused by the Balkan atrocities, the international conferences at San Stefano and Berlin, and rumours relating to movements of the British, Turkish and Russian fleets. From Cardiff, in June 1879, the *Frau Minna Petersen* sailed for Smyrna, where she arrived in August, back to Ayr by October, and from Ayr again in November to Smyrna, arriving on the 3 January, returning to Liverpool by 25 March 1880. These and subsequent voyages will be dealt with in a more detailed study of the *Frau Minna Petersen;* here it is necessary to note that it was in the spring and summer of 1880 that she first entered the Cadiz - Newfoundland - Mediterranean trade — she was at St. John's on 7 July 1880. As Basil Greenhill has explained, the three-masted schooner *Frau Minna Petersen,* like the other 'jack barquentines', *Venedocian* and *C. E. Spooner,* 'built with a view to employment in the phosphate trade from the West Indies, all in fact went almost at once into the Newfoundland trade and stayed in that business. These ships were large enough to take cargoes for South America and, too large for direct loading at the small Labrador ports, they took their fish on board at St. John's'.[26]

According to Emrys Hughes, the *Venedocian* was probably the first Porthmadog vessel to sail regularly in the Newfoundland trade. Built in 1873 by Griffith Williams, her unusual rig, as explained by Emrys Hughes, was dictated by the fact that her master only held a 'fore-and-aft' certificate. When certificates of competency were first made compulsory under the Merchant Shipping Acts of 1850 and 1854, the only types envisaged were those for the different levels of knowledge. It was soon found, however, that men were coming forward for examination who were obviously well qualified seamen, except that they had not had experience of square-rig ships. As it would be unfair and a hardship to deny such men certificates, the Board of Trade instituted an endorsement, Fore and Aft Rig only, by administrative decision. Although there were suggestions that this concession should be rescinded, for later candidates this was never done. Thus, as Mr. Greenhill has indicated,[27] in the closing decades of the nineteenth century there were three types of certificates issued by the Board of Trade: (1) Ordinary Master, who could command any vessel, steam or sail, square-rigged or fore and aft; (2) Master, fore-and-aft, who could command fore-and-aft-rigged vessels but was denied the command of square-rigged vessels; (3) Master, steamship, who was entitled to command foreign steamships only. As the definition of square-rigged vessels included full-rigged ships, barques, brigs and barquentines, it was obvious that this posed problems for shipbuilders, masters, and owners in Porthmadog. In the fifties and sixties there had clearly been two types of vessel, the coastal schooners and the deep-sea brigs and barques, and there must have been two fairly clearly defined types of masters, the majority, the coastal skippers, the fore-and-aft-rigged masters, on the one hand, and a more select class, the deep-sea masters, with a full square-rig qualification. But, as the years went by and the number of vessels increased dramatically and became more ubiquitous, so the maritime experts of Porthmadog looked for more economical rigs which could cope with the varied problems both of deep-sea work and the intricacies of navigation in restricted waters, whilst still retaining fairly large vessels capable of carrying heavy cargoes in the ocean trade. The barquentine rig would have been an obvious choice, but this called for masters with square-rig qualifications. To obtain these qualifications, intending masters would have to leave Porthmadog ships to put in a spell in large full-rigged ships just at the time when the port needed all its seamen because of the boom conditions. The importing of ' outsiders ' as masters was not to be contemplated. The obvious alternative was to so adapt the rig of the new three-masted vessel so that fore-and-aft certificate men could retain command. Thus Hugh Jones of the *Venedocian,* who only held a fore-and-aft rigged certificate, was able to command his vessel because her rig was adapted to produce a three-masted stay-sail schooner; according to Emrys Hughes, she 'was rigged like a top-sail schooner, except that instead of having a gaff foresail to the foremast she carried main staysails like a barquentine. Also, instead of having a square foresail bent on the large fore yard, she had a bent square sail on a smaller fore yard. Neither did she have a fore gallant mast'. It is significant that in the schooner port of Marstal in Denmark there were parallel developments in the rigging of stay-sail schooners in the 1870s.

Lest the reader who is not intrigued by such technicalities should become completely disenchanted, it is perhaps sufficient to note here that, as Greenhill and Emrys Hughes have explained, the staysail schooner *Venedocian* anticipated the later top gallant schooners, which became acknowledged as the most efficient and economical rig for small ocean-going ships. In the case of the *Frau Minna Petersen,* it was not the master's qualification which decided the rig, for Captain Hugh Parry had obviously previously commanded square-rig vessels, but in the same year, when David Jones built his first vessel in Porthmadog (at the south end of the new quay, Cei Newydd), the *C. E. Spooner* for Captain John Jones, Porthmadog, shipowner and retired master mariner, the rig *was* important, for, again according to Emrys Hughes's notes, Captain William Jones, her first master, only held a 'fore-and-aft' certificate. Captain John Jones, of Garth Cottage, Porthmadog, was at this time managing a number of vessels, and among those who invested in the *C. E. Spooner* was David Evans of Gelli Gaer, in Glamorgan, described as 'Headmaster of Endowed Grammar School', no doubt a relative or a former Porthmadog boy who had seen the potential of vessels built in the port — his name appears more than once in the registers among the shareholders of Captain Jones's vessels. Whilst the shipping of Porthmadog in 1878 was very much in the hands of the 'Mutual' and the professional seamen, men like Captain Hugh Parry and Captain Hugh Roberts of the *Constance,* the shipbuilders, and the slate interests, the way in which the people of the neighbourhood identified themselves with the maritime interest is exemplified in another vessel launched in 1878, and as well known in this century

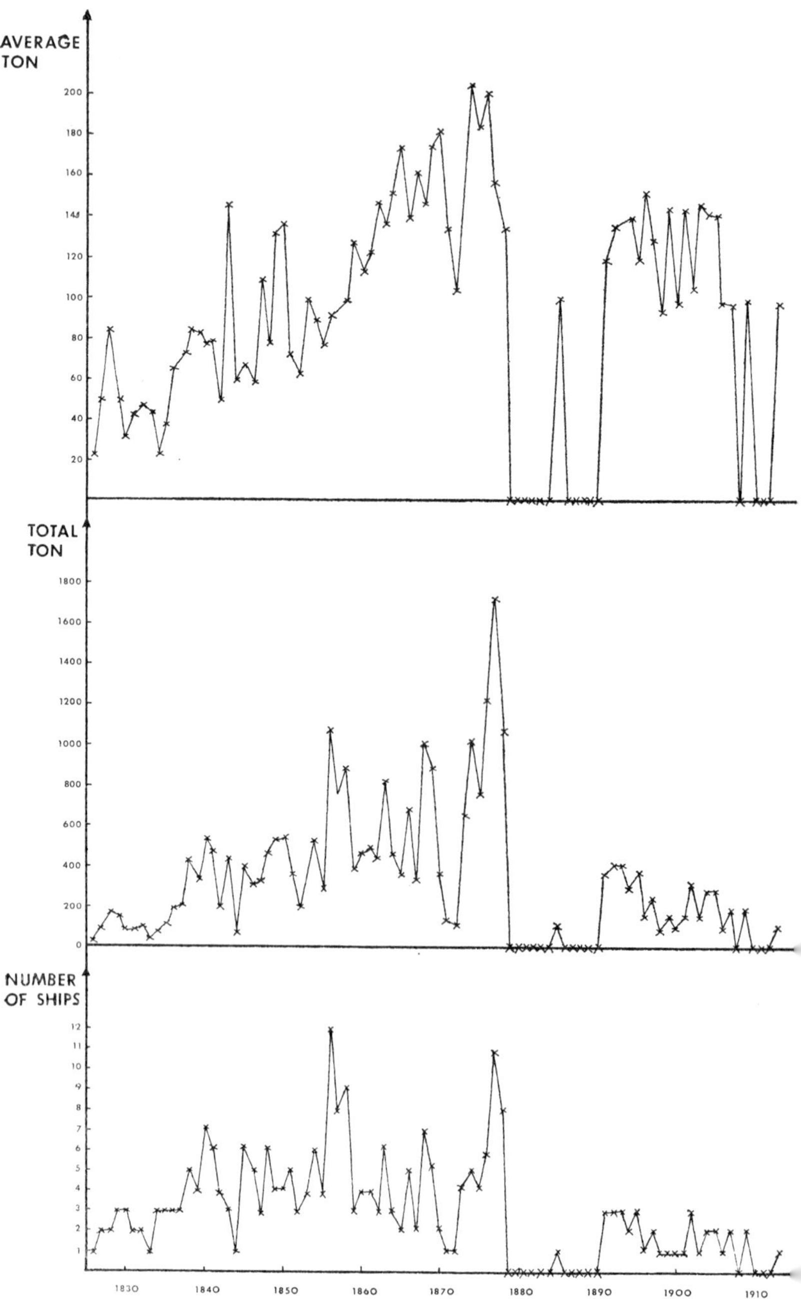


Annual totals of ship-building at Porthmadog, 1825-1913.
Sources: Registers of Shipping, Caernarfon, and D. Thomas, *H.L.S.G.*

as the *Frau Minna Petersen*. She was a smaller vessel, the two-masted *Cadwalader Jones*, built at Borth-y-gest by John Hughes for Morris Owen (Morris). The principal shareholder in her was her master, John Cadwalader, of Cricieth, master mariner, who had 20/64, having obtained a mortgage of £500 at 5% interest from William Jones, the Porthmadog sailmaker. She must have been considered a fine little vessel, for David Jones and John Watkins, both described as Surveyors of Shipping at Porthmadog, had shares in her, as well as the highly experienced Owen Morris, Porthmadog, the slate merchant. But so, too, did John Jones of Braich y Saint and Owen Jones of Pentrefelin, farmers, John Jones, Pentrefelin, coal merchant, Captain John Roberts, Borth-y-gest, master mariner, Richard Jones, Cricieth, butcher, and, for good measure, an interdenominational connection, Joseph John Williams of Pwllheli, Baptist minister, and Griffith Jones of Porthmadog, Wesleyan minister. Her subsequent history is told in Emrys Hughes's account and the extended histories of selected ships.

The busy years of 1877 and 1878 had thus produced Porthmadog ships which were truly representative of the port in that they both looked back to the earlier traditions and anticipated the future final stage of shipbuilding. The *Evelyn*, the fine brig built for Captain Hugh Roberts, and the *Marianne Greaves*, another brig, built by Simon Jones, and the barquentines *Martha Percival* and *Tony Krogmann*, both built by Ebenezer Roberts, were all very strongly built for the phosphate rock and ocean trades, comparatively large vessels in the older tradition; the *Sarah Evans*, built at Borth-y-gest in 1877 by Richard Jones, was a two-masted schooner destined to have over fifty years in the coastal and Northern European trades, and thus representative of the coastal traders, a large proportion of the vessels built over the years; the *C. E. Spooner* and *Frau Minna Petersen* were, in their design, pioneer vessels which prepared the way for the later Western Ocean Yachts, whilst the little two-masted schooner, *Cadwalader Jones*, opened up the possibilities of the Labrador coasts for small, handy vessels, thus again preparing the way for the small three-masted *Blodwen* and her sister ships.

The year 1878 was also a landmark in the history of shipbuilding for North Wales as a whole, for it marked the end of an era. At Pwllheli, eight fine vessels were built between 1874 and 1878, all of them destined for the Porthmadog trades, the *Mary Owens, Richard Owen, John Roberts, Theda, Lucy March, Charles James, W. D. Potts* and the *Carl and Louise,* but they were the last of their line. The port which had since 1786 built 463 vessels, representing a registered tonnage of 31,415 tons, had launched its last vessel. At Nefyn the story was the same. Griffith Owen built the schooner *Clara Felicia,* 90 tons, in 1874; *Walter Ulric,* 98 tons, in 1875; the three-masted *Ebenezer Parry* in 1877; and, last of all, the *Venus,* 107 tons, in 1880. At Portinllaen, the schooner *Miss Wandless,* 92 tons, 1875, and the brigantine *Annie Lloyd,* 149 tons, in 1876, both built by Hugh Hughes, brought to an end a record of shipbuilding which reached back into the eighteenth century. The story was much the same in the formerly busy Menai Straits ports: two smacks and two ketches in the seventies, the schooner *Miss Hughes,* built in 1884, and the little smack *Idris* in 1891, were the last vessels built at Caernarfon. At Bangor, the *Fomalhaut,* an 83 ton schooner, built by T. T. Parry for Captain William Williams for £1,680 in 1874, and the *Pilgrim,* a 38 ton smack, also built by Parry in 1879, were the last vessels built. In 1877 there had been great excitement at Port Dinorwic, for there the largest wooden vessel to be built in North Wales, the *Ordovic,* 825 tons, left the yard of Rees Jones and his son, W. E. Jones, on a calm Wednesday morning in February.

> 'On Wednesday, Feb. 28, the quiet inhabitants of this village witnessed the launching of the largest ship ever built in North Wales. She is a barque called "Gordfic" [*sic*], a model vessel of 1,300 tons of gross register, measuring 170 feet long, 34 feet wide, by 21 feet deep. She was built at the yard of Messrs. Rees Jones and Son, a firm owning several large vessels. The launching operations were carried on with much eclat, the weather fortunately being very calm. At 9.30 in the morning the key-wedge was struck off by Mrs. Wynn-Griffith, Llanfair Hall, and as soon as the blow was struck, the huge vessel made a steady start, and in a few seconds she was floating leisurely on the middle of the Menai Straits, in the care of her future conductor, Captain Joseph Richardson, who is a part owner, he having been in the employ of the builders firm as master for seventeen years. On her anchor being dropped she took her first start, and she was baptized in the usual manner, the ceremony being performed by Mr. W. E. Jones, the youngest partner. The builders and Captain Richardson had arranged everything so well that all passed off without accident of any kind'.[28]

Two small schooners, the *Velinheli* in 1878 and the *Miss Williams* in 1880, and the ketch *Ruby* in 1886, were launched from these yards during the next few years, but with the launching of the *Ordovic* it is clear that W. E. Jones, in common with so many of his countrymen, had decided that the future lay with the large iron sailing ships of Liverpool and Sunderland, and devoted his energies to managing the *Moel Eilian, Moel Tryfan,* and their sister ships.

Indirectly, however, it may be assumed that W. E. Jones did have an influence upon the designers of Porthmadog, for he appears to have been very able and much respected by the maritime community of North Wales. It was W. E. Jones whom William Thomas, the Liverpool ship broker, commissioned to make a model of a vessel which they agreed would be both economic and efficient in the long distance carrying trade, and, as Thomas later noted, the design of the model and specifications for such vessels as the *County of Flint, County of Denbigh, County of Merioneth, County of Pembroke, Kate Thomas, Principality, Colony* and *Province* were all by W. E. Jones, and, apart from the *County of Denbigh,* all built by Doxford, Sunderland. The design and sailing qualities of these vessels must have been of great interest to all the seafaring folk of North Wales, and none more so than to David Williams of Porthmadog, for he had himself sailed as a ship's carpenter in one of William Thomas's earlier ships, the Quebec-built *Havelock.* He had, therefore, probably served under some outstanding master mariners, including Captain Owen Jones of Cricieth, Captain John Jones of Newborough, and, possibly, the greatest sail-carrier of them all, Captain William Meredith of Ropewalk, Nefyn. David Williams returned to Porthmadog to join his uncle, Griffith Williams, in the shipyard on Rotten Tare, where, because David Jones, soon to be their arch rival, had control of the launching at the southern end, they had to launch their vessels broadside on, like Simon Jones with the *Frau Minna Petersen.* With his experience in the Cape Horn trades in the *Havelock,* David Williams could not fail to be interested in W. E. Jones's designs for the William Thomas fleet, and in the lines of his own ships, the *Ordovic* and those of the *Moel Tryfan* type. As so many of Porthmadog's later mariners, including ship's carpenters, particularly in the 1880-1914 period, also served in such ships as the *Principality* and

TONNAGE AND SHIP PRODUCTION BY RIG IN FIVE-YEAR PERIODS

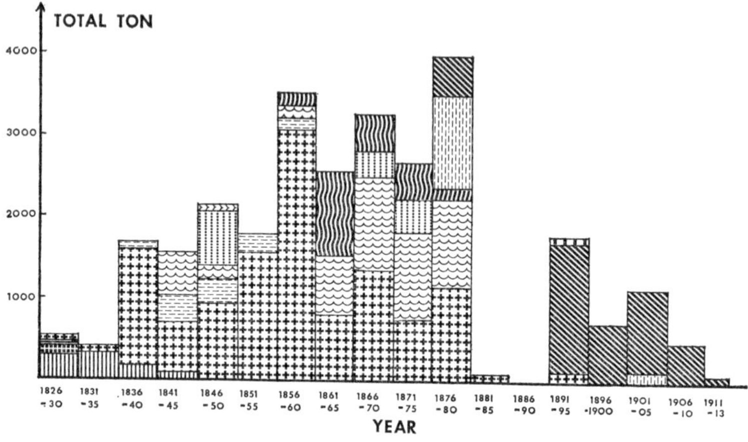


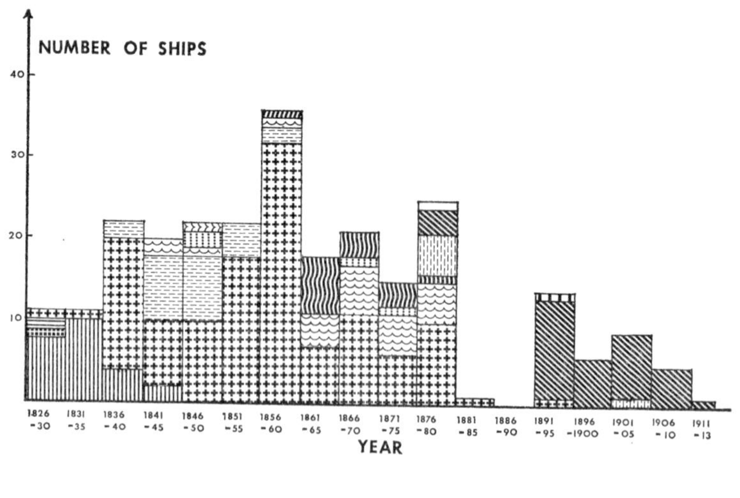


LEGEND

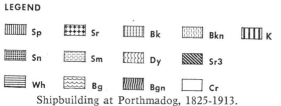

Sp | Sr | Bk | Bkn | K
Sn | Sm | Dy | Sr3
Wh | Bg | Bgn | Cr

Shipbuilding at Porthmadog, 1825-1913.
Sources: Registers of Shipping, Caernarfon, and D. Thomas, *H.L.S.G.*

the *Kate Thomas,* David Williams had plenty of experience to draw upon when building the Western Ocean Yachts.

It was David Jones, however, who built the only vessel to leave the yards at Porthmadog between 1878 and 1891, the *Richard Greaves,* launched in 1885. Henry Hughes, in *Immortal Sails,* has a wonderfully evocative description both of this period in the eighties when so much of the work was confined to repairing the storm-battered vessels, and of the builder David Jones himself. It was fitting that this energetic and very successful builder should be responsible for the first and, perhaps the best known of all the Western Ocean Yachts, the *Blodwen.* Happily, it has been possible to interview some of those who served aboard the *Blodwen* and, therefore, there are further notes about her in the selection of extended histories of Porthmadog ships. The *Owen Morris,* a larger three-masted schooner, came next from David Jones's yard; the list of her owners indicates that her building was no doubt inspired by the revival of the slate trade, for the slate shipping interests are strongly represented. The first vessel to be built by David Williams in conjunction with his uncle, Griffith Williams, was the *Dorothy,* and here again long-standing mutual interests can be seen in the names of her owners. J. E. Greaves of Bron Eifion, Cricieth, and Richard Methuen Greaves of Wern, Tremadoc, each had a quarter share, but the men who would have made certain that she was a fine sea boat were Captain Hugh Roberts, 16 Terrace Road, Porthmadog, the managing owner, and his son, Captain Thomas Roberts, Cricieth, who was to be her master, and each of them had a quarter share. The relationship between the Greaves and Roberts families went back a long way: Captain Hugh Roberts, senior, who had been master of the *Independence* and the *Constance,* had had the support of the Greaves family when the *Evelyn* was built in 1877 for his son and namesake, who remained in command of her until she was lost in 1913. The *Blodwen* and the *Dorothy* were always regarded by their builders as keen rivals, for they were the first of the group known as Western Ocean Yachts to leave the yards of David Jones and David Williams.

The spate of building which followed is rightly regarded as the high water mark for Porthmadog ships. Encouraged by the obvious success of the *Blodwen* and the *Dorothy,* the competition increased, and in 1892 the *Consul Kaestner*, ordered by Dr. J. H. Lister, proved that Ebenezer Roberts was not to be left out, even though he was now regarded as very much the veteran by his younger rivals. Captain W. H. Hughes, D.S.C., now of Holyhead, was a little boy watching all the excitement across the harbour from aboard his father's brigantine, *Geraldine*, a thirty-year-old vessel built at Barmouth in 1860, and remembers it as a very exciting day in Porthmadog, particularly for a small boy. Across at 'Eban' Roberts's yard at Station Bach, as it was known locally, there were the celebrations in connection with launching the *Consul Kaestner*, and as he wandered home, he peeped into the Town Hall where the local Volunteers in their bright uniforms were having a gargantuan meal with harassed womenfolk carrying mountainous dishes of new potatoes.[29] Nine days later, Griffith and David Williams's *Elizabeth* was registered. Her list of owners again suggested a powerful combination of local interests, for, in addition to her master, Captain Evan Jones, who had a quarter share in her (thanks to a loan of £716 from Griffith Williams, her builder), they included James McKerrow, a Tremadoc draper, David and William Morris, the ship chandlers, Jane Morris, W. F. Jones, a Pwllheli saddler, Robert Thomas, the former Nefyn schoolmaster, now of Cricieth and well on the way to becoming an influential shipowner and Liverpool shipbroker, as well as Griffith Williams himself, and, almost inevitably, Captain Hugh Parry, the shipbroker. David Jones countered by launching *The Oakleys* a month later, in which Captain Llewelyn G. Llewelyn, an experienced master mariner, had the major shareholding, a vessel to be commanded by one of the outstanding mariners of the port, Captain Griffith E. Dedwith. John Roberts, in conjunction with Ebenezer Roberts, built the *Jenny Jones* in the following year, and Emrys Hughes remembered this launch well; she, again, had been built for Dr. Lister, whose connection with the port is told by Dr. Lewis Lloyd later in this book. She was the last vessel to be built in Ebenezer Roberts's yard; henceforth all Porthmadog ships were to be built by either David Jones or David Williams. As the majority of them sailed in the days immediately preceding the First World War, there are many memories of them which Emrys Hughes, who knew them well, has been able to record. Between 1894 and 1913, no more than two vessels were built in any one year, except

1902, when the *Royal Lister, Kitty* and first *Isallt* were built. In the leaner years, only one left the stocks. Captain Griffith Roberts, O.B.E., and Captain R. Roberts, both of Borth-y-gest, Captain W. H. Hughes, D.S.C., and, indeed, all those who sailed in them who have been interviewed, stated that these late schooners were all very much alike. Yet each one had its own special qualities which had been carefully thought out by David Jones or David Williams in highly conspiratorial fashion with their customers, all of whom had their individual requirements. Basically there were the two types, the smaller vessels, like the *Blodwen, Elizabeth Pritchard* and *M. A. James,* that proved to be so successful, and the somewhat larger type represented by the *Emrys, Mary Lloyd* and the *Miss Morris.* Fuller details about them and their subsequent fate is given in the alphabetical list, but for the reader's convenience, their dimensions are summarised here:

| *Date* | *Name* | *Tg* | *Tn* | *Dimensions* | *Builder* |
|---|---|---|---|---|---|
| 1891 | *Blodwen* | 120 | 99 | 88.8/22.7/11.6 | David Jones |
| | *Owen Morris* | 168 | 139 | 102.2/23.9/12.4 | David Jones |
| | *Dorothy* | 143 | 122 | 91.2/22.9/11.7 | Griff + David Williams |
| 1892 | *Consul Kaestner* | 144 | 116 | 101/24.2/10.7 | E. Roberts |
| | *Elizabeth* | 156 | 136 | 100/22.9/11.8 | Griff + David Williams |
| | *The Oakleys* | 147 | ? | 104.5/23.8/12 | David Jones |
| 1893 | *Mary Annie* | 154 | 130 | 96.4/23.4/11.9 | David Jones |
| | *Emrys* | 164 | 151 | 102.2/23.6/11.7 | Griff + David Williams |
| 1894 | *Mary Lloyd* | 172 | 150 | 101.8/23.5/12.3 | Griff + David Williams |
| | *Mary Owens* | 150 | 130 | 97/23.1/11.9 | David Jones |
| 1895 | *Elizabeth Llewelyn* | 159 | 136 | 97.3/23.4/11.8 | David Jones |
| | *Sydney Smith* | 177 | 151 | 101.8/23.6/12.2 | David Williams |
| 1896 | *Miss Morris* | 156 | 151 | 96.5/23.5/12.3 | David Jones |
| 1897 | *David Morris* | 162 | 135 | 99.6/23.2/12.0 | David Jones |
| | *Ellen James* (1) | 139 | 117 | 92.4/22.8/11.6 | David Williams |
| 1898 | *Elizabeth Pritchard* (1) | 122 | 93 | 88.7/22.7/10.6 | David Williams |
| 1899 | *M. Lloyd Morris* | 166 | 144 | 101/23/12.3 | David Jones |
| 1900 | *M. A. James* | 124 | 97 | 89.6/22.7/10.6 | David Williams |
| 1901 | *Callidora* | 169 | 144 | 103.3/23.8/12 | David Jones |
| 1902 | *Kitty* | 124 | 98 | 90.6/22.8/10.5 | David Williams |
| | *Royal Lister* | 140 | 117 | 92.3/22/11.7 | David Jones |
| | *Isallt* (1) | 124 | 98 | 91.7/22.6/10.4 | David Williams |

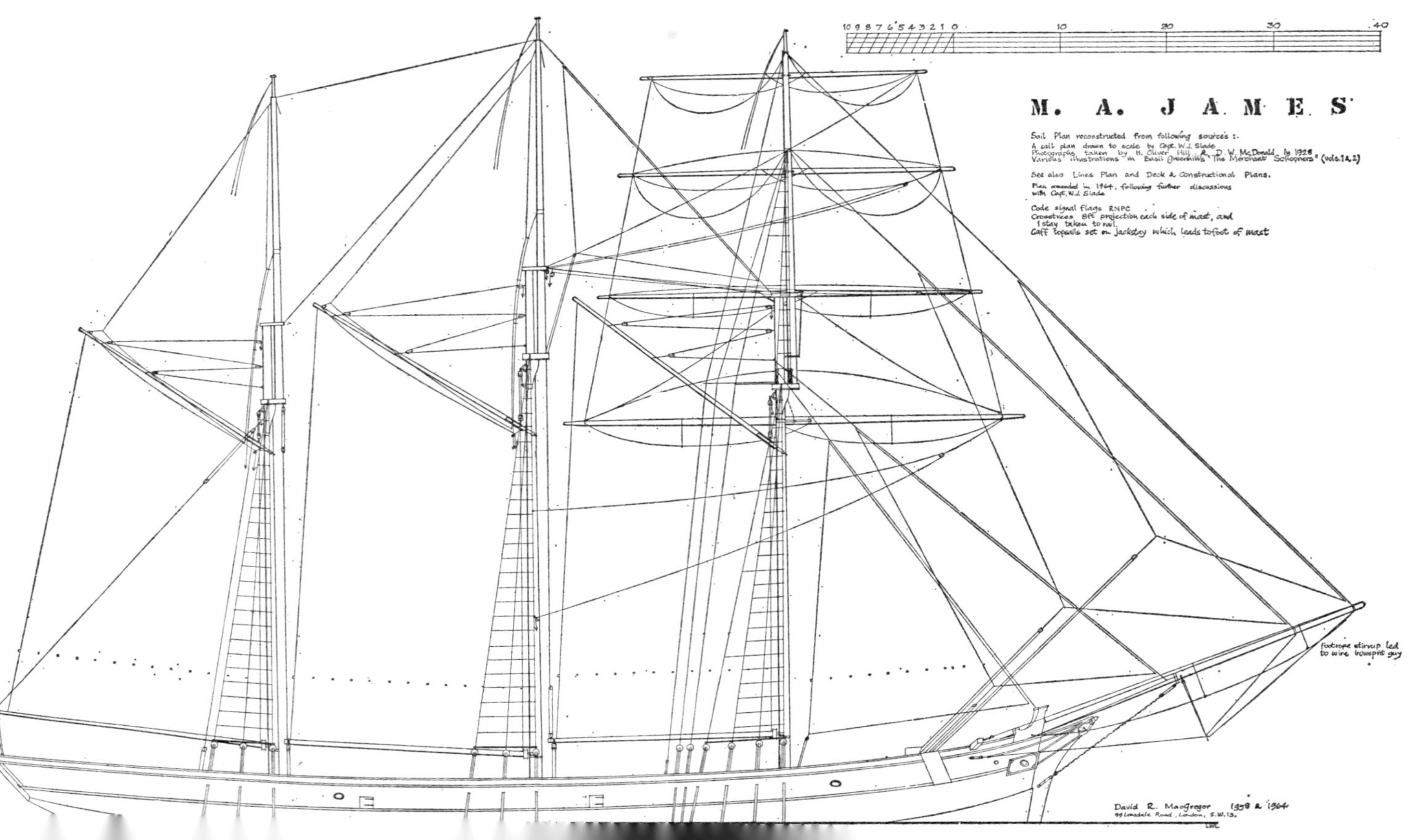
10 9 8 7 6 5 4 3 2 1 0 10 20 30 40
M. A. JAMES
Sail Plan reconstructed from following sources:
A sail plan drawn to scale by Capt. W.J. Slade
Photographs taken by H. Oliver Hill & D. W. McDonald in 1928
Various illustrations in Basil Greenhill's "The Merchant Schooners" (vols. 1 & 2)
See also Lines Plan and Deck & Constructional Plans.
Plan amended in 1964, following further discussions with Capt. W.J. Slade
Code signal flags RNPC
Crosstrees 8ft projection each side of mast, and 1 stay taken to rail.
Gaff topsails set on jackstay which leads to foot of mast
Footrope stirrup led to wire bowsprit guy
David R. MacGregor 1958 & 1964
99 Lonsdale Road, London, S.W.13.

| Date | Name | Tg | Tn | Dimensions | Builder |
|---|---|---|---|---|---|
| 1903 | *William Pritchard* | 171 | 146 | 102.2/23.7/12.4 | David Jones |
| 1904 | *Ellen James* (2) | 165 | 137 | 101.4/23.7/11.9 | David Williams |
| | *John Llewelyn* | 171 | 145 | 199.8/22.6/12.2 | David Jones |
| 1905 | *Elizabeth Eleanor* | 169 | 137 | 101.4/23.7/11.9 | David Williams |
| | *William Morton* | 169 | 142 | 104.2/23.7/11.7 | David Jones |
| 1906 | *John Pritchard* | 118 | 96 | 92.6/22.6/10.4 | David Williams |
| 1907 | *Gracie* | 127 | 96 | 92.6/23.1/10.5 | David Jones |
| | *R. J. Owens* | 123 | 98 | 91/22.6/10.4 | David Williams |
| 1909 | *Isallt* (2) | 133 | 98 | 94.3/23/10.6 | David Williams |
| | *Elizabeth Pritchard* (2) | 126 | 99 | 93.4/23/10.4 | David Jones |
| 1913 | *Gestiana* | 124 | 98 | 95/22.6/10.5 | David Williams |

Mr. David Williams, now of Largs, Ayrshire, was a boy of six when his father, David Williams, the shipbuilder, was preparing the second *Isallt* for launching in 1908. Together with his schoolmates, he wanted to be one of those heroes of the classroom who had seized a piece of the blue ribbon used in the christening ceremony, and he remembers that pieces of the said ribbon were then sold for a ½d a time in the schoolyard. Last summer, 1974, David Williams recalled those far-off days and recorded his memories of his father's yard at Porthmadog.[30] Born in 1860, his father had first gone to sea in 1879 as a ship's carpenter; the date is significant, for, as already indicated in this chapter, this was the year when shipbuilding ceased temporarily in Porthmadog. For the next eleven years, David Williams, like so many of his contemporaries, sailed in the *Havelock, Larkfield* and other large ocean-going sailing ships in the Cape Horn and Australian trades. He had attained Chief Officer's status when he came ashore in 1890, at the age of thirty, to assist his uncle, Griffith Williams, who was then building the *Blodwen*. Gradually, he took over more responsibility for the building of the vessel, so that when the *Sydney Smith* was launched in 1895 David Williams was named as the sole builder for the first time.

His son remembers the yard employing about a dozen men when the second *Isallt* was built; John Jones, the foreman, was highly experienced, and could undertake any work in the yard, but David Williams himself probably worked harder than anyone. The working day started at six a.m. and continued until six in the evening, but rather than employ another man, if the boiler needed to be lit at four o'clock in the morning to steam the planks, it was David Williams himself who was there to light it, ensuring that no time was wasted when the men arrived at six. If it had come on to blow in the night, and the ropes securing either his own vessels or vessels being repaired by him needed attention, he was down there, taking his two young sons with him to do the work.

The oak used for the frame of his vessels had almost invariably been selected by David Williams, who went out to the Maentwrog area and looked for local oak of the right shape so that he could use the natural bend of the wood for his vessels. His son remembers the considerable quantity of rock salt that was imported for seasoning wood; if there was any rock salt to spare, David Williams would sell it to local farmers or tradesmen. The iron work was all done locally, either by blacksmiths or at the Britannia Foundry, but in order to galvanize it, the iron was sent by the *Rebecca* to Liverpool, and there was some impatience waiting for its return. Pitch pine, yellow pine, mahogany for cabins, teak, were all imported, and so was very heavy gear, but sails and blocks, indeed, almost everything required for building the vessel, was obtained locally.

Leafing through the ledgers of Jones and Morris, Britannia Place, the sailmakers, one gets an impression of the prices of individual sails, the types of canvas used, and the costs of a suit of sails for a new vessel. When the second *Ellen James* was being made ready by David Williams for launching in 1904, for example, he paid the sailmakers £120, the contract price for 'New Ship's Outfit of Sails, Covers, Tarpaulins etc. Complete, made to all satisfaction of Builder and Purchaser, Lump Sum'. This seems to have been about the standard price; David Jones paid £120 for a new outfit of sail for the *Miss Morris* in 1896, for the *David Morris* in 1897, and the *M. Lloyd Morris* in 1899, a little less for the *Royal Lister,* £115 in 1902, but, not unexpectedly, more for the barquentine *Callidora,* £124.10 in 1900, and £122 for the *John Llewelyn* in March 1904. For the *William Morton,* regarded by several master mariners as 'a real clipper', David Jones paid £128 for the complete outfit in 1904. Hugh Jones, spar, pump and blockmaker, Cornhill, whose main work was obviously concerned with repairs and refitting vessels already in service, occasionally did some work on new vessels for David Jones, though David Williams's name does not appear in the ledgers — he may have patronised another blockmaker, or had the necessary work done by his own men. In June 1899, David Jones paid Hugh Jones, the blockmaker, 'per new vessel labour, making 2 round tops and fitting topmast preventers, 7/6d; New Blocks, Spars etc. for new vessel M. Ll. Morris as per agreement £47'. Hugh Jones also supplied the builder from time to time with sheaves, timber and treenails. Mr. David Williams remembers that his father had one man who seemed to spend most of his day at his bench using the square socket, rather like a very large pencil sharpener, which produced a vast amount of treenails when the yard was busy. At the saw-pit, the sawyers, one above and one below, always attracted the attention of small boys. He also remembers the many half-models strewn around the yard, all, unfortunately, long since vanished.

In the years from 1906 onwards, life was not always easy for the shipbuilders. Mr. Williams remembers his father having a schooner which he had built speculatively, about 1907, on the stocks for some time without a buyer, with consequent hardship for the builder and his employees, but usually the two banks in Porthmadog were most helpful and understanding and did much to encourage the shipbuilders. Perhaps this is why David Williams wanted his sons to enter a secure profession like banking, and strongly opposed either going to sea; in the event, one became a dentist and the other, the young David Williams, went to work at the Britannia Foundry, Porthmadog, but later trained as an engineer and went to sea himself in 1922 for some years, before taking a shore appointment in the Persian Gulf. David Williams, senior, continued to build schooners. The *Gestiana* was his, and Porthmadog's, last. He always took his schooners as far as St. Tudwal's Roads; not, he said, that he did not trust the pilot or the master — it was just that he wanted to be sure that the vessels were in good shape as they set off on a voyage that would take them to the Elbe, to Newfoundland, and to the Mediterranean. His children would take penny bets as to the length of a particular vessel's passage out across the Atlantic or back home; the young David Williams was sent by his father round to the houses of crew members in Borth-y-gest and Porthmadog when the telegram came bearing the word 'Agreeable', the code word to say that the vessel had arrived safely at the port in question. It was always a thrill to be allowed to sail with his uncle, Captain R. O.

Williams of the *Isallt*, on a coastal voyage, to take the helm; — 'Keep an eye on that lower to'gans'l there' his uncle would say — to learn to box the compass, and to hear the stories of what had happened at Cadiz, Harbour Grace or Patras. Home in Porthmadog, he loved to listen to the yarns of John Griffith, the rigger, Llyn Bach, for whom the boys in their navy jerseys used to hold the ball of marline whilst he was busy serving wire, and regaling them with stories of distant ports. Lieutenant-Commander J. Penri Davies, D.S.C., in his most interesting recently published *Blas y Môr,* recalls another John Griffiths, sailmaker, a tall, bearded man, with a voice like a foghorn and great histrionic talents, who used to thrill the boys of his generation in Porthmadog with yarns of the China tea-clippers, and remembers with affection the workshop of William Roberts, pump, block and spar maker, with its fine craftsmen, and the smithy of Richard Williams. The latter, incidentally, was a relative of John Williams, another blacksmith in Porthmadog, better known in Wales in the last century as Ioan Madog, the poet, who died in 1878 aged 66. Both he and William Roberts, Gwilym Eryri, a sailmaker by trade, won many awards at local eisteddfodau for their poetry, but Ioan Madog was also a very skilful craftsman, who is said to have invented a number of improvements for Porthmadog ships, notably a specially adapted windlass and a 'patent stopper'. Another craftsman who was a very well-known character in Porthmadog was Evan Morgan (1846-1920), better known as Llew Madog, a singer much in demand at local concerts. He was a cabinet-maker by trade, and largely employed in making mahogany cabins for the vessels built at Porthmadog. Captain W. H. Hughes remembers a day long ago when, as a small boy wandering from schooner to schooner in the harbour, he called in at Llew Madog's hut, at Trwyn y Pier — he knew him well, as he lived in Borth-y-gest. It was lunch time and Llew had gone for his pint to one of the pubs in the harbour area, so the very young boy edged his way into the fine new cabin the cabinet-maker was completing for one of the new schooners. As he surveyed a large mahogany panel, planed down as smooth as glass, his boyish eyes fell upon some fine chisels, all laid out in order. What was more natural than to carve, painstakingly, on the centre of the panel the initials W.H.H. — his friend Llew Madog would be pleased! Later that day he saw Robert Jones, who had sailed as cook with his father in the *Edward Seymour,* who called to him, saying he'd better run for his life if he saw Llew Madog approaching! The future distinguished master mariner kept well away from the harbour for many days after that little incident.

The photographs of David Jones and his men in the yard as the *Gracie* neared completion; the photographs of David Williams and his team with the *R. J. Owens* in the background; and in the hold of one of the schooners, probably the second *Isallt,* as she was in course of construction; and alongside the *Isallt* again, showing her massive oak frame and the inevitable gaggle of small boys — these, more than any words, convey the world of the shipbuilders of Porthmadog. The many photographs of their ships, at sea or in harbour, speak eloquently of the excellence of their creations.

---

14, Cornhill, Portmadoc, Nov 12th 1887

The Owners of Brigteen Tyne

To HUGH JONES,

BLOCK, PUMP & SPAR MAKER.

STEERING WHEELS MADE TO ORDER & REPAIRED.

| 1886 | | | | | |
|---|---|---|---|---|---|
| Sept 30 | To | 2. Bolts in Dbl block | | | 3 |
| | " | New stave in Bucket & gal hoops | | | 10 |
| June 13/87 | " | 1 Dozen deck plugs 3 (?) 1. 3" Block 1/3 | | 1 | 6 |
| 17 | " | Side piece on 9" Block | | | 4 |
| | " | Mole handle 6 1 gal hoop 7½ | | 1 | 1½ |
| Sept 20 | " | 2 plugs for water cask 6 ea | | 1 | 0 |
| 22 | " | remaking Kit & new bottom & hoops | | 1 | 3 |
| | " | hooping buckets | | 2 | 0 |
| | " | 1-13 ft ash oar | | 6 | 6 |
| | | | £ | 14 | 9½ |

Settled Nov 12/87
Hugh Jones

## REFERENCES

[1] Basil Greenhill, *The Merchant Schooners* (1968), 1, 58-60.
[2] J. Glyn Davies, *T. Cymm. S.*, 1948, 212.
[3] William Morris, *Plans of the Principal Harbours, Bays and Roads in St. George's and the Bristol Channels, etc.* (Shrewsbury, 1801), 15.
[4] B.R.S., 1821. The *Gomer* was the ninth vessel to be registered in 1821.
[5] O. Morris, 53. In addition to the timber, imports in 1855 included 4,000 tons of coal and 4,000 tons of limestones, from Plymouth, Cork, Limerick and Waterford, 2,000 sacks of flour, 200 sacks of bran, beans, etc., from Liverpool, 2,000 quarters of oats and barley, 300 tons of grocery, and 1,000 tons of sundry goods, including iron, powder and oil.
[6] *P.P. 1894 LXXVI*, 707. Report of timber-laden ships lost. *Hope* capsized 22 August 1892.
[7] *CN* quoting from *Halifax Herald*, August 1892.
[8] Basil Greenhill and Ann Gifford, *Westcountrymen in Prince Edward's Isle* (1967).
[9] R. S. Craig, 'British Shipping and British North American Shipbuilding in the early 19th century, with special reference to Prince Edward Isles', in *The South West and the Sea*, ed. H. E. S. Fisher, Exeter Papers in Economic History (1968).
[10] B.R.S. and C.R.S. and Bob Owen, 'Y Barque Hindoo, Caernarvon', *T.C.H.S.*, 5, 60-70.
[11] J. Glyn Davies in *T. Cymm. S.*, 1948, 211.
[12] Jürgen Meyer, *150 Jahre Blankeneser Schiffahrt*, 1785-1935 (Hamburg, 1968).
[13] Henry Hughes, *Through Mighty Seas* and *Immortal Sails* (2nd Ed., 1969), 145-154.
[14] *CN*, 14 January 1921.
[15] Henry Hughes, *Immortal Sails*, 119.
[16] Account-book of Morris E. Morris, Chemist, Druggist, Grocer and Tea Dealer, Porthmadog, now N.L.W. 7898E.
[17] C.R.O. Log book of Portmadoc National School. Other entries in 1875 refer to lessons on the West Indies, and the Baltic Sea — regions which the pupils would have heard their fathers and brothers talking about when referring to their voyages.
[18] *CN*, 19 January 1877.
[19] C.R.O. M/531, letter from Emrys Hughes to Basil Greenhill, 24 May 1947.
[20] Greenhill, *The Merchant Schooners*, 81-161.
[21] *CN*, February 1877.
[22] *CN*, 9 March 1877.
[23] *CN*, August 1877.
[24] Henry Hughes, *Immortal Sails*, 165.
[25] *CDH*, 8 June 1878.
[26] Greenhill, *The Merchant Schooners*, 1, 55.
[27] ibid., 79-80.
[28] *CN*, 9 March 1877.
[29] T.R. with Captain W. H. Hughes, D.S.C., Holyhead, August 1974.
[30] T.R. with David Williams, Esq., of Largs, Ayrshire, August 1974.

## III

## THE SEAMEN

On 24 April 1839, Thomas Jones, master of the *New Expedition*, of Porthmadog, opened his new account book to record the finances of his little vessel, and laboriously noted that he had received that day £2 from William Jones, owner of the vessel. The *New Expedition* does not appear among the hundreds that Emrys Hughes traced, nor is there any mention of her in the lists carefully compiled by Henry Parry and David Thomas, or more recently by Dr. Lewis Lloyd for the port of Barmouth. She does not appear to have been built at Porthmadog, but wherever she had come from, by 1839 she was regarded as 'of Pord Madoc' as her master proudly wrote on the first page of his account-book. The English language was foreign to Thomas Jones, as it was to so many of these early mariners of Gwynedd, but he made a brave stab at it. The record he left unwittingly for posterity is valuable in that it is one of the earliest documents recording the day-to-day work of one of the little coasting vessels of Porthmadog in those comparatively quiet years when its harbour was being carefully ruled by the first harbour master, Daniel Morris of the Ship Inn, whose tombstone in Ynyscynhaiarn is inscribed, 'To the memory of Daniel Morris, Harbour Master in Portmadoc, a strong, useful, active man, who died December 29, 1840, aged 51 years'.[1] Space does not permit for more than the first two pages of the first quarter's entries for 1839 of the *New Expedition*'s account book to be included; had they survived, the account books of the scores of little coasting vessels which plied from Porthmadog around the coasts of Britain would have probably given much the same story.

There are many other pages recording disbursements at the various ports, so it must not be assumed that there was a large profit as these pages might suggest. From Liverpool, the *New Expedition* sailed home through the Menai Straits, paying six shilling and nine pence for the pilot through the Swellies, and putting in to Caernarfon

| | | £ | s | d |
|---|---|---|---|---|
| 1839 | Abril 24th at Pord Madoc | | | |
| | Resivet of William Jones --- | 2 | 0 | 0 |
| Mey 11 | Resivet at Sudney freidu | 29 | 12 | 0 |
| June 8th | Reeved at Port Matoc freite | | | |
| | for Cargo of Cyclom Lym | 24 | 0 | 0 |
| July 3th | Resivet at Cork freite of | | | |
| | 70 tons of Sletes 9/ Per ton | 31 | 10 | " |
| 12th | at Pord madoc Resived on a | | | |
| | Cownd of Carco Leimsdon Lym | 10 | " | " |
| 25 | do. frum Daniel Moris on | | | |
| | A Count of the Leimsdon - | 5 | " | " |
| August 5 | Glousder Resived | | | |
| | freid from Port Madoc Sletes | | | |
| | 70 don at 8/6 Per don — — | 29 | 15 | " |
| August 21 | from Nuport to Leverpwl | | | |
| | with 72.15 of Torn at 8/6 don | 30 | 18 | 1½ |
| | Resived for Limston £4.9.0 £ | 167 | 4 | 1½ |

| 1839 | | L | s | d |
|---|---|---|---|---|
| Mey 14th | Swansca bey in the Bank | L | s | d |
| | do the onor William Jones swm | 17 | 0 | 0 |
| July 4th | 1 bl of sope | " | 4 | 6 |
| 1839 | Bente at the Bank in Cork | | | |
| | do the onor William Jones | 15 | " | " |
| 1839 August 10 | Nuport to Cook & Turner | | | |
| | for the owl mensel | 12 | " | 8 |
| 1839 23 August | at Lewerpwl | | | |
| | Sucar 12 at 7½ pount | " | 7 | 6 |
| | 12 haf Beind Clasus | " | 3 | 6 |
| 24th | Bey for the forsl | 4 | 4 | " |
| | sas flowar | 2 | 3 | 6 |
| 25 | do suger 12 lb at 7½ | " | 7 | 6 |
| | do the onor Wam Jones for Bwtsiar | " | 6 | 8 |
| 26 | do the onor William Jones | 14 | " | " |
| | L | 65 | 17 | 10 |

where Thomas Jones bought five pounds of beef (at five pence a pound), 'Dedus' (potatoes), butter, and herrings. He had paid seven shilling and three pence at Gloucester for 'Canfas for the scwarsel', which suggests that the *New Expedition* was square-rigged, possibly a small brig. At Porthmadog, in June, in addition to paying the blockmaker, the carpenter, and Daniel Morris for bread, he had obviously had to have the vessel surveyed, 'Mr Ellis for mesyr fesel, £1.0.0,". His own wages were £3.10.0 a month. Evan Huws, who served from April 23 to July 10 received £2.3.0 a month, and 'Howal Loid' who replaced him on July 11, 'shipped on board' at a rate of £2.5.0 The other members of the crew were paid less; Thomas Jones, £1.12.0. 'John Bowal', who joined at Gloucester, received £1.10.0 a month, Robert Jones 17/-, and David Jones 7/-. Advances were not made on a lavish scale; at Lydney Thomas Jones had had 2/6, 1/- at Swansea, £1.3.0 at Porthmadog, in mid-May, and a further 11/8 there towards the end of the mond, 12/6 at Cork, and the balance of his wages when he returned to Porthmadog in July; the boy, David Jones, had received 2/10 at Cork, 3/- at Porthmadog, and 3d at Liverpool, and the balance of 15/- for the quarter. The *New Expedition* had carried slates, culm and limestone, typical cargoes during this period, as well as seventy-two tons of iron from Newport to Liverpool.[2]

The *William* was built at Porthmadog in 1838, probably by Francis Roberts, and was one of the largest schooners to have been built in the first fifteen years of the port's history. By 1844 her master (and probable owner) was Captain Hugh Watkins, who was paid £5 a month, and, therefore, received £60 for the period from January 1 to December 31, 1844. The remainder of the crew were paid, according to the ship's account book, as follows:

| | |
|---|---|
| Evan Jones, Mate from the 27 Feb 1844 till 3 January 1835 [*sic*] | |
| 10 months 7 days at 45/- per month | £23.0.6 |
| Robert Owens, Seaman from the 29 Feb till 3 January | |
| 10 months 5 days at 40/- per month | £20.6.8 |
| John Williams, Seaman from the 29 Feb till 20 July, | |
| 4 months 21 days at 35/- and 21 July till 3 January, | |
| 5 months 13 days at 40/- | £19.1.10 |
| Watkin Parry, Apprentice Second Year the sum of £6 | £6.0.0d |
| Owen Davies, Boy from 29 Feby till 3 Jany | |
| 10 months 5 days at 10/6 per month | £5.6.8 |
| | £133.15.8[3] |

During the year 1844, the *William* sailed with a cargo of one hundred and thirty-six tons of slates from Porthmadog to London at a freight of 11/6d per ton in March, then took ninety tons fifteen hundredweight of coal tar from London to Bridgwater at 10/- per ton in April, bricks from Bridgwater to Falmouth in May for a lump sum of £42, and then returned in ballast to Caernarfon. From Caernarfon she took one hundred and thirty-eight tons ten hundredweight of slates at 10/- per ton to North Shields in June, seven hundred and eighteen quarters of barley at 1/6 per quarter from Newcastle to Gloucester in July, one hundred and forty tons of pig iron at 13/6 per ton from Gloucester to Amsterdam in August. She must then have sailed for Newcastle — there is no record of her cargo — whence she embarked six keels, three chaldrons of coal at £10.10.0 per keel for Jersey, where she arrived on September 21. By October 15 she was at Runcorn, having sailed there from Charlestown where she had embarked one hundred and thirty-seven tons of chain, stones and clay at 6/3 per ton. Welsh vessels almost invariably could get a coal cargo at Runcorn, and on November 1, the *William* arrived in Caernarfon with fifty tons of coal at 1/6 per ton. Three weeks later she had arrived at North Shields with one hundred and forty tons of slates at 12/- per ton, and her final cargo in 1844 was six and a half keels of coals at £10.10.0 per keel from Newcastle to Exmouth, where she arrived on Christmas Eve. During the year the value of freights recorded in her account book amounted to £648.18.0. Against this one can place the £133.15.8 for wages to the crew, £66.4.0½ for their victualling, £172.11.9 for port charges and £75.11.0 in the wear and tear account; the owners of the *William* could feel well satisfied with the year 1844.

Captain Hugh Watkins was probably one of the leading master mariners in the port at this time; he had been one of the first to set his hand and seal to the agreement which established the Portmadoc Mutual Ship Insurance Society, along with Evan Evans, Henry Jones and Francis Roberts, the shipbuilders, and Captain Richard Prichard, now a banker, and Captain David Morris of the *Success*. By 1853, the *William* had extended her range of sailing considerably, and although Captain Watkins is still listed as her master in *Lloyd's Register* for 1852, it is likely a new master was employed in the following year, again at £5 per month. In the *Lloyd's Register* of

1855, J. Roberts is named as master. In 1853 the mate was paid at the rate of 52/6 per month, the seamen at 45/- and 40/- and the young cook at 10/- a month; the total wages paid to the crew in the year ending 1853 was £207.0.2. This was certainly £70 more than the wages bill for 1844, but the receipts from freights had, in the meantime, almost doubled to a total of £1,017.18.4. The main reason for the considerable increase was that instead of her coastal voyages, the *William* was now sailing in the European trades. In February 1853 she had sailed with slate from Porthmadog for King's Lynn, with barley from Lynn to Neath, iron from Neath to Cardiff, and a further cargo of iron from Cardiff to Liverpool, where she arrived on April 4. From Liverpool, the *William* sailed with general cargo for Gibraltar, and there then followed a profitable voyage with wine from Cadiz to Southampton and Hull, and another in the autumn with wheat from Danzig to Le Havre, at a freight of £250.10.0. She then made one voyage before Christmas with slates from Porthmadog to Mistley and after Christmas with coal from Newcastle to Dublin. After settling the account for wear and tear, victualling, port charges, and the men's wages, the profits on the year's work amounted to £182.11.10. It would be wrong to attribute too much of the success to the longer European voyages, for most of the schooners from the Welsh ports were earning reasonable profits at this time — the *Heir Apparent,* a thirteen-year-old schooner, for example, earned for her Anglesey Captain, Owen Williams, and his fellow shareholders a profit of £95.4.1 in the first half year of 1855, and that was in the coastal trade.[4] Profits fluctuated considerably; Captain Griffith Griffiths in the *New Valiant* (a smaller schooner than the *William*), built in Porthmadog by Evan Evans in 1841, was able to pay a dividend of £40 to himself and his fellow owners, and keep £7.10.5 in 'the ships Pocket', on the year's working from 9 March 1849 to 9 March 1850. In that year, the *New Valiant* had sailed from Porthmadog to Gloucester with slate, then to Rochfort, Dunkirk, Cardiff, Liverpool, Wick, Colberg, Danzig, London, Lybster, Limerick and Liverpool again, earning in all £403.4.7 by way of freights. Port charges, victualling and wear and tear amounted to £235 and the crew's wages to £109.13.6, and £8 had to be paid to the ship's husband, and for insurance. During the year, Captain Griffiths had three mates, Robert Owen from March 10 to September

20, William Roberts from September 27 to December 12, and John Jenkins from December 12 to January 14, 1850, the first two being paid at a rate of £2.6.0 per month, and Jenkins £2.10.0 — it was, after all, a voyage over Christmas. The seamen, who had also only signed on for the individual voyages, were paid at rates of £2 and £1.5.0 respectively, and the young cook, 8/- per month. For the voyage home from Liverpool to Bangor, and from Caernarfon to Porthmadog, Captain Griffith employed 'runners' who were paid £2.5.0 and £1.4.0 respectively. The following year left a balance of £31.12.0 after the accounts were settled, a year in which the *New Valiant* had sailed mainly in the coastal trade, with one voyage to 'Flanders'; in 1851 she made a return voyage there, and also to Lisbon from Liverpool and back to London with a profitable cargo. Even the smaller schooners of Porthmadog were seizing the opportunities further afield, and each year, as indicated in the earlier chapters, more vessels were being built to compete for freights. This meant a call for more masters and mates, and, to meet the requirements of the Porthmadog Ship Insurance Society they had to satisfy the Committee of that Society of their competency: 'no person shall be employed as master of any vessel insured by the Society who shall be under the age of 21 years, unless the previous consent of the Committee for that purpose shall have been obtained and entered into the books of the Society. The master of every vessel insured in the Society who shall not have previously commanded a ship or vessel for 12 months shall appear before the Committee to be examined as to his competency'.[5] The first members of the Committee had included such men as Captain Prichard of the *Gomer,* Captain David Morris of the *Success,* Captain John Jones of the *William Alexander,* Captain Ellis Roberts of the *Lucy,* and Captain Hugh Watkins of the *William,* and the shipbuilders, Evan Evans, Henry Jones and Francis Roberts. They were not men to be trifled with, and, as they were all financially involved, they and their successors ensured that standards of competency were maintained.

The rapidly increasing number of vessels built and needing to be manned and the extension of the range of trades in which Porthmadog vessels were sailing, must inevitably have caused problems, for master mariners are not created overnight, and the 'Mutual' 's Committee would naturally have looked not only for aptitude but also for experience and 'sea-time'. But, perhaps, most difficult of all, the nature of the expanding trade called for a deeper knowledge of navigation than mere coastal pilotage, and this, according to some witnesses who gave evidence to the Commissioners appointed to enquire into the state of education in Wales in 1847, was just the problem; 'many of our Captains know nothing of navigation. They can just go to London, Hamburgh, the French coast and different ports by the help of certain clues which they have'.[6]

In *Ships and Seamen of Anglesey,* I attempted to show that there is reason to question the generally gloomy picture presented by the Commissioners in 1847 regarding the lack of navigational instructions, and their statement that 'navigation has been as much neglected as every other branch of industrial knowledge, and the same ignorance characterizes the adult sailors at Holyhead, Amlwch, Bangor, Barmouth, Portmadoc and Conway'. The school of William Francis at Amlwch, and the evidence of the work undertaken by pupils at that school, suggested that the Commissioners were underestimating the attempts being made to provide mariners with at least some basic instruction in navigation.[7] It is, however, very difficult to assess the availability and quality of such instructions. The schools were, in almost all cases, private adult schools, not connected with the British or National Schools, whose log-books are more easily available. It is only by chance that some of the exercise-books in which aspiring mariners painstakingly entered their efforts have survived. John Hughes's exercise-book at Amlwch in 1842 contained a series of graduated exercises relating to 'Chart Navigation', using local examples in Liverpool Bay and St. George's Channel, and examples of how to keep a journal at sea. The potential master mariner, however, had also to know about the world of business, for he had to be able to keep an account of freights, and, as trade extended beyond the purely local coastal traffic to more prolonged visits to foreign countries, he needed to know about exchange rates for currency, the mysteries of brokerage and a host of complex business transactions.

At Plasgwyn, near Y Ffôr (Fourcrosses), within a few miles of Pwllheli and Porthmadog, there was a 'navigation school' kept by a woman teacher, as in the case of the school of William Francis's daughter at Caernarfon. The teacher at Plasgwyn gave instruction in both navigation and what might be described as a business course; in front of me as I write is the exercise book of Daniel Jones, Drwsdeugoed, Chwilog, used at Plasgwyn about 1850.[8] He must have had another exercise book for navigation; this one is concerned with arithmetical problems, such as 'Bought 59 cwt. 2 qrs. 4 lb. of tobacco at £2.17.4 per cwt, what does it come to?' 'Bought 171 tons of lead at £14 per ton, paid carriage and other incidental charges £4.10. I require the value of the lead and what it stands me in per lb.'; and graduates to problems relating to simple interest, commission, 'If I allow my factor $3\frac{3}{4}$ per cent for commission what may he demand on the laying out of £876.5.10d?'; the purchasing of stocks, brokerage, compound interest, 'the rule of three in decimals', arithmetic and geometrical progression and 'superficial mensuration'. On several pages the name of 'Miss Ann Roberts, Portmadoc', no doubt the object of young Daniel Jones's affection, is written in the margin, and on another page 'Daniel Jones, on bord the Smack Alpha, Captain William Ellis, To be left at Post Office, Tooley Street, London'. Captain Daniel Jones eventually became master of a number of large sailing ships, including one of the 'Moel' group belonging to the Gwynedd Shipping Company.

The late David Thomas traced a number of navigation schools in South Caernarfonshire, although little is known of the nature of the classroom instruction — there was David Wilson, a former customs officer at Portinllaen, who had a school at Nefyn early in the century; Isaac Morris, at Llangybi, is said to have been a good mathematician who taught navigation, and John Thomas, a shoemaker at Llanengan, was described by his former pupil, John Owen, Bishop of St. David's, as a fine mathematician, who taught navigation to many intending master mariners.[9] William Griffith, the one-legged seaman, who had a school in Porthmadog, near Grisia Mawr, has already been mentioned; he must have taught many Porthmadog boys, as he was there in the 1830s and is recorded as being alive and holding shares in Porthmadog ships in the fifties. Another Griffith is said to have had a school in Porthmadog: Owen Griffith's school was held at the Queen's Hotel, and later at the Royal Oak. There were others in the community who must have appreciated the importance of education for seamen; William Ambrose, minister of the Congregational Chapel, Porthmadog, from 1837 to his death in 1873 was a much respected citizen whose seal is among those who originated the Mutual Ship Insurance Society and was said to be the close friend of Captain David Richards, senior, the shipowner. Such men would surely not have stood by idly to allow the situation described by the Commissioners to continue long (if, indeed, the Commissioners' evidence is reliable!): 'although the principal employment of the inhabitants is in connexion with the Shipping, no instruction is given in navigation. I was informed, by good authority, that of the crews of 50 vessels belonging to the port, not more than six men know anything of navigation except by practice, and that nothing is known of the subject as a science'.

In fairness to the 1847 Report, it must be added that the Commissioners noted with much approval the establishment in Porthmadog of a potentially useful source of self-education for adults, and that at the very centre of the activities of the maritime community.

> 'A reading room has been established at the port for the use of the middle and working classes, and especially for sailors, both captains and crews. The object is to afford rational occupation, and to withdraw these from the public houses. The low rate of payment, 1s. 6d., per quarter, places this within reach of the poor. Captains of vessels are allowed the use of the room, so long as they are in port, for a payment of 6d, and common sailors are admitted at half price. The publications consist of a daily newspaper and some weekly newspapers, in Welsh and English, and the publications published by the different denominations in Wales. There is a small library of 200 books . . . This reading-room is much frequented'.[10]

The serious-minded, religious ship-owners and master mariners who gave their support to the idea of establishing the Reading Society and, later, the News Room at Pen Cei, Porthmadog, were sharing in the enthusiasm of mid-century for self-improvement, the desire, whether they realised it or not, to inculcate the puritan values of many sections of the middle class in what was a fundamentally religious society, to stress the early Victorian age's goals of respectability and hard work. To become educated, to acquire a share of property, was an aspiration which was common to many different types of community and in this the Porthmadog seamen were exhorted to educate themselves in much the same way as, say, the Bradford

Mechanics Institute was regarded as a passport for 'the sons of working men' to rise 'to positions of responsibility which in all probability they never would have filled without its aid, and, in many cases, entering upon and pursuing a successful middle class career by the habits of knowledge, and the connections acquired in this Institute', in the words of a Bradford merchant in 1859.[11] Porthmadog shipowners needed sober, industrious and educated master mariners, there was a career open to the young man of talent, and, at the same time, it was a very worthy cause from the religious and moral standpoint. Whatever the nature of the argument, the Porthmadog Reading Society came into existence in 1842; it was called 'The Portmadoc Mariners and Mechanics Reading Society'. Subscriptions were fixed, according to the rules printed bilingually in 1847, 'at 6s. per annum, and 5s per annum for vessels frequenting Port Madoc, with FREE ADMISSION to the crews of such ships as shall subscribe: to sons (between the ages of thirteen and eighteen years of age) of annual subscribers at 10s. 6d.; and to Apprentices of master tradesmen subscribing 10s. 6d. per annum'.[12] One of the young men who benefited from the Reading Society was Richard Griffith Humphreys, son of Captain William Humphreys. He went to sea as a boy of thirteen in Porthmadog ships, but having bought some books of his own, and using the resources of such institutions as the library of the Reading Society in Porthmadog, he is said to have taught himself not only to read and write effectively, in both Welsh and English, but also acquired some knowledge of Latin and Greek. After five years at sea he came ashore to work in an office in Porthmadog, and eventually became a well-known local journalist — Rhisiart o Fadog. Years later, in the *North Wales Chronicle,* he described a navigational school which he remembered hearing about in the fo'csle of many a Porthmadog vessel — the navigation school at Mynytho in Llŷn, and the yarns of the amorous adventures of the nautical students which culminated in many a young girl from the area becoming a master mariner's wife.[13]

The careers of these early master mariners are, for the most part, very shadowy, just names — and very similar ones at that — against the name of a vessel, or occasional references in an account book. One of the few about whom a little is known is Captain Hugh Hughes, Gellidara, who later became a highly respected Methodist minister, and contributed much to the Methodist movement in the Porthmadog area.[14] Born at Pontrhydfechan, Morfa Bychan, in 1813, son of a blacksmith who had worked on Madocks's embankment, Hugh Hughes went to sea young, following in the footsteps of his grandfather, Captain Evan Owen of Tynybonc, Talsarnau, who had a high reputation in the area as master of one of the vessels engaged in the Atlantic emigrant trade. His father's death when he was a boy of ten meant that young Hugh Hughes's education (at a school kept by John Wynn in the Town Hall at Tremadoc) until he was thirteen, was paid for by Captain Owen, his grandfather, and his elder brother, William, who was already at sea. Hugh Hughes's first voyage proved eventful, for the Porthmadog vessel in which he was serving as boy was wrecked on the coast of Ireland, and he was rescued from the rigging and the yard to which he had lashed himself. He was then apprenticed to his uncle, who had his own brig plying from Porthmadog. He came ashore again after a few voyages to attend the school of William Griffith at Grisia Mawr, Porthmadog. His brother William then took him aboard his sloop *Jane,* and when William Hughes became master of the new schooner *Una,* the young Hugh Hughes was accepted to command the *Jane.* The *Una* had been built in 1840 by Henry Jones, and this became Hugh Hughes's next command when his brother moved to become master of the *Aeriel.* Captain Hugh Hughes then became master of the *Eagle,* the largest schooner that had yet been built in Porthmadog, again by Henry Jones in 1837. It is possible that he took this vessel over following the death of her master — possibly on her maiden voyage — as there is a memorial in Treflys churchyard with the inscription 'Drowned in Dublin, Captain John Richard Jones, Eagle, Portmadoc, aged 40 years, July the 7th, and was interred on the 13th, inside of the Church, 1837'.[15] Aboard the *Eagle,* he soon established a reputation among his contemporaries both for his skill as a seaman and navigator, and his remarkable religious zeal, which made the *Eagle* the regular meeting place for Welsh seamen on Sundays wherever they went. The signal that a service to be held on board was the hoisting of the Bethel flag; Captain John Roberts, master of the *Emily Jane,* in *Y Drysorfa,* the Welsh Calvinistic Methodist magazine, put on record, in February 1843, an account of a Sunday evening at Falmouth, where there were about fifty vessels from Wales at anchor.[16]

As evening approached, from one after another of them the ship's boats quietly pulled alongside the *Surprize,* where Captain Hugh Hughes, master of the *Eagle,* preached a sermon on the eleventh chapter of Paul's epistle to the Hebrews to over three hundred seamen. Back home, in Porthmadog, Captain Hugh Hughes, together with his brother, Captain William Hughes, Captain Richard Prichard, of the *Gomer,* now the banker, and John Davies, the 'shipper' whose name was the first on the list of those who had set their seal to the agreement of the Mutual Ship Insurance Society, held religious services in the sailroom overlooking the harbour. In 1847, Captain Hugh Hughes married the daughter of the farm Gellidara in Llŷn and left the sea to be a Methodist minister, but he continued to devote much of his time to missionary work among seamen.

A number of this first generation of master mariners of Porthmadog seem to have come ashore at a comparatively early age in order to devote themselves to shipowning and shipbuilding. Captain David Morris, Ceylon Villa, grandfather of Henry and Emrys Hughes, belonged to the second generation — he was master of the *Success* at the age of twenty-six, in 1849, and then became master of the *Royal Charter,* 'which was one of the few if not the only vessel built at Abergafran, Minffordd'.[17] According to his obituary notice in the *Cambrian News,* after his successful career in the *Pride of Wales,* he 'continued to take the keenest interest in shipping matters and was at one time chairman of the Portmadoc Mutual Ship Insurance Company, a director of the Steam Tug Company, and of the Caernarvon and Merioneth (Rebecca) Company. He did not mix in political or municipal affairs; but he was much attached to the Congregational Connexion and was a member of Salem'.[18] There were many like him among the master mariners, although they were not all as successful financially; sober, industrious citizens of a port which was becoming increasingly prosperous, certainly until the late seventies.

There were others who started their careers in Porthmadog ships but achieved their successes far from their native county. The 'Darkie' Williams brothers, as Emrys Hughes discovered, established themselves as important shipowners at Newcastle, New South Wales, after they had sailed there in the *Anne Mellhuish,* one of the largest vessels built in Porthmadog, in 1849, by Henry Jones. One of the most successful of all was William Williams, born at Rhiw in 1825. According to a testimonial dated January 12, 1845, from Waterford, and signed by W. J. N. Williams, the twenty-year-old William Williams had served before the mast, then as mate, and finally as master of the brig *Mystery,* 'which you have commanded on three successful voyages over to the West Indies, the next to the Mediterranean, and this last to the River Danube'. On December 11 of the same year, the author of this letter wrote to the young Captain Williams's father informing him that 'Captain William Williams of the Brig The "Mystery" of Port Madoc sailed on the 6th October last from Cork bound for the West Indies and should it be your wish to write to him a mail leaves Southampton on the 17th of this month, his direction is Capt. Williams Brig "Mystery" care of W. H. Thompson (?) . . . St. John's, Antigua'. After highly commending his service before the mast in the *Mystery,* the writer must have pleased the twenty-year-old Captain's father when he read of how he had obtained his command: 'I have great pleasure in being able to inform you that he has hitherto given me the greatest possible satisfaction and I promoted him to the Command . . . at a salary of £7.7.0 per month. He is a good honest young man and you have every reason to be justly proud of such a son'.[19] In *Ships and Seamen of Anglesey* I have attempted to outline Captain William Williams's career, from his days in command of the *Mystery,* then the barque *Ann Grant,* owned by Edward Ellis, shipbuilder, and the Reverend John Phillips (the fund-raiser for Nonconformist schools and the Normal College, Bangor), his days of service with the Davies brothers, Menai Bridge, the commendations he received from Admiral Fitzroy and the Meteorological Office for the accuracy of his observations on the effects of magnetism on the compasses of iron ships, and, finally, his days as a shipowner in Fenchurch Street, London, when he owned such famous sailing vessels as the *Commodore Perry,* the *Light Brigade* and the *Donald Mackay.* An exceptionally fine seaman, and obviously highly intelligent — there are references in his early testimonials to his ability as 'a scholar', Captain William Williams appears also to have been a shrewd business man, a Porthmadog master mariner of the mid-century period who left the port young to achieve outstanding success in the largest ocean-sailing vessels.

It is important to recognize that Porthmadog was from the early years a deep-water port, that its mariners were engaged in the ocean trades. Captain William Williams, a young man in his twenties, was sailing his brig *Mystery* to the West Indies, the Mediterranean and the Danube in the 1840s; his contemporaries continued in these trades and added to them the great North Atlantic Newfoundland trade. Their experience on deep-water stood them in good stead when it became necessary to develop such trades as the Newfoundland trade and, as already indicated, had a considerable influence on the type of vessels built in the port. A glance through the individual histories of Porthmadog ships will confirm the wide range of their activities both in the coastal and deep-water trades. They were all subject to the requirements of the same society, the Porthmadog Ship Insurance Society, whose committee obviously had to include master mariners with this breadth of experience. By 1878 the tensions between the different types of trade were beginning to appear — in an unsigned note appended to the original Agreement of 1841, referring to the time ' when the Society was first established 37 years ago ', it is stated that the constitution provided and was adapted ' to the state of things as they then existed ', but it was now felt advisable ' to divide the present somewhat overgrown Society into two — one for the large and the other for the small vessels now built '.[20] This did not come about, and, indeed, the interchangeability of vessels continued to the end — the *Cadwalader Jones* is a good example of a long-lived vessel which plied in both coastal and deep-water trades.

If there was interchangeability of vessels, there was certainly interchangeability of crews. Seamen from Porthmadog from the days of the *Lord Palmerston* in the twenties, and the *Mary Holland* in the forties, signed on for voyages which would take them to a wide range of European ports. It had been a tradition for years — the case of Captain William Jones in the *Harlech Castle* at St. Petersburg in 1796 is one that immediately springs to mind. But with the development of the trade with the German ports in the second half of the nineteenth century, Porthmadog seamen visiting Hamburg were coming into contact with the great deep-sea traffic of the full-rigged ships and barques returning from San Francisco, Australia, the Far East, and, of course, the same was true for London, Cardiff, and, more than anywhere, Liverpool. The ambitious young seaman naturally found it advisable to put in a voyage or two in a large square-rigged vessel, after which he might come ashore and study for his second mate's ticket at one of the navigation schools in London or Liverpool, thus climbing the promotional ladder. But there were no illusions; success in Board of Trade examinations did not cut any ice with the 'Mutual' — they had to pass in the eyes of the local Society before they could obtain command of one of the Porthmadog vessels. Nevertheless, in the third quarter of the nineteenth century, when the large sailing ships were being produced in considerable numbers for the long-haul voyages with bulk cargoes in the coal, iron, jute and rice trades, and as floating warehouses in the grain and wool trades, it was fairly common for Porthmadog seamen to move easily from the vessels of their own home port to the ships of the Davies brothers of Menai Bridge, or those of William Thomas, or, later still, to the Caernarvonshire Shipping Companies and the ships of Robert Thomas, Cricieth. By the eighties, when local shipbuilding came to a virtual halt, the attraction of these full-rigged ships had taken a firm hold, but, unlike the other ports of North Wales, Porthmadog men were able to continue to make a conscious choice. To illustrate, one can take some examples to suggest the career patterns of the men who sailed Porthmadog ships.

It is immediately apparent, reading through the mass of Crew Agreement Lists, or 'Articles' as they were known to seamen, that family ties were an important factor in the manning of Porthmadog ships. The master of a vessel would take his sons with him to sea as first voyagers, and, then, when the time came for the next son to want to go to sea, the older boy would perhaps move to another vessel to gain wider experience, whilst a younger brother signed as boy or cook, only to be relieved by another brother if, and when, he wanted to go to sea. Thus there is this close-knit continuity which is so marked a factor of Porthmadog, and, indeed, of most of the schooner ports in the West Country. The *Independent* (or *Independence* as she was sometimes called in Porthmadog), according to Emrys Hughes's records probably built in New Brunswick in the 1830s, was bought by J. W. Greaves, about 1841, to transport slates from the Llechwedd Quarry which he had acquired some years previously. Her first master, Captain Hugh Roberts (who was to be associated with the Greaves family for many years), sailed her in the coastal trade. Her cargo was usually about 95 tons of slates out from

Porthmadog; between 3 July 1849 and 4 June 1850 she made, according to the shipments book of J. W. Greaves and Company, fourteen voyages to Colchester with such cargoes. Thus Captain Hugh Roberts may be said to have taken part in that early expansionist phase in the history of Porthmadog when the development of London and other British cities led to an increasing demand for slate — he was sailing regularly in the coastal trade from Porthmadog at a time when Henry Jones's yard was busily turning out ships, and men like Thomas Christian, the sailmaker, were having vessels built for them. The schooner *Constance,* built in 1862, was one of the early schooners of Ebenezer Roberts, soon to become one of the leading shipbuilders of the port; she was named after a member of the Greaves family, Constance Greaves. It was natural that Captain Hugh Roberts, who had done so well in the *Independent,* should be appointed to command her: she was the largest schooner yet built in the port, and, in 1865, the Mutual Ship Insurance Society valued her at £2,580 — the new brig, *Edward Windus,* built two years later, and, therefore, less than a year old, was valued at only £70 more, £2,650.[21] The *Constance,* one of the 'maids of all work', as Henry Hughes described them, was soon busily engaged in the Baltic and Mediterranean trades of the Porthmadog vessels of the sixties. She was also to be the training-ship for Captain Hugh Roberts's three sons, Hugh, Thomas and William. Each, turn in, served aboard her. Thus, when the brig *Evelyn* was being built in Hugh Williams's yard for him in 1876, Captain Roberts sailed one of his last voyages in the *Constance,* leaving Porthmadog in late April for Kiel; his mate on this voyage was his eldest son, Hugh Roberts, aged 20, with a mate's ticket, according to his discharge certificate. The launching of the *Evelyn* has already been described; when she sailed on her maiden voyage to Stettin, in April 1877, she was commanded by Captain Hugh Roberts, senior, then aged 52, whose previous vessel, according to the 'Articles', is named as the *Constance,* but in her crew there are also the names of Thomas Roberts, aged 20, boatswain, and William Roberts, aged 15, whose previous ship, in both cases, was the *Constance.* Thus, during the 1876 voyages, Captain Roberts had had his three sons serving with him, and when he moved to take the *Evelyn* for her first few voyages, he took with him the two younger boys, making Thomas boatswain of the new ship, but left the eldest, his namesake, Hugh, as mate of the *Constance*. The latter was still with the *Constance* in 1878; a discharge certificate which has survived indicates that he was her mate when she left Porthmadog in July 1878 for Danzig, returning with her to Gloucester in the following November. Obviously the intention, as stated in the account of her launching, was for young Hugh Roberts to command the *Evelyn,* and, presumably, as soon as his father was satisfied with his new vessel, and happy that his son could take over, Captain Hugh Roberts, junior, sometime in 1879, started his long career as master of the *Evelyn,* which he commanded with great distinction for well over thirty years, until November 1913 when she was lost in the North Atlantic. It was typical that Captain Roberts, when completing his wages account for that last voyage of the *Evelyn,* should have entered the place of discharge for the remaining members of the crew as the ports at which they were landed by their rescuers, but his own place of discharge as 'lat. 50°56′N, long. 30°26′ W', the approximate position of the vessel when she finally sank after an heroic struggle (which has been described by Henry Hughes in *Immortal Sails,* based on the account given by one who sailed for many years on the *Evelyn,* Captain 'Evie' Morris, in a letter to Emrys Hughes).[22]

For many years, Captain Hugh Roberts, junior, had as his mate his brother, William, who had served as a boy with him when he himself had been mate to his father in the *Constance.* But for those first voyages in 1877 and 1878, when Captain Hugh Roberts, senior, sailed the *Evelyn* to Hamburg, Huelva and Dublin to test the quality of his new vessel, he took with him as mate his brother-in-law, Evan Morris, from Llanbedr, an experienced seaman who had first gone to sea in a small smack from Porthmadog when he was barely twelve years of age. It was the beginning of a career which, even for Porthmadog, was particularly eventful; he served in all types of sailing ships, including famous tea clippers and lowly but tough tramp steamers; he was shipwrecked off California, rescued by Red Indians, trekked to Portland, Oregon, where he obtained command of the *Sarmatian* of Quebec, and served some years in her, transporting cheap labour from Calcutta and Rangoon to the sugar plantations of Demerara. After serving as master of the full-rigged iron ship, *British Commodore,* and the Anglesey owned iron barque, *Menai*

44. David Williams, builder of 'Western Ocean Yachts', and his family.

45. A vessel in frame, *c.* 1900; David Williams (extreme right) and workmen

46. Partially 'planked up' vessel; David Williams (second from left) and workmen again *c.* 1900.

47. David Williams (with 'topi' helmet, fourth from right) with workmen inside frame of vessel, probably *R. J. Owens* or *Isallt* (II).

48. Three-masted schooner *R. J. Owens* on blocks at Rotten Tare, 1907. Dav Williams (extreme right) and workmen.

49. The *Isallt* (II) in frame, showing massive oak timbers; David Williams, th from left, and workmen (and small boys, constant and knowledgeable spectators o vessel's growth).

The *Isallt* (II) nears launching day; David Williams, extreme right in foreground.

Three-masted schooner *Ellen James* (II), built David Williams, 1904, Captain John James Jones, master, at King's Lynn.

52. The three-masted schooner *Isallt* (II) at Copenhagen. Captain R. O. Williams, master, and brother of builder, centre, and crew, including David Mark Jones (sitting inside lifebelt), who fell from rigging and was lost overboard in storm some months later. Visiting Englishman (with cricket cap!) was schoolmaster at Copenhagen.

Three-masted schooner, *John Llewelyn,* built David Jones, 1904, at St. John's, wfoundland. [Photograph given to late Emrys Hughes by Mr. A. Munn of St. John's.]

4. The *William Morton,* built David Jones, 1905, at Middlefurt, Denmark.

55. The *William Prichard,* built David Jones, 1903, at Bristol on her maiden voya

56. The *William Prichard* (centre) towing into Stettin, 1905.

7. The *Jenny Jones,* built Ebenezer and John Roberts for Dr. J. H. Lister, 1893.

58. The *Kitty*, built David Williams, 1902, at Papenburg, *c.* 1904-5.
[Dr. Jürgen Meyer Collection.]

59. David Jones's three-masted schooner, *Blodwen,* built 1891, at Harbour Grac
Newfoundland.

60. Griffith and David Williams's three-masted schooner *Elizabeth,* built 1891.

61. The *John Pritchard*, built David Williams, 1906.

The crew of *John Pritchard*: left to right, Jack Williams, mate, wearing braces, wn locally as 'Jack Klondyke', Captain John Watkin Roberts, master, Bill Payne, A.B., David Nicholas, boy, and William Morris Lloyd, Ordinary Seaman.

63. The *Elizabeth Eleanor,* built David Williams 1905, Captain J. M. Jones, mas

64. The *Miss Morris,* three-masted schooner, built David Jones, 1900, one of largest of the Western Ocean Yachts.

65. The *Dorothy*, built Griffith and David Williams 1891, towing into Bristol.

The schooner *Cariad*, built W. Date, Kingsbridge, Captain John Owen, master, which sailed from Newfoundland to Oporto in ten days.

67. The *Elizabeth* at Leghorn.

68. The *Dorothy* at Leghorn, 1875.

69. The *John Llewelyn* being towed into Bristol.

*Straits*, which went on fire off Cape Horn, and spending many days in an open boat before navigating it safely to the Falkland Islands, Captain Evan Morris returned to Porthmadog and took command of the barquentine *Ellen Lloyd*. It was while he was master of her, as Emrys Hughes has recorded, that he was washed overboard in a gale off Newfoundland and swam back aboard, only to have his leg broken by the spokes of the wheel which the helmsman had abandoned in panic. A formidable character, Captain Evan Morris was aged thirty-five when he went as mate of the *Evelyn* on her trial voyages; Captain Hugh Roberts, senior, could not have chosen a better man. Years later, young 'Evie' Morris, son of the indomitable Captain Evan Morris, went to sea with his uncle, Captain Hugh Roberts, junior, in the *Evelyn* as a boy of fourteen on a voyage to the Baltic. He remained aboard her on voyages to the West Indies, Newfoundland and the Mediterranean, and graduated from boy and cook to ordinary seaman, and then able seaman. After leaving the *Evelyn*, he served as mate of the *M. A. James*, and then went to his other uncle, Captain Thomas Roberts, who had signed as boatswain aboard the *Evelyn* when his father, Evan Morris, was mate. Captain Thomas Roberts's ship, which the young Morris joined, was the *Dorothy*, the first of David Williams's Western Ocean Yachts, another of the vessels which the Greaves and Roberts families owned.

Captain Thomas Roberts's Certificate of Competency as Master of a foreign-going ship, and his service record complete this family story. He had joined his father's ship *Constance* as a boy aged twelve in June 1869 for a foreign voyage; he was promoted to Ordinary Seaman nearly five years later in January 1874, and then to Purser and Second Mate in March 1879, and (presumably when his older brother, Hugh, moved to take command of the *Evelyn*) he became mate of the *Constance* two months later. After five years as mate, he took his master's ticket in June 1884, and in September of the same year he took command of the *Constance*. Almost nine years later, in June 1893, he became master of the *Dorothy*, just two years old, and regarded as one of the finest vessels built in the port. He remained in command of the *Dorothy* until November 1904, when she foundered following a collision off Cape Trafalgar; according to 'Evie' Morris, his nephew, who was then mate of the *Dorothy*, they were run down by the steamer *Adana* of Liverpool in a gale, but managed to get away in their own boat within a matter of minutes, and landed safely in Gibraltar. In the following year, 1905, Captain Thomas Roberts became master of the second *Rebecca*, the all-important link with Liverpool, succeeding Captain David Roberts, who had been in command of the first and second vessels of that name for twenty years. With Captain Hugh Roberts, the father, playing such an important part ashore in the deliberations of the 'Mutual' and other shipping affairs of Porthmadog, Captain Hugh Roberts in the *Evelyn*, and Captain Thomas Roberts in the *Dorothy* and then the *Rebecca*, the family surely played an essential part in the development of the shipping community of Porthmadog.

Of all the many photographs relating to Porthmadog ships and their crews, perhaps the most evocative as a group which I have seen are those relating to the Roberts family. They were not included in Emrys Hughes's vast collection but were loaned to me recently by Miss Evelyn Roberts, daughter of Captain Hugh Roberts, junior. Among them are the photographs of Captain Roberts's wedding to Miss Mary Williams, daughter of David Williams, of Borth-y-gest, late Customs Officer, Porthmadog, in February 1893. Captain Roberts's best man was William, his brother, who served as mate with him for many years, and also in the photograph are his father, Captain Hugh Roberts of the *Constance*, now one of the most influential members of the committee of the Mutual Ship Insurance Society, and his other brother, Captain Thomas Roberts of the *Dorothy*. The local newspaper reported 'all the vessels in the harbour and estuary were decked in their flags to an almost unprecedented extent. The town, too, displayed a good show of bunting, everything had put on a gay appearance — a signal proof of the great respect in which the memory of the bride's father is held by the shipping community at Portmadoc. It was a clear indication, too, how highly the family of the bridegroom is esteemed, all of whom are well known as sea-faring men'.[23]

The subsequent photographs — of Captain Roberts and his extremely young-looking bride at Antwerp; of her and her young baby daughter, surrounded by Captain Roberts and William Roberts, the mate, and other members of the crew, on the deck of the *Evelyn* at an unidentified port; of Captain Roberts and his crews, in their working clothes and in their 'Sunday best', at various ports; th postcards from different ports, including a very interesting one to Captain Roberts from Robert Lietner of Harburg, with a view of vessels discharging their cargoes at two of his yards in Harburg — all these bring to life in a remarkable fashion a world we have lost, a world of small merchant sailing ships, their crews, and the ports which they knew so well.

There were many families who were deeply involved in the ships of Porthmadog — indeed, the difficulty would be to find families who were not in some way involved. Captain Hugh Parry of Borth-y-gest, the shipbroker at Cornhill, has already been mentioned more than once. In the seventies he had sailed in command of the *George Casson* and the *Frau Minna Petersen;* he is one of the many Nefyn men who made Porthmadog and its ships their life. He had three sons, Ebenezer, Robert, and Maurice, and all three became master mariners. Captain Ebenezer Parry was lost with all the crew of the *Pluvier* when she foundered on New Year's Eve 1905 off Queenstown. She was on passage from Portugal to Porthmadog in ballast when she was overtaken by the storm that drove her ashore. When Captain Robert Parry, the master's brother, and others went over from Porthmadog to investigate, they found the ship at low tide stripped bare; two of the crew, it was said, had clambered on to some rocks, but violent seas had washed them away, and only the ship's cat survived. Captain Robert Parry himself, recorded as Ordinary Seaman aged fourteen aboard the *Frau Minna Petersen* under Captain John Ellis on voyages to Hamburg, Cadiz and Newfoundland in 1884, became her master in later years, before leaving for a career in steamers (where he earned rewards for gallantry for saving life by leaping overboard on more than one occasion to rescue drowning men) and eventually became a Superintendent of Docks at Garston. Captain Maurice Parry had moved from the *Frau Minna Petersen* and other Porthmadog ships to steamers when he returned to sail in 1905 to take command of the *Cenric,* one of the fine steel schooners built in that year by the younger William Thomas at Amlwch. When Captain Parry left Porthmadog two days before Christmas 1905 in his much-admired new vessel, he had a crew of experienced men who had served in vessels like the *George Casson,* the *Elizabeth Llewelyn* and the *C. E. Spooner.* After discharging their slate cargo at Bremen, they sailed for Belfast and then to Cardiff where the crew were paid off. With a Gothenburg man as boatswain, an A.B. from Fowey, another from Borth-y-gest, and a young first voyager from Cardiff, Captain Parry sailed from Newfoundland. On 12 June 1906 she left Twillingate with her return cargo, and was never heard of again.

One of the experienced Porthmadog seamen who had been paid off from the *Cenric* at Cardiff by Captain Maurice Parry was a member of another family much involved in Porthmadog ships in its later stages; he was a son of Captain David Roberts of the *Michael Kelly*. The latter was not built at Porthmadog, but was an iron steamer built at Preston in 1871 and converted, somewhat oddly, into a three-masted schooner; her story is told by Henry Hughes in *Immortal Sails*. However unconventional her appearance, she again became a training ship for the sons of a family: Captain David Roberts, the father, a very experienced ship rigger in the busy days of Porthmadog — he was much in demand when the new schooners were being built — was also regarded as a fine coastal master, and it was with him that Captain Griffith Roberts, O.B.E., and his brothers learned their seamanship. Captain Griffith Roberts was older than most Porthmadog boys when he went to sea, as he had already been working in the Port Office in Porthmadog, but at the age of 20 he made his first voyage in the *Cecil Brindley,* a Cardigan Bay coastal schooner which his father commanded. He then sailed in the elderly brigantine *Tyne,* owned by the Lloyds, another family with long associations with the port. After a voyage to the Baltic in the *Tyne,* Griffith Roberts went to the *Blodwen,* in which his younger brother had already sailed; his elder brother, Job Roberts, also moved from one Porthmadog schooner to another, until he went into steam and became a master in the Ratcliffe steamers out of Cardiff. Captain Griffith Roberts recalls fast passages in the *Blodwen,* which confirm her reputation for sailing across the Atlantic, but states there was little to choose in speed between her and several of the other later Porthmadog schooners in the Newfoundland trade: 'if you'd seen one of them, you'd seen the lot, they were lovely vessels '.[24] Among his contemporaries, he remembers that the *William Morton,* built by David Jones, had an enviable reputation as a fast sailing vessel, but in their turn all the Western Ocean Yachts made fast passages. So much depended on wind and tide conditions and time of the year; Captain Griffith Roberts remembers vividly one passage he made in the *Blodwen* with Captain John Richard Williams in command, when they left Fogo, Newfoundland, in fine weather, with a strong following wind, and within the fortnight they were snug in Lisbon, 'never touched a sheet, following wind all the way, in lovely weather'. Not all passages were like that.

After a spell in the *Blodwen*, Captain Roberts went to the *David Morris* and then to the *Mary Lloyd* as boatswain. Deciding that he ought to get experience in large square-rigged vessels, he then left Porthmadog ships and shipped in the barque *Gwydyr Castle*, owned by Robert Thomas and Company, Cricieth and Liverpool, on the two year voyage, after which he went ashore to take his Second Mate's ticket. He was immediately appointed second mate of the steel full-rigged ship *Talus* (described by Lubbock as a 'magnificent ship' and commanded for some years by Captain Robert Jones of Amlwch), but the pull of Porthmadog ships, and loyalty to an old friend, the master of the *M. Lloyd Morris*, made him reject this appointment: the *M. Lloyd Morris*, bound for the Baltic, was above the 100 ton register and, therefore, had to have two certificated men aboard her, so Griffith Roberts was prevailed upon to go as mate. After taking his mate's certificate, he then went into tramp steamers; Captain Humphrey Ellis Williams, the master, and Griffith Roberts, the mate, both left the *M. Lloyd Morris* at Cardiff shortly before she was lost with Captain William Hughes, Velog, his son, and all hands following a collision off the Lizard in January 1917. From tramp steamers, Griffith Roberts too his master's ticket and embarked upon the distinguished career with the Ellerman Line which culminated in those momentous years as Commodore of ocean convoys in the 1939-45 War which were deservedly recognized by the award of the O.B.E.

Captain Griffith Roberts and his friend and neighbour in Borth-y-gest, Captain Robert Roberts, remembers Porthmadog in the day of the Western Ocean Yachts, but they also knew the vessels of the seventies, the *Evelyn, Frau Minna Petersen* and the like. Captain Robert Roberts was, in fact, at one time master of one of the vessels which were launched during that surge of activity in the port in 1877. The *Sarah Evans*, a two-masted schooner of 99 tons register, was designed for the coastal trade, and plied in that trade for close on sixty years; her managing owner for her first voyage was Rees Evans, Cwmorthin Slate Wharf, and her first master was John Davies, a twenty-seven year old Nefyn man, whose last ship had been the *Margaret and Mary* of Caernarfon. She sailed from Porthmadog on what must have been the first of scores of such voyages on 31 March 1877 with a cargo of slates for Middlesborough, thence to Bristol, home to Porthmadog and away again in June for Wisbech. Two years later she was in the foreign trade, and, therefore, John Davies had to sign as boatswain and purser, with Thomas Walters, a certificated master mariner, in command for the voyage which took her from Porthmadog on 21 May 1878 to Stettin, where she arrived on 12 June, to Danzig in July, and home again to Gloucester in early August. Her owner and master by 1900 was Captain Evan W. Roberts of Trem-y-don, Borth-y-gest; on the coasting voyage which began in January 1900 and ended in April, her all-Porthmadog crew consisted of the master, the mate, aged 34, two A.B.s aged 19 and 17 respectively, and as Ordinary Seaman, he is registered as having made at least one earlier voyage — Robert Roberts, aged 12, at 15/- a month. In 1906 the *Sarah Evans* sailed with Captain Evan W. Roberts, the owner, in command, the same Robert Roberts, the master's son, as boatswain, another Robert Roberts, whose home address was Tŷ Capel, Carmel, Mynytho, as A.B., and two ordinary seamen, also from Porthmadog, for Copenhagen with slates. They arrived in mid-April and returned via Briton Ferry to Porthmadog in June 1906. By the following year, young Captain Robert Roberts had taken over as master of his father's vessel; his age is recorded for this voyage as 20, but he had, in fact, become master at the age of 19. With him for these early voyages was a certificated man, William Ellis, aged 60, and together they sailed the *Sarah Evans* to Ipswich late in 1906, and thence to Belfast. Apart from the mate, the crew were all young men; two A.B.s aged 19 and 17 respectively, the one from Pen-y-Groes, the other from Ffestiniog, whilst the Ordinary Seaman, aged 16, came from Aberdaron. Thus began the career of Captain Robert Roberts, who had, besides his time in the *Sarah Evans,* served as a seaman in the *Dorothy,* with several other master mariners' sons as crew, in the Newfoundland trade. When he left Porthmadog ships for steamers and the 1914-18 war broke out, he joined the R.N.R., and served aboard a 'Q' ship which was torpedoed in the Atlantic; Captain Roberts navigated an open boat, containing dead and dying survivors, with an oar as a makeshift mast, three hundred miles and more to the Irish coast. In the Second World War, again serving in the R.N.R., he was bombed and wounded at Namsos in the Norwegian campaign, but survived, and is, happily, living in retirement at Borth-y-gest, possibly the last of those who could say they had commanded a Porthmadog ship, just as he must have been one of the youngest to attain command.[25]

The two Captain Roberts at Borth-y-gest look forward to the visits of two other contemporaries, the brothers Captain W. H. Hughes, D.S.C., and Captain Jesse Hughes, both of whom have retired to live in Holyhead after commanding the Irish Ferry steamers to Dun Laoghaire for many years. They are the sons of Captain Harry Hughes, who commanded many Porthmadog vessels, some of which have already been mentioned. Himself the son of Lewis Hughes, the tailor from Porthmadog, who, in the seventies, invested in such ships as the *Edward Seymour* and the *Hilda,* and later bought the *Geraldine* and the *Carpasion,* the timber carrier, Captain Harry Hughes was one of the best known mariners of Porthmadog. I have outlined the career of Captain W. H. Hughes, D.S.C., in *Ships and Seamen of Anglesey.* Here it must suffice to indicate that the Hughes family were another example of the tradition of sons going with their fathers to sea. When the *Miss Pritchard* sank off Cape Wrath not long after she had left Stornoway in 1904, Captain Harry Hughes had two of his sons aboard to help to row their boat the fifteen miles to Loch Inver — all three sons, in fact, became master mariners in steamers, having served their apprenticeship in Porthmadog ships. Captain W. H. Hughes's career is particularly interesting for Porthmadog seamen in that he served both as a seaman and, later, as mate of the *Beeswing,* the only large barque owned and managed in the port in the closing decades of the nineteenth century. She was owned as a single ship company, and managed by the Pritchard brothers, the brokers at Cornhill, and although she was obviously too large to have ever visited Porthmadog, she served as an unofficial training ship for many young Porthmadog seamen who wished to gain experience in square-rigged ships, serving with men whom they knew, like Captain John Roberts of Cricieth, her master for a number of years, and W. H. Hughes, her chief officer and mate.

There was, of course, a marked contrast between the family type atmosphere of the schooners of Porthmadog (and the other West Country ports) and the large iron and steel square-riggers with their international crews, many of them the unwilling victims of the 'crimps' in Portland, Oregon, San Fransisco and the Australian ports. There was not much romance in the harsh reality of these ships in the cruel Cape Horn trades, yet boys who had little direct connection with the maritime community of Porthmadog sometimes started careers which brought them to the command of the largest of the Liverpool square-riggers by joining small ships out of Porthmadog as cooks, the first rung on the ladder of their sea-going career. Others who may have gone to sea first in the little smacks of Nefyn or the Cardigan Bay ports, moved to deep-water Porthmadog ships in the hope of starting an ocean-going career. One can only briefly give a few examples. Captain David Williams of Morfa Nefyn, born in 1866, joined the Nefyn-built schooner, *Miss Beck,* at the age of twelve, for a wage of ten shillings a month, then, in 1881, joined the schooner *The Secret,* and in the following year the *Miss Pritchard,* later to be owned by Captain Harry Hughes. He then went to serve aboard the full-rigged ship *Cambrian Queen,* managed by Captain Thomas Williams of Liverpool. Now an A.B., his next ship was the Porthmadog brig *Hugh Roberts,* followed by a period in steamers and a voyage in the *Portia,* managed by William Thomas, Liverpool. From 1903, through the 1914-18 war, he commanded the local steamships *Telephone* and *Dora.* Captain William Williams of Cricieth was born in 1878, first went to sea in 1891 as cook aboard the Porthmadog schooner *David Sinclair* at a rate of 15/- a month. As Ordinary Seaman aboard the Porthmadog barquentine *Martha Percival,* he was paid £2 a month on voyages to Hamburg, then out with 'patent fuel' to Laguira in Venezuela, then to Aruba for phosphate rock, and in later years recalled the voyage home: 'in dead of winter, with a heavily laden ship, we encountered very bad weather. Our decks were flooded practically all the voyage, and we lost quite a lot of our bulwarks. The crew were continually called up to shorten or to make sail when the weather improved. Eventually we arrived in Plymouth and discharged our cargo . . . I was very sorry to leave the old ship, as I had become very friendly with the old captain, who died on the voyage home; his name was Edward Jones of Penrhyndeudraeth '.[26] William Williams then made three voyages in another well-known Porthmadog-owned vessel, the *Albert Baltzer,* to the German and Baltic ports; he remembered that on the last of these voyages they had left Porthmadog late in October, and, going round the Skaw, bound for Copenhagen, 'we had to rig a small anchor from the end of the bowsprit to break the drift ice coming down from the Baltic Sea '. They sailed from Copenhagen for Norway to load heavy granite blocks for building a new dock at Port Talbot. There then followed voyages, now as an A.B., in the *Sarah Evans* and the *Miss Pritchard* in the coasting trade, and then he left Porthmadog ships in order to get the experience to enable him to take his second mate's ticket. A voyage in Robert Thomas's *Powys Castle* as an A.B. from Hamburg to Brisbane, thence to San Francisco with a coal cargo, which went on fire, and home to London with redwood; another passage out to San Francisco, then to Vladivostock, Portland, Oregon, and Durban during the Boer War, followed by voyages as second mate of the barque *Ednyfed* and mate of the barque *Maelgwyn,* both owned by Robert Thomas, led to his obtaining a master's certificate and his subsequent career in steam.

Captain R. Hughes, D.S.C., of Cricieth, was born in Porthmadog in 1879 and first served as a cabin boy in a coastal steamer during the school holidays, then worked in a solicitor's office for nearly two years before the call of the sea became too strong. From the Nefyn-built schooner, *Venus* — last to be built there, a very fine vessel — he went to the *Sidney Smith,* commanded by Captain R. O. Williams, brother of David Williams, the builder, as ordinary seaman, then to the schooner *Glanogwen,* commanded by Captain Rees Davies, and a further voyage in the barquentine *Martha Percival* to St. Helena and the Ascension Islands. Like the others, he then found that he had to move to the square-riggers to gain the experience to sit his second mate's examination, and, therefore, joined the four-masted barque *Bowen Hill* and a series of other large sailing ships before going to steam. He was awarded the D.S.C. for his gallant action against a German submarine, the *U-38,* in 1918. Sometimes, as experience of the large full-rigged ocean carriers became general for hundreds of North Wales seamen, and as the Welsh Shipping Companies from 1875 to 1905 continued to attract Welsh seamen, some of them drifted back to Porthmadog vessels for a spell; Captain John Jones of Bangor had served his apprenticeship in the William Thomas, Liverpool, ships, then as an A.B. aboard the Davies, Menai Bridge, company's *Flintshire* and as second mate of the *Glanivor,* owned by the Eryri Shipping Company. His next voyage as second mate was surely a very demanding experience, serving with Captain William Meredith aboard the *Dominion,* and as mate of the *Aberfoyle* from Liverpool to Australia. He then came home and did a voyage as mate to Captain Hugh Morris, master of the schooner *Robert Morris* — his first experience of smaller ships. Captain W. E. Price of Morfa Nefyn made his first voyage as deck boy aboard William Thomas's barque *County of Merioneth,* and after two more voyages in her joined the same company's *Kate Thomas* as an A.B. for a voyage from Barry to Port Pirie, Newcastle, N.S.W., Bombay and Calcutta. He had now completed more than six years' service and, therefore, decided to take the Board of Trade's 'Only Mate' examination, and as a result served as mate in the Porthmadog brigs *Phantom* and *W. W. Lloyd,* following which he qualified as master and went into steam.[27]

Master mariners from other seafaring communities in North Wales who had already achieved command of large square-rig vessels frequently came to Porthmadog when they were home on leave to have a yarn with former shipmates, particularly during the period between Christmas and March when the vessels were being refitted. There is a photograph of Captain Robert Thomas of Llandwrog, who had progressed from being a cabin boy in one of the Davies, Menai Bridge, ships, to the commander of the *Merioneth* (in which he made the record passage to San Francisco and back) and the *Afon Alaw,* taken with two of his master mariner friends in Porthmadog, all of them probably 'big ship' men.[28] Another of these visiting captains was Captain David Thomas, the remarkably young South Walian master of the full-rigged iron ship *Cambrian Monarch,* who had already had an enviable reputation when he came to Porthmadog to spend a holiday with a shipmate and his family. It was here that he met young Hannah Morris, daughter of Evan Morris, the pilot, whose strong swimming saved him when his fellow pilots were all lost when their cutter was overturned on the

Bar. Mrs. Hannah Thomas, who has a remarkable memory for a lady in her nineties,[29] remembers the young captain whom she married coming to Porthmadog in those far-off days, and so many facets of the life of the port — her brother's death in the *Ocean Wave* off Newfoundland, her father's account of his ordeal on that fateful night the *Rebecca* had taken the pilot-cutter in tow, when he swam for seemingly endless hours until he dragged himself ashore on the beach at Morfa Bychan; the boys in her class at Borth-y-gest who became masters of vessels like the *John Llewelyn,* and the harbour so full of ships that the pilots could not find berths for them.

With the ink not long dry on his newly-acquired mate's ticket, Peter Jones from Pwllffanog, on the Anglesey side of the Menai Straits, came to Porthmadog in September 1897 after four years of sailing as an A.B. in the full-rigged *Chinsura* and the *Cambrian Hills* and signed as mate of the *Martha Percival* (in which many of these outstanding captains seem to have sailed) for voyages to Aruba, Para, and Lafuyara. The next two years in the *Martha Percival* were good training for the future Captain Peter Jones, late master of the *County of Cardigan, Boadicea* and *Metropolis,* and for many years Master-Pilot at Belfast.[30] One of the discharge books loaned to me is that of W. W. Hughes, 67 High Street, Porthmadog (known locally as Wil Tynnu Lluniau): it records his service as A.B. aboard the *David Morris,* the *Ann and Jane Prichard* and *Owen Morris* between 1903 and 1906, and then as boatswain aboard the *James Kerr,* the steel four-masted barque managed by William Thomas, Liverpool. He then served again as bosun of the Porthmadog schooner *Robert Morris,* and then the two vessels in which Captain W. H. Hughes, D.S.C., also served, the *Deccan* and the *Marion Frazer,* where, under the signature of Captain Llewelyn Rees, it was recorded that W. W. Hughes was promoted second mate in April 1889.[31] Occasionally one comes across evidence from other sources; Captain Owen Owens, master of the *R. J. Owens,* noted in his Bible his ship's position when he had read certain passages. Thus when he read Paul's letter to the Ephesians, he wrote: 'Beeswing: September 9th, 1906, off Cape Horn, running before a heavy westerly gale and high seas, bound from Taltal Chile to Rotterdam with nitrate'. Three years later he was master of the *R. J. Owens,* and as he read the third chapter of Zecharaiah, he noted 'Schr. R. J. Owens. Lat. 40°N, Long. 23.19W on Sunday July 4th 1909 off Western Island bound to Punch Bowl, Labrador, 3rd voyage '.[32]

Among the seafaring community of North Wales in the early decades of this century, two master mariners were very well known, and they may serve as the final examples of the career patterns of the Porthmadog seamen who survived long enough to have careers, and were not claimed by the seass in their early youth. Captain William Roberts was born at 'Rochr, Llanengan, in 1870, and left school at the age of eleven to work in a lead mine near his home for sixpence a day. He went to sea first in the little smack *Fishguard Lass,* then another coaster, the *Industry,* and made his first Newfoundland voyage in the schooner *Charles James* from Porthmadog under the command of Captain Johnson. By 1887 he was serving aboard the full-rigged *Cambrian Monarch,* owned by Captain Thomas Williams, and commanded by another Williams from Dinas, near his home. He then served in a number of large square-riggers, including the *Cambrian Prince,* commanded by Captain Philip Davies, brother-in-law of David Lloyd George, on a voyage round Cape Horn and to Batavia and Java, before becoming second mate of the full-rigged iron ship *Forest Hall,* built by Potter's and owned by Herron. In 1898 he obtained his mate's certificate and it was then that he returned to Porthmadog ships, to become mate of the *Frau Minna Petersen* and then of the brig *John Roberts.* Following this, and having qualified as master, he returned to the ships in which he made his name, as first officer of the *Metropolis,* then as master of the *County of Cardigan,* where he appears to have been highly regarded by the young apprentice Bissett, afterwards Sir James Bissett, master of the *Queen Mary,* who was highly critical of the owners and some of the captains, but acknowledged his indebtedness to Captain Williams, whom he recognized as a fine seaman. There is little point here in tracing Captain Williams's career in larger sailing ships and in steam, but it is significant that a man of his undoubted quality had found it worthwhile to gain experience as mate of the *Frau Minna Peterson* and the *John Roberts.*[33]

There is also a link between Captain Hugh Parry, the Porthmadog shipbroker who was so closely associated with the *Frau Minna Petersen,* and the very large-framed Captain Hugh Roberts, who is remembered by many as Marine Superintendent in Antwerp for the

William Thomas Company, but who had previously commanded the *County of Flint,* the *Kate Thomas,* and the *Crocodile,* and was known from Newcastle, New South Wales, to Portland, Oregon, and San Francisco as one of the toughest and most experienced sailing ship masters. In 1892 Hugh Roberts persuaded his father to take him from his home in the slate community of Carmel in Caernarvonshire to Porthmadog to seek a berth aboard one of the Porthmadog ships. At Porthmadog they met Captain Hugh Parry, who promised young Roberts's father he would do his best to get him a ship. A few days later a telegram arrived instructing Hugh Roberts to join the schooner *Sarah Williams,* which was at Porthmadog loading slates for Kiel. After visiting Captain Parry's office at Cornhill and being told that he was to be signed as deck boy and not cook, at a wage of fifteen shillings month, Hugh Roberts made his way tentatively to report to the Captain, who appeared to be 'a very ferocious looking chap'. Captain Roberts recalled many years later that first night at Porthmadog: he had been told to go ashore to a boarding house to sleep, but when he arrived he found it so full of sailors — 'all were drunk, even the old woman and her daughter, and the old girl sitting down in the midst of it, as drunk as a fiddler' — that he fled back to the ship to spend a troublesome and uncomfortable night huddled in one of the bunks. Next day they sailed on a voyage which turned out to be full of incident, including running aground on the voyage home from Gothenburg for Yarmouth. The young Roberts was eventually paid off at an Irish port, and came home with £4 in his pocket after his first six months voyage. He then joined the *Samuel Holland,* in which he sailed to Hamburg, Runcorn, Porthmadog again, then Hamburg, Fredrikshaven, then in ballast to Norway for a timber cargo home. Compared with the confused experiences aboard the *Sarah Williams,* Roberts had very happy memories of the well-ordered ship, *Samuel Holland,* and her firm but very efficient Cardiganshire master. The lessons he learned on the *Samuel Holland* stood him in good stead later when he served on the *Cambrian Hills,* then as second mate of the *County of Flint,* and as master of the *Kate Thomas* and his other large square-rigged ships.[34]

There were many who did not live to tell of their experiences, nor even long enough to serve in more than one ship. The family connection, although advantageous in some respects, could be tragically cruel: the twenty-one-year-old smack *Hebe* (still known locally as 'Rhibie) was on passage from Newport to Porthmadog with a cargo of 'Powells house coal' when she was lost, 'not heard of since sailing 15 November 1881, 3 crew lost' was the official report, but those three crew members were the master and his two sons. The Prince Edward Island-built *Hope,* very ancient in 1891 (the vessel known as '*Hope Bach*' to avoid confusion with the timber ship of the same name) sailed from Porthmadog with a slate cargo for Cowes, and took shelter because of the weather at Milford. The *Liza Hannah* and the *Resolute* had both left Porthmadog at the same time as her, and were with her at Milford. None of them were heard of again after leaving Milford on 8 March 1891; in the wreck reports I counted twenty-seven small schooners lost in storms off the West Coast, Land's End, Milford and the Longships during the next two days. These were small coasters, but it could happen to anyone. The *Catherine Richards* was about the largest two-masted schooner in the port. She was wrecked in Brandon Bay on the Kerry coast on the night of 30 December 1891, and near the spot where she foundered is a monument to the crew who lost their lives, Robert Jones, Walter Steward Jones, William Jones, Hugh Hughes (brother of Captain Harry Hughes and son of Lewis Hughes the tailor) and two others who are unnamed. Others foundered far from home. The strongly-built *Blanche Currie* was lost off Cape Race with all hands in the storm that so battered the *Mary Lloyd* and the *John Llewelyn.* The latter's epic struggle and the reception she received in Porthmadog on her return has been very well told recently in Lieutenant Commander J. Penri Davies's *Blas y Môr.* There is a more prosaic account in the owners' letter to the London agents, John Holman and Sons, Lloyd's Avenue, requesting their opinion 'if the vessel is still liable to be called on to fulfill charter party or can we claim release because of stress of weather'.[35] Apparently the *John Llewelyn* had left Pernambuco on 12 December 1913 for St. John's and was chartered to take a cargo of codfish in drums from there back to Brazil. 'She experienced terrible weather in the Gulf stream and could make no headway for St. John's. She was struck by a heavy sea which shifted the ballast, and the vessel was on her beam ends for some hours, was badly strained, and became very leaky'. Despite many attempts, the master of the *John Llewelyn* failed to make St. John's and, therefore, decided to put across for the United Kingdom, and eventually arrived home in Porthmadog 'in a very damaged state'. Another vessel which had a violent battle with the Atlantic was the *Robert Morris* some years earlier; she failed to make Newfoundland with her cargo of salt from Portugal, running first into fog off Newfoundland, and then very heavy weather which drove her eastward across the Atlantic. She arrived in Porthmadog after one hundred days at sea; much of the salt had melted and had been pumped out during the passage.

Although the loss of vessels was a serious blow to the community, the news that the crew were safe brought great rejoicing. When the *Cambrian News* reported that the *Excelsior* had been driven ashore at Halmstadt, Sweden, on Boxing Day 1902, the account was soberly factual: 'It is feared that she will share the fate which has befallen five other vessels sailing from Porthmadog during the past two months, and become a total wreck. Of the six vessels mentioned which have met with disaster, this is the fourth insured with the Portmadoc Mutual Ship Insurance Company. It is gratifying to learn that in this instance again all the crew were saved'.[36] But the tension sometimes was almost unbearable, as the inhabitants of Porthmadog waited for news. In April 1903 there is an account of the suspense felt as the days passed and no news came from the *Rosie*, which had left a fortnight previously for Southampton.[37] 'She set out almost simultaneously with a number of other vessels, with a like sailing capacity bound for a more distant port'. News came that the vessels for the more distant ports had arrived safely, 'one of them actually making Harburg in five days. But seven, ten and thirteen days elapsed and still no news of "Rosie".' By the Saturday there was a gloom about the town, but that morning the 'glad tidings . . . spread through the town like the proverbial wildfire. Not since the day when the telegram came announcing the relief of Mafeking was there so much sincere ecstatic joy amongst the population generally as last Saturday'. Apparently the *Rosie* had encountered severe weather, taking five days to round Land's End, 'and during the remainder of the fortnight she had to keep in the English Channel, the gale which followed gale making it absolutely impossible to venture shorewards without great peril'. Her master, Captain Dedwith, had saved the day, and his skill and experience 'enabled her to weather the storms successfully hour after hour and day after day'. The reputation of Captain Griffith E. Dedwith was already almost legendary for his exploits in the *Theda,* in which he had made a record Atlantic crossing, and subsequently in the *Rosie,* details of which have been given both by Emrys Hughes in his records and in his brother's *Immortal Sails*. He had had long experience in Porthmadog ships; when the *Cadwalader Jones,* then still a very new ship, had sailed from Porthmadog with slates for Danzig, one of her A.B.s was Griffith E. Dedwith, aged nineteen, whose previous ship had been the *Francis Henry*. The *Cadwalader Jones* has received much attention because of her long career, but in order to give an indication of the type of trade in which Porthmadog vessels were engaged at the beginning of this century, I have attempted to trace her voyages for a few years in the section of additional notes on selected ships.

The hazards encountered, the complexities and danger of such trades as the phosphate rock trade, the threat from icebergs as winter approached off Labrador and Newfoundland, these are eloquently yet briefly told in the wreck reports of the individual ships traced. So, too, are the all too frequent instances of collisions, of small sailing vessels being run down by steamers; this was the fate of the *Consul Kaestner, Edward Windus, Elizabeth Pritchard,* and the *Emrys,* to name only a few of the later vessels. There was little hope for the crew of a small vessel run down by steamers on a dark night; when the *Edward Windus* collided with the S.S. *Bingo Maru* off Hastings, the only member of her crew saved by the steamer was Julius Matore, a German Ordinary Seaman, aged eighteen — Captain J. H. Williams of Llanengan, aged thirty-seven, Gustav Jones, the mate, aged twenty-two, Eleazer Oliver, the old 'shellback' who was cook and A.B., aged sixty-six, Herman Prahle, aged nineteen, and Owen Jones, of Nefyn, aged twenty-one, all vanished in the blackness of the sea. Saddest of all are the scattered references to the loss of wives and children — the loss of Captain R. Parry and all four of his family in the first *Daniel Morris* is an early example. Porthmadog people knew well that there was sorrow in the sea. Young Robert Williams of Glaneivion, Borth-y-gest, son of David Williams, the Customs Officer at Porthmadog, was twelve years old when he recorded in his diary on January 26 that his father had gone to Harlech where a vessel had gone ashore; two days later he noted that 'there are three boats ashore.[38] One with its keel up is the Miningu . . . It is supposed that in this Mrs. Wright, who was found on Morfa Beach, the Captain's wife tried to come ashore and the boat was turned'. The *Miningu,* a nine hundred and twenty-four ton full-rigged ship, was owned in Cardiff, and was one of the many ships wrecked in that storm. On the following day, young Williams wrote in his diary: 'Went with father to the Custom House. Mr. Williams Police came there with Mrs. Wright's purse, brooch, and watch case, also some bills. She had five children on board and her husband and seventeen crew were all lost'. There were also the tragedies that occurred in the harbour. One particularly poignant entry in the diary is that for February 2 in the same year: 'Went to Custom House. We heard that a little boy from Borth Aberystwyth had drowned here last night. He was in bed when his father left the ship. He must have been frightened by the rattling of the chains, and came on deck and was blown into the water. His body was found near Cwmorthin Wharf'.

Life was not all sadness. Robert Williams's diary reflects what a young boy whose father had a special relationship with the ships must have felt; on 3 January 1884 he had recorded: 'Went to the Mary and Ellen to play with Captain Evans's little boy Rowland John Evans. I also went on board the Glad Tidings Captain Williams gave me ten biscuits to come home'. The *Mary and Ellen* was in Porthmadog again in the following April and, sure enough, in young Richard's diary there is another entry: 'Mrs. Captain Evans called and asked us to go on board the Mary and Ellen for tea. We enjoyed ourselves in the ship playing on deck and watching the other ships being loaded'. The ships' biscuits which young Robert Williams and so many youngsters found exciting, 'sgedins caled', were not as welcome, perhaps, to the crew after months at sea. Whilst the food in Porthmadog ships seldom reached the abysmal depths of that 'meagre, monotonous, miserable scale of salt beef, biscuits, tea and sugar', the words which Lloyd George used to describe the food on the large long-distance sailing vessels, when he introduced the Bill to amend the Merchant Shipping Acts in 1906, there may have been justification to maintain as he did 'the cooking on sailing ships is, as a rule, wholly uncharacterized by skill'.[39] Young first voyagers who found themselves as cooks aboard Porthmadog ships could hardly have been very skilful, but they soon learned. As conditions ashore improved, and a wider range of food became available from the local ship chandlers, there is reason to believe that the food on Porthmadog ships improved — except in some notorious cases. There were 'hungry ships' in Porthmadog as elsewhere, but the merchant-schooners with their local crews, and the consciousness of the inevitable stories that would leak back into the local community about meanness or poor food created a different attitude to that in the large international Cape Horners. One senses the good relations between a master and his crew in some letters written in 1870-71 by Richard Humphrey Williams, who had recently joined the schooner *Betty,* commanded for many years by Captain Owen Lloyd, father of that other master mariner of the same name who was master of the *Tyne.* The letters, which are from Waterford, Newcastle, Boulogne, and Boness, describe the voyages of the *Betty* at the time of the Franco-Prussian War, and Robert Williams has references to the war which reflect his lively interest in all that he saw and heard.[40] The overall impression is that this was a happy ship with a captain who was kind and interested in his crew. Whilst they were at Boness, young Williams noted particularly that vegetables, herrings and bread were much cheaper there than at home in Porthmadog; at Boulogne he found the Frenchmen he met kind and considerate. The *Evelyn* was said to have been a particularly happy ship; the Canadian press reports about her visit to Halifax in March 1910 stated: 'The first full-rigged brig to be seen for more than twenty years is now in port from Trinidad, with a cargo of 500 casks of molasses. She is the Evelyn, a wooden vessel of 216 tons gross, built at Portmadoc, Wales in 1877 and under the command of Captain Hugh Roberts for the past 31 years, during which there has never been any illness aboard, nor any serious disaster. The chief mate is the master's brother, who has been in the brig for 25 years'.[41]

The ship chandlers' account books are probably the best guide to the development of a more varied diet aboard Porthmadog ships; in 1893, for example, when the *Emrys* was being fitted out, there is a detailed account of the goods, charts, and food supplied to her, ranging from the '120 lbs tins Butter at 10d', '50 lbs Rice at $1\frac{1}{2}$d',

'3 cases Rst. Beef, 6 dozen tins', '6 tins Marmalade, 42 lbs. at 4d', '6 lbs Welsh Butter at 1/3d' to '3 paint and Deck Scrubbers 5/-' and '1 Almanack 1/-'. When the *Blodwen* took on stores in 1900, shortly before her record passage, she took on £53.3.9 worth of stores, including '20 lbs Green peas at 2½d', '20 lbs. French beans at 2/4d', '60 lbs Bacon at 5d', '35 lbs Tea at 1/11d', '3 cwt Bread at 16/-' — the full list is given in the study of the *Blodwen* among the selected ships. The accounts relating to about two hundred vessels are contained in these ledgers, and deserves fuller attention than is possible in this present work.[42]

It would be unwise to assume that there were not occasions when there was trouble with the crew, that there were no grievances or misdemeanors. Life was hard aboard these vessels and there are entries in the logs which suggest that some tough customers shipped aboard them. This was particularly true at times, and in ports where captains had to sign almost anyone they could get. The *Linus* was, as Henry Hughes described her, a beautiful barquentine with 'the lovely bow, the graceful sheer and the perfect masting and rig' which enabled her to sail round Cape Horn to the guano islands and take all kinds of weather whilst still maintaining fast passages. Yet, despite her beauty, she had had her troubles. In 1874, the *Linus* was at Bute Dock, Cardiff, in July, when her master, Captain John Peter Jones, and the mate, John Jones, mustered their crew for a voyage which was to take them to the Mediterranean and thence to Hamburg.[43] The trouble started almost at once; whilst the *Linus* lay in Penarth Roads, the master recorded in the official log that he had to discharge one man for refusing to work; another, who had failed to report for duty, was taken ashore before the magistrate and threatened with fourteen days hard labour. On the Saturday night, as she sailed out of the Bristol Channel, Captain Jones entered a note that 'Patrick Horrigan shiped OS and he cannot steer nor kept his look out, and from this day out I will reduce his wages from two pound ten to two pound a month, and that will be very good wages. I ask his reply and the reply he made that his eyes was bad'. They were in the Bay of Biscay when he recorded that 'F. E. Lemman shipped as A.B. seaman and he cannot make splice over strop Block nor he dont know how to reeve studding sails gear, and from this out his wages will be reduced from £3.7s.6d to £2.10 per month'.

By the end of August they reached Palermo, and the crew went on the spree. In the log, Captain Jones reported, 'These is to certify that I went ashore at 10 a.m. with ship papers. at 4 p.m. met with Capten of the Modration barque belong to North Shields and he tould me that my criw was in awfful state in the present of Capten of the Brigantine Clara and the Capin Brigantin Eascord of Plymouth'. When he returned aboard he found those members of the crew whose wages he had reduced, and the deck boy, all drunk, having gone ashore without permission. Refusing to unload the coal, saying they were too weak to work, the malcontents in the crew went ashore for another two days, which culminated in Patrick Horrigan coming back aboard, and, according to the master's report, 'he came aft to the Cabin door and saying Fight you Buggurs fight and I went on Deck and Push him forward as far as the Main Mast', where the mate helped to overcome the fighting Irishman. After repeated incidents, a Naval Court was held before H.M. Consul for Sicily, as President, Lieutenant J. Millar, R.N., commanding H.M. Schooner *Fly,* and Robert Hall, master of the brig *George Bartram;* the four older men were all sentenced to imprisonment and dismissed the ship, the boy, who, in the opinion of the Court, 'had been led astray by his elder messmates', was treated more leniently and fined. This case is a rare example as far as Porthmadog ships are concerned. Whatever breaches of conduct occurred, they were not recorded in the official logs; almost invariably these only record accidents or damage at sea.

Apart from seamen from Porthmadog itself, the men whose names probably feature most frequently in the 'articles' of Porthmadog ships are from the ports of the Elbe and the Baltic. The presentation of the Elsinore bowls when a Porthmadog vessel first visited Copenhagen was a symbol of the close relationship between the Baltic ports and Porthmadog. Many a German boy started his career in Porthmadog ships and remained with them for many years. This was inevitable because of the close connection with Hamburg, and Welsh seamen had many friends among the maritime community there. Apart from Caesar Marquard, whose warehouse was a meeting place for Welsh seamen, and who is said to have learned Welsh himself, visiting Porthmadog on at least one occasion, there were the shoemakers where the Welshmen purchased the much sought after 'bluchers' — David Lloyd George, in a speech at Caernarfon, once referred to the way he and his boyhood companions used to be fired with ambition to go to sea as they saw the sailors home on leave from distant ports swaggering down the street in Porthmadog wearing 'yr hen flwtshars', the shoes of Hamburg.[44] Both Henry Hughes and Lieutenant Commander Penri Davies have given unforgettable and evocative descriptions of the clothes the Porthmadog seamen they remembered wore. When the 1914-18 war broke out, a number of Porthmadog vessels, including the *George Casson* and the *Frau Minna Petersen,* together with their crews, were entrapped in the Elbe. Many Porthmadog seamen remembered with affection the little German tailor who had so frequently been aboard their vessels in the days of peace, who throughout the war years visited the prisoner-of-war camp with parcels for his friends from the Welsh ships. An indication of the links with Hamburg in the pre-war days in the photograph now in the possession of Miss Evelyn Roberts of her father and the other nine Porthmadog captains in Hamburg together; another is the photograph sent by Dr. Jürgen Meyer of a model made by a German seaman who served in the *Jenny Jones.*

Mr. John F. Owen now lives in retirement with his daughter at Chester after many years of farming in Wales, but as a young man he had thought of the sea as a career, and persuaded his Liverpool Welsh parents to get him a berth aboard the *Blodwen.* Recently he read me extracts from a diary he had kept, noting his emotions as the *Blodwen* sailed from Porthmadog, and how, despite his preoccupation with his early attempts at cooking for the crew and his unaccustomed duties as a seaman in the mate's watch, one of his first impressions was that of an Australian member of the crew who was uncommonly depressed at leaving 'Marged Ann' of the Ship Inn, Lombard Street, Porthmadog. Some days later, I read in the 'articles' for that voyage of the *Blodwen,* which commenced on 7 April 1906, the names of the crew, which included John F. Owen, aged seventeen, of 11 Malta Road, Bootle, First voyage, and William Payne, aged twenty, born in Newcastle, New South Wales, but who now gave his address as 10 Lombard Street, Porthmadog. Later, in his diary,[45] he recorded the happy days he had spent in the company of two young German seamen from a neighbouring schooner when they were together at Patras, and, on another occasion, the friendship he formed with a young Eskimo called Emanuel when the *Blodwen* was loading her salt cod cargo. Like so many Porthmadog seamen, he treasures the seal-skin trophies from Labrador and the memories of sun-filled days at Patras in Greece with Captain John Richard Williams encouraging his crew to sing on a still Sunday evening — with some of the Greeks on the quay and the crew of the *Elizabeth,* which lay nearby, joining in — a stark contrast to the bitter cold and the freezing fog of the Banks of Newfoundland. In February 1901, the *Cambrian News* reported that ' last week, the " Mary Lloyd Morris " arrived in charge of Captain Jones, Penmorfa, with ballast from Greece, and the soil has been mixed with Welsh soil in the new quay, this, according to the captain, being the first occasion for such a thing to happen '.[46] A glance through the charter-party agreements which have survived from one of the ship-brokers offices at Porthmadog[47] suggests the range of the sailings, the out of the way places to which these comparatively small vessels ventured. In the first few months of 1906, for example, the *William Morton* was chartered to take a cargo of oil in casks from Messina to Falmouth for orders, the *Fleetwing* to take manure in bags from London for Martinique and then to proceed to Aruba for phosphate in bulk for London, the *William Pritchard* to take a cargo of salt in bulk for St. John's, Newfoundland, and then fish, at least 3,500 quintals, from Newfoundland to Europe, the *John Pritchard* at least 3,200 quintals from Batteau, Labrador, the *C. E. Spooner* to take 150 loads of oak logs and other timber from Stettin to Sunderland — and more and more cargoes and far-off ports. The ship chandlers' accounts also bear witness to the range of sailing; when new vessels were built, or masters intent on visiting strange ports, there are the payments for Admiralty Charts: ' 1 Brit. Isles to Coast of Africa, 12/-, 1 Belle Isle and Cape Cod, 12/-, 1 Adriatic 8/-, 1 Grecian Archipelago, 10/-, 1 chart Newfoundland 10/- '[48] and so the charts, and ports visited, multiplied.

From the mass of papers, letters, diaries, and recorded interviews, there emerges the picture of a port and its seamen who knew adventure and adversity, a community which had grown to maturity, of builders who had created beautiful ships. There was much humour — the story of the *Thomas Charles,* whose master had died and his body brought home in the ballast, and whose impressive figurehead, unshipped and stowed below decks, caused a seaman going below to faint when he mistook the figurehead for his resurrected captain; the Porthmadog master mariner who was accused of consulting gypsies, a *cause célèbre* in the local newspapers. There was genuine concern and sadness at the loss of the schooner *Twelve Apostles,* relief that the crew were safe, and uninhibited glee long after the seriousness of the event had faded about that telegram which came to Cornhill: 'Twelve Apostles making water in Hell's Mouth'. Then there was the deck boy (a future distinguished master mariner) who threw the captain's spittoon over the side in error, and the innumerable eccentricities of captains and crews — these and many more are the yarns, some, no doubt apocryphal, that will be told in Porthmadog for many years. But there was also tragedy — the captains who were bankrupted by unexpected accidents, 'unable to pay his debts in full owing to the heavy loss sustained . . . through losing his vessel by explosion'[49] — despite the existence of the 'Mutual'. Then there were the bizarre events: the sinking of the brig *Waterloo* by a whale in the North Sea, and the dramatic account of the event by Captain Evan Jones, master of the *Waterloo,* in the *Illustrated London News;* the misfortunes of the mate of the *Ida* when two cigar-smoking German merchants were inadvertently blown up inspecting stone ballast in her hold, by igniting the remains of a previous cargo of gunpowder to Hamburg; vessels like the *Pilgrim,* alleged to have been sunk by the gnawing sharp teeth of rats. There were the near tragedies, as when the *John Roberts,* homeward-bound from the West Indies with a cargo of phosphate rock for Berwick, was wrecked near South Shields, with the master lying seriously ill in his bunk. The rescuers succeeded after many attempts in getting a line aboard, and brought all hands to safety, including the master's wife, Mrs. Davies of Llanystumdwy, and her sick husband. 'Mrs. Davies showed great courage, having had no fear of being dragged through the raging surf', but 'exhibited much anxiety, however, concerning the safety of her husband' who was carried unconscious to a nearby inn.[50] There were tragedies nearer home: the drowning of the Borth-y-gest pilots out in their boat one stormy night; the accidental drownings in and near the harbour; a small boy, son of a mariner, falling in front of a waggon being wheeled by his father and other members of the crew; a young man falling from aloft on to the deck of the schooner *Jennett* within an hour of joining her, and shortly after hearing of his mother's death.[51]

All too frequently there were major tragedies, vessels and crews vanishing without trace. 'Lost with all hands', 'not heard of since leaving', the phrases remind the reader of the records of Porthmadog ships of the cost of the port's investment in ships, and, even more, in lives. And there were the smaller tragedies: the photograph of the crew of the *Isallt*[52] has, in the foreground, ironically with the lifebelt around his neck, a young ordinary seaman, David Mark Jones, of Tanybryn, Llangybi, aged fourteen when the *Isallt* left Porthmadog in April 1912, for a voyage which took her to Aarhus in Denmark, Rasvaag, Norway, Runcorn, Carbonear, Newfoundland, Merchantman's Harbour, Labrador, Gilbraltar, Patras, Trapani in Sicily, and ended at Cork in January 1913. When she was in Denmark, her master, Captain R. O. Williams, wrote a note on the back of the photograph and sent it to his young nephew, son of David Williams, the ship builder. He explained that with the crew in the photograph was an English schoolmaster in Copenhagen — one notes his cricket cap! Captain Williams was naturally delighted that the *Isallt* had made a faster passage than her rival, the *Elizabeth,* and added, probably as he was fond of the lad, who was a near contemporary of his nephew, that David Mark was just about killing himself unloading the slates. At every port David Mark had small cash advances from the master, for postcards at Plymouth, postages and cash at Carbonear, Gibraltar, Patras and Trapani, for he was buying presents to give when he came home. It was not to be. At 4.30 a.m. on 11 January 1913, when the *Isallt* was in an estimated position 47°35′N and 12°10′W, three days away from Cork and home, Captain Williams had to enter in his log 'David Mark Jones (OS) fell from the Port Side of Fore Rigging in going up aloft and outside the vessel hull into the water, and was drowned. Ship at the time under small canvas and sea running very high. We hove ropes over the side for him to try and take hold of, also a Lifebuoy, but as it was so dark, he failed to catch any of them. We did not put a boat out as the weather was so rough and too dangerous to risk other lives'. When they reached Cork, Captain Williams and the mate sadly listed and entered into the official log the balance of his wages (£1.1.0) for the voyage of eight months and twenty-seven days, and the clothes and effects of David Mark Jones. Together with the jersey, trousers, blankets, sailor's bag, muffler, sewing palm, other clothes and the treasured photo frame, were one bottle of perfume and eighteen cigars, which, it was noted, were taken charge of by the Customs.

The excitement at the launching of the *Gestiana* from David Williams's yard in 1913, an occasion many people in Porthmadog still remember, was somewhat marred by the gloomy foreboding, the universal and almost involuntary groan that went up from the crowd when the christening bottle failed to break at the first attempt. Before the year was out, the gloom of the pessimists was borne out by events. Already the victim of an earlier mishap on the Goodwins, the *Gestiana* sailed across the Atlantic from Dysart, Scotland, and then, from Carbonear, Newfoundland, bound for North Sydney, Nova Scotia, in ballast. She was overtaken by a heavy storm and driven ashore ' at Gooseberry cove, near Brig Lorraine, Cape Breton, Nova Scotia, on Saturday, the 4 October 1913, about 2 a.m. Crew rescued by Seaman J. N. Myonis jumping on cliff and getting line ashore. Vessel broke up and became a total wreck '.[53] The master's report added that there had been dense fog beforehand, and the *Gestiana* had struck a rock close inshore. She had broached to alongside the cliffs, ' where heavy seas washed over the vessel ' and ' all hands were compelled to take to the rigging, where by the aid of ropes to the cliff, secured by seaman J. N. Myonis, all hands were saved '. Myonis, a Newfoundland seaman, had joined the *Gestiana* some seven weeks previously. With the *Gestiana* went ' all important papers, books, Instructions, everything on board ship, were totally lost. Absolute nothing saved. Crew rendered helplessly destitute, being clothed and cared for by the Canadian Government '.[54] Captain Pritchard's deep despair as he wrote the above was echoed in Porthmadog. In less than twelve months, Britain was at war with Germany; Porthmadog vessels were trapped in the Elbe. The slate trade ceased.

Sailing vessels, however beautiful, and however skilful their seamen, were no match for submarines. Of the Western Ocean Yachts still trading, the *Mary Annie, Mary Lloyd, Miss Morris,*

*Elizabeth Eleanor, John Pritchard,* and *Ellen James* were all sunk by U-boats between 1914 and 1918; the *R. J. Owens, William Prichard, M. Lloyd Morris, Elizabeth Pritchard, Blodwen* and *Mary Owens* were all wrecked during those same years. Shortly afterwards, in 1919, the *William Morton* was abandoned at sea. The *John Llewelyn,* sold to Newfoundland, was lost in 1928; the *Elizabeth,* which had been converted into a Q-ship, survived and returned to Porthmadog, where David Williams, the builder and owner, allowed the public to go aboard in order to raise money for post-war charitable purposes. She was later sold, and then she, too, was wrecked on the coast of Madagascar in 1927. The second *Isallt* survived both wars, but foundered off the Irish coast in 1948. The *M. A. James,* owned by the experienced and knowledgeable Captain W. J. Slade, sailed out of Appledore from 1930 to the Second World War, when she was requisitioned — and ruined — in the balloon barrage service. In 1950 she was still afloat as a hulk in Appledore. It was there, at Appledore, that she ended her days, the last Porthmadog ship.

Dis. I.

ISSUED BY THE BOARD OF TRADE

No. 183

**CERTIFICATE OF DISCHARGE**

FOR SEAMEN DISCHARGED BEFORE THE SUPERINTENDENT OF A MERCANTILE MARINE OFFICE IN THE UNITED KINGDOM, A BRITISH CONSUL, OR A SHIPPING OFFICER IN BRITISH POSSESSION ABROAD.

| Name of Ship. | Offic<sup></sup>l. Number. | Port of Registry. | Reg. Tonnage. |
|---|---|---|---|
| "Ellen James" | 92222 | Carnarvon | 114 |

| Horse Power of Engines (if any). | Description of Voyage or Employment. |
|---|---|
| — | Foreign |

| Name of Seaman. | Age. | Place of Birth. | No. of R. N. R. Commission or Certif. | Capacity. If Mate or Engineer, No. of Cert. (if any) |
|---|---|---|---|---|
| Hermann Lemke | 17 | Germany | — | OS. |

| Date of Engagement. | Place of Engagement. | Date of Discharge. | Place of Discharge. |
|---|---|---|---|
| 18/5/98 | Sligo | 24/12/98 | Portmadoc |

I certify that the above particulars are correct and that the above named Seaman was discharged accordingly,* and that the character described hereon is a true copy of the Report concerning the said Seaman.

Dated this 24th day of Dec 1898

Jno. James Jones MASTER.

AUTHENTICATED BY W. Lewis

Signature of Superintendent, Consul, or Shipping Officer.

M. M. OFFICE — OFFICE SEAL OR OFFICIAL STAMP. 27.12.98 PORTMADOC

* If the Seaman does not require a Certificate of his character, obliterate the following Words in lines two and three and score through the Dics.

CHARACTER FOR CONDUCT.

CHARACTER FOR ABILITY.

Signature of Seaman } Hermann Lemke

NOTE.—Any Person who forges or fraudulently alters any Certificate or Report, or who makes use of any Certificate, or Report, which is forged or altered or does not belong to him, shall for each such offence be deemed guilty of a misdemeanour and may be fined or imprisoned.
N.B.—Should this Certificate come into the possession of any person to whom it does not belong it should be handed to the Superintendent of the nearest Mercantile Marine Office, or be transmitted to ...

## REFERENCES

[1] Alltud Eifion, *Y Gestiana,* 128.
[2] C.R.O. XM/1853/2.
[3] N.L.W. 12108.
[4] Account book of *Heir Apparent,* now in possession of Mrs. E. Humphreys, Tynygongl, Anglesey. cf. *Ships and Seamen of Anglesey,* 395-402.
[5] C.R.O. XM/2387.
[6] *Report of the Commissioners of Inquiry into the State of Education in Wales, 1847* (London, 1848), 525.
[7] A. Eames, *Ships and Seamen of Anglesey,* 367-374.
[8] I am indebted to Mrs. Elenora Fox of Abererch for allowing me to peruse this notebook which originally belonged to her great-uncle, Captain Daniel Jones, who was later to become master of a number of large full-rigged sailing ships.
[9] D. Thomas, *Hen Longau Sir Gaernarfon,* 162.
[10] *Report, 1847,* 526.
[11] Evidence of John V. Godwin, quoted in J. F. C. Harrison, *The Early Victorians, 1832-51* (1971), 148.
[12] C.R.O. M/531/65.
[13] *N.W.C.,* 30 November 1917.
[14] The biography of Captain Hugh Hughes contains many references to his voyages, often extracted from sermons which he had preached, e.g., on one occasion he spoke about the cholera epidemic which was raging at St. Petersburg when he was there in the *Eagle.* John Jones, *Cofiant Capten Hugh Hughes, Gellidara* (Dolgellau, 1898), 58.
[15] Alltud Eifion, *Y Gestiana.*
[16] *Y Drysorfa* (1843), 114.
[17] *CN,* 30 January 1903.
[18] ibid.
[19] Letter dated 11 December 1845 to Mr. David Williams, Porthmadog, from W. J. N.(?) Williams, now in possession of Captain William Williams's grandson, Mr. Riby Williams of Weymouth, to whom I am indebted for much of the information regarding Captain William Williams of Rhiw. cf. A. Eames, *Ships and Seaman of Anglesey,* 256-258.
[20] Unsigned note appended to original Agreement, now C.R.O. XM/2387.
[21] Report of Portmadoc Mutual Ship Insurance Society, 1865, now C.R.O. M/531/50.
[22] Henry Hughes, *Immortal Sails,* 136-139.
[23] Newspaper cuttings from English and Welsh newspapers relating to wedding of Captain and Mrs. Hugh Roberts, 15 February 1893, provided by Miss Evelyn Roberts, daughter of Captain Roberts.
[24] T.R. interview with Captain Griffith Roberts, O.B.E., Borth-y-gest, June 1974.
[25] T.R. interview with Captain Robert Roberts, Borth-y-gest, June 1974.
[26] U.C.N.W., Bangor, 11829.
[27] U.C.N.W., Bangor, 11822.
[28] I am indebted to Mr. R. Froom of Liverpool for this photograph and much information regarding his grandfather, Captain Robert Thomas, whose career I intend to trace in some detail in a future study of North Wales master mariners.
[29] T.R. interview with Mrs. Hannah Thomas, Porthmadog, November 1974.

[30] For this and much other information about Captain Peter Jones, I am indebted to Mr. H. Conway Jones of Southall, Middlesex. There is a fine slate memorial stone erected by Mr. Conway Jones at Llanenwyn, Dyffryn Ardudwy, where Captain Peter Jones and his wife are buried, which records his service at sea, and a portrait of a sailing ship, based on Godfrey's painting of the *County of Cardigan*, engraved into the slate.

[31] There papers were kindly lent by Mr. D. Hughes of Bangor, son of W. W. Hughes.

[32] Miss Mair Evans, daughter of the late Captain E. Evans, Arenig, Criccieth, kindly drew my attention to the papers of Captain Owen Owens, master of the *R. J. Owens.*

[33] U.C.N.W., Bangor, 11830.

[34] Captain Hugh Roberts lived in his years of retirement at Benllech, Anglesey; his wife sailed with him on several Cape Horn passages when he was master of William Thomas's *Crocodile.*

[35] C.R.O. M/1027. Letter book of owners of *John Llewelyn* and *William Moreton.*

[36] *CN,* 2 January 1903.

[37] *CN,* 3 April 1903.

[38] Diary kept by Robert Williams, born 4 July 1872, of Glaneivion, Borth-y-gest. I am much indebted to Miss Ennys Williams of Bangor, daughter of Robert Williams, for transcribing these extracts from her father's diary.

[39] *Parl. Debates,* 4th Series, 154, March 1906, 238-294.

[40] The letters of Richard Humphrey Williams are now in the possession of his descendant, Mrs. V. Mitchell-Rawles of Welwyn Garden City, to whom I am indebted for photostat copies of those written in 1870 and 1871.

[41] *Shipping Illustrated, Halifax,* 19 March 1910.

[42] N.L.W. 12088E - 12093E.

[43] C.R.O., Crew Agreement List and Official Log of *Linus,* July 1874.

[44] *Y Genedl,* 16 June 1930.

[45] C.R.O., Crew Agreement List, *Blodwen,* voyage commencing 7 April 1906.

[46] *CN,* February 1901.

[47] C.R.O., XM/988. These charter-party papers were deposited by Mr. H. Roberts of Menai View Terrace, Bangor, whose father was a clerk in a Porthmadog ship-broker's office, 1906.

[48] N.L.W., 12093E fo. 26.

[49] N.L.W., 12088E. Letter from O. Robyns Owen, Solicitor, Pwllheli, 4 December 1905.

[50] There was some indication in this report of the dependence of the crew on the master when it came to an emergency: 'The coastguards had great difficulty in working the rocket apparatus, and even when that was done, it was found that the men on board had not a clear knowledge of the working of the apparatus. It was afterwards learnt that the master was lying in the forecastle ill, and could not be consulted about the working of the life-saving gear'.

[51] *CN,* 13 July 1877.

[52] This photograph, and a number of others relating to the vessels built by David Williams, is reproduced through the kindness of Mr. David Williams of Largs, Ayrshire, son of the shipbuilder.

[53] The papers of the *Gestiana* were all lost, and these are, therefore, reports written by Captain Pritchard, on duplicate copies of the official log and Crew Agreement, and duly certified as correct by the Notary Public, Henry C. V. Le Vatte, of Louisberg, in the County of Cape Breton, on 11 October 1913.

[54] ibid. The *Cambrian News* had underlined the significance of the launching of the *Gestiana* for Porthmadog in its report some months previously: 'Twenty-five or thirty years ago it was no uncommon thing to see several new vessels being launched at Portmadoc, some from the Ballast Wharf, others from Harry Jones's Wharf, and at Borth-y-gest. But since then ship-launching has been almost a rare occurrence, and it was somewhat of a novelty to hear the town crier announcing in the streets on Monday that a vessel was to be launched from the ship-building yard of Mr. David Williams on Tuesday morning. We know the history of Portmadoc fairly well, and we do not remember of a forthcoming launch ever being proclaimed by a town crier before'.

1) Joined Smack Brothers of Nevin about the middle of September 1885 at Porthtinlleyn loaded at Llanbedrog for Garston & back with coal to Porthdynllaen about 2½ Months ------ Cook

2) Joined Schooner Margaret & Martha about the beggining of March 1886 trading on the coast left her about the end of June 1887 – about 16 Months.----- Cook & OS

3) Joined the Schooner John Pierce at Port Madoc the end of July 1887 loaded for Harburg thence to Havre & Port Madoc 2½ Months ------- Cook

4) Joined Barquantine Ethiis of London at Cardiff the end of November 1887 went to Campana thence to Buenos Ayres loaded hides for Antwerp thence to Cardiff left 18th September 1888 10 Months. ----- OS

Diary of Thomas Evans of Aberdaron.

5) Joined the Brig "Ephratah" of
of Carnarvon at Cardiff the
end of September 1888. went O.S.
to Santa Catherina Brazils
thence to Barbadoes for orders
and to aruba loaded Phosporate
Rock for Newcastle left the
beginning of April 1889
about 6 1/2 Months ------
6) Joined Schooner Ebenezer
of Port Madoc May 5th 1889 went
to Randers Denmark thence
to Frederickstad Norway O.S.
loaded for London loaded
there for Plymouth went to
Pwllheli & then to Port Madoc
left August 6th 1889 3 Months.
7) Joined Schooner Quarryman at
Port Madoc September 4th 1889 O.S.
went to Kolding & Aalborg Denmark
then to Frederickstad loaded for
Wexford thence to Pwllheli
left November 26th 1889 nearly 3 Months

8) Joined Schooner Rebecca Mary
of Carnarvon at Carnarvon about
1st of December 1889 trading
between Bristol & Llanaelhaiarn
Left at Cardiff about the middle
of February 1890. about 2 1/2 Months AB
9) Joined Ship Astracana of
Liverpool February 24th 1890 Joined at Barry
went to Anger Point Java
for Orders proceeded to
Nagasaki Japan thence light
to Tacoma Washington U.S.A. AB
loaded flour for Dublin
left april 1st 1891 = 14 Months.
10) Joined Ship Fred. B. Taylor of
Yarmouth N.S. at Barry Dock AB
April 24th 1891 went to Rio de Janiero
then to Seattle Washington U.S.A.
loaded for Queenstown for orders
ordered to Havre.
left april 4th 1892 = 12 Months

# Portmadoc Ships.

A brief record of vessels trading to and from the port during the greater part of the 19th century and the first quarter of the 20th century with short notes on those I have personally known and heard of.

Henry Hughes
Pen y Traeth
Borthygest. Portmadoc

IN presenting Emrys Hughes MS. XM/1559, the aim has been to preserve the essentially personal nature of the document; many of the masters and their families, as well as the vessels, were well-known to the late Emrys Hughes and his brothers, and, therefore, anecdotes and reminiscences have been retained as they appear in his notes and additional jottings. It is evident that Mr. Hughes had been compiling this material over a number of years and had jotted down new information from time to time. It has, therefore, been necessary, occasionally, to re-arrange the material in the light of his later additions and amendments. The enthusiast will find that there are still gaps, and room has been left for insertions of further information; the hope is that this will eventually lead to an even more comprehensive list.

As explained in the preface, this material was used by Henry Hughes in *Immortal Sails,* and, in order to avoid repetition, some of the entries here have been compressed where a very full account has already appeared in *Immortal Sails.* The late Emrys Hughes noted meticulously the source of the illustrations which were interspersed in the text of his notes; some of these have been re-photographed with the owners' consent and included in this book. As most of the illustrations in *Immortal Sails* were from the Emrys Hughes collection, only the most significant have been reproduced here, again to avoid repetition. In addition, however, many photographs more recently donated or on loan to the Gwynedd Archives Service have been included.

In order to indicate information which I have gleaned from other sources, new and additional material is indented in the text with, where appropriate, the source of the information. Most of this additional material has come from interviews and tape recordings, the wreck returns in the *Parliamentary Papers,* local newspapers of the nineteenth century, and the Register of British Shipping for Beaumaris and Caernarfon. In this latter context, I am indebted to Mr. Lyle and Mr. R. S. Wells and their colleagues at H.M. Customs Office, Caernarfon, and Customs House, Holyhead, respectively, for their interest and assistance in granting me access to records in their care. The following abbreviations have been used in order to present the document in a compact form; these abbreviations have also been used in the footnotes to the text of the introductory chapters and the further studies.

## ABBREVIATIONS

| | | |
|---|---|---|
| Bg. | — | Brig |
| Bk. | — | Barque |
| Bkn. | — | Barquentine |
| Bn. | — | Brigantine |
| *C.D.H.* | — | *Caernarvon and Denbigh Herald* |
| *C.N.* | — | *Cambrian News* |
| C.R.O. | — | Gwynedd Record Office, Caernarfon |
| C.R.S. | — | Registers of Shipping, H.M. Customs, Caernarfon |
| K. | — | Ketch |
| I. | — | Iron |
| *H.L.S.G.* | — | D. Thomas, *Hen Longau Sir Gaernarfon* |
| *L.R.* | — | *Lloyd's Register* |
| Ma. | — | Master (of vessel) |
| M.O. | — | Managing Owner |
| N.F.L. | — | Newfoundland |
| N.L.W. | — | National Library of Wales |
| N.M.M. | — | National Maritime Museum |
| *N.W.C.* | — | *North Wales Chronicle* |
| *P.P.* | — | *Parliamentary Papers* |
| P.R.O. | — | Public Record Office |
| P.Y.A. | — | Porth yr Aur MSS. |
| S. | — | Ship (full-rigged) |
| S.H. | — | Ship's Husband |
| Sm. | — | Smack |
| Sp. | — | Sloop |
| Sr. | — | Schooner |
| 3 mst. S. | — | Three-masted Schooner |
| Sw. | — | Snow |
| tg. | — | tons gross |
| tn. | — | tons net |
| tr. | — | registered tonnage |
| *T.Cymm.S.* | — | *Transactions of the Honourable Society of Cymmrodorion* |
| *T.C.H.S.* | — | *Transactions of the Caernarvonshire Historical Society* |
| T.R. | — | Tape-recorded interview |
| U.C.N.W. | — | University College of North Wales, Bangor |

ABEONA

Sp, 87/94 tg, 57/19/-. Built Talsarnau at Carreg Ro. 1811. R. Lloyd, ma. Reg. at Barmouth.

A vessel of this name (Captain Morris, ma.) was said to have been at Konigsberg in October, 1795. Another commanded by a Captain Evans traded to the Mediterranean also about 1795. *Daily Advertiser,* Sat., Dec. 24, 1796, quoted in U.C.N.W. Bangor MSS. 19065.

ABERKIN

Sr, Built Traeth Mawr, Capt. Owen, ma. She was at St. Petersburg in 1795 with the *Harlech Castle.*

Built 1786. Lost and Reg. 1798. Described as *Bg* in 1790. Bangor, P.Y.A. 32, 254.

ADA

*L.R. 1871:* Sr, 97t, 79.6/18.8/10.5. Built Pwllheli 1869, owned Davies & Co., L. Davies, ma, reg. at P.M. Trade — Bangor — Hamburg. D. Thomas in *H.L.S.G.* gives 1869 as date of building but states she was lost at sea in same year (1869).

ADRIA

Captain Jones, *Netherton* was once her ma. Wrecked in 1881.

At the time of the 1871 Census, she was in the harbour at Porthmadog, and had one AB aboard that night, Owen Jones, from Aberffraw, Anglesey.

AERIEL

79t, Wm. Hughes, ma. Wm. Hughes, ma, father of Wm. Hughes, Belle Vue. In 1859 Henry Owen was her ma, and John Roberts her mate.

*L.R. 1859:* Sr, 104t. Built Newport 1848, Hughes & Co., P.M. owners W. Hughes, ma.

AERON BELLE

Sr, 61tn, 55/4, 18/2, 8/2. Built Aberayron 1856, Capt. Davies, ma.

*L.R. 1871/2:* D. Evans, ma. Evans & Co., owners, Aberayron.

AERON LASS

Sr, 80tn, 62/6, 17/2, 10/2. Built Aberayron, John Jones, Borthygest. Lost off Lands End, voyage Portmadoc to Ipswich, Jan. 1906. Cargo of Slates 115 tons, 11 cwts, 2 quarters at a freight of 8/6 per ton.

*L.R. 1871/2:* P. Owens, ma, Owens & Co., Aberystwyth, owners. *L.R. 1904/5:* Built 1845, by E. Jones, Llanddewy, H. Humphreys, ma, J. Jones, owner.

AGNES (I)

Sr, John Ellis, Tregunter, Portmadoc, ma.

*L.R. 1871/2:* J. Davies, ma, 93t, 72.0/18.2/10.3. Built New Brunswick, 1845, Jones & Co., P.M. Owners.

AGNES (II)

*C.R.S.:* Bn, 199t, 106/24.2/12.6. Built Summerside, Prince Edward Is, 1874, by Angus McMillan, Watkin Owens, Criccieth M.M. 64/64ths, reg C'von, 3.3.1875. 32/64ths sold to William Williams, shopkeeper, Criccieth. Vessel run down 23/6/1879 off Ceuta.

AGNES MAY

Sr, Owen Roberts, Talsarnau, ma.

AGRICOLA

K, 'Fore and After', later Ketch. 'Hên John' ma. He mixed his seafaring life with a little farming.

AILSIE

J Hughes, ma.

3mst. Sr, 130t, 96.9/22.6/10.4. Built W. C. Paynter & Co., Amlwch, 1892. cf. *Ships and Seamen of Anglesey,* 498.500.

ALBERT BALTZER

Bn, 161tn, 91.1/23/12.7. Built P.M. 1867, Eben Roberts, Owen Morris, ma, and owner. Lost on Terschelling Bank, August 1, 1897, on Voyage from Portmadoc to Hamburg. She was carrying at the time 292 tons of slates at a freight of 9/- per ton. She was principally a Baltic Trader in my time. The crew were in the boat for 24 hours when she was lost and were landed at Calais.

ALBION

*? L.R. 1855:* Bg, 169t. Built Wales, 1852, owned Jones & Co., Aberystwyth coaster.

ALERT

Sr, 3mst., River Dee?

*Alert* Sm, 46th. Built Borthygest, 1860. Lost off Ireland 4.9.1876. *L.R. 1904/5:* 3mst Sr, (Wood) 163t., 103.8, 23.6, 11.1. Built Runcorn 1885, W. Pearce, ma; J. Waters, owner, reg. Falmouth.

ALEXANDER

*P.P. 1903, LXII:* 13 April, 1902. Alexander of Beaumaris, 41 years old. Sr, 70t, 4 crew, H. Parry, ma; Mrs. M. Parry, Bangor, owner. Voyage P.M. to Grimsby with slates. Wind force NW4, foundered 10 miles SSW of St. Anne's Head, Pembrokeshire.

ALICE CHUMLEY

Sr, 85t. Built Portdinorwic, 1857, Evan Hughes, ma, 1862/3; Wm. Hughes 1865/7. Locally known as the 'Alice Chimney'. About 150 tons d.w., Sank on the Goodwin Sands. All hands safe.

*L.R. 1870/71:* Alice Chamney. 85t, 68.5/19.5/11.0. Built Portdinorwic by Wilson, 1859. R. Morris, ma, Portmadoc + owner.

ALMA

*L.R. 1859:* Sr, built Portmadoc 1855, W. Jones, ma, owned Jones & Co., Portdinorwic. Lost off Maryport, 20 Oct. 1873.

ALPHA

Sr, 91tn. Built Salcombe, John Jones, ma. Admitted to the Club — February 5, 1904. Lost with all hands on voyage from Dublin to Amlwch, Anglesey. After leaving Dublin she was not heard of again. John Jones (Johnie 'Star') was her Master at the time. Cargo 150 tons, 8 cwts of manure @ a freight of 4/- per ton.

*L.R. 1904/5:* Sr, 99tg. Built 1865 by Vivian at Salcombe, J. R. Jones, Porthmadog, owner.

*C.R.S.:* Sr, 99tg, 79.8tr, 79.3/20.5/10.6. Built Salcombe, Devon, 1865. Owner: John Richard Jones, 20 New Street, P.M., M.M. 64/64ths. Vessel missing. Left Dublin, 2 p.m., 25 Feb. 1905, bound for Amlwch and has not been heard of since. Reg. closed 3 April 1905. Certificate of Reg. lost with vessel.

AMANDA

Bn, 154tn, 170tg, 96.7/23.5/12.5. Built Borthygest, 1864 by Owens near William Wallace Williams Shop, Robert Jones, ma. Condemned because she was eaten with dry rot.

*L.R. 1870/71:* Portmadoc/Baltic Trade. Sold Newhaven, 1889.

A. M. FOX

Sr, Built Appledore, David Davies, ma. Admitted to the Club, December 1913, afterwards lost in the Bay of Naples, all the crew were saved. She was a Newfoundland Trader.

*L.R. 1910/11:* W. Sr, 125t., 91.4/22.2/10.6 Built Appledore, 1905 by R. Cock & Sons, W. G. Fox owner, reg. Plymouth. For a detailed description of the building of Srs at the Bell Inn yard by the Cock brothers, see Basil Greenhill, *The Merchant Schooners,* Vol. 1, 81.91 (1968).

AMITY

*L.R. 1859:* Sp, 45t. Built Aberystwyth 1802, Davies & Co., Aberystwyth, owners, D. Davies, ma.

AMNER

? Sr, 81t, built Llanbedrog by Isaac Williams, 1840, and lost off Portland, 1872.

ANGHARAD

Sr, 84tn, 75.1/16.3/8.2. Built at P.M. 1853 Vaughan and other owners, Wm. Wms., ma.

Builder: Morgan Jones. Lost 1891.

ANN

*? L.R. 1880:* Sr, 67t, 76/20/9. Built Ferguson, Connah's Quay, 1866. W. Sloane, Jnr., owner of Chester.

ANNA

K, 70tn. Built Rotten Tare. Built P.M., 1895, by David Williams, sold to Belfast, Ireland, off the Blocks.

*L.R. 1904/5:* K, 86t, gross, 82.6/21.5/8.4. P.M., 1895, T. Shaw, Belfast, owners.

ANNA BRAUNSCHWEIG

Bkn with a quarter deck, 262tg, 246tn, 116.3/25.5/14.5. Built P.M., 1876, by Ebenezer Roberts, Evan Jones, ma. Lost on Buenayre Island, West Indies, Voyage Brazil to Aruba in ballast October 20, 1897. The barque *Cuerero* belonging to Capt. Morgan Jones was wrecked near the same spot.

*C.R.S.:* David Jones, P.M., Retired M.M. 36/64ths, John Jones, Braich y Saint, Criccieth, Farmer, 16/64ths, Robert Jones, Caernarfon, M.M. 12/64ths, in 1876. In 1890, David Jones, P.M., sold shares to Ebenezer Roberts, 1 Mount Pleasant, P.M., retired ship builder. Wrecked 26.10.1897, N.M.M. Wreck List.

ANN ALICE

Sr, Built Nevin, Wm. Williams, ma. Lost off Point Lynas 1877.

*L.R. 1871/2:* Sr, 98t, 78.4/21.3/10.9. Built Builth Wells 1870, W. Williams, P.M.; owner, W. Williams, ma, P.M. — Hamburg.

ANN CATHERINE

Sr. She belonged to the family of Margaret Griffiths, Terrace Road (The sister of Dick Crudd).

*L.R. 1871/2:* Sr, 110t, 76.2/21.1/11.3. Built P.M. 1860; Williams, Williams & Co., E. Williams, ma. P.M. — Baltic.

*P.P. 1886, LIX, 698:* Sr, 20 years old, not heard of since sailing 10 June 1880. Built P.M. 110t, G. Griffiths, P.M. owner, cargo of gas coal 175t. This vessel is stated to have been fitted with patent ventilators. Newcastle-on-Tyne to Viana, Portugal, 6 crew lost. Owner stated that vessel was well found in every respect, and was of opinion she must have been run down.

ANN MORGAN

*L.R. 1871/2:* Sr, 68t, 67.6/19.4/9.6. Built by Jones, Barmouth, 1861. Jones & Co., Barmouth. J. Jones, ma.

ANN PRITCHARD

David A. Pritchard, owner.

*? Ann Prichard,* Sp, 34t, lost off St. Davids, 10 April 1887.

ANN WARREN

Sr, 956. Built Aberystwyth, Morris Davies; owners, Thomas Davis, ma.

*L.R. 1859:* 95t. Built Newquay, 1857, Jones & Co., Newquay.

*L.R. 1904/5:* 4 Sr. 95tg, 75.1/10.2/10.5. Built Newquay, 1857, A. Johns, Aberystwyth.

ANN WHEATON

*L.R. 1880/1:* Sr, 3 mst. 214t, 11.0/23.7/13.9. Built Bridport 1865, by Cox E. Owen, owner and ma. reg. port. Plymouth.

ANN & SUSAN

Rhys Davis, owner, father of Rhys Davies, the pilot.

*L.R. 1859:* k, Barmouth 1826, Davies & Co., R. Davies, ma.

ANN & ELLEN

(I) *Ann & Ellen:* Sp, 40t. Built Pwllheli, 1831.

(II) *L.R. 1871/2:* Sr, 110t, 79.0/21.4/11.1. Built Wales, 1858. H. Jones, Caernarfon; J. Jones, ma.

ANN GRIFFITH

Sr, 107. Built P.M. 1859. Lost off Copanshay, 27.3.1866.

ANN GRIFFITHS

Sr, 139t, 88.4/23.4/12.0. Built P.M. 1869. Hugh Williams, T. Jones, ma. *L.R. 1871/2:* Sr, 139t, 88.4/23.4/12.0. Built P.M., 1869. Hugh Williams, Griffiths & Co., Cardiff — Mediterranean. Stranded Mexico 23.12.1881. Reregistered as *Carmen.*

ANNE MELHUISH

Bk, 376t, 107.8/24.2/17.6, Built P.M. 1849 — Henry Winch, Liverpool, merchant; John James Mellhuish, Liverpool, merchant; Robert Kent, Liverpool, merchant; Henry Jones, P.M., Shipbuilder (each 16/64ths); Canol y Clwt, Portmadoc (now Greaves Wharf). Registered at Liverpool (no. 22 in 1849) 20 January 1849. Described as a sailing vessel with one deck, three masts and a standing bowsprit, square stern no galleries, female figurehead. Carvel built. Builder Henry Jones (Harry Jones the father of William Jones, Yr Yard). He lived at Shop Newydd before it was made into a shop. Registry closed and vessel reregistered de'novo as No. 229 in 1859, Liverpool, Dimensions altered to 112/26.2/17.5, 363.15t. Transferred to Melbourne 1863 (r. of S). Her owner in Australia was David Williams, Newcastle, New South Wales. As this vessel was one of the largest vessels built at Portmadoc, and that as early as 1848, I made enquiries at Newcastle, N.S.W., Australia, concerning her career there. I wrote to Mr. Harry Hey, Secretary of the Rotary Club of Newcastle, N.S.W., to ask if he could put me into touch with anyone who could throw any light on the subject. He found two descendants of Capt. David Williams at Newcastle, viz., Ben and Cramer Robbins whose eyes sparkled with pleasure when he showed them my letter. 'Ben informed him that Capt. Williams was only 19 years old when he sailed the vessel from United Kingdom to Australia, and Cramer informed him that she traded between Australia and New Zealand. Ultimately, Mr. Hey contacted a fellow Rotarian in the Newcastle Club, Mr. Fred Steward, Superintendant of the Mercantile Marine Office in Newcastle who looked up his records and also wrote to Freemantle and Sydney and he was so good as to furnish me with the following very interesting information:

> Dimensions: Length 112 feet; Beam 26′ 2″; Depth of Hold 17′ 6½″; Crew normally carried 9. Details of Registry: Portmadoc, 1849; re-registered in Melbourne 1863; re-registered in Newcastle 1869; transferred to Wellington, N.Z. No. 1 of 1873 and re-transferred to Newcastle, N.S.W., 12.12.1883. Vessel's History: On 24.9.1863 the vessel was sold by David Williams to John Lovitt at Melbourne. On 8.7.1866, Samuel James Lindsay became part owner with John Lovitt at Melbourne. On 4.3.1867, S. J. Lindsay and William R. Williams, of Newcastle were registered as owners at Melbourne. On 7.5.1869, Mr. William A. Williams, became sole owner, on

which date the vessel was re-registered in Newcastle. On 12.12.1883 the date of final registration in Newcastle, N.S.W., the transaction was under Certificate of Sale, dated 5.12.1883, under authority of David Williams acting as attorney to William Robert Williams, owner. The Williams brothers were known in Newcastle as 'Darkie' Williams. The vessel was engaged in trading between Newcastle and Wellington, New Zealand, with outward coal cargo returning from New Zealand with timber and general cargo. The vessel subsequently proceeded to Albany, W. Australia, and was later used as a coal hulk by Messrs. Mc-Ilwraith McEachern Ltd., in Albany. The exact date of arrival in Albany is not known but she sank in Albany sheltered waters in approximately 1890 and was subsequently blown up and destroyed to clear the harbour. There is a photo of the Barque *Anne Melhuish* in the office of the Union steamship Co., of New Zealand, Watt Street. I have been verbally informed that the Williams brothers were amongst the pioneers of the Union Steamship Company of New Zealand and that they originally belonged to the Portmadoc district.

## ANNIE

Sr, 2 mst. Built Portdinorwic, David Jones, Abergafran, owner, father of Wm. Morris Jones, P.M. Lost off Rotterdam, 1863, along with *Betsy* and *Mary Hills.*

*L.R. 1859:* 75t, 61.0/19.6/10.3. Built P.M. 1856; Holland Owner.

## ANNIE HOLLAND

Sr, 137tg, 128n, 84.7/23.1/12.0. Built P.M. 1868, by Hugh Williams, father of Miss Williams, the Schoolmistress, J. E. Jones, Penmorfa, ma. Coaster and Morocco trader.

Sold Brazil 1890.

## ANNIE LLOYD

Bn, later converted into a Bkn. 161tg, 149n, 95.5/23.5/12.4. Built Nevin, 1876, David Roberts, ma. David Morris, y Cei, S.H. Lost on Fortune Island, West Indies, March 6, 1907. Cargo: 140 tons of Dur-Dur in bricks. Freight: £2 per ton. Traded in the Brazils and West Indies. I remember her new mizen mast being put in very well at Pwll Grisia Môr when the tide was out. She was one of first Portmadoc vessels to enter Newfoundland Fish Trade.

*L.R. 1880/81:* Bn, Built Hughes, Wales, 1876 — J. Roberts & Co. J. Roberts, ma.

*C.R.S.:* Vessel built by Hugh Hughes, Portinllaen. William Jones, sailmaker, P.M., subsequently had shares in her and on his death in 1883 had 54/64ths; David Roberts, of P.M., also had 4/64ths shares. Ship stranded on Hogsty Reef, Bahamas, reg. closed 7 Sept. 1907. On 6 March 1907, had become a total wreck.

ANNIE MAUDE

Bn, Mr. Edwards of the Welsh Flannel Depot at Aberystwyth was her owner, father of I. Edwards, M.P.

*L.R. 1870/71:* Snow, 136t, 88.4/22.6/11.5. Built Sunderland, 1864 — Lister, Davies & Co., Aberystwyth, Cardiff & Medit.; J. Davies, ma.

ANN JANE

Sr, 109tg, 76.7/21.5/11.5. Built Nevin 1858, Robert Jones, Barmouth. Owner: Capt. Davies, ma, (J. Evans, ma). Lost on the coast of Anglesey, Voyage London to Caernarvon, March 1898, Cargo: 175 tons of cement. Freight: 5/6 per ton. This vessel was involved in a law suit due to a collision with the *Lizzie Jane*. This action plus damage cost the Club £665.9.5.

*L.R. 1863/4:* Owned Edwards & Co. — W. Griffiths, ma. Totally wrecked C'von Bay: N.M.M. 31.12.1897. Reg. closed 17.1.1898.

ANN & JANE PRICHARD

Sr, 3mst. 139tg. Built Pwllheli, Robert Prichard, S.H.; Owen Roberts, Talsarnau, ma. During the period — September 8, 1897, and March 6, 1903, — she took cargoes of slates to the following places: Copenhagen 6 times; Aarhus and Harburg 5 times; Svenborg, Stettin and Kiel, twice. During these 16 trips she shipped 3,840 tons of slates to Germany from Portmadoc. Lost in collision with *S.S. Carndale*, June 1909. Cargo: 225 tons. Manure freight 5/6 per ton. In December 1888 she collided with the brigantine *Ariel* at Newhaven and cost the Club £59.0.0.

*L.R. 1863:* 140t, 86.0/22.3/12.6 Built Pwllheli 1859, Prichard: Williams, ma.

*P.P. 1910, LXXXI:* Collided with *S.S. Croxdale* of W. Hartlepool, off Purfleet. R. Thames voyage London to Cork with manure, 30 Dec. 1908.

ANN JONES

Sr, Evan Williams, ma.

*L.R.:* Sr. 85t, 63.5/18.2/10.0. Built Pwllheli 1852, Wms. + 6 owners, Baltic trade. Lost with reg. Humber 10.12.1888.

ANN & MARY

Bk or Bg, John Ellis, Tregunter, ma.

*L.R. 1859:* Sr, 51t. Built Wales, 1843 — Humphreys ma. Aberystwyth coaster.

ARABELLA

Bn, 147tg, 135tn, 89/22.1/12.3. Built P.M., 1871; Eden Roberts, P.M.; Owen Jones, P.M., M.M., 16/64ths shares; William Lloyd, P.M., Ships Chandler, 8/64ths; Owen Lloyd P.M., M.M., 4/64ths; John Henry Williams, P.M., Iron and Brass Founder, 4/64ths; Hugh Jones Morgan, P.M., Plumber & Glazier, 4/64ths; Peter Pugh, P.M., Butcher, 2/64ths; John Williams, Shopisaf, Llandwrog, Mason, 4/64ths; Morris Owen, Pant Glas, near Ffestiniog, miner, 4/64ths; Robert Jones, Tŷ Coch, near Maentwrog, Relieving Officer, 4/64ths; Elizabeth Roberts, Brynhyfryd, near Ffestiniog, widow, 2/64ths; Morris Thomas, Talsarnau, Mariner, 4/64ths; Robert Jones, Harlech, miner, 2/64ths; Evan Pugh, Talsarnau, M.M., 2/64ths; Hugh Edwards, 63a Great Howard Street, London E.C., Ship Broker, 4/64ths; Vessel stranded at Saffi 19 December, 1866. Owen Jones, later Evan Evans, ma. Evan Pugh commanded the *Pride of Wales* for a time.

*Lloyds Weekly Shipping Index, Dec. 31, 1886.* Saffi (by tel. dated Gibraltar, Dec. 27, 6.20 p.m.). During a hurricane from S.W. on Dec. 19, the following vessels went ashore and will probably be total wrecks . . . British Brigantine *Arabella* also German vessels *Helene* and *Johann,* both laden with sugar. No lives lost. Dec. 28, Gibraltar, 4.55. All captains' vessels reported . . . vessels totally wrecked.

ARDUDWY

Bg, 203. t, 102.6/23.9/13.9. Built Borth-y-gest, 1863, by either Simon Jones or Richard Jones, Garreg Wen. Wm. Williams, ma. Registered owners: Cadwaladr Williams, P.M., M.M., 32/64ths shares; William Jones, P.M., Ship Chandler, 20/64ths; Robert Roberts, P.M., Surgeon, 4/64ths; Robert Roberts, Tyddyn Berllan, Towyn, Merioneth, Farmer, 4/64ths; Edward Williams, Portdinorwic, M.M., 4/64ths. On 7 November 1866 William Jones sold 4/64ths shares to Bennet Williams, P.M., Ship Broker, and son of Cadwaladr Williams, above. Registry closed 28 January 1870. Lost with all hands and all official papers about 10 or 11 Sept. 1869, when on a voyage from Cardiff to Salonica. On her last and fateful voyage this fine brig was commanded by Capt. Wm. Williams of Fron Galed, Dyffryn, near Harlech. He had just given up the command of the old brig *Lord Palmerston.* At the time of the loss of the *Ardudwy* he was only 28 years old. She sailed from Cardiff to Salonica with a load of iron rails. They were difficult things to store satisfactorily. On running into foul weather, probably in the Bay of

Biscay, her cargo moved causing her to capsize and sink. She was lost with all hands 10/11 Sept. 1869. Her master during his life was Cadwaladr Williams as above, father of Bennet Williams, 1863 to 1865. Wm. Evans, for a few months, ma, then Cadwaladr Wms. 1866/1868. Wm. Williams 1868 until her loss in 1869.

ARDWY

ARGO

Sr, 120t. Built Pwllheli, Ellis Humphreys, Borth-y-Gest, ma. Lost off Smalls.

Lost near Bally Water, Ireland, 9.12.1883.

ARVON

79tg, Wm. Parry, owner. Harry Hughes, ma.

*L.R. 1865:* Sr, W. Parry, 100t, 79.5/28.1/14.6. Built Wales, 1860. W. Parry, owner. *L.R. 1880:* Sr, W. Parry, 100t, 79.5/28.1/14.6. Built Wales 1860, J. Williams, ma. Lost Capt. W. H. Hughes, D.S.C., and his father were aboard the *Arvon* when she was lost off Corton Beach, Lowestoft. cf. *Ships and Seamen of Anglesey,* 462-3.

According to her official Log, she had sailed from P.M. for Gluckstad on July 24, 1899. She subsequently sailed to Harburg, Dundee, Dysart, Tonsberg, and Fredrickstad. She left Fredrickstad on Oct. 20, 1899, and became a total wreck after being stranded on Corton Beach, near Lowestoft. Henry Hughes, the ma, of Ralph Street, Borth-y-gest, was then aged 47, and his son, W. H. Hughes, was aged 13. According to *P.P. 1901, LXVIII,* 7 Dec. 1899, the wind force at the time was SE force 7, and the *Arvon's* crew of 5 were all saved. She was carrying a cargo of timber from Fredrickstad to P.M.

A.T.

K. Built at Milford Haven, Thos. Thomas, ma.

ATALANTA

Bg, 223tn, 100.0/24.5/13.8. Built P.M. 1864 by Jones. Capt. Griffith, Barmouth, ma. Phosphate Trader. Lost in 1892.

AURORA

? Bk. Lost in Caernarvon Bay, 1850, with all hands. ? a Portmadoc Ship.

*Aurora,* Sp, 59t. Built 1782, Barmouth. cf. L. M. Lloyd, *Maritime Merioneth, The Town and Port of Barmouth,* 83.

BARMOUTH

Sp, 30t. Built P.M. by Henry Jones, 1827.
Lost off Penmaenmawr, Jan. 1863.

BEAUMONT

N.F.L. Trader.

BEESWING

I. Bk, Capt. Griffith, ma. Prichard Bros., of P.M.S.H. She never entered P.M.

*L.R. 1901/2:* Steel Bk, 1,462t, 236.5/36/21.7, built by Russell & Co, Greenock, 1893. Owned *Beeswing Sailing Ship Co.* (Prichard Bros & Co) R. Griffith, ma, since 1893. The *Beeswing* served as a training ground for many P.M. Seamen, cf. *Ships and Seamen of Anglesey,* 464-5.

BELLE OF ARFON

Built Sunderland 1876.

*L.R. 1884/5:* I. Bk, 923t, 193.1/33.2/20.6. Built Sunderland by Osbourne Graham & Co, 1876, owned by W. Griffith & Co, 28 Brunswick St., Liverpool. W. Evans, ma.

BELVOIR CASTLE

Bg, 121t. Built Traeth Mawr, 1801. Sold Liverpool, 1814.

BENJAMIN HEWSTON

Sr. Built P.M. Edward Lloyd, ma, brother to Capt. Robert Lloyd of the *Wern.* On June 19, 1849, & on August 28, 1849, she sailed from Greaves Wharf, P.M., with 180 tons slate voyage to Kings Lynn. Foundered 70 miles off the coast of Norway on April 7, 1857: crew rescued by Schooner *Betsy (1).*

Built P.M. 1849 for Thomas Christian.

BETSY (1)

Sr, 73t. Built P.M. 1827 by Henry Jones, Wm. Morris, ma, father of Dr. R. O. Morris. Lost off Rotterdam 1863, along with the *Annie* and the *Mary Hills.*

BETSY (2)

Sr, 91t. Built Conway, Capt. Evans, ma. E. Williams, S.H. Talsarnau. Lost in Cardigan Bay.

BETSY (3)

Lost off Howth, 1838?

BETTY

Sr. Reg. at Pwllheli, Owen Lloyd, owner and ma, father of Capt. Owen Lloyd of the *Tyne*. On 26 January 1850 she sailed from Greaves Wharf P.M. to Kings Lynn with 145 8/20ths t. of slates, freight 11/- per ton. Owen Lloyd ma.

*L.R. 1859:* Sr. 98t. Built Pwllheli, 1838, owned Johnes and Co., ma J. Williams.

BILLOW CREST

Sr, 200 t, (d.w.). Built Milford Haven (? Bideford) Dr. Lister, owner. Newfoundland trader. Lost June 1899. Voyage Portmadoc to Esbjerg, Denmark. Cargo 201 tons 5 cwts, at a freight of 11/6 per ton of slates.

*L.R. 1884/5:* Sr, 107t, 91.7/21.3/10.9. Built Plymouth, 1883, by Watson & Fox, owned S. B. Harvey, Plymouth.

BISPHAM

Sr, 3mst. With a 'pole' mizzen mast. Humphrey Humphreys, ma. Newfoundland trader. Bought after going ashore at Abersoch, later sold to a German firm.

*L.R. 1884/5:* Sr, 119t, 92.7/21.7/11.6. Built Appledore, by Cook, 1867, owners J. Bradshaw, Fleetwood.

*C.R.S.:* John Williams, Bryn Llewelyn, Llangian, farmer, 64 shares. Sold 64/64ths on June 22, 1900, to Daniel Jones of 16 Mersey Street, Borth-y-gest. David Richards, 51 High Street, P.M. designated S.H. Reg. Closed 15 Sept. 1900. Vessel sold to German owners.

BLANCHE CURRIE

Bg, later a Bkn. 193tg., 103.8/24.2/12.6. Built Borthygest, 1875, by Richard Jones, Garreg Wen. Prichard Bros, S.H., David Evans, ma. Named after the sister of Sir Osmond Williams (the first Baronet), of Castell Deudraeth. She was originally built as a brig for the West Indies trade in phosphate rock, but as this trade diminished she was converted into a barquentine, a more suitable rig for general deep sea trade, especially the Newfoundland fish trade to the Mediterranean, Southern Brazil and the River Plate. Lost off Cape Race with all hands. Voyage Bahia to Newfoundland in ballast. Last heard of February 4, 1914. The *John Llewelyn* commanded by Rhys Davies pilot, was in the same storm, but survived. The *Mary Lloyd* was also in the same storm and also survived it. These vessels used to carry fish from Newfoundland to Bahia and Rio Grande do Sul, packed in tubs or drums and then returned to Newfoundland in ballast. Capt. Ellis Jones, Penmorfa, commanded her on one voyage as follows — Cardiff — with Coal to Berbice, British Guiana, Fort St. Andrew, then in ballast to Georgetown Demerara — then to New York with sugar, then general cargo to Rosario, ballast to Buenos Aires then home to U.K. with hides and horns. The general cargo was discharged 200 miles up River Plate.

*C.R.S.:* Built P.M. by Jones and Pritchard. Changed to 3 mst. Sr, at Liverpool 1894. Reg. closed 29 May, 1914, Owners: Humphrey Jones, P.M. ship chandled 4/64ths shares; Thomas Casson, P.M. Banker, 4/64ths; Robert Williams, Talysarn, Quarryman, 4/64ths; Griffith Prichard, P.M. Shipbroker, 4/64ths; John Jones, Minffordd, Merioneth, M.M. 16/64ths; Robert Jones, Minffordd, Merioneth, Quarryman 4/64ths; Andreas Roberts, Cwmorthin, Quarryman 4/64ths; David Griffith Williams, Rhiwbryfdir, grocer 4/64ths; Annie Louisa Loveday Williams, Castell-deudraeth, widow 4/64ths; Thomas Jones, Minffordd, shipowner 8/64ths; Richard Jones, P.M. Shipbuilder 4/64ths.

Hugh Pugh and Robert Jones, both bankers of P.M., made available mortgages amounting to £1,200 to Robert Jones, John Jones, Griffith Pritchard and Thomas Jones, at 6% interest to enable them to purchase their shares in May 1875. Ship missing since 4 Feb. 1914, last reported off Cape Race, Newfoundland. Reg. closed 29 May 1914.

BLODWEN

Sr, 3 mst, 129 tg. Built P.M. by David Jones, 1891, Hugh Parry, owner, Capt. John Roberts, Talsarnau ma, later Capt. 'Johnie' Williams, Son-in-law of Mrs. Rees Evans, Borthygest. It was he who commanded her on her record passage to Patras. The Richards family sold their shares in March 1892 to Capt. Roberts, who in turn sold 4/64ths each to David Morris, Shipper, Owen Morris, M.M., and Hugh Parry, Shipbroker, all of P.M. She was one of the smartest of the Newfoundland Traders, and in 1901 did a record passage from Newfoundland to Patras in 22 days. Capt. Roberts was drowned on Traeth Bach. He was a nephew of Shôn Tŷ Gwyn who used to ferry across Traeth Bach. She was sold in 1916 to W. Rorke of Carbonear, Newfoundland, and was wrecked near Alicante, Spain, on her 1st voyage under her new owner in 1916.

*C.R.S.:* Sr, 3 mst, 88.8/22.7/11.6. Built P.M. 1891 by David Jones, P.M., Carvel build; with a head of a woman as figure-head. Owners: John Roberts, Talsarnau, M.M., 48/64ths shares; Samuel Richards, Criccieth, shipowner 8/64ths; Edward Richards, P.M., shipowner, 8/64ths all of P.M.

[See additional notes on *Blodwen* infra.]

BLUE JACKET

Sr, 100tn, 79.5/20.9/10.9. Built Aberystwyth 1860, Evan Robert *Economy* owner, Humphrey Humphreys, Borthygest, ma. Lost in Cardigan Bay, 1887.

BLUE VEIN

Sr, 79t, Built P.M. 1838.

Built Evan Evans 1838, J. Watkins, ma (1859). Wrecked off Dublin, 25.9.1868.

BOADICEA

Sr. ?

*L.R. 1880:* K, 72t, 74.2/19/7.1. Built Pill, 1869, owners Cooper & Co., Bristol, reg. S. Cooper, ma.

BOLINA

Sr, 76.0/21.0/10.8 Built Pwllheli, 1867, R. Jones and others, owners, Pwllheli.

Built R. & D. Prichard 1867. Wrecked Scilly Is. 1.12.1887.

BRIDGET

Sr, 56tn. 42.2/14.7/8.1. Built Borthygest, F. S. Percival, owner, H. Humphreys, ma (formerly R. Ellis).

BRITANNIA

Sr, Thos. Jones, ma.

BROTHERS

46tn. Built Cardigan, 1848, Capt. Jenkins, ma.

CADWALADER JONES

Sr, 103tg. 95n. 81.5/21.8/10.9. Built Borthygest, 1878, by John Hughes for Morris Owen, John Cadwaladr, Owner and ma of Criccieth. Reg. as *Cadwalader Jones* No. 3 at Carnarvon 1878. Built at the slip which was at the point where the car park is now. Her owners on the date of her 1st reg. were:— John Cadwalader, Criccieth M.M. 20/64ths; David Jones, P.M. Surveyor of Shipping 8/64ths; John Jones, Braich y Saint, Farmer 8/64th; Owen Jones, Pentrefelin, Farmer 4/64ths; Joseph John Williams, Pwllheli, Baptist Minister, 4/64ths; John Jones, Pentrefelin, Coal Merchant, 4/64ths; John Roberts, Borth P.M. M.M., 4/64ths; John Watkins, P.M., Surveyor of Shipping, 2/64ths; Rd. Jones, Criccieth, Shipping Butcher 2/64ths; Owen Morris, P.M. Merchant

4/64ths; Griffith Jones, P.M., Wesleyan Minister, 4/64ths. She was one of the most notable little vessels attached to the Port. She entered the Newfoundland Fish Trade as soon as she was launched and continued in it for 38 years. There is hardly a Port in the Mediterranean that she did not visit and owing to the smallness of her size and her manouverability there is hardly a fishing station on the 200 miles of the Labrador coast that she did not load at. She was sold in January 1916 and went off the Reg. of the Portmadoc Mutual Ship Insurance Society. In 1900 or thereabouts Capt. T. J. Evans of Criccieth commanded the *S.S. Iolo Morgannwg* (the vessel on which my brother Willie lost his life). He was at Huelva and found 4 Portmadoc vessels windbound there viz:— *Cadwaladr Jones, Rose of Torridge,* Evan Evans Master, *C. E. Spooner,* Robert Jones Master, and the *Linus,* E. H. Williams, Master. After spending the evening together, the Captain of the *Iolo Morganwg* offered to tow them all out to sea the next day. They finished the evening on *Cadwaladr Jones* and her master John 'Cadwalad' drew the attention of his guests to a flying fish suspended on a thread from the cabin skylight. It was pointing for a change in the wind — a fair wind. The Master of the Steamer told him not to talk nonsense. Next morning however, when Captain Evans came on deck of his steamship, all the Portmadoc vessels had left the anchorage and, when he got out to sea, he saw them all well on their way to U.K. *Cadwaladr Jones* inshore — the others well out to sea. The little *Cadwaladr Jones* arrived at her destination several days before the others. Her career after she went off the Portmadoc Reg. in 1916 is interesting. Between 1916 and 1925 I believe she was trading in the Argentine under the name of *Sophie.* In 1925 she was bought by the Countess Marcovitch and was refitted in the S.W. India Dock, London. After being refitted she was loading a general cargo for Venezuela. The Customs Officials observing an unusually large number of cases labelled 'Butter' being put on board became suspicious and 'pounced' and found the cases full of small arms and amunition intended for an insurrection that was being planned in Venezuela. The vessel was impounded and several well-known people were found to be involved when the Court proceedings took place. Capt. A. R. T. Kirby a little later bought the vessel for £130 — that being the amount of the harbour dues outstanding against her. He renamed her *Mynonie R. Kirby* after his daughter (now Mrs. Hildred). After buying her sails back for £80 from a Chinaman, who no doubt had stolen them, he sailed her to Burseldon on the Hamble River and refitted her, building a 24ft. deck house of teak, aft, which contained his cabin, dining saloon, chart room, galley and a pantry. He then took a crew of 5 and a varying number of cadets for training and traded between West Country Ports and Antwerp. China Clay out and cement in paper bags back to U.K., quite a good paying trade until freights fell from 30/- a ton to 10/-. In 1930 he laid her up at Cowes for sale and eventually sold her to a Commander Stapleton, who with some ex-naval officers tried to carry on the same trade as Captain Kirby. On their first voyage, when carrying a load of coal, they ran into bad weather off Brixham. They lost their heads and were eventually picked up by the local Lifeboat, and towed into Brixham. They were unable to pay the lifeboat's salvage claim so, after about a year, she was put up to auction. She fetched £80 and was bought by a syndicate of Germans who took her to Hamburg where she was once again completely refitted, with 2 big diesel engines, and 2 bottle screws in place of the 'Deadeye' rigging she had previously. Captain Kirby saw her soon after this at Dover in 1933; she looked 'magnificent'. She still had the white painted ports he had given her. The next thing he heard was of her loss off the Scilly Isles on her way to the South Sea Islands. He had a photograph of her taken from the air, lying in the trough of a wave having been on fire and dismasted; she was then in tow by the Dutch tug *Zwarte Zee* and looked on the point of sinking. Captain Kirby's story ends there.

> *C.R.S.: Cadwalader Jones,* carvel built, half male bust stem. John Cadwalader, mortgage for £500 plus interest at 5% a 20/64ths shares dated 12 March, 1878, to William Jones, Porthmadoc, Sailmaker, mortgagee. David Morris, Brittania Terrace, P.M. apptd. Manager by John Cadwalader, Letter dated 8 October, 1880.

CALLIDORA

Bn. Built P.M. 1901 by David Jones. Sold off the blocks to Newfoundland.

> *L.R. 1904/5:* Bkn, 169t, 103.3/23.8/12.0. Owned by J. Rorke, St. John's, Newfoundland.
>
> *C.R.S.:* Bkn, 168tg, 143tr, 103.3/23.8/12. Built P.M. 1901 by David Jones. Owner: Robert Ehlers of 61 Queen Square, Bristol. Reg. transferred to port of St. John's, Newfoundland, 26 July 1901.

CAMBRIAN (I)

> *P.P. 1905, LXXI:* 20 Dec. 1903, Sr, 43 yrs. old, 56t, 3 crew, R. Roberts, ma, Mrs. F. Evans, Pentrefelin, Caernarvonshire, owner. Voyage P.M. to Cardiff with slates, foundered 15 miles NW by W of Bishop's Rock, off Pembrokeshire, wind SSE force 6, no lives lost.

CAMBRIAN (II)

Sr, 80tn, 74.2/20.0/9.8. Built Ynyslas, Aberdovey, 1873, Thos. Williams, ma. Father of Wm. Wallace Williams, the Pilot. Lost in collision with a French trawler in the English Channel, 1907.

*L.R. 1884/5:* Sr, 80t, 74.2/20/9.8. Built Aberdovey, 1873, by Jones, T. Williams, owner, reg. Aberystwyth.

CANDANCE

*L.R. 1859:* Sr, 44t. Built Aberystwyth 1850 owned Jenkins & Co. D. Jenkins, ma.

CARADOC

Sr. Built P.M. by Ebenezer Roberts at Station Bach.

*L.R. 1859:* Sr, 91t. Built 1857 P.M., Williams, owners. Lost & reg. following collision, 1869.

CARDIGANSHIRE

Bkn, Capt. Robt. Jones, Talarfor, owner, Wm. Jones, ma. Capt. Jones bought her at Falmouth after selling the *Talarfor* to a Norwegian firm. She was a West Indies Trader and was lost on the French coast 1892. Went on fire.

*L.R. 1884/5:* Bkn, 365t, 124.0/26.4/17.0. Built Neyland 1864, owner R. Jones.

CARIAD

Sr, 22 mst. Built Salcombe, Kings Bridge, 1896, by W. Date, Dr. Lister. Owner John Owen, son of Humphrey Owen the pilot, ma. A very pretty vessel. Capt. John Owen told me that she crossed from Eurges, Newfoundland, to Oporto in 10 days when under his command.

*L.R. 1904/5:* Sr, 114t, 84.5/21.9/10.8. Built W. Date and Son, Kingsbridge, owner D. Jones, ma, E. L. Jones. Carvel built, scroll stem. Joseph Herbert Lister, Barmouth, Shipowner, sold (1) 16/64ths, March 1898, to Jane Jones, Penycei, Barmouth, wife of Evan Lewis Jones, Mariner; (2) 16/64ths, August 1899, to David Jones of Penycei, Barmouth, Fisherman; (3) 12/64ths, 5 April 1904, to David Jones of Harbour View, Barmouth; (4) 12/64ths, 5 April 1904, to Evan Lewis Jones of Penycei, Barmouth, M.M. All in turn sell to Llewellyn Griffith, 1 Garth Terrace, P.M. (Bill of Sale June 1913), and to Wm. Morris, Britannia Terrace, P.M. Shipowner, 16/64ths; John Owen, 28 Ralph Street, Borth-y-gest, 16/64ths. Reg. transferred to port St. John's, Newfoundland, 19 October 1916.

CARL AND LOUISE (1)

Bn. Built Borthygest, by Richard Jones, Garreg Wen, John Roberts, Pen Cei, ma? Traded in the West Indies and Newfoundland. Lost with all hands.

Lost R. Weser, 1877. *L.R. 1875:* 144t, 90.7/22.8/12.2. Built 1873 by Jones, owned J. Roberts & Co., J. Roberts, ma.

CARL AND LOUISE (2)

Bn, 183tg., 169tn., 100.3/24.2/12.4. Built at Pwllheli 1878 by Williams, J. Roberts owner. Traded in the West Indies and Newfoundland. William Jones, Cei Greaves, told me that about 1884 when he was an A.B. on the *Ellen Greaves* the two vessels met in the West Indies south of Barbuda. *C. & L.* had lost nearly all her crew with fever. The *Ellen Greaves* lent her one Ordinary seaman, a German, to help her along. Lost in the Firth of Forth loaded with phosphate rock. See under *Ellen Greaves.*

> *C.R.S.:* Built 1878 Pwllheli by David Williams, Pwllheli. Wrecked off Berwick, 25.1.1890. John Roberts, M.M. P.M. 44/64ths; Harry Jones, Labourer P.M. 4/64ths; David Morris, Ship Chandler P.M. 4/64ths; Thomas Hughes, Senior, Druggist, Pwllheli 8/64ths; Thomas Hughes Junior, Farmer, Pwllheli 4/64ths; Thomas Hughes, Senior, mgr. Lost off Berwick 25.1.1890.

CAROLINE

Sk, Ellis Humphreys, Borth y gest, ma. Lost on New Ferry?

CARPASIAN

Bk, formerly a Bkn, 288tg., 275tn, 131.6/26.1/12.9. Built Ayr, 1875 by Weir, Harry Hughes, Borth y gest, ma. She used to carry timber from Pensacola to P.M.

> *L.R. 1875/6:* Bkn, 288t, 131.6/26.1/12.9. Owner, W. Grieve. Did not enter P.M. often as she was of too deep draught for the approach to port. Information from Capt. W. H. Hughes, DSC, son of master.

CATHARINE (1)

Sr, 96tn, 72.7/21.1/11.3. Built at Southerly end of Cei Cwmorthin under Trwyn Cae Iago, 1856 by David Richards, Senior, for his son John in 1856. John Richards (son of David Richards), ma. Reg. at Lloyds as *Catherine.*

> Sold Aberystwyth 1873.

CATHERINE (II)

Bkn. Built Kingsbridge, 1877. John Richards of Aberystwyth was her master for a time. Tonnage @ 500t d.w. Lost in collision with *S.S. Hamburg* in the North Sea. Cargo at the time 520 tons of fuel oil @ a freight of 12/6 per ton. All hands were lost except one German boy in July 1898. Humphrey Lloyd (Junior) of Clogwyn Melwyn, was her ma. at the time.

> *L.R. 1884/5:* Bkn. 316t, 118.2/26.3/15.0. Built Kingsbridge 1877, by Date, owned Steer & Co., Salcombe.

CATHERINA

Exploded and sank in the Thames.

CATHERINE & MARGARET

Sr, 91tg, 70.4/20.5/10.8. Built P.M. 1858, Capt. Morgan Jones, S.H., John Lewis, ma, was drowned on P.M. Bar. Between January 24, 1898, and January 12, 1903, this little vessel of 170 tons d.w. did 20 voyages from P.M. as follows: 8 to London, 5 to Southampton, 2 to Aberdeen, 1 each to Newhaven, Belfast, Poole, Shoreham, Harburg. Total tonnage of slates shipped by her from Portmadoc during this period (5 years) 3,200 tons. John Lewis was brother to Capt. Thos. Rd. Lewis, Bronafon, Borthygest.

Built Hugh Williams, 1858. Condemned 2.8.1926.

*P.P. 1894, LXXCI:* 1 Dec, 1892, Sr, 34 years old, 5 crew, J. Roberts ma, Mrs. A. Evans, P.M. owner, voyage North Shields to Plymouth, with patent manure cargo. Decks swept, 1 life lost, 12 miles SW of Beachy Head, wind W by S, force 9.

CATHERINE AND MARY (1)

Sr, 90t. Built P.M. 1856 Henry Jones, owner Williams P.M. Wrecked 5.12.1873.

CATHERINE AND MARY (II)

Sr, 90tn, 69.2/20.4/10.5. Built 1858 at Newquay, David Nicholas, ma.

CATHERINE MORGAN

Sr, 80tn, 74.5/19.3/10. Built Aberdovey, 1862. Belonged to Aberystwyth.

*Celerity* Sr, 79t. Built P.M. 1840, lost Newcastle to Drogheda 8.9.1864.

CATHERINE RICHARDS

Sr, 2mst, 167t, 155tn, 95.5/22.6/12.8. Built P.M. 1874, by Hugh Williams, John Hughes ma, David Richard (Senr) S.H. Lost in 1892 off Tralee Bay, crew took to the boats but all were lost. Later the vessel was salved and the cat was found still alive. She was the largest two masted schooner in the Port. Phosphate Rock Trader.

*C.R.S.:* P.M. 1874. Built by John Owen, P.M. Carvel build, Stem: Demi Woman. Ship wrecked Porthsgadan Point, October 1891 reg. closed 28 Jan, 1892. This would appear to be a clerical error in the Register: the *Catherine Richards* was in fact wrecked in Brandon Bay on the night of December 30, 1891. John Hughes P.M. M.M. 32/64ths; Morris Evan Morris P.M., Chemist 4/64ths; Richard Owen, Tŷ Fry, Merioneth, Farmer 4/64ths; Margaret Owen, Ty Fry, Merioneth, Spinster

4/64ths; David Richards, Senr., P.M. Ret. M.M. 16/64ths; Henry Williams, Ynys Isaf, Clynnog, Farmer 2/64ths; Elizabeth Williams, Ynys Isaf, Clynnog, Spinster 2/64ths. John Hughes mortgage to North and West Wales Bank. David Richards, 147, High St., P.M. was appointed M.O. by Morris Evan Morris, on Nov. 3, 1875. Large number of subsequent transactions.

CERES

Sr, 97tn., 77.2/20.6/10.5, Reg. at Aberystwyth. On one occasion she sailed to Iceland — the only vessel trading from P.M. to do so. Built Aberdovey, 1862, by Richards; E. Humphreys, Borthygest, owner and ma.

CECIL BRINDLEY

Sr, 104tg., 94tn, 80.1/21.0/10.5. Built Aberdovey, 1871 by Richards, D. Jones and other owners. A frequent visitor to P.M.

C. E. SPOONER

'Jack' Bkn, 186tg, 172tn, 103.2/24.0/12.7. Built south end of Cei Newydd, P.M. 1878 by David Jones. Mrs. Jones, Garth Cottage, S.H. Capt. Robert Jones, ma of Cae Ednyfed, Minffordd; later she was commanded by Capt. Evan Henry Williams, of P.M. Wm. Jones, brother of Rbt. was her 1st master. He only held a 'fore and aft' certificate. One of the port's finest vessels. She crossed the Atlantic in 13 days, Shoal Bay, Labrador, to Fastnet Rock, and a little later did the return passage in 18 days. *Typical Voyage:* P.M. to Harbug with slates; to Cadiz in ballast; Cadiz to Harbour Grace, Newfoundland with salt: then to Shoal Bay, then to Liverpool. with 2000 Kentils [quintals] of fish, then to Garston to load coal for Gibraltar. Gibraltar to Huelva in ballast. Huelva to Exmouth with copper ore. Exmouth to P.M. with lime. The round passage from P.M. to P.M. would take about 10 or 11 months. Her crew consisted of six men viz:— Capt., mate, 1 A.B., 2 ord. seamen, and a steward or cook. On her record crossing her spread of canvas was: fore topmast staysail, lower top'sl., double reefed mainsail (no mizen sails). She used to be painted black with a yellow strake along the gunwale, copper bottomed with a white strake along the top of the copper. Her figure head was a torso of Charles Edwin Spooner Esq., of P.M. In May 1898, when on a voyage from Stettin to Bordeaux with a cargo of timber with deck load, Capt. Jones, during a rough crossing of the North Sea, slipped on the deck load, and suffered concussion of the brain from which he died. His body was landed at Dover. When she was about 35 years old she was sold to a Portuguese firm and renamed *Saint Juan.* She was no longer equal to her accustomed tasks. No ship more fully deserved to be 'canonised', than this one. (Capt.

Jones was a great friend of our Family). She was the last vessel to deliver 'Cod fish' to Liverpool from Newfoundland. She was sold in 1912 to a Portugese firm and renamed *Senhora de Monte* and was delivered to the Azores. (J.R.M. in *Sea Breezes,* June 1933).

*C.R.S.:* John Jones, P.M., Shipowner, 40/64ths (also M.O.); David Evans, Gelligaer, in County Glamorgan, Headmaster, Endowed Grammar School, 4/64ths; Robert Jones, P.M., M.M., 20/64ths; John Jones died Dec. 16, 1890. Catherine Jones, Garth Cottage, P.M. designated M.O. G. Prichard, Mgr., 1898. Sold 1912.

CHARLES HORSEY

Sr, John Timothy, Borthygest, ma.

CHARLES JAMES

Sr, 3mst, 148tg, 136tn, 93.0/24.0/11.7. Built at Pwllheli, 1877, Capt. Johnston, Llanbedrog, ma, Pritchard Bros. S.H. Lost April 1901. Voyage Mazagan (Morocco) to U.K. Cargo 1004 quarters of peas at a freight of 3/6 per quarter. Newfoundland trader. A regular trader to Morocco and Newfoundland.

Owners: William Johnson, M.M., Pwllheli, 32/64ths; John Jones, M.M., Llanystumdwy, 8/64ths; Griffith Johnson, Land Agent, Llandegai, 8/64ths; Llewelyn Lewis of Aber, Farmer, 8/64ths; David Williams, Stonecutter, Pwllheli, 4/64ths; David Williams, Shipbuilder, Pwllheli, 4/64ths. According to letter received from Custom House, Blyth, master made deposition that *Charles James* totally lost by foundering on 31 Jan., 1901, near entrance to English Channel, lat. 49n. long. 5.45w. All papers and effects, including certificate of Reg. went down with vessel.

CHARLES JOHNSTON

CHARLOTTE ANN

Sr, Built at Fowey, 1835, 53tn, Mr. Percival, owner, John Owen ma. Lost on Skerries.

CLARA

K.

CLARA FELICIA

Sr, later K, 97tg., 89tn, 75/21/11.2. Built at Nevin, 1874 by Owens, Rees Evans, Trwyn Cae Iago, S.H.

Sold Bridgwater 1896.

CLARE

Sr, 88tn, 75/20/10. Built Caernarvon, 1868. Foundered off Tusker with all hands.
? lost off Arklow Light, 16.12.1899.

CONCORDIA

Sr, 127tg. Built Jersey, 1856, Hugh Jones, Block maker, owner. Sr, of French origin. Went ashore inside P.M. Bar and was later towed to Holyhead for repairs.

CONFIDENCE

Sr, 109tg, 96tn, 78.8/21.4/10.7. Built at Pwllheli 1845. Capt. Wm. Lewis, ma. Renowned for her association with Garibaldi, the Italian patriot. It is said that when leaving Reggio, the *Confidence* took Garibaldi, who was making his escape from the Royalists, on board. Garibaldi, it is said, gave Capt. Lewis his red scarf and baton being the only things he had on him at the time as a token of his gratitude. Mrs. Morris of the *Phantom* used to have this scarf. It is contended by some that it was not Garibaldi that was taken on board the *Confidence* but one of his officers. I don't know which assertion is correct. Garibaldi's baton of African palm, weight 16½ ounces, is now in the possession of Capt. Lewis, grandson of Capt. Wm. Lewis' brother, (1950). A silver tankard was presented to Capt. Wm. Lewis by one of Garibaldi's supporters as a token of gratitude for a 'sevice rendered to Garibaldi at Spezia in 1862'. The facts which can be verified appear to be as follows:— (1) At Aspromonte on August 22, 1862, Garibaldi was defeated by the Royalists, wounded and taken prisoner and was transported to the Fort Varignano in the gulf of Spezia where he remained in hospital. (2) Oct. 22, 1862, he was moved to the Hotel de Milan at Spezia and on Nov. 10, 1862, he left for Pisa after a regular amnesty had been proclaimed by the Italian Government. (3) Capt. Wm Lewis visited Garibaldi whilst he was convalescent at Spezia, whether it was at the Fortress or at the Hotel is not clear, nor the date. When visiting Garibaldi Captain Lewis obtained two photographs, one of Garibaldi sitting up in a four poster bed wounded, and an autographed photograph of him. (4) 2 November, 1862, Letter from M. G. de Schwartz to Capt. Lewis asking him to allow 'the bearer' to remain on board (*The Confidence*). (5) Letter dated 1862 from C. F. Claudius, Agent for Madame de Schwartz in London to Capt. Lewis forwarding to him the inscribed silver tankard as a token of her gratitude for the services he rendered to Garibaldi at Spezia in 1862. Reference is also made in this letter to Capt. Lewis' 'noble generosity' to the poor Italian Officer, whom he had brought to England and who was then in London. (6) There is no evidence that I can find that Capt. Lewis ever rescued Garibaldi himself. Garibaldi does not mention it in his autobiography and he would hardly fail to recount such an incident in his life's story. I have also been in communication with the Assistant Director of the Museo Del Risorgimento il Vittoriano, at Rome, where the most authoritative literature on the subject was referred to, but no mention of any such incident could be found. (7) What 'the service' was that Capt. Lewis rendered to Garibaldi at Spezia remains, on the evidence available, obscure. It might be that the Officer that Capt. Lewis brought to this country was a particular friend of Garibaldi and that he had been excluded from the amnesty and that Garibaldi was particularly anxious that he should escape, therefore, he may have asked Capt. Lewis to help him in the matter, for which service he may have given to him the stick and scarf. On the other hand these two relics may have been given to Capt. Lewis by the refugee officer himself. But Capt. Lewis did obviously render a service to Garibaldi at Spezia but its exact nature is not clear.

The illuminated address presented to Capt. J. O. Morris, son in law of Capt. Wm. Lewis when the *David Morris* was at Genoa, in 1905, rather suggests that it was presented as a token of appreciation of a service rendered to Garibaldi *personally.* It is hardly likely that the Genoa Soc. would present it because Wm. Lewis had been instrumental in rescuing one of his junior officers, and *junior* he must have been otherwise he would not be seeking occupation in London in 1862. On the other hand the photograph given to Capt. Tom Evans at Leghorn (another son in law of Wm. Lewis) rather supports the view that 'the service rendered' to Garibaldi was during his incarceration in the Fortress at Spezia in 1862 after he was wounded and taken prisoner at Aspromonte in August 1862. Capt. John O. Morris commanded the *David Morris* until she was sold. For some years he commanded the brig *Phantom* of Portmadoc. He used to have the Garibaldi stick and scarf framed and hung in the cabin of the *Phantom.*

## CONFIDENCE

*P.P. 1886, LIX:* 7 July 1880, *Confidence* (36 years old) owned R. Jones, Tremadoc, in ballast Tralee to P.M. 5 crew, none lost. Head Sea, force 2, wind SSe, 22 miles E. by S. of Tuskar Rock, St. George's Channel. Ma found vessel making more water than usual, pumps were worked until they became choked. Being unable to find the leak, or to bale her out, and the water having increased, the crew took to the boats, immediately after which she foundered.

## CONSULS (Or Consols)

CONSTANCE

142tg, 90.1/22.0/12.2. Built P.M. 1862 by Roberts. Capt. Hugh Roberts, ma. Named after Constance Greaves, who later became Lady Smyth, wife of Sir Henry Smyth, at one time Governor of Gibraltar. She was sunk in collision by the barque, *Dundale* of Glasgow, 16 miles off St. Catherine's Point, at 2 p.m. on a clear day; the barque on the port tack tried to clear her and just failed. *Constance* was on the starboard tack. All hands saved. Passage London — Douglas, I.M., cargo cement. Sunk 13.5.1890.

CONOVIUM

Sr. Built Aberystwyth, 1876. W. Jones, owner.

*L.R. 1880/81:* Sr, 83t, 74.9/20.6/10.1. Built Aberystwyth, 1876, by Jones. W. Jones, Aberystwyth, owner. Foundered at sea, 1880?

CORDELIA

Sr, 110tg, 99tn, 79.4/21.8/10.9. Built P.M. 1863 by H. Williams, Samuel Richards, owner and ma. Lost at Palnachai [Balnachiel Bay?], Scotland on a voyage from P.M. to London with a cargo of 'Setts' 170 tons @ freight of 7/8d per ton, July, 1914.

CORRINA

CORWENA

Bg, 192tn, 102.5/24.2/13.2. Built P.M. 1869 by Pierce Roberts, Eben Roberts, owner, and others. M. Evans, ma. Lost in May 1889 carrying a cargo of Slates, which was worth £1,230.0.0.

Lost off Sandgate, 28.5.1889.

CRICCIETH CASTLE

Bg, 234tg, 218tn, 106/25.3/13.7. Built Borthygest, 1876 under Tai Pilots by Simon Jones for Morris Owen. John Morris, Borthygest, ma, brother of Hugh Morris of Barmouth. Lost in the Scillies with all hands in 1882 (February). Voyage Montevideo to Birkenhead cargo of hides and horns.

*Wreck Reg. N.M.M.:* Scilly, Feb. 12, 9.15 a.m. The body of a coloured man was picked up Feb. 10 in Porthgeol Bay, supposed to be James Ruban of Santa Cruz who shipped in the *Criccieth Castle* at Falmouth, Feb. 3, by the run for Liverpool. The broken wreckage washed ashore from *Criccieth Castle* was sold at an auction Feb. 10. *Scilly* Feb. 10, 8.30 a.m. It blew a very heavy gale last night from SSW with thick rain. This morning Porthcresa Bay St. Mary's is strewn with the wreckage of a vessel of about 200 tons. Part of a boat's sternpost with Carnarvon cut on it and a lifebuoy with Criccieth Castle, Portmadoc 1876 painted on it. No signs of crew or cargo. Supposed to be *Criccieth Castle* which left Fray Bentos. Nov. 10 for Channel. Arrived Falmouth, Feb. 3, and left for Liverpool. Empty sacks are washing ashore, marked with a bullock within a circle on top 'Lem. Berow, Fray Bentos' in black letters, no doubt having contained cargo from Liebig's Extract Meat Company, Fray Bentos. *R.S.* Vessel foundered off Scilly Island and totally lost 9 Feb. 1883. Reg. closed March 1883.

CONSUL KAESTNER

Sr. 3mst, 110tg, Built at Station Bach by Eben Roberts, Dr. Lister, owner, Wm. Watkins, ma. Wm. Watkins' brother, John Watkins, was Surveyor to the 'Club' for many years. I remember her launch quite well. A German eagle with wings outspread on either side of the stem formed her figure head. Lost in collision, June 28, 1902. All hands lost.

*L.R. 1894/5:* 3mst, Sr, 146t, 101/24.2/10.7. Built E. Roberts, P.M. 1892. C.R.S. 3mst, Sr, 144.71t, 101/24.2/10.7. Built by Ebenezer Roberts, P.M. 1892. When on voyage from Douglas, Isle of Man to Cadiz was run into by *S.S. Jokai* off Fiume on 28 June 1902 and went down off Cape St. Vincent. Reg. closed 25 July 1902.

CUERERO

Bk, 259tg, 239tn, 122/24.1/12.9. Built Bideford 1870, Capt. Morgan Jones, owner, Humphrey Lloyd, (sen), Clogwyn Melyn, Talsarnau, ma. Lost on Buenaire Island, West Indies, Cargo of Phosphate Rock bound for U.K.

*L.R. 1875:* Built Cox at Bideford, 1870 owned F. Troubridge & Co., Bristol.

CYFARTHFA

*Cyfarthfa* Sm. 24t, built P.M. 1846 for Thomas Christian, P.M. Lost off Fishguard, 27.9.1856. For death of ma by accident on board, *N.W.C.* Nov. 16, 1847.

CYGNET

Bn, 185tn, 102.4/24.5/11.5. Built at Prince Edward Island, 1870, Capt. Robert Thomas, Criccieth, ma. Her master died on Rio Grande Bar and was buried in the cemetery at Rio Grande. A tomb stone of Festiniog slate was taken out by a comrade and placed on his grave. Capt. Wm. Williams of Criccieth who commanded Brazilian Liners saw it there when attending the funeral of a friend.

*L.R. 1875:* Built Ramsey, Pei, 1870, owned by J. C. Roberts, Aberystwyth.

CYMRIC

Amlwch vessel.

I. Bkn. 226t, 123/24/10.8 built by W. Thomas, Amlwch, 1893, Capt. Robert Jones, Garden Cottage, Amlwch, master. cf. *Ships & Seamen of Anglesey,* pp. 308-314, + pl. 16.

CYNHAIARN

Sr, 107tg, 97tn, 80/21.8/11.1. Built at Cei Newydd, by David Jones before the *C.E. Spooner.* According to *L.R.* she was built by Hugh Williams at P.M. in 1874. W. Roberts ma, W. Ellis owner.

C.R.S.: Sr, 2mst. Built P.M. 1874 by John Owen, P.M. William Roberts, P.M., Osmond Lane, M.M. 24/64ths, (M.O.). John Owen, Osmond Lane, P.M., Shipbuilder, 8/64ths; Richard Jones, Bodawen Lodge, P.M., Gardener, 4/64ths; John Roberts, Borth, Nr. P.M., M.M. 4/64ths; William Williams, Osmond Lane, P.M., Ship Carpenter, 4/64ths; Humphrey Jones, Market Place, Ffestiniog, Grocer, 4/64ths; David Williams, Bron y Manod, Ffestiniog, Farmer, 4/64ths; Evan Thomas, Llechwedd, Quarry Agent, 4/64ths; J. Elizabeth Davies, Havod Fawr, Maentwrog, spinster, 4/64ths; Jannette Davies, of Same place, spinster, 4/64ths.

DANIEL MORRIS (1)

Sr. Built Borthygest, 1846 by Wm. Griffith. Named after the 1st harbour master at P.M. Lost on Runnel Stone, near Lands End with all hands. Capt. Parry (son in law of David Richards, Senior, and brother in law of D. Richards, harbour master) and his family were on board at the time. Mrs. Parry and her young child were found on the shore a few days later. May 30, 1855, Griffith, age 18, and Henry, aged 13, were drowned on her.

*L.R. 1852:* Sr, 83t. Built P.M. 1846. Owned by Parry and Co., R. Parry, ma. Wrecked 30.5.1855.

DANIEL MORRIS (2)

Sr. Built Borthygest 1858, for Ellis Williams of the *Lara.* Named after the brother of T. E. Morris, Barrister, P.M. Lost on the Irish Coast.

*L.R. 1875/6:* Sr. 98t, 75.4/21.0/11.0. Built P.M. 1858, E. Roberts, ma. Robert & Co., owners.

DAUNTLESS

Bn, 89½t. Built Traeth Bach, 1816, Lewis Edwards, ma. Reg. at Pwllheli. Reg. at Beaumaris, No. 20/1817.

DAVID MORRIS

Sr, 3mst. 161tg. Built P.M. 1897 by David Jones, John Morris, ma, brother of David Morris, Y Cei, Newfoundland Trader. Sold at Cardiff to a Plymouth firm of fish traders and was commanded by Capt. Partridge who had a cork leg. Lost her keel on Old King Rock near Bolsters Rock Harbour Newfoundland but managed to reach Harbour Grace. Lost Nov. 1924.

*L.R. 1904/5:* Sr, 3mst, 162t, 99.6/23.2/12.0, J. O. Morris, ma. C.R.S.: Ship totally lost on 11 Nov. 1924, off Turks Island. Advice received from M.O. and R. of S. Turks Island. Owners: John Owen Morris, P.M., M.M. 16/64ths; David Morris, P.M. Shipowner 8/64ths; Mary Lloyd Morris, P.M. wife of David Morris, 4/64ths; William Morris, P.M. Ship Chandler 12/64ths; Jane Morris, P.M. spinster 8/64ths; Owen Morris, P.M. Shipowner 8/64ths, [M.O. apptd. 25 Aug. 1897]. Thomas Jones, P.M. Shipowner 4/64ths; Dora Lloyd, P.M. widow 4/64ths. 1903 Dora Lloyd sells 4/64ths to John Owen Morris, 12 Lombard St., P.M., M.M. Thomas Jones died 15 June 1906. Owned 1923 by Newfoundland and Labrador Fish & Oil Co. Ltd., in liquidation, sold to E. A. Bowder, Coal Merchant, Queen Street, Exeter, who sold to Haver & Co., London St., Salisbury House, London Wall E.C.2.

DAVID SINCLAIR

Sr, with a single topsl. 122tn, 87/21.5/11.9. Built Brixham 1872. David Richard, S.H. Lost 17 Nov. 1901, at Frederikstadt, Norway. Voyage Denmark to Isle of Man in Ballast. She was one of the very first P.M. ships to enter the Newfoundland fish trade.

*P.P. 1903, LXII:* 17 Nov. 1901, Sr, 94t, 5 crew, O. Evans, ma, D. Richards, P.M. owner. Voyage Copenhagen to Frederikstadt, in ballast, stranded entrance to R. Glomen, Norway, wind SW force 9, no lives lost.

DDRAIG GOCH

A small tug boat, the last to function in the port.

DEBORAH

95tn. 79/20.5/10. Built Aberystwyth 1860 by Jones, John Owen, Borthygest, owner and ma. Lost in 1892 off Dungeness.

C.R.S.: Owned 1875 M. Evans, Aberystwyth. Built Derwenlas, Montgomeryshire, John Jones of Aberdovey, 1860. Llewelyn Griffiths, P.M., M.M. owner in 1885. Sold to John Owen of Borth, P.M., M.M. 32/64ths and Anne Jones of Commerce House, York, spinster 32/64ths on 6 April, 1887. G. Prichard,

Old Bank, P.M., M.O. 1887. Foundered English Channel 14 Sept. 1892.

*P.P. 1894, LXXVI:* 14 Sept. 1892, Sr, 32 years old, 5 crew, J. Owen, Borth, Caernarvonshire, owner, voyage P.M. for Harburg, slates, foundered about 12 SSE of Dungeness, Kent, no lives lost. Wind WSW force 11.

DEFIANCE

*C.R.S.:* Sk, 15t., 45.2/12.2/5.8. Built Newlyn, Cornwall, 1848. Previous reg. Aberystwyth. Vessel stated to have been broken up, and removed from reg. 1885. Griffith Williams P.M., M.M. 64/64ths. Died June 1876, probate granted to Catherine Williams, Borth-y-gest, widow who sold in Sept. 1876 to John Owen, Morfa Bychan, Fisherman.

DESDEMONA

Sr, 94tg, 88tn, 79/20/10. Built Aberystwyth 1874, Hugh Williams, ma. Stranded at Newport, Pembrokeshire, February 1906, carrying a cargo of clay 156 tons @ a freight of 4/9 per ton. Hugh Williams also commanded the *Ida* and the *Nanhoron.*

DEWI WYN

Sr, about 90tg, 49tn. 59.6/17.2/8.5. Built at P.M. 1852, J. R. Jones, owner, O. Thomas, ma.

Sk, P.M. 1852 built for Thomas Christian. Wrecked Cardigan Bay, 1861.

DINAS

16t. Built P.M. 1834.

Sp. Built by Henry Jones, P.M. 1834.

DINORWIC (I)

Bg. Built P.M. 1815?

*L.R. 1859:* Bn, 85t. Built Caernarfon, 1815, owned Ellis & Co., Caernarfon. Lost off Texel, 1861.

DINORWIC (II)

Sr. Built in 1862 by Jones. Griffith Williams, ma.

*L.R. 1875/6:* Sr, 124t, 80.3/21.0/11.5. Built Jones, Wales, 1862, owned J. Elias & Co., Bangor.

DIZZIE DUNLOP

Sr, 110tg, 99tn. 84.5/22.2/10.7. Built at Borthygest, 1878, by Richard Jones, Garreg Wen. T. E. Williams, ma. (Thos. Williams ma. 'Goodness Gracious'). Lost off St. Catherine's Point. Owen Humphreys, her master was a master mariner, and for some years held a school of navigation at Borthygest. His daughter, Miss Humphreys married the master of the *Elizabeth Prichard,* John Prichard Roberts.

C.R.S.: Sr, 110tg, 84.5/22.2/10.7. Built P.M. 1878, Jones and Pritchard, P.M. Head or Stem: Female Figure. Vessel stranded 6 April 1890, Aberfeld Ledge, Reg. Closed + Cert. cancelled 6.4.1890. *Owners*: Thomas Ebenezer Williams, P.M., M.M. 32/64ths; William Prichard, P.M. Ship Agent, 2/64ths; Richard Jones, P.M. Ship builder, 2/64ths; Henry Jones, P.M. Lime Merchant, 2/64ths; Griffith Prichard, P.M. Shipbroker, 2/64ths; Morris Jones, P.M. Shipowner, 2/64ths; David Richard, P.M. Shipowner, 2/64ths; Margery Williams, P.M. widow, 2/64ths; Owen Williams, Timber Merchant, 2/64ths; Robert Williams, P.M. Iron Founder, 2/64ths; David Williams, Tremadog, Minister, 4/64ths; Ellen Griffiths, Penmorfa, spinster, 2/64ths; Ellinor Ellis, Dolgelly, widow, 4/64ths; Richard Edward Hughes, Holyhead, Bank Inspector, 4/64ths; Elizabeth Lewis, Birmingham, widow, 4/64ths; William Prichard of 3 Cornhill, P.M. apptd. manging owner by letter dated 15 March, 1878, under hand of Thomas Ebenezer Williams, owner of 32/64ths; Thomas Ebenezer Williams, mortgage for £700 + interest dated 12 March 1878 to Hugh Pugh and Robert Jones of P.M., Bankers, Joint Mortgagees.

DORA (formerly Margaret & Mary)

Sr, 91tg, Rees Evans, S.H. (See under Margaret + Mary)

*L.R.:* Built Wales 1859.

DOROTHEA

Sr, 95t. Built P.M. 1840 by Henry Jones. Lost with all hands on passage Poole to Liverpool, 1885.

DOROTHY (1)

3mst. Sr. 142tg. Built P.M. by David Williams, Thos. Roberts, ma, H. A. Thomas, S.H. Newfoundland trader. Lost in collision in the Straits of Gibraltar, February, 1905. Voyage Labrador to Gibraltar. Cargo 4000 quintals of fish @ a freight of 2/- per quintal. Arthur Llewelyn Morris of P.M. was chief engineer on the *S.S. Adana* that collided with her. Evie Morris was mate on her at the time.

*L.R. 1904/5:* 3mst. Sr, 143t, 91.2/22.9/11.7. Built P.M. 1891 by G. Williams, owner H. Roberts, T. Roberts, ma.
C.R.S.: Sr, 142t, 91.2/22.9/11.7. Built P.M. 1891 by Griffith and David Williams, P.M., 3 mst, with female Head or Stem. Vessel sank after collision off Cape Trafalgar, 3 Nov. 1904, certificate of Reg. lost with vessel. Reg. closed 16 Nov. 1904. Owners: John Ernest Graves, Bron Eifion, Criccieth, Gentleman, 16/64ths; Richard Methuen Greaves, Wern, Tremadog, Gentleman, 16/64ths; Hugh Roberts, 16 Terrace Road, P.M., M.M. 16/64ths; [M.O.] Thomas Roberts, 10 High Street, Criccieth, M.M. 16/64ths.

DOROTHY (2) (formerly Mary Owens)

3mst. Sr, P.M. Built by D. Jones, P.M. Newfoundland trader. Lost October 10, 1912, at Fogo, Newfoundland. Cargo of fish. [See *Mary Owens*].

DOROTHY AND MARY

Sr, 72tn., 62.7/17.9/9.5. Built P.M. 1854, John Evans, Morfa Nevin, ma. Lost off Holyhead.
Built 1854 at P.M. by William Jones. Lost and Reg. 11.12.1883.

DOVEY BELLE

Sr, 85tn., 73.5/20.1/10.0. Built at Aberdovey, 1867, by Richards. A frequent visitor to P.M.
*L.R. 1875/6:* Owned J. James, Aberystwyth, J. James, ma.

DREADNOUGHT

Sr, Newquay 1866 by Davies. Went ashore at Pwllheli but was later salved.
*L.R. 1875/6:* Sr, 146t, 94.5/23.1/12.2. Built Davies, Newquay, 1866, and owned by Davies & Co., Newquay.
*P.P. 1904, LXXXVI:* 4 Dec. 1902, (43 years old), crew of 4, J. Thomas, Aberystwyth, ma., and owner, P.M. to Littlehampton with slates, foundered 5 miles NNE of Skomer Is., Pembroke. Wind SE force 3, no lives lost.

DRUID

Sr, built P.M. by Hugh Williams.
*L.R. 1871/2:* Bg, 213t, 104.6/25.4/13.7. Built P.M. 1869 by Richards, Richards & Co., owners. P.M. / Medit. trade. Wrecked Bay of Biscay, 1872.

DUKE OF CORNWALL

Sk, 15t, built P.M. 1856.

EAGLE (1)

Sr, 111t. Built P.M. 1837.

Built Henry Jones, P.M. 1837, P.M./Baltic trade. P. Jones, ma, 1859. Wrecked off Scotland, 13.2.1871. Capt. Hugh Hughes, (later Rev. Hugh Hughes, Gellidaran), was her ma. in 1840s. *'Cofiant Capten Hughes'* J. Jones, p. 114.

EAGLE (2)

Originally a Bg, then a Bkn and finally a Bn. 226tg, 110.2/24.6/13. Built Prince Edward Island, 1874, Wm. Evans, Minffordd, ma, John Owen, Ty Fry, S.H.

EAGLE EYED

Sr, 98tg, 76.0/20.6/10.6. Built Newquay 1858, R. Morris ma, Wm. Morris, Barmouth S.H. Lost off Lands End with all hands. The *Morning Star* was in the same storm, but made Falmouth safely.

EASTWARD

Sr, 67/72t, 72.5/19.1/8.7. Built Rothsay 1871 by McLean. Robert Morris of the *Eagle Eyed,* ma. Robert Morris died when giving out a hymn at the Methodist Chapel, Borthygest.

EBENEZER

Sr, 105tg, 96tn, 75/20.5/11. Built P.M. 1858. Edward Roberts, Borthygest, ma. Morgan Jones S.H. Built at Canol y Clwt, P.M. where Greaves Wharf is now, by Harry Jones.

Sold, Llanelly 1903.

EBENEZER PARRY

Bkn, 194tg, 182tn, 100.5/24.6/13.2. Built at Nevin, 1877. Lost in the Baltic and later salved. Re-named *Ellen Lloyd,* [See *Ellen Lloyd*].

Built Griffith Owen, Nefyn, 1877. Sold as *Robert Marguerite* at Fowey, 1912. Lost Havre, 1917.

ECONOMY

Evan Roberts, ma. Evan Roberts at one time owned a brigantine named *Louis Montgomery* built at Nova Scotia. On June 22, 1850, she [*Economy*] sailed from Greaves Wharf P.M. with 131¼ tons of slates to Newcastle on Tyne, Capt. Evans Roberts, ma., and on 28/6/1849 with 135 tons, and on 15/12/1849 with 130t, same destination.

*L.R. 1859:* Sr, 89t. Built P.M. 1841. Lost off Berry Head. 5.3.1866.

E.C.T.

K, John Crocker, owner.

*L.R. 1904/5:* W. Sr, 111t, 83.1/20.6/10.7. Built Falmouth, Lean, J. Crocker owner, reg. Padstow.

EDITH

Sr, Wm. Williams, Brittania, ma.

*L.R. 1859:* Sr, 87t, 63.3/19.0/10.2. Built P.M. 1851 by William Jones, owned Greaves & Co., P.M. Lost and Reg. off Kinsale, 30.1.1875.

EDITH ELEANOR

Sr, 104t. Built Aberystwyth, 1881, Wm. J. Jones, Llanbedrog, ma. Morroco trader and general coaster. In 1885 she did the following voyage: Portmadoc to Harbug, slates, in ballast to Cadiz; salt to Port Charles, Newfoundland; fish to Gibraltar for orders then to Naples; in ballast to St. Vast, salt to Penzance, then home in ballast. M. H. Foulkes was an A.B. on her during this voyage.

*L.R. 1884/5:* Sr, 96t, 80.4/21.3/10.4. Built Aberystwyth 1881 by Worrell & Co., owned D. C. Roberts & Co., Aberystwyth.

EDWARD

Sr, 140t. Built Borthygest, 1876, by Richard Jones. J. Ellis, ma. Sunk in collision 1892, off Bardsey Island, all the crew saved except the ma, Capt. John Ellis who went down with her.

*C.R.S.:* Sr, 101t, 79.5/21.8/10.8. Built Borth, P.M., 1876, by Jones & Pritchard, Caernarfonshire. Vessel lost in collision with *S.S. Phoenician* 12 May 1892. *Owners*: John Ellis, Criccieth, M.M. 24/64ths; Ellis Roberts, P.M., Shipowner, 16/64ths; John Roberts, P.M., M.M. 8/64ths; Thomas Roberts, P.M., Solicitor, 8/64ths; John Jones, Borth, Cardiganshire, M.M. 8/64ths. John Ellis Mortgage dated 30 Sept. 1876 for 24 shares: £600 and interest @ 5% — Mortgaged to John Jones of Borth, Cardiganshire, M.M. John and Ellen Roberts' shares pass on their deaths to Elizabeth Roberts, 3 Osmond Terrace, P.M.. M.O. in July 1885.

EDWARD ARTHUR

Sr, 157tg, 141tn, 95.5/22.9/12.1. Built P.M. 1877 by Williams. John Williams, Minffordd, ma, Prichard Bros. S.H. A fine little vessel. I remember her very well. Later converted into 3 masted Sr. On a voyage from P.M. to Stettin she lost her port side light off the Smalls but proceeded on her voyage without one and got there safely.

P.M. Built 1877 by Hugh Williams. Lost and reg. Jan. 1917. Griffith Griffiths of 5 Garth Terrace, P.M., apptd. M.O. by Evan Davies, M.M. 32/64ths. in Nov. 1880.

EDWARD SEYMOUR

Bkn, named after the son of J. E. Greaves, Esq., 187tg, 172tn, 100.9/24.4/13.2, Built P.M. 1876 by Hugh Williams, David Richards owner, Harry Hughes, ma, son of Lewis Hughes, Tailor, P.M. A notable vessel. She once sailed from New York to Capetown, then to Durban and Calcutta and from there to United Kingdom. She sailed the passage from Halifax, Nova Scotia to P.M. loaded with timber in 19 days. Phosphate trader. Lost in January 1903 on Anticosti Island, Gulf of St. Lawrence, voyage Cadiz to Paspebiac, cargo 308 tons of salt @ a freight of 10/- per ton.

*C.R.S.:* Bkn, 187t, 100.9/24.4/13.2. Built P.M. 1876 by Griffith Williams, P.M. Owners: Lewis Hughes, P.M., Draper, 44/64ths; Henry Hughes, P.M., M.M. 20/64ths; Lewis Hughes, 110 High Street, P.M., apptd. M.O. 1876. Lewis Hughes and Henry Hughes obtained mortgage dated 2 Nov. 1876 for £2,000 and interest at 6% to Hugh Pugh and Robert Jones, both of P.M., Bankers. In October 1877 further mortgage of £800 and interest of 5% from William Jones, P.M., Sailmaker, (on 20/64ths). On Jan. 11, 1879, Hugh Pugh and Robert Jones transfer Mortgage A for £2,000 and interest at 6% to John Owen of P.M., Shipowner, and Griffith Williams of P.M., Ship Carpenter, Joint Transferees. Reg. closed on 24 Nov. 1902, vessel wrecked on South Point, Anticosti, of which fact owner received tidings on 3 Nov. 1902.

*P.P. 1904, LXXXCI:* 29 Oct. 1902, Bkn, 26 years old, 7 crew, J. Griffiths, ma, D. Richards, P.M., owner. Voyage Cadiz to Gaspé with salt. Foundered, 1 life lost, in SW by S force 9 wind, South point of Anticosti Island, Canada.

EDWARD WINDUS

Bgn, 156tn, 90.3/23.3/12.5. Built at Borthygest, Wm. Griffiths, 1864. Capt. E. Williams, ma, Capt. Morris Jones, owner, Pritchard Bros. S.H. Lost in collision with a Japanese mail boat off Beachy Head. She was then carrying 270 tons of coal from Hull to Portsmouth at a freight of 5/- per ton, Feb. 25, 1904. The ma. was lost in the collision, only a German boy was saved.

*P.P. 1905, LXXI:* 22 Feb. 1904. Bn, forty years old, 6 crew, J. H. Williams, Borth-y-gest, owner and ma, collided with *S.S. Bingo Maru,* 5 crew drowned, in force 5 N wind, about 6 miles off Hastings, Sussex.

EDWIN

Sr, 158tg, 149tn, 97.2/22.6/12.5. Built Pwllheli 1873 by Williams. Harry Hughes, ma. Hugh Parry S.H. Two masted Sr. with a dbl. topsail. Later converted into a 3 masted Sr. Condemned 1920.

E.L. & MARGARET

Bg, 229tg, 216tn, 107.1/24.9/14.2. Built Pwllheli 1873 by Prichard. John Williams, Garreg Ro, Talsarnau, ma and part owner. Fruit trader in the Mediteranean. A well known clipper; only occasionally visited P M.

Lost with all hands off Whitby, 1891.

EIVION of Pwllheli

Sp, 53tg. Reg. no. 37 in 1824 at Beaumaris. Built at Traeth Mawr, 1824 by Wm. Williams. Owners, David Williams, Criccieth, mariner, 24/64ths shares; William Williams, Pandy, Penmorfa, Shipbuilder, 32/64ths shares; Daniel Morris, Inn Keeper, Towyn, Ynyscynhaiarn, 8/64ths shares.

Wrecked, Caernarfon Bar, 9.4.1850.

ELEANOR (1)

Sr. Built Newquay, Cardiganshire. Capt. Davies, ma, father of Jenkin Davies, pilot at P.M.

ELEANOR (2)

Bg. 128t, 68/21½/-. Built at Traeth Bach, 1813. Reg. at Pwllheli, Richard Ellis, ma.

ELEANOR (3)

34tg. Built P.M. 1829.

Sp. Built at P.M. 1829 by Henry Jones. Lost off Barmouth, 3.1.1870.

ELIZA

37t. Built P.M. 1835.

Sp. Built at P.M. 1835 by Henry Jones. Lost on passage Cardiff to P.M., December 1853.

ELIZA ANN

Sk, 32tn. Built Newquay, Cardigan: D. Evans, ma.

ELIZA BLAKE

Sr.

*L.R. 1859:* Sk, 49t. Built Thomas Christian P.M. 1848 for Holland & Co., J. Roberts, ma. Lost + reg. off Copeland, 1871. She was in P.M. harbour on Census night, 1871; her ma. was on board, John Simkins(?), a native of Borth, Cardiganshire.

ELIZA BOND

Sr, 60tn, W. Roberts, ma. Coaster.

*L.R. 1859:* Sr, 70t. Built Chester, 1856, owned Roper & Co.

ELIZA BOWEN

Bg, 171t. Built P.M. 1847 by Henry Jones reg. Liverpool. South American Trader. Lost Feb. 1866.

ELIZA & HANNAH

Sr, 80tn. Built Newquay, 1858. Ellis Humphreys, ma, Borthygest. J. Humphreys owner. Lost with all hands in 1901, Capt. and his son on board. [See under *Hope Bach*].

*P.P. 1892, LXXI, 632:* Sr, 33 years old, 4 crew, E. Humphreys, ma, owned by W. Humphreys, Borth, Caernarvonshire. Voyage Killough to Penzance with cargo of potatoes, 4 lives lost, not heard of since sailing on 9 March 1891.

ELIZA & JANE

Sr. Built in Cardiganshire, 1843, but traded from P.M. David Griffith, Penrhyndeudraeth, ma, and part owner with Mr. Christian of P.M. Coasting trader i.e. Bristol, Cardiff, Holyhead, Liverpool, Londonderry, Portland, Brixham, Troon, Ballyshannon, Killybegs, Kings Lynn, Newport, Caernarvon, Chester, Hastings, Fowery, Padstow, Waterford, Caledonian Canal, Criccieth, Mochras, Aberdaron, Rowen. (per Masters Account Book). Crew of 4, ma, mate, O.S. and a boy.

*L.R. 1859:* Has an *Eliza and Jane* Sr, 62t. Built P.M. 1839 and owned by Griffiths. A Sr. named *Jane & Eliza* 67t. Built 1838 by H. Griffiths at Pwllheli was lost off Bardsey, 19.10.1885.

ELIZA JONES

Sr, Thos. Williams, Borthygest, ma. Wrecked on Lundy Island. All hands lost. Ilfracombe Dec. 23, 1.25 p.m. 1889. Reported at noon by James Parsons, Bristol pilot N. 23, small vessel ashore on the Rattles, Lundy Island. Vessel wrecked and broken up, nothing known of the crew. One mast visible above water. Portion of sail recovered with No. 6 and what appears to be the letter " O " underneath. A boat marked on stern

" Eliza Jones " and a hatch were picked up about 1 p.m. 17 miles N.E. of Lundy by the *Norah* of Cardiff. This boat was bought by the ma of the *Blodwen*. This was the boat in which Capt. John Roberts of the *Blodwen* was drowned on Traeth Bach.

62t. Built Henry Jones, 1857, owned by J. Jones & Co.

ELIZA & MARY

Sp, 46t. Built Pwllheli 1831 by John Ellis.

ELIZA WOLSEY

Sk. John Thomas, ma of Borthygest. Coal carrier for the Foundry of Owen Isaac and Owen at P.M.

ELIZABETH (1)

Sr, 82t, 57/19/-. Built at Traeth Mawr, 1804. Ellis Roberts, ma. Reg. at Barmouth.

ELIZABETH (2)

Sr, 79½t, 55.0/19.0/-. Built at Traeth Bach, 1809. Richard Williams, ma. Reg. at Pwllheli.

ELIZABETH (3)

Sr, 84tn, 60.1/18.6/10.7. Built at P.M. 1850 by Wm Griffith. Owen Lloyd ma and owner. Father of Owen Lloyd of the *Tyne*.

ELIZABETH (4)

3 mst. Sr. 156tg. Built at P.M. 1890 by Griffith Williams. Owner, Capt. Hugh Parry. One of the most notable of the Newfoundland Traders. Not only did she carry fish to the Mediterranean but also to Bahia in Brazil. After spending about 30 years in this trade she was sold at P.M. to Capts. Coward & Coss who had her re-fitted in her old form. They took her out to the Indian Ocean under sail and traded there between Madagascar, the Seychelles, Mauritius and Re-Union Island for about 2 years. She left Portmadoc for the last time on the 3 of October, 1925 with a general cargo for Mahe in the Seychelles. In 1927 a great typhoon swept Madagascar. All the vessels in the harbour were wrecked and the *Elizabeth* was blown inland and dismasted, and came to rest in a coconut plantation where she was declared a constructive total loss. She was also a 'Q' boat in the 1914/18 war.

*L.R.:* 3mst. Sr. 156t, 100.0/22.9/11.8 Built P.M. Built by G. Williams, owner W. Morris, D. Williams, Mgr., G. Williams, ma. C.R.S.: Sr. Built P.M. 1892 Griffith and David Williams, P.M., 3mst. with head or stem of a female. *Owners:* Evan Jones, P.M., M.M., 16/64ths; James Kennedy McKerow, Tremadog,

Draper, 16/64ths; David Morris, P.M., Shipowner, 4/64ths; William Morris, P.M., Ship Chandler, 4/64ths; Jane Morris, P.M., Spinster, 4/64ths; Griffith Williams, P.M., Shipbuilder, 4/64ths; William J. Jones, Pwllheli, Saddler, 4/64ths; Robert Thomas, Criccieth, Shipowner, 4/64ths; Hugh Parry, P.M., Shipbroker, 8/64ths. M.O. 7 April 1892, Evan Jones mortgage dated 20 April 1892 for £716 and interest @ 5% to Griffith Williams, P.M., Shipbuilder. Hugh Parry, Bill of Sale of 4/64ths to Morgan Jones, P.M., Shipowner, April 1892. Griffith Williams, died 1 April 1894, probate to Ann Williams, widow. Hugh Parry died 19 Nov. 1901. William Morris, Britannia Terrace, P.M., M.O. Evan Jones, 29 April 1902. David Williams of 15 Madoc Street, P.M., M.O., 25 May 1903. Vessel altered to aux. motor steamship, Aug. 1919.

ELIZABETH & ANN

Built at Cardigan 1875, by Williams.

ELISABETH & ELLEN

Sr, 81tn, 68.0/19.7/10.1. Built at Borthygest, 1857, by Wm. Griffith under Graig y Don. Wm. Griffith was the father of Griffith Griffith 'King'. Named after Ellen, the wife of Mr. Jones, Croesor, and her sister, Elizabeth. Mrs. Rees Evans told me that she attended the launch dinner at Borthygest.

*L.R. 1878/9:* E. Roberts, owner, J. Thomas, ma. Lost and reg., collision 29.9.1892.

ELIZABETH BECK

98tn, 69.1/19.5/11.5. Built P.M. 1854.

Built Evan Evans, P.M. Lost and Reg. Skye, 11.6.1883.

ELIZABETH BENNETT

3mst. Sr, 161tg. Built in 1884, John Crocker, ma. Withdrew from the Club in October, 1916.

*L.R. 1904/5:* 3mst. Sr, 162t, 103.8/23.4/11.0. Built Runcorn 1884, owners Bon Accord Slate Merchant Co. Ltd. J. F. Wyness, M.O. M. Owen, ma.

ELIZABETH CHARLOTTE

Sr, of Carnarvon.

*L.R. 1904/5:* 3mst. Sr. 151t, 93.8/22.4/11.8. Built Holyhead 1860 owned T. Morgan & Co.

## ELIZABETH DAVIES

Built at Cardigan 1868.

*L.R. 1871/2:* Sk, 29t, 53.0/16.2/6.5. Built Cardigan, 1868 by Williams, E. Davies, ma.

## ELIZABETH ELEANOR

3mst. Sr. 168tg. Built at Portmadoc 1903 by David Williams, and launched sideways. John M. Jones, ma, of Criccieth. Torpedoed and sunk in the Bristol Channel 1917. Newfoundland Trader. Two of her voyages (not consecutive): (1) Portmadoc to Harburg with slates, Harburg to Grimsby with Oil Cake, then to Gibraltar with coal, ballast to Cadiz, Cadiz to St. Johns' Newfoundland. St. Johns Newfoundland to Pernambuco, South America, with a load of drum fish. Then in ballast to Santos, Santos to Falmouth with coffee, then home in ballast. (2) *Her last voyage.* Portmadoc to Hamburg with slates, Hamburg to the East Coast, United Kingdom, with Oil Cake, then Coal to Gibraltar, ballast to Cadiz, Cadiz to Newfoundland with salt, Newfoundland to Leghorn with fish, then to Malaga with marble, Malaga with manganese ore to Gibraltar for orders, then to Bristol. On entering the Bristol Channel she was torpedoed and sunk, having been away from P.M. for 10 months.

*L.R. 1910/11:* 3mst. Sr., 169t, 101.4/23.7/11.9. Built D. Williams, P.M., 1905, owner J. Williams. Sunk by U Boat, 13.3.1917.

3mst, Sr, 168tg, 136tr, 101.4/23.7/11.9. John Williams, 5 Market Square, Tremadog, merchant, 32/64ths; John Mathias Jones, Morvin House, Criccieth, M.M., 24/64ths; Ellen Jones of Moranedd, Borth-y-gest, P.M., spinster, 8/64ths. John Williams, 5 Market Square, Tremadog, M.O. Reg. closed 4 April 1917. Vessel sunk with gunfire by enemy submarine on 13 March 1917 in lat. 50° 47'N, long. 6° 58'W. Certificate lost with vessel.

## ELIZABETH OF HULL

Sr, 122tn, 82.0/21.0/11.6. Built at Sunderland, 1847 Edward Humphreys, Clog y Berth, ma. Edward Humphreys was related to the owner of *Lady Vaughan.*

## ELIZABETH LLEWELYN

3 mst. Sr. Built P.M. about 1904. Newfoundland Trader. Lost off Gibraltar on a passage from Gibraltar to Huelva in ballast February 8, 1912. David Richard (Bach) was then her ma.

*L.R. 1910/11:* 3mst. Sr. 159t, 97.3/23.4/11.8. Built David Jones, P.M., 1895, owned L. G. Llewelyn, D. M. Solomon, ma 09-11.

C.R.S.: Reg. closed 28 Feb. 1912. Vessel stranded near Pearl Rock, Gibraltar, and became a total wreck. Certificate of reg. lost with vessel.

*Owners:* Llewellyn Griffith Llewellyn, 1 Garth Terrace, P.M., Shipowner, 48/64ths [M.O. 26 April 1895]; Gwen Jones, Fron, Trawsfynydd, wife of William Jones, 6/64ths; Mary Lloyd Morris, The Oakleys, P.M., wife of David Morris, 4/64ths; William Morris, Brittania Terrace, Ship Chandler, 4/64ths; Sarah Williams, 2 Neptune Villa, Towyn, widow, 2/64ths. Mortgages: (1) Llewellyn Griffith Llewellyn mortgage dated 24 April, 1895, for £575 and interest @ 4% on 44 shares to John Owen, Garth Cottage, P.M., Shipowner. 2nd May 1895. (2) Llewellyn Griffith Llewellyn mortgage dated 25 April 1895, for £117 and interest nil to Hans Georg Carl Renck of Harburg, Shipbroker. (3) Sarah Williams, 24 Dec. 1896 mortgaged dated 22 Dec. 1896 for £40 and interest at 5% Richard Griffith Prichard, P.M., Marine Engineer. John Owen died 17 Dec. 1896, and according to will, William Jones of Penbryn Isaf, Talsarnau, Farmer, and John Williams of Stuntur, Minffordd, Penrhyndeudraeth, M.M., became joint mortgagees.

ELIZABETH PARRY

ELIZABETH PRITCHARD (1)

3mst. Sr. 122tg. 92tn. Built at P.M. 1898 by David Williams, John P. Roberts, Borthygest, ma. She had a double top'sl and no gallan'sl. Newfoundland Trader, Admitted to the Club 8 April, 1898. Lost in collision in 1908. Compensation awarded for her loss £2,026.18.6.

*L.R. 1904/5:* 3mst. Sr. 122t, 88.7/22.7/10.6. Built P.M. 1898, by D. Williams, owner Mr. L. Roberts, G. Prichard, Mgr. J. P. Roberts, ma., 1900.

C.R.S.: John Pritchard, 36 Madoc St., P.M., M.M., 58/64ths. Laura Roberts, 36 Madoc St., P.M., widow, 6/64ths. Griffith Prichard, 6 Cornhill, P.M. designated S.H., 31 March 1898.

John Pritchard, mortgage for £400 and interest at 4% to William Jones of Penbryn Isaf, Talsarnau, Farmer, (on 28 shares). Mortgage discharged 4 Nov. 1899. On John Pritchard's death on 3 Oct. 1900, sole executrix, Laura Roberts sold 16/64ths to John Pritchard Roberts, P.M., M.M., and 16/64ths to Elizabeth Jane Roberts, P.M., spinster. Reg. closed 12 May 1908, vessel sunk in collision off Shoreham, 4 May 1908.

*P.P. 1909, LXXVIII:* 4 May 1908, Sr, 10 years old, 6 crew, J. P. Roberts, ma, Mrs. L. Roberts, P.M., owner, voyage Aarhus to Llanelly, cargo steel turnings, collided with *S.S. Belford* of Synderland, about midway between Owens Lightship, and Beachy Head. Weather calm, no lives lost.

ELIZABETH PRITCHARD (2)

3mst. Sr, double top'sl. and a gallan'sl. 126tg, 99tn. Built at P.M. 1909. Admitted to the Club 28 April, 1909, at a valuation of £19 per ton, viz. £2,394. Newfoundland Trader. John Pritchard Roberts ma. He married Miss Humphreys who used to work for my aunt Grace Jones at Bank Place, P.M. See under *Dizzy Dunlop.*

*L.R. 1910/11:* 3mst. Sr. 126t, 93.4/23.0/10.4. Built P.M. 1909 by David Jones. Owners: J. P. Roberts, G. Pritchard. Mg. J. P. Roberts, ma. Sold Newfoundland, 1916.

3mst. Sr, 125tg, 99.04tr, 93.4/23/10.4. Built David Jones, P.M., 1909. Owners: John Pritchard Roberts, Borth-y-gest, M.M., 20/64ths; Laura Roberts, P.M., widow, 16/64ths; Elisabeth Jane Roberts, P.M., wife of Wm. Watkin Roberts, 8/64ths; Thomas Parry, P.M., Iron Monger, 8/64ths; Robert Pritchard of P.M., Shipowner, 4/64ths; Thomas Jones, P.M., Shipowner, 4/64ths; John James Jones, Borth-y-Gest, M.M., 4/64ths. Reg. of vessel transferred to Port of St. John's, Newfoundland, 11 Sept. 1916. Sold to James Ryan, Merchant, St. John's, Newfoundland.

ELIZABETH RICHARDS

Sr, 66tn, 66.0/19.2/8.5. Built at Borthygest 1858 by Wm. Griffith. William Roberts, ma. Wm. Roberts married my father's sister, Ann. His daughter has a picture of the vessel dated 1879. Lost with all hands in Sligo Bay.

ELIZABETH ROBERTS

3mst. Sr, 99tn. Built at Amlwch, 1904, Ellis Owen Roberts owner, Rhys Jones, Barmouth, ma. Left Llanelly April 9, 1913 for Oporto with a load of coal and was never heard of again. All hands lost.

Steel 3mst. Sr. Built Amlwch, 1904, by Wm. Thomas, 134t, 93.4/23.0/10.4. E. O. Roberts, owner.

ELIZABETH THOMAS

Sr, 104tg, 96tn, 73.2/21.0/10.7. Built at P.M. 1855, Richard Jones, ma. She took 9 days on a passage from Dublin to P.M. with a Cargo of wines and spirits. The crew, it is said, had consumed a good proportion of the cargo.

Built Morgan Jones, P.M., 1855. Sold Aberystwyth 1874.

ELLEN

Sr, 140tg. Built Nevin (?Conway 1858), Thos. Davies ma, John Owen, S.H. Lost on Grassholm Island, Pembrokeshire. All hands saved except the master who was later found dead on the wreck eaten by rats.

Probably *Ellen* listed *L.R. 1871* as Sr, 140t, 93.2/22.4/11.2. Built Conway 1858, owned J. Davies & Co., P.M., — Hamburg trade.

ELLEN ANN

Owned at Aberystwyth.

ELLEN BEATRICE

Sr, of Cardiganshire.

ELLEN GREAVES

Bg, 271tg, 254tn, 114/25/15. Built at P.M. 1876 by Simon Jones. Capt. R. Roberts, ma, Capt. Morris Jones, S.H. Named after the 3rd daughter of J. W. Greaves, Esq.; she later became Mrs. Williams Ellis. Lost off the coast of Aruba on voyage between British Guiana and Curacao. An infrequent visitor to her home port. Wm. Jones, who now lives on Greaves Wharf (1946), informed me of the following voyage he did on her as an A.B. about 1894. He joined her at Swansea from where they sailed to Pernambuco with coal, then to Aruba in ballast, then to Harburg with phosphate rock, to Middlesboro in ballast, to Rosario, River Plate, with railway sleepers, then to Aruba in ballast. To London with phosphate rock, then to Paysandu, River Plate, with railway sleepers. At Paysandu they met the *Evelyn* loading Coffee. Then to Aruba in ballast, and to Ipswich with phosphate rock where he left her after serving on her for 2 years during the above voyages. See under *Carl and Louise* (2).

*C.R.S.:* Owners: John Williams, Llanystumdwy, M.M., 24/64ths; Morris Jones, P.M., Shipowner, 12/64ths; David Richards, P.M., Shipowner, 8/64ths; George James Barnard, P.M., Agent, 4/64ths; Morris Evans Morris, P.M., Chemist, 4/64ths; David Jones, Tremadog, Auctioneer, 4/64ths; John Williams, Llanystumdwy, Miller, 4/64ths; Morris Jones, Dolgelley, Commercial Traveller, 4/64ths. Vessel stranded on Aruba Island, West Indies, and became a total wreck, 27 Jan. 1897. Reg. closed 6 March 1897.

*P.P. 1898, LXXXIII:* 27 Jan. 1897, 21 years old, 8 crew, W. Parry, ma, M. Jones, P.M., owner. Voyage: Aruba, Dutch West Indies to Nantes with phosphate, no lives lost, near Aruba Bar, wind SE force 4.

ELLEN JAMES (1)

3mst. Sr. Built at P.M. 1897 by David Williams. John James Jones, Borthygest, ma. Lost on Carbonear Island, Newfoundland, on passage from St. Johns, Newfoundland, to Avondale, Newfoundland, with part cargo on board, viz 3000 quintals of fish at a freight of 2/6 per quintal

March 1903. The following voyage is a remarkable record of hers, (10.3.1898): Portmadoc to Stettin with slates via the Skaggerack, Stettin to London with railway sleepers, London to Sligo with cement, Sligo to Garston with logs, Manchester Ship Canal with coal for Gibraltar. Towed to Cadiz from Gibraltar, Cadiz to St. Johns, Newfoundland with salt, for orders, then to Fogo. Fogo to Naples with fish, in ballast then to Gibraltar for orders, then to Huelva (Spain). Huelva to Exmouth with copper ore, Exmouth to Portmadoc in ballast. She left Portmadoc for Stettin in March 1898 and returned there from Exmouth, December 23, 1898. Richard Williams, now Capt. Richard Williams, was on her during this trip. The above is his testimony.

> *C.R.S.:* 3mst. Sr. 139t, 92.4/22.8/11.6. Built P.M. 1897 by D. Williams. *Owners:* John Jones, Borth-y-gest, Shipowner, 16/64ths; John James Jones, Borth-y-gest, P.M., M.M., 28/64ths; Ann Prydderch Owen, 131 High St., P.M., Ironmonger, 16/64ths; Ellen James Jones, 131 High St., P.M., spinster, 4/64ths. John Jones, 6 Ivy Terrace, Borth-y-gest, P.M. designated M.O., advice under hand of John James Jones, 26 March 1897. Reg. closed 17 Dec. 1902, vessel lost in Conception Bay, Newfoundland, on 6 Dec. 1902.

ELLEN JAMES (2)

3mst, Sr, 165tg. Built P.M. 1904 by David Williams, John James Jones, ma. Newfoundland Trader. Lost by enemy action 1914/18. All hands lost except one. R. Cadwaladr Jones was then her master, son of John Cadwaladr Jones of the *Cadwaladr Jones.*

> *L.R. 1910/11:* 3mst, Sr, 165t, 101.4/23.7/11.9. Built P.M. 1904 by D. Williams, owned J. Jones. J. J. Jones, ma. Sunk by U Boat, April 1917.
>
> *P.P. (1910) LXXI:* Comfort Bight, Labrador to Gibraltar, cargo fish. Patent reefing chain carried away and struck ma. 1 killed, 46°N, 25°W. N. Atlantic, 11 Oct. 1908.

ELLEN JONES

Bn, Wm. Williams, Garreg Wen Bach, ma. Lost with all hands, voyage from Danzig to Gloucester.

> *L.R. 1871/2:* Sr, 178t, 95.2/23.8/12.1. Built Pwllheli 1867 by Pritchard and owned by Williams & Co., Pwllheli. Lost Dec. 1876 — Danzig to Gloucester.

ELLEN LLOYD (formerly Ebenezer Parry)

Bg. later a Bkn, 194tg. Built Nevin. Evan Morris, ma, son-in-law of Capt. Hugh Roberts, *Constance.* Phosphate Rock Trader, including Rio de Janeiro and the Brazils. Lost in the Atlantic. Capt. Ellis Jones, Borthy-gest, did the following voyage on her: Runcorn to Bermuda with coal, ballast to Snooks Arm, Newfoundland, fish to Genoa, ballast to Trapani, Valentia to Ireland with salt, then home to P.M. in ballast, 8 months for the voyage. Capt. Morris, an intrepid sailor, once visited St. Helena in her at the time General Cronje was incarcerated there, during the Boer War. He used to visit Cronje and take him some tobacco and had many a happy chat with him. On one occasion, when at Trinidad, the cargo of coconuts was attacked by rats who emptied the milk out of the nuts. The cargo had to be unloaded, and the ship fumigated to destroy the rats. On another occasion, when off Newfoundland, Capt Morris was washed overboard in a gale; being a strong swimmer, he got back on board on his own. The crew, having panicked, had taken to the rigging, thinking the ship was going down as she had 'broached to'. Capt. Morris ran to the wheel which was racing; it knocked him down and broke his leg in 3 places. He removed three small bones from his leg with a pair of scissors himself, unassisted, and when he arrived home it had to be re-set. He sailed a few voyages afterwards and died at Portmadoc in 1910, 69 years old. He had commanded large deep water ships in his day and made some smart passages, once beating the mail boat from the Cape to Australia when he commanded the *Carmarthen Castle.* He lost the *Menai Straits* off the Horn, the ship having caught fire, and was 19 days in open boat and ultimately landed in the Falkland Islands. He afterwards commanded the *Sarmatian,* a large full rigged ship belonging to Quebec, engaged in carrying coolies from Calcutta to Demerara and had a serious mutiny on board. He shot the ringleader to quell it. The old *British Commodore* which he afterwards commanded is now (1945) a training ship, for the Chilean Navy at Valparaiso. The above information was given to me by Capt. Evie Morris, his son, who at one time commanded the *Venedocian.*

*L.R. 1901/2:* Bkn. 207t, 100.5/24.6/13.2. Built Nevin 1877 by G. Owen as *Ebenezer Parry,* owned (1901) by E. Morris who took command of her in 1896. C.R.S.: Hugh Roberts, 16 Terrace Road, P.M., S.H., advice under hand of E. Morris, 7 Sept. 1896. Sold at Fowey 1912, wrecked Letturre, 1917.

ELLEN PHILLIPS

ELLEN ROBERTS (1)

Bg.

ELLEN ROBERTS (II)

*C.R.S.:* Sr, 104tg, 98tn, 75.3/20.3/10.6. Built Pwllheli 1868, Joseph Roberts, ma. Owners: John Roberts, P.M., M.M., 32/64ths; David Roberts, P.M., Grocer, 16/64ths; Owen Roberts, Pwllheli, Shipbuilder, 8/64ths; Robert Thomas, Grocer, 8/64ths. She was afloat as late as 1916 to my knowledge. She sprang a leak and sank 5 miles south of Baltimore harbour, Co. Cork, 19 January 1917.

ELLEN WILLIAMS

Sr, later a K. Built Millom, 1913, Wm. Green, owner. Sold to someone at Barnstable, Cornwall.

EMILY DINGLE

Bk, 273tg. Built West Country, Morgan Jones, owner. Declared lost, April 1899, voyage from Gaspé, St. Lawrence to Rio de Janeiro, cargo 4000 tubs of fish @ a freight of 4/3d per tub; last heard of December 10, 1898. After losing her rudder in a storm, she drifted away from the usual trade routes and was abandoned in a sinking condition. The crew after taking to the boats were picked up by a Norwegian sailing ship. Capt. Humphrey Lloyd, Clogwyn Melyn and his son, Humphrey, were on board at the time and reached home safely. A story is told that the ma (H. Lloyd) kept a pig on board on long voyages — an assurance for some fresh meat. The pig once fell overboard and the vessel had to heave to and a boat was launched to save him. When hauling the pig aboard the boat capsized and rescue party was nearly lost. The pig was drowned.

*L.R. 1890/1:* Bk. 286t, 126.7/25.3/13.6. Built Cox, Bridport, 1876, owned W. W. Dingle, W. Roose, ma, 1888.

EMILY MILLINGTON

Built Amlwch. Tom Davies, Borthygest, ma. Newfoundland Trader.

*L.R. 1884/5:* Sr, 99t, 88.9/22.2/10.3. Built Banks, Selby, 1876, Owner: G. Millington reg. at Runcorn.

EMPRESS

Bn, later a Sr, 115tg, 81/21.3/11.7. Built Pwllheli 1856, Capt. Morris Jones, P.M., owner. David Davies, ma, brother of Rhys Davies, the pilot. Re-registered at Carnarvon 1878, as a schooner, with David Davies as owner. Stranded at Douglas harbour, December 6, 1882 and became a total wreck. When at Douglas a few years ago I met the Cox of the lifeboat that saved her crew. (1939).

EMRYS

3mst, Sr, 280t.d.w. Built P.M. by David Williams, and launched sideways at Rotten Tare. Capt. Griffiths, ma. Newfoundland Trader. Lost in collision in the English Channel, 15 May, 1900. Cargo 282 tons slates at a freight of 10/- per ton bound for the Elbe. She was a particularly good looking vessel. I witnessed her launch.

*L.R. 1894/5:* 3mst, Sr, 164t, 101.2/23.6/11.7. Built Williams & Co., P.M., 1893, owned D. Richards & Co., P.M. J. Griffiths, ma.

*C.R.S.:* Vessel sunk off Eddystone, 16 May 1900, after collision. Certificate of reg. lost with vessel. Owners: John Griffith, P.M., M.M., 24/64ths; David Richards, P.M., M.M., 24/64ths — (David Richards, 8 Dora St., P.M., designated M.O.); David Richards, P.M. Harbour Ma., 4/64ths; Ellen Ambrose Hughes, P.M., wife of Hugh Hughes, 4/64ths; William Ambrose Jones, P.M., Clerk, 4/64ths; Thomas Joseph Hughes, Bethesda, Chemist, 4/64ths; 1896: 4/64ths of William Ambrose Jones sold to David Richards, 146 High Street, P.M., Harbour Ma.

ENDEAVOUR (1)

Bg, (Sw) 160tdw, 128½t, 66.9/21.5/-. Built Traeth Mawr, 1802. Thomas Jones, ma, grandfather of Sir Robert Armstrong Jones, Eisteddfa. She was captured by the French in 1808. On one occasion she took a load of slates to Archangel from P.M. Oct. 1803. Cost to build £1,958.3.2.

ENDEAVOUR (2)

Sk, 46tn. Built P.M., 1845 by Richard Jones, J. H. Williams, owner, Francis Williams, Borthygest, ma.

Lost Pwllheli 8.12.1886.

ENTERPRISE

Sw, 119tn, 81.8/20.3/13.3. Built P.M. 1845, J. & J. Hodson, Whitehaven, owners. Todhunter ma.

*Enterprise*: Bg, 165t. Built P.M. Henry Jones, 1845 sold to Whitehaven owners, 1859.

EPHRATAH

Bg, 230t, 112.3/25.1/14.4. Built P.M. 1873 by Eben Roberts, Capt. Griffith Jones, Creuau, ma. Phosphate rock trader. Lost near Porto Cabello, Venezuela, in 1892 Sept. Owners: Griffith Jones, P.M., M.M. 16/64ths. Evan Jones, P.M., M.M., 4/64ths. Eben Roberts, P.M. Shipbuilder, 6/64ths. Pierce Roberts, P.M. Shipbuilder, 4/64ths. John Roberts, P.M. Shipbuilder, 2/64ths. Thomas Casson, P.M., Banker, 4/64ths. John Henry Wms. P.M., Iron Founder, 4/64ths. Robert Jones, P.M. Butcher, 4/64ths. Lewis Jones Lewis, P.M. Butcher, 2/64ths. Henry Jones, P.M. Quarryman, 2/64ths. Richard Owen, Penrhyn, Farmer, 4/64ths. John Griffith, Penrhyn, Farmer, 4/64ths. Hugh Edwards, London, Shipbroker, 4/64ths. Michael Jones Evans, Liverpool, Corn Merchant, 4/64ths.

*P.P. 1894 LXXVI:* 15 Sept. 1892, Bg, 19 years old, 8 crew, J. Davies, ma, J. Owen P.M. owner. Voyage Aruba, Dutch West Indies for Gloucester with phosphate rock, stranded off Cayo Blanco, Venezuela, Caribbean Sea, no lives lost, Wind E force 4.

EQUITY

Sr, 1858. Built Newquay.

ERMINE

Sp, 27t. Built Towyn, County of Carnarvon, 1825 by Henry Jones, Alexander Madocks, owner. Griffith Griffiths, ma of Llanfihangel y Traethau.

ESPERANZA

Sr, John Crocker, ma.

ESTHER of Pwllheli

(Reg. at Beaumaris 13/1824). Bn, 110t, 63½/20½/-. Built Traeth Bach, 1815, Thos. Jones, ma, later John Owen. Wm. & Thos, Casson had 8 shares in her.

*Esther* Sr, 110t. Built P.M. by Henry Jones, 1846. Lost 1860.

ETHELS

Bk, 254tn, 117.5/23.5/14.4. Built Kincardine, 1863, G. Griffith & other owners, Garth Terr. P.M. Wm. Evans, Madoc Street, P.M. ma.

*L.R. 1871:* Bk, 254t, 117.5/23.5/14.4.

EVELYN

Bg, 216tg, 202tn, c 350tdw, 104.9/25.6/13.9. Built Trwyn Pier, P.M. 1877 by Daniel Evans, Llety, as foreman for Hugh Williams, Capt. Hugh Roberts, ma, son of Captain Hugh Roberts of the *Constance.* H. A. Thomas, S.H. Phosphate Rock Trader. One of the Port's most famous brigs and probably the most sturdily built of them. There is hardly a port on the East Coast of S. America that she did not visit including Port Madryn in the Patagonia. Lost May, 1914. Abandoned in the Atlantic in a sinking condition after a great struggle in many days of hurricane. Capt. Evie Morris sent me a graphic account of her loss, which account appears in my brother's book, *Immortal Sails.*

[See also additional information on selected ships, infra.]

EXCEL

Sr, 98tg. 75/20/12. Built Bideford, 1850. Thos. Davies, ma, Rees Evans, S.H. Coasting Schooner. Lost with all hands off St. Ives, Cornwall. My brother, Tom, did his first voyage on her.

EXCELSIOR

Bg, 176tn, 320tdw, 99.5/23.7/12.8. Built P.M. 1868 by Eben. Roberts. David Morris (my grandfather) owner, William Hughes (my father) ma. Phosphate Rock Trader. Blown ashore and lost at Halmstadt, Sweden, Dec. 1903. A vessel with a remarkable trading record. She traded in the Brazils, West Indies, the Mediterranean and the Baltic. About 1890 she wintered at Archangel. For her story see *Immortal Sails* by my brother. In 1898 I did a voyage on her to Harburg [see under *Evelyn*]. Morris Edwards of Penrhyndeudraeth was bosun in the *Excelsior* for 4 years, and recounted to me the following voyage he made in her during 1888/89: [My brother Willie was O.S. on her during these years.] Portmadoc to Hamburg with slates; Hamburg to Bowness Alloa and then to Granton; Granton to Aruba with coal. Aruba to Falmouth for orders with phosphate rock, then to Hamburg. When off the Western Isles she ran into a heavy S.W. Gale. The vessel was hove to at 3 in the morning with the two lower topsails, the fore and main top mast staysails set. Edwards and a young boy were on deck. The master (father) and the rest of the crew were below. Suddenly when the sea was at its height the gale abated and the winds virtually stopped. The vessel was more or less helpless — a collossal lump of sea hit the vessel on the port quarter — Edwards shouted to the boy just in time to look out, whilst he himself put both his arms through the steering wheel and held on — the boy had done the same with the pump wheel. The vessel shuddered as her starboard bulwark went over board together with the 2 boats, the galley and the main top mast staysail. All hands were on deck in a very few minutes, whilst the vessel toiled in a windless sea. Shortly the wind resumed but from the N.W. before which the vessel ran with the four top sails set and two staysails and the reefed trysail. (If another sea had broken over her at this time Edwards said she would undoubtedly have foundered). They reached Falmouth safely where she was repaired and provided with 2 new boats, and then proceeded to Hamburg. From Hamburg she sailed for Laguira with her cargo. Laguira to Aruba in ballast. Aruba to Glasgow with phosphate rock. When leaving Aruba she damaged her keel and ripped much of her but reached Glasgow safely. When examined about 1/3rd of her keel had gone. Then to Portmadoc in ballast. When she was at Bowness mother and I visited her. I was then 4½ years old.

> *P.P. 1904, LXXXVI:* 25 Dec. 1902, Bg, 34 years old, 7 crew, R. Evans, ma, D. Morris, P.M., owner. Voyage: Copenhagen to Halmstad in ballast. Foundered near Halmstad, Sweden, no lives lost, wind force 9 W.

FAITH

Sr. Built Topsham, Edward Hughes, Morfa Bychan, ma.

*L.R. 1884/5:* K, 76t. Built Topsham 1860 by Homan, H. Evans, owner. [Hugh Evans, 108 Dalton Road, Barrow].

FALCON

K. Built Amlwch.

? *L.R. 1871/2:* Sr, 53t, 60.3/17.3/8.6. Built Aberdovey 1857, E. James, owner and ma. Cardigan Coaster.

FAME

Bg, of Barmouth. Reg at Liverpool. Passenger boat Liverpool.

FAIRWIND

? *L.R. 1880:* Sr, 147t, 98.3/23.8/11.1. Built Banff 1876 by Watson, A. Watson, owner.

FANNY BRESLAUER

Bk later Bkn, 295tg, 274.09tn. Altered to 261.89t in Jan., 1890. 131.4/27.1/13.2. Built Stonehouse, Plymouth, 1871, Reg. at Carnarvon (No. 1 in 1889) 4 March, 1889. (Formerly No. 37 in London in 1871, No. 50 Hull in 1876). Phosphate trader, formerly a tea trader. Wm. Prichard P.M., Shipbroker, 64/64ths, Capt. Evan Jones, Borthygest, ma, (bro. of Capt. Owen Jones, *Fleetwing*). Sold to Jersey September, 1894. Reg. closed 23/11/1914 on sale to Danish subjects.

C.R.S.: John Richard Prichard, P.M., Bank Accountant, 8/64ths; Griffith Prichard, P.M., Shipbroker, 8/64ths; David Jones, P.M., Shipbuilder, 8/64ths; Daniel Williams, P.M., Draper, 4/64ths; Owen Jones, Borth, P.M., M.M., 8/64ths; John Griffith Williams of Tanygrisiau, Merionethshire, Quarryman, 4/64ths; Janet Jane Lloyd Jones, Egremont, Cheshire, wife of Hugh Lloyd Jones, 8/64ths; Evan Jones of Borth, P.M., M.M., 8/64ths.

FLEETWING

Bg, 237tg, 226tn, 110/25/14.6. Built Borthygest, 1874 by Richard Jones, Garreg Wen. Prichard Bros, S.H., Capt. Owen Jones, ma, Borthygest. Phosphate rock trader. She also traded in the Brazils, West Indies and the Mediterranean. I remember her at P.M. about 1898 undergoing repairs. When the tide was subsiding, she went over on her beam ends and was dismasted because she listed outwards towards the river instead of inwards. The River Plate and Rio were her favourite haunts. Ellis Humphreys, Borthfechan, Borthygest, served on her as A.B. during the following two voyages. (1) Cardiff to the Island of Santa Catherina,

Brazil with coal and patent fuel. Santa Catherina to Aruba in ballast, Aruba to Leith with Phosphate rock. (2) Cardiff to Laguira with coal, then to Aruba in ballast. Aruba to Plymouth with phosphate rock, then home in ballast. Capt. Ellis Jones, Borthygest did this voyage on her as an O.S.: Cardiff to Cadiz with coal, Cadiz to Newfoundland with Salt, Newfoundland to Genoa with fish, Genoa to Sicily in ballast, then to Great Yarmouth with salt. She was ultimately sold to the Falkland Islands as a Coal hulk. Evie Morris saw her in this capacity at Port Stanley about 1932. (Sold in May 1911). Capt. Ellis Jones, Ty Mawr, Penmorfa, informed me that he commanded her for 4 years from 1897. These are some of the outstanding voyages he did with her: (1) Portmadoc to Cardiff with a small cargo of slates (on his outward tack from St. Tudwals he bumped on Sarn Badrig in a fog, two boats were launched to try and tow her off. The weight of the two boats lightened her sufficiently for her to sail off and she reached Cardiff without incident.) To Laguira, with patent fuel; ballast to Aruba; phosphate rock to Barking, fertilisers to Bay St. Francis, Martinique; Aruba in ballast; then back to Barking with phosphate rock (1901). (2) 15/8/1899. Cardiff to Ascension Island with 400 tons of coal, then to St. Johns, Newfoundland in ballast (150 tons), then 4113 drums of fish to Pernambuco @ a freight of 3/- per drum. Pernambuco in ballast to Aruba, then phosphate rock to U.K. (3) Cardiff to Maranhao, N. Brazil with patent fuel, ballast to Aruba, then phosphate rock to U.K. Capt. Jones took command of her after she was dismasted in P.M. harbour and re classed. He also commanded for a time the *W. W. Lloyd,* the *Edward Windus* and the *Blanche Currie,* and also the 3 mst. Sr. *Wm. Prichard.* He declared *Fleetwing* to be the finest vessel he had sailed in. *Fleetwing* ended her days as a coal hulk in the Falkland Islands.

## FLORENCE

Sr. Built P.M. 1878 by Hugh Williams, Wm. Jones, P.M., ma. Lost with all hands on a voyage home from Morocco. Wm. Jones, the ma, died in her at sea on a voyage from Bremen to Newcastle on Tyne. The mate buried him in the ballast. The *Excelsior* came on the scene and found chaos on board — no one could navigate the ship. Father ordered them to follow *Excelsior* to Newcastle which they managed to do.

> *C.R.S.:* Topsail Sr, 100t, 84.5/22/11.1. Built at P.M. by Hugh Williams, P.M. reg. 1878. Vessel sailed from Falmouth for Montrose, 4 Jan. 1890, and has not since been heard of, certificate lost with vessel. Reg. Closed 4 March 1890. Owners: William Jones, P.M., M.M., 48/64ths; William Evans, P.M., Brazier, 16/64ths. Wm Evans of High Street, P.M., M.O. apptd. by William Jones, Aug. 1878. Both died by 1886 — G. Prichard Mgr. 1887. [William Jones named as ma in *L.R. 1880*].

FLYING DUTCHMAN

K, Richard Williams, Criccieth, ma.

FOUR BROTHERS

35t. Built P.M. 1833.

Sp, 44t. Built Henry Jones, P.M., 1833. Lost and reg. 1860.

FRANCES

K, Hugh Jones, Blockmaker, owner in 1915.

*L.R. 1904/5: Wood K,* 89t, 83.7/20.4/9.2. Built Burt & Sons, Falmouth, & owned in 1904/5 by W. Hutchings of Falmouth.

FRANCIS HENRY

Sr, 110tn, 76.0/20.5/10.5. Built Pwllheli 1865 by Williams, Capt. Jones, Criccieth, ma. Lost with all hands shortly after leaving Newfoundland. Before leaving P.M. in this voyage her mate fell from the mast head and was killed. On one occasion she arrived at P.M. with human bones in her ballast.

Not heard of since leaving Labrador for Gibraltar, 23.10.1887.

FRANCIS HENRY

K.

FRAU MINNA PETERSEN

3mst, Sr, with a round stern and a poop, 176tg, 165tn, (altered to 153.98, Feb. 27, 1891), 102/24.3/12.6. Built P.M. 1878 by Simon Jones, Reg. Port of Carnarvon. 12/1878 (27 July). Owner, Hugh Parry, Borthygest, M.M. Reg. in Fowey in 1901 on transfer of ownership. Name changed to *Jane Banks.* Reg. closed on Sale to an Esthonian firm 6 April, 1938. She was launched sideways at Rotten Tare, and stopped half way down the slip way with part of her hull overhanging the quay. She was one of the earliest of the P.M. fish traders in Newfoundland and was also a phosphate rock trader and a great roamer. In her day she visited Calatz and Braila on the Danube with fuel and general cargo from U.K. She was sometimes referred to as a " Jack Barquentine ". In 1883 when on a passage from Grady harbour to Harbour Grace, Newfoundland she rescued the crew of the Barque *Videx* (Captain Roberts) which was foundering with a load of copper ore from Tilt Cove Newfoundland for Swansea. She was seen by a friend of mine in 1942 at Par, Devon under the name of *Jane Banks.*

R.S. Sr, 3mst, 176t, 102/24.3/12.6. Built P.M., 1878, by Simon Jones, P.M. Stem: Female bust. Reg. closed and transferred to Fowey, 1901. Owners: Hugh Parry, Borth, P.M., M.M., 64/64ths. Hugh Parry mortgage July 31, 1878, £2,200 + Int.

@ 5% to Owen Morris of P.M. Slate Merchant (Mortgagee). Owen Morris dies intestate, 18 April, 1884, letters of administration to Jane Morris, 9 Bank Place, P.M., spinster. Discharge of mortgage, receipt dated 11 Nov. 1895. Hugh Parry sold on 11 Feb. 1901 33/64ths to Robert May of Par, Cornwall, M.M., and 10/64ths to Thomas May of Port Isaac, Cornwall, Shipowner. On 12 Feb. 1901 Hugh Parry sold to Alfred Charles Parkyn, of Par, Cornwall, 8/64ths; Arthur Henry Croke of Par, clergyman, 8/64ths, and Benjamin Moss Tregaskis, of Par, Shipbuilder, 5/64ths.

FRIENDS (1)

40t. Built P.M. 1830. (A Bk of this name was built at Barmouth in 1799).

Sp, 47t. Built John Parry, P.M., 1830. Sold Aberystwyth, 1847.

FRIENDS (2)

FRIENDS AND GOODWILL

70½t, 53/18/-. Built Traeth Bach, 1809.

FRIENDSHIP

Sr. Built Newquay, 1857, D. Davies and others owners. E. Evans, ma.

FRITZ VON GADO

Bn, Robert Jones, ma, brother of Richard Jones, Garreg Wen. She used to 'Winter' sometimes at Borthygest.

*Fritz Von Gadow* 6/1883 C.R.S.: Bn, 160t, 94/23.6/11.7. Built Germany, 1879. Rees Jones, Shipbuilder of Portdinorwic owned 64/64ths in 1883. On Rees Jones's death, 18 November 1885, William Edward Jones, his son, became owner. Sold to Greek owners, 1886.

GANDAGE

Sr. Locally known as the 'Gandass' Richard Owen, ma.

GAZELLE

GEISHA

3mst, Sr. Built at Appledore. Admitted to the Club April, 1909.

Built Cock brothers, Appledore, in 1906, from same model as *Katie* and *Rose*. For details of their building, vide Basil Greenhill, *The Merchant Schooners*, Vol. 1, 81 et seq., 164.

GELERT

37t. Built P.M. 1837.

Sp. Built P.M. 1837 by Henry Jones. Lost and Reg. Douglas Bay, 15.10.1865.

GEM

*L.R. 1904/5:* W, 3mst. Sr. 174t, 102.6/22.5/12.9. Built Fowey, 1871, by Butson.

GEORGE CASSON

Bn, originally a brig, 154tg, 145tn. Built P.M. 1863 by Pierce Roberts, Robert Evans, Farm Yard, ma. Prichard Bros. S.H. Phosphate trader in her early days. Interned at Harburg, August 4, 1914. She never returned home. She spent the greater part of her life carrying slates from P.M. to the Elbe and the Baltic ports.

*L.R. 1871/2:* Bg, 154t, 92.3/22.3/12.3. Built P.M. 1863, Pierce, owned Morris & Co., P.M. — Hamburg. Capt Robert Evans was her ma., when she was interned, and David Owen (locally known as Dafydd French) was her mate. (Information from Captain Griffith Roberts, Borth-y-gest).

GEORGE HENRY

Sr, 100tg, 92tn. Built Pwllheli 1864, Hugh Jones, *Venedocian* was once her ma. Rees Evans, S.H. Traded in Newfoundland on occasion. Sold to Ireland.

*L.R. 1871/2:* Sr, 99t, 75.7/20.0/10.7. Built Pwllheli, Owens, 1864. Owen & Co., owners.

GEORGINA

? *L.R. 1871/2:* Sw, 77t, 67/19/8. Built 1861 by Jones at Rhyl, owned Liverpool.

GEORGE THOMAS

GERALDINE

Bg, later Bn, 143tn, 89.2/23.0/12.2. Built Barmouth 1869 by Jones, for Lewis Hughes. Harry Hughes of the *Edward Seymour,* ma. (Son of Lewis Hughes, The Tailor, Portmadoc). Lost the day after leaving P.M. H. Hughes, ma. Phosphate trader.

*L.R. 1871/2:* Bk, 142t, 89.2/23.0/12.2. Built Barmouth, Jones, 1860, owned Griffiths & Co., Barmouth.

GESTIANA

3mst, Sr, 124tg. Built P.M. 1913, Capt. Griffith Pritchard, Tremadoc, ma. Admitted to the Club June 5, 1913. Went on the Goodwins on her 1st outward voyage. Lost 6 miles East of Louisburg, Newfoundland in October, 1913 on her 1st voyage. Passage Newfoundland to Sidney Cape Breton Island when only 4 months old. She was the last ship to be built at P.M.

3mst. Sr, 124tg, 98tr, 95/22.6/10.5. Built David Williams, 15 Madoc Street, P.M. Owners: David Williams, 15 Madoc Street, P.M., Shipbuilder, 8/64ths; Robert Roberts, Plas Weunydd, Blaenau Ffestiniog, Physician & Surgeon, 4/64ths; William Owen of Plas Weunydd, Blaenau Ffestiniog, Quarry Manager, 4/64ths; Joseph Humphreys of Gwalia, Penrhyndeudraeth, Grocer, 4/64ths; William George, Garth Celyn, Criccieth, Solicitor, 4/64ths; Thomas Jones, Brecon Place, P.M., Solicitor, 4/64ths; William Morris Jones, Bank Place, P.M., Solicitor, 4/64ths; David Williams, Bodgwynedd, P.M., Dentist, 4/64ths; John Roberts Jones, Brynmeddyg, Penrhyndeudraeth, Physician and Surgeon, 4/64ths; Richard Bowton, Cartre, Blaenau Ffestiniog, Quarry Owner, 4/64ths; Henry Rathbone Griffith, Tanyronen, P.M., Physician and Surgeon, 4/64ths; Griffith Evan Jones, Plas y Bryn, Blaenau Ffestiniog, Quarry Manager, 4/64ths; Robert Ehlers, 61 Queen Square, Bristol, Merchant, 4/64ths; Fanny Carr, Hafanedd, Betws y Coed, private nurse, 4/64ths; Robert Thomas Williams, Bron Rhiw, Blaenau Ffestiniog, retired Quarry Manager, 4/64ths; Margaret Lloyd George, Bryn Awelon, Criccieth, wife of David Lloyd George, 1/64ths. David Williams, M.O., 4 June 1913. David Williams, sold 4/64ths on 5 July 1913 to Arthur Stephen Rendell of St. John's, Newfoundland, Merchant. Vessel wrecked 6 miles E of Louisberg on the 4 October 1913. Certificate of Reg. was lost with vessel.

GLAD TIDINGS

Sr. Built Aberystwyth, 1866, Capt. John Williams, ma. Coasting trader.

*L.R. 1871/2:* Sr, 101t, 77.6/20.6/10.5. Built Aberystwyth, 1866, by Jones. Owned Williams & Co., Aberystwyth.

GLANAVON

Bg. Built Nevin 1862, John Timothy, Borthygest, owner.

*L.R. 1871/2:* Bg, 184t, 96.0/21.0/13.0. Built Nefyn, 1862. Owners: Jarrett & Co., South American trade. Built by Owen Griffith, Nefyn, 1862. Lost R. Weser, 25.12.1884.

GLANOGWEN

Sr. Built Nevin (Aberystwyth?), Evan Jones of the *Volunteer* ma.
*L.R. 1871/2:* Bn, 145t, 82.66/20.0/12.6. Built Bangor 1855. Owners: Parry & Co. Built by John Parry. Hulk, Feb. 1915.

GLASLYN

Sr, 105t. Built P.M. 1856, Jones & Co. owners. P.M. — Hamburg. Lost voyage Nantes to Leith, 1869.

GLEAM

*Glean L.R. 1871:* Sr, 78t, 79.5/19.4/9.7. Built Shoreham 1855, W. Jones, owner, of Caernarfon. Bangor coaster.

GLEANER

'Fore + after', Moroccan trader, not a P.M. vessel.
*P.P. 1892, LXXI, 632:* Gleaner of Guernsey, Sr, 94t, 12 years old, 5 crew, R. Jones, ma. O. Jones, P.M., owner, sailed from King's Cove, Newfoundland, to Lisbon for orders, cargo of cod fish, 5 lives lost. Not heard of since sailing 13 Nov. 1890.

GLEN CABLE

Bg, Capt. John James, ma, son of John James, the Pilot, died 1871. Capt. Jenkins of the Bg. *Hope* later commanded her. Mediterranean trader. Lost in the Bay of Biscay in the same storm as that which caused Cleopatra's Needle to break adrift.
*L.R. 1875/6: Glencaple.* Sw, 166t, 99.5/22.0/13.6. Built Southwick, 1862. Owned: J. Jones. J. James, ma.

GLYN

Sr. Built Barmouth, 1865.
*L.R. 1871/2: Glynn.* Sr, 80t, 72.4/19.7/10.1. Built Barmouth, 1865, by Davies, owned Richards & Co., P.M. coaster. E. Richards, ma.

GLYN AERON

Sr. Built Aberystwyth, 1852, Thos. Lewis owner and ma.
*L.R. 1871/2:* Sr, 65t, 59/17/9.5. Built Aberaeron, 1852, owned Lewis & Co., Aberystwyth. T. Lewis, ma.

GLYNDWR

Sr, Barmouth, 1840. John Williams, ma. Lost at Tobermory, Scotland.
*L.R. 1871/2:* 94t. Built Barmouth, 1840, owned Griffiths & Co., Pwllheli. P.M. coaster. D. Davies, ma.

GLYNDYFRDWY

Sr, Bennet Williams, brother of Cadwaladr Williams, owner.

GOMER (1)

Built Minffordd 1821, Richard Prichard, ma and owner. Beaumaris Reg. No. 9/1821, Sw, 73.6/23.0/14.0 Burden 161t. Owners Richard Prichard and others, built at Traeth Bach 1821. Her Port of Reg. was Pwllheli, (P.M. was not at that time, 1821, a sub port of reg). She traded as a passenger ship between Beaumaris and New York. Lost off Great Ormes Head 1879. Richard Prichard took a leading part in the early development of maritime P.M. His two sons in law Wm. & Griffith Prichard were ship brokers at P.M. for many years.

also *Gomer* (*II*) *L.R. 1871/2:* Sr, 81t, 54/16/9. Built Pwllheli 1839, owned Richard & Co., P.M. Coaster. Lost and Reg. 3.9.1881.

GOOD INTENT

GOOD WILL

GOWERIAN

Sr, Capt. Parry, Chwilog, Evan Jones, Borth, owners. Wrecked at Abersoch (1905?) Voyage Belfast to Newport.

*L.R. 1871/2:* Sr, 109t, 79.1/21.2/11.0. Built Aberaeron 1856, owned Evans & Co.

GRACIE

3mst. Sr. 126tg. Built P.M. 1907 by David Jones. Newfoundland trader. Sold at Newfoundland Sept. 1916 Capt. O. H. Owen, Borthwen, Borthygest, ma.

3mst, Sr, 126tg, 96tr, 92.6/23.1/10.5. Built P.M., David Jones, 1907. Owners: Owen Humphrey Owen, Castle View, Talsarnau, Mer., M.M., 24/64ths; Ellen Taylor, 26 North End Ave., North End, Portsmouth, widow, 12/64ths; John Richard Williams, Glan Meirion, Talsarnau, Mer., M.M., 8/64ths; Robert Ehlers, 61 Queen Square, Bristol, Newfoundland, Merchant, 8/64ths; Ellen Parry, 5 Lombard St., P.M., spinster, 4/64ths; John Owen Jones, Penbryn Isaf, Llandecwyn, Mer., Gentleman farmer, 4/64ths; David Davies, 7 Cornhill, P.M., Shipbroker, 4/64ths. David Davies, 7 Cornhill, P.M., designated M.O. 8 April 1907. Reg. of vessel transferred to the Port of St. John's Newfoundland, 9 Oct. 1916. Sold to Wilson Garland and Arthur Garland, both of Gantois, Newfoundland, Merchant.

GREAT BRITAIN

Sr, 86tn. Built Pwllheli 1840, Robert Jones, Criccieth, ma.

Built Humphrey Griffith, Pwllheli, 1840. Lost and Reg. off Bardsey, 4.3.81.

*P.P. 1886, LIX, 698:* Sr, Pwllheli built, wood, 85t, G. Griffiths, P.M., owner. 144t of slates and slabs, P.M. to Plymouth, 5 crew, 1 lost, Wind SSE, force 9, very high sea, 14 miles NW by N of Bardsey Light. Sprang a leak during strong breeze, weather became worse, pumps were kept going but would not suck, and there being no hope of saving vessel, she was abandoned, probable cause, strength of weather.

GWEN

85t. Built P.M. 1839.

Built Henry Jones, P.M., 1839.

*L.R. 1836:* Sr, 86t, owned Edwards, P.M., Edwards, ma.

GWEN EVANS

Built Pwllheli 1842.

Bg, 305t. Built Robert Evans, Pwllheli, 1842. Lost Mediterranean? 1845.

GWEN JONES

Sr, 94tn, 64.5/18.7/10.6. Built P.M. 1848 for Thos. Christian, W. Lloyd & Co. owners. Owen Humphreys, ma. Coasting Trader. She left P.M. with a cargo of slates and was not heard of again.

*L.R. 1880/1:* E. Lewis, ma. Lost + reg. Margam 30.4.91.

G. & W. JONES

Sr, 103tn, 80.5/21.3/11.4. Built Borthygest, 1872, by Wm. Griffiths. Mr. Rees Evans, Cwmorthin, owner. Griffith Jones, ma. Lost off coast of Norway with all hands. In ballast at the time. Ma and eldest son, Wm. Jones, lost.

Lost 16.11.1888.

HANNAH

Sw. Built Prince Edward Island, 1864. Mr. Richards, owner. J. Evans, ma.

*L.R. 1880/1:* Bg, 206t, 106.7/24.2/12.6. Built Prince Edward Island by McDouglass in 1864, M. Richards, P.M., owner. J. Evans, ma.

## HANNAH AND JANE

Sr, 99tg, 92tn. Built Pwllheli 1867, John Owen, S.H. John Humphreys ma, son of J. Humphreys, Pilot. Lost near Hartlepool — voyage Sunderland to London with 165 tons of bricks @ a freight of 4/9 per ton. Only one of the crew was saved, November 13, 1901. She was stranded on Morfa Bychan beach, April, 1898.

*L.R. 1871/2:* Sr, 99t, 76/20.5/10.9. Built Pwllheli, Jones.

*P.P. 1903, LXII:* 13 Nov. 1901, Sr, 81t, 5 crew, J. Humphreys, ma, W. O. Morris, P.M., owner. Voyage: Sunderland to Grays, Essex with cargo of firebricks. Wind E force 10, stranded Blackhall Rocks, Co. Durham, 4 lives lost.

## HARLECH CASTLE

Bg, 85t.d.w. 51/20/-. Built Traeth Bach 1787. Wm. Jones, ma and owner. She was at St. Petersburg in 1795 along with the *Aberkin.* Captured by the French in December, 1796. Crew interned in France. The ma and 2 of his men escaped and landed at Hythe, Kent, where they were greeted in Welsh by men of the Flinshire Militia who were stationed there at the time.

## HARMONY

Sr. Built Cardigan, 1829.

*L.R. 1859:* Sr, 70t, owned Havard & Co., Milford.

*Harry Keslake* 2/1889 3mst, Bn, 228t, 116/25.2/12.5. Late *Aimée Marie* of France, formerly *Harry Keslake* of London. Built Turner, London, 1874, 22 March 1889, David Richards, P.M., shipowner, 64/64ths; later sold shares to Thomas Roberts of 3 Osmond Terrace, P.M., solicitor, 16/64ths; Rees Nicholas, 7 Water Street, Newquay, M.M., 8/64ths; John Jones of 3 Osmond Terrace, P.M., Retired M.M., 16/64ths, who later sold them to Ellis Owen Roberts, 65 Norwood Grove, Liverpool, Oil Merchant. Vessel lost on voyage from Burnt Island to Nickerie. Certificate of Reg. lost with vessel. Reg. closed 20 Aug. 1891.

*P.P. 1892, LXXI, 632:* Bkn, 255t, 17 years old, 8 crew, E. Williams, ma. D. Richards, P.M., owner. Voyage: Burntisland to Nickerie, Dutch Guinea, cargo coal and general, 8 crew lost, not heard of since sailing, 30 March 1891.

## HARVEST HOME

Sr, Built Liverpool 1866. Lost near Aberdaron, February 1914. Voyage Par, Devon, to Ardrossan, cargo of 170 tons of clay at a freight of 8/6 per ton. Ma had to appear before the Club but was absolved from blame for the loss of the vessel.

? Sr, 100t, 80.2/20.8/10.7. Built Liverpool 1866 by Dawson, owned T. Thomas, reg. St. Ives ? Sr, 103t, 88.4/21.4/9.6. Built Lund, Tarleton, 1882, reg. Preston.

HEATHER BELL

K, or Dandy. Built Cardigan 1873.

*L.R. 1878/9:* Dandy, 58t, 68.4/17.9/7.6. Built Cardigan by Williams also (i) *Heather Bell,* Bk, 258t, 119/24/14.4. Built Bangor 1859 by Ellis, owned Davies & Co. (iii) *Heather Bell,* Sr, 61t, 72/9.5?/8.8. Built Barnstaple, Aberystwyth (1890), by Westacott, 1870, Barnstaple coaster.

HEBEY

K, Clinker built locally known as 'Rhibie'. Lost with all her small crew voyage Newport to P.M. with coal. The ma and two of his sons went down with her.

*P.P. 1886, LXIV, 432:* Sm, 21 years old, built Castletown, H. Jones, P.M., owner, cargo Powell's house coal, voyage Newport to P.M., not heard of since 15 Nov. 1881, 3 crew lost.

HEDESSA

Sr. Built Newquay, Cardiganshire, 1853. John Williams, ma of Borthygest, father of Mrs. Roberts, Tremydon. Sunk in collision off Ramsgate, all hands saved.

*L.R. 1859:* Sr, 93t. Built Newquay 1853, owned Lloyd & Co.
*L.R. 1884:* Sr, 93t, 64.8/18.6/10.8, owned T. Owen, Aberystwyth. T. Owen, ma.

HEIR OF BRYNKIR

Sr, 60t. Built Evan Evans of P.M. 1844. Lost Ipswich to Irvine, 1846.

HENRIETTA (1)

Bg, 178tn. Built Brixham 1869. Capt Morris Jones (Lombard St., P.M.) of the *Edward Windus,* owner and ma. During the Garibaldi rebellion in Italy in the 1860s Capt. Jones brought the son of the Bishop of Naples to Hull. There was a price on the fugitive's head. It is said that Capt. Jones was well remunerated for the service rendered. It could not have been in the *Henrietta* as she was not built until 1869 and the Garibaldi war was over by this time.

*L.R. 1871/2:* Bg, 191t, 103.4/23.7/12.9. Built Dewdney, Brixham, 1869, owed Beer & Co., Darmouth — Mediterranean trade.

HENRIETTA (2)

Fore and after, later a K, Jenkin Davies, ma.

HENRY JONES

Bk, 354tn, 102.1/24.2/17.3, launched 7.9.1850. Built Henry Jones at Canol y Clwt, P.M.: reg. at Carnarvon, No. 32 in 1850. Reg. owner, Henry Jones of P.M. 64/64ths shares. Henry Jones, ma. Re-reg. at Liverpool de novo No. 24 in 1851. Same particulars except for the addition of a poop deck. John Jones, ma. Owners:— William Imrie, Wm. John Tomlinson, merchants of Liverpool trading as Imrie & Tomlinson, joint owners, 64/64ths shares. On Dec. 9 1853 Imrie & Tomlinson sold the vessel 64/64ths shares to Edward Roberts of Liverpool, stevedore. On 14 March 1854 Ed. Roberts sold the vessel 64/64ths shares to Henry Jones. Vessel re reg. No. 654 in 1854 de novo at Liverpool. John Jones, ma. On 27 Feb, 1857 Henry Jones P.M. sold vessel to Meek + Powles, Liverpool, merchants. Vessel burnt off Pernambuco, 16 May, 1857, reg. closed June 1857.

HERBERT

Sr, 94tg, 76tn. Built Nevin, 1848, John Thomas, Borthygest, ma. Admitted to the Club February 1899. She was condemned and was allowed to fall to pieces at Station Bach, P.M.

> *L.R. 1904/5:* Sr, 94t, 67.1/18.6/10.6. Built Nevin, 1848, owned D. Morris & Co., P.M. W. Jones, ma.

HILDA

3mst, Sr, or 'Jack' Bkn. 185tg, 171tn, 100.5/24/12.8. Built P.M. 1877, by Griffith Williams. Owner, Lewis Hughes, tailor, P.M. 64 shares. H. Hughes ma. Vessel stranded on the Island of Buenaire and became a total loss — 2 May, 1883.

> Hugh Hughes, brother of H. Hughes, first ma, drowned at Tralee in the *Catherine Richards*. Lewis Hughes was grandfather of Capt. W. H. Hughes, D.S.C., and Capt. J. Hughes, Holyhead.

HONOUR

K. Ellis Evans, Penmorfa, ma.

HOPE (The Larger)

Bk, 287tn, 116/26.3/12.9. Built Quebec, 1865 by Labbie. Capt. J. Jenkins, ma. Timber carrier from Quebec to P.M. She used to arrive at P.M. with her deck cargo chained down round her hull. Capsized and lost off Newfoundland. Her crew drifted about on a raft for many days in stormy weather and were ultimately saved. Wm. Rees of P.M. was one of them. Robert Hughes, Borthygest was also on her at the time but was drowned, also Richard Jones, Borth.

*P.P. 1894, LXXVI:* 22 Aug. 1892, Bk, 27 years old, 9 crew, D. Jenkins, ma. J. Evans, Aberystwyth, owner. Sailed from Dalhouse, New Brunswick, for P.M. with timber cargo. Foundered with loss of 6 lives, about 60 miles SE of Cape Race, North Atlantic. Wind SSE force 12.

HOPE (Bach or the Smaller)

Sr, 55tn, 57.5/17.5/9.5. Built Prince Edward Island, 1821 Wm. Watkins, owner, ma. Lost with all hands in the Bristol Channel after leaving Milford Haven where she had been wind bound. The *Liza Hannah* and the *Resolute* which had left P.M. with her, were both lost in the same storm. Each of the 3 vessels' masters had one of their own sons on board at the time.

NMM Wreck List: Missing since 8.3.91. Reg. closed 17.4.91. *P.P. 1892, LXXI, 632:* Voyage P.M. to Cowes with slate, 4 crew lost, not heard of since being seen after leaving Milford on 8 March 1891. [27 small schooners lost in storms off West coast, Land's End, Milford, Longships during March 9-10 period.]

HOPEWELL

28t. Built P.M. 1828.

Sp. Built Henry Jones. Lost and Reg. 1858.

HUGH & ANN

Sr, 93tn, 72.7/21.6/10.6. Built P.M. 1860 by Owens, R. Evans ma.

HUGH ROBERTS

Bg, 194tg, 171tn, 104.7/23.6/13. Built P.M. 1875 by Williams, J. Jones, ma. H. Roberts, owner. Phosphate rock trader.

Built P.M. 1875 by John Owen. Lost off S. Ronaldsay, 29.9.1880. C.R.S.: Bg. 104.7/23.6/13, P.M. 1876 by John Owen & Co., P.M. Owners: Hugh Roberts, Newcastle-on-Tyne, Shipbroker, 36/64ths; John Jones, Edeyrn, Co. C'von, M.M., 28/64ths. John Jones, mortgage to North and South Wales, Bank, Liverpool, 19 Jan. 1876. Hugh Roberts, 29 Quayside, Newcastle-on-Tyne, appointed M.O. by John Jones, 10/1/76. Hugh Roberts subsequently sells 8/64ths shares on 9 May 1876 to joint owners, viz.: Maria Roberts, Edeyrn, widow; William Parry, Llaniestyn, Saddler; Griffith Roberts, 29 Quayside, Newcastle, Shipbroker. On 28 August 1877 also sells 8/64ths to David Davies, Dean Street, Newcastle-on-Tyne, Shipowner.

HUMILITY

Sr, 84t, 79tn, 62/19.9/10.5. Built P.M. 1839, David Richards, senior, of Trwyn Cae Iago, owner. Later J. Williams, ma. P. R. Daniels, owner.

Built P.M. by Evan Evans, 1839. Lost + Reg. on voyage P.M. to London, 8.4.1868.

*Hypsipyle:* Sr, 120t. Built P.M. 1857. Lost on passage Leghorn to Queenstown, 1857.

IDA

Bkn, 194.02tg, 178.71tn. 103.5/24.2/13.4. Built Borthygest 1877 by David Jones. Owners: Hugh Williams, P.M., M.M. 40/64ths. John Jones, P.M., M.M. 8/64ths. David Jones, P.M., Ship builder, 8/64ths. Stephen Davies, Liverpool Tea Merchant, 4/64ths. Harriet Edwards, Chester, spinster, 2/64ths. Dinah Roberts, Chester, widow, 2/64ths. Phosphate Rock Trader. Lost off the Smalls, Pembrokeshire in a calm, August 8, 1890. On one occasion she took a load of gunpowder from Hamburg to Alexandria with blocks of stone as ballast. On her return to Hamburg, two German merchants entered the hold to inspect the stones with a view to buying them. They were smoking cigars and apparently some of the gunpowder had been left loose amongst the blocks of stone with the result that a heavy explosion took place killing the two Germans on the spot. The mate, Griffith Edwards, was imprisoned for nine months for negligence.

IDA BAY

IDEA

K, later a Sr, 79tg. Built Bristol, 1847. Joseph Williams, Borthygest, owner and ma. Lost in ballast at Hells Mouth, 1905.

*L.R. 1871/2:* Sr, 87t, 61.1/15.9/10.0. Built Bristol, 1847. 36/64ths: Joseph Williams, M.O.; 28/64ths: John Williams, Post Office, Borth-y-gest, June 1903. Vessel lost Porth Neigwl, broken up where she lies.

*P.P. 1900, LXXVII, 750:* K. 4 crew, J. Williams, ma and owner. Voyage: P.M. to St. Helen's, Isle of Wight, with slates. Top lift of main boom carried away, 1 life lost, 10 miles S by W off Eddystone, wind SW force 7.

IDRIS

Sr. Built Aberdovey, 1860.

*L.R. 1852:* Sr, 75t. Built Prince Edward Island 1848 owned R. Carr, Beaumaris. R. Carr, ma.

ILLYRIA

Sr, 54t. Built Miramachi, 1848, Capt. Morris Jones, P.M., owner. Lost in 1856.

*L.R. 1852:* Sr, 75t. Built Prince Edward Island 1848 owned R. Carr, Beaumaris. R. Carr, ma.

INDEPENDENT (Sometimes referred to as the Independence)

Sr, 100t. Built 1849, Richard Humphreys, the father of 'Richard o Fadog', later owned her. Capt. Hugh Roberts, *Constance,* ma. Between 3 July, 1849 and 4 June 1851 she made 14 separate voyages from P.M. to Colchester, carrying about 94 tons of slates each voyage, from Greaves Wharf P.M. at a Freight of about 5/- per ton. She was then under the command of Capt. Hugh Roberts.

Captain Hugh Roberts was ma of the *Independent* before he took command of the *Constance.* (Information from Miss Evelyn Roberts, 1974).

INDEPENTA

57tr. Built New Brunswick, 1834. Owned by J. W. Greaves in 1841.

INDUSTRY (1)

Sr. Built Gloucester, 1867, William Evans, ma. Lost on P.M. Bar having drifted there from Abersoch loaded with slate.

*L.R. 1871/2:* Sr, 84t, 79/18.6/9.1. Built Gloucester by Davies. 1884/5 owned by J. Jones. S. Jones, ma.

INDUSTRY (II)

Sk, 44tg, John Watkins, S.H.

*L.R. 1846:* Sk, 48t. Built Barmouth 1841. Owned Williams, also ma, reg. at Barmouth. On census night, 1871, she was in P.M. harbour, and Robert Edwards, her ma. and John Edwards, mate, both of Barmouth, and William Roberts, ord. seaman, from Llanfrothen, were aboard.

INTEGRITY (I)

66t. Built P.M. 1836.

Sr, Built P.M. 1836 by Henry Jones, Lost off Arklow, 9.1.1849.
*L.R. 1846:* Sr. owned Griffiths & Co., Coaster.

INTEGRITY (II)

Sr. Built Newquay 1852.

IRISH MINSTREL

Bn, 154tg. Sold to someone at Runcorn. Now a Barge (1942).

Sr, 154t, 99.1/25/11.4. Built Dundalk, 1879 by Connick, bought by Ebenezer Griffiths, Efail Fawr, Amlwch, in 1899. Richard Griffiths, ma, cf. *Ships and Seamen of Anglesey,* pp. 494/5, + pl. 48.

ISABEL

*L.R.:* Bg, 186t, 103.4/23.8/12. Built Newquay, 1865, Davies, *or* 3mst, Sr, 161t, 99/21.5/11.6. Built Whitehaven, 1880. S.B. Co. B. Tupin, owner, Hamburg trade.

ISABELLA

(I) *? L.R. 1846:* Sr, 49t. Built Isle of Man 1838, owned Griffiths, reg. C'von.

(II) Sr, 119t. Built P.M. 1854, lost + reg. off Skerries 1877. Built for D. Richards by William Jones.

ISALLT (I)

3mst, Sr, 124tg. Built P.M. by D. Williams 1902. Admitted to the Club March 12, 1903 (New). Newfoundland trader. Lost in collision with *S.S. Atlantic,* 1908. Compensation received £2393.3.7.

Lost in collision off Lizard, 1908.

C.R.S.: 3mst. Sr, 124tg, 98.3tr, 91.7/22.6/10.4. Built David Williams, P.M., 1903. Owners: David Williams, 15 Madoc Street, P.M., Shipbuilder, 20/64ths; Robert Owen Williams, 16 Madoc Street, P.M., M.M., 16/64ths; Joseph Humphrey, Gwalia, Penrhyndeudraeth, Grocer, 8/64ths; Robert Roberts, Plas Weunydd, Blaenau Ffestiniog, Medical Doctor, 8/64ths; William Owen, Blaenau Ffestiniog, Quarry Manager, 4/64ths; Catherine A. Parry, Bank Place, P.M., widow, 4/64ths; William Morris Jones, P.M., Solicitor, 4/64ths. David Williams, designated M.O. 13 March 1903. On 25 March 1903, David Williams sold 4/64ths to Thomas Williams, 16 Madoc St., P.M., Engineer. Reg. closed 12 May 1908. Ship lost in collision off the Lizard on 25 April 1908. Certificate with vessel. Advice from M.O.

ISALLT (II)

3mst, Sr, 133tg. Built P.M. 1909 at a cost of £2527. Admitted to the Club April 6, 1909. Newfoundland trader. On a passage Newfoundland to Patras she had to jettison her cargo. In 1942 she was in South Ireland as a training ship. Lost off Wicklow, 1948.

Sold Boston, 1918. Lost off Wexford, Dec. 1947.
3mst, Sr, 132tg, 97tr, 94.3/23/10.6. Built David Williams, P.M., 1909. Owners: Robert Owen Williams, 18 Ralph Street, Borth-y-gest, P.M., M.M., 16/64ths; David Williams, 15 Madoc Street, P.M., Shipbuilder, 16/64ths; Joseph Humphreys, Gwalia, Penrhyndeudraeth, Tradesman, 8/64ths; Robert Roberts, Plas Weunydd, Blaenau Ffestiniog, Surgeon, 8/64ths; William Owen, Blaenau Ffestiniog, Quarry Manager, 8/64ths; William George, Garth Celyn, Criccieth, Solicitor, 4/64ths; William Morris Jones, Bank Place, P.M., Solicitor, 4/64ths; Catherine Parry, Bank Place, P.M., widow, 4/64ths; David Williams, designated M.O. advice under hand of R. G. Williams, 8 April 1909. Reg. transferred to port of Boston, 27 February 1918, vessel having being sold by P.M. owners to George Copland of Reykjavik Iceland, Fish Merchant, who in turn sold it to Sutcliffe & Co., 32 Market Place, Boston, Lincs., both transaction in 1918.

ITHAN

IVANHOE

Bk. 347tn. 130.7/36.8/16.3. Built Aberystwyth 1871 by Evans, Lewis ma. Timber Droger. She belonged to an Aberystwyth man.

IVOR

Sr. Built Newquay.

JAMES

Sk.

*L.R. 1880/1:* Sk, 35t, 53.5/16.5/7.3. Cardigan, 1864 by Williams.

JAMES BIBBY

3mst. Sr. 100tn. Ellis O. Roberts owner. Lost on voyage from P.M. to Copenhagen. Cargo of slates 219 tons 19 cwts, @ a freight of 10/- per ton. March 1910. Stranded near Mandal. Capt Evans, ma. All crew saved, cargo lost.

*L.R. 1904/5:* 3mst, Sr, 130t, 97.3/23/10.4. Built Glasson Dock 1892, by Nicholson & Marsh, E. O. Roberts owner, reg. Liverpool, J. E. Hansen, ma.

JAMES CONLEY

A wood-built paddle boat owned by the Portmadoc Steam Tug. Co. Built at Newcastle on Tyne. Her predecessor at Portmadoc was *Wave of Life* (*The 1st*). When the Cambrian Railway was being built across

Traeth Mawr, the *James Conley* was commissioned to fetch a locomotive from Aberdovey. The locomotive had been loaded on to a barge which the *James Conley* towed to Portmadoc. The locomotive was unloaded and wheeled along the streets from Pen Cei to the Railway Station. When the *Snowdon* was bought, Lewis Jones sailed the *James Conley* to Newcastle on Tyne where he left her and brought back the *Snowdon* via the Caledonian Canal. Robert Williams was the engineer, and Simeon Thomas the fireman (1884).

JANE (1)

Bn, 124½t, 66/21/12.3. Built Traeth Bach, 1813, No. 25 Beaumaris 1813. John Richards, ma, reg. de novo as a brig, 1825. Owners: John Richards, Llandecwyn, Mariner. William Turner, Parkia, Merchant. John Jones, Criccieth, Mariner. Ellis Roberts, Beddgelert, Mariner. Wm. Casson & Thos. Casson, Festiniog, Merchants. Hugh Jones, Dolgelly, Esq. Janet Jones, Llanfihangel. Robert Roberts, Jerusalem Coffee House, London, Labourer.

JANE (2)

Sr, 94tn, 71/17.3/10.2. Built Pwllheli 1827, Robert Jones. S.H., Hugh Hughes, (Father's brother) commanded her 1855-8. He also commanded the *Twelve Apostles* 1858-75.

Built Pwllheli 1827, by Thomas Griffith. Lost at sea 1898.

JANE & ALICE

Sr, 131tn, 82/23.1/11.3. Built P.M. 1868, by Williams. Morris Lloyd, Clog y Berth, owner. Lost 1892 off Tuskar.

Built Hugh Williams, P.M., 1868. Lost and Reg. off Dungaran, 20.2.1892.

JANE & ANN

Built Nefyn by Robt. Thomas.

*? L.R. 1871/2:* has *Jane and Catherine* Sr, 74t, 66.5/20.2/10.5. Built Nevin by Thomas, 1860, owned Griffiths & Co., Bangor coaster. *Jane & Mary* Sr, 139t. Built P.M. 1853, lost off Norway, 15.10.1854.

JANE ANWYL

Sr, 52tn, 66.6/17.6/7.3. Single top'sl. and flying gallans'l. Built Barmouth 1860 by Annwyl. Mr. Percival owner, Wm. Griffith, ma. [Capt. Wm. Griffith was drowned at P.M. harbour when he was mate of the *Desdemona.*] She carried a crew of 3, Capt. mate and an O.S. — Cook. On one occasion when in the Bristol Channel the mate was at the tiller and the O.S. who was only a boy of 18 was forehand. It became necessary to take in the flying gallans'l. The mate called for the ma to take the helm whilst he and the boy went aloft, but the ma who was enjoying his sleep told him to go to hell and take in the sail himself. This he had to do whilst the boy took the helm. She traded between P.M. and Portsmouth nearly all her fairly long life. The mate, Capt. Wms, Ralph St., Borthygest was a brother in law of the ma.

JANE & CATHERINE JAMES

JANE CATHERINE

Sr, 78tn. Built Borthygest 1845 by Robert Owen. Griffith Williams, ma. Lost + Reg. off Portland, 22.11.1872.

JANE ELLEN

76tn, 72.5/18.5/9.2. Built P.M. 1863 by Griffiths, W. Lloyd and others owners, J. Evans, ma. Lost with all hands in an explosion on the Thames. The ma had 3 sons on board at the time; only one of them was saved. 1887?

JANE HUGHES

Built Nevin, 1861. R. Owens owner.

(1) Built Portinllaen 1861 by Hugh Hughes. Lost + Reg. Loch Eribold, 18.3.1881.

(2) *L.R. 1871/2:* Sr, 63t, 62.7/18.0/9.2. Built P.M. 1855 owned Hughes, reg P.M., Bangor — Baltic trade. Lost + reg. s, Whitehaven to Cardiff, 1.6.1867.

JANE MORGANS

Built Aberystwyth 1858.

*L.R. 1871/2:* Sr, 73t, 67/19.2/9.5, owned Morgans, Aberystwyth, P.M. Coaster.

JANE OWEN

Built Pwllheli 1860.

*L.R. 1871/2:* Sr, 73t, 68.2/19.7/9.3. Built Pwllheli 1860 by Evans, owned E. Roberts, Barmouth. Lost Scilly Is. 3.3.1889.

JANE OWENS

Sr. Built at Aberdovey, 1858. Capt. Jenkins ma.

*L.R. 1871/2:* Sr, 96t, 78.6/20.2/10.5, owned Lewis & Co. Built Aberdovey. Aberystwyth coaster.

JANET

Sr, 120tn, 87/20/11. Built Pwllheli 1861 Capt. W. O. Morris, owner. Lost on Horn Reef, Denmark with all hands, voyage P.M. to Stettin with 218½ tons of slates at a freight of 11/- per ton, November 9, 1910. John Davies, the son of Jenkin Davies, was her ma at the time.

Built Griffith Jones, Pwllheli, 1861.

JANET & ALICE

Sr. Built Barmouth, 1856.

*L.R. 1871/2:* Sr, 96t, 73.6/20.5/11.3. Owned Lloyd & Co., P.M. — Baltic, R. Lloyd, ma.

*P.P. 1887, LXXIV:* 26 Nov. 1884, Sr, O. Jones, ma, D. Morris, P.M., owner, voyage Plymouth to P.M. in ballast. Foundered about 8 miles off Cardigan Lightship, Cardigan Bay, 2 lives lost, wind NW force 6.

JANNET & JANE

Sr, 81tn, 66/20.1/10.6. Built P.M. 1858, M. Evans ma. [Morris (fawr)] Very leaky.

Owned R. Pritchard & Co. R. Pritchard, ma, 1875/6.

*P.P. 1904, LXXXVI:* 18 December 1902, Sr, 44 years old, 4 crew, O. Evans ma, D. Jones P.M. owner, voyage Gravesend to Lancaster with whiting, no lives lost, stranded entrance to R. Lune, Lancs., in force 10 W wind.

JEANETTE EVANS

Sr. Built P.M. 1860 by Eben Roberts.

*L.R. 1875/6: Jennett Evans.* Sr, 97t, 74.2/20.6/10.6, owned Evans & Co., J. Evans, ma. 1875. Lost Cornwall, 3.5.1875.

JENNETTE

Sr, 117t. Built P.M. 1857. Wrecked mouth of R. Plate, 1858.

JENNY JONES

3mst, Sr, 151tg. Newfoundland Trader. Built Station Bach, 1893 by Eben Roberts for Capt. Salmon Jones, Abersoch. Dr. Lister, owner. I remember her launch very well. Evie Morris was mate on her on a voyage from Glasgow to St. Johns Newfoundland. After some days out at sea the cargo took fire and they failed to put it out. The Capt., Tom Ellis developed pleurisy and ordered Evie to put back with all speed. On the way back, Evie and two men went into the hold with wet sacks over their heads and located the fire; they then bored holes in the deck and poured in water and put the fire out. Arrived at Lamlash and resailed for St. Johns a few days later. Arrived at St. Johns and left for Oporto with fish — then home to P.M. in ballast. Voyage lasted 4 months. Capt Salmon Jones died at Rio Grande and was buried there. Capt. John James Jones commanded her for a time. Sold January 1915. Coal hulk at Gibralter 1917/18.

*C.R.S.:* Sr, 150.79t, 100.2/24.8/11.1. Built P.M. 1893 by John Roberts, P.M. Head or Stem: Woman bust. Owners: Joseph Herbert Lister, Barmouth, Shipowner, 64/64ths, M.O. 17 May 1893. (1) B. of S. dated 5 May 1899, 24/64ths to Thomas Ellis of Llanbedr, M.M.; (2) B. of S. dated 12 April 1904, 40/64ths to Thomas Ellis of Llanbedr, M.M., 12 April 1904. Thomas Ellis mortgage dated 8 April to secure £650 + interest @ 5% from Eliza Griffiths, 15 East Avenue, P.M., wife of John Griffith, Sailmaker. Owen Morris, 49 High St., P.M., designated S.H. under the hand of Thomas Ellis, 8 April 1904.

JENNY LIND

Bn, of Hull, 147t, 82/19.1/13.2? Built Yarmouth, 1850? John Jones, *Nathalia,* ma.

JIM

K. John Roberts, Borthygest, ma.

JOHN

K. Wm. Lewis ma.

JOHN & ANN

Sr. Built Aberystwyth, Isaac Jones, ma. Went ashore at Talcymerau, Pwllheli in the same gale as the *Wild Rose,* etc.

*L.R. 1871/2:* Sr, 47t, -/15.6/7.8. Aberystwyth 1821. Owners: Jones & Co. I. Jones, ma. Reg. Aberystwyth, surveyed P.M.

JOHN DAVIES

Sr. Built Nevin, 1867, Owen Jones, Graig y Don, ma. Lost off Cork.

*? L.R. 1871/2:* Sr, 89t, 71/20/10. Built Ellis, 1867, owned Davies & Co., reg. C'von.

JOHN ELLIS

Large Sr. with painted ports, 99tn, 79.7/21.5/10.9. Built P.M., 1856, John Ellis, Tregunter, owner.

Built Henry Jones? Lost 11.3.1884.

## JOHN EVANS

Large Sr, 133tg, 126tn, 85.6/22.9/11.6. Built P.M., 1873 by Williams. H. Jones, ma when new, then Wm. Evans, ma. Prichard Bros, S.H.

*P.P. 1898, LXXXIII:* 8 July 1896. Sr, 23 years old, 6 crew, W. Evans, P.M., owner. Voyage: Frederikshald, Norway, to Port Talbot, cargo granite blocks. Collided with *SS Bordeaux* of London, no lives lost. Wind W by N force 2, 8 miles SSW of Brighton, Sussex.

## JOHN LLEWELYN

3mst, Sr, Newfoundland trader. 170tg. Built P.M. 1904, Capt. Rhys Evan Davies, Borthygest, ma son of Rhys Davies, the Pilot. During January 1914 she sailed from Newfoundland with tub fish to Bahia. On her return passage from Bahia to Newfoundland in ballast she encountered a hurricane off Cape Race (the *Blanche Currey* went down in it) and was driven out into the Atlantic and suffered very heavy damage; so much so, that the ma decided to make for P.M. She reached St. Tudwals, Feb. 8, 1914, during a stormy night, and the P.M. tug boat towed her to P.M. where she discharged her ballast from Bahia on the Cei Ballast. This vessel was afterwards sold to Newfoundland and was the last of the Newfoundland fish carriers. She was wrecked on the coast of Labrador in 1928; she was then owned by Harvey & Co., Newfoundland.

## JOHN & MARGARET

Sr, 90tdw, 44tn, 59/17.5/8.2. Built Barnstaple, 1857, John Jones Ffridd Newydd, Morfa Bychan owner and ma. Coasting trader only, a very spick and span little craft. Between January 13, 1898 and December 11, 1902 she did 24 voyages from P.M. loaded with slates, always down to her Plimsoll line: 19 times to Cardiff, twice to Gloucester, twice to Newport and once to Bridgwater. Total tonnage of slates shipped by her from P.M. during the period 2,160 tons. She almost invariably returned to P.M. with either coal, timber, lime, or flour. She seldom returned in ballast and plied her trade in the hazardous Bristol Channel and Cardigan Bay winter and summer alike. She ultimately caught fire and was run ashore at Llanbedrog in 1912. Her remains were sold for £5 and her anchor and chain were brought to P.M. in the *Rebecca* from Pwllheli and sold by auction.

## JOHN & MARY

Built Nevin. Locally known as 'Bwgan Lleyn'. [trans. 'The Ghost of Lleyn'].

? Sr. Built John Thomas, Nefyn, 1831, lost 1841.

JOHN PIERCE

Sr. Built Aberayron, 1860. John Hughes, ma. Lost in the Mersey.

*L.R. 1875/6:* Sr. 97t, 77.1/20.4/10.5 built Aberaeron, Jones, 1860 owned Jones & Co.

*P.P. 1894, LXXVI:* 15 Feb. 1893, Sr, 33 years old, J. P. Morgan, ma, J. Hughes, P.M., owner. Voyage: Poole to Ellesmere Port with cargo of clay, 1 passenger. Stranded Zebra Flats, Queen's Channel, Liverpool Bay, no lives lost, wind W force 5.

JOHN PRITCHARD

3mst, Sr, 118tn. Built P.M. 1906 by David Williams. Wm. Watkin Roberts, ma (brother to 'Bob Three Janes'). Newfoundland Trader. Lost by enemy action off Patras March 1916.

*C.R.S.:* 3mst. Sr, 117tg, 95.7tr, 92.6/22.6/10.4. Built David Williams, P.M., 1906. Owners: William Watkin Roberts, 36 Madoc Street, P.M., M.M., 36/64ths; Laura Roberts, 36 Madoc Street, P.M., widow, 8/64ths; John Pritchard Roberts of Borth-y-gest, M.M., 16/64ths; Robert Prichard, 18 New Street, P.M., 4/64ths. R. Pritchard designated M.O. 6 April 1906. Reg. closed 27 April 1916. Vessel sunk in the Mediterranean by an Austrian Submarine. The Commander of the sub. took possession of the Certificate of Reg.

JOHN ROBERTS (I)

Bg, 221.77tg, 207.13tn, 105.6/25.3/13.8. Built Pwllheli 1875. (Tonnage altered to 196.95 in July 1893). Owners: Evan Thomas P.M. M.M. 24/64ths. Peter Jones Jr. P.M. M.M. (retired) 6/64ths. Richard Jones, P.M. Grocer, 8/64ths. Robert Roberts, P.M. Gentleman 4/64ths. Wm. William Morris, P.M. Shipper 2/64ths. Thos. Morris, superannuated Officer of Customs, Holyhead 4/64ths. Edward Morris, Holyhead, Farmer, 4/64ths. Hugh Hughes, Pwllheli, M.M. 4/64ths. Griffiths Williams, Llanberis, Merchant 4/64ths. John Parry Jones, Llanberis, Quarryman 2/64ths. Robert Jones Griffith, Llanberis, Grocer 2/64ths. Later Captain Davies, Rhoslan, ma and prior owner. Captain Morgan Jones, S.H. P.M. Phosphate Rock Trader, also traded in Brazil and the West Indies; went ashore on Marsden Beach, near S. Shields and abandoned 14 December, 1901, on voyage Laguira to Berwick on Tweed. Cargo 360 tons Phosphate Rock at a freight of 24/- per ton. She was later salved and reg. at South Shields in 1906. In 1907 she was wrecked in collision.

*P.P. 1903, LXII:* 14 Dec. 1901, 197t, 7 crew, D. W. Davies, ma, D. Jones, P.M., owner. Aruba, W. Indies, to Berwick, cargo of phosphate rock, 1 passenger, stranded, no lives lost. Wind ESE force 10, at Marsden, Co. Durham.

JOHN ROBERTS (II)

Sr, of P.M.

JOHN WILLIAM

Built Aberystwyth. Capt. John Jones, Borthygest, owner.

*L.R. 1875/6:* 77t, 62.5/19.6/9.4, Aberystwyth, 1862, Jones & Co. owners. J. Jones, ma, 1875.

JOHN & WILLIAM

18t. Built P.M. 1839.

Sw, 23t. Built P.M. 1839 Evan Evans. Condemned 1885.

JOHN WILLIAMS

Sr, 74tn, 59/17.6/10.1. Built P.M. 1848, Hugh Davies, S.H., John Thomas, ma.

Built Wm. Griffith, P.M., 1848. Lost 25.12.1895.

JOSEPH BRINDLEY

Sr, later re-named *Thomas Owen.* John Williams, Garth, P.M. Owner. John Williams, carpenter, rebuilt the *Thomas Owen.*

*L.R. 1884/5:* Thomas Owen Sr. 81t, 71.2/21.0/10.8, P.M. 1880, Williams owner J. Williams, G. Williams, ma.

JOSEPH NICHOLSON

Sr, with a poop. 99tg. Built Nevin 1868, Rees Davies, owner of Pen Cei; David Davies, Criccieth, ma, (the father of Rees Davies the plumber). Lost off St. Tudwals Island in collision with the *Walter Ulric.* The latter survived. See *Unicorn.*

*L.R. 1884/5:* Sr. 99t, 81/20.9/10.6. Nevin, 1868 by Thomas, D. Davies owner and ma.

J. W. GREAVES

Bg, 220.89t, 107.1/25.6/14. Built P.M. 1868 by David Richards. Owners: Humphrey Jones, David Richard, Senior, David Richards, Junior, Robert Prichard, Ty Gwyn y Gamlas, and others. Phosphate Rock Trader. Lost off Imbituba (North of Santos) 16 October, 1881.

KATE

Sr, 88tn. Built Quebec 1855, P. Parry owner. H. Jones ma then Evan Lewis, ma. Evan Lewis, Clog y Berth, became a well known carpenter at P.M.

KATIE

Sr, 3mst, 124tg. Built Appledore, 1903. Wm. Griffith, Llanbedr, ma. Newfoundland trader. Withdrew from the Club 13 March 1913.

*L.R. 1904/5:* 3mst, Sr, 124t, 91.6/22.2/10.5, Appledore, 1903 by R. Cock & Sons, owner W. D. Owen, W. Griffiths, ma, vide Basil Greenhill, *The Merchant Schooners,* vol. I, p. 81 et seq., for a description of the building of the *Katie* at Appledore in the Bell Yard by the Cock brothers.

*C.R.S.:* 3mst, Sr, 124tg, 98.7tr, 91.6/22.2/10.5. Built Appledore by Messrs. Cock and Sons, 1903. Owners: William Roberts of Tan y Gaer, Corwen, co. of Merioneth, Farmer, 8/64ths; William Davies Owen, P.M., Shipbroker, 4/64ths; William Griffith of Llanbedr, co. Merioneth, M.M., 52/64ths. W. D. Owen designated M.O. 1903. William Griffith's address in 1908 is given as 'now of Quay House, Appledore, in Co. of Devon'. Reg. closed 27 May 1914. Ship totally lost on 22 February 1914 in Mona Passage, West Indies. Certificate lost with vessel.

KENRICK [Sic.]

I. Built Amlwch. Lost off Newfoundland with all hands, Maurice Parry Borthygest ma.

*Cenric.* Built Amlwch 1905 by William Thomas, vide, *Ships & Seamen of Anglesey,* 315.

KETURAH

Bn, (A clipper) 141tn, 96/21.2/12.3. Built Bridport, 1855. J. Evans, owner and ma, 1878. John Griffiths of the *Pride of Wales* was once her ma.

*L.R. 1880:* Bn, 141t, 96/21.2/12.3 new keel + some repairs 1875: part new deck 1880, surveyed 1880 at Portmadoc. A1 for 8 yrs.

KILLA LASS [Sic.]

Bg, 185tn, 99.6/24/12.0. Built Aberdeen, 1860 by Jones Morgan Jones, owner, Humphrey Lloyd, Talsarnau, ma. Lost on Anholt Island, in the Baltic. In our time H. Lloyd commanded also the *Emily Dingle, Mary Classen, Sultana Reins* and the *Cuerero.*

*Killa Lass:* O. Humphreys, ma, 1875.

KITTY

3mst, Sr, 124tg, 97tn. Built P.M. 1902 by D. Williams. Pierce Owen Williams, ma. (Son of Joseph Williams, of the *Idea*). Newfoundland Trader. Lost off Frederickstadt, Norway, December 1906. In ballast. All hands saved except the ma.

*C.R.S.:* 3mst. Sr, 123.9tg, 97.9tr, 90.6/22.8/10.5. Owners: Joseph Williams, 18 Ralph Street, Borth-y-gest, P.M., Shipowner, 8/64ths; Joseph Roberts, 98 High Street, P.M., retired M.M., 8/64ths; Pierce Owen Williams, 18 Ralph Street, Borth-y-gest, P.M., M.M., 48/64ths. Reg. closed 29 Dec. 1906. Vessel struck a reef in the Christian Fiord on the 8 Dec. 1906 and afterwards foundered. Advice for Acting British Consul at Christiana.

*P.P. 1908 XCVI:* 8 Dec. 1906, *Kitty,* Sr, 98t, 6 crew, J. Thomas, ma, J. Williams, P.M., owner. Voyage: Copenhagen to Frederickstadt, Norway. 1 crew lost, wind SW force 4, stranded Proesten, Norway.

KOH-I-NOOR

Sr, 53tn. Built Aberdovey, 1853.

LADY AGNES

Sr, later a K., 91tr. Built 1877. She is the only vessel left in the Harbour at P.M. where she is moored at Rotten Tare, condemned (1944). She was later broken up at Station Bach.

*L.R. 1884/5:* Sr, 94t, 79.1/21.5/10.1. Built St. Agnes, 1877, Hitchins.

*C.R.S.:* K, 90tg, 70tr, 79.1/21.5/10.1. Built St. Agnes, Cornwall, 1877. Owners: Joseph Williams, Idea House, Borth-y-gest, M.M., 36/64ths; John Williams of Borth-y-gest, M.M., 28/64ths. Sold 1917 to Channel Shipping Co., Cardiff.

LADY NEAVE

Sr. Built Amlwch.

Sr, 89t, 87.3/21.0/9.7. Built Amlwch, 1876, by William Thomas, vide *Ships and Seamen of Anglesey,* 303-305.

LADY VAUGHAN

Bg, Humphrey Humphreys, ma and part owner of Llanfair Hill, Nr. Harlech. Reg at Beaumaris 1827. Her reg. particulars are as follows: *Lady Vaughan* of Barmouth built at Barmouth in 1826 under the certificate of Edward Humphreys, the builder, dated 13 February 1827, H. B. Hughes, Surveyor at Barmouth. One deck, 2 masts, 65.6/21.6/12. Square rigged standing bowsprit, square stern, carvel build, no galleries, no figurehead. Owners: Humphrey Humphreys 4/64ths; Edward Humphreys 60/64ths. Tonnage 125. She was later commanded by Capt. H. Roberts, the father of Capt. David Roberts who commanded the *S.S. Rebecca* of P.M.

*Lloyd's List* April 13, 1857. 8 April, Heligoland, The Lady of Vreuan (?Vaughan), Roberts with a cargo of slates from P.M. for Hamburg, is on shore on the Wester rock, off the island. Hopes are entertained, should the weather continue fine, of getting the vessel off next flood tide. *Lloyd's List* April 16: *Lady Vaughan* 'assisted off after throwing 12 to 16 tons of cargo overboard: she is tight and will proceed as soon as weather will permit'.

*Lloyd's List,* 28 Jan. 1863, Antwerp, 27 Jan. The *Lady Vaughan,* bg, Edwards, from Newcastle to Plymouth, with coal, was abandoned in a sinking state 21 Jan. about 21 miles off Ostend: crew saved by an Ostend fishing craft.

LADY VERE DE VERE

Bk, originally a ship, 900t.d.w. Built Nova Scotia. Prichard Bros. S.H. She never entered P.M. She was at Montevideo and Rangoon 1877. John Owen ma, father of Mr. H. J. Owen, County Clerk, Dolgellau.

*L.R. 1884/5:* Ship. 999t, 187.7/36.3/22.1. Built Nova Scotia, 1873 by Smith, T. Owen, ma.

LARA

Sr. Built Borthygest.

*L.R. 1871/2:* Sw, 106t, 66.4/16.6/10.7. Plymouth, 1844, E. Williams, owner, P.M. P.M. coaster, J. Roberts, ma.

LARK

Sk, John Richards, Penrhyn, ma.

LAURA

Sk, 47tg. 48.5/16.1/8.5. Built P.M. 1845 by Owen, W. Lloyd, owner in 1878. Lost in Fishguard Bay, 14 November, 1898. Passage P.M. to Cardiff. Cargo of slates, 71 tons, 5 cwts @ 6/- per ton.

Lost Goodwins, 13.11.1893?

LAURA GRIFFITH

Sr, 100tg, 95tn, 74/20.4/10.6. Built Pwllheli 1865 Edward Williams, S.H., Edward Hughes, ma. Lost in ballast off Pencilan Head, Pwllheli, December 1909.

LAURA JANE

The grandfather of Lewis Casson, the actor, was her ma.

LEADER

Sr, 124tn, 86.8/20.2/11.6. Built Plymouth 1852. T. Jones owner, R. Davies, ma.

LEANDER

Sr, 72tn. Built South Wales, 1859, owned in Aberystwyth. Richard Jones, ma.

LEONARD HOLLIS

Sr, 93tn, 71.1/20.5/10.9. Built Station Bach 1856 by Eben Roberts, Wm. Hughes, P.M. owner. Owen Morris and other owners. Lost on the North Rock near Belfast on her way to the Baltic, North about on her second day after leaving P.M.

Lost and Reg. 4.3.1885.

*P.P. 1887, LXXIC:* 3 March 1885, Sr, J. Jones, ma, D. Morris, P.M., owner, 5 crew. Voyage: P.M. to Kolding, Denmark, with slates. Stranded South Rock, Cloghy Bay, Co. Down. Wind SE force 6, no lives lost.

LERRIE

Sk.

LILLY

LINUS

Bkn, formerly a Bg, 198tg, 189tn, 105.6/22.7/13.5. Built Nevin 1857, David Morris, Cei, S.H., Capt. Evan Henry Williams, ma. Evan Henry Williams was preceeded in her command by his father, Henry Williams, who was drowned at Lisbon. One, if indeed, not *the* Clipper of P.M. In her day she went round the Horn to Chile, and the Lobos Islands, Equador, also round the Cape of Good Hope to Calcutta. Capt. Rd. Williams told me he was on the *Sidney Smith* making for Gibraltar, and, although they had not sighted a P.M. ship whilst crossing the Atlantic, 13 of them were making for Gibraltar together when the *Linus* appeared on the horizon one morning and sped through them all, and by dusk was out of sight ahead of them. On a voyage from S. Wales to Newfoundland, she had to put back and she arrived at P.M. and had lost nearly all her sails.

Sold Lerwick, 1901. Previous reg. 1857 Bn 183t, 105.6/22.7/13.5. Built Nevin, 1857 by Robert Thomas, Nevin. Reg. Closed 19 Aug. 1901, vessel brought to Port of Lerwick. Owner: David Morris, P.M., Ship chandler, 64/64ths. D. Morris of Brittania Terrace, P.M., designated M.O.

LIVELY

LIZA HANNAH

Ellis Humphries, ma, Borthygest. Lost in the same storm as the *Hope* and the *Resolute.* See under *Hope* (Bach).

*L.R. 1875/6: Eliza and Hannah,* Sr. 80t, 70/20/9.5, Newquay, 1858. W. Humphreys owner and ma, 1875. J. Humphreys, ma, 1884.

LIZA JONES [See under Eliza Jones.]

Lost off Lundy with all hands.

LIZZIE

Sr, 110tg. Built Salcombe, 1872, David Richards Joiner, S.H., Daniel Jones, Borthygest, ma. Lost at Aland in the Baltic, January 1913. Stranded and capsized.

LIZZIE JANE

73tn, Built Aberdovey 1869, Capt Hughes, ma. Commanded by Wm. Hughes, brother of Bob Hughes of the *Edward Seymour.*

*L.R. 1884/5:* Sr. 73t, 71.4/18.6/9.8. J. Hughes, ma and owner.

LORD PALMERSTON

Bg, 111tg. Built P.M. 1828 by Henry Jones, Cadwaladr Williams, ma brother of Bennet Williams, P.M. Her reg. tonnage varied in succeeding years. Lost with all hands off Oporto Bar, 1869. C.R.S.: Built at P.M. in 1828 according to the certificate of the builders, Henry Jones, dated 12/6/1828. First reg. at Beaumaris as No. 25 in 1828. Rigged 'SNOW' with standing bowsprit — later brig. Stern, Square, Build, carvel. Reg. tonnage 137t, 66.9/22.4/12. Reg. owners:— John Roberts, Ynyscynhaearn, M.M. 25/64ths, Griffith Griffiths, Caernarvon, Tanner, 2/64ths, Henry Jones, Ynyscynhaearn, shipbuilder 4/64ths (father of Wm. Jones, Yr Yard, Lime Place, P.M.), John Pugh, Penmorfa, Maltster 2/64ths, Wm. Williams, Penmorfa, Fuller 2/64ths, Hugh Evans, Beddgelert, Farmer 2/64ths, Cadwaladr Evans, Maentwrog, Merioneth, merchant 8/64ths, Wm. Evans, Llandecwyn, Merioneth, Farmer 2/64ths, Robert Roberts, Trawsfynydd, Gentleman 2/64ths, Richard Roberts, Trawsfynydd, Farmer 8/64ths, Sylvanus Jones, Trawsfynydd, Farmer 2/64ths, John Owen, Trawsfynydd, Farmer 2/64ths, Griffith Humphreys of the City of London 3/64ths. Mas: 1829 to 1832 John Roberts (No. 1 above); 1832 to 1840, John Evans of Caernarvon M.M., 1840 to 1863; Cadwaladr Wms., Merioneth (Pant Gweinog): 1865, with breaks in between, to 1866, Wm. Williams, who left her to command the Brig *Ardudwy* of P.M.; 1866 to 1869, John Harris. Reg. closed 18 Feb. 1869.

Vessel lost with all official papers and all hands, on Oporto Bar, 10 January, 1869. The share transactions in her ownership reveal some very interesting names of local people. At all times of her life the masters held a few shares, including also local tradespeople, e.g. Wm. Jones (Yr Yard) Ship chandler, and later sail maker, and Thos. Christian, sail maker. She was a fine old ship and was the 1st brig to be built at P.M. after it received its name under the P.M. Harbour Act of 1821.

> *Lloyd's List Jan. 11, 1869.* Oporto 10 Jan. The *Lord Palmerston* brig, Jones from Girgenti, sulphur laden has been wrecked on the Filgueitra (?) rock: crew saved.

LORNE

Sr, 74tn. Built Chester, 1871, John Hughes, Aberystwyth, ma.

LOUISA (BACH)

A very small Sr, 59tn, 53.5/17.0/9.4. Built P.M. 1849, Morris etc. owners. John Thomas, ma.

> Built William Griffiths, P.M., 1849. Lost and reg. off Bishops, 4.9.1895.

LOUISA MARE

LOVE

Sr, Wm. Wms. of Criccieth, ma. Reputed to be the 1st P.M. vessel to go to the Baltic, North about, i.e. round the North of Scotland.

> *L.R. 1855:* Sk. 30t. Built P.M. 1845, owned Williams, Williams, ma. Lost + Reg. off Fishguard, 12.5.1870.

LUCY (I)

K, 130 tdw, Hugh Williams, Borthygest, owner and ma. Sold and later lost off Milford.

LUCY (II)

Sr, Ellis Roberts, ma. (father of Ellis Owen Roberts and Tom Roberts, solicitor). In 1851 she sailed from Greaves Wharf, P.M. with 151½ tons of slates for Newcastle on Tyne. Capt. Ellis Roberts, ma. I believe she was wrecked on Ynys Cyngar, P.M.

> *L.R. 1855:* Sr, 94t. Built P.M. 1840, owned Roberts & Co. Wrecked P.M. 1867.

LUCY MARCH

Bkn, 260tg, 244tn, 118.0/26.6/14.1. Built Pwllheli 1876, Capt. Morgan Jones, S.H. Henry Thomas, Criccieth, owner. Phosphate Rock trader, also traded in the Brazils, West Indies and United Kingdom. Same type of vessel as the *Anna Braunsweig.*

Built David Williams, Pwllheli, 1876. Lost + Reg. off Amsterdam, 1.3.1893.

*P.P. 1894, LXXVI:* 1 March 1893, Bkn, 17 years old, 8 crew, R. Griffiths, ma. M. Jones, P.M., owner. Voyage: P.M. to Harburg with slates. Stranded Haak Sands, Holland, no lives last, wind S force 4.

LYNAS

Bkn?, Griffith Roberts, ma. She left Plymouth 3 days before one Xmas day and was never heard of again. This happened during the '60s.

LYRA

B 380t. Built Sunderland 1867, Henry Thomas, Madoc St., P.M. owner.

*L.R. 1875/6:* 380t, 140.8/27.2/16.7 Built Sunderland, 1867, owned Penney & Co., Shoreham.

MABEL

Bn, 140tn, 87.7/22.4/12.3. Built P.M. 1864 by Hugh Williams, G. Griffiths and others owners. Named after Ellen Mabel Williams Ellis. Driven ashore and became a wreck off Saffi, Morocco, 1892. Only part Cargo on board. Capt. Evan Evans of the *Rose of Torridge* was then her ma.

Lost 11.12.1889.

MAGDALEN ANN AND SOPHIA

*L.R. 1871:* Sr, 56t, 52.8/16.3/9.1. Built Newquay in 1841, owned Davies & Co., Newquay.

*P.P. 1886, LIX, 657:* 8 Sept. 1880, *Magdalen Ann and Sophia,* Sr, 39 years old, of P.M. Built Newquay. W. Williams, Borth, Cardiganshire, owner. Cargo 105t slate, P.M. to Shoreham, crew 3. Wind SSE, force 5, smooth sea, 12 miles SW by W of St. Ann's Head, St. George's Channel. Vessel sustained damage in Broad Sound and put into Milford. After being repaired, sailed again, but, off St. Ann's Head, she sprang a leak and as water gained on pumps and vessel was fast sinking, she was abandoned, (crew saved).

MAGIC

Sr, Robert Jones, Talarfor, was once her ma. Lost with all hands on the Goodwin Sands in a gale.

MAGNA CHARTA

Bg, 190t reg. Evan Hughes, (Alice Chimney) ma. 1865/70? Father was in her command in 1868.

Built P.M. 1865. Lost Bay of Biscay, 1873.

*L.R. 1871/2:* Bg, 190t, 163.2/23.7/13.4, P.M. 1865, Roberts, Hughes & Co., owners. G. Jones, ma.

MAID OF MEIRION

Sr, 62tn. Built Aberystwyth, 1859. Wm. Blake, ma. Wrecked on Bardsey Island.

*L.R. 1871/2:* 60t, 65.2/18.4/8.6, Aberystwyth, Jacobs, 1859, S. Lewis, owner, J. Owens, ma.

MAJESTIC

Bn, 131t, 83/22.2/12.1. Built P.M. 1861, Capt. Owen Lloyd ma, father of Capt. Owen Lloyd of the *Tyne*. In a picture of her dated 1863, she is described as a 'Brig Schooner'. Owners: Owen Lloyd, P.M., M.M. 32/64ths, Lewis Griffith, P.M., M.M. 4/64ths, Morris Owen, P.M., M.M. 4/64ths, John Ellis, P.M., M.M. 4/64ths, Wm. Williams Lloyd, P.M. Shopkeeper, 2/64ths, David Lloyd, P.M. Shopkeeper, 2/64ths, Wm. Jones, P.M. Lloyds Surveyor 4/64ths, John Henry Williams, P.M. Iron Founder, 4/64ths, John Parry, Tremadoc, Tanner, 4/64ths, Robert Lloyd, Talsarnau, Merioneth, Shopkeeper, 4/64ths. After leaving Ardrossan for Marseilles in Nov. 1868 she was not heard of again. Lost with all hands.

M. A. JAMES

3mst, Sr, 124tg. Built P.M. 1900. Newfoundland trader, John Morris, brother of Evie Morris saw her on the Clyde, August 1944, sailing with the Sinn Fein flag painted on her side. Tom Ellis, Harlech, was her last ma from P.M.

Sold at Plymouth, 1918.

*C.R.S.:* 3mst, Sr, 124tg, 96.7tr, 89.6/22.7/10.6. Built P.M. David Williams, 1900. Owners: Richard Jones, Borth-y-gest, P.M., M.M., retired, 32/64ths; John Jones, Borth-y-gest, M.M., 12/64ths; John James Jones, Borth-y-gest, M.M., 8/64ths; Ann Prydderch Owen, P.M., widow, 12/64ths. Ann Prydderch Owen sold her 12/64ths to Richard Jones Glanaber, Borth-y-gest, March 30, 1916. All sold their shares to D. P. Barrett of Baltic House, Mount Stuart Square, Cardiff, on 12 June 1917, who in turn sold to the Plymouth Co-operation Society, 15 Frankfort Street, Plymouth, on 26 April 1918. Reg. transferred to Plymouth, 17 June 1918.

MANOD

MARGARET

Bkn. Built West of England, Humphrey Lloyd, the son of Capt. Humphrey Lloyd, Clogwyn Melyn, Talsarnau, ma. Lost with all hands in the North Sea.

MARGARET AND ANN PRITCHARD

MARGARET AND JANE

Sr, Peter Jones, ma. On May 2, 1850, she sailed from Greaves Wharf P.M. to Gloucester with 73½ tons of slates.

*L.R. 1871/2:* Sk, 42t, Barmouth, 1839, by Thomas, owned Jones & Co., Barmouth, P.M. coaster, P. Jones, ma.

MARGARET AND MARTHA

*P.P. 1892, LXXI:* Sr, 66t, 44 years old, 2 crew, R. Griffiths, ma. Mrs. Griffiths, Rhiw, Nr. Pwllheli, owner. Voyage: Pwllheli to Llanelly with lead ore, 2 crew lost. Not heard of since sailing, 9 March 1891.

MARGARET & MARY

Sr, later re-named *Dora* 91tn, 78.8/20.2/10.7. Built Wales, 1859, Roland Williams, Llanystumdwy, ma. R. Jones + Co. owners. Ended her days as a hulk. She once took a load of the timbers of the *Herbert,* to Holyhead in tow.

*L.R. 1884:* Sr, 91t, 73.1/20.6/10.7. Built P.M. 1856, by Jones, owned R. Jones, R. Jones, ma.

MARGARET ELLEN

Sk? Built Cardigan, 1862. T. Davies owner and ma.

*L.R. 1871/2:* Sk, 27t, 50.1/16.0/6.2. Cardigan, 1862 by Williams, Davies & Co., Cardigan.

MARGARET JONES

Sr, 80tn, 62.3/17.6/10.3. Built P.M. 1854, Evan Rogers, owner, Morris Rogers, ma.

Built Simon Jones at P.M. 1854. Owned in 1888 by Evan Jones of Port Dinorwic. Foundered near Rhoscolyn Head, Anglesey, 8 Jan. 1896. Reg. lost.

MARGARET OWEN

Sr, 99tn, 74.7/20.6/10.8. Built P.M. 1861 by Roberts, H. Williams, ma. Owen + Co. owners.

Built Eben Roberts, 1861. Lost + reg. Ardglass, 3.3.1881.

MARGARET PUGH

Built at Pwllheli 1862.

Bkn, 693t. Built Pwllheli, 1862, by William Jones. Sold France 1878. Lost at sea, on fire, Feb. 1892.

*L.R. 1871/2:* Bk, 692t, 136/32/20, Pwllheli, 1862, owned Pugh & Co., R. Jones, ma.

MARIA JANE

Sr, 99tn, 78.2/21.2/10.7. Built Wales, 1857. G. Williams owner.

MARIANNE GREAVES

Bg, with a round stern and half poop. 201.72tg, 185tn, 105.8/25.1/13. Built P.M. 1877 by Simon Jones of P.M. Named after the wife of J. E. Greaves, Esq. Owners: Thos. Williams, (Rebecca) P.M. M.M. 40/64ths, Richard Williams, his son, M.M. 8/64ths, Robert Williams, Abererch, M.M. 8/64ths, Ed. Lloyd, Festiniog, Quarryman, 2/64ths, John G. Williams, Maentwrog, Quarryman, 6/64ths. The vessel sailed from the Clyde for St. Johns, Newfoundland, 13 Oct. 1890, and was not heard of again. Lost with all hands.

*P.P. 1892, LXXI, 632:* Glasgow to St. John's, Newfoundland, with coal, 8 crew lost. W. Williams, ma. Not heard of since sailing on 13 Oct. 1890.

MARIE AGATHE

3mst, Sr, or 'Jack Barquentine', 186tn. Built P.M. 1878 by John & Eben Roberts, at P.M. Foundered in the Bay of Biscay, when two years old Her crew were rescued by a passing sailing ship and landed in New Zealand.

*C.R.S.:* 3mst, Sr, 198t, 101/24.5/13.25. Built P.M. 1878 by John and Ebenezer Roberts, P.M. Head or stem, Demi woman figure. Vessel abandoned at sea on 8 Feb. 1883. Certificate of Reg. lost: Reg. closed 1883. Owners: Ebenezer Roberts, P.M., Shipbuilder, 28/64ths; Laura Roberts, P.M., spinster, 2/64ths; John Roberts, P.M., Shipbuilder, 28/64ths; Mary Roberts, P.M., widow, 6/64ths. John Roberts of Snowdon Street, P.M., appld. M.O. by Ebenezer Roberts, dated 9 July 1878. Heavily mortgaged to William Jones, of 2 Marine Terrace, P.M., sailmaker.

*P.P. 1886, LIX, 698:* 8 Feb. 1883. Sr, 199t. Built P.M., 5 years old, J. Roberts, P.M., owner, cargo of Patent fuel, railway iron, deals and dynamite (330t) Newport (Mon) to La Guyara, Brazil, crew of 7, wind SW 10, 44°N 11°W, North Atlantic. The vessel encountered very heavy weather, she became leaky, water gained on the pumps and she had to be abandoned. Cause apparently due to stress of weather.

MARIE KAESTNER

Sr, 96tn, 83.9/21.5/10.6. Built P.M. 1877 by Simon Jones, D. Morris, and other owners. R. Pritchard ma. Launched sideways at Rotten Tare; she was the 1st to be launched this way. Lost on voyage from Liverpool to P.M. with a cargo of wheat. All hands were lost. The ma and his wife and son were on board at the time.

Lost with all hands, Liverpool to P.M., 1878.

MARIE LOUISE

MARINER

MARION

Sr, 67tn, 61.1/17.0/9.5. Built Borthygest, 1853 by Wm. Griffith, Wm. Roberts, ma. Went ashore at Criccieth loaded with lime and became a wreck. Her ma wept at the sight of her being knocked to pieces by the storm.

Lost of Criccieth, 30.9.1885.

*L.R. 1871/2:* Owned Owen & Co., W. Owen, ma.

MARQUIS OF ANGLESEY

Sr, 74tn. Built Amlwch, 1826. Wrecked on the Isle of Skye.

Sp, 65t. Built Amlwch, 1827 by Nicholas Treweek.

MARTHA

Wm. Jones Yr Yard was associated with her.

*? L.R. 1990/1:* Bg, 226tn, 104/24.4/12.9. Built Prince Edward Island, 1867. Owned Jones and Griffiths, Aberdovey.

MARTHA GERTRUDE

Sk, Thos. Jones, Britannia Ma. Evan Jones ma later.

Sk, 53t. Built Wm. Griffith, P.M., 1851. Lost with all hands 12.10.1872.

## MARTHA JAMES

Sr, Capt. John Ellis, ma. On 29 March 1850 she sailed from Greaves Wharf, P.M., with 150¾t, of slates to Hamburg, freight 13/- a ton. Also in July 1850 to Newcastle on Tyne with 151 tons.

> Sr. Built P.M. 1847, by Wm. Griffith. Lost 30.11.1874.
> *L.R. 1871/2:* Sr, 99t, 64.5/19.0/10.5. Built P.M. 1847 owned Williams & Co., E. Williams, ma, P.M. — Baltic.

## MARTHA JANE

Sk. Built Aberayron, 1862.

## MARTHA PERCIVAL

Bkn, 268tg, 249tn, 120.1/26.3/14.5. Built P.M. 1877 by Eben Roberts, Eben Roberts, S.H., Edwards Williams, Gelli Grin, ma and later she was commanded by Capt. Evan Hughes, Borthygest. Phosphate Rock Trader. She also traded in the Brazils, West Indies and South Africa. Stranded on Sylt Island, Germany, and became a total loss April 1, 1901. Cargo of 451 tons, 11 cwt. of slates at a freight of 10/6 per ton. Capt. R. (Robin) Hughes, Criccieth told me of the following voyage he did on her as an A.B. in 1900. He joined her at London and sailed to St. Helena with Government Stores and then to Ascension Island with the remainder of the cargo. Ascension to Aruba in ballast, then to Hamburg with phosphate rock, then to Galway with rock salt. Galway to P.M. in ballast. The voyage was uneventful and took 10 months. Her crew were Capt. Evan Hughes, ma, Will Thomas, Clog y Berth, mate, Bosun, 3 A.B.s, 1 O.S., and a Cook. She was a fine vessel and faced stormy weather with great compsure. My Cousin, Morris Edwards, did the following voyage on her as an A.B.: joined her at Granton (Frith of Forth), Granton to Demerara with coal ballast to Curaco, phosphate rock to Memel, then oil to London where he left her about 1882. She also made several voyages to the nitrate ports of Chile and the Horn.

> *C.R.S.:* Owners when *Martha Percival,* Reg. 11/1877. Edward Jones, M.M., of Penrhyn, Co. Merioneth, 26/64ths; Ebenezer Roberts, Shipbuilder, P.M., 14/64ths; Thomas Jones, Shipper, P.M., 4/64ths; John Evans, Farmer, Llandecwyn, 4/64ths; Gwen Ellis, widow, Talsarnau, 4/64ths; Robert Roberts, Innkeeper, Penrhyn, 4/64ths; Morgan Jones, Farmer, Talsarnau, 4/64ths; Owen Emmanuel, Labourer, Penrhyndeudraeth, 2/64ths; John Roberts, Quarryman, Penrhyn, 2/64ths.
> *P.P. 1902, XCII, 753:* 1 April 1901, W. Jones, ma, J. Jones, P.M., owner, 8 crew, voyage P.M. to Harburg, slates. No lives lost. Wind force 2 SW, stranded Rantum, Sylt Island, Germany.

MARWOOD

Sr, 103tn. Built Newquay, 1860. Sr, later a K.
*L.R. 1871/2:* Sr, 95t, 75.1/20.6/10.7. Built Newquay 1860 by Evans. Owned Jones & Co., J. Jones, ma.

MARY

Sr, John Roberts, ma.
*L.R. 1871/2:* (i) Sr, 104t, 75.0/21.0/11.0. Built P.M. 1856 owned Owen & Co., P.M. — Baltic, J. Roberts, ma. Lost + Reg. off Swansea, 23.6.1870. (ii) Sr. Built P.M. 1861 by Eben Roberts. Lost + Reg. Ardglass, 3.3.1881.

MARY ANN

Sk. Built P.M. 1826, 15t.

MARY ANNIE

R.S. 3m. Sr. Built P.M. 1893 by David Jones, for Solomon Jones, Bryn Goleu, Abersoch, who later died in Brazil. Sunk by enemy action 1917.
3mst, Sr, 153t, 96.3/23.4/11.9. Built P.M. 1893 by David Jones. Owners: John Jones, Bryn Goleu, Llanengan, M.M., 36/64ths; M.O. Solomon Jones, Bryn Goleu, Llanengan, M.M., 16/64ths; John Owens, Sorten Villa, Llanengan, M.M., 12/64ths. Sold 1900 to William Williams, Mona Street, Amlwch, M.M., 16/64ths. Thomas & Sons, designated M.O. 25 May 1900. Lewis Thomas, Amlwch, Shipbuilder, 24/64ths; William Thomas, Amlwch, Shipbuilder, 24/64ths.

MARY BARROW

Sr, Wm. Barrow, ma, later harbour ma at P.M. Reported to have brought the gateway of Tremadoc Church from Italy to P.M.

MARY CASSON

Sr, 122tn. Built P.M. 1869 by Griffith, 87/5/22.4/11.5. Thos. Parry, Timber Merchant, S.H.

MARY CATHERINE

K. formerly a Sr. Built Amlwch 1857, 76tn.

MARY CLAASEN

Bg, later Bkn, 200tg, 182tn, 104.6/25.1/13.5. Built P.M. by Hugh Williams, 1876, Mrs. Jones, Garth Cottage, S.H. D. Evans, ma. Phosphate Rock Trader, foundered and abandoned in Atlantic 12 October, 1905. Voyage Aruba to Berwick upon Tweed. Cargo 340 tons of phosphate rock at a freight of 18/- per ton. Capt. Humphrey Lloyd was her ma at the time. The crew were saved.

*C.R.S.:* Built P.M. 1877 by John Jones. Owners: Owen Evans, M.M., P.M., 28/64ths; John Jones, P.M., Shipbuilder, 12/64ths; Robert Jones, Llanfihangel y Pennal, Farmer, 4/64ths; Margery Williams, widow, P.M., 4/64ths; Owen Williams, Timber Merchant, P.M., 4/64ths; Robert Williams, Engineer, 4/64ths; David Evans, Schoolmaster, The Gelligaer Endowed Grammar School, Glam., 4/64ths; G. H. Davies, Watchmaker, Dolgelley, 4/64ths; Richard Williams, Nailer, Penrhyn, Merioneth, 2/64ths; Samuel Griffith, Surgeon, P.M., 4/64ths; Robert Jones, M.M., Penrhyn, Merioneth, 2/64ths. John Jones of Garth Terrace, P.M., M.O., 17.1.77. Certificate cancelled + reg. closed 30 Dec. 1905. Vessel abandoned in Lat. 30° 57′N (or 32N) + Long. 40° 45′W (or 48 W) on 12 Oct. in a sinking condition and is believed to have foundered. Advice received through Custom House, Bristol.

## MARY EDWARD

## MARY & ELEANOR

Sr. Built Pwllheli, 194tg., Capt. Jones, Llangwnadl, ma. Isaac Morris, S.H. Lost Feb. 1903, Cargo 205 tons 12½ cwts of slates at a freight of 9/- per ton.

Sr, 108t, 82/21.6/10.8. Built Pwllheli by David Williams, 1874. *P.P. 1904, LXXXVI:* 2 Dec. 1902, Sr, 90t, 5 crew, R. Jones, ma, G. Pritchard, P.M., owner. Voyage: P.M. to Harburg with slates, stranded in E by S wind, force 10 Jade Pt, Germany, no lives lost.

## MARY & ELLEN

Sr, 96tg., Mrs. Rees Evans, S.H.

## MARY EVANS

Bk, 258t, 118.9/35.8/14.8. Built Aberystwyth 1867, David Richards (Senior) owner. One of her voyages was as follows: London to Cardiff in ballast. Coal to Pernambuco, then sugar to New York. General Cargo for Rosario in the River Plate. Then raw hides to Falmouth for orders, then to Liverpool. She went on fire and was declared a wreck off the Coast of Brazil. David Richards was then her ma. She was later saved. During the Zulu war she did the following voyage: London to Port Natal and Quelimaine, Portugese E. Africa, then to Pernambuco in ballast, then with sugar to Greenock, where she was sold to go to Rio de Janeiro as a coal hulk.

## MARY HILLS

Sr. Lost off Rotterdam. The *Annie* and the *Betsy* were lost in the same storm. On May 31, 1849, she sailed from Greaves Wharf, P.M. with 101½ tons of slates to Copenhagen at a freight of 15/6 per ton. Capt. Simeon Roberts, ma.

Sr, 84t, Henry Jones. Built P.M. 1840, Lost + Reg. Voyage: Hamburg to Caernarfon 3.12.1863.

## MARY HOLLAND

Sw, later a Bg, one deck. 223t. 85/22.7/14.4. Built P.M. 1843 by Henry Jones, on Canol y Clwt. 1st reg. Liverpool, No. 40 in 1843. Owners: John James Melhuish, James Wilson Jeffryes, John Meek and Henry Winch all of Liverpool. Henry Jones, P.M. and William Holland of London, merchant. Reg. anew No. 513 in 1854 at Liverpool. 264t, 118.7/23.2/15.2 Square Rig. Owners: James Baines and Thomas Miller (in equal half shares) of Liverpool. Reg. anew. No. 36 in 1857 at Glasgow. 330t, 123.1/25.9/15.2, Baines and Miller disposed of their interest by Bill of Sale to William Cruikshanks and John McKillop, both of Glasgow, who became joint owners and were her owners when the vessel was lost off the Bahamas, 18 Feb., 1858.

## MARY JANE

Sr. Built P.M. John Williams, ma, father of David Williams, Shipbuilder at P.M. On one occasion there were 16 P.M. vessels weather bound in St. Tudwals Roadstead during a great storm from the S.W. Owing to the stoutness of her chains she was the only one of them that rode the storm. All the others were either blown ashore or wrecked in the vicinity. The brig *Wild Rose* was one of them.

*Mary and Jane* Sr. 100t. Built P.M. 1854 by Morgan Jones. *L.R. 1884/5:* 88t, 67.3/18.9/10.5, owned J. Owen and J. Pierce, J. Owen, ma. Out of Reg. 1894.

## MARY JONES

Bg, 226.9tg, 214tr, 110.2/25.6/14.2. Built P.M. 1869 by Simon Jones. John Roberts, Penyllyn, Morfa Bychan, was her ma for some time. He was a nephew to Richard Jones, Garreg Wen, who had an interest in her. Owners: Peter Jones (Junior) P.M. Surveyor 32/64ths, Morgan Jones, P.M. M.M. 32/64ths. Stranded and lost off Yarmouth, 3 December, 1882.

*L.R. 1871/2:* P.M. — North American trade.

MARY LLOYD (I)

Sr, 63tn, 58.1/17.0/9.2. Built Borthygest, 1852 by Isaac Lloyd. Isaac Lloyd Morris, ma and owner. She sailed for 50 years without losing a single man. Wrecked in Sept. 1893 off Lands End. Isaac Lloyd Morris was the brother of Morris Owen Morris who used to engage Simon Jones to build ships for him at Borthygest.

Wrecked off St. Ives Head, 10.10.1893.

MARY LLOYD (II)

3mst, Sr, 172tg, 150tn, 100/25/11.6. Mean draft fully laden 12′ 6″ Freeboard 21½″. Launched broadside on at Rotten Tare. Figurehead bust of a female. Built P.M. 1894 by Griffith Wms. and his nephew David. Capt. R. A. Jones, Glanva, Criccieth, ma. Owners: Mrs. Mary Lloyd, Harlech. Newfoundland trader. She was off Cape Race when the Blanche Currie was lost. Sunk by enemy raiders off Bahia, Brazil, 1917.

*C.R.S.:* Sr, 172t, 101.8/23.5/12.3. Built P.M. 1894 by David Williams and Griffith Williams, P.M. Head or stem of female. Owners: Mary Lloyd, Llechwedd Ddu, Harlech, 64/64ths, wife of John Lloyd, M.O. (1) 24 March 1894 mortgage for £500 + interest on 20/64ths Griffith + David Williams, P.M., Shipbuilders. 16 Dec. 1896 Griffith Williams dies, certificate of burial 7 Dec. 1896. Mary Lloyd, 16/64ths Bill of Sale 1905 to Robert Arthur Jones of Harlech M.M. Transferred to Port of St. John's Newfoundland 28 Oct. 1916. Memo. 16.1.1919. from Rec. of Wreck, Liverpool, vessel destroyed by fire 3 Dec. 1918, South Atlantic.

MARY ORE

Sr, later a K. Built at Glasgow.

*Mary Ore, L.R. 1871/2:* Sr, 84t, 81.8/20.7/9.7. Built Glasgow, 1868 owned Smith & Co.

*L.R. 1880/1* owned J. Thomas + Co., O. Thomas, ma.

*L.R. 1904/5:* Still reg. at Glasgow but owned by Miss L. Parry, with J. Parry, ma.

MARY OWENS (I)

2mst, Sr, 128tn, 87.5/22.7/11.8. Built Pwllheli 1874. Sunk in collision off Beachy Head: all hands saved. A very fine Sr. My brother Tom sailed on her for some time.

*C.R.S.:* 2mst. Sr, 136t, 87.5/22.7/11.8. Built Pwllheli 1874 by Robert A. Prichard. Owner: John Owens, Llanengan, M.M., 64/64ths. David Morris, Britannia Terrace, P.M., appointed manager by John Owens, 22.11.75. Sunk by collision off Beachy Head 1 Aug. 1893.

MARY OWENS (II)

3mst, Sr, later re-named *Dorothy*. 136tg. Built P.M. about 1892. David Morris (Y Cei), S.H. Newfoundland trader. Dragged her anchors and was lost at Twillingate, Newfoundland, 12 October, 1912. Cargo of Fish (See *Dorothy*).

*C.R.S.:* Sr, 150.42t, 97/23.1/11.9. Built 1894 by David Jones, P.M. Figurehead of female. Owners: John Owens, Sorton Villa, Abersoch, Ret. M.M. 64/64ths, M.O. Owens dies 10 Sept. 1904 — shares passed to Mary Owens, M.O., Sorton Villa, widow. Mary Owens sold 64/64ths 1 Aug. 1905 to William Owen Morris of East Avenue, P.M., M.O. 1 Aug. 1905. Renamed *Dorothy,* 19.6.1906. Ship totally lost at Fogo, Newfoundland, 23 Oct. 1912. Reg. closed 27 Dec. 1912. Certificate with the vessel. Advice from R.S. St. John's, Newfoundland.

MARY WATKINS

Sr, later a Bn. 169tn, 91.0/23.3/12.7. Built at Nevin 1850, Capt. Watkins, Criccieth, ma.

Sr. Built Owen Jones, Nefyn, 1850. The Mary Watkins was lengthened from 73′ to 91′ in 1865. Lost Cape Calvoiero, 1888.

MARY AND ALICE

Sr, 84tn, 71.0/19.5/9.9. Built P.M. 1857, J. Hughes owner and ma.

Lost voyage P.M. to London 1868.

MARY AND JANE

Sr, 88tn, 67.3/18.9/10.5. Built P.M. 1854, E. Roberts, owner and ma.

Out of Reg. + converted into hulk 1894?

MAY QUEEN

Went ashore at Mochras and was brought to Borthygest for repairs.

MELA

Sr. Built Appledore, 1864.

*L.R. 1871/2:* Sr, 76.9/19.5/9.9. Built Appledore by Cock, 1864, owned Evans & Co., Newquay. Cardiff — Mediterranean trade.

MENAI PACKET

48t. Built P.M., 1838.

Sr, 64t. Built by Henry Jones, P.M. Lost + Reg. 10.2.1865.

MERCY

Sr, Owen Williams, Borthygest, ma.

MERIDIAN (I)

Sr, 93tn. Built Aberystwyth, 1858.
*L.R. 1871/2:* Sr, 92t, 83/20/10 Aberystwyth 1858, R. Francis owner and ma.

MERIDIAN (II)

Bg, or Bk. David Richards, ma. She was at Port Natal, South Africa, during the Zulu War, then to Quelimane, Portugese, East Africa, then Mozambique — Pernambuco — Queenstown, U.K.
Not a P.M. vessel.
*L.R. 1880/1:* Bk. 389t., 127.5/28.7/17.6. Built Sunderland 1866 by Pickersgill, owned J. Gibson, J. Smith, ma.

MERMAID

Sr, Built Pwllheli 1842.
88t, owner E. Jones.

MERVINIA

Sr, of Aberdovey, 1878.

MESSENGER

Sr, with a poop. 82tn. Built Aberystwyth, 1841? Capt. Williams, ma.
*C.R.S.:* Also *Messenger.* Sk, 28t, 43.5/14.8/7.3. Built Barmouth, 1841, owned in 1886 by Henry Parry, Bryn Chwilog, Aberdaron, M.M./Certif. cancelled and Reg. closed 4 Jan. 1907. Vessel converted into a dwelling at Abersoch. Advice from owner. Reg. no longer required.

MICHAEL KELLY

3mst, 1Sr, 142tg, 52tn, 112/20.1/9.9. Built Preston 1871. Ellis Owen Roberts, owner, David Roberts, ma. An old iron steam ship converted into a sailing vessel. vide *Immortal Sails,* 232-235.

MILO

Bn, 125tn, 87.5/20.4/10.5. Built Plymouth, 1861, Capt. Williams, Pentrefelin, ma. also Bob of the *Eagle Eyed.*

MINERVA

Newfoundland trader.
? Bgn. Built Borth-y-gest, 1866 + lost off Sicily, 1870.

MINNA ELKAN

Sr, 137tg. Built Beaumaris, David Griffith, S.H. Lost in the Elbe, March 1900, voyage Harburg to Ipswich with 230 tons of Oil Cake @ a freight of 9/- per ton. She ran into ice and sank.

*L.R. 1894/5:* 3mst, Sr, (ex *Planet*) 149t, 91/23.3/11.6. Built Nefyn, Owen, 1872 owned T. Griffith, O. Griffiths, ma. 1894.

MINNIE COLES

Sr, of Barmouth. 115tn, 80.6/21.0/11.1. Built 1867, R. Jones and others owners.

MISS BECK

Sr, 120tn, 82.4/22/11.5 Built in Wales, 1857, H. Roberts, owner. Lost at Porthdinllaen, 1881.

Built Nefyn, 1857 by Robert Thomas, Hulk Liverpool, 1914. also *Fanny Beck* Bn, 153t, Nefyn, 1864 by James Owen. Lost with all hands, Patagonia, Dec. 1879.

MISS HUGHES

Sr, Wm. Jones, ma.

*L.R. 1884/5:* Sr, 65t, 72/19.2/8.6. Built Caernarfon, 1884 by H. Hughes, H. Hughes & Co., owners, O. Owens, ma, 1888. Sold to Aberystwyth owners, 1898.

MISS HUNT

Sr, 88tn. Built Caernarvon, 1861.

*L.R. 1880/1:* Sr, 88t, 75.6/20.4/9.9. Built Caernarfon by Williams, 1861, owners in 1880 O. Roberts & Co., E. Evans, ma. Lost + Reg. off Hartland Point, 13.12.1907.

MISS MADDOCKS

Sm, 42t. Built P.M. 1843 by Henry Jones. Condemned, 1876.

MISS MORRIS

3mst, Sr, 156tn. Built P.M. 1896. W. O. Morris, East Ave., P.M., ma. Newfoundland Trader. Sunk in the Mediterranean off Spain by enemy action by U.35 (off Almeira) 1917.

*C.R.S.:* 3mst, Sr, 156.25t, 96.5/23.5/12.3. Built P.M. 1896 by David Jones, P.M. Owners: Thomas Jones, 33 Snowdon Street, P.M., M.M., 32/64ths; Jane Morris, Bank Place, P.M., spinster, 8/64ths; Catherine Morris, The Oakleys, spinster, 4/64ths; William Morris, Brittannia Terrace, P.M., Ship Chandler, 8/64ths; David Morris, The Oakleys, Slate Shipper, 8/64ths;

John Williams, 3 Marine Terrace, Slate Shipper, 4/64ths. John Williams, 3 Marine Terrace, designated M.O. advice under hand of Thomas Jones, of 33 Snowdon Street, Mg. 1896. John Williams, died 1899. David Morris, The Oakleys, designated. M.O. 1906 on death of Thomas Jones.

MISS THOMAS

Sr, 127tg. Built Nevin 1864, Evan Griffith, S.H. Penmorfa, John Jones, (Johnie star), ma for a time. 2mst single tops'l and a flying gallan'sl. Morocco Trader, also the Elbe and the Baltic. On one occasion she was driven ashore on the Skaw but managed to reach Landskrona (Sweden) where she had to be re keeled.

*L.R. 1871/2:* Sr, 127t, 80/21.5/11.8. Built Nefyn, 1864 by Robert Thomas, E. Jones, ma 1871.

*P.P. 1898, LXXXIII:* 3 Nov. 1896, 5 crew, J. R. Jones, P.M. owner, at anchors off Greenhithe, R. Thomas, in ballast, collided with steam tug *Wasp* of London, no lives lost, vessel lost + reg.

MIZPAH

Bn, 145tg, 142tn, 97.6/23/11.8. Built P.M., 1874 by Williams, R. Roberts, ma. E. Roberts and others owners.

*C.R.S.*: Bn. Lost 19 April 1878: Certificate of Reg. lost with vessel. *Owners*: Robert Roberts, M.M., 32/64ths; Evan Roberts, Retired, M.M., 20/64ths; Hugh Williams, Shipbuilder, 4/64ths; John Ellis, Retired, M.M., 4/64ths; Thomas Casson, Banker, 4/64ths. All of P.M. Thomas Casson 28 April 1875 transferred by bill of sale to Evan Roberts, 4/64ths. M.O. Evan Roberts, 13 Bank Place, P.M., appointed M.O. by John Ellis, 30.10.75.

M. LLOYD MORRIS

3mst, Sr, 166tg. Built P.M. 1899. Wm. Hughes, Morfa Bychan, ma. Newfoundland Trader. Lost off the Lizard with all hands. Wm. Hughes and his son were on board. See under *Venedocian.*

*C.R.S.:* 3mst, Sr, 165.97t, 101.0/23.0/12.3. Built P.M. 1899 by David Jones, P.M. Owners: John Etheridge Jones, Penmorfa, M.M., 32/64ths; David Morris, P.M., Slate Shipper, 16/64ths; William Morris, P.M., Ship Chandler, 12/64ths; Margaret Jones, Penbrynisaf, Talsarnau, wife of William Jones, Farmer, 4/64ths; David Morris, The Oakleys, P.M., app. M.O. 5 June 1899. Robert Prichard, of Ynysfan, New Street, P.M., designated M.O. 23 Jan. 1911. J. E. Jones, sells 16/64ths to Humphrey Ellis Williams, of Penmorfa, Caernarfonshire, M.M., 28 June 1911.

[Humphrey Ellis Williams was Capt. Etheridge Jones's nephew — information from Capt. G. Roberts, Borth-y-gest, who sailed as mate aboard her. Both H. E. Williams, the ma and G. Roberts, the mate left her shortly before she was sunk in 1917. Her ma on the last voyage was Capt. Wm. Hughes, Velog.] Reg. closed 26 Feb. 1917, vessel sunk off the Lizard on 17 Jan. 1917. Certificate with vessel.

MORNING STAR

Sr. Built Cardigan Bay. Two masted, double top sail, no gallan'sl. On one occasion on being driven into Falmouth in a storm found that 2 other P.M. vessels that left P.M. with her had gone down in the storm.

*L.R. 1904/5:* Sr. 11t, 79.1/21.1/11.1. Built 1877, Aberystwyth, by Jones, owned J. Thomas, reg. Aberystwyth, surveyed P.M. 1903.

MOUSE

K. Capt. Williams, Tremadoc, ma.

MY LADY

Sr, West of England built. Newfoundland trader.

*L.R. 1904/5:* Sr, 110t, 84.5/21.3/10.6. Built W. Date, Kingsbridge, 1889, owned J. Westcott. Reg. Plymouth.

MYSTERY

Sp. Massey Williams, ma, 1845.

*L.R. 1846:* Bg, 140t. Built Conway, 1843, Williams, owner, Capt. W. Williams ma. vide: *Ships and Seamen of Anglesey,* pp. 256-258.

NANHORON

Bn, 147tn, 92.6/22.7/12.2. Built Nevin, 1858. Capt. Hugh Williams, ma, and owner. Lost on Wangeroog near the Elbe January 1899. Voyage Hamburg to Londonderry, cargo 233 tons of salt at a freight of 10/3 per ton.

*P.P. 1901, LXVIII:* 13 Jan. 1899, Bn, 40 years old, 6 crew, H. Williams, P.M., ma and owner. Voyage Hamburg to Londonderry with cargo of manure and salt. Stranded Wangeroog Island, Germany, no lives lost, wind NW force 10.

NATHANIEL

Sr, 98-106t, 76/21/11.1. Built P.M. 1858 for John Jones, ma. and owner: T. Davies, ma. and owner, 1878. Sold for £1000 to pay, it is said, some of the expenses for divorcing his wife.

NETHERTON, Brigantine    Phosphate trader.
Built at Salcombe 1872
199 ~~202~~ tons Gross, 188 Net.    Sold to a German firm.
Capt. John Jones, Owner 103/-23/3,12/9
and Master.    Ref. 5 and 7.
In January 1898, on a voyage from Liverpool to PARA with coal she
was driven back from the Atlantic to Holyhead in distress. Ref. 5.

NEW BLESSING (1).

Built at Traeth Bach 1815.
John Roberts, master.
Length 59'0" Beam 20'0".
Reg. at Pwllheli.

NEW BLESSING (2). Brigantine later a schooner ~~Schooner~~.    Lost on the Goodwins in 1864. ?
John James, later the pilot
at Portmadoc, was her owner. but
when she was built she belonged to J. Watkins & others
with W. Watkins as her master
She was built at P.M. 1865 by Griffiths. 158 net. 93/9, 23/1, 12/7.

NEW DOVE. Ketch. formerly a schooner    Liverpool trader.
Built at Barmouth 1831
63 net 57/2, 19/2, 9/6.
Roberts & others owners. / Rhys Barrow Thorpe, a well known
tenor singer at Portmadoc, told me that his grandfather Rhys Barrow
of Barmouth was the owner & master of this vessel when she
was a fairly new vessel. W R. B. Thorpe's mother used to tell
him that Capt Rhys Barrow master of the "New Dove" brought
the Gothic Arch now at the entrance to Tremadoc Church
in the "New Dove" from Italy for Alexander Madocks' Exors:
who erected it where it now stands. — EH. August 1953

*A page from Emrys Hughes MS. XM/1559.*

NATURE

NESTA

Sr, 104tn, Prichard Bros. S.H., Capt. H. Williams, ma. Capt. Williams lost his life on her, fell overboard and was killed at Oporto. He had formerly commanded the *Linus.* Abandoned in the Atlantic in a sinking condition. Voyage Cadiz to Twillingate, Newfoundland Cargo, 151 tons of salt @ 8/- per ton.

> W.Sr. built 1878 by William Thomas, Amlwch, 88/21.3/10.8 & originally owned by S. R. Platt, Oldham, vide *Ships & Seamen of Anglesey,* 293.
>
> *P.P. 1905, LXXI:* 26 Oct. 1903, foundered in N. Atlantic, 49° 15′N, 30°W, wind WNW force 11.

NEPTUNE

Sr. An old tub.

NETHERTON

Bn, 188t, 103.0/23.3/12.9. Built Salcombe, 1872. Capt. John Jones, owner, and ma. Phosphate trader. In January 1898, on a voyage from Liverpool to Para with coal she was driven back from the Atlantic to Holyhead in distress. Sold to a German firm.

> Restored Portmadoc 1896 & owned in 1904/5 by J. W. Finch of Teignmouth.

NEW BLESSING (1)

59/20/-. Built Traeth Bach, 1815, John Roberts, ma. Reg at Pwllheli.

NEW BLESSING (2)

Bn, later a Sr, 158tn, 93.9/23.1/12.7. Built P.M. 1865, by Griffiths. John James, later the pilot at P.M., was her owner, but when she was built she belonged to J. Watkins and others, with W. Watkins as her ma. Lost on the Goodwins?

> In 1883 stranded on South Mull and salvaged by Capt. Macdonald, at Tobermory. Sold Liverpool, 1903.

NEW DOVE

K, formerly a Sr. 63tn, 57.2/19.2/9.6. Built Barmouth, 1831, Roberts and other owners. Liverpool trader. William Barrow Thorpe, a well known tenor singer at P.M., told me that his grandfather Rhys Barrow, of Barmouth was the owner and ma of this vessel when she was a fairly new vessel. W. B. Thorpes' mother used to tell him that Capt. Rhys Barrow ma of the *New Dove* brought the Gothic Arch now at the entrance to Tremadoc Church in the *New Dove* from Italy for Alexander Madocks' Exors. who erected it where it now stands. (E.H. August, 1953).

NEW LIBERTY

138t, 70.0, 22.0. Built Traeth Bach, 1810. John Prichard ma. Reg. at Beaumaris No. 22 in 1816 as a Sw, Richard and Robert Prichard owners. Sold to Limerick Nov. 1821. (The year *Gomer* was built).

*New Valiant* Sr, 74t, built Evan Evans, P.M., 1841. Capt. G. Griffiths, ma and owner. Lost on passage Londonderry to Liverpool.

NORINE

Bn, 188t, 104/24.8/12.9, round stern. Built Souris, Prince Edward Island, Gulf of St. Lawrence in 1875. Henry Jones, Tremadoc, Farmer, 64 shares. Vessel abandoned at sea 21st March, 1879. Capt. Robert Jones, Garth Terrace, P.M., ma. (Lloydie Jones' Grandfather). He later owned the Lime Kiln at Cefn Rodyn, P.M.

*C.R.S.:* Bn. Previous Reg. Charlotte Town. 199t, 104/24.8/12.9, Souris, P.E.I., by A. W. Owen, Charlotte Town, P.E.I. Owners: Henry Jones, Tremadoc, Farmer, 64/64ths who transferred by Bill of Sale Sept. 1876 to Richard Griffith Prichard, P.M., Commercial Traveller, 4/64ths; David Morris, P.M., Ship Chandler, 4/64ths; Robert Jones, P.M., M.M., 28/64ths. William Prichard, 3 Cornhill, P.M., M.O. Vessel abandoned at sea, 21 March 1879.

NORTH WALES

Bg, 1852.

*L.R. 1855:* Bg, 238t. Built P.M. 1852 by Henry Jones, R. Pritchard, ma, in South America trade, 1855.

NUGGET

Sr. 73t, 68.3/20.0/9.6, Built at Trwyn Cae Iago, 1865 by Owen. (At the end of Cei Cwmorthin, by David Richards (Senior)). J. Wms., owner, R. Jenkins, ma.

*L.R. 1871:* Built 1865 by Owen, Richards & Co., owners.

THE OAKLEYS

3mst, Sr, 147tg. Built at P.M. 1892 by David Jones, Prichard Bros S.H., Newfoundland trader. Her figure head was the coat of arms of the Oakley family. Lost in the Mediterranean on her 2nd voyage between Cephalonia and Patras. Capt. Griffith Evan Dedwith was her ma. She was wrecked on the Island of Zante, Greece, 1893.

*C.R.S.:* 104.5/23.8/12. Built P.M. by David Jones. Llewellyn Griffiths, P.M., Shipowner, 34/64ths; Griffith E. Dedwith, P.M., M.M., 22/64ths; Mary Lloyd Morris, P.M., wife, 4/64ths; Gwen Jones, Trawsfynydd, wife, 4/64ths. Llewelyn Griffiths, 1 Garth Terrace, P.M., M.O. Llewellyn Griffiths, mortgage dated 25

May 1892 on 34/64ths shares for £700 and interest at 5% from Morris Jones, P.M., Shipowner. Griffith E. Dedwith, mortgage dated 28 May 1892, on 22/64ths for £385 and interest at 5% from John Owen of P.M., Shipowner. Vessel stranded and became a total wreck at Cacava, Is. of Cephalonia, Greece, 7 Dec. 1894. Reg. closed 18 Dec. 1894.

OCEAN BELLE

Capt. R. Williams, Aberystwyth, ma.

*L.R. 1871:* Sw, 188t, 104/23/12.8. Built 1859 at Sunderland by Pile, owned James & Co., Aberystwyth, J. Williams, ma.

OCEAN CHILD

Bk, 300t, 120/29/12. Built in Nova Scotia, 1863. Capt. Edwards Morfa Bychan, ma John Henry Williams, owner. Timber Drogher. She used to carry timber to P.M. from Quebec. Her deck cargo used to be chained down round her hull. Her Capt. died at sea having drunk paraffin oil by mistake.

*L.R. 1871:* Built 1863 by McLennon, Nova Scotia. Owners: Williams & Co., M. Davis, ma.

OCEAN MONARCH

Sr, 61t. Built at P.M. 1851 by Simon Jones. David Morris of the *Pride of Wales,* ma and owner. He sold her in 1862 to his brother-in-law, Thos. Edwards, Penrhyn, who later sold her to Wm. Humphreys of P.M., 1867. On June 25, 1851, she sailed from Greaves Wharf, P.M. with 110 tons of slates. Destination not stated.

*L.R. 1871/2:* Sr, 60t, 54.1/16.7/9.1, owned Humphreys & Co., P.M. coaster, Wm. Humphreys, ma. Lost & Reg. 8.12.1872.

*Ocean Queen:* Sm, 21t, built Henry Jones, P.M., 1846. Lost & Reg. 9.10.1857.

OCEAN RANGER

268tn, 125/25.1/13.9. Built at Appledore, 1875, J. H. Hocken, owner in 1878, Capt. Davies, P.M., ma. Newfoundland and Brazil trader.

OCEAN WAVE

Sr, 157tn, 96.8/22.9/12.2. Built Milford, 1876. Capt. Meuric Ellis, ma and owner. Phosphate trader, foundered in Bay of Biscay with cargo of marble. Meuric Ellis Served at one time on the brig *Gomer.* Owen Griffith, son of Margaret Griffith, 'Gomer', when he was her ma died at Fishing Ships Harbour, Labrador, Capt. Tom Roberts of the *Dorothy* took a blue slate gravestone to place on his grave from P.M.

*L.R. 1890/1:* Sr, 167t, 96.8/22.7/12.2. Built by Howell at Milford, 1876. J. Davies, ma since 1889, owner M. Ellis, reg. Caernarfon.

*P.P. 1898, LXXXIII:* Sr, 157t, 6 crew, J. Jones, ma, M. Ellis, P.M., owner, voyage Huelva to Exmouth, sulphur ore, 6 lost. Not heard of since passing Sagres Point, Spain on 21 Feb. 1897.

OLEANDER

*P.P. 1886, LIX, 698:* 17 November 1880, *Oleander,* bq, 9 years old. Built Yarmouth, 1871, wood, 396t, G. Griffith, P.M., owner. Wheat cargo, 609t, (549t in bags, 60t in bulk). Valparaiso for Falmouth for orders, 11 crew. Wind SSE to SSW, force 9 heavy seas, 33°S, 76°W, South Pacific. *Oleander* was struck by a heavy sea which opened the lee waterways and side of deck to such an extent that water pumped down, and vessel filled and sank. Court of Inquiry found that vessel was fully laden, though not overladen, and justified master and crew in abandoning her.

OLGA ELKAN

Sr, 131tn, 90.6/22.5/11.9. Built 1877 by Roberts, D. Griffiths and others owners, T. Griffith, ma. Lost off Cuxhaven, 1882.

OLIVE

OLIVE BRANCH

Sr, E. Griffith, ma.

*L.R. 1890:* Sr, 118t, 85.4/21.7/11.5. Built Aberdovey by Richards, 1880. O. Williams, owner. E. Griffith, ma.

*Onyx:* Sm, 59t. Built Henry Jones, P.M., 1851. Lost off Cape Clear, Feb. 1861.

OSPREY

*C.R.S.:* 7/1878. Cr, 7t., 33.6/10/5. Built at P.M. 1878 by Robert Ellis, P.M. Owned by Richard Young of Borth, P.M., gentleman and a member of the Royal Wales Yacht Club, 64/64ths. Sold 1879 and again in 1885 to Jane Latchford Edwards, Hawarden Villa, South Town, Dartmouth. Reg. transferred to Dartmouth.

*Owen:* Sr, 114t. Built P.M. 1857 by ? Roberts. Lost 1859.

OWEN MORRIS

3mst. Sr, 167tg. Built at P.M. by David Jones, Owen Morris of *Albert Baltzer*, S.H. Newfoundland Trader. Lost on Black Rock, Criccieth, Dec. 1907, voyage Genoa to P.M. in ballast. She had done the passage in 21 days. Capt. David Roberts of the *Annie Lloyd* was then her ma.

*C.R.S.:* Built David Jones at P.M. in 1891, 102.2/23.9/12.1. Owners: Owen Morris, P.M., Shipowner, 16/64ths; Jane Morris, P.M., spinster, 16/64ths; Robert Pritchard, P.M., M.M., 16/64ths; David Morris, P.M., Slate Shipper, 12/64ths; John Williams, P.M., Clerk, 4/64ths; Owen Morris, 36 Madoc Street, P.M., designated M.O., 20/3/1891. John William dies intestate 25 July 1899, shares retained by Margaret Mary Williams, 3 Marine Terrace, P.M., widow. Reg. closed 16 Dec. 1907, vessel went ashore at Trip Point, close to Graig Ddu, Morfa Bychan, Tremadog Bay, and was dashed against the rocks, and smashed to pieces. Vessel wrecked on 8 Dec 1907, crew rescued by Criccieth lifeboat.

*P.P. 1909, LXXVIII:* 9 Dec. 1907, Naples to P.M. in ballast, stranded under cliffs at Craigddu, off P.M. Bar, six crew, no lives lost.

PALESTINE

Bg, 210.6t, 109.3/24.8/14.9. Built Portdinorwic, 1870. Reg at Carnarvon. Capt. Robert Williams, S.H. Phosphate trader. Lost off the Coast of Africa 5° South of the Equator, Voyage Manchester Ship Canal to Cape Town, Cargo 379 tons 5 cwts of coal @ a freight of 21/9 per ton, Oct. 27, 1892. It is said that rats bored holes in her causing her to 'spring a leak' and sink. Capt. Owen Parry of Criccieth and his wife were on board at the time. Owners Robert Williams, Llanbedr, M.M. 20/64ths, Jane Jones, Dolgelley, widow, 8/64ths, David Homfray, P.M., Gent. 8/64ths, Wm. Jones, Dolgelley, Gent. 8/64ths, Rd. Williams, Dolgelley, Merchant, 8/64ths, Griffith Davies, Dolgelley, Watchmaker, 4/64ths, Rowland Jones, Dolgelley, Merchant, 4/64ths, Griffith Griffiths, Dolgelley, M.M. 4/64ths.

All crew saved.

PATRA

Bg, later a Bkn, 184tn, 101.4/23.5/12.7. Built Brixham, 1864 by Dewdeny. David Richards (Harbour Ma), S.H.; Capt. David Richard Morgan, was her ma for a time. Phosphate trader. Collided with a light ship in the Elbe, April, 1886 but was not lost.

*C.R.S.:* Bought in 1899 by D. Richards, 48/64ths; Thomas Ellis, Harlech, 16/64ths in 1899. Reg. closed 2 May 1901, vessel transferred to Fowey. Sold to Joseph Grigg Coode, Jesby Cottage, Port Isaac, Cornwall.

PATRIOT

Sr, 137tn, 97.4/21.9/11.4. Built Trwyn Cae Iago near the end of Cei Cwmorthin by David Richards, senior, in 1859. W. Richards, ma.

Lost off Gibraltar, 1883.

PEARL

Sr, owned in Borthygest and lay rotting there for many years under Tai Pilots.

PETER VARKEVISSER

K, John Croker, owner. Lost in collision with *S.S. Boilian,* passage London to Cardiff cargo of 110 tons of cement at a freight of 5/- per ton. November 1897.

*C.R.S.:* K., Kingston upon Hull. Built in 1875 by W. and J. McCann, Kingston upon Hull. Hugh Jones, P.M., Blockmaker, 64/64ths, M.O., 12 Sept. 1895. Vessel sunk after collision off Beachy Head, Reg. lost with vessel Aug. 7, 1897. Reg. closed 8 July 1898.

PHANTOM

Bg, later Bkn, 249tn, 11.2/24.2/14.5. Built Salcombe 1867 by Evans, Capt. Hugh Parry, S.H., Capt. John Morris, ma. (R. H. Sladun original owner). Torpeodoed and sunk off Guernsey 1914/18 war. Griffith Roberts was then her ma. After being in the water for some time he was picked up by a British war vessel.

According to *C.R.S.*: Owned in 1888 by Hugh Parry, Shipowner, Borth, P.M., 16/64ths; David Morris, Shipowner, P.M., 16/64ths; William Morris, Ship Chandler, P.M., 16/64ths; John Owen Morris, Mariner, P.M., 16/64ths. Vessel sold to a subject of Argentine Republic, 12 June 1897.

PHYSICIAN

Sr, 2mst, 79tn, 79.2/20.6/10.7, single top sail and flying Gallans'l. Built Pwllheli, 1861 by Roberts, Capt. Jones, Chwilog, ma. She later belonged to Capt. John Williams, Borthygest, Hugh Williams of the *Lucy* was also once her mate. Lost in ballast in the North Sea. Sand from the ballast had choked the pumps. All hands saved.

*P.P. 1898, LXXXIII:* 19 June 1896, 36 years old, 5 crew, J. H. Williams, P.M., ma + owner, voyage Geestemunde to P.M. in ballast, foundered, no lives lost, about 80 miles E by N of Spurn Point, North Sea, wind ESE force 9.

PICTON

Sr, 111t, 81.5/21.4/11.9. Built Trwyn Cae Iago at the end of Cei Cwmorthin P.M. 1858 by David Richards, Senior. David Richards, S.H. Lost off the coast of Norway, 1900. Capt. Hansen was then her ma. A pretty vessel.

*P.P. 1901, LXVIII, 651:* Sr, J. A. Hansen, ma, owned D. Richards, P.M., voyage Shoreham to London with carbolic acid, stranded Shingles Sand, Thames Estuary. No lives lost, wind SW force 8.

PIKE

? *Pilgrim* (*I*) Sr, 131t. Built Richards, P.M., 1861.
? Lost & Reg. off Algeria 11.8.1884.

PILGRIM (II)

Sr, 159tg, 92.4/23.4/12.4. Built Trwyn Cae Iago, end of Cei Cwmorthin, P.M. 1866 by David Richards, Senior. Evan Pugh, ma. Lost with all hands off the Isle of Wight about 1900. On a previous occasion she collided with the ship *Braekka* and cost the Club £1235.16.10.

PIONEER

K. Built Milford.

PLANET

Sr. Built Trwyn Cae Iago, at the end of Cei Cwmorthin, P.M. by David Richards, Senior, John Roberts, ma.

PLANET

Bn, 134t. Built Pwllheli 1860 by Roberts.

*L.R. 1871:* Bn, 134t, 81.7/21.7/12.2, owned Hughes & Co., Pwllheli, J. Roberts, ma. P.M. — Bremen trade. Lost & Reg. off Llandudno, 7.11.1890.

PLANET

Sr, 138tn. Built Nevin, 1872.

Later named changed to *Minna Elkan.* Lost & Reg. R. Elbe, 15.12.1899.

PLEIDES (? Pleiades)

Sr, 149tn. Built Aberayron, 1866.

*L.R. 1871:* Sr, 149t, 97.1/21.7/12.5. Built Jones, Aberaeron, 1866, owned Rees & Co., D. Rees, ma.

PLINLIMMON

Small steam ship trading in Cardigan Bay and Liverpool, a frequent caller at P.M.

PLUVIER

Sr. Built Fowey. Ebenezer Parry, son of Capt. Hugh Parry, ma. Lost in ballast off Queenstown with all hands, passage Figueira, Portugal to P.M. The *Snaefell* was out in the same storm, and the *C. E. Spooner.* Two of her crew had clambered on to a ledge of rock with no means of getting at them. They were ultimately washed away and drowned. She was a very good looking vessel.

*L.R. 1894/5:* Sr, 120t, 89.8/22.1/10.7. Built Plymouth, 1889, by W. S. Kelly, owner T. Davies, G. Prichard mgr. T. Davies, ma. 1893 surveyed P.M. Mrs. Gwen Jones of P.M. daughter of the mate, Francis Henry Jones, has recalled that she was five years old when the *Pluvier* was lost on New Year's Eve 1905/6 off Cork, and remembers that three experienced seamen from P.M. went to investigate the state of the wreck which could be reached at low water. Robert Parry, the ma's brother (later Capt. Parry, of Garston Docks), R. Roberts, his brother-in-law, and R. Jones found that the vessel had been stripped bare by the time they arrived, and everything of any value stolen. [Information from Miss Evelyn Roberts, P.M.].

POLLY PRESTON

Sr, 131tn, 89.6/22.6/11.7. Built Nevin, 1863 by Thomas. Lost with all hands in the North Sea. David Nicholas was then her ma.

Lost Bremerhaven to Scotland? 2.9.1903.

PRICILLA

Sr.

*? Priscilla L.R. 1884/5:* Sr, 110t, 81/22.4/10.9. Built Sunderland, 1871 owned W. Vickers, Chester, J. Vickers, ma.

PRIDE OF WALES

Bk, 299tg, 288tn, 125.3/26.5/14.6. Built Borthygest, 1870 (1869 L.R.), by Simon Jones. Capt. David Morris, (My grandfather) ma, and owner. For her story see *Through Mighty Seas* and *Immortal Sails* by my brother, Col. Henry Hughes. She traded between Rangoon and Ceylon and Sourabaya and was also a Phosphate trader. Abandoned in the Atlantic in a sinking condition. When at Santos in 1876, Thos. Edwards her mate died. Evan Pugh was then her ma, Grandfather having retired 1876. Morris Edwards son of Thos. Edwards was then 9yrs old.

*P.P. 1894, LXXVI:* 5 Jan. 1893, Bk, 23 years old, 9 crew, J. Griffiths, ma, D. Morris, P.M., owner, voyage Monte Cuyo, Mexico, for Fleetwood with logwood. Foundered 40° 40′N, 37° 20′W, North Atlantic, no lives lost, wind SE force 12. Cargo of about 350 tons logwood, but no deck load. Abandoned leaky and unmanageable after encountering a hurricane and losing bowsprit, starboard bulwarks, and rudder, and having two of the main deck beams broken, hatch coamings started, etc.

PRINCE LLEWELYN

Sr. Built P.M.? Lost off Norway, 1903.

*L.R. 1871/2:* Owned E. Williams, R. Prichard, ma.

*L.R. 1894:* Sr. 111t, 78.3/21.3/11.3. Built Caernarfon 1860 by Barlow, E. Roberts, owner and ma, reg. Caernarfon.

*P.P. LXXI:* 21 Aug. 1903: Prince Llewelyn (43 years old) of P.M., E. Roberts, Borth-y-gest, owner and ma, foundered. Voyage: Aarhus to Fredrikstad, in ballast, no lives lost, NW, force 12. Stromstad, Sweden.

PRINCE OF WALES

Sr. Lewis Roberts, Borthygest, ma owner.

PRINCESS

*L.R. 1878/9:* BKn, 223t, 115/25.2/12.5, P.E. Island, 1872. Owned G. Williams & Co. Reg. Caernarfon, G. Owens, ma.

PRINCESS ROYAL

Sr, 96tn, 74.1/20.3/10.6. Built Barmouth, 1858, Prichard Bros. owners.

*L.R. 1871/2:* J. Owens, ma.

PRINCESS OF WALES

Bn, 163.8tr, 91.5/22.8/13. Built P.M. 1863 by Hugh Williams, Thomas Jones, Brittania, ma. Owners: Henry Jones, P.M., M.M. 16/64ths, Griffith Griffiths, P.M., M.M. 24/64ths, Hugh Williams, P.M. Ship Builder 4/64ths, Hugh Williams, P.M. Iron Founder 4/64ths, Owen Williams, P.M. Clerk 4/64ths, Catherine Griffith, Tremadoc, widow 4/64ths, John George Johnson and Charles Lathy Limpricht, Newcastle on Tyne, jointly 4/64ths. Vessel stranded and lost at Varde, Denmark, 19 Dec., 1884.

*P.P. 1887, LXXIV:* 10 Dec. 1884, Bg, 164t, 6 crew, G. Jones, ma, D. Griffith, P.M., owner. Voyage: Fredrikstad to Newry with boards. Abandoned 20 miles E of the Leman and Owers, North Sea, no lives lost, wind SW force 9

PROSPECT

PROSPERITY

Sp/Sm, 41tn, 53.5/18.0/8.3. Built P.M., 1850, for Jones & Co. Wrecked Llanddwyn, 1845.

Wrecked off St. Tudwal's 1874.

*C.R.S.:* Re-registered 6/1878, rebuilt Caernarfon by Hugh Hughes, Ship Builder, 1878. Re-registered and rebuilt anew, 4/1904 Hugh Jones, Ship Builder, Caernarfon.

PROVIDENCE

80t, 53.0/19.0. Built Traeth Bach, 1783, Richard Roberts, ma. Reg. at Caernarvon.

PWLLHELI PACKET

20tr. Built P.M. In May 28, 1850 she sailed from Greaves Wharf P.M. for Cardiff with 35 tons of slates at a freight of 5/- per ton. Capt. Morris Williams, ma.

Built P.M. 1830 by Evan Evans. Wrecked Caernarfon Bar, 30.9.1873.

QUARRYMAN

Sr, 104tg, 99tn. Built Pwllheli, 1840, Capt. Hugh Parry owner, Wm. Williams, ma. Lost with all hands off Lands End.

*L.R. 1884/5:* 99t, 73.8/20.7/10.9, R. Williams & Co., owners. E. Williams, ma, reg. Caernarfon. Lost on voyage Falmouth to Cork, 15.11.1893.

QUEEN

Bg, Built at Canol y Clwt, P.M., 1859 by Harry Jones, (Cei Greaves) Owen Jones, Britannia, ma. Traded in the Brazils and the West Indies.

Bg, 162t, 91/23/12.7. Built P.M. 1859 by Henry Jones, O. Jones, ma. Lost Cattegat, Sept. 1875.

QUEEN EMMA

Bg, with a round stern. 193tn, 103/23.5/12.9. Built at Quebec, 1866. Capt. Evan Rogers, owner, Roberts & Griffiths P.M. owned her in 1878. Phosphate rock trader. Later a timber drogher from the Baltic. Sunk in the North Sea near the Straits of Dover after being in collision with a Cross Channel steamer.

QUEEN OF THE WEST

Sr. ? of Milford. Built at Salcombe, 1849, John Crocker, ma.

*L.R. 1878:* Sr, 119t, 82.6/18.6/12.1. Built Salcombe, 1849.

QUEEN VICTORIA

Timber Drogher, Capt. Wheeler, ma.

REBECCA (I)

Sr, formerly a Bn, 104tg, 99tn, 78.0/20.4/11.2. Built Prince Ed. Island, E. Jones, owner and ma.

Built P.E. Island 1859 by Orr. R. Thomas ma in 1880.

REBECCA (II)

174tg, 138tn, 136.2/19.1/10.4. A small steamship with a cut water bow, built in 1859 at Greenock. 40h.p. First came to P.M. in 1864. Her 1st ma was Capt. Thomas Williams. Traded in General merchandise twice a week between P.M., Pwllheli, and Liverpool. Capt. David Roberts, ma, from Dec. 1885. In 1895 a vessel named *Krageroe* went aground on St. Patricks Causeway, off Harlech. *Rebecca* went to her rescue and in doing so went so close that her propeller was fouled in a submerged wreck and was damaged. A claim for salvage and damage was made by her owners for the amount of £300, but only £75 was awarded. In 1896 having become unequal to her job and uneconomic to run, she was sold for £1,000, and was replaced in the same year by a new vessel of the same name.

REBECCA (III)

A small steamship built in 1895/6 by Messrs. Ross & Duncan of Glasgow at a cost of £6,000 to replace the above and carry on the same trade. She was sold in 1917 by her owners for £9,200. The owner of the above two Steamships was the Caernarvonshire & Merionethshire Steam Ship Co. Ltd. First formed in 1864. The following were the first directors of the company: Samuel Holland, Esq., Glanwilliam, Maentwrog (Chairman), David Homfray, Esq., P.M., Mr. David Roberts, Grocer, P.M., Mr. Wm. Lloyd, Draper, P.M., Mr. Wm. Jones, Tallow Chandler, P.M., Mr. J. H. Williams, Iron Founder, P.M., Mr. Evan Richard, Draper, Ffestiniog, Mr. Wm. Davies, Merchant, Ffestiniog. R. M. Greaves, Esq., of Wern, Tremadoc, was later chairman of the Company and my Grandfather, Capt. David Morris of Garth was a prominent member of the board for many years. A dividend of 10% was paid at the end of the 1st year of the Company's career. The Company was wound up voluntarily in February 1917 after a useful and successful life of 53 years.

*C.R.S.:* 3mst. Sr, Screw Steam Ship. Clench/Clinker build. 140.3/23.1/11.0. Built Paisley, 1895 by J. Fullerton & Co., Paisley. Engine Room Length 33.3. Caernarfonshire Steam Ship Co. Ltd., Cornhill, P.M., 64 shares. William Prichard of Cornhill, P.M., Mortgage on behalf of owners. Reg. transferred to Port of Belfast 3 Feb. 1917.

RED JACKET

*L.R. 1871:* Sr, 131t, 88/20/12. Built Brixham, 1857.

REGISTER

She was at Monte Video in 1876.

RESOLUTE

Sr, 67tn, 56.3/16.4/9.5. Built Wales, 1850, D. Jones, ma. Belonged to Aberystwyth. Lost off Lands End with all hands. The ma and his son were on board. See *Hope.*

REVIVAL

Sr, 96tn. Built Wales, 1860 by Hughes, H. Roberts owner.

*L.R. 1871:* Sr, 96t, 76.4/21.6/10.4. Bangor coaster.

RESOLVEN

Bg, 143tn. Built Prince Edward Island, 1872, John James, ma.

*L.R. 1878/9:* Bg. 143t, 96.3/23.6/11.0, owned Mrs. J. Griffiths, Aberystwyth.

RHEIDIOL VALE

Sr, 90tn, 77.6/19.6/10.2. Built Aberystwyth, 1859, D. Thomas, owner.

RICHARD GREAVES

Sr. 118tg. Built P.M. 1885 by David Jones. Capt. Richard Davies, ma. J. K. McKerrow, S.H. Newfoundland trader. She once sailed the passage from Naples to Plymouth in 12 days. Sold to Newfoundland and was lost in the Atlantic on a passage from Cadiz to Newfoundland with a cargo of salt. In a lawsuit at Newfoundland she was landed with very heavy legal costs — so much so that she had to be sold there. Messrs. Ryan Bros., of Trinity Newfoundland, bought her and were her owners when she was abandoned in the Atlantic in a sinking condition. A grand little ship.

*C.R.S.:* 86/22.8/11.2. Built P.M., by David Jones, P.M., Head or Stem: Bust. Owners: Margaret Lloyd, wife of John Lloyd, Shipbuilder, P.M., 16/64ths; Catherine Edwards, Pwllheli, widow, 4/64ths; John Davies, Borth, P.M., M.M., 24/64ths; John Ellis, P.M., Ret. M.M., 4/64ths; J. K. McKernow, Tremadog, Draper, 16/64ths. Henry Arthur Thomas of the Wharf, P.M., appt. M.O. by John Davies, John Ellis and Margaret Lloyd, June 1885. Sold 1907, Newfoundland. Wrecked 1908.

RICHARD OWEN

Bg, 183.9tk., 169.6tr, 99.5/25.2/12.8. Built Pwllheli, 1875, David Roberts of the *Rebecca,* owner. Phosphate trader and Newfoundland trader. Lost in collision off the coast of Newfoundland 24 July, 1884. The mate and Capt. were saved, the others were lost. A Norwegian Barque ran into her. Owners: David Roberts, P.M., M.M. 32/64ths, David Williams, Pwllheli, Shipbuilder, 4/64ths, Robert Owen, Ffestiniog, Quarry manager, 4/64ths, Robert Davies, Hafod Fawr, Maentwrog, Farmer 8/64ths, Evan Richard, Ffestiniog, Draper, 16/64ths.

RICHARD AND MARY

R. J. OWENS

3mst. Sr, 123tg., 98tn. Built P.M., 1907. Capt. Owen Owen ma., son of Humphrey Owen the pilot. Newfoundland Trader. Sold to Newfoundland.

> *C.R.S.:* 3mst, Sr, 122tg, 97.5tr, 91/22.6/10.4. Built David Williams, P.M., 1907. Owners: Owen Owens, Borth-y-gest, M.M., 32/64ths; Humphrey Owens, Borth-y-gest, Trinity Pilot, 8/64ths; William Morris, P.M., Ship Chandler, 8/64ths; Griffith Prichard, Bodhyfryd, Penrhyndeudraeth, Mer., Shipbroker, 4/64ths; John Thomas Jones, P.M., Bank Manager, 8/64ths; John Owens, Borth-y-gest, P.M., Mariner, 4/64ths; Griffith Prichard, Bodhyfryd, Penrhyndeudraeth, designated M.O. 25 April 1907. Sold to James Ryan of St. John's, Newfoundland, June 20, 1916, reg. transferred to St. John's, Newfoundland.

ROBERT

Sr, Wm. Williams, ma. ? of Bideford, 1835.

ROBERT JONES

Bq, 287tn, 114/24/14.7. Built Barmouth 1866 by Owen. Wm. Pritchard, ma, R. Rees owner in 1878.

ROBERT MORRIS

3mst, (originally a 2mst. Sr.). Sr, 146tg., 135tn, 92.7/22.2/11.8. Built P.M. 1876 by Williams, David Morris, Y Cei, S.H., Capt. D. Davies, ma. In the Autumn of 1898 on a voyage from Lisbon to Newfoundland with salt, she failed to make Newfoundland due to fog; she was driven out into the Atlantic by heavy weather and ultimately made for P.M. She arrived there on the 11 of November 1898, having been at sea 100 days and discharged her cargo at Mathews' Wharf. Much of it had melted and disappeared through the pumps. She then took a load of slates for Aberdeen and left P.M. December 14, 1898. Returned to P.M.

March 3, 1899 and sailed for Koenigsburg with a load of slates on March 14, 1899. Returned to P.M. May 30, 1899 in ballast from Great Yarmouth and reloaded what was left of the salt and took it to its destination St. Johns, Newfoundland. Left P.M. June 10, 1899. Lost by enemy action off Ushant, November 20, 1917, voyage Cardiff to Oporto. Fired on by enemy submarine, then boarded and sunk with bombs. The commander of the German submarine observing the old age of her ma, asked him if there was anything on the ship he would like to take away; the ma said he would like to take the ship's compass. He was allowed to take it.

> *C.R.S.:* 3mst. Sr, 145.9t, 92.7/22.2/11.8. Built P.M., 1876, by Hugh Williams, P.M. *Owners*: Thomas Jones, P.M., M.M., 28/64ths; Owen Morris, P.M., Shipper, 24/64ths; David Morris, P.M., Shipper, 4/64ths; Henry Jones, P.M., Labourer, 4/64ths; Ellen Jones, P.M., widow, 4/64ths. In 1884 David Morris of Brittania Terrace, P.M., appointed M.O. Owen Morris died intestate 18 April 1884: Letter of administration to Jane Morris, spinster, of P.M. Thomas Jones died 15 June 1906. Sunk 1917.

ROSA HARRIETE

Sr, of Carnarvon. 117tn. Built Newport 1864? Evan Humphreys, Borthygest, ma.

> *L.R. 1878/9:* Sr, 117t, 84/26.6/11.7. Built Newport, 1864, owned J. Lindsay & Sons, Montrose, survey Bangor, 1877, O. Roberts, ma.

ROSE

Sr, 92tn, 71.7/17.7/9.2. Built Nova Scotia 1846, J. H. Williams & Sons owners. Condemned and was left to rot at Station Bach. On June 22, 1849 she sailed from Greaves Wharf P.M. with 156½ tons of slates to Lubeck. Capt. William Humphreys ma, and on June 5, 1850 she took 150 tons to Hamburg.

> *Roseina:* Sr, 91t. Built P.M. 1851, sold Aberystwyth, 1855.

ROSETTA

K, Ludwig K. Anderson, owner.

> *L.R. 1894/5:* K, 74t, 76.3/19.5/8.7. Built Plymouth, 1890 by Watson and Fox, owned J. Rice, Tope, ma. 1890. [T. Hewell ma, 1898].

ROBERT WILLIAMS

Sr, 64tn, 62.7/18.8/9.3. Built Wales, 1864, W. Evans, owner.

> *L.R. 1878/9:* Sr, 64t, 62.7/18.8/9.3. Built Wales, 1864 by Ellis, W. Evans, owner, reg. Caernarfon and surveyed P.M., 1876.

ROSIE

2mst. Sr, with signel tops'l. 89tr, about 170td.w., Capt. Griffith Evan Dedwith, owner and ma of Borthgest. A beautiful little vessel with a coppered bottom and a thick fore topmast (Dedwith found the previous ones inadequate for his rather large top'sl). *Rosie* was built at Bideford and was owned by Mr. R. Cock of Appledore. In 1894 she went ashore on the coast of Labrador but was later salved and bought by Capt. Dedwith in 1894/5. Before buying the *Rosie,* Dedwith had commanded the new 3mst. Sr. *The Oakleys* which he lost on her 2nd. voyage on the island of Zante, Greece. Prior to commanding *The Oakleys* Capt. Dedwith had commanded with great distinction for 5 years, the 3mst. Sr. *Theda.* In the *Theda* he sailed the record passage from Cape Charles, Newfoundland, Gibraltar in 12 days. Capt. Dedwith was a capable and fearless seaman and for 18 years the little *Rosie* crossed the Atlantic in the Newfoundland Fish trade during all seasons of the year, sometimes doing two trips from Europe to Newfoundland in one season. In the three vessels above mentioned this redoubtable sailor put in 30 years in this hazardous trade. Late in 1912 *Rosie* was sold to the Hudson Bay Co., when she was divested of her yards and converted into a Ketch with an auxiliary engine. For some years she did service in the bleak and rough coast of Northern Labrador. She was again sold to the Sabellum Trading Co. of London. I am told that her wonderful little hull now lies on the shore near Milford Haven (1942).

*Note of an Interview with Capt. Lewis Williams, Snowdon St., P.M., 17/7/1950:*

Capt. Williams denied that *Rosie* was ever sold to the Hudson Bay Co. Dedwith sold her to the Sabellum Trading Co. of London, a mushroom Co. formed to exploit the fur trade of Hudson Bay. This Co. converted 'Rosie' into a Ketch and put an auxiliary engine on board. Her bow was specially sheathed with teak for ice breaking. After 3 years in this rather dangerous trade, based on Baffin and Davis Straits, Hudson Bay, the Co. went into liquidation, and when at Peterhead in this country she was bought by a Capt. Brodick who used her in the home Coasting trade. About 1933 when at Truro, Capt. Wms bought her as she then was (a K. minus her engine) and continued to use her in the coasting trade. When on a voyage from Garstang to Falmouth she ran into foul weather in the Irish Sea and proved unequal to the elements — leaking so badly that she was compelled to run into Milford Haven where she now lies on the tide there. She was 160 tons d.w. and Capt. Wms told me that when Dedwith owned her she did 3 passages out to Newfoundland and back to Lisbon and Oporto in 12 months and she frequently did two. She was in the Newfoundland trade for 18 years.

For further details of the Dedwydd (Dedwith) family, vide Lewis W. Lloyd, *The Town & Port of Barmouth (1565-1973)*, pp. 33 & 91.

ROSE OF TORRIDGE

Sr, 114tg, 104tn, 88.5/21.1/10.6. Built Bideford? 1875 by Cox. Capt. Evan Evans, ma. Newfoundland Trader. Went ashore at Turnavik, Labrador 1892. Declared lost but was later salved.

*C.R.S.:* Sr. 3mst, 88.5/21.1/10.6. Built 1875 in Bideford, Devon. Previous reg. Fowey, 2/1883, Cardiff 18/1875. Caernarfon 1891. Owners 1891: Richard Hughes, P.M., Shipowner, 32/64ths, M.O.; Evan Evans, P.M., M.M., 16/64ths; William Evans, P.M., Ironmonger, 16/64ths; William Evans, P.M., Painter, 64/64ths + M.O. in 1895. In August 1914 Ann Roberts of Borth-y-gest, P.M., wife of Edward Roberts, P.M., becomes owner + M.O. Ann Roberts in June 1915 sells 16/64ths to Humphrey Francis Roberts of Borth-y-gest, P.M., M.M. Reg. closed 1917. Vessel said to be seriously damaged at Cadiz + that repairs would cost more than double her insurance value. Vessel sold to a Spanish subject.

*P.P. 1894, LXXVI:* 29 July 1892, Sr, 27 years old, 5 crew, E. Evans, ma. R. Hughes, P.M., owner. Voyage: St. Ubes, Portugal, for Windsor Harbour, Labrador, with a cargo of salt. Stranded entrance of Turnavik Harbour, Labrador, no lives lost, wind SW force 2.

ROYAL CHARTER

Sr, 119tn, 82.5/22.3/11.4. Built Abergafran, Minffordd, 1858, Capt. David Morris, ma and owned (My Grandfather). He sold her in 1869 to R. Jones who later sold her to Wm. Evans and others of P.M. Her cabin was made of Bird's eye Maple. I have a little box in my possession made with what was left over of the maple. Lost off Bardsey. Tom Evans, brother of Evan Evans, tinman, was then her ma and part owner about 1880.

Lost & reg. off Craig Maen Mellt, Llŷn, 3.3.1881.

ROYAL LISTER

3mst. Sr, 140tg, 117tn. Built P.M. 1902 by David Jones. Newfoundland Trader. Lost off Cape Spartel, near Tangier, March, 1913, voyage Runcorn to Gibraltar, 211 tons, 10 cwts of coal at a Freight of 16/- per ton. Capt. reprimanded.

*C.R.S.:* 3mst. Sr, 140tg, 116tr, 92.3/23/11.7, J. H. Lister of Barmouth, 64/64ths. On 26 July 1904, Lister sold 8/64ths to Henry Llewelyn Jones of 11 Snowdon Street, P.M., Coal and Iron Merchant; 2/64ths to Grace Thomas of 35 Cambridge Road, Seaforth, Liverpool, spinster, and on the same date 38/64ths to Llewelyn Griffith Llewelyn, of 1 Garth Terrace, P.M., Shipowner, who was designated M.O. under hand of J. H. Lister on 29 July 1904. On Nov. 18, Ll. G. Llewelyn transferred 4/64ths to Richard John Thomas, 35 Cambridge Road, Seaforth, M.M., and on 3 April 1905 J. H. Lister sold 16/64ths to William Griffith of Liverpool House, Barmouth, M.M. Registry closed 14 April 1913. Vessel stranded on coast of Morocco on 27 Feb. 1913 and sold by underwriters to a foreign subject as a total wreck.

RUBY

Sr, 81tn, 69/19.8/10.8. Built Newquay, 1856, Capt. Thomas, ma, father of Simeon Thomas, of the *Wave of Life*. The ma fell dead on deck at Milford Haven, 1873. Newfoundland Trader.

SABRINA

Sr, 95tn, 76.3/21.2/10.8. Built Pwllheli, 1864, Capt. Prichard, ma.

SAGE

K. Lost off Port Talbot.

*P.P. 1908, XCVI:* 1 Jan. 1907. K, 40 years old, 25t, 3 crew, E. Evans, ma, E. Evans, Senior, P.M. owner, voyage P.M. to Port Talbot with slates, no lives lost, stranded $\frac{1}{4}$ mile S. of breakwater, Port Talbot, wind force 7.

THE SAINT

Sr, with a round stern. 118tg, 107tn, 87.2/21.3/10.7. Built Drogheda, 1870, Capt. David Roberts, ma. Dr. Lister, owner.

Built by Grendon at Drogheda, 1870.

SAINT HELEN

*P.P. 1886, LIX, 698:* 1 March 1883, Bn. Built Caernarfon, 39 years old, 134t, Ellis, Barmouth, owner, cargo 200 tons of slates, P.M. to Harburg, crew of six, wind ENE, force 6, 8 miles NE of South Bishop, St. George's Channel, sprang a leak during moderate weather; water gained on pump at rate of 6 in. per hour. She was abandoned with the water even with her deck. Cause of leak unknown.

SALEM

Sr, 100tn. Built Pwllheli, 1838, Capt. Harry Williams, ma. He later commanded the *Linus*. Morris and others owners.

Built Pwllheli, 1838 by William Jones. Lost 16.8.1884.

SAMUEL HOLLAND

2mst. Sr, later converted into a 3mst. Sr. Double topsail and a gallan yard across. 159tg, 151tn, 92.4/23.1/12.5. Built P.M. 1867 by Griffiths. Capt. Hugh Parry, S.H., John Williams, Minffordd, ma. (Later of the *Ed. Arthur*). John Williams, Borth? was her ma when a three masted schooner.

Owned J. Williams, G. Evans, ma 1878/9. Lost 1903.

SARAH

Sr, 113tg, 100tn, 79/23/11.6. Built P.M. 1866 by Wm. Griffiths, Capt. John Ellis owner, Tom Ellis, Tregunter, ma. Lost on the coast of Denmark, Oct. 1898. Voyage P.M. to Harburg. Cargo 217 tons 4 cwts. 3 qrs. of slates at a freight of 10/- per ton. Wm. Roberts of Trip Farm was then her owner.

W. Rowlands, ma, 1893.

SARAH BRIDGET

Sr, 126tn, 86.4/22.5/11.8. Built Bangor, 1858. O. Roberts, ma.

Sr. Built Bangor, by Edward Ellis, Re-registered Aberystwyth: Condemned Runcorn, 1936.

SARAH DAVIES

Sr, 90tn, 77/20/10.2. Built Aberdovey, 1870, J. Williams, ma.

SARAH EVANS

Sr, 110tg, 98t, 82.5/22.4/10.8. Built Borthygest, 1877 by Richard Jones. Rees Evans, Trwyn Cae Iago, owner, Capt E. W. Roberts, ma. Sold, but afterwards wrecked north of Lands End.

Wrecked 30.10.1932.

SARAH JANE

Sr, of Hull? or Bangor, 1861. J. Thomas, ma.

*L.R. 1871/2:* Sr, 73t, 70.1/19.5/9.5. Built Bangor, 1861 by Owens, owned Simon & Co. Reg. Beaumaris, Bangor coaster.

SARAH & MARY

Built Wales, 1852, belonged to Aberystwyth — 1878.

*L.R. 1871/2:* Sr. 76t, 61.1/16.6/10.0. J. Davies, ma. P.M. coaster.

SARAH PRITCHARD

Bn, Edmund Humphreys, ma.

SARAH ROWE

Sr. Built 1872. Reg. at Milford. Believed to have been built at Llanbedrog? Capt. Owen Jones, Llanbedrog, ma.

*L.R. 1878/9:* Sr. 63t, 73.8/18.9/9. Built Cochstn, 1872 owned by W. Rowe & Co.

SARAH WILLIAMS

Sr, 118tn, 80.5/21.5/11.4. Built Barmouth 1859 by R. Jones.

SCOTIA

Bkn/Sr. Built New Brunswick, 1837, Mrs. S. Parry, owner, in 1878. Her ma was the son of Thos. Richards, the brother of David Richards senior.

*L.R. 1878/9:* Sr, 55t, 84.1/15.7/7.4. Reg. Caernarfon.

SECRET

K, 60tn, 67.2/17.2/9.6. Built Rye, 1857, R. Williams, owner in 1878. Capt. Owen Williams, *Industry,* Borth, ma. Lost on Rathlin Island.

SEVEN BROTHERS

Hugh Williams, (of the *Lucy*) Borth, ma; later his brother, Capt. Wms., Ralph St., Borthygest. 'Fore and after,' built at Beaumaris, with 'out of door' rudder. Her bottom was nearly flat, 8ft. draught, when fully laden, crew of 3. Capt. Williams, Ralph St., was her ma for 10 years. Lost off Aberayron.

SIDNEY SMITH

3mst. Sr. 176t. Built P.M. 1895 by D. Jones, Capt. R. O. Williams, ma. Lost in Twillingate Harbour, Newfoundland, December, 1912. The following is a notable voyage of hers: June 6, 1899, Preston to Gibraltar with coal, Gibraltar to Cadiz in ballast, Cadiz to St. Johns, Newfoundland, with salt, then to Long Tickle, Labrador, in ballast, — Long Tickle to Gibraltar for orders. Gibraltar to Patras, Greece, Patras to London with valonia loaded at Dragonesto. London to Falmouth in ballast. Stranded on the North Bank at Falmouth for 4¼ hours. Repairs at Falmouth — then to Gibraltar with granite blocks loaded at Penryn, Cornwall, for the new dock at Gibraltar. Then Gibraltar to Cadiz in ballast, — Cadiz to St. Johns again for orders, then up the coast to Double Islands, North of Hope Dale, loaded part cargo of fish there and completed loading at Square Island (October 18, 1900) then to Malaga, Malaga to Cadiz — Cadiz to Rio Grande du Sol. From there to Falmouth with a cargo of raw hides (a stinking cargo). Took stores on board at Falmouth and proceeded to St. Petersburg, arrived there May 17, 1901. Left there in Sept. 1901 with a cargo of linseed oil cake for Perth, Scotland. Then coastwise to P.M. Richard Williams, Terrace Road, P.M., served on her during this voyage as an Ordinary

Seaman. He later became her ma as Capt. Rd. Williams. On her 1st arrival at Gibraltar Capt. Williams told me that 13 P.M. vessels arrived there 24 hours after the *Sidney Smith;* they had not sighted one another during the passage across the Atlantic from Newfoundland.

*C.R.S.:* 3mst. Sr, 176.62t, 101.8/23.6/12.2. Built P.M. 1895 by David Williams, P.M. Owners: David Williams, P.M., Shipbuilder, 24/64ths; Griffith Williams, P.M., M.M., 16/64ths; Sidney Smith Twort, Clynnog, Gentleman, 8/64ths; Thomas Joseph Hughes, Bethesda, Chemist, 4/64ths; William Morris, P.M., Ship Chandler, 4/64ths; David Roberts, P.M., Grocer, 4/64ths; Richard Owen, Machynlleth, Timber Merchant, 4/64ths. David Williams, 15 Madoc Street, M.O. 24 Aug. 1895. Lost Newfoundland 12.12.1913.

SIRUS (Or Sirius)

Sr, Capt. Evan Humphreys, Borthygest, ma. (See under *Ceres*).

SIX BROTHERS

Sr, 76tn. Lost on Ynys Cyngar, P.M. Part of her hull can yet be seen at very low tides. John Owen Morris, ma Borthygest, (Brother of Isaac Lloyd Morris of the *Mary Lloyd*) grandfather of Katie Morris. He lived at the shop where Wm. Wallace Williams now lives. (1942).

*L.R. 1852:* Sr. 44t, owned Williams, P.M., Williams, ma. also ? Sr, 66t. Built P.M., 1841 by Evan Evans. Lost P.M., Bar, 1867.

SNAEFELL

Sr, 79tn, 83.4/21.5/9.2. Built Barnstable, 1876, Capt. Evan Evans, Llanbedrog, ma. Newfoundland trader. Lost off Jutland, December, 1906. On one occasion when at St. Johns, Newfoundland, the crew deserted her. The ma and mate set out coastwise to try and find a fresh crew. A strong N.W. wind sprang up so they decided to have a shot at crossing the Atlantic by themselves and did it.

*C.R.S.:* Sr, 89tg, 77.6tr, 83.4/21.5/9.2. Built Barnstaple 1876. Owners: Robert Marks of Glangors, Llanbedrog, M.M., 64/64ths. He died intestate on 5 April 1904, letters of administration granted to Lizzie Evans of Llanbedrog, wife of Evan Evans, mariner. Mrs. Evans thus became owner of 64/64ths. Certificate cancelled and reg. closed 25 Dec. 1906. Vessel stranded on the Danish coast on 1 November 1906, and afterwards became a total loss.

*P.P. 1908, XCVI:* 1 Nov. 1906, *Snaefell,* Sr, 78t, 5 crew, R. Owens, ma. Mr. L. Evans, Llanbedrog, Caerns., owner. Voyage P.M. to Middlefort, Denmark, with slates, stranded about 4 miles E of Hirtshal Lighthouse, Denmark. Wind force 7, E, no lives lost.

SNOWDON (I)

K, Wm. Rees, ma.

SNOWDON (II)

Steam Tug Boat at P.M., Built Newcastle upon Tyne, at a cost of £2,000 (1884). Rhys Jones, ma.

*L.R. 1894/5:* I. Paddle S, 106t, 96.0/18.7/9.5. Built S. Shields, 1885 by Lawson & Eltringham. P.M. Steam Tug Co. Ltd. owners.

SNOWDONIA

Bk, 419tg, 402tn, 138.2/28.9/17.2. Built Tai Pilots, Borthygest, 1874, by Morris Owen. John Hughes, Llanbwll[?] designed her hull and supervised her construction as foreman. Roberts & Griffiths, owners, 1878. The largest vessel built at Borthygest that made P.M. her home port. Lost with all hands near Holy Island, Berwick on Tweed, loaded with phosphate rock. The body of her ma Capt. Roberts was recovered and brought to P.M. for burial. Capt. Joseph Roberts of the *Ellen Roberts* was his brother. Quatrain by Ioan Madog on beholding her figure-head at Pen Cei.

'Delw hardd uwch ben y dŵr,
Delw Hudolus i longwr
Ymholais fel ymwelwr
O ble daeth yr hen hwr.'

*L.R. 1878/9:* 402t, 138.2/28.9/17.2, J. Roberts, ma. Lost with all hands, Fern Island, Oct. - Nov. 1881.

SOLWAY LASS

I Sr/K. Anderson, owner, Son-in-law of Rd. Williams, the Ship Smith.

SOPHIA

*P.P. 1887, LXXIC:* 16 Aug. 1884, Sr, 63t, of Caernarvon, 3 crew, owned by D. Roberts, P.M. Voyage: Thurso to Greenock with pavement cargo. Foundered off Cape Wrath, Sutherlandshire, wind SSE 6, no lives lost.

STAR

K. Thos. Jones, ma.

SUCCESS (1)

Sp, David Morris, of Pant y Wrach, ma. David Morris my grandfather later commanded (1) *The Royal Charter,* (2) *The Ocean Monarch,* (3) *The Pride of Wales.* The *Success* was his 1st command.

SUCCESS (2)

Sp, 30t, 32.6/13.0/6.6. Built Traeth Bach, 1772, No. 184 Beaumaris Reg, 1876. Owner, Griffith Francis of Llanfihangel Merioneth, mariner. Ma: Llewelin Francis 1795?, David Griffith, 1806, Francis Griffith, 1809. Reg. de Novo at Aberystwyth, 26.6.1810.

SULTANA REINA

Bn, 129tn, 82/20.2/12.5. Built Yarmouth, 1857 Capt. Morgan Jones, owner. Capt. Humphrey Lloyd, Talsarnau, ma. Sunk at the mouth of the Elbe in collision with *S.S. Holderness,* Nov. 1898. Cargo 200 tons of Oil Cake at a freight of 10/- per ton. She had a reputation for making the most of bad weather.

SUMMER CLOUD

Sr, Built Burton S. 1863.

*L.R. 1880/1:* Sr, 92t, 78/20.2/10.2. Built by Wray, at Burton Stather in 1863, owned T. Lewis, Aberystwyth. T. Lewis, ma.

SUSANNA

16t. Built P.M., 1836.

Sp, 23t. Built P.M. 1836 by Evan Evans, out of Reg. 25.7.1876.

SUSAN & ELLEN

Sr, 106tn. Built Pwllheli, 1834. H. Jones, ma, H. Roberts, owner.

Built Pwllheli, 1834 by John Prichard. Lost with all hands, left London, 15.1.1879, not heard of since.

SYDNEY GRACE

Sr, of P.M. 124tn, 87.3/22/11.6. Built P.M. 1875 by Wms. H. Jones, ma, J. Jones, etc., owners. Lost with all hands voyage South Shields to Dublin.

*C.R.S.:* Sr. 132.4t, 87.3/22.0/11.6. Built P.M. 1875 by Hugh Williams, P.M. Owners: Henry Jones, Penrhyndeudraeth, M.M., 24/64ths; John Jones, Llanfrothen, Ret. M.M., 12/64ths; Richard Owen, Ffestiniog, Quarryman, 4/64ths; John Jones, Garth Cottage, P.M., Ret. M.M., 4/64ths; John Prichard, Quarry Clerk, Beddgelert, 4/64ths; John Ellis, P.M., Ret. M.M., 4/64ths; William Hughes, Beddgelert, Farmer, 4/64ths; John Henry Roberts, Beddgelert, Quarry Agent, 4/64ths; Humphrey Prichard, Beddgelert, Farmer, 4/64ths; John Jones, Garth Cottage, P.M., appt. M.O. by John Ellis, 29/10/75. Henry Jones, on 16/64ths shares. Mortgage A date 5 March 1875. £300 and interest @ 5% from William Jones of P.M., Sailmaker. Vessel sailed from Newcastle for Dublin, 13 Oct.

1881, and has not since been heard of. Reg. closed Dec. 1881. *P.P. 1886, LXIC, 216:* Sydney Grace, built P.M., J. Jones, owner, P.M. Cargo of 220t. of Hebbwn gas coal. The weather was showery at time of shipment. Vessel had no ventilators. Not heard of since sailing 13 Oct. 1881, voyage Newcastle on Tyne to Dublin, 6 crew lost. The vessel is supposed to have foundered during the heavy gale of 14 Oct. 1881. [One of 12 vessels similarly accounted for on that date, including *Nantglyn* of Amlwch.]

SYDNEY & JANE

Bn, 178tn, 97.2/24.4/12.5. Built Pwllheli, 1841, Wm. Jones, Yr Yard, S.H., J. Davies, ma. R. Griffith etc. owners.

Built Pwllheli, 1840 by Robert Evans.

SYDNEY JONES

Sr, Capt. Morris Jones, owner.

Sr, 80t. Built P.M. 1856. Lost off Heligoland, 1869.

*L.R. 1859:* Sr, 79t, owned Jones & Co., P.M. M. Jones, ma.

TAFF VALE

Sr. Originally a Sp, 64tr. Built P.M. 1841 by Lewis Williams. Robert Roberts, owner and ma. (Father of Mrs. Rees Evans, Bronavon). Capt. Evan Williams of the *Mercy* later commanded her. Lost 1866.

*L.R. 1852:* Sk. 46t, P.M., 1841. Owned Griffith & Co., P.M.

TALARFOR

Sr, 133tr, 123tn, 85/21.6/11.9. Built P.M., 1861, by Hugh Williams, Capt. Robert Jones, Criccieth, ma and owner. Lost off the Smalls with all hands. Uncle Evan Hughes commanded her 1863/64.

*C.R.S.:* Owners: Simon Robert Ellis, Nevin, M.M., 64/64ths. 1891 Thomas Morgan of Brynllwyd, Amlwch, designated Manager advice under hand of Simon Robert Ellis, 5 Dec. 1891. Vessel missing. Left Falmouth for Runcorn, 17 Dec. 1903, seen by a passing vessel on 18 Dec. 1903. Not heard of since. Reg. Closed 9 March 1904.

TAY & TEES PACKET

Sr, 59tn, 60.2/16.7/9.8. Built Dundee 1845, Ellis Humphreys (Talarock) ma. Mr. F. S. Percival owner.

TECWYN

1 Sr. Built Goole, Ellis Roberts owner.

*L.R. 1910/11*: Steel Sr, 132t, 95/22/9.7. Built J. Scarr & Son, Beverley, E. O. Roberts, owner, J. H. Lewis, ma. [Ellis Owen Roberts, Richmond Buildings, 26 Chapel Street, Liverpool.]

TELEPHONE

Sk, later a K. Built Padstow, Capt. James ma.

*L.R. 1904/5:* Sk. 51t, 59.7/19.1/8.5. Built Barnstaple 1878 by Westacott, owned S. James, Mrs. A. James, ma.

TEST

Bn, 154tg, 129tr, 90.7/22.6/12.5. Built Trwyn Cae Iago at the end of Cei Cwmorthin, 1862 by David Richards, senior. Owner Rees Davies Richards, Caernarvon M.M., 64/64ths. She was the 1st Bn built at P.M. with a double top sail. D. Jones, ma. Sold to Glasgow 28 Sept. 1920 and re named *Sannox*. Foundered in the Atlantic, 1922.

Out of reg., 1920.

THEDA

3mst. Sr, or Jack Bkn, 100/23.6/12.4. Built at Pwllheli, 1876 by Pritchard. Owner, Mrs. Jones, G. Jones, ma. Newfoundland Trader and Phosphate trader. Lost on Sunderland Bank, Morecambe, Nov. 1903. The vessel was a well known clipper and once sailed the passage from Belle Isle, Labrador to Gibraltar in 12 days. Capt. Griffith Evan Dedwith was then her ma (Oct. 1888).

In 1887, on failing to obtain a full cargo in Labrador, was compelled to return to Harbour Grace with 140 fishermen as passengers, — an old planter, the master of the harbour, being amongst them. He was a chronic rheumatic and was brought aboard on a stretcher. He demanded to sleep on the cabin table but Dedwith would not let him, so he slept under the table, throughout the passage. It cured his rheumatism, so he was able to walk off the ship on arrival in Port. One of the women passengers also gave birth to a baby girl during the passage — she was named Theda Gannet, *S.B.* June 1933. Her [Theda] first ma was Griffith Arthur Jones, the father of R. Arthur Jones. He only held a 'fore and aft' certificate. Capt. R. A. Jones, Glanva, Criccieth served on her from March 1888 to June 1892. Here is one of her typical voyages. Cadiz to Harbour Grace with salt, then to Cape Charles, to Gibraltar with fish for orders, then to Genoa. Genoa to Patras in ballast, then to Casablanca with beans, then to Newcastle on Tyne. Dedwith was ma of Theda for 5 years.

Lost Fleetwood, 1896.

THETIS

Sr, 62tn, 52.6/17.4/10.3. Built Nevin, 1830, R. Wms. and other owners, R. Jones, ma.

Built Pwllheli? Thos. Griffith. Lost & Reg. Plymouth Sound, 27.10.1880.

THOMAS CHARLES

Sr, Robert Hughes, ma, son of Lewis Hughes, the tailor, at P.M.

*L.R. 1875/6:* Sr. 82t, 69.5/20.0/10.7. Built P.M. 1868 by Griffiths, owned Hughes & Co., H. Hughes, ma.

THOMAS OWEN

Sr. Built Borthygest, by John Williams, her owner; Tom, his son, ma. Morocco trader. Lost in the N. Sea. All hands saved except the ma, Thomas Williams.

Sr. Built Borth-y-gest, 1880 by John Wms. vessel's rig altered to K, 1889 87t, 71.2/21/10.8, owned by John Williams, P.M., Shipbuilder, 64/64ths. Vessel lost in North Sea on 14 June 1890. Certificate lost with vessel reg. closed 18 Sept. 1890.

THREE BROTHERS

Sr, 92tn, 64.8/21.3/10.8. Built Nevin 1845, J. Roberts, owner, W. Jones, ma.

THREE JANES

Sr, 96tg, 79/20.9/10.8. Built Conway 1858 by Roberts, O. Morris & Co., owners, 1878. Wm. Watkins, ma. David Morris, Cei, S.H. Lost in collision off Lands End, 1895.

THREE SISTERS

*L.R. 1884/5:* Sp, 33t, 55/17/17.2. Built Cei Bach, Newquay, 1882, by E. Davies. Owned T. Thomas, Cardigan.

TONY KROGMANN

Bg, later Bkn, 271tg, 251tn, 119/26/14.7. Built P.M., 1878 by Eben Roberts. Phosphate trader. Left the West Indies for U.K. and was not heard of again. Capt. Evan Williams, husband of Mrs. Williams, Confectioner, was then her ma. Some of her wreckage was found on the Scottish coast. On one occasion she did this voyage: he joined her at Newport, S. Wales, to Dakar with coal; Dakar to Aruba in ballast, then to Memel, Russia with phosphate rock, then to Pembroke Dock, U.K. with timber. Wm. Jones, Cei Greaves was an A.B. on her during this voyage, 1891, which took about 6½ months. C. Napier Henry, R.A., made a painting of her at Falmouth, 1887.

*C.R.S.:* Owner: Ebenezer Roberts, Shipbuilder, 64/64ths. Ebenezer Roberts, 1 Mount Pleasant, P.M., M.O. Vessel sailed from Aruba, W. Indies, on or about 31 Oct. 1888, and has not since been heard of. Reg. closed 26 April 1889.

TOPAZ (Locally Tobas)

K, 46tn, 50.6/15.6/8.6. Built P.M. 1851 by Evans, W. Lloyd and others owners. Wm. Roberts, ma. Liverpool Trader.

Lost + Reg. Fishguard, 14.10.1881.

TRADER

32t, Built P.M., 1837.

Sp. Built P.M. 1837 by Henry Jones. Lost all hands off Liverpool, 1848.

TREBISCIN

K. Probably formerly a Sr, probably built at Padstow, 1859. Clement Evans, owner, brother of Wm. Henry Evans, (Fawr).

*L.R. 1871/2:* Sr, 69t, 75.3/17.5/8.7. Built Padstow 1859 by Bennet, owned Martyn, Padstow J. Bate, ma.

TRUE LOVE

Sr, 69t. Built Henry Jones at P.M. 1860. Lost on passage Glasgow to Dieppe, December 1868.

TRURO

Sr, John Crocker, ma.

TWELVE APOSTLES

Sr, 118tn, 86.2/22.2/11.4. Built Pwllheli 1858. H. Hughes and others owners. Capt. John James Jones, ma and later Rd. Jones, his brother. Owen Morris, S.H. Her figure head was a bust of St. Paul. Hugh Hughes, father's brother commanded her 1858/75. Lost at Hell's Mouth, near Pwllheli, November 23, 1898, in ballast.

TWO BROTHERS (I)

Sk, No. 32 1824. Reg. 22/6/1824 at Beaumaris. Built Traeth Mawr (Canol y Clwt), by Harry Jones by his certificate dated 3/6/1824. Owners: Wm. Parry, Mariner, 52/64ths, David Hughes, slate loader, 4/64ths, Daniel Parry, farmer, 8/64ths.

TWO BROTHERS (II)

Sr, 76tn, 60.7/17.7/10. Built Pwllheli 1851 D. Pritchard, owner.

TYNE

Bn, 157tg, 92.1/22.4/12.5. Built S. Shields in 1867 by Winlo. Owen Lloyd, owner and ma. She once broke from her moorings at P.M. and was stranded near the embankment loaded with slates. She was due to sail for Copenhagen.

*C.R.S.:* Transferred from North Shields 1890 6/1890. Owen Lloyd, 5 Dora Street, P.M., M.M., 64/64ths, 11 Oct. 1890. Owen Lloyd died 1891, then owners: Owen Lloyd, Mariner; David Lloyd, Shipbroker; Elizabeth Lloyd (died 1894). Owen Lloyd, died 1895: David Lloyd sold *Tyne* to Thomas Biddey Jones of St. Dogmell's, Pembrokeshire, Shipowner, April 27, 1916, transferred reg. to Jersey, 30 June 1917.

UNDAUNTED

UNA

Sr, 52tn, 52.2/17.4/9.1. Built P.M., 1840, G. Edwards owner and ma.

Built P.M., 1840, by Henry Jones. Lost off Skerries, 28.2.1881. Capt. Wm. Hughes, brother of Capt. Hugh Hughes (later Rev. Hugh Hughes, Gellidara) was ma of her in 1841.

UNICORN

Sr, 119tn, 71.2/19.9/12.1. Built Caernarvon, 1840. E. Davies owner and ma 1878. David Davies ma, the son of Rhys Davies, shopkeeper at Pen Cei. Rhys Davies used to sit in the pew in front of us in chapel. I once shoved one of my sister's hat pins into his bottom during prayers and caused a great commotion. Lost on the Goodwin Sands, Cargo of Coal. There was a carving of a unicorn on her stern.

Lost 1912?

UNITY

125t, 67/21/-. Reg. at Barmouth. Built Traeth Bach, 1813. Ed. Edwards, ma.

U-LARSING

Sr, 95tg. Built Borth by John Hughes. Capt. W. O. Morris, ma. of P.M. Her figure head was the head of a negro. She was named after a foreign missionary. Lost on a voyage from Harburg to Great Yarmouth on the Leman and Nore Bank, N. Sea, loaded with Oil Cake at a freight of 8/6 per ton.

*C.R.S.:* Reg. trans. from Aberystwyth, 1888. Sr, 75.5/20.2/10.6. Built Traethgwyn, Cards. by Thomas Davies, Traethgwyn. Owner: William Owen Morris, P.M., M.M., 64/64ths. Morris Owen Morris of 7 Amanda Terrace, Borth, P.M., M.M., designated S.H., May 1887. William Owen Morris, 31 East Ave., P.M., designated M.O., 13 Nov. 1895. Stranded 13 Nov. 1897 and then foundered. Cert. of reg. lost with vessel.

VALIANT

VELOCITY

Sr, fore and after. Of Pwllheli 1825, but belonged to Aberystwyth. 65tn, 64/17.6/9.7, W. Edwards ma and owner.

VENEDOCIAN

3mst. Sr, of Jack Bkn, 180tg, 170tn, 102.8/22.8/12.7. Built P.M., 1873 by Griffith Williams. Capt. Evan Jones of *Fanny Breslauer,* ma. Prichard Bros. S.H. (Capt. Hugh Jones was her 1st ma.). Phosphate trader and Newfoundland trader. Capt. Evie Morris of the *Ellen Lloyd* and Grandson of Capt. Roberts of the *Constance* sailed the following voyage in her when she was 38 years old: Crew; Evie Morris (Age 24), ma; Harry Foulkes, mate, who had not been to sea for 11 years previously; Hugh Roberts, Grisia Mawr, A.B.; 2 Ordinary Seamen viz: Will Graig Don and Will Bach Gandage, and a Dane as a Cook, 6 all told. The ma was the only certificated man on board. On April 1, 1907 she and the *M. Lloyd Morris* left P.M. on the late evening tide. *Venedocian* bound for Kiel and Stettin and the *M. Lloyd Morris* for Aalborg, Denmark. A bet was laid at P.M. as to which would pass Beachy Head first. Each vessel had separate tugs, but the hawser of *Venedocian* snapped and the *M. Lloyd Morris* got a nice start. At daybreak they were together in face of a stiff S.W. breeze, off Lands End; *Venedocian* lost her main top mast. After taking it down and splicing it, it was put up again. On turning the Longships, *Venedocian* had to give way on opposite tack and lost good ground. They sailed up the Channel in a stiff southerly gale with as many sails as they could carry. Prudence really demanded a 'heave to' but on they went. *Venedocian* passed Beachy Head 2 hours before *M. Lloyd Morris.* A strong Northerly wind was met in the North Sea, but *Venedocian* made for the Elbe. She was held up in Brunsbuttel Canal by the *Hohenzollern,* the Kaiser's Yacht, for 2 hours. *M. Lloyd Morris* had gone round the Skaw and was well beaten in the race (She was only 2 years old.) From Stettin the *Venedocian* took a load of timber to Pornic, France. The deck cargo was jettisoned and rafted into the harbour. Pornic to Cadiz in ballast; Cadiz to Harbour Grace, Newfoundland, with salt, then to Song Harbour and back to Harbour Grace. Then with fish to Gibraltar for orders to Malaga, then to Setubal in ballast; Setubal to Newlyn, Cornwall with salt. Ran into a N.W. gale in the Bay of Biscay. Turned round at great risk, and made for Lisbon just in time to run her on the mud, as she was leaking badly and her pumps were choked with salt. The Club at P.M. sent Capt. Pritchard from the *Owen Morris* which was at Lisbon to inspect. Part cargo discharged and copper stripped in order to trace the leak Ultimately sailed to Newlyn uneventfully. The *Venedocian* was sold at Newlyn to an Irish firm in 1908 and ceased trading to Newfoundland. When crossing from Cadiz to Harbour Grace, Capt. Morris, when sleeping in his bunk was awakened by the sound of water near his head. He forced open the old disused locker and found it full of water. After emptying it he found water streaming in through the hull. It was patched up with lead and felt for the rest of the passage. The above is Evie Morris's testimony. Her rather unusual rig was 'Fore and aft' certificate. The holder of such a certificate was not qualified to command a vessel with a square rig on the Fore, like a Bn or Bkn. The *Venedocian* was rigged like a tops'l schooner except that instead of having gaff foresail to the foremast, she carried main staysails like a Bkn. Also instead of having a square foresail bent on the large fore yard, she had a bent squaresail on a smaller fore yard. Neither did she have a fore gallant mast. She spent nearly the whole of her P.M. career of 35 years in the Newfoundland Fish Trade. She was I believe the 1st P.M. vessel to enter this trade.

## VENUS

Sr, 120tg. Built at Nevin, 1880, Capt. Pierce Owen, ma, Mrs. Hughes, S.H. Lost near Lisbon, voyage Labrador to Portugal, cargo 3,200 quintals of fish at a freight of 2/- per quintal. She was the last vessel to be built at Nevin. Joseph Williams was her managing owner. In 1897 she did the following voyage; P.M. to Cadiz in ballast; Cadiz to Fogo Newfoundland with salt; Fogo to Naples with fish; Naples to Bari, Italy, in ballast; Bari to Goole with olive oil; Goole to Southampton with coal; Southampton to P.M. in ballast. 11 months from P.M. to P.M.

*L.R. 1884/5:* Sr. 107t, 83/22.1/11.5, owned H. Hughes, ma, in 1884. Built Griffith Owen Nefyn, 1880.

*P.P. 1902, XCII, 753:* 21 Dec. 1900, when 20 years old, stranded entrance to R. Tagus, Portugal, P.O. Williams, ma, J. Williams, P.M., owner. Voyage: Fogo, Newfoundland to Lisbon with cod fish. Crew of 5 saved.

## VICTORIA

I 3mst. Sr. Ellis Owen Roberts, owner.

Capt. Lewis ma, Job Roberts mate.

*L.R. 1904/5:* Steel 3mst. Sr., 165t, 165.1/22.7/10.6. Built W. H. Lean, Falmouth, 1897, E. O. Roberts, owner, E. Lewis, ma.

VIGILANT

Bk. ? (Bkn. of Banff). Built in the West Country, Capt. Morgan Jones, owner.

*L.R. 1884/5:* Bn, 303t, 125.4/25.4/14.9. Built by Geddie at Kingston, 1871. H. Jones, owner, Port of reg. Banff, T. Hughes, ma.

VILLAGE MAID

Sr, Capt. Morris Evans, ma. Capt. Lloyd of P.M., owner.

*C.R.S.:* Built Inverness 1864 by Stewart Bros. Sr. 139t, 88.7/22.4/11.9. Bought by Robert Lloyd of P.M. M.M. & Reg. Caernarfon 4/1886 on 14 July 1886. Sold 1903 by Robert Lloyd to John Hoban, M.M., Back Jobling Street, Sunderland. Lost 1910.

VITAL

48½t, 45/16½/-. Built at Traeth Bach, 1810, Reg. at Pwllheli, John Richards, ma.

VOLUNTEER

Sr, 116tg, 81.1/21.7/11.5. Built at Borthygest by Griffiths, 1863, Capt. Evan Jones, Borthygest, ma, Prichard Bros. S.H., J. Jones and Co. owners, 1878. Lost on the Goodwin Sands, Voyage Dunkirk to Sligo, Cargo of slates at a freight of 12/- per ton. She was a fast sailing little vessel and Evan Jones was a very daring sailor. He later commanded the *Glanogwen.*

Lost Goodwin Sands, 1903.

WALTER ULRIC

Sr, 98t, 85.8/22.5/10.9. Built at Nevin 1875 by Owens. Capt. Evan Williams, ma and owner, Rees Evans, S.H. Morocco and Baltic Trader. Sunk by enemy action 1914/18 War, off Lands End.

*C.R.S.:* Sr, 98tn, 85.8/22.5/10.9. Built Nevin, 1875 by Griffith Owen, Nevin. Owners: Richard Hughes, P.M., M.M., 20/64ths; Rees Evans, P.M., Slate Agent, 16/64ths; Robert Roberts, P.M., Clerk, 16/64ths; John Farmer Sims, P.M., Quarry Manager, 4/64ths; William Evans, Junior, P.M., Grazier, 4/64ths; Charles Nicholson, Slate Merchant, of the town and county of Newcastle on Tyne, 4/64ths. In Feb. 1894 64/64ths shares to Evan Williams, Borth, P.M., M.M., who had bought the other owners out. Sold to Cornish Traders Ltd., Commercial Chambers, Falmouth, 12 July 1916. Reg. closed 24 April 1917. Vessel reported missing since 24 March 1917, stated to have been sunk.

WATERBIRD

Sr, 97tn, 83.2/21.7/10.3. Built at Fraserburgh, 1868, Mrs. Williams, S.H. A bonny little vessel.

WATERLOO

Bg, of P.M., 1850. 104tn, 69.7/18.5/10.8. Built at Nevin 1815. Evan Jones, ma. Lost 21st March, 1855, 50 miles N. of Lowestoft. Capsized and sunk after colliding with a whale. Passage Kings Lynn to Schiedam with barley. All hands saved and taken to Calais.

For account of ' astonishing sinking of a sailing-vessel through an attack by a whale ', vide *Illustrated London News, April 7, 1855.*

WAVE (I)

*Wave (I):* Bn. 146t. Built Wm. Griffith, P.M., 1862. Lost 1867.

WAVE (II)

Bn, 149tn, 94/23.4/12.5. Built at Borthygest 1868 by Wm. Griffith, Capt. Meuric Ellis, owner. Lost off the Smalls with all hands. Meuric Ellis's brother was then her ma.

*P.P. 1886, LXIV: Wave* Bn, of Caernarfon. Built P.M., 159t, owned M. Ellis, P.M., cargo 275t of steam coal from Swansea to Catania (Sicily). Vessel is stated to have been fitted with patent ventilators, not heard of since sailing on 6 Feb. 1881, 7 crew lost. The *Wave* is stated to have been a smart little vessel and well found. Heavy weather prevailed immediately after she had sailed.

WAVE OF LIFE (1)

A wood built paddle boat with a single engine. The first tug boat at P.M. She was replaced by the *James Conley* another wood built paddle boat. Came to P.M. August 1862 and was succeeded by the *James Conley.*

WAVE OF LIFE (2)

102tg, 91.3/17.9/9.2. Built at Newcastle on Tyne, by Hepple, 1872. Iron built twin engined paddle boat belonging to the P.M. Steam Tug Co. She succeeded the *James Conley.* Lewis Jones ma. She was rebottomed at Hugh Jones, Block's yard at Pen Cei, a job that took many months. On her relaunching my mother performed the launching ceremony with a bottle of port wine, bought by my grandfather at Mr. Barnard's shop in High St., slung on a red ribbon. She was ultimately sold by Auction for £150 having done a wonderful period of service to P.M. vessels both over the Bar and in Tremadoc Bay in all weathers.

## WERN

Bn, 188tg, 174treg. 102.2/24.2/13.2. Built at P.M. 1876 by Eben Roberts and his brother John. Mrs. Jones S.H., Minffordd, Ty Canol. E. Lloyd & Co. owners. One of the port's most notable Bn. She did many voyages between Tilt Cove, Newfoundland and Swansea with copper ore. John Richard Williams, commander. She was later commanded by his sons, Jack and Dick. In 1903 Evie Morris joined her as an A.B. at P.M. Greaves Wharf, Capt. Tom Jones was then her ma. (Twm bach Dre). Passage to Stettin with slates. In collision off Dungeness, bowsprit and foretopmast carried away, bow badly knocked in. Evie nearly killed in his bunk. Towed into Dover. Later proceeded on her voyage and ran on a sand bank in the Baltic, she was kedged off and ultimately arrived at Stettin. Tom Jones was an excellent navigator, but was always dogged by bad luck. On returning to Portsmouth all the crew left her. In the late Autum of 1898, she was sailing from Bahia, Brazil to Newfoundland in ballast. She encountered fearful storms and icebergs. During one storm the whole ship froze. The rudder became one block of ice. Dogged applications of boiling water failed to set it free. Forced to beardown for tropical weather, eventually reached the Azores, as the Newfoundland season was well advanced. The owners ordered her to come home to P.M. She arrived there on March 1, 1899 and discharged her ballast from Brazil on Cei Ballast. She was lost in collision (Feb. 1906) with the pilot steamer, *Leonard Spear* of Liverpool, bearing S.E., 3 miles from Point Lynas. Owners: Robert Lloyd Talsarnau, M.M., 32/64ths, Edward Lloyd P.M. retired M.M. 32/64ths.

## WHITE STAR

Mercantile Marine Reg., 1861 has *White Star* of Caernarvon, 166tons. Lloyds Reg. of 1861 has *White Star*, Bkn, built in Prince Edward Island in 1857. 166tons. Owned by Lloyd & Co., P.M. George Sorrell states in his book '*THE MAN BEFORE THE MAST*'. 'My fifth ship was the *White Star* of Port Madoc, Wales, Brigantine - rigged. Date of engagement 4 Aug., 1862, and discharge 18 Feb. 1863. From Ardrossan we sailed to Cette in the south of France with a cargo of pig-iron. This was my second appearance in the Mediterranean Sea. From Cette we sailed in ballast for Beyrout, Syria, the Holy Land of Scripture. From Beyrout we sailed north to Latakiveh — Laodicea I believe it is called in the Bible where St. Paul once preached. At Latakiveh we loaded up with millet seed and our instructions were to proceed to Falmouth for orders. On our homeward passage we called at Malta, also at Cagliari in the island of Sardinia. Between the latter place and Gibraltar I passed my third New Year's Day at sea. (1863). At the "Rock" we were detained some days on account of head winds for the current running through the Straits into the Mediterranean is so strong that few ships, if any, can beat their way out into the Atlantic without a fair wind. The passage home from "Gib" was rather stormy. On arriving at

Falmouth we had to wait for our orders; but when they came to hand they were to the effect that we were to proceed to Lynn in the east of England, where I left the *White Star* and took passage in a small steamer to Hull '.

*L.R. 1871:* Bn, 166t, 95.5/23.4/12.2. Built P. Edwards Is. 1857, E. Lloyd, owner, W. Parry, ma, P.M. — Hamburg.

WHY NOT

Sr, with painted ports. 93tn, 76/21.2/10. Built at New Brunwick, 1859. Francis Williams, ma.

WILD ROSE

Bg. Driven ashore at Afonwen and was bought by Mr. S. P. Owen and others of P.M. She was then used for carrying timber from Pensacola to P.M. See *Mary Jane.*

*C.R.S.:* Bg, 251.85t, 102.2/25.9/15.7. Sunderland, 1863. Caernarfon Reg, 1887. Previous Reg. A Norwegian wrecked vessel recovered, certificate of Seaworthiness granted Liverpool, 1887. Owners: Samuel Prydderch Owen, P.M. contractor, 64/64ths, M.O. July 1887. Owen dies 17 Oct. 1887. Ann Owen executrix sell 32/64ths to William Jones, sailmaker, P.M., who also received 32/64ths by way of mortgage. Vessel lost off Para, Brazil, 19 June 1889: Cert. lost with vessel.

WILLIAM

Sr, 87tr, 66.6/19.6/10.9. Built at P.M., 1838, John Roberts, ma. Later commanded by Capt. Hugh Watkins. During 1850 she sailed from Greaves Wharf, P.M., to Hamburg with 133⅓ tons of slates.

Built Francis Roberts, 1838. Lost off Abersoch, 12.5.1866.

WILLIAM ALEXANDER

Sr, 89t. Built at P.M., 1839, William Jones, P.M. ma.

Lost with all hands, North Sea, 3.10.1860.

WILLIAM EDWARDS

Sr, 51tn. Built at St. Helens, 1834, H. Jones, ma. H. Hughes, owner.

W. D. POTTS

Sr, with a double top'sl. 97tn, 83/22/10.4. Built at Pwllheli 1878 by Williams, Capt. Williams (Brandy Mawr) ma. Issac Ll. Morris, S.H. She and the *Carl & Louise* were the last vessels to be built at Pwllheli.

*C.R.S.:* Built by David Williams, Pwllheli, owned Robert Williams, M.M., on his death 1893 John Williams + Hugh Williams, mariners, owners. Hugh Parry, 7 Cornhill, P.M., S.H.,

1893. Sunk by U-Boat, Irish Sea, 1.5.1917? There is a model of the *W. D. Potts* in the City of Liverpool Museum, made by Capt. W. J. Slade of Appledore, who was her ma when she was sunk in 1917.

WILLIAM JONES

Sr, (2mst), 79tn, 77.1/19.8/10.3. Built Borthygest by 1870 by Wm. Griffiths, Thos. Humphreys, ma., the son of John Humphreys the pilot. The original ma was W. Evans and E. Owens, owner. Lost near Dungeness voyage Great Yarmouth to Llanelly, cargo of rails, 139 tons 8 cwts. 2 qrs. @ a freight of 6/- per ton.

WILLIAM KEITH

Sr, 99tg, 79.5/22.2/10.7. Built Portdinorwic, 1859 by Jones. Capt. Jones Barmouth ma.

WILLIAM AND MARY

WILLIAM MORTON

3mst. Sr, 167t. Built P.M., 1905 by David Jones, Capt. Lewis Lloyd, ma. Newfoundland trader. Abandoned at sea, 1919.

Sold Newfoundland, 1918.

*C.R.S.:* 3mst. Sr, 168tg, 142tr, 104.2/23.7/11.7. Built David Jones, P.M., 1905. Owners: Lewis Lloyd, Clogwyn Melyn, Talsarnau, M.M., 24/64ths; Robert Owen, 28 Brunswick Street, Liverpool, Shipbroker, 4/64ths; William Morris, 1 Britannia Terrace, P.M., Ship Chandler, 6/64ths; John Jones, Netherton House, Bank Place, P.M., Shipowner, 6/64ths; Hugh Morton of Meadow Bank, Coppice Road, Moseley in Co. of Worcester, Gentleman, 12/64ths; William Morton of Irvine Dale, Oakland Road, Moseley in Co. of Worcester, Gentleman, 12/64ths. John Jones of Netherton House, Bank Place, P.M., designated M.O. 5 May 1905. Reg. transferred to Port of St. John's, Newfoundland, 2 March 1918.

WILLIAM OWEN

2mst. Sr, 96tn, 72.6/20.5/11.0. Built at P.M., 1858, Morris & Co. owners, O. Roberts, ma. (L.R., 1878). She was condemned about 1898, and lay rotting on Traeth Cocos, for many years. She was ultimately broken up at Station Bach.

WILLIAM PRICHARD

3mst. Sr, 170tg, 146tn, 280td.w. Built at P.M. 1903 by David Jones, Prichard Bros., P.M., managing owners, Capt. Ellis Jones, Ty Mawr, Penmorfa, ma. Launched Feb. 14, 1903. Newfoundland trader. The launching ceremony was performed by Miss Nesta Prichard, daughter of

Mr. Griffith Prichard one of the owners. The following details of this vessel were given to me by Capt. Ellis John her ma. Total crew 6, Figurehead, a bust of Wm. Prichard, the shipbroker. *Free board* 20 inches, *Bowsprit* 14″ × 15″, between partners, heel to partners 13ft. *Fore Mast* Heel to deck, 12ft. 8inch., girth 14½in., deck to hounds 38′ 4″. Masthead to hounds 10ft. 61ft. overall (lower mast). *Fore top mast.* Heel to hounds 20ft., Gallant mast (part) 10ft., pole (or spare mast) 3ft., total length 35ft. *Overall length deck to truck* 83ft. 4in. *Main Mast. Deck to truck* 84½ft. *Mizen mast, Deck to truck* 81½ft. *Fore boom* 25ft. 1in. *Gaff* 23ft. *Main boom* 26ft. 9″. *Gaff* 25ft. 1in. *Mizen boom* 26ft. 9in. *Gaff* 21ft. *Stunsail booms,* 20ft. each overall. Patent reef to main and mizen sails only. *Fore Yard* 49ft. overall, *lower tops'l yard* 40ft, *upper tops'l yard* 37ft., *gallant yard,* 28ft. *Anchors, Port bower,* 6¾ cwt., stock 1½ cwts., total 8¼ cwts. *Starboard bower,* 10½. Whilst the vessel was commanded by Capt. Ellis Jones, i.e during the period she belonged to P.M., 1903 to 1916, she was almost wholly engaged in the transport of dried cod fish from Newfoundland and Labrador to Europe. During these 13 years she crossed the Atlantic 28 times (twice each voyage) and on one occasion she took a cargo of fish in drums from Newfoundland to Rio Grande do Sol in Southern Brazil and then took a cargo of raw hides to Falmouth for orders. On another occasion she sailed from Cadiz with salt for Rio Grande do Sol and returned to Hamburg with a load of hides (Oct. 1910). The *Jenny Jones Ellen Lloyd* and *Sidney Smith* carried out this last voyage at about the same time. When crossing the Bar at Rio Grande the *Wm. Prichard* grounded and suffered a severe shaking so much so that her riggings were loose and almost useless. This damage was repaired at sea, and she got across the Atlantic quite safely. In 1916 the vessel was sold to Newfoundland and resold to an Irish firm a little later, and during a N.E. gale she was blown ashore on the East Coast of England and was declared a 'constructive total loss'. Capt. Ellis Jones is a grandson of John Ethridge, one of Alexander Maddocks's right hand men; for 4 years from 1897 he commanded the brig *Fleetwing.* For short periods he also commanded the *Edward Windus, W. W. Lloyd* and the *Blanche Currie.*

> *C.R.S.:* 3mst. Sr, 169tg, 92.18tr, 102.2/23.7/12.4. Built David Jones, P.M., 1903. Owners: Ellis Jones of Penmorfa, co. Caernarfon, M.M., 24/64ths; Richard Griffith Prichard, Llwyn Onn, P.M., Shipowner, 16/64ths; Griffith Prichard, Bodhyfryd, Penrhyndeudraeth, Ship Broker, 8/64ths; Owen Jones of Borth-y-gest, Shipowner, 4/64ths: David Jones of P.M., Ship Builder, 12/64ths. On 9 Feb. 1903 David Jones sold 8/64ths to John Getheridge Jones of Penmorfa, M.M. David Jones died intestate December 5, 1910, letters of administration granted to Margaret Jones of 19 Lombard Street, P.M., widow. P.M.

owners all sell shares on 6 June 1916 to Robert Ehlers of 61 Queen Square, Bristol, described as Newfoundland Produce Merchant.

WILLIAM RUTTS

WILLIAMS (1)

K, 37t. Built at P.M., 1837.

WILLIAMS (2)

Sk, (Known as *Williams bach*). Morris Williams. Built Morfa Bychan, ma. *L.R. 1871/2:* Sk, 28t, 41.4/13.4/7.3, Pwllheli, 1840 owned Morris & Co., P.M., R. Jones, ma. Built by John Williams, Bardsey? Lost near Criccieth, 2.8.1881.

WINIFRED

Bg, 189tg, 173tn, 99.3/23.9/13.1, Built at P.M., 1866, by Hugh Williams. Reg. at Caernarvon, 10 Oct. 1866. Owners: John Owen, Ty Fry, P.M., M.M., 56/64ths, William Owen, Ty Fry, Merioneth, Farmer, 2/64ths, Rd. Owen, Ty Fry, Merioneth, Farmer, 4/64ths, Margaret Owen, Ty Fry, Merioneth, spinster, 2/64ths. Phosphate rock trader and Newfoundland trader. Stranded and became a total wreck in Almeira Bay, Spain. 23 November, 1898 on a voyage from Labrador to Genoa with a cargo of 4,100 quintals of fish at a freight of 2/3d. per quintal. Robert Evans, Farm Yard, P.M. was then her ma.

WRESTLER

Sr. Built at Borthygest and wrecked on her 1st voyage.

W. W. LLOYD

261tg, 244tn, 116/24.5/14.4. Built at P.M., 1875 by Eben Roberts, Owen Lloyd of the *Tyne* and others owners. Capt. John Owens, ma. Phosphate trader. She once crossed from Aruba to Liverpool with phosphate rock in 27 days. Capt. Owen Parry was then her ma. Lost near Port of Spain, voyage Trinidad to Rotterdam, March, 1900. Cargo 388 tons of Asphalt at a freight of 19/- per ton. She was later re'floated and sold to someone from Jersey. Mr. John Prichard Williams (son in law of Evan Morris pilot) served on her as an A.B. on the following voyage, 1893/4: P.M. to Cardiff with a small cargo of slates; Cardiff to Santa Catherina with coal; Santa Catherina to Aruba in ballast; Aruba to Glasgow with phosphate rock; Glasgow to Cardiff in ballast. Again to Santa Catherina with coal; Santa Catherina to Aruba in ballast; then to Plymouth with phosphate rock where he left her. 12 months later he rejoined her as bosun, 1895. P.M. to Harburg with slates; Harburg to Dundee, then to

Waterford, then Cardiff in ballast. Cardiff to La Guira coal; then to Aruba in ballast; Aruba to Barking with phosphate rock, where he left her. Capt. Owen Griffith was her ma on these voyages. Mr. Williams, testifies that she was a splendid ship especially in rough weather.

> *C.R.S.:* Bg, 252.89t, 116/24.5/14.4. Built P.M. 1875, by Ebenezer Roberts & Co., P.M. Owners: John Owens, Gellidywyll, Maentwrog, M.M., 26/64ths; Robert Thomas, Pantnewydd, Llanfrothen, Farmer, 4/64ths; John Owens, Gellidywyll, Maentwrog, Farmer, 4/64ths; John Roberts, Snr., Gellidywyll, Maentwrog, Farmer, 4/64ths; John Roberts, Jnr., Gellidywyll, Maentwrog, Farmer, 2/64ths; Pierce Jones, Garth, Maentwrog, Farmer, 2/64ths; Robert Parry, Ffestiniog, Bookseller, 2/64ths; Morgan Jones, Plasnewydd, Penrhyndeudraeth, Farmer, 2/64ths; Owen Lloyd, P.M., Shipowner, 8/64ths; William Lloyd, P.M., Ship Chandler and Draper, 4/64ths; Mary Lloyd, P.M., Spinster, 4/64ths; Jane Ellen Lloyd, P.M., Spinster, 2/64ths; John Owens transferred 8/64ths by b. of s. to Owen Lloyd of P.M., M.M., on 23 Dec. 1879. Various exchanges but David Lloyd, Dora Street, M.O., in 1891. Reg. closed 27 Aug. 1900. Vessel wrecked in West Indies and re-registered at Bridgetown, Barbados as being passed seaworthy.

ZEDULOUS

(Locally Sedulous). Sr, 74tn. Built at Nevin, 1849 by R. Thomas. Lost on P.M. Bar loaded with copper ore and dynamite, 1882. One of her masts stood above water for many years. I passed it with *Cwch Pink* many times.

> Lost 3.1.1882, P.M., bar.

ZION HILL

> *Zino Hill:* Sr, 114t. Built 1856? Henry Jones, lost off Morecambe 7.12.1877.

# FURTHER STUDIES

## A PROFILE OF THE SNOW-BRIG *DEPTFORD* (1810-1844)

THE *Deptford* was launched on the Mawddach river in 1810 and was immediately armed with 4 guns to ward off the attentions of French privateers in the English Channel. Several other Barmouth vessels were armed (though lightly) in this period for the same reason,[1] as masters and owners were not prepared to confine their vessels within the relatively protected waters of the Irish Sea. These guns (probably 6- or 9-pounders) were removed in 1815 at the conclusion of the Napoleonic Wars. At 121 tons, the *Deptford* was of average capacity, though several larger vessels were built on the Mawddach at this time.[2] The first master was Capt. John Williams of Barmouth and the vessel was owned by Capt. Williams and others, though, until 1839, the port of registry was London.[3]

In the absence of any surviving logs, disbursement books or the like, the details of 'destined voyages' in *Lloyd's Register* provide some impression of the vessel's movements:

Destined Voyages of the Snow-Brig *Deptford* (1811-1844).

| *Year* | *Destined Voyage* | *Year* | *Destined Voyage* |
|---|---|---|---|
| 1811 | London-Cork | 1828 | Cork |
| 1812 | London-Dublin | 1829 | Plymouth Coaster |
| 1813 | London-Dublin | 1830 | Plymouth Coaster |
| 1814 | Cork | 1831 | Dublin Coaster |
| 1815 | London-Dublin | 1832 | Topsham Coaster |
| 1816 | Waterford-Dublin | 1833 | Hull Coaster |
| 1817 | | 1834 | London-Newcastle |
| 1818 | London-Dublin | 1835 | London-Newcastle |
| 1819 | London-Dublin | 1836 | London-Newcastle |
| 1820 | London Coaster | 1837 | London-Newcastle |
| 1821 | London-Cadiz | 1838 | Shields-Dublin |
| 1822 | London-Dublin | 1839 | Beaumaris-Lynn |
| 1823 | Plymouth-London | 1840 | Liverpool Coaster |
| 1824 | Falmouth-London | 1841 | Liverpool Coaster |
| 1825 | Cork-London | 1842 | London Coaster |
| 1826 | London | 1843 | London Coaster |
| 1827 | Plymouth-Wales | 1844 | London Coaster |

The end came in about 1844 when the *Deptford* was condemned as unseaworthy.[4]

These details indicate that, like most of the smaller brigs and snows of local build, the *Deptford* generally engaged in coastwise voyages to and from London and that trading links with Irish Sea ports enabled the vessel to return to 'home waters' for cargoes of slate from the Caernarvonshire ports for London and elsewhere.[5] The voyage to Cadiz in 1820-1 appears to have been exceptional, but the evidence derived from *Lloyd's Register* is so limited that it must be treated with caution. During the 1830s, when the *Deptford* was commanded by Capt. Lewis Dedwydd (Dedwith) of Barmouth, coal was carried from Newcastle to London. In short, the *Deptford* was a typical coastwise trader employed, no doubt, in a variety of trades, though slate and coal were probably the principal freights.

THE VESSEL'S RIG. — The *Deptford* was variously described in *Lloyd's Register* as a brig or snow; as a snow between 1811 and 1815, in 1818 and from 1820 to 1823, and as a brig in all other years. This distinction cannot be treated too seriously as the two rigs were very similar. Both brigs and snows were two-masted vessels, square-rigged on both masts. The only real distinction was that snows (properly so-called) had a mast or spar aft of the main-mast, the 'snow mast', upon which was set a fore-and-aft sail, called the 'snow sail'.[6] All that can be said with confidence is that the snow rig was favoured at Barmouth when the *Deptford* was built in 1810 and that it remained popular until the 1820s when square-riggers were ousted by smacks and schooners. Until the opening of Porthmadog in 1824, the Mawddach shipbuilders were the square-rig specialists of North Wales with over 100 vessels to their credit.[7] Yards at Pwllheli and Porthmadog thereafter assumed a commanding lead in this department.[8]

REPAIRS. — *Lloyd's Register* suggests that the *Deptford* sustained no really serious damage, but the vessel was repaired and re-fitted at various times. In 1833 the vessel was lengthened and thoroughly repaired. Major repairs were also effected in 1837 and a new deck was fitted in 1838. Small repairs were made in 1843, shortly before the vessel was condemned as unseaworthy. It is likely that much of this work was done at Barmouth, which was a port of survey for the purposes of marine insurance.[9]

THE VESSEL'S TONNAGE. — From 1811 to 1826, the tonnage was given as 120 or 121; from 1827 to 1833 as 113; from 1834 to 1837 as 114; and from 1838 to 1844 as $^{114}/_{107}$. Without going into the technicalities, tonnages in the 19th century were variously rendered as tonnage burden, registered tonnage, gross tonnage and under-deck tonnage. It is sufficient here to note that the *Deptford* was of average tonnage (and, hence, capacity) for a locally-built square-rigger and that few vessels built in North Cardigan or Tremadog Bay exceeded 200 tons (this may be compared with the *Cutty Sark* of 900 tons register, now preserved at Greenwich).[10] Many similar vessels were built for the slate trade and for general trading to, from and within the Irish Sea. The significantly larger vessels, it seems, were built for Liverpool owners in the main.[11]

MASTERS AND OWNERS. — The first master of the *Deptford* was Capt. John Williams of Barmouth. He was also part-owner from launching to at least 1833.[12] I have not been able to trace Capt. Williams in the parish registers as yet, but he may have been associated with the Williams family of Henddôl, a farm situated near the southern shore of the Mawddach estuary, near the modern township of Fairbourne.[13] Capt. Williams retained command until about 1825, when he was succeeded by Capt. Lewis Dedwydd (1792-1859) of Barmouth. Capt. Dedwydd (Dedwith or Deadwith) was a member of one of Barmouth's most distinguished seafaring families. He was a son of Capt. Griffith Dedwydd (1756-1826) of Maesafallen (Llanaber parish) and, as such, a grandson of Capt. Griffith Dedwydd (1706-1783), who was a native of Nevern parish in Pembrokeshire. His grandfather settled in Barmouth in 1747 upon his marriage to Jane Owen, heiress of Gorllwyn Fawr. Capt. Lewis Dedwydd married Anne Owen at Llanaber in 1826, and this marriage produced at least four children.[14] A son, Capt. Griffith E. Dedwydd (1827-1902), distinguished himself, when master of the three-masted schooner *Theda* by sailing from Labrador to Gibraltar in just over 11 days.[15] Like many other mariners from Barmouth, this Griffith Dedwydd moved to Porthmadog and was associated with that port throughout his sailing career. His father, on the other hand, remained at Barmouth, where he died in April 1859 aged 67.[16] He commanded the *Deptford* from 1825-6 to the undignified end in 1844, and he was part-owner of the vessel from at least 1834 onwards.[17]

London remained the port of registry until 1838, when the *Deptford* was registered at Barmouth.[18]

THE *Deptford* AND THE PORTHMADOG SLATE TRADE. — Capt. Lewis Dedwydd and other Barmouth masters quickly appreciated the new trading opportunities presented by the opening of Porthmadog harbour in 1824, although they continued to frequent the other major slate ports of Caernarfon and Bangor (Port Penrhyn). The shipment of slates from Porthmadog in the early years was on a fairly modest scale until the completion of the Ffestiniog tramway in 1836, but the harbour records indicate that Capt. Dedwydd loaded slates there in 1826 and 1828. In each case, 113 tons of slate were received and £1 17s. 8d. was paid on each occasion by way of harbour dues calculated at the rate of 4d. per ton.[19] Porthmadog soon joined the more established Caernarvonshire slate ports as a vigorous competitor and as the focal point of maritime activity in North Cardigan or Tremadog Bay.

## REFERENCES

[1] About 20 such vessels are recorded in *Lloyd's Register*. They included the snow *Belinda* (6 guns); the snow *Brothers* (2 and later 4 guns); the snow-brig *Cambria* (6 guns); the brig *Catherine* (4 guns); the snow *Ceres* (4 guns); the snow *Eliza* (2 guns); the snow-brig *Fame* (6 guns); and the snow *Friends* (2 guns). Many privateers, on the other hand, fairly bristled with guns, and lightly-armed merchantmen like those above were no real match for them.

[2] They included the ship *Betsey* (202 tons); the snow *Ceres* (190 tons); and the snow *Mervinia* (173 tons).

[3] *Lloyd's Register*, 1811-1839.

[4] ibid., 1844. The registration year was 1843-4.

[5] In other words, the slate trade generated a complex trading cycle which comprised major English ports like London, Bristol and Liverpool and both Irish and Scottish ports. Trade with Europe steadily increased.

[6] See, for example, George Goldsmith-Carter's *Sailing Ships & Sailing Craft* (Hamlyn, London, 1969), p. 101. The snow is there described as 'a brig-type coastal trader'.

[7] Some 105 square-riggers were built on the Mawddach from 1750 to 1827, and most of these were launched during the first two decades of the 19th century. The list has been compiled from *Lloyd's Register*.

[8] The Pwllheli yards produced a number of large square-riggers (over 300 tons) — mostly barques and fully-rigged ships. The Porthmadog yards also produced several larger square-riggers during the early decades.

[9] In other words, vessels could be surveyed at Barmouth and repaired in accordance with the stringent standards applied by Lloyd's. Vessels had to be surveyed every few years to retain a Lloyd's classification.

[10] Thus local vessels were miniatures, but this did not seriously restrict the trades in which they engaged. Builders had to work within the limits set by the difficult coastline and small harbours of Wales.

[11] Many vessels were built for Liverpool owners and were destined for deep-water voyages. Thus, for example, the ship *Betsey* (202 tons), built on the Mawddach in 1803, traded to the West Indies and South America. She was lost, without trace, having sailed from Rio de Janeiro for London on September 22nd, 1813 (*Lloyd's List,* Friday, March 26th, 1813).

[12] *Lloyd's Register,* 1811-1833: owners variously given as Capt. & Co. and Williams & Co. John Williams seems to have retained his interest when Capt. Dedwydd assumed command in 1825.

[13] For this interesting family, see *The Old Order* (based on the Diary of Elizabeth Baker, 1778-1786), ed. Ben Bowen Thomas (Cardiff, 1945).

[14] Llanaber Parish Registers.

[15] Henry Hughes, *Immortal Sails* (2nd. Ed., Prescot, Lancashire, 1969), pp. 168-171.

[16] He was buried at Llanaber and the details are taken from his gravestone.

[17] *Lloyd's Register,* 1834-1844.

[18] ibid., 1838-44.

[19] Porthmadog Harbour Papers, N.L.W. MS. 513. Slate remained the principal export throughout, though small quantities of manganese and copper were exported. The copper ore came mainly from the Beddgelert district.

## A PROFILE OF THE BRIG *LADY VAUGHAN* (1826-1863)

BUILT on the Mawddach in 1826,[1] this brig of 125 tons appears to have been named in honour of Lady Vaughan of Nannau, wife of Sir Robert Williames Vaughan (1768-1843). The vessel was commanded by a series of local masters and was owned outright by Capt. Humphrey Humphreys (1802-1863) of Barmouth. In the absence of any surviving logs or other detailed records, the entries in *Lloyd's Register* provide a general impression of the vessel's movements:

Destined Voyages of the Brig *Lady Vaughan* (1828-1863).

| *Year* | *Destined Voyage* | *Year* | *Destined Voyage* |
|---|---|---|---|
| 1828 | Liverpool-Riga | 1846 | Barmouth Coaster |
| 1829 | Liverpool-Riga | 1847 | Barmouth Coaster |
| 1830 | London-Riga | 1848 | Barmouth-Hamburg |
| 1831 | Plymouth Coaster | 1849 | ........................ |
| 1832 | Plymouth Coaster | 1850 | Barmouth |
| 1833 | Plymouth Coaster | 1851 | ........................ |
| 1834 | ........................ | 1852 | Not registered |
| 1835 | London-Bangor | 1853 | ,, ,, |
| 1836 | London-Le Havre | 1854 | ,, ,, |
| 1837 | London-Le Havre | 1855 | Porthmadog |
| 1838 | London-Le Havre | 1856 | Porthmadog-Harburg |
| 1839 | London-Le Havre | 1857 | Porthmadog-Harburg |
| 1840 | Beaumaris-London | 1858 | Porthmadog-Hamburg |
| 1841 | Beaumaris-London | 1859 | Porthmadog-Hamburg |
| 1842 | Beaumaris-London | 1860 | Porthmadog Coaster |
| 1843 | Beaumaris-London/ Cardiff Coaster | 1861 | Not registered |
| 1844 | Cardiff Coaster | 1862 | ,, ,, |
| 1845 | Cardiff Coaster | 1863 | ,, ,, |

The above list suggests that the brig *Lady Vaughan* did not become closely associated with Porthmadog until the 1850s, though the vessel was registered at that port from 1847 onwards — this runs counter to what Henry Hughes had to say about the *Lady*

*Vaughan* in his book *Immortal Sails*.[2] It appears that this brig was initially registered at Beaumaris; in 1839 the port of registry was Barmouth, but the *Lady Vaughan* was again registered at Beaumaris from 1840 to 1847. Thereafter, Porthmadog remained the port of registry until 1863, when the vessel was lost:

> 'Antwerp, 27th Jan. — The 'Lady Vaughan' (brig), Edwards, from Newcastle to Plymouth, with coal, was abandoned in a sinking state 21st Jan., about 21 miles off Ostend; crew saved by an Ostend fishing craft'. ('Lloyd's List' January 28th, 1863.)

The evidence suggests that the *Lady Vaughan* was primarily a slate trader from the northern ports of Caernarvonshire and, later, from Porthmadog.

REPAIRS. — Various repairs were effected. In 1845 a new keel and keelson were fitted; a new deck was fitted in 1847; small repairs were made in 1849 and large repairs in 1854 when the vessel was surveyed and classified AE/1; and damage repairs were effected in 1858. Much, if not all, of this work was done at Barmouth, in the shipyard, perhaps, where the vessel was originally fitted out in 1826.

MASTERS AND OWNERS. — The first master of the *Lady Vaughan* was Capt. Humphrey Humphreys (1802-1863), a son of the brig's original owner, Capt. Edward Humphreys (1761-1833). His father was a significant shipowner in local terms. At his death in 1833, Edward Humphreys owned 15½/16ths of the brig *Hope* of Barmouth, a vessel which he commanded from its launching in 1803 until 1830; a share (1/16th) of the sloop *Meirion;* 4½/16ths of the sloop *Anna Susan*; and the brig *Lady Vaughan* outright (16/16ths).[3] He also owned a farm called Caeau'r Hafod in Llanynys parish, Denbighshire, and Ffriddfechan in the parish of Llanaber. Humphrey Humphreys was left 15/16ths of the brig *Lady Vaughan* in his father's will.[4] The vessel was then valued at £23 per 1/16th (£368 in all), so that Humphrey Humphreys's interest was worth £345. He remained master of the vessel until about 1839, when he was succeeded by Capt. David Davies of Harlech. Having married Jane Humphreys (1806-1867) of Llanfairuchaf, he retired from the sea to live at 'Llanfair Hill', Llanfair, where he carried on business as a 'merchant' (or shopkeeper). He died in the same year as his vessel was lost and was buried at Llanaber in August 1863, aged 61. Some of his descendants, notably the Pughs of Llanfair, were mariners.

Capt. David Davies, who succeeded Capt. Humphrey Humphreys in about 1839, was master of the *Lady Vaughan* until 1848, when Capt. H. Roberts took over.[5] Capt. Davies lived at Pentref, Harlech.[6] Capt. H. (Humphrey) Roberts was succeeded by Capt. J. Roberts in about 1855 and, finally, the vessel was commanded by a Capt. Edwards when she was abandoned off Ostend. There is reason to believe that Humphrey Humphreys of 'Llanfair Hill' remained almost outright owner of the *Lady Vaughan* from 1833 to the end in 1863 — this was quite unusual, as owners were not generally associated with one vessel over such a long period.[7]

THE 'PROTEST' OF 1851. — Whilst no logs or disbursement books appear to have survived for the *Lady Vaughan*, one document pertaining to the vessel, now preserved in Coleg Harlech Library, deserves some consideration. This is an 'Attestation & Protest' made known by Capt. D. Davies on February 9th, 1841, before one Simon Ring, a 'Notary and Tabellion Public' of Cove in the county of Cork. Capt. Davies, as master of the brig *Lady Vaughan* of Barmouth, recounted how his vessel, laden with slates and bound from Bangor to London, sustained damage and loss at sea. On 23 February, Capt. Davies and two of his crew, Aaron Roberts ('Chief Mate') and Rees Edward ('Seaman') appeared before Simon Ring and swore to the following account of the damage sustained. Having completed the lading at Bangor, the vessel unmoored in charge of a pilot on Monday, 25 January, and was brought to anchor off Garth Point, where they remained until Monday, 1 February. At 3 p.m., the wind being ESE and the pilot having come aboard, they made sail over the Bars and proceeded on their voyage on 2 February. They swore that their vessel was 'then tight, and staunch well and sufficiently found with Chains, Anchors and other materials, her Cargo well and carefully stowed and secured, and Hatches secured'. The *Lady Vaughan* encountered strong breezes and snow on the following day, 3 February, and at 7 a.m. they 'got the length of the longships'. The weather proved too thick to run for Scilly on 4 February, and the wind continuing strong Capt. Davies put into Whitesands Bay, Cornwall, for shelter where he anchored in 12 fathoms of water. At this time they had 70 fathoms of chain out. On 5 February it was still blowing strong, so they sent down the yards and got their best Bower chain ready to let go. In spite of these precautions, the vessel continued to drag. The best Bower chain proved insufficient, and by 4 a.m. on 6 February they were two miles offshore and still dragging the anchors. The anchors later held, but on Sunday, 7 February, 'the vessel rode heavily' and sprung a leak, which they found to increase. Sunday was a day of 'tremendous Gales, and Squalls, with thick weather', and the vessel again dragged her anchors and drove right out of the Bay. The appearers said that 'it was dangerous to be on deck, the sea washing over them, they deemed it requisite and advisable to Slip both Cables, and set the Maintopsail close Reefed, and hove to with Ship's Head to North East . . . ' The wind veered to ESE and SE and they wore ship and kept away for Scilly, but the weather thickened that afternoon. At 8 a.m. on 8 February 'it becoming more moderate they made Sail for Cork Harbour for Shelter, and to procure Anchors and Cables, as also to have the leaks stopped. And upon the next day (February 9th), having received the assistance of a Pilot, and Boats crew, they arrived in Cork Harbour and ran their vessel on a Bank, and where Surveys upon the damages were held'. They declared that this was a true account of the mishap and protested 'the aforesaid bad Weather, Gales, Storms, accidents and occurences' as being the entire cause of the damage sustained.

The Protest was signed by David Davies, Aaron Roberts and Rees Edwards and by Simon Ring as Public Notary of Cove in the Barony of Barrymore. The Cornish coasts claimed numerous Welsh vessels in the 19th century, but, fortunately, they were denied their prey on this occasion. Capt. Davies of Harlech remained in command of the brig until 1848. Rees Edwards of Barmouth, a grandson of Capt. Rees Edwards (1757-1837) of the sloop *Unity*,[8] later transferred to the *Jane Brown of Barmouth*.[9] Whilst this incident possessed certain unusual features, it can be taken as being fairly typical of the kind of hazards encountered by the slate traders of North Wales, and it is fortunate that the Protest has survived to provide this brief insight into such hazards on the Bangor-London slate run. As we have seen, the *Lady Vaughan* survived for another 20 years or so until she was abandoned in January 1863. She was then a matronly vessel of some 37 years. Capt. Humphrey Humphreys, the owner, had good reason to lament the passing of a vessel which he first took to sea in the 1820s when brigs and snows ruled the waves. The sense of loss may even have hastened his own demise just six months later.

## REFERENCES

[1] *Lloyd's Register,* 1828. Apart from the brig *Merioneth,* which was launched in the following year, the *Lady Vaughan* was the last square-rigger built on the Mawddach until the 1850s. This may well have been due to developments at Pwllheli and Porthmadog.

[2] Henry Hughes, *Immortal Sails* (2nd Ed., Prescot, Lancashire, 1969), plate 3, where it is said that the brig was Porthmadog's first. It is also said at p. 34 that the *Lady Vaughan* was launched to the order of Capt. Humphrey Humphreys and that she was 'probably one of, if, indeed, not the first, square-rigger vessel to carry the name of Portmadoc to foreign lands and distant seas'.

[3] Will of Edward Humphreys of Barmouth, Bangor Probate Records, N.L.W., Aberystwyth. Such outright ownership was unusual in Gwynedd as indicated in the writer's essay: 'Maritime Merioneth: The Town and Port of Barmouth, 1565-1973'.

[4] Will of Edward Humphreys, 1833. The remaining 1/16th of the *Lady Vaughan* was left to Humphrey Humphreys's brother, Richard Lloyd Humphreys (an elder brother).

[5] *Lloyd's Register,* 1848.

[6] Llandanwg Parish Registers. According to the Tithe Commutation Award for Llandanwg of 1840, Capt. Davies owned a small parcel of land called 'Pentre' in Harlech. It comprised some 5¾ acres and included two marsh allotments on the Morfa.

[7] Most of the Barmouth square-riggers which survived beyond their prime were sold to English owners (some in the West Country) for routine coastwise work. In other cases, masters bought out other shareholders as shares fell in value with depreciation. A modest shareholder could never have felt quite the same about a vessel as Capt. Humphreys is likely to have done.

[8] See the writer's study of Barmouth and the forthcoming essay: 'Mawddach Sloops and the *Unity* of Barmouth, 1781-1799'. The Edwards were a noteworthy seafaring family.

[9] The Disbursement Book of the *Jane Brown* of Barmouth, which contains entries for the period 1841-1850, is preserved at the Dolgellau Archives. The vessel traded to London from Caernarfon and Port Penrhyn. Rees Edwards (1817-1877) was subsequently master of the schooner *Owain Glyndwr* of Barmouth, another slate trader.

## ELSINORE BOWLS

WHEN a Porthmadog vessel went to Copenhagen for the first time, it was customary for the Master of the vessel to be presented with a bowl by the brokers who had arranged the charter on arrival at Elsinore. The name of the vessel's master, and sometimes his wife, was inscribed in gold on the bowl, and sometimes a picture of the same rig of vessel would appear on the bowl.

These bowls are very beautifully made in Danish china. There are many of them in the Porthmadog district.

Illustrated on Pl. 10 from left to right:

(1) Presented to 'Capt. Griffith Roberts master of the schooner Laura' of Porthmadog. Inscribed as follows: 'Capt. Griffith Roberts from Major Wright & Co., Elsinore 1852'. 'Success to the Laura of Portmadoc'.

Now in the possession of Misses L. and D. Jones, Tegfryn, Borth-y-gest, grand-daughters of Capt. Griffith Roberts and sisters to Griffith Roberts Jones, D.D., of Pwllheli, 1954.

(2) Presented to Griffith and Sarah Williams, Borth-y-gest — Inscribed 'Griffith and Sarah Williams' with a picture of schooner. Capt. Williams was master of the schooner *Jane Catherine* of Porthmadog, 1842-1872.

Now in possession of Mrs. Tom Davies, Ralph Street, Borth-y-gest.

(3) Presented to Capt. Owen Lloyd, master of the schooner *Betty* of Porthmadog. He also commanded the schooner *Elizabeth* (3) and the brigantine *Majestic*. He was father of Capt. Owen Lloyd of the *Tyne* of Porthmadog.

The bowl is inscribed as follows: 'Schooner Betty [1873]' (the date is obscure). 'Capt. Owen Lloyd from Major Wright & Co., Elsinore'.

Now in possession of Miss Lloyd, Dora Street, Porthmadog, grand-daughter of Capt. Owen Lloyd.

(The *Betty* was built at Pwllheli 1938 and was lost 1871.)

The brig *George Casson,* Captain Hugh Parry, master, entering the Bay of Naples, 5 December 1868.

71. The brig *Fleetwing,* Captain John Roberts, master.

72. The steel barque *Beeswing*, built Greenock 1893, Captain R. Griffiths, ma

73. The barquentine *Martha Percival*, built Ebenezer Roberts, 1877.

74. Captain R. Griffiths and members of the crew of the *Beeswing* at Portland, Oregon. Top, left to right, W. Paul, cook; P. Williams, first mate; Captain R. Griffiths; J. Lewis, second mate; R. Roberts, steward. Second row, G. Davies; W. Woodrow, apprentice; A. J. Owens, apprentice; T. O. Jones, boatswain. Bottom row, J. Soly, T. Jones, J. Thomas, J. Williams, R. H. Roberts, M.(?) Jones.

75. The schooner *Dizzy Dunlop*, built 1878, being re-keeled at a Scandinavian port. Captain Thomas E. Williams.

The brigantine *Edward Windus*, built 1864, at Harburg, shortly before she was lost through collision in English Channel, 1904, with only one survivor.

78. Figurehead of *Cadwalader Jones*, at Brixham, August 1931.
[Grahame E. Farr Collection.]

87. Launching day for three-masted schooner *Gestiana*, last vessel built at Po madog, in 1913. A cry of dismay came from assembled crowd when the christer bottle failed to break at first attempt on bows of ill-fated vessel.

88. The *Gestiana* launched ‘broadside on’ at Rotten Tare, Porthmadog.

89. The *Gestiana* safely launched at Porthmadog.

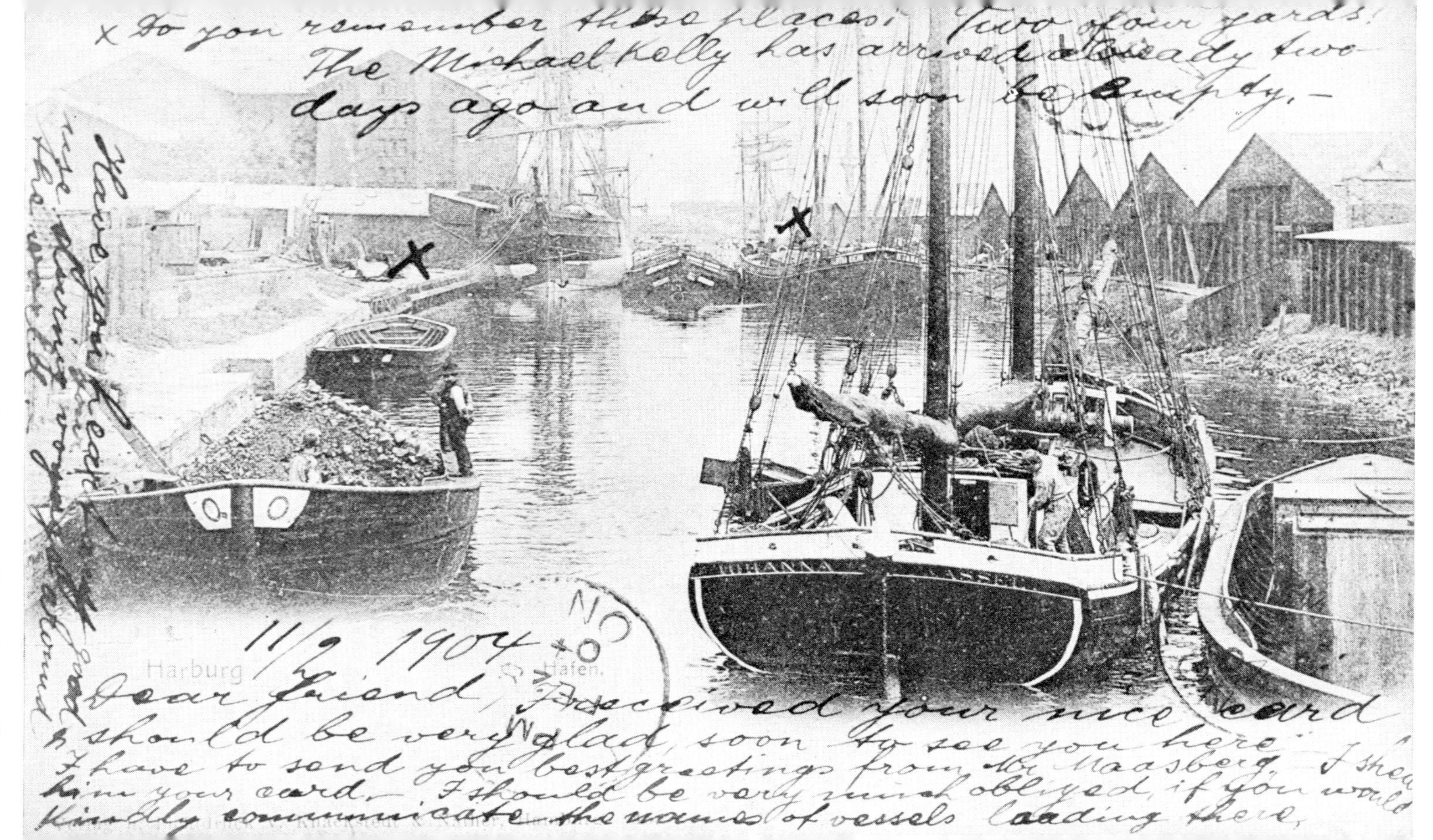
x Do you remember those places? Two of our yards!
The Michael Kelly has arrived already two
days ago and will soon be empty. –
Harburg Hafen.
11/9 1904
Dear friend, I received your nice card
& should be very glad, soon to see you here.
I have to send you best greetings from Mr Maasberg, I shew
him your card. – I should be very much obliged, if you would
kindly communicate the names of vessels loading there,
Have you heard any good
use during voyage around
the world.

91. The German connection (2). Ten Porthmadog master mariners have their photograph taken at Hamburg, where their vessels were unloading slate at the same time. (Left to right, standing) Captain R. A. Jones, *Mary Lloyd;* Captain Lewis, *Mary Casson;* Captain W. Green, *Tyne;* Captain R. Jones, *M. A. James;* Captain H. Roberts, *Evelyn;* Captain John T. Jones, *Mary Annie;* (seated) Captain J. Morris, *David Morris;* Captain David Roberts, *Michael Kelly;* Captain Owen, *Edwin*; and Captain Roberts, *Ann and Jane Pritchard*.

92. Safe arrival: the *Wave of Life* tows two homeward bound vessels over the into Porthmadog on a peaceful evening.

## THE BRIGS *GEORGE CASSON* AND *FLEETWING*

AMONG the best known of all Porthmadog vessels were the *George Casson,* built there in 1863, and the *Fleetwing,* built at Borth-y-gest in 1874. The *George Casson,* a brig of 154 tons gross, was commanded in the Mediterranean trade in her early years by Captain Evan Rogers of Harlech, with John James, a young Porthmadog man, as his mate. They were followed, in 1867, by Captain Robert Roberts, who had Humphrey Lloyd as mate, and, later, in November of the same year, Captain Hugh Parry, the future shipbroker, took command. He was then aged 27 and had previously served in the *Fanny Beck;* his mate was Ellis Roberts, also aged 27, who came from Criccieth. Their first voyage was not without incident: at Gibraltar, in December, Hugh Parry entered in the 'Articles': 'Richard Baham deserted from this day and never was found'. Captain Parry had reason to assert his authority a few weeks later as the *George Casson* sailed northwards off the Spanish coast. On 8 January 1868, at 11.50 a.m., when they were in an estimated position 38°25′N 10°W, he entered in the log: 'Thomas Jones, Boatswain, refused to come on deck to take in sails, which cause them to split. Same day refuse to do his duty, when I told him to go down to the forecastle, and that he was to live on bread and water until he would come to his work'. It must have been with quiet satisfaction that the young Captain Parry recorded in the log next day that the boatswain had 'turn to his work again'.

The following year saw the *George Casson* sailing from Porthmadog to Stettin and Hamburg, and also from Cardiff to Naples (where the almost inevitable painting of her entering the bay was duly obtained). The vessel had been named after one of the Casson brothers, the bankers who had made a considerable contribution to the development of Porthmadog shipping, and no doubt it was they who had originally found the money to finance her building. By 1870, when she was registered *de novo* at Porthmadog, the Casson brothers were no longer shareholders, although William Pierce, described as ' Bank Manager ', had a mortgage in respect of his four shares with George and John Casson, bankers. George Casson himself died in the late sixties; his will, dated 18 July 1865, appointed John and W. G. Casson as his executors. By 1870 the shareholders in the *George Casson* were Hugh Parry, her master, who held 16/64 shares, William Pierce, bank manager, 4/64, Robert Morris, slate shipper, 8/64, Robert Jones, merchant, 4/64, John Parry, joiner, Tremadog, 4/64, Humphrey Prichard of Beddgelert, coachman, 4/64, John Jones of Llanllyfni, quarryman, 4/64, John Owen of Ffestiniog, Quarry Agent, 8/64, John Richard, also of Ffestiniog, shopkeeper, 4/64, Edward Williams of Elwy House, Wrexham, mine agent, 4/64, and Jane Jones of Penybryn, Dolgellau, widow, 4/64.

Captain Parry had Evan Ebenezer Parry, also from Nefyn (probably his brother), as mate for the voyages to the Baltic and Elbe ports and the Mediterranean throughout the early seventies, and in 1878, when Captain Hugh Parry moved to take command of his fine new schooner, the *Frau Minna Petersen,* Evan Ebenezer Parry of Well Street, Nefyn, became master of the *George Casson,* which he commanded for the next nine years. Throughout his period as master, a preponderance of Nefyn men served aboard the *George Casson* on voyages from Hull to Malaga, Irvine to Algiers, the Tyne to Tarragona, from Swansea to Smyrna, and, of course, regularly to Hamburg and Stettin. On 17 April 1882, Robert Parry, aged 12, of Borth, signed as boy for his first voyage to sea from Porthmadog to Stettin at £1.0.0 a month. One of Captain Hugh Parry's sons, Robert Parry later commanded the *Frau Minna Petersen,* as already mentioned, and, according to his friend, Captain W. H. Hughes, D.S.C., who often saw him in his later years at Garston, Captain Robert Parry was one of the few Porthmadog seamen to take his Extra Master's Certificate. When Captain E. E. Parry left the *George Casson* in 1887, he was succeeded by Captain John E. Jones, Pen-y-bryn, Penmorfa, then aged 28, who commanded her for the next ten years, mainly in the European trades.[1] In 1901, Captain Thomas Richard Lewis became master of the *George Casson,* and it was with him that the young William Henry Hughes (later the Captain W. H. Hughes who deservedly gained the D.S.C. at Dunkirk) served aboard the *George Casson.* Captain Hughes remembers as clearly as yesterday how he used to wait for Captain Hugh Parry to come from his shipbroker's office in Cornhill at tea time so that he could sail with him in the shipbroker's small yacht, *Helena* — he was aged eight at the time, and his father, Captain Harry Hughes, of the *Edward Seymour,* was a great friend of the Parry family. So when young W. H. Hughes, a few years later, wanted to leave Porthmadog ships to join the large full-rigged ship *Pengwern* sailing out of Liverpool,[2] it was not surprising that his mother should turn to Captain Hugh Parry to get him a berth aboard the *George Casson,* saying that Hamburg was far enough for anyone to sail. Young William Henry at this time had already survived the wreck of the *Arvon,* his father's schooner, near Lowestoft in 1898, as well as some bizarre experiences aboard the *Cambrian,* as the only member of the the large, formidable, bearded Captain Roberts's crew, so that his mother's concern was no doubt justified. Captain Hughes remembers the *George Casson*'s voyage clearly; she had long since been converted to brigantine rig, but her main sail was still very large and heavy to handle, and, like the *Edward Windus* and his father's schooner, the *Edwin,* made heavy demands on her crew. The young Hughes's career was destined to be full of incident, for not long after leaving the *George Casson* he served in the *Excelsior* and was one of the crew compelled to take to the rigging when she dragged her anchors in a fierce gale and was driven ashore near Halmstadt in Sweden on Christmas Eve 1902. Nearly fifty years afterwards, when Captain W. H. Hughes met Captain R. Evans, the master of the *Excelsior* on that fateful night, at Porthmadog harbour, the latter's first words were 'Wil bach, 'rwy'n clywed sŵn dy draed ti yn dod i ddeud ein bod ni'n dragio' (I can hear your footsteps now as you ran to tell me that we were dragging anchor).

It was this Captain Robert Evans who later commanded the *George Casson.* After the loss of the *Excelsior* and a spell in command of the *Laura Griffith,* Captain Evans became master of the *George Casson* from 1907 until she was interned in the Elbe at the outbreak of the 1914 war. She had been sailing regularly in the German slate trade; in the first six months of 1913, for example, her 'articles' indicate the dates of her arrival and departures at the following ports:

| | | | |
|---|---|---|---|
| Depart | Porthmadog 23 March 1913 | Arrive | Harburg 10 April |
| | Harburg 25 April | | Penryn 10 May |
| | Penryn 15 May | | Plymouth 16 May |
| | Plymouth 27 May | | Porthmadog 31 May |
| | Porthmadog 18 June | | Harburg 27 June |
| | Harburg 15 July | | Bristol 3 August |

Porthmadog seamen of those far-off days remembered with gratitude that, at the first news of the outbreak of the war in August 1914, some German tug-masters, who had over the years become very friendly with Porthmadog master mariners, whose vessels they had towed so often in and out of harbour, acted on their own initiative in those first hours of war. They towed out of the Elbe a number of Welsh sailing ships, including the *Wern* (which was almost awash and submerged because of the hurried nature of the tow) lest they should be interned and their crews made prisoners of war.[3] The *George Casson,* however, could not be one of the fortunate ones, as she was alongside the loading quays and too closely under official eyes. When the *George Casson* was interned, Captain Robert Evans, the mate, Lloyd Williams, and the crew, including Jack Edmunds, serving as 'boy', were imprisoned with several thousand others at Ruhleben, a former race-course. Among them were many other Porthmadog seamen, including the crew of the steamer *Saxon,* commanded by Captain Rowland Humphreys, and several Amlwch men. David Owen, 'Dafydd French' as he was known locally, one of the crew of the *George Casson,* who was a good soccer player, was a member of a very successful football team organised among the prisoners, who had good reason to be thankful to some of the friends they had made in the days of peace among the shipping community of the Elbe ports. The *Frau Minna Petersen,* the other vessel in which Captain Hugh Parry and his family had been so involved in the closing decades of the nineteenth century, was also captured by a torpedo-boat in the early days of the war and taken into Emden. After the war, re-named *Jane Banks,* she was to be a familiar sight, and, as already indicated, survived well into the second World War.

According to the entry in the Caernarfon Register of Shipping, the *George Casson*'s registry was finally cancelled locally on 21 June 1920, but an Admiralty telegram had been received more than a year before, on 27 January 1919, which bore the terse statement 'Vessel sunk in Kaiser Wilhelm Canal'. In fact, the *George Casson* was acquired by Amandus Breckwoldt of Hamburg after the war, and, following a lengthy refit, she was surveyed and placed in Class A of the German Lloyds, for four years from February 1920 for voyages in the North Atlantic region. Renamed the *Katharina*, she sailed 16 March 1920 for Bergen with a cargo of 300 tons of salt, but she never reached her destination. She was sighted on 13 March, but on 6 April the fishing vessel *Kehdingen* came upon the empty ship's boat of the *Katharina* in an estimated position 57°25′N 3°20′E. The maritime authorities and underwriters of Hamburg accepted in September 1920 that although the *Katharina* had in all respects been seaworthy when she sailed, she must now be presumed lost. One possibility canvassed at the time was that she had struck a mine, relic of the 1914-18 war.[4]

A little over a hundred years ago, in 1874, Borth-y-gest witnessed the launching of two fine vessels, the ill-fated *Snowdonia*, the largest vessel ever built there, and the brig *Fleetwing*, a larger vessel than the *George Casson*, but equally solidly built, with fine lines and the high bow so typical of the best Porthmadog vessels. After her initial voyages under the command of Captain Owen Evans, the *Fleetwing* was commanded from July 1876 by Captain Owen Jones, then aged 26, a native of Harlech, formerly of the *Winifred*, whose first voyage in her was from Cardiff to Pernambuco, with Emmanuel Williams of Pwllheli as mate. Voyages to Naples, Girgenti, Oporto, Stettin, Dakar, Buenos Aires, Rosario, Cape Town, Demerara followed in rapid succession; in 1881 Griffith E. Dedwith, who had previously served aboard the *Evelyn*, joined Captain Owen Jones as his mate — he was then 21 years of age. Whilst Dedwith was aboard as mate, voyages were made to Dakar, Bahia and Demerara, as well as the usual slate voyages to the Baltic and the Elbe. A number of Merioneth men followed Dedwith as mate during the next few years, but Robert Roberts of Barmouth remained as boatswain for nearly all the voyages in the 1880s; he was aboard her when she sailed from Newport to Santa Caterina, Brazil, in late August 1887. They arrived at Santa Caterina on 31 October, at Parakyba on 11 January 1888, at New York on 1 May, at Natal on 20 August, at Hamburg on 7 December, and Middlesborough a few days before Christmas 1888, a voyage of sixteen months.

It was at Middlesborough early in the New Year 1889 that Captain Richard Griffiths took command of the *Fleetwing*. A native of Aberdaron, then aged 33, Captain Griffiths had Robert Williams, formerly of the *George Casson* as mate and Owen Lloyd of Llanbedr as boatswain, but Robert Roberts remained, this time signing as cook/steward. For the next three years Captain Griffiths sailed the *Fleetwing* mainly in the phosphate and South American trades; his crews contained many well-known Porthmadog seamen, including Owen Humphreys, a Merioneth man, as boatswain, Hugh Ellis and Ellis Humphreys. He must have pleased the Prichard brothers, the ship-brokers who managed the *Fleetwing*. When they formed the single ship company to buy the steel barque *Beeswing*, 1,462 tons, built by Russell and Company, Greenock, in 1893, it was Captain Richard Griffiths whom they appointed to command their fine new vessel, which, although ultimately unsuccessful as a financial venture, nevertheless proved a most valuable training ship for so many Porthmadog seamen. The photograph taken at Portland, Oregon, of Captain Griffiths and the crew of the *Beeswing* is not only typical of the ship's company photographs sold to thousands of sailing-ship seamen at ports ranging from San Francisco to Newcastle, New South Wales, but it also includes photographs of several of the men who had served with Captain Griffiths in the *Fleetwing*.[5] Both managed by the Prichard brothers, the crews of the *Beeswing* and the *Fleetwing*, as the years went by, contained a significant number of the same names, and when Captain Griffiths finally left the *Beeswing* he was replaced by Captain John Roberts of Criccieth, who had taken command of the *Fleetwing* in May 1903, when he was aged 28, and remained as master until April 1907, when he went to the *Beeswing*, and was himself replaced as master of the *Fleetwing* by John Humphreys of Castle View, Talsarnau. Captain W. H. Hughes, who served in the *Beeswing* as an able seaman with Captain Griffiths, and as chief officer with Captain John Roberts, remembers them both as fine seamen, who moved easily from the command of the comparatively small *Fleetwing* to the steel barque *Beeswing*, for their experience in the former and the wide range of her cruising had served them well.

Before taking command of the *Fleetwing,* John Roberts had sailed as her first mate and purser in 1902, with Captain William Pritchard as master, and W. Ellis Jones of Havelock House, Criccieth, aged 20, as second mate, on a voyage from Ipswich to Barbados and Martinique. The young second mate had already had considerable experience, having first served with Captain Thomas Roberts of the three-masted schooner *Dorothy,* and had then had a fourteen-month voyage in the barque *Ednyfed* as A.B., following which he took his second mate's ticket at the age of 18. He was the son of Captain Owen Jones of the *Havelock,* the full-rigged ship managed by William Thomas, Liverpool; Captain Jones's wife used to sail the seas with him, and two of W. Ellis Jones's brothers had been born when the *Havelock* was in South America, the one at Callao and the other at Pisco. After this voyage in 1902 in the *Fleetwing,* W. Ellis Jones obtained command of the *Sidney Smith,* a three-masted schooner built by David Williams in 1895 and previously commanded by the latter's brother, Captain R. O. Williams, who became master of the newly-built *Isallt.* Captain W. Ellis Jones sailed the *Sidney Smith* to the Baltic, Spain, Newfoundland, Labrador, and the Mediterranean, and then, on his return to Porthmadog, bought shares in another of David Williams's vessels, the *Elizabeth,* which he commanded for a number of years; the shipbuilder's son, Mr. David Williams, recalls that the young Captain W. Ellis Jones, who was still in his early twenties, was very highly regarded by his father and the sternest critics among Porthmadog's maritime community.[6]

In 1911, the *Fleetwing* was bought by the Falkland Islands Company, 61 Grace Church Street, London. The days of sailing ships, particularly in the types of trades in which the *Fleetwing* had been engaged, were almost over, and no doubt the financial difficulties of the *Beeswing* (which the Prichard brothers were soon to sell to J. B. Walmsley, the Liverpool shipowner), were a contributing factor in the decision to sell the *Fleetwing,* then nearly forty years old. On 18 July 1911, J. D. Parsell, a Bootle man, and a Liverpool crew signed articles for a voyage from Liverpool to the Falkland Islands: 'The vessel to be left in the Falkland Islands and the wages of the crew payable until arrival back in Liverpool, the return passage to be provided by the owners'. And it was there, at Port Stanley, that many Porthmadog seamen last saw the *Fleetwing.*

# REFERENCES

[1] It is apparent from the transactions recorded in the Registers that the new masters of the *George Casson* bought and took over the shares of their predecessors — Evan Ebenezer Parry bought the majority of Hugh Parry's shares when he assumed command, and he, in turn, sold his 16/64 in her to John Etheridge Jones of Penmorfa when the latter took command of the *George Casson* in 1887. (Bill of sale dated 19 July 1887). Captain John Etheridge Jones was one of the descendants of John Etheridge, the London-born Scot who was one of W. A. Madocks's agents, and invented some of the slate quarrying machinery which his late employer, Mr. Mathews of Wern, developed with much success.

[2] The *Pengwern*, an iron ship of 1,648 tons, had been bought by William Thomas, the Liverpool shipbroker, from D. W. Davies and Company, and was commanded by a Captain Jones, with Griffith Jones of Borth-y-gest as mate — hence, young Hughes's wish to join her. According to Basil Lubbock in the *Last of the Windjammers*, I, 226, she was one of the vessels that had had to seek shelter at Port Stanley after the unusually bad weather off the Horn in 1900, so that young W. H. Hughes may have had reason to be thankful that he went to the *George Casson* instead. The *Pengwern* suffered a severe buffeting again in 1905 when she was one of the ships which, as Alan Villiers has vividly described, were compelled to join 'The flight from the wet battlefield of Cape Horn that bitter winter, with its forever snarling storms and never-ending onslaught of the sea'. Alan Villiers, *The War with Cape Horn*, 52. The *Pengwern* was later lost with all hands approaching the Elbe.

[3] Information from Captain W. H. Hughes, May 1975.

[4] For fuller details of the *George Casson*'s history as the *Katharina*, Dr. Jürgen Meyer, *150 Jahre Blankeneser Schiffahrt*, 196-197.

[5] Captain W. H. Hughes provided both the photograph of the *Beeswing* and much information about her voyages.

[6] *SB* 27, Jan. 1959, 374-6. It will be recalled that David Williams, the shipbuilder, had sailed in his earlier years aboard the *Havelock*, so that the link with Captain W. Ellis Jones was probably a natural development between the shipbuilder and the young master mariner, son of his old captain in his sea-going days.

## THE BARQUENTINE *MARTHA PERCIVAL*

THE square-rigged vessels built by Ebenezer Roberts at his yard, just a stone's throw from where the thousands of tourists today commence their journey on the Ffestiniog Narrow Gauge Railway, were justifiably regarded as among the finest of Porthmadog ships. The brigs *Ephratah, W. W. Lloyd,* the brigantine *Wern,* and the barquentines *Anna Braunschweig, Martha Percival,* and *Tony Krogmann* were all built by him during the boom period 1873-1878. Their story, and that of the other phosphate-carriers of Porthmadog, has been told by Henry Hughes; the *Martha Percival* may be taken as a fair representative of the group.[1] She was owned by Ebenezer Roberts himself, who had 14/64 shares in her, Edward Jones, her first master, who had 26/64 (he may be the 'Edward Williams, Gelli Grin' whom Emrys Hughes mentions in his notes), Thomas Jones, described as 'shipper', who had 4/64, the remaining shares being divided between a Llandecwyn farmer, an innkeeper, a labourer, and a quarryman, all from the birthplace of Captain Edward Jones, which is given as 'Penrhyn' in the articles, and two Talsarnau men. In July 1877 Captain Edward Jones (whose previous ship had been the *Geraldine*) sailed her with her first cargo of slates for Hamburg. The crew were Merioneth or Caernarvonshire men, all young but already experienced; the mate was a Nefyn man, William Meredith, Ropewalk, aged 26, who had just left the Liverpool barque *Culdee,* commanded by Captain O. Evans. William Meredith remained as mate for the voyages from Hamburg to Christiana, thence to Glasgow, and from Glasgow to Oporto and Huelva, and back to Berwick by the end of October, a busy and profitable three months for the *Martha Percival,* and very good experience for the young Meredith, who was soon to take his master's ticket and earn for himself a formidable reputation as master of the large Cape Horners in the fleet of William Thomas, Liverpool, moving from the *Havelock* to the *County of Merioneth,* the *Dominion* and, finally, the *Annie Thomas.*[2] His wife, Mary Ann, daughter of Castellior, Llansadwrn, on the banks of the Menai

Straits, died at sea in August 1894 when the *Dominion* was homeward bound from Tacoma with 3,788 tons of wheat for Hull; Captain William Meredith and all his crew were lost five years later in the *Annie Thomas* on passage from Cardiff to Acapulco with coal, 'not heard of since spoken to 57°25'S, 70°30'W, 19 October 1899'. The *Martha Percival* was to outlive him by two years, but all this was in the distant future as William Meredith stood on the new barquentine's decks in Porthmadog harbour — she was every bit as impressive there as the large steel four-masters which he later commanded in vast harbours like San Francisco — in 1877 the *Martha Percival*, as she sailed into Oporto, Christiana and the Clyde, was a vessel of which her young mate was justifiably proud.

The papers of the *Martha Percival* for the next three years are not available in the local archives, but in 1881 she was sailing from Cardiff to Dakar with coal, with Captain Edward Jones still her master, a new mate, Humphrey Roberts of Porthmadog, and Benjamin Jones, who had sailed as boatswain in her since her first voyage. In the 80s Captain Jones took the *Martha Percival* to Demerara, Pernambuco, Bahia, Santos, Barbados, Buenos Aires, Curacao and Santa Caterina, Brazil. In 1890 he was suceeded by John Roberts, who had been mate for several voyages, had previously served in the *Tony Krogmann*, and whose address, 1 Mount Pleasant, Porthmadog, was the same as that of Ebenezer Roberts, so it is not unreasonable to assume that he was the ship-builder's son or near relative.

Edward Jones was again master in 1892 for the voyage from Hamburg to Maracaibo, with Morris Hughes of Harlech, aged 25, as mate, and Ellis O. Paul from Porthmadog, aged 21, previously serving aboard the *Frau Minna Petersen* as boatswain. By 1897 Captain Evan Hughes had become master. A 26-year-old Porthmadog man, living in Osmond Lane, Captain Hughes had as his new mate, Peter Jones, aged 23, whose home address is given as Moel-y-Don Ferry, Anglesey, and whose previous ship had been the *Cambrian Hills*. Like Captain Meredith before him, Peter Jones was to have a distinguished career as master of full-rigged ships and four-masted barques after his spell in the *Martha Percival;* Ebenezer Roberts's barquentine was only a tenth of the tonnage of the vessels they were later to command, yet it is likely that both

Captain Meredith and Captain Peter Jones regarded their period as mate of the *Martha Percival* as an all-important formative experience, which stood them in good stead in their later careers. Peter Jones sailed as mate in the *Martha Percival* to Puerto Cabello and then on a voyage from London to Dublin, home to Porthmadog, then to Garston for a cargo for Para, then to Bremerhaven and back to Cardiff. For the next voyage from Cardiff to La Guayra, Venezuela, Peter Jones took with him as ordinary seaman his younger brother, Ishmael Jones, whose address is also given as Moel-y-Don Ferry; like Peter Jones, he had also served in the small coaster *Pride of the Dee*. The *Martha Percival*'s next voyage to St. Helena, Ascension, Aruba, Hamburg and Galway has been described in some detail by Henry Hughes from the account of Captain R. Hughes of Cricieth; Evan Hughes was still in command for this voyage of about 17,000 miles in ten months, but Peter Jones had left her to become mate of the very well-known and beautiful four-masted barque, the *Principality*.

Most of these voyages are recorded in the barest outline in the official logs and have to be augmented with the occasional detail which emerges from the crew agreement lists. The voyage of 1891 under Captain John Roberts was one of the few exceptions. Similar incidents to those recorded may well have taken place on many other voyages, but Captain Roberts was one of the few who put pen to paper. The *Martha Percival* had sailed from Rochester at 7.30 a.m. on 4 September 1891 with a full cargo; she was drawing 13′9½ forward and 14′2½ in. aft, with a freeboard amidships of 2′6½—not much when one considers that she was bound for a westward passage across the Atlantic to Ceara on the Brazilian coast. Nine days out, Captain Roberts recorded in his log that when the *Martha Percival* was in an estimated position 30°20′N and 17°37′W, at six in the evening, Albert Estdohl, one of the A.B.s 'went to lay up, with swollen legs, being unable to walk about', so the master gave him 'some opedeldoc to rub them with'. A little over a week later, Captain Roberts ruefully recorded in his log 'Albert Estdohl still laying up, having used all the opedeldoc on board the ship', adding 'but his legs are much better being able to work a little on the sails under decks'. Ten days later, as they approached the South American coast, a little north of the Equator, in 0°15′N 32°26′W, the master noted that the sick A.B. was still unable to come on deck, but 'continues working a little on the sails under deck'. The *Martha Percival* arrived at Ceara on the 5 February at 8 p.m., and the next morning Captain Roberts sent the sick man ashore, where he remained for the next three weeks, but was sent back aboard on 26 February, 'the Doctor . . . saying he was alright but when he went on board he refused to work, complaining with his eyes, so on the 27th to (*sic*) him ashore again to see the Consulate, who, being a medical man himself, examined him and sent him on board saying he would be alright in a day or two'. But the man was obviously sick, and when the *Martha Percival* was ready to sail from Barbados, her next port of call, in mid-March, Albert Estdohl was put ashore again, 'the doctor pronouncing him unable to proceed in the vessel, left his clothes at the Harbour master's office, also balance of wages due £5.4.6.' On the same day as the *Martha Percival* set sail for 'St. Francois, Guadeloupe', Captain Roberts entered in his log 'This day shipped Olaf Olsen, A.B.' to replace the man put ashore.

There had been other troubles. At 5 a.m. on 22 January, when the *Martha Percival* was sailing towards Ceara in a position estimated to be 14°11'N 27°37'W, the cook/steward was 'layed up, complaining with his shoulder, saying he had fallen down on deck'. Three days later he was reported to be better, but at 5.30 a.m. on 1 February, Captain Roberts noted in his log, the cook 'tried to commit suicide, by tying a rope round his neck, with the other end fast around his trunk, which he through overboard, and followed himself after it'. The other sick man, Albert Estdohl, 'saw him going, and called the boatswain'. Captain Roberts himself 'was immediately called on deck and managed to throw a bowline around him and got him safe on board, the wind being very light at the time'. Towards evening the deranged cook threatened 'to do the same again first chance' and so Captain Roberts decided to 'put him in Irons and fast to a chain . . . will keep him fast until I'll get the British Consul's opinion of him on arrival at Ceara, all his effects went astray owing to his trunk being smashed also his bed and bedclothes he threw overboard at 5 a.m.' As if all this was not enough, at Ceara another member of the crew was taken ill, and although he made a temporary recovery, he was ill again on the passage to Barbados, and yet again on the voyage from Guadeloupe to St. Nazaire Roads. Captain Roberts recorded in the log: 'as far as I can make out he's suffering from consumption, best strengthening medicine supplied to him'. Two days later the ailing seaman turned to again, and appears to have survived until the *Martha Percival* finally docked at Swansea on 3 June 1891.

In November 1900 the *Martha Percival* was at anchor at Cuxhaven; as her crew prepared to get the vessel under way, 'the *George Casson* was coming down the river and she came across our Bow and carried away our jibbom, then cleared doing us no further damage'. Captain Hughes was later asked to give his reasons in writing why he had failed to enter the details of this collision in his log-book; his answer was forthright enough, 'As the collision and damage done to my vessel was so slight . . . I did not think it was necessary for me to enter it in my Official Log Book'. Captain John Jones of Netherton House, Porthmadog, the managing owner in 1901, appointed William Jones, aged 33, of Porthmadog to be the next master of the *Martha Percival*. His command was not long lived. The *Martha Percival* left Porthmadog in mid-March for Hamburg, but ran aground in thick fog when making for the Elbe: Captain Jones noted on the Crew Agreement, 'The vessel went on shore thick fog, wind S.W. on 1st April: after being carried by the current 40 miles to the Northward of the dead reckoning. Lead was kept going, soundings at 11.30 on the 31st was 12 fathoms, Dark Sand. At 2 a.m. on the 1st vessel ashore on Sylt Island, bumping heavily, left the ship at 7 a.m. on account of the wind increasing'. Ten days later the *Martha Percival* was a total wreck buffeted by westerly gales. The crew were sent home to Britain, but Captain Jones remained a little longer, and the British Consul General in Hamburg noted in the 'Articles': 'The Master who stayed some time at the place of the wreck has also returned to the United Kingdom: but had no funds to pay the Consular Fee (2/-) due for the Endorsement, which therefore has not been stamped'. Although the Gomerian Freight and Outfit Mutual Insurance Society of Porthmadog eventually won their legal battle with the Hamburg underwriters, it was a dismal end to a notable vessel in which some of Gwynedd's finest seamen had served their apprenticeship.

# THE SCHOONER *CADWALADER JONES*

THE two-masted schooner *Cadwalader Jones,* built by John Hughes for Morris Owen at Borth-y-gest in 1878, was destined to become one of the best known of all Porthmadog ships. As indicated in the introduction and in Emrys Hughes's notes, she had an eventful career of over fifty years and there is little doubt that her first shareholders, who included two surveyors of shipping at Porthmadog, two master mariners, together with farmers and tradesmen, and a Baptist and Wesleyan minister, had seen to it that they had invested in a soundly-built little ship. The major shareholder was John Cadwalader of Criccieth, who had raised some at least of the money to buy his own shares by way of a mortgage from William Jones, the sailmaker, son of Henry Jones, the first Porthmadog shipbuilder. John Cadwalader was to sail his little ship for the next thirty years, and, according to the 'Articles', hardly missed a single voyage. The cargo book, which he kept for several years, has passed to Mrs. A. Evans, Menai View Terrace, Bangor.[1] By combining this notebook with the Crew Agreement lists of the *Cadwalader Jones,* it is possible to give some indication of the range of her sailing, the cargoes she carried and the men who manned her.

The *Cadwalader Jones,* she was registered thus, and John Cadwalader signed his name with an -er, although she was often referred to as the *Cadwaladr Jones* — according to Emrys Hughes's notes, 'entered the Newfoundland trade almost as soon as she was launched and continued in it for 38 years'. I have been unable to find evidence to confirm this in the early crew agreement lists, which indicate, in fact, that, to the contrary, her early voyages were confined to the Baltic and German ports, and in the coastal trades. In March 1879 she sailed from Porthmadog with slates for Danzig or Königsberg under the command of Captain David Rees, aged 53, a native of Aberaeron, with John Cadwalader, aged 36, of Criccieth, as boatswain; two A.B.s, Cadwaladr Williams of Criccieth, aged 28, and Griffith E. Dedwith of Towyn, aged 19, who had previously served in the *Francis Henry;* and Owen Jones, aged 17, of Criccieth, as cook and seaman. Having returned to Porthmadog in October, the *Cadwalader Jones* left again for London in November with another cargo of slate, and this time John Cadwalader is named as master, and remained in command for the subsequent voyages in 1880 in which he took his ship to Dublin, Hamburg, Itzhoe, Dunkirk, Newcastle, Waterford and home to Porthmadog on Boxing Day 1880. The young Griffith E. Dedwith, the future master of the *Theda, Oakleys* and *Rosie*, remained with Cadwalader for most of these early voyages. It is evident that Cadwalader had no master's certificate, and for one of the 1880 voyages, to Danzig from Porthmadog in May and back to Great Yarmouth, he had to revert to the role of boatswain and purser, at a stated wage of £4, whilst Captain Ellis Griffith, formerly of the *Florence,* is named as master. For the 1881 voyages, from Porthmadog to Rotterdam, Scarborough, Newcastle, Youghal and home again to Porthmadog, John Cadwalader resumed command as they were in the coastal trade, but in May 1881, for the voyage with slate from Porthmadog to Aarhus, Fredrikstad and back to London, an elderly master mariner, Captain William Jones, aged 63, was appointed, with John Cadwalader as boatswain, but he was master again for the voyage from London back to Porthmadog.

This pattern of command continued throughout the 80s, with different 'ancient mariners' appointed as nominal master for foreign voyages to the Baltic ports, with John Cadwalader sailing as boatswain, although purser, his role in practice, was probably unchanged; within the limits of the coastal trades, Cadwalader was always listed as master. From the 'Articles' available in the Gwynedd Record Office, it would seem that the first voyage to Newfoundland took place in 1890: in May the *Cadwalader Jones* sailed from Goole for Cadiz, thence to Harbour Grace, Newfoundland, where she embarked salt fish for Naples, arriving in mid-November, returning to Liverpool and, eventually, Porthmadog by April 1891. For this voyage, Captain Ellis Evans of Caernarfon was master, with Cadwalader again as purser, at £5 a month. After a month's refitting at Porthmadog in June 1891, she sailed again with Captain Robert Griffith of Barmouth, formerly of the *Netherton,* in command, with Cadwalader as boatswain at £5, and among the crew young Ellis Jones, aged 14, of Criccieth, 'First voyage, boy, 12/-'. According to the *Cadwalader*

*Jones*'s crew agreement list, her papers were delivered to the consul or vice-consul on her arrival at Cadiz on 12 July; at St. John's, Newfoundland, 13 August; at Naples, 13 November; at Zante, 20 November; at Cagliari, 9 February, and at Liverpool, 11 May 1892.

For the next ten years the *Cadwalader Jones* sailed regularly in the Newfoundland trade, sometimes with a young master mariner in command, sometimes a very elderly man, but ever present was John Cadwalader as boatswain and purser. It was just as well. In 1898 the master was Edward Taylor of Saltcoats, whose age was recorded as 66 in the 'Articles'; ages were notoriously misrepresented, and he may even have been older. On 23 December 1898, as the *Cadwalader Jones* made ready to depart from Patras, Captain Taylor deserted, but John Cadwalader then signed Karl Knudssen, a Norwegian A.B., in his place and brought the vessel home from Patras, leaving early in January and arriving at Bridgwater in April 1899. Captain William Williams of Talsarnau, aged 60, formerly of the *George Casson*, was employed as master for the Cadiz-Malaga-St. Ubes-Lisbon voyage in the spring of 1900, but John Cadwalader was listed as master for almost all the voyages, including those to Newfoundland, from 1900 to 1909 (when the crew agreement lists held locally cease) — he was aged 68 when he took the *Cadwalader Jones* into Appledore in 1909 — but occasionally one finds him still sailing as boatswain, as in 1907 when Captain Hugh Pugh, one of Porthmadog's outstanding master mariners, commanded the *Cadwalader Jones* on her voyage to Copenhagen. Often enough his crews were, apart from himself, comparatively young — on the 1908 voyage from Porthmadog to Papenburg his mate was a 23-year-old Swede, and the remainder of the crew were young seamen from Porthmadog, aged 20, 16 and 14 respectively.

In order to give some impression of the nature of the voyages which John Cadwalader and his crews undertook during these years, the voyages are briefly recorded in simplified tabulated form extracted from the cargo book of the *Cadwalader Jones*:

| *Sailed* | *Cargo* | *From* | *For* | *Delivered* |
|---|---|---|---|---|
| 1902 | | | | |
| 31 March | 170 tons manure in bags | London | Duncannon and New Ross | |
| 24 April | Ballast | | Porthmadog | |
| 12 May | 185 tons slate | Oakleys, P.M. | Calais | 17 May |
| 5 June | Ballast | Calais | Cadiz | |
| 26 June | 77 last of salt | Cadiz | King's Cove, NFL | |
| 23 September | 2,000 Quintals Codfish | Bateau | Gibraltar for orders ordered to Malaga | |
| 24 November | Ballast | [Malaga] | Larache | |
| 1903 | | | | |
| 5 January | | Larache | orders | |
| 17 January | Ordered at Falmouth for London | | | 30 January |
| 13 February | 173 tons manure | London | Cork | 7 April |
| 12 April | Ballast | Cork | Porthmadog | 13 April |
| 27 April | 185 tons slate | Porthmadog | London | 6 May |
| 16 May | Ballast | London | Hamburg | 22 May |
| 14 June | General cargo | Hamburg | St. John's, NFL | 23 July |
| 30 August | — | St. John's | Emily Harbour, Labrador | |
| 28 October | Codfish and Codoil | Emily Harbour, Labrador | Bristol | 16 November |
| 30 November | Ballast | Bristol | Porthmadog | 9 December |
| 23 December | slates | P.M. | London | 11 January |
| 1904 | | | | |
| 22 January | Manure | London | Londonderry | 26 February |
| | [Ballast?] | Londonderry | P.M. | 15 March |
| 1 June | slates | P.M. | Poole | 13 June |

| *Sailed* | *Cargo* | *From* | *For* | *Delivered* |
|---|---|---|---|---|
| 20 June | ½ cargo slates | Poole | Guernsey | 21 June |
| 30 June | Ballast | Guernsey | Cadiz | 19 July |
| 26 July | 168 tons salt | Cadiz | St. John's | 1 September |
| 31 December | Ballast | St. John's | Catalina (to load fish) | — |
| 1905 | | | | |
| 15 January | 2,000 Quintals codfish | Catalina | Alicante | 20 February |
| 7 March | Ballast | Alicante | Cadiz | — |
| 6 April | salt | Cadiz | Newlyn | 4 May |
| — | Ballast | Porthleven | P.M. | 20 May |
| 17 June | 190 tons slates | P.M. | Copenhagen | 8 July |
| 17 July | Ballast | Copenhagen | Thorsokell, Norway | 29 July |
| 5 August | 170 tons stones | Thorsokell | Exmouth | 18 August |
| 30 August | Ballast | Exmouth | P.M. | 3 September |
| 28 September | 194 tons slates | P.M. | Copenhagen | 12 November |
| 27 November | 172 tons Burnt ore | Copenhagen | London | 9 January |
| 1906 | | | | |
| 27 January | 165 tons manure | London | Dungarvan | — |
| 12 May | 200 tons slates | P.M. | Copenhagen | 29 May |
| 19 June | 173 tons oilcake | Copenhagen | Plymouth | 30 June |
| 12 July | Ballast | Plymouth | P.M. | 17 July |
| 8 August | 200 tons slate | P.M. | Copenhagen | 22 August |
| 4 September | 172 tons oilcake | Copenhagen | Great Yarmouth | 15 September |
| — | Ballast | Great Yarmouth | P.M. | 25 October |
| 20 December | 173 tons slates | P.M. | London | 31 December |

| *Sailed* | *Cargo* | *From* | *For* | *Delivered* |
|---|---|---|---|---|
| 1907 | | | | |
| 9 January | 170 tons manure | London | Angle | 7 February |
| — | Ballast | Angle | P.M. | 8 March |
| 2 April | slates | P.M. | Copenhagen | 23 April |
| 1 May | —? | Copenhagen | Gemlle Sound | — |
| 22 May | —? | Gemle Sound | Ellesmere Port | 3 June |
| 18 June | — | Ellesmere Port | P.M. | 23 June |
| 23 July | slates | P.M. | Harburg | 3 August |
| 24 August | — | Harburg | Ayr | 14 September |
| 27 September | — | Ayr | Penzance | 7 November |
| — | — | Penzance | P.M. | 23 November |
| 1908 | | | | |
| 4 February | 180 tons slates | P.M. | London | — |
| 28 February | 170 tons cement and whiting in bags | London | Kirkcudbright and Whitehaven | — |
| 16 April | 65 tons large house coal | Whitehaven | P.M. | — |
| 17 June | 174 tons slate | P.M. | London | — |
| 15 July | 168 tons manure | London | Waterford | 25 July |
| 5 August | (? Ballast) | Waterford | P.M. | — |
| 11 September | 188 tons 15 cwt slates | P.M. | Papenburg | 29 September |
| 20 October | 165 tons bogore in bulk | Delfzijl | Newport | 30 October |
| 14 November | 170 tons coal | Newport | P.M. | 25 November |
| 1909 | | | | |
| 7 January | 178 tons slate | P.M. | Poole and Guernsey | — |
| 26 February | 166 tons stones | Guernsey | London | — |
| 27 March | 170 tons cement | London | Swansea | 10 April |

| *Sailed* | *Cargo* | *From* | *For* | *Delivered* |
|---|---|---|---|---|
| 27 April | 173 tons coal | Swansea | St. Sampson's | 1 May |
| 12 May | 166 tons stones | St. Sampson's | Chatham | 16 May |
| 28 May | 170 tons cement | Chatham | Kirkcudbright | 12 June |
| — | — | Kirkcudbright | P.M. | 28 June |
| 3 August | 174 tons slates | P.M. | London | — |
| 30 August | 170 tons cement in casks and bags | Swanscombe, London | Newport | 10 September |
| 28 September | 130 tons flour | Cardiff | P.M. | 2 October |
| 30 October | 174 tons slates | P.M. | London | 10 November (at Gravesend) |
| 24 November | 170 tons manure | London | Appledore | 5 January |
| 1910 | | | | |
| 31 January | 145 tons gravel | Appledore | Swansea | — |
| 12 February | 166 tons coals | Swansea | Annan | 26 March |
| — | Ballast | Annan | P.M. | — |
| 7 July | 178 tons slate | P.M. | Poole | 17 July |
| 5 August | — | Poole P. | P.M. | 12 August |
| 25 August | 184 tons slates | P.M. | Papenberg | — |
| — | Ballast | Papenburg | Delfzjil | 16 October |
| 22 October | 127 tons paper | Delfzijl | London | 27 October |
| 31 October | 168 tons manure | London | Waterford | 24 December |
| 1911 | | | | |
| 7 January | 55 tons ballast | Waterford | London | 10 January |
| 1 February | 180 tons slate | P.M. | Sunderland | 1 March |

| *Sailed* | *Cargo* | *From* | *For* | *Delivered* |
|---|---|---|---|---|
| 10 March | Tug boat Kate took us to Newcastle to load. | | | |
| 1 April | 167 tons coals | Newcastle | Skiboreen | 11 April |
| 4 May | Ballast | Baltimore | P.M. | 8 May |
| 13 June | 184 tons slate | P.M. | Poole | 20 June |
| 4 July | 170 tons clay | Poole | Runcorn | 15 July |
| 26 July | 90 tons coals | Runcorn | P.M. | 31 July |
| 25 August | 178 tons slate | P.M. | Cork | 4 September |
| 17 September | 60 tons limestones | Cork | P.M. | 20 September |
| 25 October | 172 tons slates | P.M. | Ipswich | — |
| 1912 | | | | |
| 23 January | 170 tons manure | Ipswich | Kinsale | 29 January |
| — | Ballast | Kinsale | P.M. | — |
| 6 April | 178 tons slate | P.M. | Harburg | 19 April |
| 3 May | 170 tons salt in bulk | Harburg | Balnackie | 26 May |
| — | Ballast | Balnackie | P.M. | 30 May |
| 1 August | 184 tons slates | P.M. | Harburg | 18 August |
| 2 September | 170 tons salt in bulk | Harburg | Balnackie | 8 October |
| 28 October | Ballast | Balnackie | P.M. | 5 November |
| 28 November | 184 tons slate | P.M. | Poole | — |
| 1913 | | | | |
| 18 February | 168 tons clay | Poole | Runcorn | — |
| 18 April | 102 tons coal | Runcorn | P.M. | — |
| 4 June | 174 tons slate | P.M. | Harburg | — |
| 12 July | 170 tons salt in bags and loose | Harburg | Balnackie | 8 August |

| *Sailed* | *Cargo* | *From* | *For* | *Delivered* |
|---|---|---|---|---|
| 27 August | Ballast | Balnackie | P.M. | 29 August |
| 5 September | 185 tons slate | P.M. | Papenburg | — |
| 13 October | 170 tons Bog ore | Delfzijl | Guernsey | — |
| 20 December | 165 tons stones | Guernsey | Fareham | — |
| 27 December | 170 tons whiting | Fareham | Dublin | — |
| — | Ballast | Dublin | P.M. | — |
| 1914 | | | | |
| 10 April | 185 tons slate | P.M. | Dunkirk | — |
| 20 May | 130 tons slate | Dunkirk | Southampton | — |
| 2 June | Ballast | Southampton | Poole | — |
| 15 June | 170 tons clay | Poole | Weston Point | — |
| 1 July | 85 tons house coals | Runcorn | P.M. | 7 July |
| 6 August | 181 tons slate | P.M. | Poole | — |
| 5 September | 170 tons clay | Poole | Runcorn | 29 September |
| — | 119 tons house coal Lancashire district | Runcorn | P.M. | — |
| 14 November | 173 tons slate (Oakley) | P.M. | Poole | — |
| 1915 | | | | |
| 23 January | 170 tons clay in bulk (Pike Bros.) | Poole | Runcorn | 2 February |
| 13 March | 162 t. 2 cwt House coals | Runcorn | Penryn | 29 March |
| 22 April | 168 t 2 cwt China clay | Falmouth | Weston Point | 3 May |
| 11 May | 98 tons coals | Runcorn | P.M. | — |

From the above it will be seen that Emrys Hughes's statement regarding her 38 years involvement in the Newfoundland trades has to be modified. The crew agreement lists suggest that she did not sail regularly to Newfoundland until 1890, and it is evident from her cargo book that from 1906 to 1915 her voyages were again confined to the European trades. It is possible that by 1906, John Cadwalader, now in his sixties, did not wish to involve himself, nor the vessel to which he was devoted, in arduous Atlantic voyages which meant long absences from Porthmadog, particularly as he could find freights enough in the Baltic, German and coastal trades. It is also likely that by 1905 the *Cadwalader Jones* had much competition from the Western Ocean Yachts, particularly the smallest of them, like the *Elizabeth Pritchard, M. A. James, Kitty, Blodwen* and the first *Isallt,* which could compete with her for the trade with the small harbours of Labrador, whilst larger vessels were confined to St. John's. So she was spared the worst Atlantic gales, particularly those of 1911 and 1912, which caused many losses among the Newfoundland schooners. Still valued as a vessel in the first class in the books of Porthmadog Mutual Ship Insurance Society, she was value at £927 for insurance purposes about 1910, when the much newer and larger three-masted schooners *Elizabeth Pritchard* (2), *Gracie,* and *Isallt* (2) were each valued at well over £2,000, and the *Ellen James, Elizabeth Eleanor, John Llewelyn, William Pritchard* and *William Morton* at £2,667.[2]

The story of the *Cadwalader Jones* after she was sold by her Porthmadog owners in 1916 is told in Emrys Hughes's notes. In the interest of space, I have omitted from Emrys Hughes's notes an account which he gives (repeated in Henry Hughes's *Immortal Sails,* 209) of his meeting with Captain Ellis Jones of Borth-y-gest in 1943, who told him that the *Cadwalader Jones* or *Mynonie R. Kirby* as she was later known, was in the Firth of Forth in 1942. In *Sea Breezes,* February 1947, Harry Barrett, coxswain of the St. Mary's, Isles of Scillies, lifeboat, recorded that he was awarded the R.N.L.I.'s bronze medallion for rescuing the crew of six and a dog from the *Mynonie R. Kirby* off the Scillies in November 1933, and that the vessel had been taken in tow but had later sunk off Fishguard. Captain C. Haug of Lonsheim contributed a fuller account, based on the master's report on the loss of the *Mynonie,* which was published in the November 1947 issue of *Sea Breezes*: 80 miles off Ushant, on 27 November 1933, she was dismasted, the towing tug, *Zwarte Zee*, battling against wind and swell, tore out the windlass of the sailing vessel from her deck, and wrecked her bows, and in a full gale the St. Mary's lifeboat took off the *Mynonie's* crew. There is an obvious difficulty in reconciling the account of her sinking in 1933 with Emrys and Henry Hughes's account of her being seen in 1942. Her career as a Porthmadog ship had, however, come to an end in 1916; from 1878 she had sailed regularly from Porthmadog with slates, and her cargo book testifies to the variety of her other cargoes and ports visited. From the day Shôn Edwards of Borth-y-gest carved her imposing and well-known figurehead, the *Cadwalader Jones* was regarded with particular interest in Porthmadog, and during the thirty years and more that she sailed from the port she trained many of its outstanding seamen, but there was no one more closely associated with her than the man for whom she was first built, and who sailed in her on nearly every passage for all those years, John Cadwalader.

## REFERENCES

[1] I am indebted to Mrs. Evans for allowing me to have the cargo-book on loan, and also to her and to Mr. Evans, who himself served at sea, for their information regarding Porthmadog ships.

[2] The list of valuations and the sums for which vessels were insured at this time is included in E. Davies, *Hanes Porthmadog*, 27.

# COUNTING THE COST

It is not possible in this present work to enter into a detailed analysis of the financing of the shipping industry of Porthmadog, but a few reflections may stimulate further research into this aspect of the story of Porthmadog ships. An examination of the Register of Shipping indicates that shares in them were held by people from a wide range of occupational groups and industries. It has already been indicated that the slate quarrying industry was well represented among the shareholders, from influential quarry owners and managers like Samuel Holland and the Greaves family, to slate shippers, quarrymen and quarry agents; so, too, were the shopkeepers, ship chandlers, brokers, sailmakers, and the other members of the maritime community. The mortgages raised by master mariners from banks and the more prosperous members of the community, men like William Jones, the sailmaker, give some indication of the value of a vessel, and so, too, do the annual reports of the Portmadoc Mutual Ship Insurance Society, which contains lists of the vessels insured with the Society, their valuation by the Society's surveyors, and the amounts the vessels were actually insured for at a particular date. A few representative vessels may be taken as examples: the two-masted schooner *William,* some of whose early voyages and accounts have been quoted in the introduction, had been built in 1838 by Francis Roberts, and in 1865 her master was John Cadwalader, later to be associated for many years with the *Cadwalader Jones;* on 1 April 1865 she was valued at £950 and insured for £713 with the Portmadoc Mutual Ship Insurance Society. A year or so later she was lost off Abersoch. The *Confidence,* Captain Thomas Lewis's vessel, which became linked with the Garibaldi legend, recounted by Emrys Hughes, was valued in 1865 and 1868 at £1,125; the *Constance,* Captain Hugh Roberts, senior, was valued in 1865 at £2,500 and insured for £1,935. The highest valued vessel in the reports of the sixties was the *Atalanta,* a 223 ton brig built at Porthmadog in 1864; she was valued at £4,000 and insured for

£3,000 with the Society, whilst the brig *Ardudwy* and the brigantine *Amanda,* also built in 1863-4, were valued at £3,300 and £3,000 respectively. The brigantine *Edward Windus,* a smaller vessel which was to have a longer career than either of them, was valued at £2,650 and insured for £1,988. If the valuation of the sixties are compared with those of vessels in about 1912, it will be seen that the Western Ocean Yachts, which were, of course, smaller than the brigs and brigantines mentioned above, were valued at well under £3,000. In 1911/12 the largest of them, the *John Llewelyn,* about seven years old, the *William Prichard,* eight, and the *William Morton,* six years old, were all valued at £2,667 and insured for £2,000, whilst the *R. J. Owens* and the *Gracie,* smaller but built in 1907 and, therefore newer, were valued at £2,268 and insured for £1,701. A long-lived vessel like the *Tyne,* built in 1867 at South Shields, which was bought by Captain Owen Lloyd of Dora Street, and eventually transferred from the North Shields register to Porthmadog, had slipped into the second class category by 1911, and was valued at £936 and insured for £524, whilst the *Walter Ulric,* built at Nefyn in 1875, and the *W. D. Potts,* built at Pwllheli in 1878, were valued at £964 and £1,000 respectively. The *Cadwalader Jones* and the *Sarah Evans,* built in 1878 and 1877, were still in the first class in 1911 and were valued at £927 and £980 respectively. They both had many years sailing still ahead of them.

Although details of bills of sale and the transfer of shares are recorded in the registers of shipping, the actual prices paid for shares (which are included in the bills of sale themselves) are not shown in the registers, and, therefore, these details are somewhat elusive. Captain Evan Pugh of Cae Gwyn, Penrhyndeudraeth, according to a bill of sale dated 20 September 1877, paid Captain David Morris, Ceylon Villa, £540 for an 8/64 share in the *Pride of Wales.*[1] The mortgages raised on shares, or to pay for shares, are one source of information regarding comparative prices. The settlement of accounts of vessels lost are another. The account books of individual ships, and the reports of the Mutual Ship Insurance Society, record the costs of repairs, of the wear and tear on vessels, as well as the money earned from freights, and the wages and victualling accounts. The reports of the Society, which were printed and published in Porthmadog, and obviously carefully read by all those interested in

# THE TREASURER'S ACCOUNT,

*From the 30th November, 1862, to the 1st December, 1863.*

**Dr.**

| | £ | s. | d. | £ | s. | d. |
|---|---|---|---|---|---|---|
| To Balance at Banks .... .... .... .... | | | | 944 | 15 | 4 |
| — 31st Call due 1st March, 1863, at 1½ per cent. .... .... .... .... | | | | 1726 | 9 | 6 |
| — "Ellen and Mary," Law Suit .... | | | | 160 | 0 | 0 |
| — "Ann," (T. J.) Average .... .... | | | | 62 | 19 | 8 |
| — "Princess of Wales," First Entrance | 56 | 13 | 4 | | | |
| — "Charles Sauchey," do. | 12 | 10 | 0 | | | |
| — "Salem," do. | 10 | 6 | 3 | | | |
| — "Volunteer," do. | 43 | 15 | 0 | | | |
| — "Jane Ellen," do. | 22 | 2 | 6 | | | |
| — "Gwen Jones," do. | 3 | 16 | 4 | | | |
| — "George Casson," do. | 59 | 6 | 3 | | | |
| — "Industry," do. | 3 | 16 | 6 | | | |
| — "Cordelia," do. | 45 | 18 | 8 | | | |
| | | | | 258 | 4 | 10 |
| — "Catherine and Mary," Extra .... | 19 | 6 | 7 | | | |
| — "Westmoreland," do. .... | 13 | 19 | 9 | | | |
| — "Mary and Jane," do. .... | 24 | 0 | 0 | | | |
| — "John Ellis," do. .... | 30 | 0 | 0 | | | |
| — "Elizabeth Thomas," do. .... | 14 | 5 | 0 | | | |
| — "Alice Chamney," do. .... | 4 | 10 | 0 | | | |
| — "Catherine & Margaret," do. .... | 6 | 15 | 0 | | | |
| — "Margaret," do. .... | 1 | 19 | 3 | | | |
| — "Jennett and Jane," do. .... | 6 | 3 | 9 | | | |
| — "Betsey," do. .... | 7 | 2 | 6 | | | |
| — "William Owen," do. .... | 6 | 13 | 1 | | | |
| — "Salem," do. .... | 3 | 7 | 6 | | | |
| — "Annie," do. .... | 5 | 12 | 6 | | | |
| — "Lord Palmerston," do. .... | 6 | 15 | 0 | | | |
| — "Daniel Morris," do. .... | 7 | 4 | 9 | | | |
| — "Mary Hills," do. .... | 3 | 15 | 0 | | | |
| — "Ann Griffith," do. .... | 6 | 15 | 0 | | | |
| — "White Star," do. .... | 21 | 12 | 0 | | | |
| — "Pilgrim," do. .... | 25 | 7 | 3 | | | |
| — "Zion Hill," do. .... | 6 | 11 | 3 | | | |
| — "Enterprise," do. .... | 13 | 17 | 6 | | | |
| — "Jane," do. .... | 3 | 18 | 8 | | | |
| | | | | 239 | 11 | 4 |
| — Interest received at Banks .... .... | | | | 43 | 3 | 4 |
| | | | | £3435 | 4 | 0 |
| To Balance at Banks .... .... .... .... | | | | £877 | 6 | 10 |

**Cr.**

| | £ | s. | d. | £ | s. | d. |
|---|---|---|---|---|---|---|
| By "Ellen and Mary," Loss (Balance) | 200 | 7 | 9 | | | |
| — "Eliza Ann," do. .... .... | 495 | 13 | 2 | | | |
| — "Lady Vaughan," do. .... .... | 725 | 13 | 6 | | | |
| | | | | 1421 | 14 | 5 |
| — "Europa," Law Suit .... .... | 105 | 0 | 0 | | | |
| — "Miss Sarah," do. .... .... .... | 26 | 13 | 1 | | | |
| — "Elizabeth & Ellen," Assistance, &c. | 93 | 4 | 4 | | | |
| — "Emulation," do. | 28 | 7 | 4 | | | |
| — "Fossile," Repairs .... .... .... | 7 | 18 | 7 | | | |
| — "Sydney Jones," Assistance.... .... | 43 | 7 | 4 | | | |
| — "Ann," (J. W.) do. .... | 29 | 13 | 5 | | | |
| — "Margaret & Jane," do. and Repairs | 74 | 6 | 7 | | | |
| — "Star," Chain and Anchor .... .... | 6 | 17 | 6 | | | |
| — "Eliza Ann," Repairs .... .... | 9 | 6 | 8 | | | |
| — "Harriett & Jane," do. .... .... | 100 | 0 | 0 | | | |
| — "Albion," do. .... .... | 29 | 19 | 1 | | | |
| — "Margaret Jones," do. .... .... | 14 | 10 | 11 | | | |
| — "~~Ann," (T. J.)~~ do. Advance | 130 | 0 | 0 | | | |
| — "Rose," do. .... | 25 | 0 | 0 | | | |
| — "Caroline," Assistance .... .... | 30 | 0 | 0 | | | |
| — "Aerial," do. .... .... | 52 | 0 | 0 | | | |
| | | | | 806 | 4 | 10 |
| — Surveyor's Expenses.... .... .... | 127 | 10 | 0 | | | |
| — Adjusting Claims.... .... .... .... | 16 | 1 | 0 | | | |
| — Barmouth Surveyors .... .... | 2 | 2 | 6 | | | |
| — Secretary's Salary .... .... .... | 70 | 0 | 0 | | | |
| — Do. Stamps, Telegrams, &c. | 10 | 4 | 8 | | | |
| — Surveyor's Salary.... .... .... .... | 50 | 0 | 0 | | | |
| — Subscription to Life Boat.... .... | 10 | 0 | 0 | | | |
| — Rent of Town Hall .... .... .... | 5 | 0 | 0 | | | |
| — Do. Office .... .... .... .... | 5 | 0 | 0 | | | |
| — Fittings, &c., for new Office .... | 9 | 10 | 6 | | | |
| — Coal for Office and Town Hall, &c. | 2 | 12 | 8 | | | |
| — Printing and Stationery .... .... | 12 | 6 | 2 | | | |
| — Lloyd's Book .... .... .... .... | 3 | 3 | 0 | | | |
| | | | | 323 | 10 | 6 |
| — Bank Commission.... .... .... .... | | | | 6 | 7 | 5 |
| — Balance at Banks .... .... .... | | | | 877 | 6 | 10 |
| | | | | £3435 | 4 | 0 |

WILLIAM OWEN, } *Auditors.*
OWEN MORRIS, }

## THE TREASURER'S ACCOUNT,

*From the 1st day of December, 1863, to the 1st day of December, 1864.*

**Dr.**

| | £ | s. | d. | £ | s. | d. |
|---|---|---|---|---|---|---|
| To Balance at Banks.... .... .... .... | | | | 877 | 6 | 10 |
| — 32nd Call at 5 per cent., first Instalment of 2 per cent due March 1st, second do. of 3 per cent. due May 1st .... .... .... .... .... | | | | 5840 | 9 | 11 |
| — 33rd Call at 1½ per cent. due Dec. 1st | | | | 1918 | 4 | 3 |
| — "Charlotte Ann" First Entrance .... | 22 | 6 | 3 | | | |
| — "Atalanta," do. .... | 75 | 0 | 0 | | | |
| — "Maria," do. .... | 2 | 1 | 6 | | | |
| — "Eliza Wolsley," do. .... | 4 | 6 | 7 | | | |
| — "Amanda," do. .... | 65 | 12 | 6 | | | |
| — "John Ernest," do. .... | 65 | 12 | 6 | | | |
| — "Comet," do. .... | 8 | 6 | 8 | | | |
| — "Maria," do. .... | 2 | 10 | 0 | | | |
| — "Ann Catherine," do. .... | 5 | 0 | 0 | | | |
| — "Betsey," do. .... | 39 | 0 | 6 | | | |
| — "Miss Madocks," do. .... | 0 | 15 | 3 | | | |
| — "Jenny Lind," do. .... | 32 | 16 | 3 | | | |
| — "Edward Windus," do. .... | 49 | 13 | 6 | | | |
| | | | | 373 | 1 | 6 |
| — "Europa," Law Suit .... .... .... | 683 | 10 | 0 | | | |
| — "Alpha," Proceeds of Wreck .... | 0 | 16 | 6 | | | |
| — "Ann," Average .... .... .... .... | 40 | 12 | 1 | | | |
| — "Jane Brown," Proceeds of Wreck | 32 | 3 | 6 | | | |
| — "Aerial," Balance .... .... .... | 53 | 19 | 2 | | | |
| — "Lord Palmerston," do. .... .... | 47 | 10 | 6 | | | |
| — "Ann Griffith," do. .... .... | 194 | 14 | 10 | | | |
| | | | | 1053 | 6 | 7 |
| — "Mary Jane," Extra .... .... .... | 12 | 0 | 0 | | | |
| — "Elizabeth Thomas," do. .... | 14 | 5 | 0 | | | |
| — "Caradoc," do. .... .... .... .... | 13 | 2 | 5 | | | |
| — "Daniel Morris," do. .... .... | 14 | 9 | 7 | | | |
| — "Jannett and Alice," do. .... .... | 13 | 4 | 2 | | | |
| — "Volunteer," .... .... .... .... | 7 | 10 | 0 | | | |
| — "Westmoreland," .... .... .... | 13 | 19 | 11 | | | |
| — "Elizabeth and Ellen," .... .... | 10 | 15 | 5 | | | |
| — "Alice Chauncey," .... .... .... | 4 | 10 | 0 | | | |
| — "Atalanta," .... .... .... .... | 45 | 0 | 0 | | | |
| — "Quarry Man," .... .... .... .... | 5 | 18 | 11 | | | |
| — "Phoenix," .... .... .... .... | 28 | 14 | 9 | | | |
| — "Rose," .... .... .... .... .... | 6 | 19 | 10 | | | |
| — "Jenny Lind," .... .... .... | 19 | 13 | 7 | | | |
| — "Great Britain," .... .... .... .... | 2 | 13 | 7 | | | |
| — "Catherine," .... .... .... .... | 7 | 2 | 6 | | | |
| — "Dorothy and Mary," .... .... .... | 4 | 2 | 6 | | | |
| — "Glaslyn," .... .... .... .... | 7 | 8 | 6 | | | |
| — "Ann Griffith," .... .... .... .... | 6 | 15 | 0 | | | |
| — "Leonard Hollis," .... .... .... | 6 | 7 | 6 | | | |
| — "Zion Hill," .... .... .... .... | 14 | 17 | 2 | | | |
| — "Confidence," .... .... .... .... | 16 | 17 | 6 ✓ | | | |
| — "Edith," .... .... .... .... .... | 4 | 2 | 6 | | | |
| — "Enterprise," .... .... .... .... | 13 | 17 | 6 | | | |
| — "Pilgrim," .... .... .... .... .... | 25 | 7 | 4 | | | |
| — "Sarah Williams," .... .... .... | 22 | 10 | 0 | | | |
| — "Shields," .... .... .... .... .... | 20 | 5 | 0 | | | |
| — "Jane Brown," .... .... .... | 4 | 19 | 8 | | | |
| — Interest received at Banks .... .... | 26 | 4 | 3 | | | |
| | | | | 393 | 14 | 1 |
| | | | | £10456 | 3 | 2 |

**Cr.**

| | £ | s. | d. | £ | s. | d. |
|---|---|---|---|---|---|---|
| By "Anne," Loss .... .... .... .... | | | | 1118 | 2 | 5 |
| — "Betsey," do..... .... .... .... | | | | 1371 | 4 | 5 |
| — "Catherine and Mary," do..... .... | | | | 1083 | 2 | 1 |
| — "Mary Hills," do. .... .... .... | | | | 721 | 13 | 11 |
| — "Valiant," do. .... .... .... .... | | | | 259 | 3 | 4 |
| — "Jane Brown," do. .... .... .... | | | | 167 | 0 | 0 |
| — "Celerity," do. .... .... .... .... | | | | 610 | 0 | 1 |
| — "Miss Sarah," Law Suit .... .... | 59 | 3 | 11 | | | |
| — "Ellen and Mary," .... .... .... | 3 | 0 | 0 | | | |
| — Witnesses in the case of "Miss Sarah and Europa," .... .... .... | 42 | 14 | 0 | | | |
| | | | | 104 | 17 | 11 |
| — "Ann," Repairs .... .... .... .... | 55 | 4 | 8 | | | |
| — "Caroline," .... .... .... .... | 30 | 0 | 0 | | | |
| — "Rose," .... .... .... .... .... | 241 | 8 | 10 | | | |
| — "Margaret," .... .... .... .... | 6 | 13 | 10 | | | |
| — "Aeriel," .... .... .... .... .... | 200 | 0 | 0 | | | |
| — "Confidence," .... .... .... .... | 217 | 5 | 6 ✓ | | | |
| — "Dolphin," .... .... .... .... .... | 33 | 0 | 0 | | | |
| — "Louisa," .... .... .... .... | 31 | 10 | 3 | | | |
| — "Jane," .... .... .... .... .... | 13 | 14 | 8 | | | |
| — "Salem," .... .... .... .... .... | 265 | 0 | 0 | | | |
| — "Hope," .... .... .... .... .... | 22 | 8 | 11 | | | |
| — "Betty," .... .... .... .... .... | 11 | 3 | 4 | | | |
| — "Ann Griffith," .... .... .... .... | 890 | 6 | 7 | | | |
| — "Williams," .... .... .... .... | 14 | 18 | 10 | | | |
| — "Edith," .... .... .... .... .... | 100 | 0 | 0 | | | |
| — "Martha James," .... .... .... | 7 | 7 | 0 | | | |
| — "Economy," .... .... .... .... | 15 | 0 | 0 | | | |
| — "Ann Jones," .... .... .... .... | 42 | 3 | 6 | | | |
| — "Ann and Susan," .... .... .... | 4 | 10 | 10 | | | |
| — "Maria Louise," .... .... .... | 13 | 14 | 5 | | | |
| — "Lord Palmerston," .... .... .... | 115 | 0 | 1 | | | |
| — "Great Britain.... .... .... .... | 36 | 5 | 6 | | | |
| — "John Ellis," .... .... .... .... | 146 | 12 | 9 | | | |
| — "Fossile," .... .... .... .... | 25 | 0 | 0 | | | |
| — Auditors .... .... .... .... .... | 5 | 0 | 0 | | | |
| — Adjusting Claims .... .... .... | 21 | 15 | 0 | | | |
| | | | | 2565 | 4 | 6 |
| — Secretary's Nine Months' Salary .... | 52 | 10 | 0 | | | |
| — Surveyor's One Year do. .... | 80 | 0 | 0 | | | |
| — Surveyor's Expenses .... .... .... | 195 | 6 | 3 | | | |
| — Secretary's Incidental Expenses | 29 | 16 | 2 | | | |
| — Life Boat Subscription for 1864 .... | 10 | 0 | 0 | | | |
| — British Consul attending Evidence in Norway .... .... .... .... | 38 | 6 | 7 | | | |
| — Bank Commission... .... .... .... | 19 | 9 | 8 | | | |
| — Balance at Banks...... .... .... | 2030 | 5 | 10 | | | |
| | | | | 2455 | 14 | 6 |
| | | | | £10456 | 3 | 2 |

*Examined and found Correct.*

WILLIAM OWEN,<br>OWEN MORRIS, } *Auditors.*

# TREASURER'S ACCOUNT,

*From the 31st day of December, 1866, to the 31st day of December, 1867.*

| Dr. | £ | s. | d. | £ | s. | d. |
|---|---|---|---|---|---|---|
| To Balance at Banks.... .... .... | | | | 360 | 2 | 0 |
| Do. in Secretary's Hand .... | | | | 4 | 15 | 7 |
| 38th Call @ 1 per Cent., due February 1st .... .... | | | | 1409 | 12 | 7 |
| 39th Call @ do. due June 1st.... .... .... | | | | 1390 | 0 | 6 |
| 40th Call @ do. due October 1st .... .... | | | | 1464 | 6 | 3 |
| "Janet," First Entrance .... | 31 | 5 | 0 | | | |
| "Ann Morgan," do. .... | 18 | 0 | 0 | | | |
| "Margaret," do. .... | 13 | 6 | 6 | | | |
| "Adria," do. .... | 48 | 15 | 0 | | | |
| "Margaret & Jane," do. .... | 7 | 10 | 0 | | | |
| "George," do. .... | 22 | 10 | 0 | | | |
| "Betty," do. .... | 11 | 0 | 0 | | | |
| "Ellen Jones," do. .... | 68 | 18 | 0 | | | |
| "John Davies," do. .... | 31 | 14 | 6 | | | |
| "Samuel Holland," do. .... | 59 | 9 | 6 | | | |
| "Ardudwy," do. .... | 61 | 17 | 6 | | | |
| "Zenobia," do. .... | 35 | 12 | 6 | | | |
| "Twelve Apostles," do. .... | 23 | 11 | 0 | | | |
| "Albert Baltzer," do. .... | 64 | 2 | 0 | | | |
| "George Henry," do. .... | 8 | 1 | 6 | | | |
| "Caroline," do. .... | 5 | 7 | 0 | | | |
| "George Canning," do. .... | 6 | 0 | 0 | | | |
| "Leander," do. .... | 58 | 4 | 0 | | | |
| "Minnie Coles,,' do. .... | 37 | 10 | 0 | | | |
| "Elizabeth," do. .... | 20 | 12 | 6 | | | |
| "Hannah Jane," do. .... | 43 | 15 | 0 | | | |
| "Janet," do. .... | 7 | 4 | 0 | | | |
| | | | | 684 | 5 | 6 |
| "Pilgrim," Extra Calls .... | 21 | 15 | 0 | | | |
| "Jenny Lind," do. .... | 19 | 13 | 7 | | | |
| "Mabel," do. .... | 49 | 17 | 6 | | | |
| "Lara," do. .... | 10 | 13 | 8 | | | |
| "Hannah Jane," do. .... | 8 | 15 | 0 | | | |
| "Minerva," do. .... | 9 | 19 | 6 | | | |
| "Samuel Holland," do. .... | 11 | 17 | 11 | | | |
| "Martha James," do. .... | 2 | 14 | 5 | | | |
| "George Casson," do. .... | 20 | 6 | 5 | | | |
| "Phoenix," do. .... | 23 | 18 | 2 | | | |
| "Winifred," do. .... | 38 | 0 | 6 | | | |
| "Westmoreland," do. .... | 4 | 0 | 0 | | | |
| "Sarah," do. .... | 32 | 12 | 4 | | | |
| "Francis Henry," do. .... | 30 | 0 | 0 | | | |
| "George Henry," do. .... | 6 | 9 | 2 | | | |
| "Albert Baltzer," do. .... | 25 | 12 | 10 | | | |
| "Royal Charter," do. .... | 6 | 18 | 10 | | | |
| "Janet & Alice," do. .... | 23 | 5 | 2 | | | |
| "Patriot," do. .... | 6 | 15 | 0 | | | |
| "Elizabeth," do. .... | 4 | 2 | 6 | | | |
| "Adria," do. .... | 29 | 5 | 0 | | | |
| "Edward Windus," do. .... | 9 | 18 | 9 | | | |
| | | | | 396 | 11 | 3 |
| "William," Salvage .... | 100 | 0 | 0 | | | |
| "Margaret Owen," do. .... | 17 | 16 | 6 | | | |
| "Rose," do. .... | 67 | 17 | 1 | | | |
| "Wave," do. .... | 15 | 14 | 4 | | | |
| | | | | 201 | 7 | 11 |
| Sundry Cash received Secretary | | | | 75 | 3 | 0 |
| Interest from Banks .... .... | | | | 21 | 10 | 5 |
| | | | | £6007 | 15 | 0 |

| Cr. | £ | s. | d. | £ | s. | d. |
|---|---|---|---|---|---|---|
| By "Six Brothers," Lost .... | 297 | 5 | 8 | | | |
| "Lucy," do. .... | 645 | 2 | 0 | | | |
| "Wave," do. .... | 1743 | 7 | 2 | | | |
| "Gem," do. .... | 198 | 0 | 0 | | | |
| "Charles Souchey," do. .... | 495 | 0 | 0 | | | |
| "Jane Hughes," do. .... | 526 | 13 | 5 | | | |
| | | | | 3905 | 8 | 3 |
| "Jane Eliza," Repairs .... | 35 | 0 | 0 | | | |
| "Moelwyn," do. .... | 62 | 1 | 2 | | | |
| "Love," do. .... | 23 | 10 | 3 | | | |
| "Confidence," do. .... | 7 | 18 | 5 | | | |
| "Mary Ann," do. .... | 10 | 0 | 0 | | | |
| "Laura," do. .... | 10 | 16 | 4 | | | |
| "Sydney & Jane," do. .... | 28 | 12 | 6 | | | |
| "Great Britain," do. .... | 26 | 6 | 10 | | | |
| "John & William," do. .... | 2 | 8 | 10 | | | |
| "Taff Vale," do. .... | 12 | 6 | 0 | | | |
| "Sophia:' do. .... | 9 | 14 | 3 | | | |
| "Westmoreland," do. .... | 59 | 16 | 2 | | | |
| "Elizabeth," do. .... | 20 | 0 | 0 | | | |
| "Majestic," do. .... | 300 | 0 | 0 | | | |
| "William," do. .... | 136 | 17 | 6 | | | |
| "Volunteer," do. .... | 80 | 15 | 6 | | | |
| "Betsey," do. .... | 81 | 2 | 4 | | | |
| "Jane Hughes," do. .... | 20 | 0 | 0 | | | |
| "Fossil," do. .... | 91 | 1 | 11 | | | |
| "Progress," do. .... | 125 | 0 | 3 | | | |
| "Jane Ellen," do. .... | 15 | 14 | 2 | | | |
| "Margaret Owen," do. .... | 17 | 16 | 6 | | | |
| "Hope," do. .... | 36 | 18 | 4 | | | |
| "Planet," do. .... | 51 | 14 | 6 | | | |
| "Prince of Wales," do. .... | 14 | 4 | 5 | | | |
| "Ann Jones," do. .... | 12 | 9 | 9 | | | |
| "Mabel," do. .... | 82 | 7 | 6 | | | |
| "Sydney Jones," do. .... | 53 | 6 | 8 | | | |
| | | | | 1428 | 0 | I |
| Surveyor's Salary .... .... | 80 | 0 | 0 | | | |
| Stationery.... .... .... .... | 8 | 4 | 4 | | | |
| Sundries .... .... .... .... | 21 | 6 | 6 | | | |
| Different Surveyor's Travelling Expences .... .... | 138 | 16 | 0 | | | |
| Rent of News Room .... .... | 5 | 0 | 0 | | | |
| Adjusters of Claims .... .... | 21 | 7 | 6 | | | |
| Secretary's Salary .... .... | 70 | 0 | 0 | | | |
| Lloyd's Book & Auditor 1866 | 8 | 3 | 0 | | | |
| Average Adjusters .... .... | 4 | 14 | 6 | | | |
| Rent of Office .... .... .... | 4 | 7 | 0 | | | |
| Revaluers of Ships .... .... | 11 | 15 | 0 | | | |
| Life Boat Subscription ... | 10 | 0 | 0 | | | |
| | | | | 383 | 13 | 10 |
| Interest and Commission at Banks.... .... .... .... | | | | 27 | 19 | 11 |
| Cash at Banks .... .... .... | 226 | 13 | 8 | | | |
| Do. in Secretary's hand .... | 35 | 19 | 3 | | | |
| | | | | 262 | 12 | 11 |
| | | | | £6007 | 15 | 0 |

*Examined and found Correct this 30th day of January, 1868, shewing a balance of £262 12s. 11d. in favour of the Society.*

OWEN MORRIS, } *Auditors.*
JOHN THOMAS, }

local shipping, have, for the most part, disappeared; the Treasurer's accounts reproduced on adjoining pages may be taken as examples of the way in which the Society's business was carried on in the busy sixties.[2]

The complex transactions involved in the repairing of vessels both in home ports and abroad took up much time for masters of vessels, ships husbands, the surveyors of the Mutual Ship Insurance Society, and the correspondence which has survived reflects this aspect of the life of the port. Leafing through the papers of just one vessel, for example, something of their concern becomes apparent. The elderly brigantine *Tyne,* well over thirty years old, was in collision on 15 April 1904, 'about 3.20 a.m. (Greenwich time) . . . Texel bearing about E by S 11 or 12 miles'; in the papers of the Lloyd family, who owned and managed her, are the account of repairs at Falmouth and the amount of demurrage claimed. Two months later, the Shipowner Protection and Indemnity Association, managed by John Holman and Sons, London, reported to D. Lloyd and Company, shipbrokers, Cornhill, Porthmadog, that they believed they had 'been able to discover the name of the steamer which was in collision with the "Tyne" on 15 April last . . . we do not wish at present to name the steamer because it has only been made known to us in a private and confidential way. We think we can do something with the owners'. Two days later, Holmans suggested that it 'would be as well to keep the stanchion as it will no doubt be useful to identify the steamer', and although the underwriters asked 'for opportunity of perusing the Logbook of the "Tyne",' it was agreed that the steamer was the *Juanita North.* After protracted correspondence, the owners of the *Tyne* received their compensation settlement.

The master of a vessel involved in collisions or damaged in any way found himself involved in much correspondence. Seven years after her collision with the *Juanita North,* the *Tyne* was again damaged in a collision with a steamer near Aarhus, and Captain William Greene, her master (who had served for some time as mate to Captain Hugh Roberts in the *Evelyn*), wrote to David Lloyd, the Porthmadog shipbroker, reporting the progress of his negotiations with the Danish surveyors and 'the parties representing the steamer'. Captain Greene, obviously a shrewd realist, wrote:

'I daresay they will offer a lump sum for the job, but how much is enough for it is hard to tell . . . I think about £300 would more than make it up at home, and I would not like to accept anything under, and if they offer anything under that I shall tell them to make her up as she was before. I know they will always try to beat one down as much as they can as it is quite the way with us all. I daresay they will want to know her value. I will tell them that you have refused 900 pounds for her and that you are not open to sell her as they have use for her'.

A week later, Captain Greene reported that the surveyor had been to inspect the *Tyne*.

'They were not stingy in allowing things, but I fancy they were pricing the work too low. The surveyors estimate for Carpenter Work is Kr. 4135, which is about £216, which I think is not enough for what they have marked out'.

Captain Greene had had a telegram from Porthmadog 'From the *Club* saying if I had not already had a settlement to get surveyor to help me', but he had already done this and had himself carefully calculated the costs of repairing the damages either at Aarhus or risking a passage home to Britain where he thought more satisfactory and cheaper repairs, in the long run, could be carried out:

'The agents of the steamer called me in to their office at noon this day and said that a carpenter here had offered to do the work for Kr 2800 (which I dont believe) and that he would finish the work in 5 weeks. I told them to start on the job at once if they thought they could do it for that price, as we couldn't do it. Then he said what sum would I take so I told him that I would not take less than Kr. 10,000. He then telephoned to Copenhagen to the party who is over the Insurance of the steamers, and up to 3 p.m. I have not heard anything further. There is no slip here . . . when they want to see the bottom they heave them down and there are very few carpenters here either'.

After promising a full report in his next letter, and recording the fact that one of his crew, named Ellis, had 'not been well since he came here', Captain Greene concluded:

'The output of slate is 280 tons. There were next to no breakages, haven't seen less from Greaves before' . . . 'What made me ask for Kr 10,000 is so that I can come down a little. I know they will not give it as it is close on 550 pounds'.

Claims and counter-claims all cost time and money. When the *Tyne* was being towed out of Porthmadog harbour with a cargo of slates for Copenhagen on 7 July 1914 by the tug *Ddraig Goch,* the pilot and Captain Greene were much concerned 'when in the first turning, just below the lower quay, the ship grounded in the fairway and remained fast in spite of every effort to tow her off, and at last the hawser broke, the tide was now ebbing and ship sitting upright as the tide left her'. Despite all efforts at pumping and discharging cargo, on the next day 'the ship suddenly listed to starboard, with very heavy list, causing ship to strain very badly and making water that she sank at high water'. The detailed account of the subsequent discharging of cargo, attempts at salvaging the vessel, and the costs of all the work are recorded in the legal documents relating to the various claims of surveyors, underwriters' reports, even to the washing down of the salvaged slates 'to rid them as far as possible of salt water, sand and seaweed'. Other mishaps and disasters are recorded in the minutes of the 'Clubs', though naturally not in as great detail as in the occasional legal documents: the *Catherine* 'lost in collision with steamer Hamburgh in the North Sea' in 1898, the *Billow Crest* lost on a voyage from Porthmadog to Esbjerg with a cargo of 200 tons of slate in 1899, and, in the same year, the *Emily Dingle* on a voyage from Gaspe St. Lawrence to Rio de Janeiro with a cargo of tub fish.

The most detailed sources of every day information are the account books and bills of individual ships: those of the *Tyne* start in 1871 with the wages paid to Captain John Thomas and his crew for the voyage to Newcastle, Porto Torres, Huelva, Pomaron and back to Newcastle, the expenses incurred for food, stores, port charges, freights received, cash advanced, and payments made to Captain Lloyd and the other owners. The bundles of bills record payments to various suppliers: in the bundle for 1887, for example, are payments to Richard & Jones, sailmakers, Cornhill, Porthmadog, the Ballast Bank Company, R. Jones, Porthmadog, for beef, Hugh Lloyd, coal merchant and provision dealer, for vegetables, William Roberts, shipsmith, Edmund Humphreys for loading slates, Thomas Parry, timber merchant, Hugh Williams, shipbuilder, John Davies, Bread and Biscuit baker, Hugh Jones, Block, pump and spar maker, John H. Williams, Britannia Foundry, William Roberts, sailmaker, the Portmadoc Steam Tug Company, D. Morris, Ship Chandler, Grocer and Provision Dealer, and William Evans, ship chandler and tinplate worker. Together with the charter-party agreements, which record the cargoes carried, it is possible to reconstruct the financing of these vessels which plied regularly in the coastal and oceanic trades.

When David Williams and his mate, Griffith Williams, completed the *Emrys* in 1893 — she was destined to be lost by collision in the English Channel within seven years of her launching — accounts of the ship chandlers indicate the costs of the equipment and stores put aboard when she was being fitted out. On 4 April 1893, the charts were supplied, and obviously reflect the intended trade of the vessel:[3]

| | | £ | s. | d. |
|---|---|---|---|---|
| April 4 | 1 Chart English Channel and Dir. 12/- 1 Irish and Bristol Chl. 14/- | 1 | 6 | 0 |
| | 1 East Coast Engl. & Scotland Dir. 12/- 1 West Coast & Isl. of Scotland | 1 | 4 | 0 |
| | 1 Coast of Ireland 12/- 1 North Sea General Chart 10/- | 1 | 2 | 0 |
| | 1 South Part N. Sea + dir. 12/- 1 chart Sleeve 8/- Baltic Sea + Dir of East of England 10/- | 1 | 10 | 0 |
| | 1 Kattegat, Sound and Belts, Dir. 12/- 1 Sheet Sound 2/9 | | 14 | 9 |
| | 1 France, Spain and Portugal 10/-, North Atlantic 8/- | | 18 | 0 |
| | 1 West and 1 East of Mediterranean Sea 24/-, 1 Coast of Labrador, 8/- | 1 | 12 | 0 |
| | 1 Gibraltar to Mogador 8/- 1 Newfoundland 10/- | | 18 | 0 |
| | 1 Log Book 3/6, 1 Chart Thames and Medway + Dir. 8/- | | 11 | 6 |

A week later, together with the first of the food supplies — e.g., 6 lbs. Welsh butter came the general stores:

| | | £ | s. | d. |
|---|---|---|---|---|
| 11th | 1 skin S. Twine 9d Pepper 1d, 1S. Palm ½, Sail & Needles 4½ | | 2 | 4½ |
| | ½ cwt Bread 8/3, 12lb sugar, 2/-, 1 lb coffee 1/6, 1 lb tea, 2/- | | 13 | 9 |
| | Binding charts 4/-, Tape etc. 1/6, 6 Paint Brushes + 2 C. Hair 9/3 | | 14 | 9 |
| | 20 lbs soap @ 3p. 5/-, 28 lbs soda 1/3, 3 Paint and Deck Scrubbers 5/- | | 11 | 3 |
| | 1 Scouring Brush 11d, 1 Hard Brush 9d, 6 Bass Brooms @ 1/4, 5/- | | 9 | 8 |

| | | | |
|---|---|---|---|
| 3 lbs comp. candles 12 at 8d, 2/-; 1 Gross Matches 2/3, 2 tins Blkg. | | 4 | 9 |
| Blk Lead 8d, 1 Bail Bucket 1/4, 5 lbs Boat nails asstd @ 6d, 2/6, 2 lbs scupper Nails @ 6d, 1/- | | 5 | 6 |
| 4lbs. tallow @ 5d 1/8, 2 lb cotton waste @ 4d, 8d, 2 Bath bricks 3d, 5lbs oakum 1/8 | | 4 | 3 |
| 4lbs Pitch @ 2d, 8d; 2 key rings 3d, 1 file 6d, 1 Divider 1/3, 1 H.C. Pump tax 1/6 | | 4 | 2 |
| 1 Roping Palm 2/6 seaming needles 10, 1 Siccors 1/- | | 4 | 10 |
| 1 Oil Funnel 10d, 1 ditto 5, 2 Padlocks @ 8d, 1/4, 1 Almanack 1/- | | 3 | 7 |
| a/c books 10d, 2 doz. l/c glasses @ 2/6, 5/-, 1 gall Colza, 3/6, 6 Galls blk. varnish @ 10d, 5/- | | 14 | 4 |
| 3 yds L/c wicks @ 2d, 6d, 2 yds ditto ¾″ at 1½d, 3d ditto ⅝, 1½, 20 galls Paraffin @ 8d | | 14 | 8½ |
| 2 Fishing Lines @ 1/3, 2/6, Snood 6d, Hooks 6d, 2 leads at 8d, 1/4 | | 4 | 10 |

Finally, on 23 April, the bulk of the food stores came aboard:

| | | | | |
|---|---|---|---|---|
| 23rd | 21 lbs Tea @ 1/3, 26/3, Bond 2/6, 6 lbs. best coffee @ 1/8, 10/-, 10 lbs. Ground ditto @ 1/3, 14 ditto @ 1/6 | 3 | 19 | 9 |
| | 2 doz. Swiss Milk @ 6/3, 12/6, 3 tins cocoa @ 1/-, 3/-, 2½cwt. sugar @ 18/3, 45/7 | 3 | 1 | 1 |
| | 28 lbs. currants @ 3d, 7/-, 14 lbs Raisins @ 4½, 5/3, 50 lb Rice @ 1½, 6/3, 5lbs sago @ 4d, 1/8 | 1 | 0 | 2 |
| | 10 lbs. pearl barley @ 2½, 2/1, 56 lbs Split Peas @ 1½, 30 lbs French beans @ 2½, 5/-, 1 Bg. Flour 16/- | 1 | 10 | 1 |
| | 28 lbs. Oak Meal @ 2d, 4/8, 4 cwt. Bread @ 7/-, 68/-; 120 lbs tins butter @ 10d, 100/- | 8 | 12 | 8 |
| | 29 lbs. Bacon @ 7d, 16/11; 1 Ham, 18 lbs. @ 8½, 12/9; 3 cases Roast beef, 6 doz tins 49/6 | 3 | 19 | 2 |
| | 1 Tirce Ex. I. Mess. Beef, 85/6; 3½ lbs cheese @ 8d, 2/4; 6 tins salmon 4/-; 6 lobster 6/- | 4 | 17 | 10 |
| | 6 tins Marmalade 42 lbs @ 4d, 14/-; 3 galls vinegar @ 1/6, 4/-; 6 pickles @ 11d, 5 & 6, 2/6 | 1 | 1 | 10 |
| | 6 sauce @ 6d, 3/-, 18 lb Molassus @ 2d, 3/-; 2 lb. D/S Mustard 2/- 2lbs. pepper | | 12 | 6 |
| | 200 salt Herrings @ 4/-, 8/-; spices 1/3; 2 tins 3 powder 1/- ½lb Ginger, 12 lbs onions @ 2d, 2/- | | 12 | 10 |
| | Total Cost= | £45 | 8 | 11½ |

| | | | |
|---|---|---|---|
| Settled May 24, 1893 by cheque | £43 | 10 | 0 |
| Disc. | 1 | 18 | 11½ |
| | 45 | 8 | 11½ |

The account was settled on May 24, a payment by cheque of £43.10.0 allowing for a discount of £1.8.11½. The *Emrys* next obtained supplies, according to the ledgers, in March and April 1894 — that is, when she had returned to Porthmadog after the typical voyages of about a year to the Baltic, Newfoundland and the Mediterranean.

Dr. Lewis Lloyd has outlined the way in which the Lancashire-born Dr. J. H. Lister became a Porthmadog shipowner, with interests in several of the best-known vessels in the last decade of the nineteenth century. As befitted a professional man, Dr. Lister's accounts were carefully kept; they give some indication of the financial implications of the operations of the Western Ocean Yachts at the turn of the century. The *Jenny Jones,* built by Ebenezer Roberts in 1893 and named after the young daughter of Captain Evan Lewis Jones of Barmouth, was commanded in the early years of the century by Captain Thomas Ellis. Lister sold 24/64 shares in the *Jenny Jones* to Captain Thomas Ellis in 1899, and the remaining 40/64 in 1904. The accounts of the *Jenny Jones* for the years 1899-1903, which Lister entered into a school-type red exercise book, suggest that Dr. Lister's investment in Porthmadog ships had brought him a reasonable return. During the year ending in March 1900, the *Jenny Jones* had made an overall profit which was satisfactory; the next three years were better still, although it must be remembered that these accounts only record the gross profit without any indication of such items as vessel depreciation, etc.:[4] (See pp. 325-8.)

Captain Thomas Ellis sold the *Jenny Jones* soon after the outbreak of the 1914-18 war to the Tregaskis family, shipbuilders and shipowners of Par, who, in turn, sold her to Newfoundland. In this the *Jenny Jones* was not untypical — several of the later Porthmadog vessels were sold either to the West Country or to Newfoundland. Porthmadog's slate trade with the Elbe ports had ceased completely because of the war with Germany, thus destroying the very *raison d'etre* of the port and its ships. The *Blodwen, William Prichard, R. J. Owens, Gracie,* and the *John Llewelyn* were among those sold to Newfoundland owners; ironically, few of them survived long after they had left Porthmadog. It was also ironic that the Germans, who had been largely responsible for stimulating the building of the Western Ocean Yachts in which several of their countrymen had served, should have also been responsible for the destruction of a number of the finest examples, sunk by U-boats. The Porthmadog Ship Insurance Society, backbone of the financial affairs of the port, which had 137 ships on its books in 1880, had only 44 by 1912; the war soon decreased the number even further. In 1915 there are payments recorded in the ledgers for a new lifeboat and a new jolly boat, for the *Blodwen,* both built by William Roberts, and expenses incurred at Leghorn, but she was sold soon afterwards. In January 1916, there are payments on behalf of the *Elizabeth* for new sails and caulking parts of the deck at La Rochelle, and a few months later it was decided to transfer any amounts outstanding for the *George Casson,* 'This vessel being interned at Harburg', to the managing owner of the *George Casson* pending a decision at the end of the war. There were still 29 vessels on the registers in 1916: in 1872 the valuation of the ships registered was £243,240, in 1916 it was £54,256. Robert Ehlers of Bristol, described as a 'Newfoundland Produce Merchant' in the Registers of Shipping, bought the *William Prichard* on behalf of Newfoundland owners in June 1916, and so the numbers diminished each month either by sale or sinking. In 1917 the Port Madoc Mutual Ship Insurance Society closed its doors for the last time.

## REFERENCES

[1] I am indebted to Mr. Ifan Pugh, Pwllheli, for this and other information regarding his grandfather, Captain Evan Pugh, master of the *Pride of Wales.*

[2] The Reports for 1862-3, and 1863-4, are at the C.R.O., MS. M/531/50. The Report for 1866-67 is reproduced with the kind permission of Mr. Owen Lloyd, Dora Street, Porthmadog, to whom I am indebted also for the papers relating to the *Tyne* quoted in the pages which follow.

[3] N.L.W. MSS. 12090E.

[4] The accounts of the Lister vessels are housed at the Gwynedd Record Office at Dolgellau, Z/M, 753, cf. Dr. Lloyd's notes on the Lister vessel, infra.

Mar. 15th 1899 - Mar. 1st 1900

| | | | | | £ | s. | d. |
|---|---|---|---|---|---|---|---|
| Freight | Harburg | | | | 155 | 12 | 5 |
| | Southampton | | | | 62 | 10 | 9 |
| | St. Johns | 192 | 13 | 0 | | | |
| | | 93 | 0 | 0 | 99 | 13 | 0 |
| | Leghorn | | | | 472 | 10 | 0 |
| | Irvine | 1015 | 8 | 1 | 225 | 1 | 11 |
| Average | Brest | | | | 28 | 8 | 0 |
| ,, | Leghorn | | | | 46 | 13 | 4 |
| Discounts Bank Interest &c. | | | | | 6 | 6 | 1½ |
| | | | | | £1096 | 15 | 6½ |

| | | | | | £ | s. | d. |
|---|---|---|---|---|---|---|---|
| Port Charges | Owner | 11 | 7 | 0 | | | |
| | Master | 185 | 8 | 7½ | 196 | 15 | 7½ |
| Victualling | Owner | 15 | 1 | 8 | | | |
| | Master | 58 | 1 | 2½ | 73 | 2 | 10½ |
| Wages | Crew | | | | 157 | 11 | 2 |
| | Master to March 4th, 1900 | | | | 87 | 4 | 6 |
| Insurance | | | | | 172 | 0 | 9 |
| Ship's Stores, Repairs | Owner | 211 | 15 | 6½ | | | |
| | Master | 59 | 16 | 10 | 271 | 12 | 4½ |
| Bank charges 14/2, Petties 17/10½ | | | | | 1 | 12 | 0½ |
| Balance Gross Profit | | | | | 136 | 16 | 2½ |
| | | | | | £1096 | 15 | 6½ |

Examined and found correct — Thomas Ellis

## BALANCE SHEET FOR THE YEAR 1900 - 1901

Mar. 1st 1900 - Feb. 28th 1901

| | | £ | s. | d. |
|---|---|---|---|---|
| Freights &c. | Harburg | 159 | 10 | 4 |
| do | Swansea | 76 | 1 | 0 |
| do | Madeira | 141 | 2 | 9 |
| do | St. John's | 129 | 12 | 6 |
| do | Genoa | 505 | 13 | 4 |
| do | Newport | 156 | 15 | 0 |
| do | Portmadoc | 6 | 17 | 1 |
| Returns | Insurance Premium | 2 | 11 | 3 |
| do | Short delivery | 19 | 2 | 6 |
| Bank Int 2.16.2. Discts 2.18.2½. Cariad 12.6 | | 6 | 6 | 10½ |
| Demurrage &c in Genoa £1 | | | | |
| | | £1203 | 12 | 7½ |

| | | | | | £ | s. | d. |
|---|---|---|---|---|---|---|---|
| Port Charges | Owner | 12 | 1 | 0 | | | |
| do | Master | 201 | 2 | 7 | 213 | 3 | 7 |
| Victualling | Owner | 29 | 15 | 9½ | | | |
| do | Master | 49 | 11 | 3 | 79 | 7 | 0½ |
| Wages | Crew | | | | 162 | 4 | 4 |
| do | Master to March 4th, 1901 | | | | 96 | 0 | 0 |
| Insurance | | | | | 142 | 14 | 8 |
| Ship's Stores, Repairs | Owner | 82 | 1 | 3 | | | |
| | Master | 29 | 3 | 7 | 111 | 4 | 10 |
| Short delivery charges Genoa | | | | | 25 | 11 | 6 |
| Bank charges 1.2.6. Petties &c 6.16.4½ | | | | | 7 | 18 | 10½ |
| Balance Gross Profit | | | | | 365 | 7 | 9½ |
| | | | | | £1203 | 12 | 7½ |

E&OE

Examined and found correct — Thomas Ellis.
Mar. 1st, 1901.

## BALANCE SHEET FOR THE YEAR 1901 - 1902

Mar. 1st 1901 - Mar. 7th 1902

| | | | | | | £ | s. | d. |
|---|---|---|---|---|---|---|---|---|
| Freights | Stettin | | | | | 188 | 18 | 4 |
| | London | | | | | 96 | 15 | 3 |
| | Cardiff & Barry | | | | | 55 | 2 | 6 |
| | Gibraltar | | | | | 121 | 6 | 3 |
| | St. John's | Salv. | 208 | 19 | 9 | | | |
| | | Cost | 79 | 6 | 8 | 129 | 13 | 1 |
| | Genoa | | | | | 525 | 7 | 10 |
| | Burry Port | | | | | 137 | 11 | 1 |
| | Dublin | | | | | 63 | 18 | 6 |
| Insurance Claims £3/10/-, Ret. & Com$^n$ £2/17/9 | | | | | | 6 | 7 | 9 |
| Discts 16/5, Bank Interest £3/2/3 | | | | | | 3 | 18 | 8 |
| | | | | | | £1328 | 19 | 3 |

| | | | | | £ | s. | d. |
|---|---|---|---|---|---|---|---|
| Port Charges | Owner | 13 | 18 | 9 | | | |
| do | Master | 296 | 8 | 4 | 310 | 7 | 1 |
| Victualling | Owner | 34 | 2 | 8 | | | |
| | Master | 52 | 8 | 10 | 86 | 11 | 6 |
| Wages | Crew | | | | 179 | 4 | 6 |
| | Master | | | | 96 | 0 | 0 |
| Insurance a/c | | | | | 137 | 5 | 11 |
| Ship's Stores, Repairs &c | Owner | 50 | 17 | 0 | | | |
| | Master | 41 | 16 | 1 | 92 | 13 | 10 |
| Petties £1/0/5. Management £5/-/-. Bk. charges £1/3/10 | | | | | 7 | 4 | 3 |
| Balance Gross Profit | | | | | 419 | 12 | 2 |
| | | | | | £1328 | 19 | 3 |

## PROFIT & LOSS & DIVIDEND A/C.

| | | £ | s. | d. |
|---|---|---|---|---|
| Mar. 1st, 1901. | Balance in hand | 33 | 15 | 5 |
| | Balance Profits | 419 | 12 | 2 |
| | | £453 | 7 | 7 |

| | | | | | £ | s. | d. |
|---|---|---|---|---|---|---|---|
| Income Tax | | | | | 8 | 16 | 2 |
| Dividend £26 per 1/16 less tax | | | | | | | |
| | T. Ellis | 156 | 0 | 0 | | | |
| | | 3 | 6 | 1 | 152 | 13 | 11 |
| | J. H. Lister | 260 | 0 | 0 | | | |
| | | 5 | 10 | 1 | 254 | 9 | 11 |
| Mar. 7th, 1902. Balance in hand | | | | | 37 | 7 | 7 |
| | | | | | £453 | 7 | 7 |

| Mar. 8th, 1902 | | £ | s. | d. |
|---|---|---|---|---|
| Freights | Harburg | 142 | 13 | 9 |
| | Londonderry | 94 | 19 | 6 |
| | St. John's | 93 | 12 | 0 |
| | Hamburg | 257 | 13 | 6 |
| | St. John's | 89 | 16 | 0 |
| | Carthagena | 416 | 10 | 2 |
| | Swansea | 105 | 2 | 7 |
| | Portmadoc £1211.7.6 | 11 | 0 | 0 |
| Returns £14.5.0. Insurance claims £66.7.1 | | 80 | 12 | 1 |
| Discounts £1.9.6. Bank Interest £3.8.4 | | 4 | 17 | 10 |
| | | £1296 | 17 | 5 |

| | | £ | s. | d. | £ | s. | d. |
|---|---|---|---|---|---|---|---|
| Port charges a/c | Owner | 44 | 4 | 4 | | | |
| | Master | 257 | 13 | 10 | 301 | 18 | 2 |
| Victualling a/c | Owner | 33 | 8 | 3 | | | |
| | Master | 50 | 0 | 3 | 83 | 8 | 6 |
| Wages | Crew (£1/10 R. J. Morris) | | | | 169 | 13 | 2 |
| | Master | | | | 96 | 0 | 0 |
| Insurance a/c | | | | | 147 | 2 | 2 |
| Ship's Stores, Repairs &c | Owner | 61 | 2 | 2 | | | |
| | Master | 137 | 3 | 9 | 198 | 5 | 11 |
| Short delivery £8.18.3. Disct Carthagena £5 | | | | | 13 | 18 | 3 |
| Petties £2.6.0. Management £5. Bank charges £1.6.1 | | | | | 8 | 12 | 1 |
| Feb. 28. Balance Gross Profit | | | | | 277 | 19 | 2 |
| | | | | | £1296 | 17 | 5 |

Feb. 27, 1903. Thomas Ellis.

## BALANCE SHEET FOR YEAR 1903 - 1904

Mar. 1st 1903 - Mar. 16th 1904

| | | | £ | s. | d. |
|---|---|---|---|---|---|
| Freights | Stettin | | 177 | 9 | 0 |
| | L'Orient | | 92 | 10 | 3 |
| | St. John's | Salt 10/- | 127 | 10 | 0 |
| | Glasgow | | 219 | 19 | 9 |
| | St. John's | Coal 8/- | 79 | 4 | 0 |
| | Leghorn | | 453 | 17 | 6 |
| Returns Insurance claims | | | 16 | 18 | 0 |
| Discounts £1.15.0. Bank Interest £2.9.1 | | | 4 | 4 | 1 |
| | | | £1171 | 12 | 7 |

| | | £ | s. | d. | £ | s. | d. |
|---|---|---|---|---|---|---|---|
| Port charges a/c | Owner | 10 | 2 | 7 | | | |
| do | Master | 242 | 15 | $9\frac{1}{4}$ | 252 | 18 | $4\frac{1}{4}$ |
| Victualling a/c | Owner | 14 | 12 | $5\frac{1}{2}$ | | | |
| | Master | 69 | 14 | 0 | 84 | 6 | $5\frac{1}{2}$ |
| Wages of Crew | | | | | 203 | 1 | 8 |
| do | Master | | | | 96 | 0 | 0 |
| Insurance a/c | | | | | 104 | 15 | 6 |
| Ship's Stores, Repairs &c | Owner | 57 | 5 | $6\frac{1}{2}$ | | | |
| do | Master | 43 | 18 | $2\frac{3}{4}$ | 101 | 3 | $9\frac{1}{4}$ |
| Petties &c £6.14.$1\frac{1}{2}$. Bank charges £1.0.5 | | | | | 7 | 14 | $6\frac{1}{2}$ |
| Balance Gross Profit | | | | | 321 | 12 | $3\frac{1}{2}$ |
| | | | | | £1171 | 12 | 7 |

## PROFIT & LOSS & DIVIDEND A/C

| | | £ | s. | d. | | | | | £ | s. | d. |
|---|---|---|---|---|---|---|---|---|---|---|---|
| Mar. 16, 1903 | Balance in hand | 27 | 6 | 9 | Income Tax | | | | 12 | 18 | 9 |
| 16, 1904 | Balance profits | 321 | 12 | 3½ | Dividend £20 per 1/16 | | | | | | |
| | | | | | T. Ellis | 120 | 0 | 0 | | | |
| | | | | | less tax | 4 | 17 | 0 | 115 | 3 | 0 |
| | | | | | J. H. Lister | 200 | 0 | 0 | | | |
| | | | | | less tax | 8 | 1 | 9 | 191 | 18 | 3 |
| | | | | | Balance in hand | | | | 28 | 19 | 0½ |
| | | £348 | 19 | 0½ | | | | | £348 | 19 | 0½ |

## BALANCE SHEET

| | £ | s. | d. | | £ | s. | d. |
|---|---|---|---|---|---|---|---|
| Mar. 1st, 1904 | | | | | | | |
| Balance in hand | 27 | 6 | 9 | Port Charges a/c | 10 | 2 | 7 |
| Remittances | 768 | 12 | 4 | Victualling a/c | 14 | 12 | 5½ |
| Returns Insurance claims | 16 | 18 | 0 | Wear & Tear a/c | 57 | 5 | 6½ |
| Discounts | 1 | 15 | 0 | Insurance a/c | 104 | 15 | 6 |
| Bank Interest | 2 | 9 | 1 | Petties £6.14.1½. Bank Charges £1.0.5 | 7 | 14 | 6½ |
| | | | | Cash, Wages, Acceptances &c. | 286 | 10 | 2 |
| | | | | Balance in hand | 336 | 0 | 4½ |
| | £817 | 1 | 2 | | £817 | 1 | 2 |

## CAPT. THOS. ELLIS IN A/C WITH MANAGING OWNER

| | £ | s. | d. | | £ | s. | d. |
|---|---|---|---|---|---|---|---|
| Freights as per a/c | 1150 | 10 | 6 | Post charges a/c | 242 | 15 | 9¼ |
| Cash £22.10/0, £90.10/0. Glasgow £25.15/11 | 138 | 15 | 11 | Victualling a/c | 69 | 14 | 0 |
| Drafts Cadiz £21.16.0. Gibraltar £16.7.1 + 10/- | 38 | 13 | 11 | Wear & Tear a/c | 43 | 18 | 2¾ |
| Allotments &c. | 59 | 10 | 0 | Wages Crew | 203 | 1 | 8 |
| Draft St. John's | 34 | 0 | 0 | do Master to Mar. 4th | 96 | 0 | 0 |
| Balance due Capt. Ellis | 2 | 11 | 8 | Remittances | 768 | 12 | 4 |

# LOADING THE SLATES

THE photographs of slates being loaded into the vessel at Greaves Wharf, Pl. 9, epitomises one essential aspect of the life of Porthmadog. Mr. David Williams, son of the shipbuilder, and many of his contemporaries have described to me how, as young boys, they used to watch with fascinated eyes the slates sliding rapidly down the glass-like surface of the plank, to be halted by the specially designed wad in the hands of a man at deck level, who would, in turn, transfer them down into the hold. There, other men were ready to pass them from hand to hand until they were finally wedged into place by the large round mallet, which can be seen in the picture, on the left shoulder of the large bearded man. Considerable expertise was involved; the tightly stowed slates, kept in place by straw and wooden battens, could easily be broken and the timbers of a slate ship could be badly strained if the slates were not stowed properly. It used to be said that 'foreign' built vessels could only load at flood tide, but that Porthmadog-built vessels were so stoutly built that they could stand the strain of loading slates at any state of the tide

The men who loaded the slates were experts in their own way; they worked a long day, from six in the morning until six at night when there were vessels to be loaded. In the busier days of the port, the network of rails for the slate trucks, the stacked slates, both on the open wharves and in the long low sheds, the quarry owners in their tweedy suits talking to bowler-hatted foremen, and the 'hobblers' and ships crews weaving their way between the trucks and stacked slates, all gave the harbour an air of bustle and activity. Elderly gentlemen in Porthmadog today remember crossing two or three vessels alongside as they delivered their errands — meat from the butchers, paint and miscellaneous goods from the 'tinmen' — and always having to keep a wary eye on the moving slate trucks. There were 'characters' among the hobblers, and among the best remembered quayside figures of an earlier age were two coal merchants, Mrs. Catherine Roberts, 'a slightly built little woman, of dark complexion and always wearing a black dress and a black bonnet', and Mrs. Dolly Thomas, 'a stout little woman, always wearing clogs, and hat or cap, a short home-spun skirt, and a large blue-striped apron'.[1] As Mrs. Thomas stood on the quay above the ship which had brought her a cargo of coal, she would give orders where the coal was to be sent, but would all the time keep on with her knitting. 'She kept no account books — her accounts were kept in her retentive memory'.

The tonnage of slates loaded into the ships indicates the labour involved — an average tonnage of 11,012 tons for the years 1825-1830, increasing to 74,733 tons in the 1861-1865 period, to the maximum of 116,567 tons shipped in 1873. There are some discrepancies in the totals given by W. M. Richards, David Thomas and E. Davies, but they agree that 1873 was the year when most slates were shipped out of Porthmadog. The quarterly returns preserved in the Dolgellau Record Office give the totals of tonnage by sea and rail in 1873 appears on the next page.[2]

Mr. S. C. Evans of Osmond Terrace, Porthmadog, who worked for many years in the offices of the slate quarries in Porthmadog harbour, has kindly provided the following statistics based upon his own research into the records of the Harbour Office and the Slate Quarry Associations. The group of quarries known later as the Oakley shipped slate from Porthmadog in the pre-rail period 1825-1869 as follows:

| | |
|---|---|
| Welsh Slate Company (chairman, Lord Palmerston) | 681,973 tons |
| Rhiwbryfdir (Mathews) | 313,634 tons |
| South Holland (Holland's) | 334,690 tons |

Between 1870 and 1878 the Rhiwbryfdir Quarry shipped 119,086 tons, and 21,915 tons by rail, and the South Holland shipped 112,125 tons, and 18,423 tons by rail. Both quarries then became part of the Oakley group; the Welsh Slate Company, which continued independently until 1887, shipped 597,698 tons between 1870 and 1887 and sent 98,944 tons by rail. Between 1878 and 1948 the Oakleys group sent 1,126,281 tons by sea and 996,297 tons by rail, so that between 1825 and 1948 Mr. Evans estimated the totals as 3,285,487 tons shipped and 1,135,579 tons by rail. The records of the 'Votty'

| | Quarter Ending March 31, 1873 | | Quarter Ending June 30 | | Quarter Ending Sept. 30 | | Quarter Ending Dec. 31 | |
|---|---|---|---|---|---|---|---|---|
| | *Sea* | *Rail* | *Sea* | *Rail* | *Sea* | *Rail* | *Sea* | *Rail* |
| Welsh Slate Co. | 10668 | 1593 | 16102 | 1097 | 12957 | 1700 | 8073 | 1609 |
| Samuel Holland | 4214 | 410 | 4374 | 923 | 3826 | 1235 | 2490 | 1020 |
| Rhiwbryfdir Co. | 3248 | 568 | 4459 | 566 | 2929 | 1042 | 2119 | 1401 |
| J. W. Greaves | 3874 | 222 | 4560 | 172 | 3879 | 215 | 2395 | 306 |
| Percival & Co. | 1329 | 429 | 1445 | 278 | 1399 | 212 | 1142 | 236 |
| Diphwys Casson & Co. | 1457 | 582 | 1085 | 765 | 945 | 624 | 698 | 547 |
| Festiniog Slate Co. | 1280 | 310 | 1136 | 298 | 811 | 412 | 866 | 393 |
| Croesor Co. | — | 532 | 60 | 397 | — | 322 | — | 360 |
| Rhosydd Co. | 584 | 273 | 325 | 80 | 364 | 233 | 186 | 233 |
| Maenofferen Co. | 455 | 44 | 261 | 373 | 381 | 482 | 155 | 533 |
| R. Williams & Co. | 9 | 9 | 44 | — | 33 | — | 10 | — |
| Cwt y Bugail Co. | — | 245 | 261 | 398 | 222 | 546 | 345 | 600 |
| Craig Ddu Co. | 146 | 62 | 127 | 99 | 7 | 200 | — | 62 |
| Cwmorthin Co. | 1924 | 572 | 2702 | 546 | 2635 | 681 | 1384 | 506 |
| M. Lloyd | 169 | — | — | — | — | — | — | — |

(Bowydd or Percivals) were only available from 1856: from 1856 to 1948, 371,212 tons were shipped by sea, and 379,170 sent by rail.

Among the papers of the Slate Quarry Companies are many agreements made with ships' masters or ship-brokers to transport the slate to ports in various parts of the world. In 1884, for example, the Greaves Company's records show that early in the New Year the *Cadwalader Jones* was chartered to take a slate cargo to the Baltic, and John Cadwalader, her master, agreed to load a complete load of slates at Greaves Wharf and to deliver them at a Baltic port 'at 14/- shillings per ton computed weight'.[3] In the same month, Edward Roberts, master of the *Ebenezer,* was chartered to take slates to the Baltic ports, Hamburg or Harburg, 'at Going Freight': two years later, in 1886, Owen Lloyd, master of the *Tyne,* took slates to Harburg at 8/- a ton, and William Watkins, master of the *Hope,* of Aberystwyth, was paid 6/6 a ton for a cargo for Cork. John Williams, master of the *George Henry*, took cargoes to 'kolching and another neighbouring port' at 10/- in July 1886, and to Odense in April 1887 at a similar rate. Obviously the freight rates fluctuated according to the state of the market and the location of the port of discharge, as well as the size of the vessel. The ports most frequently visited by Porthmadog slate ships appear to have been London, Hull, Liverpool, Ayr, Bristol, Gloucester, Runcorn, Gosport, Glasgow, Aberdeen, Sunderland, South Shields, Swansea, Cardiff and Southampton in the home trade, and, obviously, Hamburg, Stettin, Copenhagen, Danzig, Malmö, Rotterdam and Flensburg in the European trades. Emrys Hughes followed the voyages of four Porthmadog schooners during the 1898-1903 period,[4] and calculated that the small coasting schooner *John and Margaret* transported in twenty-four voyages 2,160 tons of slate to South Wales and neighbouring ports, the larger *Catherine and Margaret* in twenty voyages carried 32,000 tons to more distant coastal ports like Aberdeen and London, the *Walter Ulric* took 3,400 tons in seventeen voyages, thirteen to Germany and four coastwise, and the largest of the four, the three-masted schooner *Ann and Jane Prichard,* 3,840 tons in sixteen voyages to Germany and the Baltic during this five-year period. The dates of their sailings from Porthmadog and their destinations (not including any intervening voyages) were as follows:

| *John and Margaret* | | *Catherine and Margaret* | | *Walter Ulric* | | *Ann and Jane Prichard* | |
|---|---|---|---|---|---|---|---|
| 13.1.98 | Cardiff | 24.1.98 | London | 28.10.97 | Bremen | 8.9.97 | Copenhagen |
| 19.3.98 | Cardiff | 22.4.98 | London | 7.3.98 | Bremen | 22.2.98 | Copenhagen |
| 7.5.98 | Gloucester | 4.7.98 | Poole | 18.6.98 | Stettin | 6.7.98 | Aarhus |
| 6.7.98 | Cardiff | 18.8.98 | Newhaven | 30.12.98 | London | 3.10.98 | Copenhagen |
| 6.8.98 | Cardiff | 19.10.98 | Harburg | 11.4.99 | Kiel | 13.3.99 | Harburg |
| 23.9.98 | Cardiff | 10.3.99 | Southampton | 28.7.99 | Belfast | 22.6.99 | Copenhagen |
| 8.11.98 | Cardiff | 12.5.99 | Southampton | 19.8.99 | Kiel | 21.9.99 | Copenhagen |
| 24.1.99 | Cardiff | 21.7.99 | Shoreham | 2.12.99 | Belfast | 31.3.00 | Svenborg |
| 27.4.99 | Gloucester | 28.8.99 | Aberdeen | 30.1.00 | Faversham | 15.8.00 | Stettin |
| 16.6.99 | Cardiff | 18.12.99 | Folkestone and London | 3.4.00 | Papenburg | 9.3.01 | Harburg |
| 19.8.99 | Cardiff | | | 22.10.00 | Harburg | 14.6.01 | Kiel |
| 24.10.99 | Cardiff | 11.10.00 | London | 17.4.01 | Bremen | 12.9.01 | Kiel |
| 30.1.1900 | Cardiff | 4.2.01 | Southampton | 1.8.01 | Harburg | 25.2.02 | Harburg |
| 17.3.00 | Cardiff | 16.4.01 | Aberdeen | 30.9.01 | Bremen | 23.6.02 | Copenhagen |
| 7.9.00 | Cardiff | 1.8.01 | Southampton | 28.10.02 | Bremen | 8.9.02 | Harburg |
| 27.11.00 | Newport | 24.9.01 | Belfast | 5.3.03 | Harburg | 6.3.03 | Harburg |
| 11.3.01 | Cardiff | 11.1.02 | London | | | | |
| 6.6.01 | Cardiff | 1.3.02 | London | | | | |
| 20.8.01 | Cardiff | 18.7.02 | London | | | | |
| 22.1.02 | Cardiff | 26.8.02 | London | | | | |
| 22.5.02 | Cardiff | 12.1.03 | Southampton | | | | |
| 16.7.02 | Bridgwater | | | | | | |
| 8.9.02 | Cardiff | | | | | | |
| 6.11.02 | Newport | | | | | | |

Portmadoc, 5 Jany 1884

I, John Cadwalader Master of the Cadwalader Jones of Carnarvon hereby agree with JOHN W. GREAVES and SONS, (subject to the Merchants' approval) to Load a complete Cargo of Slates from their Wharf, at Portmadoc, and deliver the same at any Baltic Port at 14/- Shillings
Call for orders at Elsinore
per Ton computed weight. The Vessel to be loaded in turn, and to sail first fair wind.

The Master to advise the Merchants if Wind Bound during the Voyage.

Classed A1
Tons Register 94
Tons Burthen 200

John Cadwalader

The best source for details regarding the cargoes are the shipment books of the quarry companies and the ship-brokers' copies of charter party agreements. Emrys Hughes referred to Hugh Parry's charter-party agreements and he had obviously had access to them, but they appear to have since disappeared. By a fortunate chance, most of the charter-party agreements in one of the Porthmadog ship-brokers' offices, the Pritchard Brothers, for one year, 1906, were kept by one of the clerks and these were later deposited by his son, Mr. H. Roberts of Bangor, at the Record Office, Caernarfon.[5] The bare outline details have been extracted from the charter-party agreements and are here presented in tabulated form, as they give some indication of the range of cargoes and ports visited. It should be remembered that by 1906 the shipments of slate had been very considerably reduced, and this particular group of papers which have survived from one office represent the last phase, the era of the Western Ocean Yachts, when the ships had been compelled to seek alternative employment to the slate trade.

## REFERENCES


1 'Voices from the past', a series of articles 'Along the Cambrian Coast' in *CN* 14 Jan. 1921, et seq.
2 Dolgellau Record Office, MS. 1199.
3 C.R.O. J. W. Greaves MSS. 219.
4 C.R.O. MS. M/531/22.
5 C.R.O. XM/988.

## CHARTER-PARTY AGREEMENTS

| *Office No.* | *Date* | *Ship Brokers* | *Charterer/ Agent* | *Ship* | *Owner/Age* |
|---|---|---|---|---|---|
| (1) | 17 Jan. 1906 | Chessell & Co., Bristol | Messrs. J. C. Harter & Co., Manchester | *William Morton* | John Jones |
| (2) | 20 Jan. 1906 | Charles Johnson & Co., 46 Leadenhall St. [London] | The Anglo-Continental (late Ohlendorff's) Guano Works, London Agency | *Fleetwing* | Messrs. Prich Bros. & Co. |
| (3) | 19 Jan. 1906 | Charles Johnson & Co., 46 Leadenhall St., London | Isaac & Samuel of London, as Agents of the Aruba Phosphaat Maatschappy of Curacao | *Fleetwing* | Messrs. Prich Bros. & Co. |
| (5) | 15 Feb. 1906 | Prichard Bros. & Co., Portmadoc | [Prichard Bros. & Co., Portmadoc] | *Lizzie* | Capt. David Richards |
| (6) | 13 Feb. 1906 | C. T. Bennett & Co., Bristol | Messrs. A. Goodridge & Sons, of St. Johns, Newfoundland | *William Prichard* | Messrs. Prich Bros. & Co. |
| (7) | 13 Feb. 1906 | C. T. Bennett & Co., Bristol | Messrs. A. Goodridge & Sons of St.Johns [Newfoundland] | *William Prichard* | Messrs. Prich Bros. & Co. |
| (8) | 22 Feb. 1906 | C. T. Bennett & Co., Bristol | Messrs. John Rorke & Sons of Carbonear | *Elizabeth Pritchard* | Messrs. Prich Bros. & Co. |
| (9) | 22 Feb. 1906 | C. T. Bennett & Co., Bristol | Messrs. A. Goodridge & Sons of St. Johns, Newfoundland | *John Prichard* | William W. Roberts |
| (10) | 22 Feb. 1906 | C. T. Bennett & Co., Bristol | Messrs. A. Goodridge & Sons of St. Johns, Newfoundland | *John Prichard* | William W. Roberts |
| (10) | 22 Feb. 1906 | C. T. Bennett & Co., Bristol | Messrs. A. Goodridge & Sons of St. Johns, Newfoundland | *John Prichard* | William W. Roberts |

| Now at | To take Cargo at | Cargo | For |
|---|---|---|---|
| tagena | Messina | Oil in casks | Queenstown, Falmouth or Fowey for orders to discharge at safe port in the United Kingdom |
| nouth, nd London lischarge | London (River Thames, alongside the Peruvian Guano Wharf, near Victoria Docks) | Manure in bags | Martinique |
| : in London lischarge | Saint Nicolaas on the eastern part of the Island of Aruba, West India | Phosphate in bulk | London |
| passage to ıcorn | Runcorn | Coal, 150-160 tons | Portmadoc |
| ding | Cadiz | Salt in bulk | Saint Johns, Newfoundland |
| ding | Saint Johns, Newfoundland | Fish, at least 3,500 quintals | United Kingdom, Portugal, Spain (Seville excepted), Italy, Malta, Sicily, the Ionian Islands, or Athens |
| ding | Carbonear, Newfoundland | Fish in bulk, at least 3,500 quintals | United Kingdom, Portugal, Spain, Italy, Malta, Sicily, the Ionian Islands, Syra or Athens |
| tmadoc | Cadiz | Salt in bulk | Batteau, Labrador |
| tmadoc | Batteau, Labrador | Fish in bulk, at least 3,200 quintals | United Kingdom, Portugal, Spain (Seville excepted), Italy, Malta, Sicily, the Ionian Islands, Syra or Athens |
| tmadoc | Cadiz | Salt in bulk | Batteau, Labrador |

| Office No. | Date | Ship Brokers | Charterer/ Agent | Ship | Owner/Age |
|---|---|---|---|---|---|
| (11) | 6 Mar. 1906 | Renck & Hessenmüller, Harburg, a./Elbe | Paul Klembt Esq. of Hamburg | *William Prichard* | E. Jones |
| (12) | 8 Mar. 1906 | Renck & Hessenmüller, Harburg, Elbe | Paul Klembt Esq. of Hamburg | *George Casson* | Tom Lewis |
| (13) | 10 Mar. 1906 | Lüdke & Marquardt, Stettin & Swinemünde | Messrs. Baltzer & Schumacher of Stettin | *C. E. Spooner* | Capt. William |
| (15) | 13 Mar. 1906 | C. T. Bennett & Co., Bristol | Messrs. John Rorke & Sons of Carbonear, Newfoundland | *Elizabeth Pritchard* | Messrs. Prich Bros. & Co. |
| (20) | 20 Mar. 1906 | Lloyd Lowe Ltd., London | The Lantaro Nitrate Co. Ltd. | *Beeswing* | Messrs. Robe Thomas & Co |
| (23) | 22 Mar. 1906 | Prichard Bros. & Co., Portmadoc | Portmadoc Flour Mill[s] Co. | *William Prichard* | Messrs. Prich Bros. & Co. |
| (24) | 3 April 1906 | Prichard Bros. & Co., Portmadoc | Messrs. Kellow & Co. | *Cambrian* | Capt. William |
| (25) | 4 April 1906 | James Prentice, Sunderland | Messrs. G. Newington & Co. of Lewes | *C. E. Spooner* | Messrs. Prich Bros. & Co. |
| (26) | 4 April 1906 | ?G. Furneaux | Messrs. John Freeman, Sons & Co. Ltd. | *Sidney Smith* | Mr. David Williams |
| (27) | 20 April 1906 | Prichard Bros. & Co., Portmadoc | Portmadoc Flour Mills Co. | *George Casson* | Messrs. Prich Bros. & Co. |
| (29) | 2 May 1906 | Evan Jones & Co., Cardiff | Société Commerciale D'Affrétements et de Commission | *Elizabeth* | Evan Jones & Co. |
| (30) | 3 May 1906 | Huntly Bros., Sunderland and Newcastle-on-Tyne | Huntly Brothers | *Isallt* | W. J. Burdis, Esq. |

| *Now at* | *To take Cargo at* | *Cargo* | *For* |
|---|---|---|---|
| :burg | Harburg | Salt in bulk and/in bags, 280 tons | Lisahally and Londonderry |
| rburg | Harburg | Salt in bulk and/in bags, 250 tons | Lisahally and Londonderry |
| ttin | Stettin | logs and ends and remainder of fir square timber, and at merchants' option, 10 loads of oak crooks | Sunderland |
| ding | Cadiz | Salt in bulk | Carbonear, Newfoundland |
| passage to quimbo | Taltal | Nitrate of soda, 2,150-2,350 tons | Queenstown, Falmouth or Plymouth for orders to discharge at a safe port in the United Kingdom or on the Continent |
| ady [to] sail m Harburg Londonderry | Londonderry | Grain in sacks | Portmadoc |
| :diff | [Cardiff] | Coal, about 120 tons | Portmadoc |
| nderland | Hetton ? Drops, River Wear | Small coals | Newhaven |
| penhagen | Ulebergsham, Sweden | Granite curb | Greenwich, London for orders, to discharge at 2 ports if required |
| ndonderry | [Londonderry] | Grain in sacks, about 90 tons | Portmadoc |
| passage to rdiff | Cardiff (West or East Dock) | Coal | Cadiz Bay |
| ading | Walker Staithes, River Tyne [Newcastle] | Coals | Concarneau |

| Office No. | Date | Ship Brokers | Charterer/ Agent | Ship | Owner/Agen |
|---|---|---|---|---|---|
| (31) | 8 May 1906 | Davies, Jones & Co., 47 Mark Lane, London | John Allan & Sons of London | *Elizabeth Pritchard* | Messrs. Pricha Bros. & Co. |
| (32) | 10 May 1906 | Prichard Bros., & Co., Portmadoc | Messrs. The Oakleys Slate Quarry Co. | *Cambrian* | Capt. William |
| (33) | 14 May 1906 | Davies, Jones & Co., 47 Mark Lane, London | The Devon Trading Co. Ltd. | *Lucy* | Davies Jones & Co. |
| (34) | 18 May 1906 | J. C. Peacock & Co., Glasgow and Greenock | Messrs. Baine Johnston & Co. of St. Johns, Newfoundland | *Ellin Lloyd* | Messrs. Pricha Bros. & Co. |
| (35) | 1 June 1906 | Prichard Bros. & Co., Portmadoc | New Rhosydd Slate Co. | *P. M. Wilcock* | Capt. Evan Jones |
| (36) | 18 June 1906 | A. Treche, Kirkcudbright | Messrs. J. & T. Williamson of Kirkcudbright | *George Casson* (of Caernarvon) | Messrs. Pricha Bros. & Co. |
| (37) | 19 June 1906 | Davies, Jones & Co., 47 Mark Lane, London | Messrs. Ernest Matthews & Co. | *Janet* | Messrs. Pricha Bros. & Co. |
| (38) | 21 June 1906 | The New-foundland and Labrador Fish & Oil Co.,Ltd., Exeter, Bristol and Plymouth | The Newfoundland and Labrador Fish and Oil Co. Ltd., Exeter | *Edward Arthur* | Messrs. Pricha Bros. & Co. |
| (39) | 21 June 1906 | „ | „ | „ | „ |
| (40) | 26 June 1906 | H. Stadtlander, Bremen | Messrs. Matthias Rohde & Jörgens | *Edith Eleanor* | Capt. Richard Jones |
| (42) | 7 July 1906 | H. Stadtlander, Bremen | Messrs. Matthias Rohde & Jörgens | *Morningstar* | [The Capt. for Prichard Bros. & Co.] |
| (43) | 10 July 1906 | John Schildt & Co./Renck & Hessenmüller, Harburg, Elbe | Clemens Müller Esq. of Hamburg | *Dorothy* | Messrs. Pricha Bros. & Co. |

| Now at | To take Cargo at | Cargo | For |
|---|---|---|---|
| – | Goole, Hull or Grimsby | Coals | Rozia Bay, Gibraltar |
| rtmadoc] | [Portmadoc] | Slates | London |
| tmadoc | Portmadoc | Slates in bulk, about 120 tons | Teignmouth |
| e at ganwy | Troon | Coal (with option of up to 30 tons freestone) | St. Johns, Newfoundland |
| tmadoc | [Portmadoc] | Slates | London |
| tmadoc | Harburg | Kainit (waste salt), 250 tons in bulk | Kirkcudbright |
| tmadoc | Portmadoc | Slates in bulk, about 220 tons | Ipswich and Lowestoft |
| passage to wfound] d | Already taken at Cadiz | Salt in bulk | St. Johns for orders, thence to Winsor Harbor, Labrador |
| passage to wfound]land | Dark Tickle, Labrador | Fish in bulk, at least 3,200 quintals | United Kingdom, Portugal, Spain, Italy, Malta, Sicily, the Ionian Islands, Syra or Athens |
| tmadoc nd for estenssinde | Bremen Sicherheitshafen or Freihafen | Rock asphalt, 175/180 tons | Magheramorne |
| tmadoc nd for nen | Bremen Sicherheitshafen or Freihafen | Rock asphalt, 195 tons | Magheramorne |
| ding | Harburg | Slag in bulk, 250-260 tons | Honfleur |

| Office No. | Date | Ship Brokers | Charterer / Agent | Ship | Owner / Age[nt] |
|---|---|---|---|---|---|
| (44) | 11 July 1906 | Cutbill, King & Co., 25 Nicholas Lane, London | The La Guayra & Curacao Rly. Co. Ltd. | *Fleetwing* | Messrs. Prich[ard] Bros. & Co. |
| (45) | 11 July 1906 | Charles Johnson & Co., 46 Leadenhall St., London | Isaac & Samuel of London, as agents of the Aruba Phosphaat Maatschappy of Curacao | *Fleetwing* | Messrs. Prich[ard] Bros. & Co. |
| (46) | 21 July 1906 | Prichard Bros. & Co., Portmadoc | Mr. Shaw | *Mabel* | Messrs. Owe[n] Evans & Son |
| (48) | 31 July 1906 | Prichard Bros. & Co., Portmadoc | Messrs. J. W. Greaves & Son Ltd. | *Andree* | F. Cabon |
| (50) | 16 Aug. 1906 | H. Stadtlander, Bremen | Messrs. Matthias Rohde & Jörgens | *Janet* | Capt. —— [Pritchard B[ros.] & Co.] |
| (51) | 5 Sept. 1906 | LETTER: O. Evans & Son at 10 Slate Quay, Carnarvon, to Me[ssrs.] to proceed to Rhiw to load for Mostyn. | | | |
| (52) | 11 Sept. 1906 | H. Stadtlander, Bremen | Messrs. Matthias Rohde & Jörgens | *Edith Eleanor* | Capt. Richar[d] Jones |
| (53) | 12 Sept. 1906 | Prichard Bros. & Co., Portmadoc | Messrs. H. Owen & Son, Carnarvon | *Glanogwen* | Messrs. Prich[ard] Bros. & Co. |
| (54) | 15 Sept. 1906 | Prichard Bros. & Co., Portmadoc | [? Prichard Bros. & Co.] | *Seven Brothers* | Capt. Hugh Williams |
| (56) | 2 Oct. 1906 | Robert Owen, 28 Brunswick St., Liverpool | Tharsis Sulpher and Copper Co. Ltd., Glasgow | *C. E. Spooner* | Robert Owen Esq. |
| (57) | 3 Oct. 1906 | Robert Owen, 28 Brunswick St., Liverpool | John Allan & Sons of London | *C. E. Spooner* | Capt. E. H. Williams |
| (58) | 2 Oct. 1906 | A. S. Rendell & Co., Saint John's, Newfoundland | Messrs. Baine, Johnston & Co. of St. John's | *Blanche Currey* | John Jones |

| *Now at* | *To take Cargo at* | *Cargo* | *For* |
|---|---|---|---|
| ıe in London discharge | Port Talbot | Coals and/patent fuel; option: 20 tons smithy coal and 10 tons coke | La Guayra |
| ıe in London discharge | Saint Nicolaas on eastern part of Island of Aruba, West Indies | Phosphate in bulk | London, Ipswich or Garston |
| ɔersoch | Port Nigel (weather permitting) | Ore | Mostyn |
| ɔrtmadoc | [Portmadoc] | Slates, about 90 tons | Guernsey |
| ɔrtmadoc ɔund for :emen | Bremen Sicherheitshafen or Freihafen | Rock asphalt, 200 tons | N/Magheramorne |

:itchard & Co., Portmadoc, confirming wires exchanged that day fixing the 'Mabel'

| | | | |
|---|---|---|---|
| ɔrtmadoc ɔund for :emen | Bremen Sicherheitshafen or Freihafen | Rock asphalt, 175 tons | Magheramorne |
| Kiel | Gothenburg | Flooring boards with deck load, and sufficient ends for broken stowage and 5 standards of laths | Carnarvon, New Dock |
| ?ortmadoc] | Portmadoc | Slates | Cardiff |
| ıverpool to load ɔr Gibraltar, ıd expected :ady at Huelva ɔout ıid-December | Huelva, Spain | Cupreous sulpher ore and/other minerals and/metals, about 300/315 tons | Exmouth or Penryn |
| iverpool | Garston | Coals | Rozia Bay, Gibraltar |
| t. John's | St. John's | Codfish in drums and half drums | Pernambuco or Bahia direct, or Pernambuco for orders, and thence to Bahia, Maceio, Rio Grande-de-Norte or Paraiba |

| Office No. | Date | Ship Brokers | Charterer/ Agent | Ship | Owner/Agent |
|---|---|---|---|---|---|
| (60) | 19 Oct. 1906 | [? Anglo-N'fld Fish Exporting Co. Ltd.] | Anglo-N]ewfound[-land Fish Exporting Co. Ltd. of Liverpool | *C. E. Spooner* | [Prichard Bros & Co.] |
| (61) | 19 Oct. 1906 | [? Anglo-N'fld Fish Exporting Co. Ltd.] | Anglo-N'fld Fish Exporting Co. Ltd. | *C. E. Spooner* | [Prichard Bros & Co.] |
| (—) | 26 Oct. 1906 | Mordey, Jones & Co., Newport, Mon. and Cardiff | G. M. Taccone, Esq., of Genoa | *M. A. James* | John Jones |
| (62) | 19 Oct. 1906 | Renck & Hessenmüller, Harburg | Messrs. F. Thörl's Vereinigte Harburger Oelfabriken Act.-Ges., Harburg | *George Casson* | Capt. Tom Lewis |
| (65) | 30 Oct. 1906 | Mordey, Jones & Co., Newport, Mon. and Cardiff | G. M. Taccone, Esq., of Genoa | *Elizabeth Pritchard* | Prichard Bros. & Co. |
| (66) | 1 Nov. 1906 | C. L. Vasey & Co., London | Henry Hills & Son, Walker, Tyne | *William Prichard* | Messrs. Prichar Bros. & Co. |
| (67) | 16 Nov. 1906 | David Jones & Co., 47 Mark Lane, London | Messrs. Ernest Mathews & Co. | *Sarah Evans* | Capt. Roberts |
| (68) | 23 Nov. 1906 | Charles Johnson & Co., 46 Leadenhall St., London | Isaac & Samuel of London, as agents of the Aruba Phosphaat Maatschappy of Curacao | *Ellin Lloyd* | Messrs. Prichar Bros. & Co. |
| (70) | 20 Dec. 1906 | Prichard Bros. & Co., Portmadoc | Messrs. The Oakleys Slate Quarry Co. Ltd. | *Mary Edwards* | Messrs. Prichar Bros. & Co. |
| (71) | 22 Dec. 1906 | Davies, Jones & Co., 47 Mark Lane, London | Messrs. Ernest Mathews & Co. | *Michael Kelly* | E. O. Roberts |

| Now at | To take Cargo at | Cargo | For |
|---|---|---|---|
| ding | Labrador | Fish in bulk, at least 3,800 quintals | United Kingdom, Portugal, Spain, Italy (West Side), Malta, Sicily, the Ionian Islands, Patras, Syra or Athens |
| ding | Cadiz | Salt in bulk | Harbor Grace, Newfoundland |
| at Leghorn ischarge | Genoa | Slate and/slate slabs and/other lawful merchandise | Newport, Mon. |
| burg | Harburg | Oilcake in bulk, 220 tons | Bristol |
| passage to oa to harge | Genoa | Slate and/ slate slabs and/other lawful merchandise | Newport, Mon. |
| assage to oa | Pomaron on the Guadina, Portugal | Cupreous sulpher ore, or other mineral/s and/ metals in bulk of in bags or in barrels, about 275 tons | Amlwch, Anglesey, N. Wales |
| madoc | Portmadoc | Slates in bulk, as per specification sent to shippers | Ipswich |
| a | Saint Nicolaas, on eastern part of Island of Aruba, West Indies | Phosphate in bulk | Londonderry or Ghent |
| tmadoc] | [Portmadoc] | Slates, about 120 tons | Belfast, Cork, or Dublin |
| madoc | Portmadoc | Slates in bulk, about 230 tons | Exmouth and Lowestoft (not more than 100 tons for Exmouth) |

| *Office No.* | *Date* | *Ship Brokers* | *Charterer/ Agent* | *Ship* | *Owner/Age* |
|---|---|---|---|---|---|
| (—) | 7 Dec. 1906 | Charles Johnson & Co., 46 Leadenhall St., London | Isaac & Samuel of London, as agents of the Aruba Phosphaat Maatschappy of Curacao | *Sidney Smith* | Messrs. Prich Bros. & Co. |

*Attached* to above:

8 Dec. 1906 AGREEMENT: made between (1) W. O. Morris of East Ave Portmadoc, and (2) David Williams of Madoc Street, Portma re placing the *Sidney Smith* to substitute the *Ellin Lloyd* f charter, Aruba to Ghent or Londonderry. Consideration: £20 completion of charter, and agreement to pay deduction in fr if any made in consequence of vessel's not reaching Arub 15th March 1907 and not 1st March as specified in charter.

| *Now at* | *To take Cargo at* | *Cargo* | *For* |
|---|---|---|---|
| passage to nambuco | Saint Nicolaas on eastern part of Island of Aruba, West Indies | Phosphate in bulk | Londonderry or Ghent |

) 9 Dec. 1907 CIRCULAR LETTER: Prichard Bros. & Co., representing the *Beeswing* Sailing Ship Company Ltd., at Cornhill, Portmadoc, reporting loss of £1,217.8.2 after Voyage No. 10, due to the scarcity and low rates of freights. The outlook for freights has improved, however, and the *Beeswing* is now loading coal at Newcastle, N.S.W., to West Coast of America at a much increased rate of freight. The loss should soon be defrayed if the present rates continue. The cost of Lloyd's Classification Survey No. 3, which was passed in the last Annual Meeting to be executed, will appear in the current voyage account. Statement of accounts for Voyage No. 10 submitted [not present].

[XM/988]

# THE 'JACK' BARQUENTINES: THE TRANSITION FROM THE SQUARE RIG TO THE THREE-MASTED SCHOONERS

As the brigs became out-dated, many of them were converted into barquentines like the *Blanche Currie* and the *Mary Classen,* but the barquentines, in turn, also became out-dated. A vessel, therefore, had to be designed that could be run more economically and also take part successfully in the Newfoundland fish trade, which was about the only profitable trade left to them. The 'Jack Barquentine', sometimes referred to as the 'bastard barquentine', was the outcome. Their rig was about half-way between the regular barquentine and the three-masted schooners that were built some years later. They carried on the foremast a bent foresail to the fore yard, two top sails and a fixed top gallant sail, with no top gallant mast. They also had staysails to the main mast instead of a fore and aft foresail to the foremast, and fore and aft sails to the main and mizzen masts. It was a very successful rig and could be commanded by a master with only a 'fore and aft' certificate.

They were the obvious forerunners to the orthodox three-masted schooners which later followed them from the shipyards of Portmadoc. Five of them were built at Portmadoc, viz.:

The *Venedocian,* 1873.
*Marie Agathe,* 1876.
*Hilda,* 1877.
*C. E. Spooner,* 1878.
*Frau Minna Petersen,* 1878 (later converted into a three-masted schooner).

EMRYS HUGHES.

## TWO PHOTOGRAPHS: THE SCHOONER *DIZZY DUNLOP* AND THE BRIGANTINE *EDWARD WINDUS*

THE undated photograph of the *Dizzy Dunlop* being re-keeled, probably at a Scandinavian port, is not only intrinsically interesting, but is also a visual reminder of the relationship between a master/owner and a sailing master. It was sometimes the case in Porthmadog, as at many other schooner ports, that the real owner and master of a vessel was not qualified to sail his vessel outside the limits of the coasting trade and, therefore, in order to meet the requirements that a foreign-going vessel should have a master with the appropriate certificate of competency, ' sailing-masters ', as they were known, signed for the voyage, with the real master/owner signing as mate, or boatswain/purser. Sometimes a young man who was the son of the owner, like ' Johnnie Blodwen ', John Richard Williams, sailed as boatswain with an older man like Captain Hugh Pugh as master for the *Blodwen*'s record run; sometimes an older master was signed for the first part of the voyage, to comply with the regulations, and then was conveniently taken ill at Cadiz or Lisbon before the vessel sail for Newfoundland. Another way was to have the master and mate alternating their roles according to whether the vessel was engaged in the coasting or foreign trades, and this appears to have been the arrangement for the two members of the *Dizzy Dunlop*'s crew, who can be seen standing on the vessel's side as she was being re-keeled. In the foreground, standing on the rudder is Captain Thomas Williams, a bearded figure, with a balaclava-type knitted cap, and on his left, nearer to the men working on the keel, is Captain Owen Humphreys, sporting a splendid tall straw hat. Captain Thomas Ebenezer Williams had the controlling shares, 32/64, in the *Dizzy Dunlop*, and invariably commanded her in the coastal trade, but for the official record, whenever the vessel was engaged in the foreign trade, as designated by the Board of Trade, Owen Humphreys, who on other occasions signed as mate, became master, as he had a master's ticket.

The *Dizzy Dunlop* was built at the yard of Jones and Prichard, Borth-y-gest, and was launched on 26 January 1878. According to the local newspaper, 'like the vessels usually turned out of this yard', the new vessel was 'a very fine schooner of 110 tons register, length of keel 76 feet, breadth of beam 21½ feet, and depth of hold 11 feet'. Calculated to carry about two hundred tons, the vessel was christened by Mrs. Dunlop of Maentwrog, wife of Mr. Dunlop of the Oakley quarry; the name of the vessel was, in fact, *Daisy Dunlop*, but in the Register of Shipping she is entered as the *Dizzy Dunlop*, and this was obviously the name she was known by locally. What Mrs. Dunlop thought of this is not recorded, but the local newspaper reported that the 'figurehead attracted much attention, and was pronounced to be an excellent likeness of Mrs. Dunlop'. A Borth-y-gest launching in 1878 was an important event: 'A stage was erected and carpeted for the accommodation of Mrs. Dunlop and party. Notwithstanding the rough weather, there was a large attendance of spectators'.

For the early voyages, Captain Thomas E. Williams was named as master in the 'Articles' as they were all in the Hamburg and coastal trade, but when, in 1881, it was intended to sail for Stettin with slates, Captain Williams must have persuaded an old shellback to put to sea again, for Thomas E. Williams sailed as purser/A.B. with Captain Thomas Parry, aged 71, of Llaniestyn as master, and Thomas Davies as mate. Captain Thomas E. Williams, who came originally from Fourcrosses, and was aged 44 in 1882, resumed command for the Elbe voyages, but in the following year was compelled to sign again as boatswain/purser, with Captain Owen Humphreys (born at Harlech in 1830) as master, for the voyage to Kiel and Gottenburg, and, later in the year, to Copenhagen and Fredrikstad. This arrangement continued for the next six years, until the vessel was lost in 1890; each time the *Dizzy Dunlop*'s voyages were to Hamburg and not beyond, Captain Williams signed as master, and Owen Humphreys as mate, but when they were chartered to go further afield they reversed their roles on voyages to places like Konigsberg, Malmo, Fredrikstad, and Aarhus. In November 1887, with Captain Humphreys as master and Captain Williams as boatswain/purser, they were at Nakstov, on the Danish island of Lolland, having left Kiel a week previously.

In April 1890, the partnership between Captains Williams and Humphreys came to an end when the *Dizzy Dunlop* was stranded and became a total wreck on Atherfield Ledge, Isle of Wight. The crew were all saved, and Owen Humphreys, whose address is given in the 'articles' as 7 Ivy Terrace, Borth-y-gest, and who was then aged sixty, probably started his 'navigation' school at Borth-y-gest. Captain W. H. Hughes remembers how the young seamen went to Owen Humphreys for instruction, and how his father, Captain Harry Hughes, was given some canvas-covered 'epitomes' by his friend Humphreys to replace those he had lost when one of his vessels foundered.

The photograph of the *Edward Windus* at Harburg is another which is evocative of so much of Porthmadog's history. The *Edward Windus,* a near contemporary of the *George Casson,* was built at Borth-y-gest in 1864 and sailed from Porthmadog for forty years and must have visited the Elbe scores of times. In the photograph one can see the familiar lighters astern of the *Edward Windus* into which cargoes were discharged for further transportation along the inland waterways of Germany and central Europe, and one can almost feel the heat of that summer's day so long ago. Judging by the dress of the crew of the *Edward Windus* and the agents, stevedores and onlookers, it is likely that the photograph was taken shortly before the vessel was lost. The bowler-hatted gentleman holding an oar and accompanied by a fairly large dog in the boat may be the master of the *Edward Windus,* Captain J. H. Williams, but his face is in shadow; above him, on the foc-sle, is an uniformed figure, surely a German, with, on his right, three members of the crew, and on his left, a bowler-hatted man with a white shirt or apron, and two straw-hatted gentlemen who may have been agents. Towering above them are the sturdy masts and, aft in the waist, are three other figures who by their dress may have been crew members ready to go ashore.

The sailings of the *Edward Windus* had not been confined, of course, to European ports. Like many of the brigs and brigantines built in the sixties and seventies, she was also a familiar sight in South American waters. Selecting from her Official Log and 'articles' at random, in the year 1874 she returned to Porthmadog in March at the end of a voyage which had commenced at Middlesborough on 27 May 1873. Her master then was Captain Ellis Roberts, whose address is given as Maentwrog, Merioneth; John Richards, the mate, Edward Roberts, the boatswain, Owen Humphreys, the cook/seaman, William Jenkins, A.B., John Roberts, ordinary seaman, all appeared to have been local men, with one 'foreign' A.B. to make up the crew, David McFarline. It is apparent from the Official Log that Captain Ellis Roberts had some problems with his crew. In October he entered in the log 'John Roberts, O.S. Deserted 9 a.m. Oct 6th in Ariog Negro River Plate been send with another seaman in the Boat ashore for Freas Beef and did not return and he was seen afterwards at Paysandu about 18 miles up the river'. One is tempted to speculate — did he succumb to the hazards facing those who deserted in unhealthy foreign ports, did he settle in South America, or did he get another ship to return, like so many of these nineteenth century seamen, to his home port long after he had been given up for dead, or did he, like many others, die of the 'yellow fever'? The sombre record of Porthmadog seamen who died of small pox and yellow fever in ports like Rio and Santos is a grim reminder that it was not only the sea that took its toll; Hugh Parry, one of the sons of Captain Hugh Parry, the shipbroker, was one of those who died of yellow fever in a South American port, whilst the case of Captain Daniel Jones, whose school exercise book has been described earlier, is an example of a master mariner who contracted yellow fever, presumably in a foreign port, but died, of all places, at Torquay. When the *Edward Windus* arrived in Le Havre in February 1874, the A.B. William Jenkins could not wait to get home, and Captain Roberts entered in his log: 'William Jenkins Deserted at Havre on the 18 February 1874 and sailed in the Barque Ocean Wave for Cardiff'.

There had been incidents of a different nature on the voyage; in August 1873, as the *Edward Windus* approached Montevideo in a strong north-easterly wind, Captain Roberts noted that he had, at 2 a.m., just 'hauled the vessel on the wind on Starboard Tack and Foreyards Aback a crie was heard on the Ley bow. The Helm immediately was put hard down when we saw a smack rigged craft alongside with Deck load of timber, which we saw by the light they brough from below at the time'. Captain Roberts noted that the vessel was a steamer 'with no lights ower lights burning well', and recorded the damage done to the *Edward Windus*'s rigging and yards by the mast of the other vessel, which he believed to be undamaged.

Home in Porthmadog by March 1874, the *Edward Windus* soon sailed again with slates, and was at Antwerp in early June. Captain Roberts had been replaced by Captain Evan Hughes, with John Richards still serving as mate and two 'locals', an ordinary seaman, William Jones, and Goronwy O. Williams, cook. But the three 'foreign' A.B.s signed at Antwerp proved to be a troublesome crew, and on 3 August, when the *Edward Windus* was at Reggio, Captain Hughes noted in the Official Log that William Rose, James Martin and John Hance had gone ashore and returned aboard in a violent drunken mood:

> 'Being Drunken Rioters fighting and beating the mate fearfull and the above named Seaman William Rose threatening to kill Mee i was oblidge to Leave my Cabin and to the Boat for my Life as he was after mee with a Blaying pin threatening to take My Life'.

William Rose, who appears to have been the ring-leader, and had already been logged for drunkenness, bad language, 'insulting Master and Mate and threatening to pitch me overboard', was fined and paid off at Girgenti with the sanction of the resident British Consul. There was no further trouble, and the *Edward Windus* arrived safely at Leith where the remainder of the crew were paid off on 7 October 1874. For the next thirty years the *Edward Windus* was sailed hard by a succession of able master mariners in the South American and Mediterranean trades, in the phosphate rock trade of Aruba, and, above all, in the Elbe and Baltic slate trade.

In February 1904, the *Edward Windus*'s long career came to an end. She had sailed from Porthmadog on 4 January, arriving in Southampton on 29 January; leaving Southampton on 5 February, she was at Hull on 9 February, and left ten days later with a cargo of 270 tons of coal for Portsmouth. But on 22 February, about six miles off Hastings, she was run down by the Japanese mail boat S.S. *Bingo Maru*. Captain J. H. Williams, the master, of 1 Amanda Terrace, Borth-y-gest, aged 37, a native of Llanengan, Gustav Jones, the mate, a Porthmadog man, aged 22, Eleazer Oliver, aged 66, a native of Aberystwyth, the cook/A.B., Herman Prahl, a nineteen-year-old German A.B., and Owen Jones, aged 21, from Nefyn, A.B., were all drowned. Julius Matare, aged 18, a German ordinary seaman, was the only survivor, who returned to Porthmadog in March, where he was formally discharged eleven days after the tragedy. It is fairly certain that some, at least, of those in the undated photograph at Harburg were among those drowned.

## THE THREE-MASTED SCHOONER *BLODWEN*

ON a fine Tuesday morning in February 1891, the reporter of the *Cambrian News* was one of the large crowd who witnessed the launching of the three-masted schooner *Blodwen* from the yard of David Jones, shipbuilder, Porthmadog. 'The launch was in every way successful, and as the vessel reached the water there was great cheering from the spectators. The vessel was christened "Blodwen" by Miss Maggie Richards of Bryntirion Terrace, Criccieth'. Miss Richards was a member of the family of Messrs. Richards and Company, shipowners and shipbrokers of Porthmadog, who, together with Captain John Roberts, Glanmeirion, Talsarnau, had placed the order for the new vessel with David Jones. There was much enthusiasm at the launching ceremony, for, after the hectic building of the seventies, there had been this lull in the eighties, with only one vessel, the *Richard Greaves,* built. The yards had had to be content with repairing the considerable fleet which had been launched in the preceding decades. No doubt the revival in the fortunes of the slate quarries and the consequent call for ships had given the Richards family the confidence to order the building of the *Blodwen.* As the enthusiastic reporter viewed the scene, he shared the excitement of the crowd . . . 'It is about five years since the last new vessel was launched at Portmadoc, and this caused a much greater attendance of spectators than the event normally brings together. There are now two other vessels on the stocks. Messrs. Richards and Co. are also having two steel vessels built at Ardrossan for the Portmadoc Slate Trade'.

Samuel Richards of Criccieth and Edward Richards of Porthmadog had 8/64 shares each in the *Blodwen,* but Captain John Roberts, her master, had the major holding, 48/64; all three had raised the money with the help of mortgages from the National Bank of Wales at Porthmadog. Some six weeks after her official launching, the *Blodwen* sailed from Porthmadog for Stettin with her first cargo of slates. Captain John Roberts, who had previously commanded the *Wern,* had a crew of four; John Hughes, a Pwllheli man, previously serving aboard the *Mary Lloyd* (1), was engaged as boatswain at £4.5.0 a month, the two A.B.s, John Williams of Porthmadog, who had previously served in the *Winifred* of Caernarfon, and William Jones Williams, another Caernarvonshire man, whose last ship had been the *Three Janes,* both signed on at the rate of £3.10 a month, whilst the youngest member of the crew, sixteen-year-old William Williams from Pwllheli, who was signed as Cook and Ordinary Seaman at £1.10 a month, had previously served in the *Volunteer* of Aberystwyth.[1] The *Blodwen* arrived in Stettin on 15 April 1891, proceeded to Memel in May, and on 3 June the crew were paid off on their return to London.

John Williams, the Porthmadog A.B., remained with Captain Roberts for the next voyage, but on this occasion he signed on as boatswain and received £4.5.0 a month; the other members of the crew, all signed in London, were new to the *Blodwen;* an experienced old shell-back from Caernarvon, Thomas Williams, previously serving in the *Euphemia,* two young ordinary seamen, both from Porthmadog, who had previously sailed in the Porthmadog vessels *Samuel Holland,* and *U. Larsing,* and a fifteen-year-old boy, born in Kent, who signed as cook. They sailed on 20 June for Cadiz, arriving there on 8 July, then sailed a week later for Newfoundland, arriving at St. John's on 8 August.

They must have then proceeded to the Labrador fishing stations, for the 'articles' record the desertion of the young cook, Alf Everett from Kent, at Packs Harbour, Labrador, on 5 October. Perhaps the thought of crossing the Atlantic in wintry seas was too much for him. In the event, he missed a swift passage, for the *Blodwen* was at Gibraltar by 24 October, where a German A.B. signed on for the passage to Genoa, only to desert the ship at that port on 29 November 1891. The Welsh members of the crew, however, remained with the ship for the next stage to Huelva and until she returned to home waters. The boatswain, the elderly A.B. and one ordinary seaman were paid off at Amlwch on 20 January, whilst the master and one ordinary seaman remained with her till the termination of the voyage at Porthmadog on 8 February 1892.

The Richards family sold their shares in the *Blodwen* in March 1892 to Captain Roberts, who, in turn, interested some of the leading members of the Porthmadog shipping community in his fine new vessel, first of the Western Ocean Yachts, tough enough to withstand Atlantic storms, yet small enough to enter the most tricky harbours. In April, 4/64 shares each were taken by David Morris, described as 'shipper', Owen Morris, master mariner, and Captain Hugh Parry, shipbroker, of 7 Cornhill; Captain Parry was appointed managing owner. The *Blodwen* was kept busy: she had sailed from Porthmadog on 14 March, arrived at Harburg on 13 April, and, back home in Porthmadog in early May, sailed on 12 May again for Harburg. Apart from an A.B. from St. Thomas, who had previously served in the *Ephratah,* the crew were all, like the master himself, Merioneth men. Captain Roberts was now aged forty, his new mate, Owen Humphreys, who had come from the *Fleetwing,* was eight years his senior; David Evans, a twenty-year-old A.B. who had previously served in the *Theda* (surely a good training school under Captain Dedwith), Charles Jones, a seventeen-year-old from Ffestiniog, who signed as cook and ordinary seaman, and Morris Isaac, a fifteen-year-old from Llanfrothen, who had already served aboard the *Louisa* and was rated ordinary seaman, made up the remainder of the crew, who all stayed with the vessel until she returned to Porthmadog on 28 March 1893. Their eleven month voyage was fairly typical of the trade in which the *Blodwen* was to be engaged; arriving 23 May at Harburg with slates, she was at Cadiz on 24 June, across the Atlantic to St. John's, where she arrived on 25 July, a return passage to the Mediterranean, arriving Genoa 20 November, and sailing again for Liverpool in December. She was at Liverpool in March, and returned to Porthmadog by the end of the month.

The pattern of the *Blodwen*'s voyages remained much the same during the nineties: the German slate trade, south to Cadiz for salt, across the Atlantic to Newfoundland and Labrador, returning to the Mediterranean with salt fish, and then home again to the U.K. with a variety of cargoes. Captain John Roberts died intestate on 28 March 1895 and probate was granted to his widowed daughter, Janet Williams of Glannau Meirion, Talsarnau, and it was she who held her father's shares in the *Blodwen.* The Morrises retained their shares in the vessel until 1902; in March 1902, David and Owen Morris sold their eight shares to Mrs. Janet Williams's son, John Richard Williams, well known in Porthmadog as 'Johnnie Blodwen'. Frequent references have been made to the *Blodwen*'s record passage

4 *Name*

| Reference No. | SIGNATURES OF CREW. | Age. | * Nationality. (If British, state birthplace.) | (1) Port of Engagement Address, and (2) Home Address. N.B.—Both to be inserted. The *Home* Address is the one to which communications should be made in the event of the death of the Seaman. | PARTICULAR… Ship in which he last served, and Year of Discharge therefrom. Year. | State Name and Official No. or Port she belonged to. | Date and place of signi… this Agreement. Date. | Place. |
|---|---|---|---|---|---|---|---|---|
| | 1 | 2 | 3 | 4 | 5 | 6 | 7 | 8 |
| 1 | Master to sign first. T. Jones | 34 | Portmadoc | (1) 3 Madoc St. (2) Portmadoc | 1901 | Same Ship | 18/3/01 | Portm… |
| 2 | Evan R. Jones | 25 | do. | (1) 8 Hill St. (2) Carnarvon | " | "Jenny Jones" Carnarvon | " | " |
| 3 | Richard Richardson | 23 | Kalmar Sweden | (1) — (2) Kalmar, Sweden | " | "Blodwen" Carnarvon | " | " |
| 4 | William Prowse | 28 | Kingsbridge | (1) Pencei, Portmadoc (2) " " | " | "Consul Kaestner" Carnarvon | " | " |
| 5 | Charles Stowe | 17 | Rugby | (1) — (2) The Straits Dudley. | " | "James Bibby" Liverpool | " | " |
| 6 | Robert Owen Jones | 17 | Pwllheli | (1) 45 North St (2) Pwllheli | " | "Mary Owens" Carnarvon | " | " |
| 7 | Hugh Pugh | 54 | Merioneth | (1) 5 Mount Pleasant (2) Portmadoc | " | [illegible] | 23/5/07 | Portm… |
| 8 | John R Williams | 22 | Do | (1) ~~Portmadoc~~ (2) Talsarnau Merioneth | " | Norfolk Island Carnarvon | 6/6/1907 | Do |
| 9 | Robert Lloyd Lewis | 18 | Pmadoc | (2) 7 [illegible] Tce Barmouth | " | David [illegible] Glasgow | " | " |
| 10 | | | | (1) (2) | | | | |
| 11 | | | | (1) (2) | | | | |
| 12 | | | | (1) (2) | | | | |
| 13 | | | | (1) (2) | | | | |
| 14 | | | | (1) (2) | | | | |
| 15 | | | | (1) (2) | | | | |
| 16 | | | | (1) (2) | | | | |
| 17 | | | | (1) (2) | | | | |
| 18 | | | | (1) (2) | | | | |
| 19 | | | | (1) (2) | | | | |
| 20 | | | | (1) (2) | | | | |

* If a British Subject, state Town or Country of Birth, and if born in a foreign

† The capacities of Engineers not employed on the Propelling Engines and Boilers should be described here and in Dis. 1 as Engine Drivers, Donkeymen, Refrigerating Engineers, Electrical

‡ If the advance of wages is *not* conditional on going to sea, the

§ If any Member of the Crew enters Her Majesty's Service, the Name of the Queen's Ship into which he enters is to be stated under the head of "*Cause of leaving*

Ship *Blodwen* 5

| OF ENGAGEMENT. | | | | | | | PARTICULARS OF DISCHARGE, &c., *To be filled in by the Master upon the Discharge, Death, or Desertion of any Member of his Crew.* | | | | RELEASE. | | |
|---|---|---|---|---|---|---|---|---|---|---|---|---|---|
| In what Capacity engaged.† | No. of Certificate (if any), and No. of Reserve Commission or R.V.2 (if any). | Date and Hour at which he is to be on board. | Amount of Wages per Week or Calendar Month. | Amount of Wages advanced upon or at the time of Engagement.‡ | Amount of Weekly or Monthly Allotment. | Signature or Initials of Official before whom the Seaman is engaged. | Date, Place, and Cause of leaving this Ship, or of Death. Date. | Place. | Cause.§ | Balance of Wages paid on Discharge. | We, the undersigned Members of the Crew of this Ship, do hereby release this Ship, and the Master and Owner or Owners thereof, from all Claims for Wages, or otherwise in respect of this Voyage, and I, the Master, do hereby release the said undersigned Members of the Crew from all claims in respect of the said Voyage. Signatures of Crew (each to be on the Line on which he signed in Col. 1). | Signature or Initials of Official before whom the Balance of Wages was paid and Release signed and Date. | Reference No. |
| 9 | 10 | 11 | 12 | 13 | 14 | 15 | 16 | 17 | | 19 | 20 | 21 | |
| 024173 Master | [illegible] | on Board | — | — | — | LOP | 9/5/11 | at sea | Dead Drowning | — | | | 1 |
| Bos^n | X 644 | " | 4 . . | 1 5 | 2 . . | LOP | 6/3/02 | Portmadoc | Dis | 12 2 8 | Evan R. Jones | LOP | 2 |
| AB | — | " | 3 5 . | — | — | LOP | 23/5/01 | PORTSMOUTH | Dis | 5 1 5 | Richard Richardson | [illegible] | 3 |
| AB | — | " | 3 5 . | — | 1 15 . | LOP | [illegible] | — " — | — " — | 3 11 8 | William Prouse | [illegible] | 4 |
| OS | — | " | 1 5 . | — | — | LOP | 6/3/02 | Portmadoc | Dis | 16 — — | Charles Stowe | LOP | 5 |
| Cook & OS | — | " | 2 5 . | . 16 6 | — | LOP | do | do | do | 16 16 6 | Robert Owen Jones | LOP | 6 |
| 035785 Master | o/c | at once | — | — | — | [illegible] | do | do | do | — | Hugh Pugh | LOP | 7 |
| Bosun | " | " | 5 0 0 | | — | [illegible] | do | do | do | 10 — — | John R. Williams | LOP | 8 |
| OS | " | " | 1 15 . | | | [illegible] | do | do | do | 5 6 5½ | Robert Lloyd Lewis | LOP | 9 |
| | | | | | | | | | | | | | 10 |
| | | | | | | | | | | | | | 11 |
| | | | | | | | | | | | | | 12 |
| | | | | | | | | | | | | | 13 |
| | | | | | | | | | | | | | 14 |
| | | | | | | | | | | | | | 15 |
| | | | | | | | | | | | | | 16 |
| | | | | | | | | | | | | | 17 |
| | | | | | | | | | | | | | 18 |
| | | | | | | | | | | | | | 19 |
| | | | | | | | | | | | | | 20 |

Country, state if a natural born British Subject or naturalized.
Engineers, or Winchmen, and not merely as Engineers. Boys entirely employed in connection with the work of Cooks and Stewards should be described as Cabin Boys, not merely as boys.
words "not conditional" should be inserted above the entry of the amount.
*the Ship,*" thus, "H.M.S. Revenge;" and the other Causes of leaving the Ship should be briefly stated thus, "Discharged," "Deserted," "Left Sick," "Died."

[*Eight Pages.*

from Newfoundland to Patras in 22 days, but memories are notoriously fickle, and there are different versions of the story regarding her master on that particular passage. Working through the 'articles', the crew agreement lists for the period in question, it is possible to trace her voyage and the names of the men who served in her. According to Henry Hughes's account in *Immortal Sails,* her master on her record passage in 1901 was Captain Roberts,[2] but this cannot be, as Captain Roberts had died in March 1895; Emrys Hughes states in his notes that her master on her record passage was Captain John Williams, 'Johnnie Blodwen'. From the crew agreement lists, it seems likely that, if the record voyage did in fact take place in 1901 as stated in both the above accounts, then the master was Captain Hugh Pugh, brother of Captain Evan Pugh of the *Pride of Wales.*

The 'articles' indicate that the master of the *Blodwen* from November 1899 to March 1901 was Captain Thomas Jones, 3 Madoc Street, Porthmadog; during these years he sailed her to Copenhagen, and Frederikstad twice, to Lisbon, Cadiz, King's Cove, Newfoundland, Malaga and Mazagan. From Mazagan the *Blodwen* sailed for Leith, and arrived home at Porthmadog via Dysart and Morlaix on 3 February 1901. On 18 March Captain Thomas Jones, with Evan R. Jones of Caernarfon, formerly of the *Jenny Jones,* as boatswain, 2 A.B.s, an ordinary seaman and a cook-ordinary seaman, sailed from Porthmadog with slates for Kiel, where she arrived on 3 April, and proceeded to Frederikstad, whence she sailed on or about 9 April 1901. On 9 May Captain Thomas Jones was drowned at sea, and his death was duly reported at the Merchant Marine Office, Portsmouth, on 14 May, when the *Blodwen* arrived there. Captain W. H. Hughes remembers that he was at Kiel in his father's *Miss Prichard* at the same time as the *Blodwen.* Whilst the one vessel proceeded to Frederikstad and the other to Fredrikshald, they met again at Gibraltar waiting for orders, when the *Miss Prichard* returned from Domino Run, Labrador. According to Captain Hughes, the cause of Captain Jones's death (which is only stated as 'Drowned at sea' in the articles) was a collision in the English Channel with a fishing boat. Apparently, in the ensuing confusion and darkness, the unfortunate Captain Jones, whilst attempting to push the two vessels apart, fell between them from the deck of the *Blodwen* and was drowned. The *Caernarvon and Denbigh Herald* for 17 May 1901 reported the funeral service back at Porthmadog: 'The funeral of Captain Thomas Jones of the Blodwen took place on Wednesday, at the cemetery, where the Rev. R. Môn Hughes officiated'.[3] The boatswain and the two A.B.s who had served under him were paid off at Portsmouth on 23 May, the day when Captain Hugh Pugh, aged 54, of 5 Mount Pleasant, Porthmadog, whose previous ship had been the *Rose of Torridge,* and John Richard Williams of Talsarnau, aged 22, formerly of the *Norfolk Island,* signed as master and boatswain respectively. Both had travelled down to Portsmouth from Porthmadog to replace the drowned master and the paid-off members of the crew. Robert Lloyd Lewis, an 18-year-old Barmouth Ordinary Seaman, also joined the vessel at Portsmouth, whilst Charles Stowe and Robert Owen Jones, the two 17-year-olds who had sailed as Ordinary Seaman and Cook — Ordinary Seaman with Captain Thomas Jones on his last voyage to the Baltic, remained to complete the voyage under the new master and boatswain. It appears that Mrs. Janet Williams of Talsarnau, the owner, had determined that her son, John Richard, was to make his first voyage as boatswain of the *Blodwen* under the very experienced eye of Captain Pugh as 'sailing master'.[4] It was probably this crew that made the record passage. The *Blodwen* was at Cadiz on 23 June 1901, but unfortunately for precise dating, the Articles were not stamped at any of the Newfoundland ports — according to Henry Hughes, she left Indian Tickle, Labrador, but she may have called at any one of the fishing stations where there was no Custom House or Consular Service to stamp the articles. The next entry, in fact, is for 2 November 1901, when the vessel arrived at Patras. In the following February the *Blodwen* was at Teignmouth, and Captain Pugh and his crew were all paid off at Porthmadog on 6 March 1902, the end of the voyage for which the crew agreement had been signed at its commencement by Captain Thomas Jones and at its conclusion by Captain Hugh Pugh.

Within sixteen days of returning from her twelve month voyage, the *Blodwen* sailed out of Porthmadog again on 22 March 1902, with Captain Owen Hughes of Rhostryfan, aged 52, and Owen Lloyd of Llanbedr, aged 44, as master and mate respectively, on a voyage to Copenhagen, where she arrived in late April. John Richard Williams,

9

**LOG BOOK**

ON THE COASTS OF THE UNITED KINGDOM.

In order that entries may be made, if necessary, when the Agreement is deposited at the Consulate, pages see page 2 of the cover.

*Ship* Bledwen

| Date and Place of Occurrence. | Date of Entry. | ENTRY. |
|---|---|---|
| Nov. 29th 1902 (River Exe) Exeter | 29/11/02 | Effects of deceased J. Roberts: O.S. & Cook<br>1 Suit of Oilskins & S Wester. 2 pair of Seaboots<br>1 Macintosh 1 pair of leggings 1 pair of Shoes<br>1 dungaree Jumper & 2 pants. 1 New Suit of Cloth<br>1 Front & tie 3 pair of pants 1 coat & Vest.<br>1 Jersey. 4 shirts 1 pr. drawers 2 singlets<br>6 pairs of Stockings 1 Quilt 1 Blanket<br>1 Pillow. 3 caps. 3 mufflers 1 Pack Sun Soap<br>3 bars of soap. 3 pks of Cocoa. Box of<br>Letters. 2 pairs of Boot Laces. 4 Books<br>2 pairs Mittens, 1 towel, 1 pipe<br>Wages from Nov. 15th to Nov. 28th 1902<br>at £1"15 per month s d<br>(14) days. 16" 4<br>Extras. 1" 1<br>17" 5<br>Money deceased had on Board 11" 0<br>Total. £1" 8" 5 |
| | | John R. Williams Master<br>Owen Hughes Mate<br>A Norman - OS |

Wages and Effects of John Roberts (Cook & O.S) deceased have been received at this Port of Exeter by me

(Letters sent with W.E.'s to Reg. Gen'l)

[illegible] Meche
D.M. Supt



(576w)

the owner's son, relieved Owen Lloyd as mate at Falmouth in May, and with Captain Hughes as master and one A.B. from Newfoundland, another from Sweden, and another Talsarnau man, Robert Williams, also A.B., and John Roberts, a young first voyager aged 16, as 'boy' (and obviously cook), made the voyage to Cadiz and Labrador, eventually returning to Exeter in November 1902. The Newfoundland A.B. had been replaced by a countryman, Archibald Norman of Conception Bay, joining his first ship on 25 August at Comfort Bight, Labrador. It was nearly his last. John Richard Williams, who had taken command of the vessel at Exeter for a 'coastal' voyage, with Captain Owen Hughes still aboard, but signing as mate, had an unenviable first entry to make in his log. He affixed a cutting from the *Western Times* of 29 November 1902 giving details of the death of John Roberts, the young Ffestiniog boy who had signed for his first voyage at Porthmadog some eight months previously. Apparently Archibald Norman, the Newfoundland seaman, and John Roberts had returned to the *Blodwen*, 'now lying at the Quay, Exeter, discharging fish', with two members of the crew of the *Ocean Wave* of Fowey, near midnight, and had taken the ship's boat to row across to the *Ocean Wave*. Unfortunately, with the river in flood, the boat was carried rapidly down stream: 'Three of the men were standing up in the boat and the fourth was rowing. The night was dark, and the men either did not know or had forgotten about the St. Thomas ferry, and they drifted down upon the ferry rope, which struck against the men who were standing up with such force that the boat was overturned. She filled and sank immediately'. Norman, who could not swim, managed to cling to the ferry rope, and struggled ashore, as did one of the crew of the *Ocean Wave*, but John Roberts and the other man, Frederick Olsen, were drowned. When the master and mate listed John Roberts's belongings, Norman's signature was beneath theirs bearing witness to the accuracy of the list of effects and also the details of the accidental death of his shipmate. The listed belongings of the young boy from Ffestiniog may be taken as representative of what the hundreds of young lads from Porthmadog took to sea with them. Whilst there are many similar entries to the page reproduced here, it is still apparent that the loss of individual members of a crew was much rarer in Porthmadog ships than in the larger four masters;

the loss of a man was similar to the loss of a member of the family in Porthmadog ships.

Captain Owen Hughes, Robert Williams, Talsarnau, and Norman remained aboard the *Blodwen* for her voyages from Looe to Gibraltar and Cadiz in December and January 1902-3, but John R. Williams missed this voyage — possibly to gain a further certificate of competency — but he was back as mate for the voyage from Porthmadog to Harburg in March 1903. He left the vessel again for a spell in 1905-06 before finally returning as her fully qualified master in May 1906. For the voyage from Falmouth to Cadiz and thence to Newfoundland, commencing in June 1905, the *Blodwen* had a completely new crew; the master, William M. Jones, of 23 Snowdon Street, Porthmadog, had just completed his time aboard the fine full-rigged iron ship *Clackmannanshire,* one of the Glasgow 'shire' vessels operated by the Law family, vessels which have been described with enthusiasm by Basil Lubbock in *The Last of the Windjammers;*[5] the mate, a 43-year-old Falmouth man, E. F. Perry, had last served aboard the *Vincent* of Falmouth, one A.B. came from the *Alert* of Falmouth, another A.B. from the *Emma and Esther,* the cook/A.B., a Talsarnau man, from the *Ann and Jane Prichard,* and the young Ordinary Seaman, also from Falmouth, from the *Lavonia,* of Newport. William Turner, the Plymouth A.B. who had previously served in the *Alert,* was paid off at Avondale, Newfoundland, on July 31; the *Blodwen* cleared customs at Avondale bound for Dark Nickle, Labrador, with salt and provisions, but it was not until she reached Leghorn in November that Turner was replaced by a German seaman. The *Blodwen* was at Huelva from 10 December till 2 January 1906 and her crew were finally paid off at Amlwch on 25 January, Captain Jones remaining with the ship to sail her with 'runners' to Porthmadog, where he, too, left her to make way for Captain 'Johnnie', the owner's son, who now took command.

The diary of the young John Owen, who sailed as ordinary seaman/cook on the voyage of 1906, has already been referred to — it is full of details which bring to life the experience of young first voyagers in the late Porthmadog vessels, from that Monday evening in May when he took a train from Lime Street station, Liverpool, bound for Porthmadog, and found himself aboard the *Blodwen* next morning washing out the galley under the critical but kindly eye of the lame Captain Evans, too old now for the sea, but still employed aboard the ships as a kind of caretaker between voyages.[6] Under the guidance of the old captain, the young Owen had learned many bends and hitches before the remainder of the crew staggered aboard on sailing day; he remembers clearly the impression the young Captain J. R. Williams made as he stepped aboard at lunch-time from the package-filled boat which had brought him across the estuary from Talsarnau. Two days out to sea, the young cook was astonished to discover that his very impressive master was, in fact, sea-sick; his own feeling of superiority vanished within a day or so, however, when he himself was overtaken by the same malady as the *Blodwen* rolled and pitched in teeming rain and blustery winds as she made for shelter in the Solent. In the fair weather that followed, young Owen perked up, and increased his range of cooking skills whilst his shipmates painted ship. After seven days at sea they drew abreast of the *Janet*, an elderly Porthmadog schooner — the crew of the *Blodwen* threw tobacco to the *Janet*'s crew and exchanged greetings before the *Blodwen* trimmed her sails and drew rapidly away — with young Owen marvelling at the speed and grace of his own vessel as she left the *Janet* far behind. Soon after passing a full-rigged ship outward bound, a fine sight, John Owen took his first trick at the wheel, under the guidance of one of the experienced A.B.s, and was so pleased with himself that, as he walked away from the wheel, he whistled to himself. His exuberance was short-lived — Captain Williams reprimanded him, saying that no member of the crew was allowed to whistle at sea — it only brought ill-luck and foul weather.

John Owen had a talent for drawing, and soon he was painting pictures of the *Blodwen* on the inside lid of the sea chests of some of the crew as they approached the Skaw. On 25 May they arrived in Aarhus. Owen's first impressions were the cleanliness of the quay-side, the hordes of bicycles, and the cake shop where all the sea-sickness and the somewhat experimental sea-dishes he had prepared for a generally tolerant crew were all forgotten. Within a couple of days, young Owen found himself playing for a Danish football team, but this delight was soon forgotten when he and the other members started to load copper ore for Hull — the dust of this cargo permeated everywhere and, as a result, one of the A.B.s and Owen both started bleeding through their noses. Although ready to sail, Captain

Williams, as always, would not depart on a Sunday, so the crew had a well-earned rest day before they left for Hull. Having discharged her cargo at Hull, the *Blodwen* sailed for Gibraltar with coal. Two nights later found the *Blodwen* hardly moving in light airs, and a steamer, looming out of the blackness, heading straight for them; Owen remembered how the *Blodwen*'s crew, who had all scrambled up on deck, watched helplessly as the steamer bore down on them, and how Nell, the little bitch, had run to the foc-sle and barked so violently that they all believed that this had caused the steamer's officer of the watch to alter course at the last moment. The limp sails of the *Blodwen* had obliterated her own port light so that she had not been seen from the steamer's bridge until the barking dog had been heard. After a wild day hove-to in the Bay of Biscay, the *Blodwen* reached Gibraltar in late June; young Owen exchanged a bar of soap for twenty large yellow peaches — his stomach suffered for it next day. The coal cargo was discharged and ballast loaded for the passage to Cadiz, where a cargo of salt was embarked on 2 July. Despite contrary winds when they sailed from Cadiz, young Owen was excited at the thought of crossing the Atlantic, and paid little heed to the gloomy forecasts of the other foc'sle hands as they viewed the sun setting on 6 July. The master and mate, too, were uneasy as they contemplated the falling barometer and prepared for the blow by seeing to it that everything was firmly secured and battened down. Soon the crew were fully occupied taking in and reefing sails, but finally lying hove-to for a couple of days. But John Owen came to realise that he preferred rough weather to the eerie progress through the thick fog of the Banks; on 20 July they sailed out of the fog to find themselves some 15 miles off St. John's, and Owen noted in his diary, 'go dda ynte ar "dead reckoning"' (good going on dead reckoning!). A couple of days in St. John's and the *Blodwen* sailed for Comfort Bight, Labrador: they had to stand out to sea because of the rough weather for a day or so, and Owen counted 22 icebergs. On 25 July they were safely in the anchorage, but a day or so later, in freshening winds, Captain Williams ordered his crew to leave the chain lockers open and to pay out more cable lest they should drag. That night, in the gale, the crews of the other two schooners anchored in the bay lost their vessels and were taken aboard the *Blodwen;* very many vessels were lost on that night —

but, as always, Captain Williams and the mate had anticipated trouble, had smelt the weather and, inevitably, they were prepared to meet the emergency. It was the end of July before they were able to start the loading of the salt cod, and it was then that John Owen made friends with the young Eskimo, Emmanuel, who wished to exchange sea-skin boots for the book of cartoons by Phil May, which was one of Owen's treasured possessions.

Soon after leaving Comfort Bight with a full load of salt cod, John Owen counted 27 icebergs as he stood at the wheel of the *Blodwen* — but the wind was favourable and it was not long before the heavy coats and sea boots were shed as the *Blodwen* neared the Gulf Stream. Despite a violent storm, Captain Williams pressed on across the Atlantic with the *Blodwen* hurled onwards by strong winds and mountainous following seas — the mate told Owen he thought the master had made up his mind to beat the record passage. It was a fast but not the fastest passage; from Gibraltar they sailed for Patras, where the *Elizabeth* of Porthmadog was already berthed. On the return voyage from Patras to Huelva the *Elizabeth* kept down to the African shore and avoided the frustrating tacking to and fro in unfavourable conditions off Malta that the *Blodwen* experienced, and was easily home first. John Owen left the *Blodwen* at Plymouth after chronicling a voyage which many Porthmadog seamen undertook but few bothered to record.

John Owen's first voyage was, according to the evidence of the Crew Agreement Lists, the first long distance oceanic voyage for Captain John Richard Williams to be in command. In April 1906, Captain John Richard Williams, then aged 26, took command of the *Blodwen* on the voyage, described in John Owen's diary, to Aarhus, Hull, Gibraltar, Cadiz, Harbour Grace, thence to Labrador, and back across the Atlantic to Patras and Huelva — John Ellis Davies, known in Porthmadog as 'John Bach Tregunter', was mate/boatswain on this voyage. For the next voyage, from May to December 1907, Edward Humphreys was Captain Williams's mate, and Griffith Roberts had replaced his brother David as a member of the crew — the future Commodore of Convoys in World War II had reason to remember with pleasure his first voyage aboard the *Blodwen*, particularly the return voyage across the Atlantic. The crews of the *Blodwen* changed from voyage to voyage over the next few years, but Captain 'John Richard' remained, certainly until 1912, when the locally held crew agreement lists cease.

As already indicated, John Owen and Griffith Roberts served as cook/ordinary seamen aboard the *Blodwen,* as did so many young men embarking upon a sea-going career in Porthmadog ships. They themselves would say that the cooking varied, but although the fare was undoubtedly monotonous and, according to the conditions, sometimes meagre, it was probably infinitely better than on some of the large vessels sailing in the Cape Horn trades. The ship chandlers' accounts give some indication of the way the Porthmadog vessels stocked up with food and stores in March before they left on their annual voyages to Hamburg, Cadiz, Newfoundland and back to the Mediterranean. One can take, for example, the stores put aboard the *Blodwen* in March 1900 when the ill-fated Captain Thomas Jones was in command.

| March 1. | £ | s. | d. |
|---|---|---|---|
| 3lbs leather @ 1/10, 2 ½lb Wire nls. 3″ | | 5 | 8 |
| 1 G. Bolt 7/8. 3½lbs @ 7½ 1 ring, 35 lbs tea @ 1/11, 3 doz S. milk @ 5/9 | 4 | 5 | 0½ |
| 2 tins Fry's Cocoa 1/8, 6lbs sugar @ 2½, 3½ cwt sugar @ 15/9 | 2 | 18 | 0 |
| 28 lbs currants @ 3½, 28 lbs raisins @ 4½, 4 Stons of Flour @ 1/9 | 1 | 5 | 8 |
| 60 lbs Rice @ 2, 4 loaves 2/-, 6 lbs Pearl Barley @ 2½ | | 13 | 3 |
| 20 lbs Green peas @ 2½, 1 cwt split peas 13/6 | | 17 | 8 |
| 20 lbs French beans @ 2, 10 pkgs. Q. oats @ 6 | | 8 | 4 |
| 3 cwt Bread @ 16/-, 120 lbs Margerine @ 8½, 12 lbs lard | 6 | 19 | 0 |
| 60 lbs Bacon @ 5, 51 lbs ham @ 7½, 9 c beef | 3 | 6 | 8 |
| 9 Brawn 9/-, 6 doz. Rst. Beef @ 12/6, 1 Tierce Beef 16/9 | 9 | 0 | 9 |
| 6 doz Bd Mutton @ 13/9, 3½ lbs cheese @ 8d, 1 doz Salmon 7/9 | 4 | 12 | 7 |
| 6 tins syrup 3/-, 1 doz Sardines 7/6, 1 Box reds No. 1 3/6 | | 14 | 0 |
| 9 Jars Jam @ 10½, 14 lbs Marmalade @ 4 | | 12 | 6½ |
| 3 galls vinegar @ 4/-, 12 pickles 6/-, 9 sauce @ 6 4/6 | | 14 | 6 |
| 2 pots ex of meat 2/6, ¼ lb mustard 6, 1lb pepper 1/- | | 3 | 6 |
| 4 tins B. powder 2/6, 8 tins P. spice 2/-, 2 cwt Potatoes @ 4/9 | | 13 | 6 |
| ½ cwt swedes 1/3, 5 bars soap @ 10, 20 lbs soda, 1/- | | 6 | 5 |
| 3 lbs Putty @ 6, 2 Blbkg. brushes 1/6, 6 lb Camp Candles 3/6 | | 5 | 6 |
| 9 doz matches @ 1/10½, 1 tin Blkg, 10 lbs wire nls. @ 4d | | 5 | 4½ |

| | £ | s. | d. |
|---|---|---|---|
| ½ lb pump tacks 10, 4½ lbs flick @ 2/3, 5 lbs Cotton waste 1/8 | | 4 | 9 |
| 2 Bth Bricks 3d, 10 lbs Oakum @ 4, 10 lbs Pitch @ 2 | | 5 | 3 |
| 1 sail hook 1, 1½ doz sail needles 1/1, 4 rope needles 10d. | | 2 | 1 |
| ½ doz glasses 1/6, ½ do 1/3, 1 Ruby dioptric Globe 13/6 | | 16 | 3 |
| 1 En. Bak. dish 1/3, 1 En tea pot 2/6, Log Book 3/- | | 6 | 9 |
| 4 shts. Em. paper 3, 2 Ballast shovels 5/- | | 5 | 3 |
| 1 doz screw, 1 pr Iron Butt hinges 3, 4 tea spoons 6d. | | | 11 |
| 2 c/s glasses 8, 56 lbs. whit. zinc @ 3¾, 56 lbs whit. lead @ 3¼ | 1 | 13 | 4 |
| 18 lbs Blk. Paint @ 3½, 7 lbs blue @ 4d, 14 lbs green @ 4½ | | 12 | 10 |
| 15 lbs umber @ 3½, 10 lbs Mast Color @ 3½ | | 7 | 4 |
| 3 tins chrome yellow @ 1/6, 10 lbs Red Ochre @ 3 | | 4 | 0 |
| 1 Gall. Machine Oil 2/6, 1 Cask 42 galls paraffine @ 8½ | 1 | 12 | 3 |
| 10 galls Bd. Oil @ 2/10, 12 galls Raw Oil @ 2/8, ½ gall turps | 3 | 2 | 10 |
| 1 gall. Br. Varnish, 5 galls Bl varnish @ 1/- | | 6 | 10 |
| 1 gall. Hd. Oak varnish @ 11/6, ½ coil 2¾ manilla 3qrs 2lb. 49/11 | 3 | 1 | 5 |
| 1 log line 9/6, 1 fire shovel 4½, 6 Balls S. Twine @ 1/6 | | 18 | 10½ |
| 3 Balls rope twine @ 1/6, 2 lbs wire nts. | | 5 | 2 |
| 1 Book Lights of the World | | 8 | 0 |
| | 53 | 12 | 3 |
| By 1 Red Lamp 11/6 | | 11 | 6 |
| | 53 | 0 | 9 |
| 1 Ad. Chart for Bonavista including King's Cove and postage | | 3 | 0 |
| | 53 | 3 | 9 |

June 29/1900
Settled by cheque 51.10.0
33/9 Disc.

A year later, in February and March 1901, shortly before she sailed on the voyage which was to include Captain Hugh Pugh's record passage, the *Blodwen* again took on her stores, including paint, paper, log books, saucepans, ropes, account books, a wider range of food (could this have been John Richard Williams's influence?) and an Admiralty chart for 'Boulter Rock to Dominic', at a total cost of £72.16.10, a bill which was incurred in March 1901 but not settled until December 1901, presumably after the owners had received their freight charges for at least most of the voyage. The 1902 accounts again indicate a wider variety of foods, with pickles, piccallili, Dutch cheese, tinned salmon and sardines, tins of tongue, in addition to the usual boxes of raisins, currants, tins of cocoa and a case of Swiss milk — a total cost of £83.16.3 incurred in March 1902, and settled by cheque for £82 on 8 December 1902, the £1.16.3 being deducted as discount. The bills for the *Blodwen* for 1903, after discount had been deducted, were £65; for 1904, settled in March 1905, £82.15.0, and again for May 1905, settled in November 1905, settled by cheque for £53. These, of course, were only the costs of stores obtained at the start of the voyage — if bad weather prevailed and unfavourable winds, they had to put in to replenish their supplies, and this, naturally, meant additional expenditure. One can, however, get a fair indication of the type of food provided in the various ships of Porthmadog by glancing through the ledgers of the chandlers; on their evidence it would seem that the *Blodwen* was a well-run, efficient ship, with a reasonably well fed crew. Not many desertions are noted in her crew lists — the *Blodwen* was, by all accounts, a happy ship.

## REFERENCES

[1] Details relating to the *Blodwen* are based on the vessel's crew agreement lists and official logs now housed at C.R.O.
[2] Henry Hughes, *Immortal Sails*, 183.
[3] *CDH*, 17 May 1901.
[4] According to interviews with several master mariners, it was not unusual to have a 'sailing master' appointed when the owner's son was too young or unqualified to be master.
[5] Basil Lubbock, *The Last of the Windjammers*, I, 370-376.
[6] The account which follows is based upon the diary and an interview with Mr. J. F. Owen at Chester in the autumn of 1974.
[7] N.L.W. 12092E.

# THE THREE-MASTED SCHOONER *MARY LLOYD* (II)

THE second *Mary Lloyd* was built by Griffith Williams and his nephew David in 1894, and followed the *Dorothy, Elizabeth* and *Emrys* from the blocks. She was possibly intended to replace the first *Mary Lloyd,* built at Borth-y-gest in 1852, and owned by Isaac Lloyd Morris, brother of the 'Morris Owen' who was responsible for financing the building of many Borth-y-gest vessels, most of them built by Simon Jones. According to Emrys Hughes's notes, the old *Mary Lloyd* had sailed for forty years and more without losing a man before she was wrecked off Lands End in 1893. The Register of Shipping indicates that the sole owner of the second *Mary Lloyd* when she was first registered was Mary Lloyd of Llechwedd Ddu, Harlech, so that it may be that the name was simply given because the previous vessel of that name had been lost in 1893 and the new owner was, therefore, free to name her new ship after herself in 1894. One of the *Mary Lloyd* (2)'s voyages, in 1895/6, was from Glasgow to St. John's, thence to Oporto, Valencia, Alicante, Huelva and back to Falmouth. Her master on this occasion was Captain Robert Roberts, aged 57, of Porthmadog. The managing owner was named as Mrs. Mary Lloyd of Belle Vue, Harlech, and the mate and purser for the voyage was Robert Arthur Jones, aged 21, whose address was also given as Belle Vue, Harlech, as was that of another member of the crew, Thomas William Jones, Ordinary Seaman, aged 16. For the coastal voyage from Penrhyn to Barry Dock, in early May 1896, Robert Arthur Jones, who then had an 'only mate' ticket, took command of the vessel. For the voyage from Barry to Newfoundland, starting 1 May 1896, R. A. Jones reverted to mate and purser, with Captain Griffith Williams taking command, but by September their roles were reversed, with R. A. Jones as master, with a certificate number at St. John's; the Marine Office at St. John's recorded this change, together with Captain R. A. Jones's new certificate number. He was then aged 23 and remained in command of the *Mary Lloyd,* missing only an occasional voyage for the next fifteen years. In 1905, Captain R. A. Jones bought a 16/24 share in the vessel from Mrs. Mary Lloyd, who still retained the major holding and was registered as managing owner. For many of his voyages in the Newfoundland and Baltic and Mediterranean trades, Captain Jones had R. R. Morris of Porthmadog as mate, the berth filled in 1904/5 by Griffith Humphreys of Borth-y-gest, and in 1905/1906 by Job Roberts of Osmond Lane, Porthmadog, both of whom appeared to have served in several Porthmadog ships. Shortly after acquiring a quarter share in the *Mary Lloyd,* Captain R. A. Jones commenced the log of his vessel's voyages in 1905 and 1906; by a fortunate chance, the abstract of this log was given to Emrys Hughes by Captain Jones some years ago. I have since checked the log book against the Official Log and the 'Articles' for these voyages; it is, therefore, possible to reconstruct in brief a voyage which must have been not untypical of scores of similar voyages made by the Western Ocean Yachts during this period.

On Wednesday, 22 March 1905, the *Mary Lloyd* sailed from Porthmadog with a cargo of 315 tons of slates for Stettin. She was towed out at 8 a.m. in light easterly winds, with the sea smooth and the weather hazy. Twelve hours later she was some six miles from St. Tudwal's Light when Captain Lloyd set the log. By midnight, steering WSW in fresh southerly winds, he recorded that Bardsey bore NNE twelve miles, and at 4 a.m., with the wind increasing and the sea rough, they tacked ship. With Cardigan Bay Light vessel bearing ENE, they again tacked ship at 9 a.m. and again at 3 p.m. in very strong winds and heavy rain. Two hours later, Captain Jones recorded South Bishop in sight. The wind suddenly shifted to NW and, steering a course inside of the Smalls, at 10 p.m., Captain Jones again set the log on a bearing of St. Ann's Light ENE 12 miles. By midnight on Friday the Wolf Rock Light bore SSW at a distance of one mile, and by 5 a.m. on the Saturday morning the Lizard light bore NNE four miles — so the entries record the passage, past St. Catherine's Light, the *Royal Sovereign* Light Vessel, Dungeness, Dover, the East Goodwin Light Vessel, the North Foreland, and, of course, the *Mary Lloyd*'s position at noon each day. A little before midnight on the 30 March the *Mary Lloyd* passed the Skaw Light Vessel and, on the following day, came to anchor 'close to Middle Fort in 7 fathoms'; since passing Elsinore, the winds had been light and unsteady, and Captain Jones had been 'tacking to best advantage'. Early next morning, in strong westerly winds, the *Mary Lloyd* proceeded through the Drogden Channel, passed Falsterboro Light Vessel and Jasmund Point, and by eight at night Captain Jones recorded 'close off Greifswald Light' and then hove to, to await daylight. At six the next morning, with a pilot aboard, they obtained a tug to tow them into Swinemunde, and moored on the buoys there, to be taken in tow the following morning by the steam tug *Otto* up to the new harbour at Stettin, where they were ready to discharge their cargo at 7 p.m. on Monday, 3 April, eleven days after leaving Porthmadog.

The return voyage, from Stettin to Grimsby, took ten days, and after nearly three weeks at Grimsby, the *Mary Lloyd* was towed to Hull to embark 250 tons of coal for Kingsbridge, a passage of four days, which ended when she beat up to the Bar at 8 p.m. on 6 June, and was then towed by a tug up to Salcombe, where she 'moored with two Anchors, abreast of town'. Three weeks later she left Kingsbridge in ballast for Cadiz; according to her Crew Agreement List, the crew then consisted of Captain R. A. Jones, aged 31, of Belle Vue, Harlech, Job Roberts, aged 26, of Osmond Lane, Porthmadog, the mate, N. Holste, aged 19, of 2 Berg Street, Harburg, A.B., E. Warne, aged 30, of Ipswich, A.B., A. Roberts, aged 17, of Frondeg, Corwen, a native of Harlech, who signed as cook/steward, and H. Timeri, aged 19, of Wyborg, Finland, Ord. Seaman. The mate was paid at a rate of £5.5.0 per month, the two A.B.s £3.5.0, the Cook/Steward £2.0.0, and the young Finnish Ordinary Seaman £1.15.0.

The passage to Cadiz was uneventful, with variable winds, a strong westerly swell running, and overcast skies; Captain Jones recorded hot, hazy weather as they approached Cape St. Vincent ten days after leaving Kingsbridge, and three hours after sighting Chipiona Light on Saturday, 5 July, he ordered the 'Small sails' to be taken in, and at 2 a.m. on the 6th he hove his ship to, with Cadiz Light some seven miles SE by E. Four hours later, having taken a pilot aboard, he dropped anchor in Cadiz harbour, 'with 30 fathoms on each bower'. At Cadiz the *Mary Lloyd* embarked '134 lasts Salt, 285 tons', and on 15 July, in baffling light winds and sultry hot weather, she sailed for St. John's, Newfoundland. The very light, variable winds continued, and it was three days later that Captain Jones recorded in his log 'Took departure Cape St. Vincent E/N 12 miles', and set a WNW course.

With moderate to fresh winds, and then a period of light, unsteady winds and calm seas, the *Mary Lloyd*'s progress westwards varied considerably from day to day, and the entries in the log are terse statements, 'Fresh wind, sea confused', 'light, unsteady wind, confused sea, sultry weather', occasionally relieved by sighting of other vessels: 'Friday, 28 July, 6 a.m. sighted a vessel presumed to be the "Electra" which sailed same day from Cadiz'.

On Monday, 31 July, the wind backed southerly, with a 'gloomy sky', and at 8 p.m. Captain Jones recorded 'strong [wind], heavy rain, high sea, taking in sails'. Next day the gales came. The morning watch on 2 August found the *Mary Lloyd* 'labouring heavily' in a 'turbulent rough sea', but the winds moderated again and on Saturday, 5 August, at 8 a.m. another schooner was sighted; at 10 a.m. 'a boat came alongside from Schr "Arabia" of Gloucester wished to be reported all well, bound to fishing grounds'. As they approached the Banks, more fishing vessels were sighted; almost inevitably as the *Mary Lloyd* approached the coast of Newfoundland she became enveloped in fog. On 8 August Captain Jones noted in his log: 'foggy weather at times clear; clear interval, sighted land vicinity St. John's dist. about four miles, made out Signall Hill and Steered for Narrows, 7 p.m. got a tug and towed in. 8 p.m. arrived in St. John's, 24 days passage'.

A week later the *Mary Lloyd* sailed from St. John's for Battle Harbour, Labrador. On 15 August, at noon, she rounded the north of Belle Isle and at 2 p.m. signalled to Battle Harbour for a pilot. But as Captain Jones noted in his log, '2.30 no pilot, got ship ready and sailed into the harbour, moored temporary for the night, alongside the wharf', and so ended the record of the passage from Cadiz to the Labrador fishing stations.

The *Mary Lloyd* remained at Battle Harbour until 14 October 1905; when she sailed out into a very rough sea, she had a cargo of 200 tons of salt fish (Captain Jones merely quoted '200 tons' in his log), and at noon the master recorded 'took departure Battle Isle W/N 12 miles, set log, Lat. 53°21′N, Long. 55°15′W'. For the first week of the homeward passage gale followed gale, and the *Mary Lloyd* fairly sped along, but the single line entries for each watch 'Mod. gale, rough cross sea, ship tumbling about', 'mod. gale, severe squalls, terrific high sea' are interrupted on the fifth day by a longer note by Captain Jones, which speaks for itself:

> Thursday, 19th October, 8 a.m., course SE/S, . . . Fore and aft sails down. Fresh breeze blowing, squalls at times. Lat. 47°51′N, long. 37°15′W. 8.45 H. Timperi O.S., fell overboard from off Topmast riggin, hove ship to wind, but failed to rescue him, high sea running, boat side was stove in trying to launch it, kept ship up for two hours, 11.00 bore away. Noon Lat. 47°46′N, Long. 36°57′W.

The severe squalls, high seas, continued for some days, and then, as the *Mary Lloyd* approached European waters, the winds moderated, the miles logged in each watch decreased, and what might have been a very fast passage now developed into steady, average progress, with Cape St. Vincent Light being sighted at midnight on Tuesday, 31 October. On 2 November, whilst passing the Tarifa Light Vessel at 6 a.m., the *Mary Lloyd* 'Spoke Schr. Richard Greaves' — the log does not indicate where the other Porthmadog vessel was bound for, but by evening the *Mary Lloyd* had sighted the lights of Malaga. In heavy rain, with nothing more than gentle breezes and 'ship drifting with current', early next morning she sailed into the harbour, and moored to the quay, the end of a twenty days passage. Eight days later, at noon on 11 November, the *Mary Lloyd* received orders to sail for Kalamata, Greece, and at half-past two that afternoon, under an overcast sky, with fresh westerly breezes, she sailed out of Malaga.

The passage to Kalamata was accomplished in thirteen days; the *Mary Lloyd* sailed into the harbour at 5 p.m. on Friday, 24 November, 'and anchored close to Custom House', and 'made fast to quay'. Captain Jones went ashore to pay the balance of the drowned Finnish sailor's wages, £4.12.0, to the acting Consul, and the signing of a replacement, a 21-year-old Newfoundland A.B. who had 'signed at sea off Malaga', was duly noted. The salt fish cargo was discharged by 21 December, and at daybreak the *Mary Lloyd* sailed in ballast for Bari, a slow passage with little wind but some rough sea, and Captain Jones noted in his log 'ship tumbling about', on Christmas Day, with 'no wind', but 'showery weather, turbulent sea'. As they sighted Corfu to the North East on 28 December, the wind freshened, and soon the

Italian coast was sighted; on the 29 December they were abreast of Brindisi at 4 a.m. and sailed into the harbour of Bari where the *Mary Lloyd* 'moored in berth' at 5 p.m. A month later, with a cargo which is not specified in the log, the *Mary Lloyd* sailed for Nantes, unmooring at 6 a.m. on 30 January, but the breeze which enabled her to clear the Mole soon fell light, 'vessel drifting along shore to the SE$^{rd}$. Noon becalmed, 3 miles off the shore'. In very unsettled weather the *Mary Lloyd* tacked frequently to make the best of the light airs, then when the North Westerly winds increased to a fresh gale, Captain Jones ordered sails to be taken in, and at midnight on Saturday, 3 February, was compelled to wear ship in high, rough seas with 'severe squalls at times', 'lightning to S.W. and S.E. threatening appearance'. At 9 p.m. on the Sunday he noted in his log 'a terrific squall passed over lasting 15 minutes blowing with great force'. During the forenoon watch of the following day, 5 February, with Malta bearing SE, at a distance of about 20 miles, the sea was recorded 'still very rough', and so the unsettled weather continued, with 'ship labouring heavily, terrific squalls'. Captain Jones noted on the 6th 'P.M. run ship before gale to clear Keith Reefs', and later that evening he 'hove ship too, wind blowing a terrific gale with rain, very high rough sea'. Early next morning the 'gale abated suddenly, ship labouring fearfully', but within a matter of three hours the 'strong wind from NW increased to a gale of a fierce force' with a 'high dangerous sea'. Day after day the unsettled weather caused problems — on the 9th Captain Jones noted 'a fierce gale blowing unable to carry any sail, ship drifts to leeward considerably, terrific squalls at times" — and time and time again the *Mary Lloyd* approached Maritime Island, Cape Bon and Pantelleria Island, only to lose ground again, and had to come up to them again, perhaps two days later. It was not until Wednesday, 7 March, that the *Mary Lloyd,* after much tacking and battling in difficult weather conditions, came to an anchorage at Gibraltar in order to get provisions, and sailed out again within a couple of hours.

The weather in the Atlantic was not much better, alternating between 'fresh, high northerly sea' and moderate gales to 'gentle breeze, rough confused sea, sultry depressing atmosphere'; on 15 March Captain Jones was no doubt pleased to record meeting another Porthmadog vessel soon after daybreak, 'Spoke with Elizabeth, all well', and at noon, in fresh breezes, and a heavy westerly swell, under a clear sky, 'exchanged time with Elizabeth'. But there were three weeks more of battling with the rough, confused seas of the Bay of Biscay ahead of them before the *Mary Lloyd* finally reached Nantes; on several days Captain Jones noted 'ship hove to', 'sea rough and dangerous', and, on another occasion, 'ship laying to with close reefed main and foresail', when the constant battering had obviously caused some of the cargo to shift, and one can imagine the complex and highly dangerous problems involved in the single line entry 'casks were heard to be loose; managed to get down and secured them', this with a strong northerly gale blowing at the time. At long last, at 7 p.m. on Friday, 6 April, they sighted Belle Ile Light at an approximate distance of 30 miles NE/E, but in the moderate easterly winds it was noon on the next day when they picked up a Nantes pilot some 10 miles off Belle Ile. It must have been a tired Captain Jones who recorded in his log book the last few hours of the passage, sailing towards the Loire, passing between the shoals with the flood tide making and tacking up the channel before coming to an anchor abreast of St. Nazaire on 'a clear moonlight night'.

Three weeks later the *Mary Lloyd* sailed for London, arriving at Gravesend after a six days passage on Sunday, 6 May. On Monday, 28 May, she sailed for Belfast with 283 tons of cement, and ten days later, at 8 p.m., Captain Jones noted that Holyhead was visible, bearing E/N½N. But now there came the daunting calms and variable light airs, 'ship hardly moving, hazy weather', and it was not until Tuesday, 12 June, that the *Mary Lloyd* entered Belfast Lough and made fast to the buoys shortly before midnight. A fortnight later, having discharged her cargo, the *Mary Lloyd* sailed in ballast for Holyhead, but after good initial progress there must have been more frustration for Captain Jones and his crew, as the *Mary Lloyd,* like so many homeward-bound vessels, approached Bardsey in fine style, only to be thwarted by very light airs and a flood tide, '10 p.m. close to Bardsey, flood tide, calm, ship drifting back'. Next morning, 28 June, the wind freshened, and Captain Jones 'steered round Bardsey and sailed close hauled up the Bay', and ended his entries in the log, 'noon, Tug came out for us and towed us in. Arrived safely home, weather fine'. The *Mary Lloyd* had been a little over fifteen months away from Porthmadog. Just one out of hundreds of similar voyages in Porthmadog ships. For them all, as for Captain R. A. Jones and his crew, the months of heavy work, hard living conditions, all the frustrations in light airs and the buffeting in boisterous seas, were more than compensated for in those final words in the log: 'Tug came out for us and towed us in. Arrived safely home, weather fine'.

Log of "Mary Lloyd" from Battle Harbor to Malaga for orders

Wed 18th Octbr

| Hrs | Course | Dist | Wind | | |
|---|---|---|---|---|---|
| 4 | SE, S | 34 | WSW | Mod gale, rough cross sea. ship tumbling about | 7 |
| 8 | SE½S | 35 | West | Do do squally. cloudy sky | |
| Noon | SE. | 33 | WSW | Mod gale, Lat 48.30 N Long 39.47 W. | |
| 4 | SE | 29 | WSW | Mod gale heavy squalls and rain | 6 |
| 8 | SE | 27 | WNW | Fresh gale. boisterous weather. high rough sea. | 9 |
| 12 | SE/S | 31 | WNW | Mod gale. severe squalls terrific high seas | 2 |

Thurs 19th Octbr

| Hrs | Course | Dist | Wind | | |
|---|---|---|---|---|---|
| 4 | SE/S | 27 | WNW | Less wind squally & rainy high rough sea. | 5 |
| 8 | SE/S | 26 | NW | Fore & aft sails down. Fresh breeze blowing squalls at times Lat 47.51 N Long 37.15 W | 7 |
| Noon | SE/S | 12 | | 8.45 H. Lumber O.S. fell overboard from off topmast rigging hove ship to wind but failed to rescue him high sea running, boat side was stove in trying to launch it. Kept ship up for two hours. 11.00 bore away. Noon Lat 47.46 N Long 36.59 W | 9 |
| 4 | SE/E | 11 | NW | | |
| 8 | SE/E | 18 | NW. | squally heavy rain. sea rough confused | |
| 12 | SE/E | 23 | NW | | |

# A LINK BETWEEN BARMOUTH AND PORTHMADOG: THE LISTER SCHOONERS (1890-1904)

MANY links developed between Barmouth and Porthmadog, but none was more interesting than that which resulted from the decision of a young English doctor to relinquish his practice and to set himself up in a shipping business at Barmouth. This was in about 1890, and one wonders why he selected Barmouth rather than Porthmadog, as the latter was clearly the more buoyant port at this time. Whatever the reasons which prompted his selection, Dr. Joseph Herbert Lister (1858-1929) came to Barmouth and purchased, between 1890 and 1902, 5 schooners, 3 of which were representatives of Porthmadog's famous sequence of three-masted schooners or 'Western Ocean Yachts'. It is most fortunate that this business venture is thoroughly documented in the Record Office at Dolgellau.[1] An attempt will now be made to convey the interest which lies in these Lister Shipping Records, though it is hoped that a fuller analysis will be published in due course.[2]

THE SHIPOWNER: DR. JOSEPH HERBERT LISTER (1858-1929). — Joseph Herbert Lister was born on February 26th, 1858, at Littleborough in the parish of Rochdale. His father was Bryan Lister, a surgeon and apothecary, and his mother was Jane Susanna Cox Pugh.[3] His mother's maiden name suggests some Welsh associations and may provide some explanation for her son's interest in this part of Wales. Even the name Cox suggests local associations.[4] Be this as it may, young Joseph was destined to follow his father in a medical career. The Royal College of Surgeons of England's Records contain an entry to the effect that he qualified L.S.A. (Licenciate of the Society of Apothecaries) and M.R.C.S. in 1882. At this time, he gave his address at 23 Huntley Street, Bedford Square, London, W.C.[5] Again, for reasons which are not apparent, Joseph Lister ceased to communicate with the Medical Directory and Medical Register in 1886, and his last communication with the College was when he moved to Barmouth.[6] It appears that he never practised medicine again.

At Barmouth, Lister formed a close and lasting association with Capt. Evan Lewis Jones (1851-1920) of Pen-y-cei. Capt. Jones, an experienced master mariner, became Lister's commodore-skipper in that he commanded most of the Lister schooners on their proving voyages. It is also significant that, when Lister commissioned his first Porthmadog three-master in 1893, the vessel was named after Capt. Jones's young daughter, Jenny Jones (1882-1969). Soon after this, in about 1895, Jenny Jones became a pupil at the new Barmouth County Intermediate School[7] and she proceeded to gain a First Class Honours degree in English at the University College of North Wales at Bangor some years later.[8] In 1904, Lister sold his two remaining vessels, and, just three years later, on October 23rd, 1907, he married Jenny Jones at the Welsh Presbyterian Church, St. Pancras.[9] He was then a bachelor of 49 years and 'Of independent means', whilst his bride was scarcely half his age. They lived thereafter at Llwyngwril, where Joseph Herbert Lister died in 1929, though he was buried at Llanaber.[10]

Joseph Lister was clearly a wealthy man. He appears to have owned his vessels outright, and the evidence suggests that his three-masted schooners each cost in the region of £2,000.[11] It is equally clear from the documentary evidence that his shipping venture was not a philanthropic exercise, as careful accounts were kept, and the owner expected to make a profit. The venture appears to have made a profit, and, in a risky business, Lister took care to insure his vessels with the Portmadoc Mutual Ship Insurance Society, and cargoes were insured whenever possible.[12] However, both the beginning and the end of the venture are shrouded in mystery. There is no obvious reason why Joseph Lister decided to pull out in 1904 so soon after his purchase of the three-masted schooner *Royal Lister* in 1902. He was then about 46 years old. Perhaps he anticipated the inevitable decline of maritime commerce under sail or wished to enjoy a lengthy retirement. He clearly enjoyed sailing for pleasure as witnessed by his purchase of the cutter *Kittiwake*.[13] One thing is clear, however, he showed a remarkable faith in the seamanship to be found in the old port of Barmouth. Most of his skippers and the bulk of his crews were Barmouth men. Almost single-handed he revived and sustained seafaring at Barmouth for a brief but vital period.

PORTHMADOG IN 1890. — By 1890, Porthmadog was the unchallenged focal point of maritime activity in Tremadog Bay. Lister chose quite a good year to begin his venture, as the port was just emerging from the recession of the 1880s. Photographs of the period illustrate, as no words of mine can, the hectic bustle on the waterfront. On the harbour were situated the increasingly busy yards of David Jones and David Williams, arch rivals in the last phase of shipbuilding, though a number of other yards existed at the time.[14] The long low sheds of the slate companies were served by a network of narrow-gauge tracks from the Harbour Railway Station. In other words, the slates were transported directly from Blaenau to the quays and thence loaded on board the waiting vessels, which were often moored three and four abreast. Apart from the Harbour Master's Office, the Pen-y-cei, or Cornhill district, near the harbour was crowded with sailmakers, chandlers and other tradesmen and merchants. Virtually everything required to build, equip and victual a vessel could be procured in the immediate vicinity. The sights, sounds and smells associated with busy sailing ports the world over were to be encountered in these few acres of concentrated activity. Beyond, along the wide main street and its spacious offshoots, pubs vied with chapels and shops to attract the attentions of ' shellbacks ' and novices alike and to the sounds of Welsh and English might be added the stranger accents of Scandinavia and Germany. Some of the sailing masters were soberly attired, though others might be seen ashore rigged in their best gear, their wives clad in the finest furs of Canada. Whilst a cosmopolitan element was not entirely lacking, the mariners were mostly Welsh and were drawn principally from Llŷn, Eifionydd and Ardudwy. This was also true in the case of the shipbuilders, chandlers and others associated with shipping. Englishmen in the town were generally connected with the quarry companies and the railways. Scandinavians and Germans sometimes served on Porthmadog vessels, whilst others visited the port on vessels carrying timber from northern Europe.

Such was Porthmadog in 1890 when Joseph Lister sent his newly-purchased vessel, the schooner *Billow Crest*, to the port to receive her first cargo of Ffestiniog slates. She was then commanded by Capt. Evan Lewis Jones, and this trim West Country vessel must have aroused some critical attention as she tied up on Porthmadog's waterfront. Her master, however, was probably no stranger to the port or to the bystanders who witnessed her arrival.

THE LISTER SCHOONERS. — The Lister vessels are best recorded in the order which Lister purchased them. Most of the details have been kindly provided by Lloyd's of London.[15]

(a) *The Schooner 'Billow Crest'*. This vessel of 116 tons register was built by Watson and Fox at Plymouth in 1883. Her dimensions (in feet and tenths) were as follows: length 97.7, breadth 21.3, and depth 10.9. The vessel's moulded depth was 11 ft. 6 inches, and freeboard amidships was 1 ft. 7 inches. Significantly, the *Billow Crest* was sheathed in 'yellow metal' in 1894-5. Her official number was 86513 and her code letters were JLTV.

Lister bought this schooner in about 1890 and, as noted, her first master was Capt. Evan Lewis Jones of Barmouth. He remained in command until 1893/4. The other masters were: H. Parry (1894-6), J. Williams (1896-7), R. Roberts (1897-9) and W. Watkins. The *Billow Crest* was wrecked at Lochboisdale (57.09N 7.19W) in the Outer Hebrides on 12 April 1899 when commanded by Capt. Watkins.

(b) *The 3-Masted Schooner 'Consul Kaestner'*. This vessel of 146 tons register was built by Ebenezer Roberts at Porthmadog in 1892. Dimensions: 101.0/24.2/10.7. Moulded depth 11 ft. 6 inches and freeboard amidships 1 ft. 5½ inches. The vessel's official number was 92206 and code letters were MNJR. The *Consul Kaestner* was sheathed in 1898. Lister bought this vessel off the stocks and the name, presumably, commemorates a consul in one of the Baltic ports, Hamburg perhaps.

The successive masters were: H. Jones (1892-6), H. Parry (1896-7), J. Williams (1897-9), and W. Watkins (1899-1904). The *Consul Kaestner* collided with another vessel, the S.S. *Jokai,* off Sagres (near Cape St. Vincent, southern Portugal) on 28 June 1902, and subsequently sank. The master was the hapless Capt. W. Watkins.

(c) *The 3-Masted Schooner 'Jenny Jones'*. This vessel of 152 tons register was also built by Ebenezer Roberts at Porthmadog. She was launched in 1893 and named after the daughter of Lister's commodore-skipper Captain Jones, who was to become his wife some

14 years later. Dimensions: 100.2/24.8/11.1. Moulded depth 11 ft. 9 ins. and freeboard amidships 1 ft. 6½ inches. Official number 92213.

The successive masters were: E. L. Jones (1892-6), R. Williams (1896-7), W. Jones (1897-9), and S. (or T.) Ellis (1899-). The *Jenny Jones* was sold to Capt. Thomas Ellis in 1904, who sold it to R. B. Tregaskis in 1914. The schooner was bought by W. S. Munroe of St. John's, Newfoundland (Munroe & Co.) in 1916 and was reported in collision with an unidentified vessel 40 miles off Cape Spartel (Morocco, 35.48N 5.50W) on January 1st, 1918. The cargo was cod-fish. It is presumed that the vessel was condemned and broken up with collision damage as she was deleted from the Register Book for 1919-1920.

(d) *The Schooner 'Cariad'*. Lister again went to the West Country for this vessel. The *Cariad* was built by W. Date & Sons at Kingsbridge, Devon, in 1896. Her registered tonnage was 114. She was copper sheathed and fixed with copper from the outset. Dimensions: 84.5/21.9/10.8. Moulded depth 11 ft. 8 inches and freeboard amidships 1 ft. 6½ inches. Official number 92220 and code letters PG FC.

The successive masters were: W. Williams (1896-9), W. Ellis (1899), and E. L. Jones (1899-1903). The *Cariad* was sold by Lister in 1903 to D. Jones of Caernarfon, who sold to Ll. G. Llewelyn of Caernarfon in 1913. Llewelyn sold the vessel to J. Ryan of St. John's, Newfoundland, in 1916. The schooner *Cariad* was wrecked near Batteau, Labrador, with a cargo of fish, on November 14th, 1919.

(e) *The 3-Masted Schooner 'Royal Lister'*. This vessel of 140 tons gross was built by David Jones of Porthmadog in 1902. Dimensions: 92.3/23.0/11.7. The registered tonnage was 116.55 and the vessel's official number was 109736.

The master of the *Royal Lister* was Capt. William Griffith (1871-1949) of Meirion House, Dyffryn Ardudwy.[16] Lister sold this vessel in 1904, having obtained a certificate from the Portmadoc Mutual Ship Insurance Society to the effect that he was outright owner (64/64ths) and that the vessel was insured for £1,997.[17] The *Royal Lister* was stranded on the coast of Morocco (Morruo) on February 27th, 1913, and was taken off the register.

It remains to notice that three of these vessels had simple scroll heads, whilst the *Consul Kaestner* had an eagle head and the *Jenny Jones* a woman's bust head.

To sum up, the venture began with the schooner *Billow Crest* in 1890 and developed to comprise four schooners with the purchase of the *Consul Kaestner* in 1892, the *Jenny Jones* in 1893 and the *Cariad* in 1896. The *Billow Crest* was lost in 1899 and the *Consul Kaestner* in 1902. Lister then bought the *Royal Lister* in 1902, sold the *Cariad* in 1903, and, finally, sold both the *Jenny Jones* and the *Royal Lister* in 1904. The following list indicates these changes:

| *Vessels*: | *Billow Crest* | *Consul Kaestner* | *Jenny Jones* | *Cariad* | *Royal Lister* |
|---|---|---|---|---|---|
| 1890 | * | | | | |
| 1891 | * | | | | |
| 1892 | * | * | | | |
| 1893 | * | * | * | | |
| 1894 | * | * | * | | |
| 1895 | * | * | * | | |
| 1896 | * | * | * | * | |
| 1897 | * | * | * | * | |
| 1898 | * | * | * | * | |
| 1899 | Wrecked | * | * | * | |
| 1900 | | * | * | * | |
| 1901 | | * | * | * | |
| 1902 | | Wrecked | * | * | * |
| 1903 | | | * | Sold | * |
| 1904 | | | Sold | | Sold |

VOYAGES AND TRADES. — The Lister schooners were typical of Porthmadog schooners of the period, so far as voyages and trades were concerned. Regular voyages to the Baltic with slates were followed by a variety of voyages from Hamburg and other great ports to Cadiz, the Mediterranean and elsewhere. The Cadiz trade was particularly significant, as salt was carried thence to St. John's, Newfoundland, and the harbours of Labrador for use in the fishing industry. Another interesting cargo was valonea (acorn cups) from Greece, which was used in the tanning industry. One trade which the Lister vessels appear to have avoided was the carriage of phosphate rock.[17] A few examples will suffice to illustrate the diversity of trades:

*Account Book of the 'Royal Lister' 1902-4.* 1902: Porthmadog - Stettin - Christiansand - Barry Docks - Gilbraltar - Cadiz. The freights included slates (to Stettin); rye (from Stettin to Christiansand); and pit props (Christiansand to Barry Docks). 1902-3: Porthmadog - Harburg - Wexford - Cadiz - Harbour Grace & Grady (Labrador) - Gibraltar - Patras - Marathonisi - Falmouth - Bristol - Porthmadog. The freight from Marathonisi to Falmouth was valonea. 1903-4: Porthmadog - Harburg - Bristol - Cadiz - St. John's and Labrador - Gibraltar - Malaga - Pomaron - Amlwch - Porthmadog. The cargo from Amlwch was copper ore. February-June 1904: Porthmadog - Stettin (slates) - Christiansand (rye) - Barry Docks (pit props).

*Account Book of the 'Jenny Jones' 1896-1904*. 1902-3: Porthmadog - Harburg - Londonderry - Ayr - St. John's - Harbour Grace - Salcombe - Hamburg - Swansea - Porthmadog. 1903-4: Porthmadog - Stettin - Swansea - L'Orient (a Breton port) - Cadiz - St. John's - Harbour Grace - Glasgow - Villefranche - Leghorn - Gilbraltar - Porthmadog.

In general, towards the close of the 19th century, sailing vessels were obliged to take what freights could be procured. These often involved dangerous and unpleasant trades which the steamships were either obliged or prepared to ignore. Insurance became an increasing problem as insurers were anxious to get out of the sailing business since the risks were unacceptably high. Porthmadog's efforts to remain in business at this time were truly heroic (and ingenious) and the main credit for this must go to the mariners, both masters and men, who were prepared to assume such risks as loading corn off the dangerous coast of Morocco or carrying salt to the rocky and secluded harbours of Labrador. The Lister vessels and the men who manned them played their part in this risky if not desperate enterprise.

PROFITS AND LOSSES. — As noted earlier, although a wealthy man, Dr. Joseph Herbert Lister does not appear to have been a philanthropist. He operated his vessels to make a profit. Whilst short-term losses could be offset against profits made by other vessels in his small fleet, this would not have been tolerated for long. The financial accounts in the Lister Records provide some insights into the general trading position, though the full picture does not emerge from them as no account was taken of vessel depreciation (which was rapid), the cost of new vessels and the like. The accounts merely rendered a gross trading profit by setting the routine expenses (wages, insurance, harbour dues, lading charges, repairs, refits, victualling, etc.) against the income from freights. Let's just look at the year 1897 when the Lister fleet comprised four vessels, though one year's figures must be treated with caution:

| *Vessel* | *Freights* | *Wages: Crew* | *Master* | *Insurance* | *Profi* |
|---|---|---|---|---|---|
| *Billow Crest* | £1208 15 5 | £150 16 5 | £86 | £84 1 11 | £175 11 |
| *Consul Kaestner* | 861 15 1 | 161 8 10 | 82 2 | 153 1 5 | 47 18 |
| *Jenny Jones* | 994 4 11 | 186 1 10 | 102 11 4 | 58 10 6 | 75 12 |
| *Cariad* | 954 14 10 | 177 10 4 | 83 | 137 7 4 | 214 5 |
| | | | | | £513 7 |

Thus the combined gross trading profit for 1897 was £513 7s. 3½d. This may well have been a good year. It is worth noting that the *Consul Kaestner* returned a 'Balance Loss on Trading' in 1898 of £75 17s. 0½d. On the other hand, the *Jenny Jones* alone that year returned a profit of £361 1s. 6d., and the other two vessels had a profitable year. On the whole, it can be said, with some confidence, that the Lister schooners provided their owner with a fair, if uncertain, income, though the possibility must remain that Lister could have put his money to more profitable use elsewhere. Perhaps the philanthropist did inhabit the man of business, or perhaps the good doctor from Rochdale was a romantic at heart.

MASTERS AND CREWS. — It has already been noted that most of the masters of the Lister vessels were Barmouth men. This was certainly the case with Capt. Evan Lewis Jones, who commanded the *Billow Crest from* 1890 to 1893/4, the *Jenny Jones* from 1893 to 1896, and the *Cariad* from 1899 to 1903. Capt. William Griffith (1871-1949) of the *Royal Lister* also came from the Barmouth district. Capt. Thomas Ellis (1867-1942), who bought the *Jenny Jones* from Lister in 1904, was a Harlech man and a brother of Capt. Frank Ellis of Harlech, who, at his death a few years ago, was one of the last men in Britain to have held a square-rig master's ticket. Capt. W. Watkins of the *Billow Crest* and *Consul Kaestner* may also have been born in Ardudwy, if not in Barmouth. The name William Watkins (and Watkin Williams) was borne by a number of Barmouth mariners. Other masters of these vessels may well have been Capt.

John Williams (1840-1907) and Capt. Hugh Jones (1842-1920), both of Barmouth.

The Wage Accounts amongst the Lister Records indicate that Lister paid his masters the basic rate of £8 per month. For this, they were expected to exercise their skills as seamen; to procure stores at economic rates and good freights; to control their small but sometimes disgruntled crews; and, generally, to carry out their duties in a thoroughly seamanlike manner. An occasional and modest bonus was the only additional inducement they might reasonably expect.

The crews of the Lister vessels contained a number of Barmouth men, though the lists include the names of a few Scandinavians and Germans. The latter included Knut Carlson, Hans Herricksen, Max Harold, Herpe Juin, Frite Saar and Henry Steinmajer. A few English names are also recorded, and amongst them was Edgar Lowe, who was brought up in Barmouth. He was an ordinary seaman on board the *Royal Lister* in 1903. As a junior officer on board the *Titanic,* he later achieved fame for his work in rescuing passengers of the stricken ship and was thereafter known in his home town as 'Lowe of the Titanic'. But Welsh names predominated: David and Edward Pugh, Thomas J. and John Jones, Humphrey Roberts, Edward Evans, Robert Hughes, Morris Roberts, William H. Williams and so on.[18]

At the turn of the century, a mate might earn £5 per month, whilst A.B.s received £3 5s. and O.S.s £2 5s. or £2 10s. There was some flexibility, as Knut Carlson was paid £2 15s. per month as an A.B. on board the *Royal Lister* in 1903. Some crewmen jumped ship. Thus Joseph Jones, an A.B. and cook on the *Royal Lister,* deserted at Harburg after just 20 days service. Wages were paid at somewhat irregular intervals, and the wages books record the deductions from pay made by masters. Such deductions were in respect of cash advances, stamps, matches, shoemaker's bills, tailor's bills, and, very commonly, tobacco. After a long voyage there can have been little left in the kitty for seamen fond of tobacco and alcohol on little more than 10s. per week. Food on board and living quarters left much to be desired. Life at sea under sail should never be romanticised.

THE END OF THE VENTURE. — Perhaps on account of falling freights and their increasing rarity, added to the loss of the *Consul*

*Kaestner* in 1902, Joseph Lister decided to pull out. As noted, he sold his three remaining vessels in 1903-4. The insurance on the vessels lost and a good price for the *Royal Lister* provided him with some fiscal compensation. Sailing for a living was nearing its end, though the decline was fairly slow in the western parts of Britain. Joseph Lister retired to his home at Llwyngwril (' Gwelfor '). He was content thereafter to sponsor and participate in local regattas and to cruise in his motorised cutter *Kittiwake*. Letters for Lister from far away places like St. John's Newfoundland, Cadiz and Marathonisi no longer came to Barmouth Post Office. He died at home on January 24th, 1929, a full decade after the last of his vessels disappeared from the face of the waters.

## REFERENCES

[1] ZM/1/753. They comprise several bundles of documents (letters, chandlers' bills, insurance papers, etc.), and a number of account books, plus an interesting collection of photographs. They were deposited at Dolgellau after the death of Mrs. Jenny (Jones) Lister in 1969.

[2] As part of the writer's series of essays entitled *Maritime Merioneth.*

[3] Birth Certificate of Joseph Herbert Lister, The General Register Office, Somerset House, London.

[4] A family called Cox Paynter were associated with the Traeth Bach district from the late 18th century onwards. One member, Joseph Cox Paynter, was Customs Officer at Porthmadog from the opening of the harbour in 1824. His father, Andrew Paynter, was a Customs Officer in the same district many years before. In addition, a Joseph Cox was Comptroller of the Customs at Pwllheli in 1748 when Lewis Morris compiled his Plans of Harbours, Bars, etc., in St. George's Channel (Cox was listed as a subscriber).

[5] These details are contained in a letter from E. Mitchell, Secretary to the Librarian of the Royal College of Surgeons of England, 35-43 Lincoln's Inn Fields, London. The assistance is gratefully acknowledged.

[6] ibid. The letter does not make it clear whether Lister's last communication was in 1886. Perhaps he did move to Barmouth in that year and his shipping venture may have taken some four years to mature.

[7] Barmouth. County Intermediate School Register, Dolgellau Record office.

[8] ibid

[9] Marriage Certificate of Joseph Herbert Lister and Jenny Jones, The General Register Office, Somerset House, London. The minister was Peter Hughes Griffith, and witnesses were Jenny Jones Williams, Tom Throup and E. Jones.

[10] In Llanaber Churchyard. His widow, Jenny (Jones) Lister, was buried in the same plot some forty years later in 1969. The churchyard contains the graves of many masters and crewmen of the Lister vessels.

[11] An insurance certificate issued by the Portmadoc Mutual Ship Insurand Society in 1904 indicates that the *Royal Lister*, built in 1902, was then insured with the Society for £1,997 (ZM/1/753). In addition, a surviving copy of an agreement for the building of the three-masted schooner *M. A. James*, dated April 27th, 1899, gives the purchase price as £2,000, of which £600 was to be paid by instalments before launching and the remainder on completion. This agreement was between the shipbuilder, David Williams of Porthmadog, and Capt. John Jones of Borth-y-gest.

[12] Porthmadog vessels were generally insured with the Portmadoc Mutual Ship Insurance Society. This appears to have been the case with the Lister vessels. The insurance of cargoes was a more complex matter and insurers were increasingly reluctant by the end of the 19th century to insure goods carried by sailing vessels. When insurance cover could be obtained, the agreements often included special protective clauses in the interests of insurers.

[13] This cutter (official number 118510) was built at Crossens in 1905 and was converted into a motor vessel on April 21st, 1926 (The Caernarfon Shipping Register).

[14] The Porthmadog yards extended to Borth-y-gest. David Jones and David Williams were the best-known builders of three-masted schooners, though the three-masters *Consul Kaestner* and *Jenny Jones* were built by Ebenezer Roberts of Porthmadog.

[15] I am most grateful in this respect to Mr. R. J. Pryde of Lloyd's, 71 Fenchurch Street, London. Other details have been taken from *Lloyd's Register* (Gregg International Reprints).

[16] His son, Capt. William Griffith (formerly of the Elder Dempster S.S. Co.), of Dyffryn Ardudwy, has a fine portrait of the *Royal Lister* in his home. The painting was made in Flensburg.

[17] For this arduous trade, see Henry Hughes, *Immortal Sails*, passim.

[18] According to the Wages Account of the *Royal Lister* for 1903 (ZM/1/753), the crew consisted of a mate, 2 or more A.B.s and 2 or more O.S.s, i.e., 5 or 6 men, apart from the master: Capt. William Griffith; Griffith Jones (mate); Humphrey Jones (A.B.) from April 9th-June 1st; Edgar Lowe (O.S.), April 1st-June 1st; Robert Lewis (O.S.), April 2nd-June 1st; Manuel Evans (A.B. and Cook), who served for 7 days; Joseph Jones (A.B. and Cook), who served for 20 days and deserted at Harburg; and Knut Carlson (A.B.), May 1st-June 1st. Wages were paid at Wexford on this occasion. Griffith Jones, Humphrey Jones, Edgar Lowe, Robert Lewis and Knut Carlson remained with the vessel and were joined by Herpe Juin (or Juim) (A.B.). Robert Lewis (O.S.) took on the apparently unenviable task of cook from June 1902 to February 1903!

## THE THREE-MASTED SCHOONERS, *GRACIE* AND *R. J. OWENS*, 1907

SPRING 1907 saw two three-masted schooners being completed at the yards of David Jones and David Williams, the *Gracie* built at the southernmost part of Rotten Tare and the *R. J. Owens* a little distance away, inshore, to the north, by David Williams. Very similar in dimensions, both vessels were registered at Caernarfon in April 1907, the *Gracie* on 2 April and the *R. J. Owens* on the 25 April; they were both sold from Porthmadog to Newfoundland in 1916, the *R. J. Owens* on 20 June 1916 to James Ryan of St. John's, and the *Gracie* on 9 October to Wilson and Arthur Garland, both of Gantois, merchants. Both were good examples of the Western Ocean Yachts, and may be taken here as representative of the later vessels. For most of the time at Porthmadog they were commanded by the master mariners for whom they had presumably been built, men who had obviously taken much interest in their building as they themselves were to be the principal shareholders.

The *Gracie,* very slightly the larger of the two, was built for and owned by Owen Humphrey Owen of Castle View, Talsarnau, Merioneth, who held 20/64 shares, Ellen Taylor, 26 North End Avenue, Portsmouth, described in the registers as 'widow' (possibly a sister or near relative of Captain Owen), who held 12/64; another well-known Talsarnau master mariner, Captain John Richard Williams, who had recently finally taken over command of his mother's highly regarded schooner, the *Blodwen,* had 8/64 shares in the *Gracie,* as did Robert Ehlers, of 61 Queen Street, Bristol, the Newfoundland merchant who had much to do with the later Porthmadog schooners. Ellen Parry, of 5 Lombard Street, spinster, John Owen Jones of Penbryn Isaf, Llandecwyn, and David Davies, the Cornhill shipbroker, who had taken over from the late Captain Hugh Parry, all for 4/64 in the vessel, which was to be managed by David Davies, the shipbroker.[1]

Some photographs of the *Gracie* illustrate different stages in her history: there is the very faded photograph of her in course of construction at David Jones's yard, with David Jones himself in the centre of the picture (in bowler hat), and nine of his workmen and the boy on the extreme left — one of the men is Robert Griffith, the rigger. Very dimly one can see a vessel in the background, a two-masted schooner, the tilt of her masts suggesting that she is aground directly opposite the end of the shipway of David Jones's yard. This photograph, with the scaffolding and ladders around the vessel, and the trenails much in evidence, was taken in 1906; the next shows the *Gracie* a stage nearer launching day with bowsprit and figurehead shipped and David Jones to be seen dimly up for-ard aboard the newly-painted vessel and three of his workmen in the foreground.[2] On 31 January 1907 the *Gracie* was launched, and the next photograph shows her at sea with 'moon-sail' up. The photograph of the crew of the *Gracie* is reproduced from a postcard-photograph taken at Great Yarmouth, probably in May 1913; the postcard was from Captain Owen and addressed to 'Miss F. Owen, Head's House, Lancing College, Shoreham by Sea'. Captain O. H. Owen and the mate have both got their hands on the wheel in this carefully posed photograph, with probably the two A.B.s on either side and the young ordinary seaman and the boy outside them. Every detail of this photograph is evocative of a whole generation of Porthmadog seamen.

Captain Owen Humphrey Owen, of Castle View, Talsarnau, was a comparatively young man of 27 when he took the *Gracie* on her maiden voyage in the Spring of 1907. With him sailed William Owen, aged 66, his father, as boatswain, William Hughes, also aged 27, of Porthmadog, as cook/A.B., David Williams, aged 18, of Tyn y Gelert, Criccieth, as ordinary seaman, and two A.B.s who had signed in at the 'Ship on Launch', Porthmadog, Konrad Gotz, aged 21, a native of Dresden, whose previous ship had been the *Jenny Jones,* and Charles Bach, aged 22, a native of Liban(?), Russia, who had last served in the *Cadwalader Jones*. In May 1907, when the *Gracie* was at Svendborg, Denmark, the 'articles' contained the following entry: 'William Owen being the Father of the Captain is left behind in the hospital here on account of sickness, 7 May 1907'. But it took more than a temporary illness to stop the ancient mariner from sailing with his son — in April 1908 he rejoined the *Gracie* at Appledore, and in the following year sailed in her, with his son as master, from Swansea for Cadiz. Arriving at Cadiz on 19 June, they were at St. John's on 18 July, Fogo Island 22 September, Naples on 10 November, and arrived home in Porthmadog on 1 February 1909. The *Gracie* continued in this trade, sailing regularly in the Hamburg slate trade and the Newfoundland/Labrador salt fish trade. Captain Owen Humphrey Owen had Griffith Roberts, a native of Portdinorwic, as mate for the March voyage of 1912; for the coastal voyages that followed in May, Griffith Roberts sailed as master and William Owen, at the stated age of 70, sailed as mate in the absence of his son, Captain Owen. He may well have been over 70, for his age had remained conveniently static at 66 for at least two years in the period 1907/8; Captain O. H. Owen returned to command the *Gracie* for the next voyage in 1912, with Griffith Roberts of Port Dinorwic again as mate. They sailed from Swansea in July 1912, were at North Sydney, Cape Breton, on 19 September, at Fogo on 7 October, at Gibraltar on 6 January 1913, Alicante 21 January, at Plymouth on 10 March, Dundalk on 5 April, and returned to Porthmadog on 11 April 1913. No Crew Agreement lists of the *Gracie* are held locally for the period 1913-1916; on 9 October 1916 she was sold, like so many of her 'sister ships' to Newfoundland. Not long afterwards she was wrecked; the photograph of the *Gracie* on her beam ends ashore near Cadiz was photographed by the late Emrys Hughes from a photograph in the possession of Mrs. Owen, widow of Captain O. H. Owen, who had made his home at Borthwen, Borth-y-gest.

When the *Gracie* was built in 1907, there is an entry in the ledgers of Jones and Morris, the sailmakers, of Britannia Place, relating to David Jones's account: 'March 1907, To contract New Outfit of Sails, Course, Tarpaulins, etc. as per specification, all complete for the lump sum price of £118.0.0'. A few days later, on 3 April, there is another account for the owners of the *Gracie*, for '1 New Cover for loading salt, made 27 yards, No. 3 Canvas, at 1/4d, £1.16.0, 1 bolt long flex canvas, 43 yards at 1/1d, £2.6.7", and in May a further 'New Flying Jib Cover painted' was provided for 9/6d. Just as the provision of the canvas cover 'for loading salt' indicated the nature of the trade for which the *Gracie* was intended, so, too, did the charts supplied on 25 March 1907 for the new vessel to David Jones, the shipbuilder, for a total cost of about £14. They included charts of the English Channel, Thames, St. George's Channel, East Coast of England, West Coast of Ireland, West Coast of Scotland, 1 North Sea General, 1 North Sea, S. part, 1 S. part of Baltic, 1 N. part of Baltic, 1 Skagerak, 1 Kattegat Sound and Baltic, 1 North Atlantic, 1 South Atlantic, 1 British Isles to Coast of Africa, 1 W. part of Mediterranean, 1 E. part of Mediterranean, 1 Adriatic Sea, 1 Grecian Archipelago, 1 Newfoundland, 1 Labrador, 1 Flemish Cap to Cape Cod, 1 Gibraltar to Mogador, 1 Brazil, 1 Admiralty Sheet to St. John's, Newfoundland, 1 Admiralty Sheet Harbour Grace, 2 sheets Belle Isle to Labrador. It was customary for the local ship chandlers to provide not only stores, food and charts, but also a host of small items — for example, when the *William Prichard* was first being made ready for sea in 1903, payments were made by her owners for binding charts, four memo books at 2d each, one ship's account book at 1/-, blotting paper at 3d, one bottle of blue ink and one bottle of red ink, blacklead pencils, steel pens, and a wide range of items, including a spring balance at 1/4d and an enamel spitoon at 1/3d.

Jones and Morris, the sailmakers, presented an identical contract price to David Williams in April 1907 to that which David Jones had been charged for the *Gracie*: David Williams, on 19 April 1907, settled the account relating 'to contract New Outfit of Sails for the New Three masted Sr. building, all complete with covers, Tarpaulins as per speicification at Lump sum price £118'. These sails were obviously for the *R. J. Owens*, built by David Williams for Owen Owens of Borth-y-gest, who was to be her master and had a 32/64 share in her. The remaining shares were held by Humphrey Owens, described as a 'Trinity pilot', of Borth-y-gest, who had 8/64, William Morris, the Porthmadog Ship-Chandler, 8/64, Griffith Prichard of Bod Hyfryd, Penrhyndeudraeth, the ship-broker, 4/64, John Thomas Jones, described as 'bank manager', of Porthmadog, 8/64, and John Owens of Borth-y-gest, mariner, who had a 4/64 share. The Register of Shipping thus records the names of the shareholders, but does not indicate that, in fact, the *R. J. Owens* was very much a 'family' ship: Humphrey Owens, the pilot, was the father of Owen Owens, and John Owens was his brother, so that between them they held 44/64 shares. The rivalry between the owners of the *Gracie* and the *R. J. Owens*, already reflected in their being built by the rival shipbuilders, was probably accentuated by the fact that whilst David Davies of Cornhill, the shipbroker, was the appointed managing owner of the *Gracie,* the rival shipbroker, Griffith Prichard, similarly had shares in, and was appointed managing owner of the *R. J. Owens.*

Owen Owens was well qualified to take command of his beautiful new schooner. As already mentioned earlier in this book, Captain Owen Owens carefully noted in the margin of his Bible the name of the ship in which he was serving and her position at the time he read particular passages. By cross-checking these references with Captain W. H. Hughes, D.S.C., who sailed with Owen Owens in the *Beeswing,* it has been possible to trace the latter's career. Born in 1870, Owen Owens first went to sea in the large Nefyn built two-masted schooner *Miss Thomas,* engaged in the Baltic and Moroccan trades; by 1895, he was serving aboard the *Venedocian,* and it was aboard her, at Gibraltar, that he started to enter his notes in his Bible — on 30 October 1895 he recorded that he had read the fourth chapter of Malachi. There are a number of entries in the years 1897-8 which refer to his service aboard the *Laura Griffith* and then the *Dorothy,* Captain Thomas Roberts's three-masted schooner, the first of the Western Ocean Yachts in which Owen Owens served. In August 1898 he recorded reading the twelfth chapter of Daniel aboard the *Dorothy* at St. John's, Newfoundland — he had previously entered notes relating to reading the first chapter of the Book of Ezekiel at Cape St. Vincent and Cadiz in early June, and later chapters 'off the Western Islands' on 28 June. By October 1898, Owens recorded reading the first chapter of Amos when the *Dorothy* was at Black Tickle, Labrador, and so one can trace the *Dorothy*'s progress on that 1898 voyage. A brief voyage in the *Excelsior* early in 1899, and then Owen Owens joined the *Beeswing* as A.B., and in November 1899, according to his Bible, he was reading Hosea at Taltal, Chile, and, appropriately enough, amid all the stench and flies, the Lamentations of Jeremiah, when the *Beeswing* was loading the foul-smelling guano at Lobos d'Afuerra in January 1900.

The entries in Owen Owen's Bible cannot be followed in detail here, but they indicate that, following his service in the *Beeswing,* he joined the *Norfolk Island* (a 1,360 ton steel barque, built by Russell and Company at Port Glasgow in 1898, commanded by Captain R. Thomas since 1891) as Second Mate — he may, in fact, have had

John Richard Williams, later master of the *Blodwen,* as one of his shipmates in this 1900 voyage. In December 1900, when the *Norfolk Island* was at Victoria Dock, Melbourne, Owen Owens recorded that he had started re-reading the New Testament, and on the passage home to Queenstown there are references to the ship's position whenever he started reading an epistle or a particularly significant chapter. His next ship was a much smaller Glasgow vessel, the *Edith Mary,* a 349 ton iron barque, in which he sailed to the West Indies for phosphate — he noted that on 23 December 1901 he started re-reading the New Testament again at Aruba aboard the *Edith Mary.* Although owned in Glasgow, the *Edith Mary* was commanded by a Borth-y-gest man, Captain R. Hughes, brother of Hugh Hughes, schoolmaster at Borth-y-gest when Captain W. H. Hughes was a boy there. Owen Owens then moved to another vessel commanded by a local man, Captain Marks, who was master of Robert Thomas and Company's *Ednyfed,* for which Owen now signed as mate. Again Owen Owens faithfully recorded his readings on the passage of the *Ednyfed* out to Newcastle, New South Wales, and then across the Pacific to Salaverry on the West Coast of South America during 1903. There do not appear to be any entries for 1904, but in 1905 Owens was back as mate of the *Beeswing.* As Captain W. H. Hughes was then an A.B. aboard this Porthmadog-owned steel barque, he remembers very clearly both Captain Griffiths, the master, and the mate, Owen Owens, particularly the latter, who lived in his own home village, Borth-y-gest. The mate recorded the voyages out to Melbourne, then from Newcastle, N.S.W., to Coquimbo and the return voyage[3]; on 9 September 1906, for example, when he started reading Paul's Epistle to the Philippians, he noted that the *Beeswing* was 'off Cape Horn running before a heavy westerly gale and high seas bound from Taltal, Chile to Rotterdam with nitrate'. Captain W. H. Hughes remembers very clearly how, when they had returned home, he was very interested to see the new schooner built by David Williams for the erstwhile mate of the *Beeswing,* and although he himself soon joined Captain Llewelyn Rees as second mate of the *Deccan,* he also remembers that for the maiden voyage of the *R. J. Owens,* Captain Owen Owens had Humphrey Owens, his brother, and Bob Morris, son of Evan Morris, the pilot, in the crew, with 'Jack Ship' as mate.

For the *R. J. Owens*'s first voyage in what was to be her regular Atlantic trade, Captain Owen Owens had Griffith Roberts, a native of Portdinorwic, now living at Ivy Terrace, Porthmadog, as boatswain — his previous ship had been the *M. A. James* and, as noted above, he was later to serve as mate of the *Gracie.* A twenty-three year old A.B. from Abersoch, an eighteen year old ordinary seaman from Hamburg, Otto Rasch, whose address is given as 2 Osterstrasse, Hamburg, and two sixteen year old Criccieth boys, next door neighbours living in Marine Crescent (one of them on his first voyage to sea), were the other members of the crew. The *R. J. Owens* was at Papenburg in May, Oporto in June, thence to Cadiz and across to St. John's, Newfoundland, by 24 July. From the Bible of Captain Owen Owens, it is possible to trace her voyage — she was off Cape St. Francis, Labrador, on 5 August, and her master noted reading the first book of Samuel and the third chapter of the Proverbs at Punch Bowl, Labrador, on the 15 and the 21 September 1907 respectively. The *R. J. Owens* arrived at Lisbon on 12 October, and proceeded to Patras, where she berthed on 11 November; Captain Owens recorded reading the second chapter of the Epistle of James when his ship was bound from 'Patras, Greece, to Seville, Spain, 36°35′N 17°51′ E'. The date of arrival at Seville is not noted in the 'Articles', but on 26 January 1908, when Captain Owens read the third chapter of Mathew, the *R. J. Owens* was in an estimated position '40°18′N 11°1′W, Seville to Amlwch'. On 20 February 1908 she arrived at Amlwch.

The next few years, those restless last years of peace before the outbreak of the First World War, saw the *R. J. Owens* sailing regularly in the Newfoundland-Mediterranean trades; Captain Owens remained, but most of the other members of the crew changed each year. In May 1909, the *R. J. Owens* sailed from Hull for Gibraltar, Cadiz, Newfoundland, Labrador, Genoa, Huelva and home to Porthmadog in March 1910, and in her crew were William Payne, aged 24, born at Newcastle, N.S.W., who had already served in the *Blodwen* and the *Rose of Torridge,* and Charles A. Payne, aged 24, born Launceston, Tasmania, both of whom gave their present address as 2 Limekiln Lane, Porthmadog. Also in the crew was Edward Morrison, aged 19, born in Sydney, N.S.W., formerly serving in the *Edwin;* both he and the younger Payne deserted at Genoa in December on their return from Labrador. Captain Owens's Bible indicates that the *R. J. Owens* had visited Shoal Bay, Labrador, on this voyage — they were there on 29 August 1909, when he had read the twenty-sixth Psalm. On the voyage starting at Llanelli in June 1911, a new name appears in the crew list, 'Ellen Mary Owen, aged 24, of Brookside, Criccieth' (the same address as the master), who signed as 'First Ship, Stewardess'. The master's wife left the *R. J. Owens* at Lisbon shortly before she sailed for Cadiz, thence for Nippers Harbour, Newfoundland, back to Gibraltar, Patras, Civita Vecchi, Preston, and home to Porthmadog in April 1912.

Captain Owens commanded the *R. J. Owens* for two more yearly voyages to Newfoundland and through the Mediterranean to Patras, in 1912-1913, but in January 1914 Captain Evan Evans of Pwllheli, formerly master of the *Tecwyn,* took his place, and with the outbreak of war the locally held crew agreement lists of the *R. J. Owens* cease. On June 20, 1916, she was sold to James Ryan of St. John's, Newfoundland, only to be wrecked shortly afterwards, in July 1917. Ironically enough, Captain Owen Owens, who had moved into steamers, probably during the early years of the war, was killed in the same year as his beloved *R. J. Owens.* He was found dead on the deck of the steamer in which he was serving, having fallen from the quayside down to the ship below at low water. He was then aged thirty-eight. His brother, John, who had joined him in 1907 in investing in the *R. J. Owens,* had also become a master of a Porthmadog vessel, the *Cariad,* built at Kingsbridge by the well-known firm of W. Date and Sons in 1896. Captain John Owens is, in fact, credited with the fastest crossing of the Atlantic by a Porthmadog vessel when the *Cariad,* under his command, sailed from Newfoundland to Oporto in ten days. In October 1916 the *Cariad,* too, was sold to Newfoundland owners, and Captain John Owens, in common with his contemporaries, moved to the world of steamers.

2

# SCALE OF PROVISIONS

## TO BE ALLOWED AND SERVED OUT TO THE CREW DURING THE VOYAGE.

NOTE.—The quantity and nature of the Provisions are a matter for agreement between Master and Crew, but the Board of Trade recommend the adoption of the scale drawn up by the Mercantile Marine Committee, 1902.

The scale agreed upon is in addition to the Lime and Lemon Juice and Sugar, or other Anti-Scorbutics, in any case required by the Act.

3 quarts Water
1/8 oz Tea
1/2 - Coffee
2 - Sugar
1 lb Bread
} Daily

1 1/2 lbs Beef. Sunday. Tuesday. Thursday. Sat.
1 1/4 - Pork. Monday. Wed. & Friday
1/2 - Flour. Sunday. Tuesday. & Thursday
1/3 - Pint Peas. Monday. Wed. & Friday
1/2 - Rice Saturday

Substitute & Equivalents
at master's option

# BILL OF FARE.

NOTE.—The Act does not require these particulars to be given, but the Table may be filled up if desired.

| | BREAKFAST. | DINNER. | SUPPER. |
|---|---|---|---|
| Sunday .. | | | |
| Monday ... | | | |
| Tuesday .. | | | |
| Wednesday | | | |
| Thursday... | | | |
| Friday ... | | | |
| Saturday... | | | |
| Articles supplied daily | | | |

Scale of Provisions on the voyage of the *R. J. Owens* from Porthmadog to Papenburg, 1907.

## REFERENCES

[1] Details relating to both vessels are from the Crew Agreement Lists, Official Logs at C.R.O., and from the Register of Shipping at Custom House, Caernarfon.

[2] In am indebted to Mr. Ronald Owen of Borth-y-gest for allowing us to rephotograph some of the prints of the *Gracie* which Mr. Emrys Hughes had originally photographed from Mrs. Owens's collection.

[3] Captain W. H. Hughes recalls that on this voyage the *Beeswing* sailed from Newcastle, N.S.W., to Caleta Coloso, where they had a long wait for freights in common with many other ships, eventually returning to Newcastle, N.S.W., and then sailing back for Coquimbo. During the voyage they also called at the Pitcairn Islands.

## THE BRIG *EVELYN*, 1877-1913

So much has already been written about the *Evelyn*, both by Henry Hughes in *Immortal Sails* and in the preceding pages of this present work, that it may appear unnecessary to include more details about this vessel. But, like the other vessels included in these further studies, the *Evelyn* may be taken both as a representative of a group, the last, in fact, of the fine brigs built in the sixties and seventies, and also as a vessel which, like the *Martha Percival* and the *Fleetwing*, proved to be a ship in which many of Porthmadog's finest mariners gained their early experience of seamanship. Like that other fine brig, the *Blanche Currey*, she had a long career of well over thirty years during which she sailed many thousands of miles in the oceanic trades, manned invariably by Porthmadog men; there was a dramatic and symbolic character to her final struggle in mid-Atlantic which Henry Hughes quite rightly seized upon in his account of her in *Immortal Sails*.[1]

The launching of the *Evelyn*, on 17 January 1877, and her early voyages, commanded by Captain Hugh Roberts, senior, the much respected former master of the *Constance*, have already been described in the introductory chapters, and it is evident from the Crew Agreement lists that Henry Hughes's description of her as 'y llong bwdin' (the pudding ship), renowned for the high standard of the food provided, is borne out by the way in which the same crews signed on voyage after voyage. Captain W. H. Hughes and his contemporaries all recalled the reputation that the *Evelyn* had for a well-fed ship's company, and the lame but very excellent cook who had suffered a serious injury to one of his legs aboard a steamer, who sailed for many voyages with Captain Hugh Roberts. In a letter to Emrys Hughes, in August 1944, Captain 'Evie' Morris, who had sailed many times with his uncles aboard the *Evelyn*, wrote 'there is no doubt that the old "Evelyn" was a bit outstanding among them as a favourite, and I've heard that she turned out more Captains from among those who served in her than any other ship of her size'.[2]

Contemporaries regarded the *Evelyn* as perhaps the most strongly built at Porthmadog. According to 'Evie' Morris, 'she was reckoned to be the strongest ship built there, having been built of greenheart, oak and teak, with pitch pine spars. She had twelve heavy cross beams in her hold, and a heavy platform which could be used as dunnage on a tween deck'. On one voyage in which he sailed in her, the cargo of heavy granite blocks from Hedestrand, Sweden, to Devonport broke loose; 'the blocks, some of about 7 tons, were thumping against her sides, and one sawed through one of the heavy beams, and the old ship was hardly leaking'.

The *Evelyn*'s commander was the kindly Captain Hugh Roberts, junior, as tough as the timbers of his sturdy vessel. From February 1878 to that stormy Sunday in mid-Atlantic nearly thirty-five years later, when he jumped from the quarter of the water-logged *Evelyn* into the rescuing boat, Captain Roberts sailed his ship with great skill — it is not without significance that until her last year of sailing he had not lost a man at sea through accident or illness, nor had the *Evelyn* suffered any serious damage throughout all those years of hard sailing. Inevitably the *Evelyn*'s reputation as a happy ship — and a lucky one — and the high esteem in which Captain Roberts was held by his fellow master mariners, resulted in a constant flow of applicants for a berth aboard her. One of the many photographs of the *Evelyn*'s crews is that taken in 1898/9; according to her 'articles', the crew signed on at Cardiff in July 1898 for a voyage which took them to Puerto Cabello, Venezuela in August, returning to Ipswich by October, where they all signed for a further voyage in November to sail for Demarera. Arriving there in January, the *Evelyn* was back in London on 18 April 1899, at Plymouth on 8 May, and the crew were finally paid off at Porthmadog on 27 May 1899. On those two voyages, each member of the *Evelyn*'s crew, all of them from Porthmadog, were the sons of master mariners: Captain Roberts himself; the mate, David Richard Morgan, Clog y Berth (who later became a master in the Pacific Steam Navigation Company), then aged 24; John P. Roberts, aged 21, the second mate, whose previous ship had been the steel barque, *Conway Castle,* owned by Robert Thomas and Company; William Roberts, brother of the master, who signed as boatswain; Hugh D. Humphreys, the cook/A.B., from Borth-y-gest; Ted Jones, A.B., who was later killed when master of the *Ellen James* by a block falling from aloft; another A.B., Johnny Williams, and Evie Morris, ordinary seaman.

As in the case of many other Porthmadog ships, the stipulations of the Board of Trade regarding master and mate's qualifications had a bearing on the composition of the crew. For voyages within the confines of the coasting trade and those between Brest and the Elbe, William Roberts, the master's brother, served as mate, as another certificated man in addition to Captain Roberts himself was not required, but for voyages beyond these limits, William Roberts reverted to the role of boatswain, with a mate and even, occasionally, a second mate being signed, as in the case of the two voyages to the West Indies in 1898/9 already mentioned. A number of well-known Porthmadog seamen served as mate to Captain Roberts. In 1892, for example, William Greene, formerly of the *Edward Windus,* the future master of the brigantine *Tyne,* signed for the voyage which commenced in Porthmadog at the end of February, took the *Evelyn* to Stettin in March, back to Belfast in June, and home to Porthmadog by 13 June. William Roberts signed on as boatswain for this voyage, with William Ralph Jones as cook/ordinary seaman, Rees E. Davies, formerly of the *Mary Lloyd,* ordinary seaman, and John Richard Eames, aged 14, first ship, who signed as 'boy' at a wage of 5 shillings a month. On their return to Porthmadog, Greene remained with Captain Roberts and his brother for the voyages in 1893/4 to Hamburg, Stettin, Memel, Santa Caterina, Brazil, and Buenos Aires and back to Antwerp in May 1894, where Captain Roberts's young wife must have joined him, for there is a photograph of them taken together in Antwerp in Miss Evelyn Roberts's collection. Unfortunately for himself, young J. R. Eames, the boy, did not sign for these voyages, but moved to another ship in which he was drowned at the age of sixteen. When the *Evelyn*'s crew returned to Porthmadog in June 1894, William Greene's balance of pay was £49.4.5, William Roberts, who had signed as cook/A.B. for this voyage, received £33.1.4, Ellis Humphreys and Robert Humphreys, both of Amanda Terrace, Borth-y-gest, both A.B.s, aged 27 and 23 respectively, received £28.1.11 and £26.2.6, Owen Williams, aged 20, of 9 Osmond Lane, A.B., had a balance of £25.14.1 due to him, and William Paul, aged 21, of Lombard Street, also A.B., received £24.15.8 for what was virtually a voyage of just under a year, starting on 22 June 1893, when they sailed from Liverpool to Santa Caterina, and ending at Porthmadog on 13 June 1894. A little over a fortnight later, the *Evelyn* sailed again for Copenhagen and Frederikstad, with Evan Hughes, formerly of the *Dorothy*, as mate, and William Roberts again as boatswain, and William Ralph Jones, returned as Cook/A.B., having made a voyage in the intervening period in the Davies, Menai Bridge's brand new steel four-masted barque, *Afon Alaw*.

Reading through the *Evelyn*'s crew lists over the years, one cannot but be impressed by the way in which the same men returned from time to time to serve with Captain Roberts after serving a spell in the large Liverpool ships and four-masted barques — Owen Ellis, previously serving aboard the *Principality*, was mate in 1895, and in the crew were William D. Williams, who had served in the *Cambrian Hills*, and Evan R. Williams, formerly of the *Gwynedd*. In 1897, R. O. Williams, brother of David Williams, the shipbuilder, served as mate of the *Evelyn* on a voyage to Flensburg and Stromstad. His previous vessel had been the steamer *Cambay* of Newcastle, and it would seem that he was sailing with Captain Roberts to prepare himself for his new command, the *Sidney Smith*, the three-masted schooner built at his brother David's yard. From the *Sidney Smith*, he moved to the newly-built *Isallt*, and when she was lost in collision with S.S. *Atlantic* in 1908, he took command of the vessel of the same name built in 1909 to replace her — his photograph with the crew at Copenhagen and the ill-starred young first voyager, David Mark Jones, is included as Plate 52.

Captain R. O. Williams was not the only master of the later Porthmadog three-masted schooners to serve under Captain Hugh Roberts in the *Evelyn*, and among those who sailed as his mate were Rees E. Davies of Pilot House, Borth-y-gest, Thomas Williams of the same address, R. I. Morris, previously serving in the *Jenny Jones*, and Maurice Parry, son of Captain Pugh Parry, the shipbroker. In 1902, when he was aged 23, Maurice Parry moved from the *David Morris* to serve as mate in the *Evelyn* for a voyage which took them to Harburg, Aberdeen, South Shields, Galway, Cadiz, St. John's, Lisbon, Huelva, returning to Amlwch in January 1903. It may well have been at that date that Maurice Parry met William Thomas, the Amlwch shipbuilder, and began the negotiations which led to his being appointed master and part shareholder in the new steel schooner, *Cenric,* built at Amlwch, which left Porthmadog with its first slate cargo two days before Christmas 1905. Captain Maurice Parry and all hands of the *Cenric* were lost some seven months later when she left Twillingate, Newfoundland, on 12 June 1906, and nothing more was ever heard of her.

Another feature of the *Evelyn*'s crews that is immediately apparent from reading through the ' articles ' is the way in which crews tended to be interchangeable with the crews of the *Dorothy,* commanded by Captain Thomas Roberts, brother of the master of the *Evelyn.* The future master of the *Isallt,* R. O. Williams, had served for several voyages aboard the *Dorothy,* with Captain Thomas Roberts, before he went to steamers, and then returned to be mate to Captain Hugh Roberts in the *Evelyn;* the Humphreys brothers of Borth-y-gest, William Morris, brother of Evie Morris, and Benjamin Welch, a native of Llandudno, who served as cook/A.B. for many years in either the *Evelyn* or the *Dorothy,* are examples of this tendency. It would be injudicious to exaggerate this, however, for it must be remembered that seamen signed articles for one voyage at a time, and then the mutual obligation ended, and the seaman had to find another ship. Thus ' Evie ' Morris, who served many years with his uncles in the *Evelyn* and the *Dorothy,* also served in a number of other Porthmadog ships; he was mate of the *M. A. James* in 1903 when she had several sheets of copper ripped off her bottom through sliding on to the ledge of an iceberg off Labrador; at the age of 24 he was master of the *Venedocian.* In 1944 Evie Morris wrote to Emrys Hughes describing that voyage in the *Venedocian,* then thirty-eight years old, ' and leaking like a sieve. No other certificated man aboard but myself, the crew being Harry Ffoulkes, mate — hadn't been to sea for 11 years — Hugh Roberts (Huwcyn Ponc), A.B., and two boys, Wil Graigydon, and Wil bach Gandage, and a Dane cook '. But with that crew the *Venedocian* sailed from Harbour Grace to Gibraltar in thirteen days, ' and after ran from the Bay of Biscay to Lisbon almost sinking with pumps choked with salt from the cargo, and [I] was just in time to beach her '.

As one after another of her contemporaries was wrecked or sold, the *Evelyn* attracted more and more attention whenever she visited ports long since accustomed to seeing only steamers; in March 1910, the Halifax, Nova Scotia, newspapers contained headlines which read 'A Unique Craft Now in Halifax Harbour — Evelyn is one of two full rigged British Brigs afloat and has been commanded by one man for 30 years', and bore various accounts of interviews with Captain Roberts. The *Echo*'s reporter stated that 'Hundreds of people took the opportunity yesterday of viewing the first full rigged brig that has been seen in Halifax harbour for twenty years or more. The brig, the Evelyn of Wales, arrived from Trinidad with a cargo of molasses for the Dominion Molasses Company after a tempestuous voyage of thirty days'. The *Shipping Illustrated* of March 19, 1910, contained similar accounts of the *Evelyn*'s arrival, adding that the vessel had been 'under command of Captain Hugh Roberts for the past 31 years, during which there has never been any illness aboard her nor any serious disaster. The chief mate is the master's brother, William, who has been in the brig for 25 years'. The *Echo* reported that Captain Roberts had stated that the only other full-rigged British brig that he knew to be afloat was the *Fleetwing*. The passage to Halifax with 500 casks of molasses had been an unusually tempestuous one, particularly in the last ten days, because of heavy gales and head seas; after discharging her cargo of molasses, the *Evelyn* was to load a cargo of deals for England. Another undated newspaper cutting bears an account of the visit of Captain Roberts and some of his crew to the Baptist Sunday School at Dartmouth, Nova Scotia, where a large audience had congregated: 'A feature of the evening was the presence of Captain Roberts and three of his men from the Welsh brig Evelyn. Three beautiful Welsh songs were rendered by them, and the programme was brought to an end by the singing of the national anthem in Welsh, Rev. and Mrs. Price joining the mariners in singing this'.

The *Evelyn* continued to sail in a variety of trades without mishap from 1910 to 1913; as an example of the range of her sailing, a page from Captain Roberts's official log-book for the voyages from July 1911 to January 1913 is included, indicating the dates of arrival at and departure from each port, with the free board and draught of water.

1913 was, however, to be the year when the *Evelyn*'s luck changed. Within three days of leaving Porthmadog, a most unusual event aboard the *Evelyn* occurred when she was some twenty miles SE of the Seven Stones Light Ship; Gabriel Jones, one of the hands, went

7

## LOAD-LINE AND DRAUGHT OF WATER.

POSITION OF DISC.

* The centre of the disc is placed at 2 feet ½ inches below the upper deck-line marked under the provisions of the Merchant Shipping Act, 1894.

* POSITION OF LINES USED IN CONNECTION WITH THE DISC.

**SAILING SHIP.**

Maximum load-line in fresh water, — feet 3 inches above the centre of the disc.
Maximum load-line in winter, North Atlantic — feet 3 inches below the centre of the disc.

**STEAM SHIP.**

Maximum load-line in fresh water___feet___inches above the centre of the disc.
Maximum load-line in Indian summer___feet___inches above the centre of the disc.
Maximum load-line in summer the centre of the disc.
Maximum load-line in winter___feet___inches below the centre of the disc.
Maximum load-line in North Atlantic winter___feet___inches below the centre of the disc.

* These particulars are to be taken from the certificate of approval of the position, or alteration of the position, of the disc, and the words which are not applicable should be erased.

## DATES OF ARRIVAL AT AND DEPARTURE FROM EACH PORT TOUCHED AT,

WITH THE

## FREE-BOARD AND DRAUGHT OF WATER

**Upon every occasion of the Ship proceeding to Sea.**

| FROM | | | | | | TO | |
|---|---|---|---|---|---|---|---|
| (1) Date and Hour of Departure. | (2) Dock, Wharf, Port or Harbour from which the Ship departs. | (3) Draught of Water in salt water at time of proceeding to sea. Forward. ft. in. | Aft. ft. in. | (4) Free-board amidships corresponding to foregoing draught. Port. ft. in. | Starboard. ft. in. | (5) Date of Arrival. | (6) Dock, Wharf, Port or Harbour. |
| 5/7/11 | Old Dk. Newport Mon | 13.0 | 14.0 | 2.0½ | 2.0½ | 30/7/11 | Cadiz |
| [illegible]/8/11 | Cadiz | 13.0 | 14.0 | 2.0½ | 2.0½ | 19/9/11 | Charlottetown P.E. Island |
| 10/10/11 | Charlottetown | 11.0 | 12.0 | 2.0½ | 2.0½ | 27/10/11 | St. Johns N.F. |
| 4/12/11 | St. Johns | 11.0 | 12.0 | 2.0½ | 2.0½ | 28/1/12 | Bahia |
| 13/2/12 | Bahia | 9.0 | 10.0 | 2.0½ | 2.0½ | 22/2/12 | [illegible] |
| 23/3/12 | Bahia | 9.0 | 10.0 | 2.0½ | 2.0½ | 24/4/12 | Barbados |
| 9/5/12 | Barbados | 13.0 | 14.0 | 2.0½ | 2.0½ | 2/6/12 | St. Johns |
| 11/7/12 | St. Johns | 10.0 | 11.0 | 2.0½ | 2.0½ | 1/8/12 | Grady (Labrador) |
| 27/9/12 | Grady Labrador | 11.0 | 12.6 | 2.0½ | 2.0½ | 21/10/12 | Gibraltar |
| 22/10/12 | Gibraltar | 11.0 | 12.6 | 2.0½ | 2.0½ | 25/10/12 | Valencia |
| 1/11/12 | Valencia | 9.0 | 10.0 | 2.0½ | 2.0½ | 2/11/12 | Huelva |
| 1/12/12 | Huelva | 13.0 | 14.0 | 2.0½ | 2.0½ | 21/12/12 | Falmouth |
| 4/1/13 | Falmouth | 9.0 | 10.0 | 2.0½ | 2.0½ | 29/1/13 | Portmadoc |
| | | | | | Hugh | | Roberts |

In the Northern Hemisphere the Summer months are April to September inclusive, and the Winter Months October to March inclusive. In the Southern Hemisphere the Summer and Winter freeboards should be used during the corresponding or recognised Summer and Winter months respectively.

The additional free-board specified for the North Atlantic trades is to apply to vessels sailing to, or from, the Mediterranean or any British or European Port, which may sail to, or from, or call at, Ports in British North America, or eastern Ports in the United States, North of Cape Hatteras, from October to March inclusive.
The reduced free-board allowed for voyages in the Fine Season in the Indian Seas only applies to vessels trading between the limits of Suez and Singapore.
The Fine Weather Season in the Indian Seas is defined as prevailing east of Tuticorin from the 15th November to the 25th May, and west of Tuticorin from the 1st September to the 25th May.

Page from Official Log Book of *Evelyn*, July 1911 to Jan. 1913

7

*Name of Ship* Evelyn

| Date and Place of Occurrence. | Date of Entry. | ENTRY |
|---|---|---|
| Mar 28th 1913 20 miles SE of Seven Stones Lightship | Mar 29th 1913 | In a fresh Gale from the SE in taking Main upper topsail Gabrielle Jones fell from aloft and took him down the Cabin and found him not seriously hurt and used the best treatment that could be given April 1st Still pain in his Hips but came on deck & Steered Hugh Roberts Master Thomas Jones Mate |
| April 11th 20 miles NE by E of East Goodwin Lightship | April 12th | Wind increasing we had occasion to take in the Main topgallantsail when Robert Jones AB & Thomas Jones OS went up to furl it @ 8.30 PM when in about 10 or 15 minutes afterwards Robert Jones sang out that Thomas Jones had gone down but did not see him fall or any of us on Deck as it was thick Rain and very Dark hauled the Ship up and kept in the vicinity seeing it useless and dangerous gale increasing kept vessel on her tack thinking that so much time had elapsed & being so thick and Dark it was hopeless to find Him Hugh Roberts Master Thomas Jones Mate |
| | | B of T 1 + Inq 9 |

Dy Supr Newhaven 14/4/13

aloft to take in the main upper topsail in a fresh south-easterly gale, but fell to the deck below. Miraculously, he was not badly hurt, but worse was to follow on 11 April when the *Evelyn* was twenty miles NE by E of the East Goodwin Light Ship. On a dark, rainy night, as the winds increased, the main topgallant sail was taken in, and two hands were aloft furling it when the more experienced of them, Robert Jones, A.B., shouted to Captain Roberts and those on the deck below that his companion, Thomas Jones, Ordinary Seaman, had disappeared. No one had actually seen the unfortunate man fall or heard any cry in the howling gale of that dark night. Reluctantly, Captain Roberts had to abandon the search for the only man he had ever lost overboard, as the conditions worsened and all hope of finding him faded. Two days later, the *Evelyn* was compelled to put into Newhaven, where Captain Roberts reported Thomas Jones's death.

From Newhaven the *Evelyn* sailed ten days later for Harburg, whence she sailed on 13 May for Boston, Lincolnshire. There the crew were paid off, and it may have been significant that the Porthmadog men did not sign for the next voyage, apart from Captain Roberts himself and Thomas Jones of East Avenue, the mate, so a Dane, two Norwegians, a German, and a local seaman were signed at Grimsby for the voyage to Cadiz and Newfoundland. Already the stories of the *Evelyn*'s uncharacteristic misfortunes had spread to Porthmadog, and much was attributed to the ill-luck associated with Thomas Jones, the mate (Twm Bach y Dre), who was recognized as a fine seaman who, unfortunately, had some kind of 'hoodoo' about him. 'Evie' Morris served as A.B. with Thomas Jones when he was master of the *Wern,* when a steamer collided with her off Dungeness and he and a shipmate were nearly killed in their bunks — there is a photograph of the *Wern* with her damaged bows much in evidence soon after the collision. Writing in 1944, Evie Morris remembered that he was glad to leave the *Wern* and the unfortunate Captain Jones — 'he certainly was unlucky, although a good master and a grand seaman, bad luck was his share'. The Porthmadog men aboard the *Evelyn* may have had this very much in mind when they left the ship at Boston after the death of one of the crew, and what could have been a serious accident to another. But Captain Roberts had no doubts, and with his alleged 'jonah' as a mate, and an

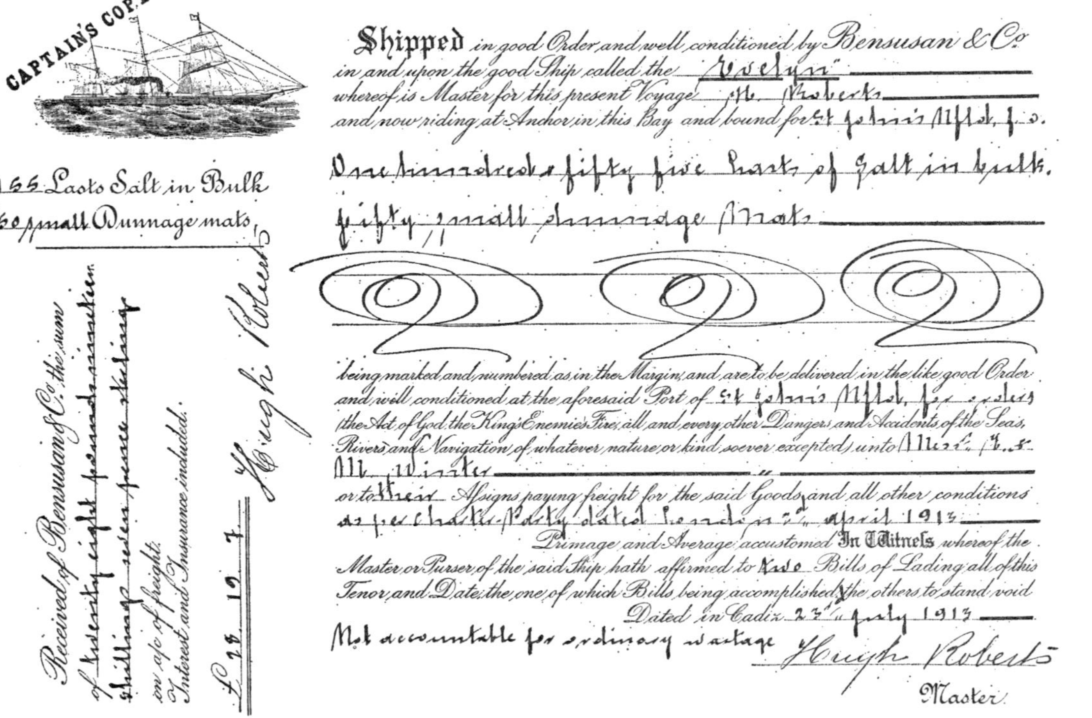

CAPTAIN'S COPY

155 Lasts Salt in Bulk

50 small Dunnage mats

Shipped in good Order and well conditioned by Bensusan & Co in and upon the good Ship called the "Evelyn" whereof is Master for this present Voyage H. Roberts and now riding at Anchor in this Bay and bound for St John's Nfld. f.o.

One hundred & fifty five Lasts of Salt in bulk.

fifty small dunnage Mats

being marked and numbered as in the Margin, and are to be delivered in the like good Order and well conditioned at the aforesaid Port of St John's Nfld. for orders (the Act of God, the King's Enemies, Fire, and all and every other Dangers and Accidents of the Seas, Rivers and Navigation, of whatever nature or kind soever excepted) unto Messrs [illegible] Winter

or to their Assigns paying freight for the said Goods and all other conditions as per Charter Party dated London 2nd April 1913

Primage and Average accustomed. In Witness whereof the Master or Purser of the said Ship hath affirmed to two Bills of Lading all of this Tenor and Date, the one of which Bills being accomplished the others to stand void.

Dated in Cadiz 23rd July 1913

Not accountable for ordinary wastage

Hugh Roberts

Master

Received of Bensusan & Co the sum of twenty eight pounds nineteen shillings seven pence sterling on a/c of freight. Interest and Insurance included.

£28 19 7

Hugh Roberts

**Shipped** in good order and well conditioned by Baine, Johnston & Co, in and up. the good Brig. called the "EVELYN" whereof Hugh Roberts. is Master, and now riding at anchor in this Port, and bound for Glasgow via Beaverton. to say

M. C.

Murray & Crawford Ltd.

SEAL OIL

TWO HUNDRED AND SIXTY TWO CASKS CONTAINING

FORTY FIVE TUNS AND FIFTY EIGHT IMPERIAL

GALLONS OF S E A L O I L.

| | T. H. G. | | T.cwt.Qrs.Lbs. |
|---|---|---|---|
| P.S. (No.115 to 276) = 162 casks contg. | 29. 0.46 | or | 30. 4. 3. 14 |
| S.S. (No.277 to 376) = 100 casks " | 15. 3.52 | or | 16.19. 0. 11 |
| 262 casks | 45. 0. 58 | or | 47. 3. 3. 25 Nett. |

THIS COPY NOT NEGOTIABLE

being marked and numbered as in the margin, and to be delivered in the like good order and well conditioned at the aforesaid Port of Glasgow. (The act of God, Fire and all and every other dangers and accidents of the Seas, Rivers, and Navigation of whatever nature or kind so ever excepted) unto Messrs. Murray & Crawford or to their Assigns, he or they paying Freight for the said goods.

"TWO CASKS IN DISPUTE " if on board to be delivered.

As per Charter Party

and average accustomed. In Witness whereof the Master or Mate hath affirmed to one Bills of Lading all of this tenor and date, one of which being accomplished the others to stand void.—
Dated in St John's, Newfoundland.

October 15th 1913.

Contents unknown.

"The Act of God, Perils of the Sea, Fire, Barratry of the Master and Crew, Enemies, Pirates, assailing Thieves, arrest and restraint of Princes, Rulers, and People, Collisions, Stranding, and other accidents of navigation excepted; even when occasioned by the negligence, default or error in judgement of the Pilot, Master, Mariners, or other Servants of the Shipowner."

Sold by DICKS & Co
Booksellers & Stationers.

Shipped onboard of the "Brig Evelyn"
2655 sacks of Guano weighing
Gross Sck weight Nett
397325. 6637 390688 =
Tons cwt qr lbs
174 8 . 1 4

Received on a/c of within freight
Thirty-eight dollars (38 00)

Hugh Roberts
Master

**Shipped** in good order and condition by The Rosiere Whaling Coy of Beaverton Newfoundland, in and upon the good ship or vessel called the Evelyn whereof H Roberts is master for this present voyage now lying in the port of Beaverton N. F. L. and bound for Glasgow Scotland

With Two thousand six hundred & fifty-five (2655) sacks of Guano weighing
lbs Tons cwt qr lbs
390688 = 174 8 . 1 . 4

being marked and numbered as per margin and are to be delivered in the like good order and condition, at the aforesaid port of Glasgow (all and every the dangers and accidents of the seas and navigation of whatsoever nature or kind excepted) unto order or to their assigns, he or they paying freight for the said goods ~~at the rate of~~
and all other conditions
As per Charter Party

with per cent. primage and with average accustomed, In witness whereof the master or purser of the said ship or vessel has affirmed to three Bills of Lading all of this tenor and date one of which being accomplished the rest to stand void.

Dated in Beaverton N. F. L. this First day of November 1913

Not accountable for weight or quality

Hugh Roberts
Master

Shipped on board the "Brig Evelyn"
104 packages of Gillbone weighing
lbs Tons cwt qr lbs
17127 = 7 12. 3 19 (by 2240lbs)

**Shipped** in good order and condition by The Rosinus Whaling Coy of Beaverton Newfoundland, in and upon the good ship or vessel called the Evelyn whereof H Roberts is master for this present voyage now lying in the port of Beaverton N. F. L. and bound for Glasgow Scotland

With One hundred & four packages of Gillbones (104) weighing -
lbs Tons cwt qr lbs
17127 = 7 12 3 19

being marked and numbered as per margin and are to be delivered in the like good order and condition, at the aforesaid port of Glasgow (all and every the dangers and accidents of the seas and navigation of whatsoever nature or kind excepted) unto Rosinus Whaling Coy Ltd, Glasgow or to their assigns, he or they paying freight for the said goods ~~at the rate of~~
and all other conditions
As per Charter Party

with per cent. primage and with average accustomed, In witness whereof the master or purser of the said ship or vessel has affirmed to three Bills of Lading all of this tenor and date one of which being accomplished the rest to stand void.

Dated in Beaverton N. F. L. this First day of November 1913

Not accountable for weight or quality

Hugh Roberts
Master

international crew, sailed the *Evelyn* to Gibraltar and Cadiz in July, where one of the Norwegians was paid off and replaced by G. Romero Perez, a Spanish seaman from Cadiz. On 3 September the *Evelyn* arrived at St. John's and proceeded to the fishing stations to discharge her salt cargo — Captain Roberts's copy relating to the 155 lasts of salt in bulk and the 50 small Dunnage mats is reproduced here.

The *Evelyn* was ready to sail again by the beginning of November: aboard were 260 barrels of oil, 2,655 sacks of guano and 104 packages of Gillbones which had been shipped by the Rosiree Whaling Company at Beaverton, Newfoundland, for Glasgow. Despite all the subsequent trials, Captain Roberts kept all the papers relating to the voyage (some which are reproduced here), together with the clearing certificate for the *Evelyn* from the Customs at Herring Neck, Newfoundland, on 1 November 1913. The *Evelyn* sailed three days later, on 4 November, soon running into foul weather conditions. The two Norwegians had left the ship at St. John's in October, and although one replacement had been obtained there, a young Reading man, William Aslett, who signed as cook/A.B., the *Evelyn* was short-handed: in addition to Captain Roberts and the mate, Thomas Jones, there were two A.B.s, Perez the Spaniard, and Boucher, a Grimsby man, the newly-signed cook/A.B., and Rudolf Schafer, an eighteen-year-old ordinary seaman whose home address was given in the 'articles' as Weinweg, 56, Berlin. Henry Hughes, in *Immortal Sails,* has given a graphic account of the next three weeks aboard the *Evelyn;* Captain Hugh Roberts's own account of what happened also appeared in many newspapers following the dramatic rescue in mid-Atlantic. When he returned to Porthmadog, Captain Roberts was again interviewed, and this is the version reproduced here.

> 'From the very start, after leaving Newfoundland, the weather was very dirty. On November 7th a tremendous sea struck our ship and filled her up to the cabin floors. The same sea struck the galley, tearing it from the deck and sweeping it into the ocean. A corner of the galley caught the lifeboat and carried it away as though it were only a toy. In the meantime, all the sails had been blown away or so damaged as to render them of no use. We were unable to get below to obtain the sails stowed there, and even if we could have got them we could not have bent them to the yards, owing to the heavy seas and the rolling of the vessel. Later on, the forecastle was carried away and the crew of six were quartered in the cabin, though

sleep was almost out of the question from November 7th until the 28th. Throughout those weeks we struggled against the elements, but seemingly all to no purpose, for the ship was absolutely unmanageable. The cargo, which comprised about 260 barrels of oil and a large quantity of guano, broke adrift, and stove in the partition between the hold and the cabin, with the result that the guano was swept into the freshwater tank in the cabin, rendering the water useless for drinking purposes. We were in a pitiable plight from November 7th. We sighted in the distance several steamers between the 7th and the 28th, and some of the crew wanted to leave the "Evelyn", but, in my opinion, bad as the position was, had I left her then it would have amounted to a premature abandonment. My earnest hope was that the weather would moderate and then I might have been able to have got my ship to a point where salvage might have been probable. We did our level best, but the weather was against us all along. On the evening of November 28th, the Glasgow steamer "Invergyle" hove in sight. We were then in an awful plight and had been for several days constantly engaged at the pumps. The "Invergyle" at once responded to our signals of distress and sent a boat to our assistance. Three of my crew, in their determination to leave the "Evelyn" jumped into the water and were rescued by the "Invergyle's" boat, which was then carried from the vicinity of the brig by the heavy seas. The "Invergyle" stood by throughout the night, but next morning got under way and proceeded on her voyage, leaving the mate (Mr. Thomas Jones, a fellow townsman), a German seaman, and myself the sole occupants of the "Evelyn". We had gone through a terrible time prior to that, but worse was in store for us. When the "Invergyle" approached us we had been for some time without fresh water, for we naturally abstained from using the contaminated water left in the tank. For three whole days we were absolutely without any fresh water or anything else to drink, except coffee and tea made with salt water. We had neither time nor the opportunity to try to convert the sea water into a semblance of fresh water. The galley had been swept away and all we had left was a small stove and a few kitchen utensils. Luckily, we had plenty of provisions such as preserved beef. For seven days and nights the mate and I kept constantly at the pumps and the water was gradually gaining on us. Our hands were in a painful state as the result of the skin being worn away. On Sunday morning, November 30th, after being three days without fresh water, and when we were nearly dead with thirst, we sighted a west-bound steamer and made signals of distress; but received no answer. We were then in awful straits, for the water was gaining on us and it was clear that it would not be long before the brig would sink under the waves. We had given up all hopes of rescue when about two p.m. on Sunday I saw a

> vessel on the horizon away to the westward. Full of hope once more, I ran up my distress signals and also the code letters " N.I." to indicate that I had lost my boats, wanted immediate assistance, and asking for a lifeboat to take us off. The vessel turned out to be the C.P. liner " Monmouth " bound from Montreal for Bristol with a general cargo. She at once responded to our signals, and soon a boat came along and rescued us. The rescue was affected with some difficulty for there was still a big swell on. As soon as the boat approached the " Evelyn " we assembled on the quarter deck. From there we jumped into the boat, waiting until the boat was brought as near to the level of the " Evelyn " as possible. The first thing we saw in the boat was a small cask of water, and with thankful hearts we satisfied within reason our terrible thirst. The joy of the time when we boarded the " Monmouth " I shall never forget. I cannot describe my feelings. The " Evelyn " was fast sinking when we left her, and in a few hours would, I feel certain, have disappeared under the waves. And even had the brig kept floating, we would have died from the thirst had our rescue been prolonged another day'.

As a footnote to this newspaper report, the Porthmadog correspondent could not resist adding: 'This is the third time in two years for Mr. Thomas Jones to be ship-wrecked'. The *Invergyle* landed the three crew members she had rescued, Aslett, Perez, and Boucher, on one side of the Atlantic, whilst the master, mate, and the German ordinary seaman were landed on the other at Avonmouth when the liner *Monmouth* docked there. The first news of the loss of the *Evelyn* had come to Porthmadog via Lloyds signal station, which had received a wireless message from the *Monmouth*: 'Monmouth, steamer signalled by wireless 5.20 p.m. that on November 30 she rescued the crew of the Brig Evelyn of Portmadoc, Carnarvon, sinking derelict lat 50°56'N long 30°23'W — Capt. Roberts, the mate Jones both of Portmadoc, ordinary seaman Schafer a German, and 3 others taken by steamer Invergyle'.

Back home at Haulfryn, Porthmadog, Captain Roberts carefully made up his wages accounts for that unlucky year 1913. (Page 416.) A few weeks later he met his nephew, 'Evie' Morris in Liverpool; thirty years later Captain Morris wrote 'I met Uncle Hugh some time after in Liverpool, and there were deep scars on the palms of his hands where the iron handles of the pumps had chafed through the flesh'. Within a few months came the outbreak of the war which brought even deeper scars to the maritime community of Porthmadog.

| Names | Rank | Where Shipped | Date Joined | | Date Discharged | | Where Discharged | Mths | Days | Rate of Pay per Mth | | | Total Earned | | |
|---|---|---|---|---|---|---|---|---|---|---|---|---|---|---|---|
| Hugh Roberts | Master | Portmadoc | 5/2/13 | | 30/11/13 | | Lat. 50-50 N Long 30-26 W | 19. | 26 | £9 | - | - | 88 | 16 | 0 |
| Thomas Jones | Mate | do | March | 25 | June | 10 | Boston. | 2 | 17 | 5 | 10 | - | 14 | 2 | 4 |
| Edward Edwards | C. & AB | do | March | 17 | do | - | do | 2 | 25 | 4 | 2 | 6 | 11 | 13 | 9 |
| Gabrielle Jones | AB | do | March | 17 | do | - | | 2 | 25 | 3 | 10 | - | 9 | 18 | 4 |
| Robert Jones | AB | do | March | 19 | do | - | do | 2 | 23 | 3 | 10 | - | 9 | 13 | 4 |
| Thomas Jones | OS | do | Mar | 19 | April | 11 | Deserted | | 24 | 2 | 10 | 0 | 2 | 0 | 0 |
| Thomas H. Williams | OS | do. | Mar | 17 | do | - | do | 2 | 24 | 1 | 10 | . | 4 | 4 | 0 |
| James W. Jones | AB | Newhaven | April | 16 | June | 4 | Do 3rd passage | 1 | 20 | 4 | 0 | 0 | 7 | 13 | 0 |
| Thomas W. Jones | Mate | Boston | June | 16 | Nov | 30 | Portmadoc | 5 | 15 | 6 | 0 | 0 | 33 | - | - |
| Peter Kristiansen | Cook | do | June | 16 | July | 15 | Gibraltar | 1 | – | 4 | 5 | 0 | 4 | 5 | 0 |
| Olaf Carlsen | AB | do | June | 16 | Sept | 15 | St. Johns | 3 | – | 4 | 5 | 0 | 12 | 15 | 0 |
| Carl Reiersen | Cook AB | do | June | 16th | Oct | 20 | St. Johns | 4 | 5 | 4 | 0 | 0 | 16 | 13 | 4 |
| Rudolf Schafer | OS | do | June | 16 | Nov | 30 | Avonmouth | 5 | 15 | 1 | 2 | 6 | 6 | 5 | . |
| James Boucher | AB | do | June | 16 | Nov | 27 | Grimsby | 5 | 12 | 4 | - | - | 21 | 12 | - |
| Guillermo Perez | AB | Cadiz | July | 23 | Nov | 27 | Glasgow | 4 | 4 | 4 | . | . | 16 | 10 | 8 |
| William Aslett | Cook & AB | St. Johns | Oct | 15 | Nov | 27 | Glasgow | 1 | 12 | 4 | 10 | . | 6 | 6 | - |
| | | | | | | | | | | | | | £265.7.9 | | |
| | | | | | | | | | | | | | 2 | 14 | 4 |
| | | | | | | | | | | | | | 268 | 2 | 1 |

| | s d |
|---|---|
| Insurances | 14.4 |
| passages | £2.0.0 |
| | £2.14.4 |

## REFERENCES

[1] Henry Hughes, *Immortal Sails,* 136-139.

[2] Letter from E. Morris, Glaslyn, North Sunderland, Seahouses, to E. Hughes, August 1944. When Captain Morris had obtained his master's certificate and took command of the *Venedocian* as a young man of 24, he invested in a new sextant, and Captain W. H. Hughes, D.S.C., remembers that he bought his old sextant from Morris at this time.

[3] The details which follow are from the *Evelyn*'s Crew Agreement Lists and Official Logs, now housed at Caernarfon, and from newspaper cuttings and papers which Miss Evelyn Roberts of Porthmadog kindly allowed me to have on loan.

# INDEX

NOTE: (i) The Index of Persons is selective.
(ii) The Index of Vessels named in the text also directs attention to any 'extended study' in the appendix.

## (i) PERSONS

S



T



W

**Y**



## (ii) VESSELS IN TEXT

Barque.

Barquentine.